RAPE AND RACE IN THE NINETEENTH-CENTURY SOUTH

RAPE & RACE *in the*
Nineteenth-Century South

DIANE MILLER SOMMERVILLE

The
University
of
North
Carolina
Press
Chapel Hill
and London

© 2004 The University of North Carolina Press
All rights reserved

Designed by Jacquline Johnson
Set in Minion
by Keystone Typesetting, Inc.

Manufactured in the United States of America

Portions of this book have appeared, in slightly different form, in the
following publications by the author and are reused here by permission:
" 'I Was Very Much Wounded': Rape Law, Children, and the Antebellum
South," in *Sex without Consent: Rape and Sexual Coercion in America*, edited
by Merril D. Smith (New York: New York University Press, 2001), 136–77; "Rape,
Race, and Castration in Slave Law in the Colonial and Early South," in *The Devil's
Lane: Sex and Race in the Early South*, edited by Catherine Clinton and Michele
Gillespie (New York: Oxford University Press, 1997), 74–89; and "The Rape Myth
in the Old South Reconsidered," *Journal of Southern History* 61 (August 1995):
481–518.

The paper in this book meets the guidelines for permanence and durability of
the Committee on Production Guidelines for Book Longevity of the Council
on Library Resources.

Library of Congress Cataloging-in-Publication Data
Sommerville, Diane Miller.
Rape and race in the nineteenth-century South / Diane Miller Sommerville.
p. cm.
Includes bibliographical references and index.
ISBN 0-8078-2891-2 (alk. paper)—ISBN 0-8078-5560-x (pbk.: alk. paper)
1. Rape—Southern States—History—19th century. 2. Southern States—Race
relations—History—19th century. I. Title.
HV6564.S68S66   2004
364.15′32′097509034—dc22
2004008917

cloth   08 07 06 05 04   5 4 3 2 1
paper   08 07 06 05 04   5 4 3 2 1

This book is dedicated to my father,
Dean Myers Miller,
and to the loving memory of my mother,
Donna Jean Smith Miller

CONTENTS

TABLES

ACKNOWLEDGMENTS

The immensity of this project eluded me until the first time I compiled the final manuscript in preparation for publication. Somewhat in disbelief I stared at the large stack of pages, the tangible manifestation of a decade-long gestation. As I was worked in the trenches, crafting narratives, framing historiographical debates, and honing analysis, it somehow failed to dawn on me that tracing rape and race over the swath of the American South and over the expanse of more than a century could end up as anything other than a mammoth project. And as one would expect, my debts are proportionately large and wide-ranging.

Support for this project began with Rutgers University, which came through time and again with funds enabling me to finish my dissertation, the germ of this book. The graduate chairs of the History Department during my tenure—Paul G. E. Clemens, T. J. Jackson Lears, Virginia Yans, and Steven Reinert—deserve thanks for tracking down stipends and channeling them my way. Several institutions, including the American Historical Association, the Virginia Historical Society, and the North Caroliniana Society, awarded me financial grants to support my travel to archival sites. Princeton University, Lafayette College, and Fairleigh Dickson University supported conference trips where I tested the waters with my preliminary research. My current academic home, Fairleigh Dickinson University, also came through with much appreciated released time from teaching to support my research and writing.

I benefited enormously from the learned assistance of skilled librarians, archivists, and their support staffs. The Interlibrary Loan Department at the Alexander Library, Rutgers University, provided invaluable help by processing my seemingly endless requests. I would also like to acknowledge the professional and hospitable staffs of the Library of Virginia, the Virginia Historical Society, and the North Carolina Department of Archives and History. Sandy Treadway, Brent Tarter, and John Kneebone of the Library of Virginia graciously allowed me to draw on their collective knowledge of Southern history while occasionally sharing a story or two about grad school days or offering a tutorial on Virginia politics. The staff there, especially Minor Weisiger and Conley Edwards, patiently tolerated an endless stream of research queries; Vincent Brooks provided very useful and timely research at long distance. The staff at the Virginia Historical Society just across town was equally gracious. Especially helpful were Frances Pollard, Nelson Lankford, and Janet Schwarz. A number of folks who knew of my research topic shared priceless nuggets of research with me over the years, including Philip Schwarz, Henry Wiencek, Barry McGhee, Gary M. Williams, Daniel Crofts, Betsy Glade, Charlene Lewis, Byron Grizzle, and Harold Forsythe. Debbie Robertson proved herself a most efficient and expert research assistant and her contribution is much appreciated.

A number of historians took a crack at reading portions of my work and offering helpful suggestions and criticisms: Dirk Hartog, Eliza McFeely, Mitchell Snay, Suzanne Lebsock, Deborah Gray White, Norma Basch, Thomas Slaughter, David Goldfield, James Goodman, Nell Painter, Lisa Lundquist Dorr, Joshua Rothman, Clement Alexander Price, Mary Block, Alice Carter, and Sharon Block. I am especially grateful to Dirk—now—for pushing me to clarify my arguments. Fitz Brundage, Jane Dailey, Michael Perman, Edward Ayers, and Glenda Gilmore kindly and thoughtfully responded to pointed questions in their areas of expertise. I am also grateful to those reviewers and commentators whose criticism I made every attempt to integrate into my analysis: Jane Turner Censer, Sandy Treadway, Leon Litwack, James Marten, Joel Sipress, Martha Hodes, and Drew Gilpin Faust. Portions of this manuscript have appeared earlier in print, and I have benefited from the editorial direction of John Boles, Evelyn Thomas Nolen, Catherine Clinton, Michele Gillespie, and Merril Smith. Friends and colleagues in the profession have lent crucial emotional as well as intellectual support at key moments in the development of this project, among them Eliza McFeely, Scott Sandage, Jon Earle, Steve Aron, Jacqueline Miller, Grace Elizabeth Hale, and Mitchell Snay, whose sense of humor and compassion have buoyed me in rough seas and in calm.

Without a doubt, the greatest intellectual debt I owe is to Jan Lewis. As fate would have it, even though we were both part of the larger Rutgers family, we didn't meet until I unknowingly but fortuitously plunked myself down next to her at a session of the Southern Historical Association gathering in New Orleans in 1991. While the topic of that session has long since escaped me, I vividly recall that it was over a drink in the French Quarter that I first opened up a dialogue about rape and race with Jan. From that moment, Jan embraced me and my work with characteristic warmth and exuberance. I have tapped her for more advice than I have had a right to do. She has remained an unwavering booster and good friend.

But it has been the circle of family and friends outside the academe that has provided the ballast of life, the delightful distractions and loving support without which this book means little. I have been blessed with a wonderful sister, Debbie Bills, though I daresay I didn't always feel that way. Having shared a bed with her for most of my childhood, I wondered at times if we both would survive adolescence. We did. And we are the better for it. Her and her family—Rob, Steven, and Ryan—and the time we spend together mean a great deal to me and my family. My brothers Glenn Miller and Dan Miller, who have inherited the Miller family tradition of storytelling, serve to keep me connected to my past. Mildred Barna, aunt extraordinaire and second mother, has taught me much about life and family, about courage and spunk, and I admire her greatly. Marion and Arthur Sommerville still probably don't understand what it is that I do, but they've been there over the last quarter-century to offer up support in many ways. Nancy McGlynn, Katie Sommerville, and Susan Rennie define loyalty and friendship. We've shared much, including shoulders. Finally, I can scarcely begin to repay the patience and support required of my immediate family throughout this project. Shannon and Jackson cannot remember a time when I wasn't working on "the book." So here it is, and as proud as I am of it, it pales in comparison to the joy and pride I take in their lives, who they are, and who they will become. My husband and life partner, Donny, decidedly not a member of the academe, has provided emotional and material sustenance throughout this protracted process and had faith that I would see this project to fruition. He has not typed a single word or detected a split infinitive, yet his mark on my work, as in my life, is as indelible as any other.

The lives of my father, Dean Myers Miller, and my mother, Donna Jean Smith Miller, are monuments to the values of hard work and integrity, even in the face of misfortune. My mother was a strong, bright woman whose own aspirations were stifled by the conspiracy of the time and place in which she was raised, then later by the demands of her own family. I know, therefore, that this achievement by her eldest daughter would have given her great joy and fulfillment, as it does my dad. It is to her memory, and to my father, that I happily dedicate this work.

RAPE AND RACE IN THE NINETEENTH-CENTURY SOUTH

INTRODUCTION

In 1918 the historian Ulrich B. Phillips, citing 105 cases of slaves accused of raping white women, challenged the "oft-asserted Southern tradition that Negroes never violated white women before slavery was abolished."[1] Phillips was writing at a time when the rape, whether real or imagined, of white women by black men was highly politicized. Turn-of-the-century radical racists, to use Joel Williamson's term, who lobbied against black education and for disfranchisement of African Americans, seized on what historians would call an "invented tradition," the idyllic antebellum plantation. They evoked a slave South in which "the natural trust and affection subsisting between the two races" made relations between master and slave sublimely harmonious.[2] Troubled by the less deferential "New Negro," increases in the black population, and an unprecedented political threat, many white southerners waxed nostalgic about the cross-racial plantation "family."[3] A strand woven into this romantic tapestry was the steadfast loyalty of slaves, best demonstrated by the absence of a sexual threat to the master's female family members. During the antebellum era, these southern apologists argued, illiterate, unschooled slaves rarely raped white women, and rape remained rare even during the Civil War when white male protectors were absent and slaves had opportunity. John Roach Straton, a professor at Mercer University in Macon, Georgia, crowed that the slave's "fidelity and simple discharge of duty during the Civil War, when the whites were away fighting against his liberty, have challenged the admiration of the world."[4] A former justice of the Alabama Supreme Court, Henderson M. Somerville, boasted that slave rape was unheard of, "even during the Civil War, when the white women of the cotton States were left comparatively unprotected."[5] It was this invented tradition, of denying the threat of slave rape, that Phillips challenged.

Phillips revealed that bondsmen at times had raped white women and received fair trials, as part of his attempt to depict slavery as so paternalistic an institution and planters as so benevolent that even black rapists received justice. In his own way, Phillips was an apologist for the slave South, and when later historians and race "liberals" challenged his interpretations, they also ignored or dismissed his evidence about rape. Hence, such an acknowledgment, that blacks raped white women and some of them received fair trials, became nearly untenable if unfathomable. Phillips's documentation of slave rape, by most accounts, seems to have been forgotten or overlooked by later scholars. Sickened by gruesome lynchings of black men, many for ostensibly sexual assaults on white women, and critical of a popular culture that eagerly embraced racist stereotypical images of black rapists, race liberals in the decades after Phillips wrote could not contemplate the possibility of black-on-white rape, convinced that such suggestions emanated from white southerners' racism and one of its corollaries, the adulation of white female purity.[6] The consummate race liberal Wilbur J. Cash, for one, gave white women greater odds of being struck by lightning than being raped by a black man.[7] To concede that black men on occasion had raped white women would have been tantamount to validating racist diatribes about black men's lust for white women. In short, black rape had become so politically charged that dispassionate historical treatment of the topic was all but impossible for much of the twentieth century.

Consequently, even scholarly works that have tackled "interracial" rape in the nineteenth-century South typically have sidestepped black-on-white rape, instead focusing almost exclusively on white-on-black rape. Politicization of the black rapist image combined with sensitivity among historians to the sexual exploitation of female slaves has rendered many historians blind to even the possibility of black-on-white rape. In essence, historical treatments of interracial rape have often failed to consider that black men, especially slaves, could also cross racial boundaries and coerce a white woman or girl into having unwanted sex. To contemplate a male slave as an aggressor, an assailant of a white person, would seem to require an ideological inversion of major proportions. A theoretical staple of race history in America is that it is whites who possessed power used to oppress and assail blacks, not the other way around. Of course slaves have always assaulted whites, sometimes overtly, other times surreptitiously, whether through arson, poisonings, or assault. But historians have usually heralded such criminal activity as resistance to the slave regime and therefore deemed such acts as heroic.[8] Viewing slave rape of white females in this same light is obviously problematic, so problematic that scholars have been reluctant to wrestle with the historical and theoretical issues that it raises.

Take, for instance, a relatively recent essay on the historical foundations of rape and sexual assault by Patricia Donat and John D'Emilio.[9] In a discussion of "racial aspects of rape," the authors point out that rape of black women has served as a means of racial control for whites. When inverting the interracial rape scenario to consider black rapists of white women, the authors veer away from focusing on actual experiences of rape and instead revert to a discussion of the *rhetoric* of rape, the "rape myth." The implication, of course, is that white men raped black women, but the rape of white women by black men was the lurid fantasy of whites obsessed with an irrational fear of black sexuality. In many classic and important works on the South, "interracial" sex has really meant white men having sex with enslaved women, forcefully or otherwise.

The "rape myth," one of the hallmarks of a distinctive southern society, has thus bequeathed to us two potent and enduring assumptions. The first is that white southerners throughout their entire history have been preoccupied (some would say obsessed) with black male sexuality. A related and concomitant assumption is that black men and slaves never raped white women at all and, hence, claims that they did were based on fear, not reality. These twin assumptions have book-ended us into a largely unexamined debate about rape and race in the South. Once we acknowledge that neither position is tenable, we are free to engage in an in-depth study of how race, class, and gender interacted in local settings when charges of black-on-white rape were aired. An important aim of this book is therefore to strip away the various layers of constructed notions of race and sexuality—dare I say *deconstruct* the rape myth and its political and cultural trappings? But the endgame here is not merely to undercut the assumptions sustaining the rape myth. That is simply my starting point. Looking beyond the rhetorical and ideological morass of black rape in the South, we find the opportunity to examine anew accusations of black-on-white rape and, stripping them of the paternalistic myth in which Phillips encased them, to take them—and their meanings—seriously. Individual incidents of black-on-white rape (or attempted rape) as played out in courtrooms, therefore, are a window through which to view the day-to-day interactions of southerners, black and white, privileged and poor, and to explore how southerners regarded one another, at least under the peculiar circumstances of a rape charge. Studied over time, cases of black rape and responses to them also lay bare important societal changes and developments that took place in the American South.

In short, I argue throughout this work that rape is an important historical marker of race and gender relations in the American South. Historians, sociologists, and laypeople have long argued that rape, in imagination and in reality, has yielded valuable clues about southern society. Hence, the use of black rape as a historical marker is nothing new. The flaw in employing rape as a means to analyze a region, its people, and its history has been that the attendant analysis has been obfuscated by politics, ideology, and fear, and rooted in untested assumptions and preconceptions—so much so that its chronological and theoretical guideposts have been misplaced, thus misdirecting much of the understanding about rape and race in the South. The crucial charge of this work is the historical reconstruction of rape and race in the American South. With that correction, we can better and more accurately map the contours of southern society and address compelling questions about the region that are central to an understanding of southern history.

M y intent is to move beyond black rape as an "invented tradition," which was constructed and utilized for explicitly political purposes, and which permeated and stubbornly dominated popular and scholarly discourses throughout much of the last one hundred or so years, and to visit a time and place when the so-called rape myth exercised little sway. In essence, I ask, what was the South like before it had become gripped with fears of the alleged "black-beast-rapist"? Who levied charges against black men? What were the reasons for charging black men with rape? Were women and girls responding to actual acts of assault, or were they merely attempting to "cover up" illicit behavior with black men? How did antebellum southern communities react when slaves and free blacks were charged with sexually assaulting white women and girls? And what do those reactions reveal generally about southern slave society?

One of the fundamental empirical lessons of the book is that in most cases in which a white female charged a black male with sexual assault, southerners overwhelmingly submitted willingly to legal processes, abiding by the outcomes. Given the reputation that the South has cultivated for antilegalism and vigilantism, this finding is significant. Most white southerners, when faced with a charge of black rape in their community, deferred to the judicial process, even when it apparently challenged racial hegemony. The critical question is, why? This book sets out to answer that question.

White community members did not always line up on the side of the white female accuser. Rather, communities often divided over whom to support during black-on-white rape trials. In fact, towns and neighborhoods were frequently racked with discord as black rape trials played out. Typically, these splits fell along class lines. In charging a slave with rape or attempted rape, a white female was, on some level, challenging the social hierarchy, impugning the mastery of the slave's owner, particularly his ability to control his slave. More importantly, a white woman's charge that a slave had raped her, a capital crime, exposed a slave to execution by the state. Thus a master whose slave stood accused of raping a white female risked personal, financial, and perhaps even emotional loss if the slave was convicted and executed. Thus it should not be surprising that masters routinely engaged the services of lawyers to plead the cases of accused slave-rapists. Guided foremost by economic self-interest, slave masters used their wealth and status to press their claims for their slaves' innocence of rape charges. Nineteenth-century rape trials thus expose the limits of whiteness as a common interest and allow us to consider a more nuanced relationship among southern whites, one that entertains contention and divergent interests.

Contention among whites, frequently divided by class, was the order of the day in many black-on-white rape cases. A common scenario that played out in antebellum southern communities where an accusation of black rape was levied was that a white master hired defense counsel for his slave who stood accused of sexually assaulting a white female. The slave's attorney generally made use of the legal arsenal available to him, as he would have for any white client, and gathered exculpatory evidence, along with character and alibi witnesses, but also interrogated the reputation of the white accuser. The latter stratagem often irritated or offended the friends and family of the accuser, typically members of the middling or poor strata of society. The ensuing fallout might yield indignation at the master's self-interest in trying to spare his slave from the gallows. Perceived acts of selfishness, and the manipulation of legal institutions to effect an accused black rapist's exoneration or pardon, sometimes did not sit well with members of the nonslaveholding class who on occasion openly challenged the motives of the slave master and thus rallied behind the female accuser, demanding that she be offered the protection generally accorded elite white women.

Class interests often combined with misogyny to forge a formidable obstacle to an expedited, successful prosecution and execution of a black man for rape. Most of the white females who officially charged black men with rape or attempted rape fell outside the circle of elite, slaveholding women. Poor and middling females made up the vast majority of rape complainants. Their inferior social status sometimes constituted a significant barrier to the successful prosecution of their attackers, although they were white and their alleged rapists black. Females of the lower social order had to work harder to make their claims of sexual assault seem credible to the community and to the courts, the leaders of which at times exhibited considerable contempt for these women. A hybrid of misogyny and class prejudice guided the deliberations and actions of many white southerners confronted with the allegation that a black man had assaulted a white female. In contrast to the fictional white but poor Mayella Ewell in *To Kill a Mockingbird*, whose charge of rape against a local black man was taken at face value by most whites, the mere whiteness of an accuser could not guarantee a conviction or execution when a black man was accused of rape in the antebellum South.

In truth, much of the ill will aimed at these accusers can be understood as a response to purported social indiscretions committed by the female accusers. Many of the accusers who appear in the rape trials in the forthcoming pages routinely acted outside the boundaries of accepted behavior, engaging in relationships and activities deemed illicit or indiscreet by southern society, thus inviting scrutiny and derision. These "unruly women," as they have been so aptly called by Victoria Bynum, many without male providers and protectors, struggled to maintain and support households. Lacking adequate resources, ties to wealthy and influential neighbors, and, importantly, a vital place in the economy of the slave South, these women operated on the fringes of antebellum southern society, adrift and unprotected in a patriarchal state. Testimony from antebellum rape trials reveals the existence of isolated households made up of unmarried women, many of whom had children, sometimes outside the bonds of marriage. At times mothers, possibly widowed or abandoned by their husbands, lived with daughters or sisters, scraped together a living, occasionally or routinely by serving wagoneers passing through or by engaging in prostitution.

Largely discarded and ridiculed by more elite whites, poor white women, unprotected and unsupported, were less constrained by racial decorum and less reticent about maneuvering across the color line. Black-on-white rape trials generated a great deal of circumstantial evidence suggesting a significant measure of interracial interaction on numerous fronts. In practice, the worlds of poor whites and blacks, both slave and free, converged in economic, social, and sexual arenas. Racial boundaries were crossed in numerous ways, as when the women bartered food for a pair of sewn trousers, or performed farm chores side by side, providing ample opportunity for companionship, romance, or animus. The marginal position of poor white women in antebellum southern society, in one sense, secured them a level of privacy, and so their illicit activities were often ignored though not necessarily condoned. That is, until they did something that could be ignored no longer. Accusations of black rape attracted the attention and response of the entire community, and thus shifted these marginalized women to center stage, a place unfamiliar to most of this station. Local notables, court officers, and elites, wary of the power of any woman "crying rape," but especially a poor white woman, fell back on the traditionally gendered evidentiary assumptions and practices of the law, insisting that rape charges be corroborated with additional evidence that sometimes included defamatory testimony against the accuser herself. So while statutes seemed to promise the death sentence or castration for convicted black rapists, the reputation and social status of the accuser held considerable weight in the adjudication process and often in the amelioration of the sentence of a convicted black rapist.

While this book is not legal history per se, it does rely upon many legal sources. It also sheds light on the relationship between the law and the people and on how the law functioned in everyday life in a southern community. Members of an antebellum southern community in the throes of a black rape trial struggled to make sense of the law as they understood it. The language in black rape statutes was unequivocally harsh, with no room to accommodate extenuating circumstances. In virtually every slaveholding state, a black man convicted of rape or attempted rape of a white female faced the death sentence or castration.[10] Yet community members found myriad ways to inject local custom into the legal process, which had the effect of softening the harsh rape laws. This study mirrors the recent findings of Ariela Gross's work on civil litigation involving slaves, in which she found that "social practices overwhelmed formal legal rules." In other words, ordinary folks helped shape "the law" and often successfully maneuvered around the strict penalties that it prescribed for black rape. Whether testifying about the rumored promiscuity of the accuser, or affixing their signatures to a petition requesting a convicted slave-rapist's pardon, white community members insisted on having their say in the legal arena. This book, then, is a study of law as it was experienced by ordinary inhabitants of southern towns and neighborhoods, demonstrating, in the words of Gross, that law is not created merely "by judges and legislators, but by the litigants, witnesses, and jurors in the courtroom."[11] One of the most salient ways, for example, in which community members sought to insert local mores into black rape trials was to scrutinize the reputations of poor white women who charged black men with rape, in the process revealing to us the existence of pervasive misogyny and class prejudice. This pattern of behavior—of locals soft-pedaling the "crime" of black "rape" (or sex with white women) because of the status of the white accuser—continued until well after the end of Civil War, though admittedly with some adjustments.

A study of rape and race in the nineteenth-century South thus highlights the limitations of statutory law as an analytical tool. If all we looked at were statutes and the letters of elite men, the South would crystallize as a dichotomy of race and status, a world of black and white, of free and unfree. Laws defined "white" according to some incontestable, objective mathematical formula. Sexual relations and marriage across racial boundaries were forbidden. Privileged men and women of the plantation South of course knew that despite these proscriptions, interracial sex abounded, especially between slaveholding men and slave women.[12] Yet it was in their interest to deny its existence or at least ignore it. Two worlds were separated by little or no geographical space, but segregated completely and wholly by social space. It was, in the words of one eminent historian, a case of "white over black."[13]

For much of the twentieth century, southern historians relied heavily on this racially dichotomous paradigm, framed by statutory law, in their analysis of the region's history. Southern historians have long used race as their starting point, a robust tradition that has tended to mute the inherent contradictions and collapse the divisions of antebellum white southern society. A recent spate of historical works in southern history, however, has argued convincingly that rigid racial categories, so neatly laid out in law, were in fact porous, anemic, and mutable in everyday life. Recent scholars have been far less convinced than their predecessors of the purported separation between the races. Collectively, their works have laid bare disparity and contradiction, revealing a disconnect between the prescribed and the lived, between the rhetoric and reality. Laws, however unequivocal, however authoritatively written, simply did not prevent interracial sex. The boundaries erected by "law" to keep the races apart did not in fact do so. The works of Martha Hodes, Victoria Bynum, Thomas Buckley, Joshua Rothman, and Laura Edwards, though they tackle slightly different subjects, render a history of the South that embraces complexity and nuance and that goes beyond "lazy characterizations in the singular" of the sort criticized by Nell Irvin Painter.[14]

This work follows in that vein. It joins the recent trend of works in southern history that do not see race as monocausal. Race as the only or even primary cause of behavior has lost its potency and appeal. A study of rape and race over the nineteenth century shows that the response of white communities to charges of black rape is not easily catalogued or understood. After a black man was charged with rape, whites did not automatically support the white accuser. In fact, southern whites often targeted one another in the fallout of a black rape trial. Peculiar cross-racial alliances such as the ones played out in these rape cases underscore the complex web of contested loyalties confronting antebellum southerners, loyalties that too often have gone underappreciated in historical studies of the South. Race mattered a great deal, but it was only one of a number of factors that shaped the responses of community members to a charge of black rape. This book finds that among these factors class was central in shaping the outcome of black rape trials. Admittedly, race and class at times were inextricably entwined, but sometimes class trumped race in determining the nature and degree of community response to black rape.

The centrality of class in shaping a white community's response to a charge of black rape continued even after the end of slavery. Southern historians have long treated the Civil War and Reconstruction as the fault line of southern history. While the tendency to neatly compartmentalize, using Civil War and Reconstruction as the dividing line, is appealing and understandable, the result of doing so has been to cast most historical studies of southern subjects as either antebellum or postbellum. This periodization shortchanges us in some ways because it does not fully allow us to track problems and subjects across the chasm of Civil War and Reconstruction.[15] Pulling back and getting a broader picture better informs the historian who struggles to make sense of his or her subject in the larger context. With this in mind, I show that black-on-white rape cases, studied over time in the South, reveal much about the structure and dynamics of southern society and reflect the changes that rippled (or in some cases, crashed) through the region. One can see, for example, that the creation of the myth of the black rapist is a relatively recent phenomenon, one simultaneous with the rise of white supremacy and black disfranchisement, and with the transformation of ideas about sexuality, specifically women's sexuality.[16]

Shifting the origins of white rape fears to the end of the nineteenth century forces a dramatic reassessment of some of the weighty notions about the history of the South, most particularly about the extent of change in the aftermath of emancipation. If one believes that white anxiety about black rape prevailed in much of the nineteenth-century South, then the subsequent racial polarization and white supremacy of the postwar period seems inevitable. On the other hand, if it can be established that fears of black rape exercised little sway throughout much of the nineteenth-century South, one becomes free to see points of contingency and greater fluidity in the state of race relations in the South. This more nuanced periodization of the rape myth allows us to understand the horrific state of white supremacy that emerged as not necessarily preordained. Nor was it universally accepted and practiced by all white southerners. Postbellum rape cases yield fascinating accounts of late-nineteenth-century white toleration for miscegenation, and of whites who continued to support accused black rapists, all the while denigrating the white accuser. The willingness of some whites in the antebellum South to extend procedural fairness to accused black rapists, and in some cases to work for their exoneration or pardon, did not abruptly end with emancipation. In part, this was because many of the ideological strains about race, gender, and class making up the worldview of the white South were so deeply rooted that it would take some time to displace them and establish new ones. Fundamentally, most white southerners believed that slaves were innately docile. On the rare occasion when a slave was charged with raping a white woman, they struggled to make sense of the charge. He must have been seduced. He must have been drunk. He must not have any sense. These racialized constructions did not precipitously and entirely end with the coming of Civil War and emancipation. Reconstruction black-on-white rape cases show continued white apprehension about newly freed slaves who tried to make it on their own without the paternalistic guidance of ex-masters. Black men, it was believed by many, were ill equipped to maneuver among disreputable whites who would surely take advantage of their naïveté and worldly ignorance. Many accusations of black rape by white women were viewed in this light. In freedom, many black men cultivated patronage relationships with respected white men, some of whom came to view freed blacks as being in need of their continued guidance and protection. Paternalistic bonds linking planter class elites to black laborers were not entirely severed with war's end.

Nor were ideas about the depravity of poor white women immediately dislodged. White elites continued to display considerable contempt for wily women who would entrap unwitting black men in their web, thus revealing their own misogynistic identification with the plight of the accused black rapist throughout much of the postbellum era.

A survey of black-on-white rape over the nineteenth century thus makes a compelling albeit qualified case for "continuity" between the antebellum and postbellum periods in the South. The line from slavery's demise to the white supremacist South was not a straight one. Rather, as Jane Dailey spells out in her recent work *Before Jim Crow*, "the path from emancipation to Jim Crow was rockier than is sometimes realized, with many detours and switchbacks along the way."[17]

The rape cases marshaled here illuminate a second central historiographical debate in southern history: that over southern distinctiveness, which has long occupied historians of the South. As suggested earlier, rape has been employed as an important historical marker in southern history. The prevalence of white fears of black sexuality, rabid and universal, has been held up to bolster arguments for regional distinctiveness. The rape myth has long been touted as a distinguishing feature of the American South. The evidence put forth here, however, questions whether the rape myth was a significant characteristic of much of the nineteenth-century South. And with this pillar of southern distinctiveness dismantled, does the case for a peculiar South remain as compelling as some have suggested? Witness the reaction of "respectable" southern community members to allegations of black rape. The community's generally callous indifference to the women who said that black men had raped them parallels the gender wars fought in nineteenth-century northern cities in the arena of sexual conflict. Among the laboring classes of New York City, for example, antagonism between the sexes pervaded social and family relations. Men's sexual abuse or exploitation of women was widely regarded as a male prerogative. Misogynistic notions of women as parasitical, corrupt, and frivolous validated the rough treatment of nonconsenting women whom men sought as sexual partners. To a certain degree, violence or coercion in the pursuit of sexual relations was deemed acceptable.[18] After all, men's need to assert sexual dominance over women was seen largely as natural.[19] Viewed in this light, gender and class relations do not seem to vary all that much between North and South. In both regions, studies of rape and sexual assault reveal pervasive misogyny and a striking lack of sensitivity for victims of sexual crimes. Men of means in the South and the North appear to have shared a disdain for middling and poorer women that manifested itself in a fundamental indifference to females who suffered sexual assault. For most men, the sexual purity of women (other than their own wives and daughters) was simply unimportant and inconsequential. Only with national Progressive reforms spearheaded primarily by women, which focused on girls' and women's sexuality and men's violation of it, did much of the nation begin to find violence or forceful coercion in the pursuit of sexual relations distasteful or unacceptable. It was not until the turn of the century, when female moral reform made significant strides on rape law reform, that southern white men begin to consider rape a distinctive wrong. And here is where the case for southern distinctiveness gathers steam—the raised consciousness about rape occurred at the same time that popular literature was churning out stereotypes about the "black-beast-rapist."

Not all historians would agree that anxiety about black rape emerged so late in the South's history. There is a vigorous and resilient tradition in southern history suggesting that whites worried, to a greater or lesser degree, about black sexual aggression since even before the first European settlers arrived in the seventeenth century. Winthrop Jordan, in his seminal work *White over Black*, traced stereotypes about black sexuality to early English contact with Africans.[20] Jordan's study marked the first historical treatment of the southern "rape complex," the term used to describe a mass psychosis, the fear that black men were predisposed to raping white women. White women were central in his analysis. Englishmen, he argued, focused undue attention on the role of white women, an outgrowth of their efforts to populate and colonize New World settlements. Jordan argued that "white women were, quite literally, the repositories of white civilization. White men tended to place them protectively upon a pedestal and then run off to gratify their passions elsewhere."[21] Jordan further theorized that guilt-ridden white men, who sexually exploited slave women and who were jealous of presumed black male potency, in turn projected their own sexual desires onto slave men, in the process creating an irrational fear of black male sexuality. "It is not we, but others, who are guilty. It is not we who lust, but they."[22] The white image of black males as sexual predators was further enhanced, Jordan argued, by the association of the black male with superhuman potency, a perception that had its origins in initial English contacts with Africans. The coincidental and simultaneous discovery of the African and the ape sparked the imaginations of curious Europeans. Englishmen grafted their early impressions of Africans to the particulars of slavery. Partial nudity, resulting from ill-fitting clothing, gossip about the size of genitalia, and divergent forms of sexuality between white southerners and their African slaves further fueled white beliefs about black licentiousness.[23]

Jordan's conjectures on the ties between race and sex have had an enormous influence on studies in southern and African American history. Later historians took their Freudian cues from *White over Black* and expanded upon projection as the cornerstone of the rape myth, building upon Jordan's contention that white views about black male sexual potency existed during slave times.[24] Peter Wood, for one, saw broad societal implications of the rape fears in colonial South Carolina when he reasoned that "the increasing white obsession with physical violation . . . must be taken as an integral part of the white minority's struggle for social control. . . . Slaves were becoming a more numerous and distinctive group, and their very real efforts toward social and economic self-assertion prompted the anxious white minority to fantasies of ravishment."[25] More recently, and attesting to the staying power of Jordan's theories on antebellum white perceptions about black male sexuality, Peter Bardaglio, relying largely on the law, has claimed that antebellum white southerners, "both inside and outside the legal system, widely shared the belief that black men were obsessed with the desire to rape white women."[26] The rape of white females by black men in the antebellum South, he writes, provoked "profound rage."[27]

In recent years, historians have begun to chip away at the notion that fears of black rape were pervasive during slavery. Most pointedly, Martha Hodes's important work on sexual relations between white women and black men in the South demonstrates that putative legal and customary racial boundaries proved inadequate in keeping blacks and whites from engaging in consensual sexual relations, in the process revealing a degree of white "toleration" for such relationships or behavior. The willingness of some white southerners at certain times and in certain places to tolerate sex between white women and black men suggests that not all white southerners were obsessed with rape fears. Had they been, greater violence and a harder line on miscegenation surely would have been the result. Challenging the historiographical tradition of white intolerance for black-white sexual relations, her work leads Hodes to conclude that "white southerners could react in a way that complicates modern assumptions," observing, for example, myriad circumstances in which black men and white women shared carnal intimacy—marriage, adultery, and premarital sex. Rather than find communities repulsed and appalled, Hodes documents a number of instances where white citizens looked the other way when confronted with evidence of illicit cross-racial sexual relations.[28]

Hodes and others in her wake have been able to upend many of the conclusions about race and sex in the South that have been taken at face value for decades, in no small measure because historians have now begun to interrogate different kinds of sources, which has permitted us to ask a different set of questions. Throughout this study I privilege the sources and methodology of the social historian. It is my position that cultural sources have been given undue consideration in previous studies of rape and race. Most of what we know, or think we know, about rape and race in the South, comes to us by way of rhetoric or the written law. And I have given those sources their due consideration in this work. Studies that focus on the ideological and the prescribed (or proscribed) are important in their own right, but they cannot claim to represent accurately everyday living. I am more interested in learning how neighbors reacted when hearing that a slave was accused of sexually assaulting a white child. How did they respond? How unified were those responses along race lines? Along class lines? What factors shaped their responses? Gossip? Personal grudges? Racism? Sexism? Class prejudices? Friendships? Paternalism? Compassion? Only a close reading of local records and the testimony of community members can reveal the many competing and conflicting individual interests and feelings, as played out in black-on-white rape trials.

I focus exclusively on rape trials, which would have required a woman to swear out a formal complaint against a black man, thus engaging the legal apparatus. Obviously this tack excludes instances of coerced sex or rape that went unreported or were reported and dismissed for lack of evidence or for administrative or technical reasons. In all, over 250 cases of sexual assault by black males on white women or girls came before the courts in the twelve southern states from 1800 through 1865, as located in archival records or secondary sources.[29] Although this book focuses on Virginia and North Carolina, admittedly two of the northernmost slaveholding states, secondary sources as well as published primary sources such as appellate decisions reveal similar patterns throughout the slave South.[30] In Virginia alone there are over 150 cases from 1800 through 1865 of African American men, free and slave, condemned to die for allegedly sexually assaulting white women or children.[31] Nearly half of these condemned black rapists escaped their sentences of execution, suggesting, I argue, that antebellum white southerners felt less compelled than postbellum white southerners to exact death from a black man accused of sexually violating a white female. The argument here is that the rape trials of dozens of black southern males demonstrate that antebellum white southerners were not nearly as consumed by fears of black men raping white women as their postwar descendants were. As Eugene Genovese has written, the "titillating and violence-provoking theory of the superpotency of that black superpenis, while whispered about for centuries, did not become an obsession in the South until after emancipation."[32]

The overarching organization of this book is largely chronological, though each chapter within the chronological framework is topical. The book begins with an examination of cases where white women officially accused a slave of rape or attempted rape in Old South communities. It traces the varied responses among whites to cases of slave rape and explores the factors that shaped the behavior of whites and forged their positions. Central to this chapter is the analysis of class. White neighborhoods and communities often divided sharply in response to accusations of slave rape, and usually the divisions fell along class lines. Moreover, it was poor to middling women, not female members of the slaveholding class, who brought forth charges of slave rape, and I examine the reasons why. In addition, class merged with gender in fashioning ideas about poor women's sexual nature. This ideology, signaling the impurity and dishonesty of poor women, proved a critical component in the deliberations of slave rape trials and figured prominently in shaping the outcomes of these cases. Distrust of women in many instances weighed more heavily as a concern and overcame any anxiety about the sexual threat of black men.

These same patterns are repeated in chapter 2, which focuses on white female children who charged black men or boys with sexual assault. Contrary to much of the prescriptive literature of the era, not all girls were romantically viewed as innocent, and hence claims of rape, especially those made by girls living in poor families, were interrogated and the girls' histories (and those of their families) scrutinized. Girl accusers faced an obstacle that adult females who charged rape did not, namely that their youthfulness left many court observers especially dubious about their testimony. Locals and court officials carefully weighed the youthful status of the accuser in seeing that black men were not wrongly accused. Nonetheless, when a community was persuaded that a black man was in fact guilty of raping a young girl, the punishment was usually swifter and more severe than when a black man was accused of raping a white woman.

Chapters 3 and 4, while still focusing on rape and race, shift the loci of attention to the more familiar and well-trodden political and elite sources, to the framers of statutory and appellate law, the legislatures and appellate courts. Traditionally historians who have written about rape and race have looked to the written law as codified by the lawmakers and justices to fashion generalizations about how whites regarded black male sexuality, particularly the threat that it posed for white women. Chapter 3 traces the history of black rape statutes and grounds the laws in their historical context. Material and practical considerations, not purely ideological ones, guided lawmakers in designing laws to punish black men convicted of sexually assaulting white females. Those historians who have found evidence of widespread white anxiety about black rape in these statutes, I find, fail to adequately consider a number of factors that informed legislators in their lawmaking process, not least financial considerations related to compensation expenses for executed slaves. Moreover, while the language of black rape statutes was indeed draconian, the legal system was pliable enough to allow government officials to avoid implementing the harshest punishments. Specifically, state executives were given the power to review black rape cases and many exercised this prerogative liberally, again bypassing the harsh penalties prescribed by law. Likewise, in Chapter 4 we observe that elite jurists in southern states heard appeals from condemned black rapists and in many cases overturned their convictions, signifying yet another way in which officials could bypass the mandated execution for black men convicted of raping white women. Appellate judges, in their reasoning, revealed judicial paternalism writ large and tremendous gendered identification with the black men accused of rape, while simultaneously subscribing to highly misogynistic stereotypes about the depravity and dishonesty of poor white women. Fashioning themselves as patriarchal protectors of last resort, state appeals judges seemed intent on policing any local prejudices and correcting juridical missteps on the local level that could have resulted in a miscarriage of justice for an African American accused of a rape-related crime.

Accusations of slave rape, and the attempts by some in the community to obtain exoneration or reprieve for those charged or convicted, reveal much about the interactions of race, class, and gender in southern communities. Cases that made their way through the legal process also reveal the various ways in which court and state officials could intercede on behalf of slaves. In both cases, the value of a slave as property goes far in explaining the motivations of white southerners. But what happened in instances where the bonded status no longer protected a black man confronted with a capital crime like rape? Chapter 5 explores the treatment of free men of color to discern how far financial self-interest goes in explaining the white response to black-on-white rape. Surprisingly, free black men accused of raping white females also received a fair share of support from certain whites. Here we see that while free black men lacked financial value as investment property, they did perform valuable services and work for local white patrons, who at times, out of loyalty to their lesser charges, or because the services of those free blacks were deemed necessary, petitioned the courts and governors in behalf of accused rapists who were free black men. Because the status of these alleged black rapists is free, I move into a brief discussion of white-on-white rapists so that I can better gauge the experiences of their African American counterparts.

Chapters 6 through 8 are crafted with the broader aim of determining the extent to which the Civil War and Reconstruction fundamentally altered white perceptions about race, sex, and class. A strong case for continuity through the chasm of war and its wake can be extrapolated from the fallout of black rape cases from this era. White southerners, even in the anxious and uncertain setting of war, manifested no great concern that their slaves posed a sexual threat to women left alone by men fighting the war. Two longstanding antebellum trends persisted throughout most of the war: the continued identification of poor, marginal women with promiscuity and duplicity, and class divisiveness that percolated to the surface in some wartime slave rape trials. Still, an important departure from antebellum slave rape cases surfaced near war's end. Leniency and reprieve suddenly disappeared from the final cases of slave rape that came before the Virginia courts. Portending important changes that would crystallize in the Reconstruction years with the emancipation of slaves, developments in the years immediately following the war made clear that the demise of slavery, and the diminished financial worth of blacks in southern society, would affect how white southerners would come to view rape and race.

Not willing to take the continuity argument too far, I note two salient changes regarding rape and race that appeared after the war, and these are the subject of Chapter 7. Southern lawmakers were forced to redefine rape and make it race neutral. Important consequences resulted. For one, women of color could now bring official charges of rape. African American women and girls latched on to this right, and used it to combat men, ironically mostly men of their own race, who coerced sex from them. The sudden empowerment of African American women proved most disconcerting to men, both black and white, but especially to white men who could, for the first time, be prosecuted for sexually assaulting women of color. Revised rape laws also allowed black men to escape execution for the attempted rape of white females. The second area of considerable change in the legal landscape of rape after the Civil War was the way southern whites came to view "the law." Reconstruction politics, including the contest over control of local courts and the administration of criminal justice, played no small role in cultivating doubts in whites about the efficacy and equity of dealing with black rapists through properly established legal channels. Once content to let local courts try black criminals, including rapists, southern whites edged toward a rationalization of extralegal violence, which came to be invoked regularly by century's end. This development is critical in understanding the spasm of lawlessness and lynching that gripped parts of the region in the last two decades of the century. It is here where we observe one of the most important changes over time: the relationship of law to southern society was forever altered, and the newly recast rape laws were at the center.

In examining the final decades of the nineteenth century, I struggle to situate the continued cases of measured leniency and toleration for interracial sex, specifically accusations of black-on-white rape, alongside the more familiar terrain of lynch mobs, sensational trials, and legal executions and try to make sense of these purported exceptions. The turn-of-the-century white South was far less tolerant of perceived acts of sexual transgressions by black men than at any previous time in the region's history. It becomes clear that many southern whites had abandoned earlier constructed ideas on racial difference, namely that of blacks as complacent and innocuous, and were all too willing to embrace the notion of the black man as dangerous. Whereas in the antebellum South whites sought explanations for anomalous behavior such as rape, by century's end stories of menacing black men no longer seemed anomalous. North Carolina penitentiary records stingily reveal some shards of evidence about the changing ideas toward rape and race at the dawn of the twentieth century, among them the universalization of the sexual threat among all black men. It is at this juncture where the notion of black docility, so embedded in white minds from slave days, seems to have been displaced by the belief that virtually all black men, even well-educated, middle-class, professional black men, posed a sexual threat.

Leniency no longer characterized white responses to allegations of black sexual assault at the beginning of the twentieth century. Nonetheless, isolated cases of whites responding to black rape of white females with measured indifference are still observable. The long-standing custom of doubting the integrity of a poor, white woman whose behavior fell outside the boundaries of respectability proved so resilient that at times it continued to be invoked at the height of white supremacy in cases where black men stood accused of sexually violating white women.

I end the book with an appendix, an expanded essay on the historiography of the rape myth. The essay is designed so that it can stand alone, without the preceding foundation and without the distraction of my own evidence and arguments. Therefore, some of the passages may be redundant and may recapture some of the points I make here and throughout the text. But my aim is to make the convoluted story of rape and race in the South, as imagined and recounted by historians, authors, and politicians, more accessible and comprehensible. Indeed, that is the very objective that underpins this project: to depoliticize, demystify, and deconstruct the rhetoric of black rape in order to better understand how sexuality, race, and class played out and evolved over the long nineteenth century, in the process suggesting new ways of looking at southern history.

NOT SO HEINOUS AS AT
FIRST MIGHT BE SUPPOSED
Slave Rape, Gender, and Class
in Old South Communities

1

n early June 1848, three Virginia slaves went on trial in Gloucester County for the rape of a white woman, Caty Smith. Piecing together information put forth by various prosecution witnesses, including Caty Smith herself, we learn that on a Saturday night in March, two slaves owned by Edward Hale, Tom and Kit, along with a third slave, Edmund, property of Peter W. B. Hughes, passed some time socializing at Hayes's Store with at least one other slave. No doubt the three slaves were exercising what little freedom their bonded status allowed them at the end of a long week of toil for their masters. Others present at the store claimed to have overheard Kit bragging about plans of the three for a night of carousing that included looking "for girls." Advised that there were no black girls "down there," an undaunted, impish Kit replied that "there was Caty Smith and old Aunt Edy and they were going to give old Caty Smith something that night."[1]

According to testimony, the three slaves broke down the door to Smith's home about nine o'clock, when Smith was already in bed for the night. Although Smith's husband was not home at the time, "Old Aunt Edy," "an old negro woman," was there with her. The intruders appear to have tried to disguise their identities by claiming to have been from New York. But Smith recognized her intruders, whom she claimed to have known since they were "knee high." According to Smith, Edmund made known his purpose, and though she protested that "there was nothing for them," he took her in his arms, threw her on her bed and instructed Tom to pull her bedclothes over her head and to restrain her arms. In Smith's words, Edmund then ravished her. After he had finished, Tom got into bed with Smith while Kit positioned himself to hold Smith's arms. Although her own nightclothes, which had been pulled over her head, greatly muffled her screams, Smith managed to cry out loudly enough to alert two male passers-by, Joseph Tilledge and William

Teagh, who responded to her cry for help. When the two men opened the door, the intruders escaped, despite the best efforts of the would-be rescuers.[2]

Edmund proved the only one of the three slaves whom either of the two men could identify with certainty. In fact, much of the defense's questioning at trial focused on the difficulty that the eyewitnesses had in identifying the defendants. Old Aunt Edy, with only one good eye, was convinced of Edmund's identity, but unsure about the other two. Unsure, that is, until she later heard what the three had purportedly said at Hayes's Store, after which she became certain of their identities.[3]

Perhaps because of this doubt, after hearing the evidence and deliberating the jury exonerated Kit. Edmund and Tom were not so fortunate. The jury found them guilty and sentenced them to hang. But their story does not end there: 182 empathetic residents of Gloucester County petitioned the governor of Virginia for clemency on behalf of Edmund, citing mitigating circumstances. First was the "notoriously bad character" of Caty Smith. It was, they wrote, "rather from the temptations offered by . . . Caty Smith than from wickedness of purpose that the unfortunate boy formed a connection with Caty Smith which has resulted so tragically for him."[4]

Second, the petitioners contended that a death sentence in this case would not necessarily deter future acts of slave rape. Edmund's hanging, his supporters predicted, would not "have the effect intended by the terrible exercise of that power." Finally, the petitioners lauded Edmund's character, and conduct that heretofore had been good. Edmund's youth (his age is never stated in the records) and his "ignorance of the awful consequences of the act for which he now awaits his final doom" also were presented as mitigating factors. Importantly, the petitioners never pronounced the slave, in their words the "unfortunate boy," innocent of the alleged offense. Nor is there even a hint of remorse conveyed by the convicted slave felon. Rather, the petition advises that the offense for which Edmund was convicted was "not so heinous as at first might be supposed." Instead of death, the white Virginians pleaded with their governor to commute Edmund's sentence to transportation out of the state.[5]

In the end, not one of the three black men, all slaves, who stood accused of either sexually assaulting a white woman or aiding another in the act, died at the hands of an executioner, or a mob for that matter.[6] That white Virginians seized a pen instead of rope and fagot to deal with accused slave rapists seems irreconcilable with our image, largely the product of the postbellum period, of lawless, unrestrained lynch mobs bent on vigilante "justice" and retribution. Not only did the three men receive a trial, presumably attendant with certain procedural rights, but at least one became the object of many white citizens' sympathies and concern.[7]

The collective white fear and anxiety about black sexual assault that loomed large in postbellum southern society is conspicuously absent in the rape case of Edmund, Kit, and Tom. In fact, the vast majority of antebellum cases in which white females officially charged slaves with rape or attempted rape proceeded rather calmly through proper legal channels. Only rarely did vigilantes attempt to supplant the authority of local courts and officials. Furthermore, although convicted black rapists faced execution for their crimes, many took advantage of procedural rights accorded them and appealed their convictions.[8] Once judicial avenues of appeal were exhausted, slaves facing the death penalty—or, probably more accurately, whites acting on their behalf—could marshal white community support to solicit the governor for executive pardon or commutation of the sentence to transportation out of the state, which state executives regularly granted.[9] That slaves, convicted of raping or attempting to rape white women or girls, stood a reasonable chance of escaping capital punishment belies claims that the rape myth exercised considerable sway in antebellum southern society. Simply put, the image of the menacing black rapist did not become the obsession of the southern white mind until sometime after emancipation.[10]

Although rape laws unequivocally spelled out harsh penalties for black men who sexually assaulted white females, some white female accusers had an easier time than others in convincing juries of the truthfulness of their claims and seeing their alleged rapists punished to the fullest extent of the law.[11] Poorer females were more likely than wealthier females to face a hostile courtroom and dubious white community. Females without male protectors appear to have been treated more shabbily than those with fathers, husbands, or other male kin acting on their behalf. And women who deviated from accepted sexual codes of behavior could find themselves as much on trial as their alleged attackers.

White witnesses often broke ranks (if ever any existed) with a dubious white accuser and testified for the alleged rapist or questioned the integrity of the white female accuser, especially if her past actions smacked of libidinous indiscretion. In the case of Edmund, Kit, and Tom, their white intercessors alluded to Caty Smith's "notoriously bad character," suggesting that the sexual infractions committed by at least one of the accused had been encouraged by "temptations offered by . . . Caty Smith" herself. Sarah Sands of Henry County,

Virginia, like Smith, found that her whiteness failed to shield her from probing and embarrassing questions about her most intimate conduct. Sands claimed she had been raped by a slave named Jerry, owned by Edward Osborne. Jerry was tried in the local court in 1807, found guilty, and sentenced to be hanged. A petition to the governor by Jerry's legal counsel, Peachy R. Gilmer, purported to reflect the sentiments of others who attended the trial, and argued for a reduction in sentence from execution to transportation.[12] Gilmer based his request on Sands's "very infamous character," a reputation she no doubt earned living as another man's concubine. And if questionable character were not enough to erode Sands's credibility, the petition also noted her size. Gilmer portrayed Sands as "large and strong enough to have made considerable resistance if she had been so disposed, yet there was by her own confession no mark of violence upon any part of her."[13] Nineteenth-century legal standards required unequivocal proof of physical resistance by women accusing men of rape.[14] Without such evidence, jurists would likely doubt claims of rape, even in cases where the accuser was white and the accused black.

Undoubtedly Jerry's counsel presented this same evidence at trial but the jury, for whatever reasons, rendered a guilty verdict. In this case, testimony about the deviant sexual behavior of the accuser appears not to have convinced the jury that Jerry should get off scot-free. Guilty verdict notwithstanding, some white members of the community did not feel the taking of a rapist's life, even a slave's, commensurate with the offense, given what they clearly believed to be extenuating circumstances. Consequently, a number of them took action and successfully presented their case to the governor, who granted Jerry a reprieve. Jerry, like Edmund, had stood accused and been convicted of raping a white woman in the antebellum South. And though the law prescribed the noose, both escaped it.[15]

White women who flouted prevailing sexual mores, especially those who crossed racial boundaries willingly to have sex with black men, often faced derision by the white community and courts. White southerners could turn viciously on white female accusers who were believed to have broached racial sexual boundaries. A group of Virginians, for instance, made an appeal in 1803 on behalf of Carter, a slave found guilty of raping a poor white woman, Catherine Brinal, who, like Sarah Sands, had a reputation for cavorting with African American men. Illicit sex with white men was cause enough for social ostracism, but when a white woman crossed the color line, the transgression was much more egregious.[16]

The petitioners, including some jury members, conceded that Carter had committed the rape upon Brinal, a fact that had compelled the jury to find him guilty. Yet facts in evidence warranted a reduced sentence. For one, it appeared that Catherine Brinal was "a woman of the worst fame, that her character was that of the most abandoned in as much as she (being a white woman) has three mulatto children," all, by her own admission, fathered by different negro men.[17]

Further mitigating Carter's actions, according to the petition, was that Brinal had "no visible means of support." In short, she was a poor, single, unmarried mother. The petitioners further suggested that Brinal had permitted Carter to have "peaceable intercourse with her, before the time of his forcing her."[18] If true, and of course there is no way to know for sure, it is entirely possible that Brinal had been bartering or selling sex with a slave to support her family, an act that would have surely earned her the scorn of the community.[19] And in the eyes of the community, once Brinal consented to "peaceable" sexual relations with Carter, she effectively forfeited her right to deny him sex at any future time. Brinal, and white women like her, who transgressed prevailing sexual conventions about race and sex paid a heavy price—their right to reject prospective sexual advances, even those of a slave. Carter, having cheated the executioner, was transported out of the state.[20]

The pattern in many of the black-on-white rape cases is that a jury found the accused slave guilty of rape but followed up with a recommendation for leniency. It should not be surprising that all-white juries in antebellum slave rape trials felt obliged to render guilty verdicts in most cases of slave rape brought before them. Harsh rape statutes for slaves left little to no room for juries to exercise leniency.[21] Convinced of mitigating circumstances, such as a dubious sexual history on the part of the accuser, many juries nonetheless sought to circumvent the letter of the law by advising governors to issue pardons. This was the case in the trial of Winky and Dennis, two slaves in Virginia convicted in 1800 of raping Ann Bacchus, a widow of "infamous" character. Jurymen, as well as other community members, showered the governor of Virginia with requests for pardons. According to several of the petitions, Ann Bacchus had been "for more than thirty years a woman of abandoned character and infamous practices." The defense had presented similar evidence at trial, specifically that Bacchus had been in the habit of "intimate intercourse with Negroes." The jury manifested its conflicted deliberations by in effect handing down a guilty verdict with extenuating circumstances. The jurymen apparently believed that the two slaves had had sex with Ann Bacchus, but they held her partially culpable. In other words, the slaves' sexual affront, if there had been any, was entirely understandable in light of Bacchus's shady past. The jury's compromise was to issue a guilty decision while requesting pardons for the two, which were granted.[22]

Similar issues occupied court officials, including magistrates and the prosecuting attorney, in Hanover County, Virginia, in 1808 after the conviction of Peter, a slave, for the attempted rape of Patsey Hooker. Although the court sentenced Peter to be castrated, fifty-seven petitioners presented the governor with a formal request to waive the prescribed punishment.[23] One letter accused Hooker of being a "common strumpet." Another described her as a "common prostitute" who had given birth to several "bastard children." Hooker, unable to deny having had sex outside marriage, did nonetheless deny having been intimate with black men.[24]

A slave in Halifax County was convicted of a violent sexual attack in 1860 on a white woman named Mary Jane Vaughn but was pardoned by the governor and eventually transported out of Virginia.[25] The mitigation of the death sentence was due at least in part to the defense attorney's attack of Vaughn, the accuser. Under cross-examination Elisha Barksdale, George's legal counsel, demanded to know how many times she had been to the home of Mary Dewes, George's owner, who lived about two miles from Vaughn. Defense counsel also sarcastically wondered out loud how Vaughn could have been so sure of details, such as the design of her attacker's pants, at nighttime, without the aid of light: "Please explain how it is that you had the leisure to examine very small stripes in his britches." Though Barksdale adeptly avoided any direct question that touched on inappropriate sexual behavior by Vaughn, he seemed to be trying to capitalize on her family's illicit past. Sally Vaughn, the accuser's sister, had an eleven-year-old daughter and no husband. The child, it would seem, had been born outside marriage, thus tainting the entire family and casting doubt on Mary Jane's claim to having been raped.[26]

Although not all rape convictions of African Americans led to reprieves or pardons, the defense could be counted on to raise questions about the character of a white female accuser. In the rape case in 1829 of Lewis, another Virginia slave, two witnesses impugned the reputations of the accuser, Amy (Amey) Baker, forty-five, and her housemate, alleging debauchery and sexual impropriety.[27] Community opinion was split, however, as five other witnesses took the stand to defend the reputations of the two women.

As Baker and her live-in companion, "old Mrs. [Drucilla] Kirkland," recounted, in the hours before daybreak on May 23, Lewis came to Baker's house demanding to be let in. After the women refused him entry, he broke down the door. They claimed that Lewis brutally raped Amy Baker four times over a two-hour period while Mrs. Kirkland hid under the bed. Soon thereafter the accused dozed off, and the two women fled to the home of a neighbor, Burwell Coleman, whose son, Richard Coleman, returned with them to their house.

Coleman groped blindly in the dark and found the intruder still lying on the bed only partially clad. After a brief struggle Coleman subdued Lewis and demanded to know what had driven him to such unthinkable behavior. Lewis confessed that he did not know but reckoned he had been drunk.[28]

Court-appointed defense counsel faced an uphill battle, since the accused had been apprehended partially naked at the scene of the crime. Lewis's attorney, Alexander G. Knox, appears to have crafted and executed a three-pronged defense strategy. First, he challenged the women's ability to identify the accused by pointing out that the assault had taken place entirely in the dark. Upon cross-examination Baker flip-flopped a bit, at first claiming that there had been sufficient moonlight to identify the rapist but then contradicting herself somewhat by admitting that as dawn broke the light had not carried to him. Despite the darkness, however, upon seeing Lewis the next day she was confident he had been her assailant.[29]

The presence of an eyewitness other than the accuser was rare in a rape case, since most rapists preyed on unaccompanied females in desolate or distant locations, out of earshot of bystanders. The testimony of Mrs. Kirkland must therefore have been considered crucial to the prosecution's case,[30] and discrediting it was the second prong in Knox's strategy. At first glance Mrs. Kirkland would seem to have been an unlikely eyewitness to the crime, since by her own admission she spent the entire ordeal hiding beneath a bed. She claimed, however, that at some point she emerged from her hiding place and "at the risque of her life" made up a light by which she was able to identify the assailant, who was on top of Amy Baker. Knox, evidently skeptical of this testimony (Baker made no mention of Kirkland's putting on a light), then took another tack with Kirkland, springing a trap of sorts. He inquired about her marital and maternal status, knowing full well that she was neither married nor had children. By this ploy Knox appears to have insinuated Kirkland's sexual ignorance and established the unreliability of her testimony that sexual intercourse had taken place in her presence. This deft defense maneuvering placed Kirkland in an awkward position. If she admitted to intercourse outside marriage, jurors might dismiss her testimony as unreliable because of her bad character. If she denied having had intercourse, she lent weight to the defense claim that she might not have known intercourse if she saw it. Kirkland appears by her answer to have been vexed by Knox's intimation and replied rather indignantly that while she had never married or borne any children, she nonetheless "had seen such acts of [intercourse performed] and knows very well that the prisoner was in the act of enjoying Mrs. Baker."[31]

The third prong of the defense strategy was to assail the characters of Amy

Baker and her housemate, Drucilla Kirkland, and by implication their veracity. One of only two witnesses who testified to Baker's dubious history was William Coleman, who claimed that he "had been to the house of Mrs. Baker for the purpose of unlawful intercourse with females" and had "known others to do so." Coleman reported that other neighbors were suspicious of Mrs. Baker. Nor did he consider her to be a "respectable woman" and would not believe her "as soon as he would a respectable woman." Alexander Pritchett, the second defense witness, never admitted to engaging in illicit sexual relations with women at the Baker house as did Coleman, but he recalled two occasions when he had observed several Negro men on the premises, by insinuation up to no good.[32]

The prosecution summoned five character witnesses to rehabilitate Baker and Kirkland. Prosecution witnesses' testimony variously described Baker as "industrious," "always correct," and of "good character." Samuel Farrar, for example, claimed never to have heard anyone speak ill of Amy Baker and doubted allegations that she had cavorted with black men, reflecting that had Baker "been in the habit of entertaining slaves" he would have heard about it.[33]

Perhaps the sheer number of witnesses who testified to Amy Baker's good character gives us good reason to doubt claims that she "entertained" slaves—which, even if true, obviously do not prove that she lied about being sexually assaulted. But Knox's having found even one witness willing to admit publicly to having had "unlawful" sexual intercourse with women at Baker's home lends credence to his testimony. Public acknowledgement of illicit sexual relations under oath is most surprising given the likely fallout in the community. Such an admission by a white male is indeed atypical; in most antebellum Virginia rape cases the "proof" of a woman's bad character was gleaned indirectly from the secondhand testimony of people who had merely heard about the alleged victim's reputation through the neighborhood gossip network.[34]

Quite possibly the most revealing evidence pertaining to Baker's status in the community is her own testimony, which is striking for its explicit, graphic details and bawdy language. Typically transcribed testimony contained language that was carefully couched. Drucilla Kirkland, for instance, testified to the intruder's bellowing that he "was sent there for *it* and was told that there was a plenty of *it* there."[35] Amy Baker's testimony defied such conventions. Her testimony reveals a virtual lack of inhibition in retelling the details of the crime that she alleged. She repeated verbatim what the accused had said upon entering the house: "He came for cunt and cunt he would have, that he had been told that there was a plenty of it there and he would have his satisfaction before he left." Nor did Baker mince words when describing a rather brutal sexual assault. She testified that the prisoner penetrated her four times and during one instance threw "her head over the bedstead and forced her legs over the prisoner's shoulders and used such violence in the penetration of the act as almost to have deprived her of her life." He also threatened to stab her with his dirk, a small knife, should she try to escape.[36]

Baker's choice of language in retelling her account of the assault suggests a conscious effort to forgo any pretense about her status in her community. Nor did the court transcriber feel compelled to "clean up" her deposition. At the very least the evidence suggests that Baker lived on the margins of respectability in the eyes of this white community. She may even have been a prostitute of sorts. In any event, the guilt or innocence of Lewis the slave at times seems to have taken a back seat to the contesting of Amy Baker's reputation. Baker and her housemate, Drucilla Kirkland, fought tenaciously for protection by the courts as well as for an acknowledgment of their perceived status, despite their obvious standing on the periphery of respectability.

In the end, the court remained unswayed by allegations of Baker's past sexual improprieties and found Lewis guilty of rape. Possibly Lewis's admission that he had been drunk at the time of the alleged assault made the attack seem more plausible to the jury. Or perhaps the documented brutality of the assault and the threat of assault with a deadly weapon ruled out Baker's compliance.[37] These factors, combined with Lewis's capture at the scene, most likely explain the jury's guilty verdict and decision to impose a death sentence with no attendant recommendation for mercy. In contrast to cases previously discussed, this case demonstrates that not every incident involving an accused black rapist led to reprieve or pardon.[38] Considering the weight of the evidence against Lewis, however, what is surprising is not so much his conviction and subsequent hanging as the vigor with which his defense was conducted.[39] Moreover, the case accentuates an archetypal defense used long before and after in rape trials, that of the woman as seductress. The counsel for slaves accused of raping white women were permitted to make use of this strategy even though it sometimes required an ambitious attack on the character of the white accuser.

The sexual history of women who accused men of rape was an important factor in rape trials well into the twentieth century.[40] In the Old South, white women who accused men of rape could expect to have their backgrounds searched for clues of past sexual indiscretion, even if their alleged attackers were black males. All-male, all-white juries, animated by misogyny as well as the age-old fear of false accusations of rape, usually required that female accusers prove the veracity of their charge. Believability was directly linked, in the minds of these men, to proper sexual conduct.[41] If a female accuser had behaved badly in the eyes of society, some reasoned, the woman was fair game for rape.[42] In this view, such women assumed partial or full responsibility for their own rapes. Purity in white females who filed charges of rape against black men was not essential for a successful conviction, but impure females faced a much greater battle persuading juries of the truthfulness of their claims.

Sometimes the mere tainting of female kin, as in the Vaughn case, was enough to cast doubt on a rape charge by a white woman. In the case of Buck in 1827, the defense called witnesses to testify to the bad character of the mother of the accuser, Susanna Alderson. The implication, of course, was that if the mother had misbehaved so might have the daughter.[43]

Purity and class were very much linked in the minds of better-off whites in the Old South. Southern ladies of the planter class personified the virtues of self-sacrifice, deference, charity, piety, and submissiveness, and were also expected to be pure, innocent, moral, and some would say without passion.[44] Conversely, members of the elite considered poor white women given to debauchery and sexual immorality.[45] One historian has even suggested that before the Civil War the notion of poor women's promiscuity was rooted more deeply in the minds of white southerners than that of black male sexual aggression.[46] Catherine Clinton has put it more starkly: "Southern planters divided women into two classes: ladies, always white and chaste; and whores, comprising all black women . . . and any white woman who defied the established social constraints on her sexual behavior."[47]

The successful intervention of white southerners on behalf of slaves convicted of raping white women should not obscure a countervailing trend: mobs occasionally threatened the lives of accused black rapists. Most slave rape cases proceeded calmly through established legal channels; however, sometimes disgruntled factions within white communities, leery of biases in the courts, threatened to take matters into their own hands and derail the proceedings.

At times discontented community members, often relatives of the accuser who were frustrated with defense tactics and court actions, threatened violence. Samuel F. Gregory from Prince Edward County, Virginia, grew exasperated at several continuances that were granted to the slave accused of attempting to rape his wife. Gregory managed to come up behind the prisoner at one point and tried to slit his throat. The slave survived and eventually was found guilty and transported out of the state.[48] Public sentiment in Mathews County, Virginia, ran so high during the trial of George in 1856 for the attempted rape of

Nancy Weston that a rumor of his acquittal prompted a "general determination
. . . to hang him notwithstanding his supposed acquittal."[49] In Rowan County,
North Carolina, a slave went on trial for the attempted rape of one Mrs. Bryant
in 1859. The court found him guilty and sentenced him to death. However, the
Charlotte Whig reported, locals had been so impressed by the woman's "irre-
proachable character" and her steadfast, unwavering testimony under cross-
examination that had the jury not convicted the accused, "the negro would have
been shot before he left the prisoner's box."[50] Angry citizens in Jefferson
County, Virginia, threatened violence in 1838 when a slave, convicted of attempted rape and sentenced to death, was granted a reprieve by the governor
and his executive council, on the grounds that the evidence was "insufficient to
warrant death." Unflinchingly, state officials stood their ground and called up
sixty volunteers to quell the disturbance.[51]

The politics of abolitionism and antislavery appear to have contributed to
the reaction of locals in Jefferson County, Virginia, neighbors of Mrs. Mathilda
Miller (Miler), who assembled in late summer of 1860 after hearing that she, in
the company of her grown married daughter and a third woman, had been
accosted by a local slave, Bill, while the three were on their way home from a
fair. Despite the official charge of attempted rape, it seems more likely that the
incident was a failed robbery attempt. Like many other whites who lived near
Harpers Ferry, Miller may have been jittery about the events of the previous
fall, when John Brown led an aborted attempt to incite slaves into armed
rebellion. Miller herself confessed that she was unsure whether she had actually been pushed by Bill during the attack or rather "fell from fright."[52]

Toting guns and making threats, a posse corralled Bill at his master's home
and escorted him to the "calaboose," where the justice of the peace persuaded
him to "confess." Miller's social standing, in addition to the tense racial and
political atmosphere, probably played a role in the quick vigilante response of
her neighbors.[53] Miller testified at trial that at the time of the assault she was
sporting a gold watch and a silk cape, both uncontestable symbols of material
wealth. The social status of Miller, coupled with her marital status and an
apparently pristine character (no questions were raised about her integrity or
personal conduct), prompted the locals to display their intolerance of Bill's
aberrant behavior, even if it meant taking the law into their own hands. They
did not have to. The trial proceeded calmly and yielded a guilty verdict.[54]

Though the threat of mob action in these cases did not result in the extralegal deaths of the accused, there are documented instances in which slaves
accused of sexually assaulting white women were lynched. A slave in North
Carolina believed to have raped the daughter of a slaveowner was burned

alive.[55] A group of white Mississippians hanged two slaves in 1843 because they suspected the men of having raped a white woman.[56] Nonetheless, while southern mobs occasionally lynched suspected black rapists, the usual course of action was to allow the case to proceed to trial.[57]

Despite these few notable exceptions, when slaves stood accused of raping or attempting to rape white girls and women, the courts typically proceeded unhampered by riled masses. That is not to say that courts were impervious to threats or rumbles within the community. But by and large, even in especially heinous cases, lynching tended not to supplant local authority. Witness the case of Jim, a slave in Virginia who in 1833 admitted to murdering a white woman, Millie Dees. He had gone to her home, he confessed, because he had heard that "negroes were intimate with her." When she rebuffed his proposal to sleep with her, he wielded an ax and delivered a terrific blow that nearly decapitated her. Then, in an attempt to conceal his crime, he set fire to Dees's house with her body inside. Despite the outrage that this gruesome crime must have elicited among whites, a lynch mob did not seize Jim, and his case proceeded through legal channels.[58]

As Samuel Gregory's attempt to murder the accused rapist of his wife reveals, at times some community members resented the ways in which slaveholding masters could "work the system" to win an acquittal or reprieve for a slave who was accused of rape or attempted rape. Lower to middling classes of southern whites could not have been unmindful of the disdain and contempt exhibited by the planter elite, community leaders, and court officials for poor, white women in the rape trials of black men. On the one side were the slaveowners who frequently hired attorneys, sometimes very expensive, skillful ones, who would manipulate the judicial system to secure acquittal or reprieve for their property. Most slaveholding states reimbursed masters, at least in part, for slaves convicted of capital crimes. The rates varied widely over time and from state to state. But generally, slaveowners could not expect to receive full compensation for legally executed slaves.[59] It seems reasonable, therefore, to conclude that many slaveholders could have been motivated by economic self-interest when they tried to spare the lives of slaves accused of sex crimes.[60]

Nonslaveholding whites at times openly displayed disgust at what some saw as blatant economic behavior by a master trying to exonerate his slave from the charge of rape. Especially when the accuser was a poor woman or girl, lowerclass whites exhibited resentment toward slaveholders who befriended slaverapists, pushing the limits of tolerance of the common folk. This is evident in the rape case of Dick, a slave belonging to Hamilton Rogers. Dick was charged in 1831 with attempting to ravish Pleasant Cole, wife of Peter Cole, from Leesburg, Virginia. Pleasant Cole successfully fought off her attacker, struggling with him for about fifteen minutes before a friend, hearing her screams, frightened off Dick. Cole managed to scratch Dick's face, a fact entered as evidence by the prosecution. Cole boasted that she "kept him off by catching [Dick] by his privates."[61]

Throughout the trial, witnesses described Cole as a "woman of truth." One witness swore that he made some inquiries of Cole's character "to do justice to the prisoner" and found that everyone spoke "in the highest terms of her character."[62] The jury found Dick guilty and ordered his execution. As a last resort Dick's owner, Hamilton Rogers, and his defense counsel Burr W. Harrison fired off letters to the governor requesting a reduced sentence, a task made all the more difficult since the jury had made no recommendation for leniency. Harrison and Rogers cited mitigating circumstances, including uncertainty about the identity of the perpetrator and discrepancies in the testimony of various prosecution witnesses. Harrison also cited Dick's age (which he did not state) and the absence of "actual injury . . . sustained by the object of his attempt." Little mention was made of Mrs. Cole's character with the exception of a single, unexplained reference to her "indiscretion."[63] Harrison's and Rogers's appeals aside, at least one other petitioner who identified himself as "a member of the court who found [Dick] guilty" concurred that extenuating circumstances, above all the very severe punishment, warranted mercy.[64]

Other community members, probably friends of the Coles, got wind of the letter-writing campaign on Dick's behalf and put to pen their own angry grievances. They accused Dick's master of cronyism; he had reportedly used a sheriff, a relative of Rogers, to investigate the character of Mrs. Cole. To the delight of the petitioners, the inquiry revealed only that she was a woman of "unblemished character." They stood appalled at the naked self-interest of the slaveholder. Venting class discord, the petitioners pondered the future safety of the community if Dick were set free, especially for "females in the humble walks of life, who have not thrown around them the protection of wealth and influential friends," an obvious dig at the well-off Hamilton Rogers. These folks, who seemed to identify more closely with people from the "more humble walks of life" than with Rogers, observed that protection was conferred on the basis of class.[65] Pleasant Cole, decidedly not a member of the slaveholding class, lacked money and powerful friends, but she did have her reputation and supportive, sympathetic neighbors. Cole's followers were outraged not only at the greed of a slaveholder more interested in his pocketbook than in justice and community safety but also at the appearance of the legal system's apparent favoritism toward the rich.[66] No doubt aware that the case had produced a political hornet's nest that he was not eager to stir, the governor denied Hamilton Rogers's appeal and the death sentence stood. Dick was executed and his owners had to settle for $400 in compensation from the state, unquestionably less than his market value.[67]

Class chafing is also evident in a letter to the governor of Virginia after the trial in 1846 of Anthony, a slave in King George County. The petitioner wrote, "[S]uppose for instance that [the alleged victim] had been of a rich family . . . you know [the accused rapist] would never have gotten to gaol, but just because she is poor she must suffer."[68] The obvious implication was that elites would never have allowed their womenfolk to appear publicly in court and testify in shocking detail about having suffered a sexual assault. The offender would have been dealt with privately. Poor women, however, did not have that luxury. The governor was unmoved by the plea and had Anthony transported out of the state.[69]

Class discord surfaced in Mathews County, Virginia, in 1856 when George, a slave owned by Thomas D. James, was accused of assault with intent to commit a rape upon Nancy Weston, who had been on her way home from church. James, an elderly man, may have insulted the Weston family when after hearing the allegation he attempted to bribe the Westons with ten dollars, promising also to whip the errant slave "to her satisfaction" if Nancy Weston dropped the charge. Much of the community appeared to have sided with the Westons. When a rumor of a pending acquittal circulated, the town quickly devolved into a "mad phrenzy." "A general determination was had to hang him notwithstanding his supposed acquittal." The reaction of residents to a possible acquittal may have frightened the jurymen into finding George guilty, but the split in the community over George's proper fate did not end there. The two camps took their cases to the governor of Virginia. Thomas James hired an attorney to draft his appeal on George's behalf. The letter, citing humanitarian motives, noted the personal suffering of James, who had raised George "almost as one of his own children." James "seems to suffer a great deal at the idea of the boy being hung."[70]

James's grown daughter, who appears to have been named Elizabeth F. Borum, pleaded her father's case, begging for executive mercy. Demonstrating negligible sympathy for Nancy Weston, she wrote, "My father raised the negro and he has always been faithful and obedient—this is the first fault he has ever been known to be guilty of. We of course can't help feeling sympathy for him."[71] She explained that George's attack had been a case of mistaken identity.

He mistook Nancy Weston for a "coloured woman" and once he learned she was white, he immediately left her.[72]

Opposition to the pardon efforts mounted in response. George Bibb, who drafted a letter denouncing the pardon, alluded to a petition being circulated among the community seeking a pardon for the condemned slave, though other than the two letters forwarded from Thomas James and his daughter no petition has been found. Bibb made every attempt to discredit the appeal by alleging that James's petition had only "very limited circulation" and was probably "presented only to the few known by the master of the slave." Truth be known, Bibb continued, nine-tenths of the county residents, "if it was thought expedient or necessary would sign a counter petition." Perhaps the "nine-tenths" figure persuaded Governor Henry Wise that he could not afford politically to grant Thomas James's request for a pardon. George hanged.[73]

Discord among white residents during the rape trial of a slave had also materialized in Davidson County, North Carolina, thirty years earlier. The oft-cited case of Jim and his alleged rape of a young white servant in 1825 also strikingly reveals class divisions among southern whites.[74] The numerous documents that this case generated permit a rare glimpse into what quite plausibly had been consensual sex between a poor white servant woman and a slave, one that was tolerated until the resulting pregnancy forced the community to confront the "taboo" relationship.[75]

Polly Lane, a white servant about eighteen years old, and Jim, a slave, both worked in the home of Abraham Peppinger, an elderly man. Jim was one of several slaves owned by Peppinger. According to Polly Lane's testimony at Jim's subsequent trial, one morning in mid-August 1825 Jim overtook her, forced her to drink brandy, and then raped her several times. Because Jim had threatened her, she explained, she did not call out until well after dark. Polly's version of events was challenged by the testimony of a slave named Dick, who after hearing the commotion sneaked to where Polly and Jim were. Dick claimed that he had heard Jim implore Polly to quiet down and then heard Polly say, " if I am left in the fire I am now in I shall surely die." Dick then made himself known to the couple, whereupon Polly accused Jim of assaulting her and implored Dick not to tell the Peppingers of the attack. She also confided to Dick that she was "big" and offered him a dollar to "get her something to destroy it." The inference to be made, of course, was that Polly and Jim had been having an affair, she became pregnant, and she then feigned the rape upon discovery, realizing that the only way out of the compromising situation was to deny that consensual sexual relations had ever taken place with Jim.

Several witnesses challenged her account, however, by testifying that they had seen Polly and Jim together intimately on numerous occasions.[76]

Members of the jury, which convened in October, apparently believed that the evidence weighed more heavily in favor of Polly Lane. They convicted Jim and set the date for his execution later that year, on December 23, despite suspicions that Polly was pregnant at the time of the trial, which she flatly denied.[77] As the execution date neared, Lane was no longer able to conceal her pregnancy, which by this time had caused considerable commotion in the community. Had Jim, not Polly, told the truth? Had Polly been trying to conceal their consensual relationship? Was she so desperate to ward off ostracism from family and community that she would risk seeing Jim die for a crime he had not committed? The white community was very divided and contentious in its response to these and other questions.

One faction seemed convinced that the prudent course would be to stave off Jim's pending execution until lingering questions could be resolved. Six white male petitioners asked the governor to transport Jim out of the state, or at least grant a reprieve until the birth of Polly Lane's child.[78] Alexander Gray, a juror who had voted for conviction, defended the jury's guilty verdict in the face of weak evidence presented by the defense. While Gray acknowledged, "in that neighborhood a greater intimacy existed between the blacks and whites than is usual or considered decent," Jim's attorney failed to prove that Jim and Polly had had an illicit sexual relationship. Gray resolutely believed that the correct verdict had been rendered, but he nonetheless wanted to hedge his bets and requested that the governor postpone the execution, which he did. A second letter by Gray in March, though, reveals an about-face: by that time Lane's advanced pregnancy had all but unraveled her lie, and Gray expressed outrage that she had knowingly perjured herself by denying consensual sex with Jim before the night of the alleged rape. "If this is the case and she knew it at the time [of the trial], no part of her testimony ought to be believed."[79]

As the birth of Polly Lane's child approached, fewer and fewer of her supporters, such as Alexander Gray, remained in her camp. But even as late as March 24, Jim's legal counsel, James Martin, feared that "many persons in the county . . . would execute this negro."[80] Martin also worried that the birth might be concealed to expedite Jim's hanging. Martin's qualms appear not to have been unfounded, for when local officials attempted to serve bastardy papers on Polly Lane, she could not be located. On advice of those "anxious for the execution" of Jim, she had concealed herself.[81]

Polly Lane's mixed-race baby was born on April 7, thus bolstering Jim's claim that she had already been pregnant in mid-August when Lane claimed to have been raped. In light of the exculpatory evidence, Alexander Gray concluded his thoughts on the matter by writing to the governor: the birth of Polly Lane's baby proved, he wrote, that "she must have knowingly and willingly sworn to a falsehood in saying . . . she was not pregnant [at the time of the trial. The] presumption naturally arises that the rest of it [her testimony] ought not be entitled to credit."[82]

Even in the face of irrefutable material evidence, however, some white community members stubbornly refused to desert Polly Lane, shifting instead to different ground in arguing for Jim's execution. Steadfastly denying that Lane's baby was of mixed race, John Smith denounced Jim's character as "one of the worst in my memory." As one correspondent explained, some residents of the county "are anxious for his execution not because they believe the conviction rightful but on account of general bad character." In other words, now that Polly Lane's claim of sexual assault proved baseless, some residents were forced to craft new grounds for Jim's execution. Jim was a troublemaker pure and simple, reason enough to kill him.[83]

Amid this cacophony of advice, pleas, and protestations, the governor found that the arguments for sparing Jim's life outweighed those for executing him. Instead of being hanged, Jim was transported out of North Carolina.[84] But weighty questions remain. What accounted for such a bitter and protracted dispute among these white citizens? What was at stake for the various players? Surely some simply wanted to see justice done. That would explain why some who favored Jim's execution at the outset were eventually persuaded to lobby for a reprieve in the face of exculpatory evidence. But more than any other single factor, class divisions seemed to have shaped the behavior and motives of many of those involved in the case.

Polly Lane came from a poor family. She worked as a servant in a white man's home alongside slaves, thus occupying a physical space with slaves but a social space just above them. Her family owned no land.[85] But while the Lane family could lay no claim to property, they could and did demand the respect they believed they were due as members of the white race. Their adherence to a code of honor is evidenced by their defiant attempt to shield Polly from probing community members bent on ascertaining the truth about very private and intimate matters. It is also imaginable that the Lanes saw themselves challenged and insulted by a propertied slaveholder, Abraham Peppinger, whose financial stake in saving Jim's life required that he and his friends malign the honor, of their daughter and, by extension, the Lane family. Peppinger, owner of nine other slaves, was wealthy enough to hire two of North Carolina's finest barristers, John Motley Morehead, who later served two terms as governor, and James Martin. Though Peppinger was not among North Carolina's richest men, he had nonetheless harnessed the state's legal apparatus for his own benefit.[86]

Ties of kinship and friendship, inextricable from class, probably also shaped the principals' behavior in the unfolding drama. One magistrate, John Smith, characterized by the historian Bertram Wyatt-Brown as a "semi-literate member of the clan to which Polly Lane belonged," refused to sign a bastardy warrant against Polly Lane, yet the magistrate Jesse Hargrave, himself the owner of twenty-eight slaves, did sign.[87] Other motives vied for attention as well: humanitarianism and personalism (Peppinger's emotional attachment to Jim; community members unwilling to see an innocent man, black or white, go to the gallows); financial interests (Peppinger's financial loss if Jim were executed; Peppinger's promise to reward the attorneys with Jim if they won the case); and perceptions about gender and sexuality (proof of Polly Lane's licentiousness and dishonesty that negated her claims of sexual assault).

And what should be made of Polly Lane's ploy of "crying rape" to hide a consensual relationship with a slave? Such histrionics were hardly typical, but the motive may have inspired some black-on-white rape cases. Though very difficult to discern, there are a few cases in which the evidence points in that direction, for example the rape case in 1825 of a North Carolina slave, Warrick, who was owned by a resident of Anson County, Pleasant Diggs. Diggs's mother-in-law, "Widow" Hensen, lived on Diggs's property in a small house that she shared with Mary Dunn.[88] Dunn claimed that one night while the Widow Hensen was gone, Warrick came to her bed and raped her. Though she testified to having struggled and called for help, neither of the two female slaves sleeping about five feet from her bed, nor Warrick's brother, who was ten feet away in the kitchen, claimed to have heard her cries. After the attack, Dunn testified, Warrick left the house, inexplicably managing somehow to fasten the lock behind him, which required placing a bar across the door.

The county court heard the case quickly, so quickly that Pleasant Diggs complained about only having a few days to gather evidence. Just as quickly, and despite some significant discrepancies in Dunn's testimony, the court returned a guilty verdict. One jury member described the verdict as having resulted from the "honest Indignation with which our white population view the highest impertinence of a slave to them or any approach towards a connection with a white woman even by her consent."[89]

Warrick's supporters wasted no time piecing together their appeal for a pardon. The heart of the solicitation turned on Mary Dunn's behavior before the alleged rape. Numerous witnesses came forth with stories of injudicious conduct between Dunn and Warrick. A neighbor, Mrs. Giddy, recalled that once, during a visit to the Hensen house, Mary Dunn had gone upstairs with Warrick and claimed to have "wound a ball of thread." Giddy must have appeared to Dunn to be harboring suspicions, because when Dunn returned she revealed rather defensively to Mrs. Giddy that Warrick had come to her bed the previous night. But Dunn begged Giddy not to tell Mr. Giddy, her husband, as he was a "drinking man" who might report the episode, and that would not bode well for Dunn's character.[90]

Mrs. Giddy believed that Dunn's demeanor that day, which she character- ized as "cheerful," belied any accusation of reckless advance by Warrick toward her. Dunn's machinations failed to fool Mrs. Giddy, who observed everything with suspicious eyes, for she had previously observed Dunn in the "negro house" alone with Warrick. Warrick and Mary Dunn were "too thick," she had warned Mr. and Mrs. Charles Hensen, the "Widow" Hensen's son and daughter-in-law. Hensen concurred, replying that Dunn surely would be "de- bauched by a negro" if she had not been already.[91]

As in the trial of Polly Lane and Jim, Warrick's jury seemed to have given Mary Dunn the benefit of the doubt during the trial. Her whiteness, after all, gave her some status, privileging her word over that of a slave. But when all the evidence was made public, some only after Warrick's conviction, certain com- munity members, including six jurors, became convinced that Warrick should be pardoned. They actively sought his reprieve from the governor, who ac- quiesced.[92]

Mary Dunn and Polly Lane were typical of the women who swore out complaints against slaves for sexual assault. Neither had a husband. They were poor, occupying the lowest station in antebellum white society. As a result of their low social status, Mary Dunn and Polly Lane came in close daily contact with slaves, sharing responsibility for some household and farm tasks, which helped to dissolve whatever barrier may have existed between these two groups. Evidence strongly suggests that Dunn and Warrick, like Lane and Jim, were lovers, but fear of ostracism led both women to "cry rape," in so doing sacrificing their lovers, who only narrowly escaped death sentences.

Unlike poor white women, elite women seldom swore out com- plaints against slaves for sexual crimes. Most complainants tended to be women, like Mary Dunn and Polly Lane, outside the slaveholding class. Despite the shared physical space between a slave and his master's female family members, slave-rapists seemed to have steered clear of choosing them as victims, or as lovers who would betray them to save face. Of 123 incidents in which white females in Virginia, or those on their behalf, swore out complaints against a slave or slaves for rape or attempted rape from 1800 to 1859, only 8, or 7 percent, can be identified as related to the accused's master.[93] One possible explanation is that male slaves came to view these women as part of their plantation families and instead sought out strangers or near-strangers. More plausibly, however, slaves understood that retribution for assaulting a master's wife, mother, or daughter would be swift and fatal. Of the eight slaves convicted of the rape or attempted rape of their masters' female kin, only two (25 percent) are known to have been transported rather than executed.[94] This compares to an overall transportation rate of 42 percent in all cases of slave rape (including slaveholding females) in Virginia from 1800 to 1859.[95]

Cases of white women crying rape to mask consensual, illicit relationships with slaves should not eclipse the reality that white women on occasion were sexually assaulted by slaves. But the question remains: Why did so few elite women bring charges against slave men for rape? Susan Brownmiller has argued that rape is a crime of opportunity and "opportunity knocks most frequently in a familiar milieu."[96] Certainly, Lane and Dunn were part of a slave's social milieu; elite white women, part of a slave's physical milieu. Yet slave men appear to have gone out of their way to avoid making sexual overtures, coercive or not, to elite women. The question then becomes why, given the proximity of planter females, women outside the slaveholding class leveled charges of slave rape in such disproportionate numbers.

Nonelite, poor white women, unlike women of the master class, proved much likelier victims of sexual assault for a number of reasons. For one, slaves may have observed, and for that matter, internalized, their masters' contempt for poorer whites and reasoned that it was possible to get away with the crime. Furthermore, lower-class white women, unlike women of the planter class, frequently traveled unchaperoned, making them easier targets.[97]

Many rape accusers were also vulnerable in another way: they lacked male protectors. Accusers were quite often widowed or single, sometimes living in the company of other females.[98] Finally, there may have been greater social contact between slaves and poor whites that effectively blurred traditional social and racial boundaries. In effect, slaves shared social space, if not physical space, with many of the women who would eventually charge them with rape. Regular social and economic intercourse occurred between many poor white women and black men. There are even strong hints that these women bartered sexual acts with slaves. Recall the observation of one participant in the imbroglio surrounding Polly Lane and Jim: "in that neighborhood a greater intimacy existed between the blacks and whites than is usual or considered decent."[99] Some slaves may have interpreted such familiarity with poor white women as a license to take sexual liberties, forcefully if necessary. Lastly, in some cases it appears that charges of rape grew out of consensual relations between white women and slave men, as with Polly Lane and Mary Dunn. At least a few women were willing to sacrifice the lives of their lovers for the vestiges of their reputations.

The validity of the claims of poor white women who filed charges of slave rape is bolstered, to a certain degree, by the communal and official scrutiny that inevitably followed. Women who brought charges knew that their sexual history would be made public, which may lead us to believe that many of their claims of slave assault had merit. Admittedly, though, in cases where pregnancy or some other event threatened to reveal a clandestine interracial relationship, the prospect of an intrusive trial was little compared to the social and familial ostracism that would surely follow.

If one thing is certain, it is that slaves did not rape members of the slaveholding elite as a systematic form of retribution. Revenge simply was not the motive. The chance circumstances of many assaults as well as the overwhelming representation of victims from the nonslaveholding class suggest that slave rape was not politically motivated.[100] Resistance took forms other than the sexual assault of females of the slaveholding class. Slaves did not manipulate whites through fears of rape, as many seem to have done through threats of poisoning.[101]

As the cases described above and numerous others demonstrate, judicial vindication for white females who claimed to have been sexually assaulted by slaves in the Old South was neither certain nor unconditional. White women who alleged sexual violation by slaves sometimes sought redress from the courts. They may or may not have received it. Although most of the cases presented here resulted from the conviction of black men for the rape or attempted rape of white females, it is worth noting that not all charges resulted in conviction. Two slaves in Halifax County were tried for rape and attempted rape, one in 1842, the other in 1856, and both were acquitted.[102] A black slave driver from Georgia was also found not guilty in 1824 for the attempted rape of a white woman. Ten years later court officials discharged a slave accused of attempting to rape a white woman, Rebecca Long.[103] Although a three-justice court in Elbert County, Georgia, found Wesley, a slave belonging to James Carpenter, guilty in the attempted rape of Nancy Fleetwood, an illiterate white woman who lived alone, the Inferior Court, to which all capital cases involving slaves were referred, acquitted him.[104] A judge in Alabama dismissed the rape case of a slave in 1860 when the accuser failed to show up in court and the judge learned from several witnesses of the "notorious bad character" of the complainant.[105] An all-white jury in Davidson County, Tennessee, failed to agree on a verdict in the attempted rape trial of Henry. The case was held over for retrial until the next term, and the attorney general ultimately dropped the charges.[106]

Occasionally, juries handed down rather lenient sentences for purported heinous acts by slaves against white women. In 1845 a court in New Orleans found Jeffrey, a twenty-five-year-old slave, guilty of attempting to rape an elderly Bavarian immigrant woman. As the woman peddled cakes and eggs along a road, Jeffrey threw two dollars into her basket, which he followed up with a "diabolical proposition." Rebuffed, the slave allegedly tried to force the woman into sexual relations. The jury sentenced Jeffrey to five years in the penitentiary and one hundred lashes, a far cry from the hangman's noose.[107] A white jury in Alabama in 1819 acquitted a slave of attempted rape, falling back instead on conviction of a lesser offense that brought with it the penalty of thirty-nine lashes and the branding of the left hand with the letter "R".[108] After Mary McManus of Spartanburg, South Carolina, complained that a slave named Tom had accosted her "with his private parts entirely exposed and expressed a desire to have Intercourse with her Saying he would give her a dollar," the magistrate filed an indictment, not for attempted rape but for "rude and insolent behavior." The remedy? Twenty-five lashes.[109] Another South Carolina slave was ordered to receive five hundred lashes over a five-week period, a harsh punishment to be sure, to be followed by banishment from the state after he was convicted not of rape but of a "high misdemeanor." The accuser had been a woman of diminished capacity who could not even tell the court her age.[110]

White communities in the antebellum South thus did not blindly and dogmatically side with white accusers in slave rape cases. Whites in the Old South appear not to have been so blinded by fear of black male sexual assault as to deny procedural rights to the accused. Nor could it be said with assurance that death was the certain outcome for a slave accused or even convicted of sexually assaulting a white woman.[111] A court or community's decision to extend support or leniency to an accused black rapist hinged on any number of factors, not the least of which was the accuser's compliance with socially acceptable behavior. Deviant conduct severely undercut a white woman's claim to protection in the Old South.[112] Those white females who failed to respect the established code of race and gender conventions, or whose female kin did, may have found their road to protection strewn with obstacles.

In confrontations between two marginalized groups in the South, poor white females and male slaves, race proved not to be the sole factor shaping the outcome or the responses of white observers. Instead, any one of a myriad of motives could have predominated in the development and outcome of these rape cases. Masters, motivated by economic self-interest, repeatedly utilized the judicial system to keep their most valuable investments from the gallows.[113] In cases such as these, the slave's status as property worked effectively to save his life. By embracing their property, however, slaveholders turned their backs on women who shared their race but not their class, thus baring, at times, sharp class divisions. The actions of these slaveholders, and of other members of white communities, remind us that slave rape trials were infused not only with racism, which has long been documented by southern and legal scholars, but also with sexism, which has been less visible.

A MANIFEST DISTINCTION BETWEEN A WOMAN AND A FEMALE CHILD
Rape Law, Children, and the Antebellum South

2

If whiteness did not inoculate women who accused black men of sexual assault against rough treatment by neighbors and courts, neither did whiteness shield girl accusers from questions about integrity and character. No sentimental attachment to childhood, no extraordinary sensitivity to the special needs of children, immunized young girls from scrutiny when they brought forth accusations of black sexual assault. A child's family history or even perceived missteps by a young girl herself opened the door to interrogation and ridicule in the face of a rape charge. The social standing of a young girl accuser not only shaped the community's response to her charge that a black had sexually assaulted her, thus influencing whether local whites would support her or the accused during the trial, but actually put a female child at greater risk for sexual assault. Children of middling and poorer classes in the antebellum South were frequently sent off on errands near and far, thus exposing them to encounters with men, some of whom exploited the circumstances and sexually assaulted the girls.

Class functioned in two important ways when girls in the Old South accused blacks of sexual assault. First, it put them in harm's way, making them more vulnerable to sexual attacks. Second, once a claim of sexual assault was leveled against a black man, the girl might very well suffer social opprobrium, or at the very least be subjected to interrogation resulting from suspicion. Girl accusers, however, faced an additional disadvantage not faced by adult women. In some ways, youthfulness jeopardized the successful prosecution of an alleged black rape. When a young girl claimed that a black man had sexually assaulted her, those around her, even family members, typically doubted her account in whole or part. Children were simply not regarded as being as reliable as adults when presenting claims of sexual assault. A fundamental wariness about children's credibility was further complicated by eyewitness testimony elicited about the sexual assault itself. Children, without knowledge or experience of sexual relations, sometimes offered confused, even contradictory, statements about the assault, leaving some juries doubtful about the alleged crime, and hence inclined to find in favor of the accused rapist.

Finally, many young girls found themselves largely unprotected from what today we would call statutory rape. The age at which most antebellum Southerners considered children capable of offering consent in sexual relations was far lower than the typical twentieth-century standard. In the eyes of the law and the community, only very young girls, under the age of ten, were believed unable to offer consent to sexual relations. For all these reasons, young girls in the Old South who came forth with an accusation against a black man for rape could face an uphill battle in prosecuting the claim.[1]

This chapter explores how antebellum southerners viewed childhood and sexuality, as seen through rape law and child rape cases. By examining these cases, it is possible to see how the institution of slavery, as well as the factors of race and class, shaped the way whites viewed rape and children in the rural, slaveholding South. Finally, a consideration of child rape cases tests the extent to which youthfulness—specifically, idealized notions about the innocence of children—operated in antebellum southern society, especially when held up against deeply entrenched and pervasive beliefs about the innate depravity of poor, white women.[2]

The legal definition of rape throughout antebellum America turned on the use of force and the lack of consent.[3] Practical application of the legal requirements for rape, though, could prove difficult, cumbersome, and perplexing. The best way to prove use of force and lack of consent was to produce evidence of a victim's resistance. In many cases, however, such evidence did not exist. Presumably when rapists used or threatened to use force, interpreters of the law reasoned, many women, for their own safety, willingly submitted to the act. So an exception was generally granted when the prosecution was able to substantiate that a rape victim succumbed to an assault for fear of her life or safety. But there were other extenuating circumstances in rape cases that sometimes confounded the courts. For example, some men stood accused of administering drugs to facilitate sex with unwilling women. Did this constitute rape? Some courts ruled not. Still other men impersonated the husbands of their victims under cover of darkness. Did this constitute rape? Again, many courts felt bound by the letter of the law, and ruled that such cases, lacking force, fell outside the definition of rape.[4] Complicating the legal definition of rape was the customary understanding, in many sectors of nineteenth-century America, that a man was justified in employing a certain level of coercion or even violence in sexual relations. Many men subscribed to the notion that no did not really mean no, and that resistance by women, especially those on the fringes of respectability who demurred from having sex initially, was part of sexual ritual. Thus, in daily life, the distinction between forced and consensual sex was quite blurred.[5]

Another problematic area for antebellum courts hearing rape cases involved accusers too young to be considered women. Prosecution for the rape of children did not depend on proof of force, as it did with adult women, since it was felt that children were unable to understand and therefore give informed consent. Moreover, children were believed incapable of rendering good judgment when it came to sexual relations. Children "lacked the instinctive intelligence to comprehend the nature and consequences of this atrocious act," noted Judge Joseph Henry Lumpkin of the Georgia Supreme Court.[6] Consent of the child therefore became an irrelevant factor in rape cases of children.

Carnal abuse of an infant, as sexual intercourse with an underage child was generally known, had been a crime at common law throughout all of British colonial America.[7] After the Revolution, most southern lawmakers enacted legislation that established an age threshold, below which force need not be proved and consent was irrelevant. But the legal communities throughout the South were not uniform or always specific in establishing the legal definition of a child. The age of consent was typically ten years, but it varied from state to state and over time. By the time of the Civil War, only Virginia, Missouri, and Kentucky had raised the age of consent to twelve.[8] Arkansas maintained no specific age requirement, but recognized the onset of puberty as the age of consent.[9] Curiously, Tennessee and Mississippi maintained two different ages of consent on the basis of the male's race. Both states established ten as the age of consent in cases of white males accused of statutory rape, but twelve for cases in which the rapist was a slave (Mississippi later raised this to fourteen). Though the motive for the disparity is not explicitly stated in the statutes, one can imagine that lawmakers sought to be more diligent in policing the sexuality of slaves who might have sex with young girls while preserving the sexual license of white males. In practice, this meant that an eleven-year-old white girl from Tennessee would have been deemed legally incapable of understanding consent in the context of sexual relations with a slave, but perfectly capable and hence responsible for having sexual relations with a white male.[10] The racial disparity in the definition of statutory rape grew even wider when in 1857 the Mississippi legislature raised the age of consent in the slave statute to fourteen.[11]

Race obviously played a much greater role in the crafting of statutory rape laws in the antebellum South than elsewhere in the nation. Most salient of the racial differences was the disparate punishment for those convicted of the crime of child rape. In Arkansas, Mississippi, Tennessee, Texas, and Virginia, slaves found guilty of having carnal knowledge with white female children could receive the death penalty, while white men were to serve sentences in the penitentiary from five to twenty-one years.[12] Missouri punished white offenders with a minimum prison term of five years whereas slaves were to be castrated.[13] In both Carolinas, by contrast, white and slave men convicted of statutory rape would be condemned to death.[14]

A few states even appear to have explicitly established statutory rape as a crime for whites but not slaves. However, it seems clear that legislators in those states meant for the rape statutes to encompass underage sexual relations as well. A number of southern states, Alabama for instance, punished whites guilty of having sex with girls under ten with a term of life imprisonment, the exact punishment held out for rape of females over ten. Since slaves, and free blacks for that matter, suffered the death penalty for rape and attempted rape of white women, it seems logical to assume that legislators believed slaves to be encompassed under the existing legislation.[15] Similarly, Georgia courts could punish white men for having unlawful sex with girls under ten with solitary confinement up to six months, or hard labor for ten to twenty years. Slaves guilty of rape or attempted rape of a white female suffered death.[16] Kentucky retained a distinction between the "rape . . . of an infant under the age of twelve years," which was punishable by death when committed by whites, and "carnally knowing a white girl under the age of ten years," a lesser offense, presumably because no force was employed, which warranted a prison term of ten to twenty years. The earliest rape statutes in Kentucky did not specify the race of the victim; however, by 1852, reflecting that state's deeper commitment to the institution of slavery, legislation became race specific.[17]

Despite a veneer of rather unambiguous criteria established by state legislatures for underage sexual assault, gray areas abounded and stymied some judges. Both appellate and local courts at times struggled with the murky ground of biological age and consent, reflecting a rather widespread confusion about age, consent, and coerced sex. In 1850, for example, the supreme court of Arkansas heard an appeal, following the conviction of a slave named Charles of assault with intent to ravish. Not only the age but the level of maturity was deemed of material interest to the high court. Witnesses testified that the accuser, Almyra Combs, was about thirteen or fourteen years of age, "not a woman," and had "not attained the age of puberty," that state's criterion for statutory rape. Combs had been sleeping with six other girls in the same room when the defendant allegedly entered, grabbed her by the shoulder, and tried to turn her over, presumably to have sex with her. A startled Combs grabbed the intruder, discovering that he was a partially dressed man. (Combs delicately explained that she "found the portion of the undressed person to be that portion of which I cannot decently speak.") Charles, who had been apparently hired out to Michael Summerron, explained to his master that he had merely tried to summon Mr. Summerron to investigate an intruder in the barn. It had all been a misunderstanding.[18]

Charles's attorney zeroed in on a technicality, an apparent loophole in the law. He argued that white men found guilty of "carnally knowing or abusing unlawfully, any female child under the age of puberty," the statute upon which Charles's indictment was based, faced a prison term.[19] Section 9 of the same law modified the punishments for African Americans, substituting death sentences for prison terms. But here Charles's attorney saw a possible legislative oversight. The provision for blacks read that "if such negro or mulatto shall attempt to commit any of such offenses, although he may not succeed, on a white *woman*, he shall suffer death."[20] The accuser, having not yet reached puberty, was therefore not a woman and hence fell outside the purview of the legislation.[21] The high court interpreted the statute more broadly, however, ruling that the law was intended to embrace young girls incapable of consent, and thus rejecting the defense argument. Nonetheless, a second defense exception proved more persuasive. The defense argued that because Charles had not used force—he had intended to have sexual relations with the girl while she slept—he was not guilty of a capital offense. The court conceded that the accused had not used force, in fact had no intention of using force. Having sexual relations with a female while she slept was not a crime, let alone a capital offense. The high court reversed the lower court conviction.[22]

Attorneys defending slaves from charges of sexually assaulting young girls, as in the case of Charles, exploited the gray area of consent and age in southern rape law. One lawyer presented an especially innovative, if ultimately untenable, line of reasoning in an appeal in 1844. The appeal centered on a Louisiana slave who had been sentenced to die for attempting to commit a rape on a six-year-old white girl. Citing a definition of "woman" as a female at least ten years old, he argued that the accuser was too young to have been a "woman" and that the act therefore fell outside the statute. The Louisiana high court was not swayed and upheld the conviction.[23]

The Tennessee Supreme Court heard a similar appeal in the case of Sydney in 1842, but ruled very differently. Defense counsel argued that "a female infant only six years of age is not a woman within a statute which makes it a felony . . . for a slave to make an assault with an intent to commit rape on a 'free white woman.'" The rape law for slaves encompassed only women. And although a statute enacted in 1829 made it a felony to have carnal knowledge of a child under ten, the legislature had neglected to take children into account when crafting the provision concerning assault with intent to commit a rape. The Tennessee legislature hastily rectified the oversight by passing legislation while the case was making its way through the appeals process, aiming to "include all and every white female" whom a slave had attempted to rape. Passage of the legislation came too late, however. The high court ruled that Sydney could not be convicted under the amended law, which was passed after his indictment and conviction. Because there was "a manifest distinction taken between a woman and a female child" and Sydney's victim was not a woman, his alleged crime was not even an indictable, let alone a capital, offense.[24]

Confusion over age, consent, and sexual assault statutes seems to have plagued local officials whose responsibility it was to bring forth indictments. In another Tennessee case, local officials in 1829 leveled two charges against a white man, one for rape, the other for carnal knowledge with a female under the age of ten. The uncertainty of a child's age, frequently not officially established, coupled with a lack of understanding of the nuances of sexual assault law, may have prompted the justice of the peace in this case to cover all bases. The defendant, who was convicted of the rape charge, protested, but to no avail. In the ruling, the court decided that the strategy of filing more than one charge in a single indictment was lawful.[25]

Sometimes the confusion over age and sexual assault carried over into questions about the age of the alleged rapist. In 1864 the North Carolina Supreme Court heard the case of Sam, a fourteen-year-old slave charged with the rape of a four-year-old white girl. Sam's defense argued that he had not yet reached puberty and thus could not have committed the act of rape. The jurists agreed. Citing ample precedent in English common law, they recognized that boys who had not yet reached puberty were physically incapable of committing rape. The court conceded, however, that "a large portion of our population is of races from more southern latitudes than that from which our common law comes," who reach puberty at an earlier age. The court accordingly urged the lawmakers of the state to consider lowering the age for which boys, especially slave boys, would be accountable for rape.[26]

Most of the published appellate opinions in the cases described above are silent about the relationship between the young female accuser and the accused. By shifting to records of trials in southern communities, however, we can divine more about the local circumstances of alleged offenses, in particular the nature of the association between the accused and the young girl who charged him with sexual assault. Despite living and working in such close proximity to slaveholding females, children (or wives, for that matter) of the planter class only infrequently leveled accusations of rape against a slave. Slaveholding children at first glance may seem to have been obvious targets for slaves seeking convenient and vulnerable victims; there were simply more opportunities for encountering unaccompanied children in some remote recesses of a farm or plantation. Opportunistic motives aside, sexual assault of a master's daughter could have satiated pent-up hostility and resentment. What better way for a slave to exact retribution? Notwithstanding opportunity and motivation, however, slaves rarely assaulted young members of the master's family, according to extant sources, possibly out of fear of the consequences. Only seldom did members of the elite bring charges of rape or attempted rape against their slaves. But on the few occasions when they did, local courts generally exacted the harshest punishment available.[27] Still, justice for the alleged black rapist was allowed to proceed without threat of extralegal violence.

One such illustration is the rape case of Dick, a slave in Southampton County, Virginia, owned by Charles and Jane Briggs. On Halloween in 1808, Jane Briggs shooed her four-year-old daughter, Sally, out of the house so that her husband, who had not slept well the previous night, could rest peacefully. About two hours passed before Jane Briggs heard her young daughter crying. She sent an older daughter, Polly, to investigate. As Polly opened the door, there stood Dick holding Sally. The child's legs and feet were covered with blood. Polly shouted, "Good Lord, Mama! Sally is ruin'd!" The child was unable to walk. Jane Briggs could find no apparent wound, despite Dick's explanation that Sally had fallen.[28]

After a fair amount of coaxing by her mother, Sally Briggs reluctantly revealed that it was Dick who had hurt her, then threatened to kill her. After her mother's assurance that she was safe, Sally led her mother to where she claimed Dick had hurt her. Sally charged that Dick had laid her on a log, covered her mouth, then "tore her with his fingers." The log appeared wet to Jane Briggs, as if it had been recently washed, although a few droplets of blood could be discerned. Sally then guided her mother to the spot where she said Dick made her wait while he fetched some water to wash herself up. Jane Briggs kicked up some sand and found a "good deal of blood" underneath. Sally then threw her arms around her mother's neck and cried, "Oh! Mama, you don't know how I was hurt." She further recounted that Dick had grabbed a chunk of wood and threatened her if she told anyone of the assault.[29]

As enraged as Sally's father surely must have been upon learning that one of his own slaves had sexually violated his four-year-old daughter, he resisted any impulse he might have felt to defend his and his daughter's honor through personal retribution. Briggs would have been painfully aware that the cost of exacting private vengeance through lynching would have been high indeed. While the state would have partially compensated him for a slave convicted in court of a capital offense, he would have received nothing for a slave executed extralegally.[30] Whatever Briggs's motive, he allowed the court to decide Dick's fate.

There is no evidence that Sally herself testified at trial; as a young child she would not have been permitted to swear an oath. Her mother, however, did relay to the court what Sally had told her about the assault.[31] Several of Briggs's other slaves also testified, suggesting that Dick seemed to have been obsessed with the young girl for quite some time. Davey, a slave about sixteen or seventeen years of age, reported that Dick had fantasized aloud about having sex with the young Sally. Dick told Davey that "after doing of it to her once or twice that he could do it to her at any time he pleased afterward, that she would be big enough." Davey also overhead Dick try to entice the young girl with the promise of a red apple.[32]

Another teenaged slave, Sam, also testified that Dick had confided to him that he planned to have sexual intercourse with Sally "two or three times if she would not be large enough." Celia, another Briggs slave, recalled that she had overheard Dick ask "Miss Sally" if she wanted to be his wife and "the child said yes." None of these three slaves, though they had reason to suspect Dick of trying to sexually assault young Sally, ever reported their observations to their master or mistress.[33] Dick was found guilty and executed.[34]

A slave accused of sexually assaulting his master's young daughter, as Dick was, had very little hope of reprieve. In the eyes of the law and white society, he had committed two of the most egregious transgressions imaginable: the rape or attempted rape of a white female child, and the rape or attempted rape of a member of his master's family. Master and slave inhabited the same physical space. Living in such close proximity required tremendous trust in one's bondsmen. A severe breach by a slave, such as the sexual assault of a member of the master's family, jeopardized the linchpin of the institution of slavery and demanded severe retribution. For these reasons, in most cases in which slaves were found guilty of sexually assaulting girls of the master class, reprieves and pardons were not generally forthcoming, as they sometimes were when the young accuser was not wealthy. Antebellum Virginia communities, courts, and elected officials vigorously prosecuted and punished slaves accused of raping or attempting to rape young girls.

Despite the high rate of execution for slaves convicted of raping children of owners, there are two cases in which the convicted slaves escaped death sentences. These exceptions merit consideration, for they suggest that sometimes the courts considered other factors in adjudicating a case, even though slaves believed to have been guilty of sexually assaulting a master's young female relative were usually treated harshly. A court in Henrico County, Virginia, ruled in 1860 that Patrick had indeed attempted to have carnal knowledge of his master's niece. Nonetheless, the jury spared his life. Patrick belonged to Charles Vest but resided and worked at the home of his son, Dr. N. A. "Gus" Vest. We know little about Patrick, except that he was probably somewhat old and crippled—he was frequently referred to as "Old Uncle Patrick." He also had a "hump" on his back from having broken his back at one time.[35]

As witnesses recounted for the court, one night in late November the Vest household had retired for the night. Dr. and Mrs. Vest were asleep in their bedchamber. Two young girls slept upstairs. One, Lelia Wingfield, was the eleven-year-old niece of the Vests and had been staying with them for several months to attend school. The other girl, Adelaide Kidd, aged twelve years, was a boarder. The two shared a bed.[36]

Not long after Mrs. Vest had retired for the night, she was awakened by noise that she assumed was made by an intruder. She distinctly heard someone open the outer door, then crash into the opened door of a nearby medicine chest. Alarmed, she awakened her husband, who was seemingly annoyed at having been awakened and surmised the noise must have been made by the dog. "I told him the dog could not open the door," his wife sarcastically testified, obviously perturbed by her husband's indifference. A few minutes later, screams from upstairs pierced the darkness. Reflecting his continued insensitivity, the doctor sent a servant to investigate the disturbance. The Vests' niece, Lelia Wingfield, was quite shaken up. She asserted that "Old Uncle Patrick" had entered her room. Again, her own uncle dismissed the commotion as the antics of the family dog. Even though Lelia continued to insist that the noise had been made by Patrick, Vest wrote off the episode as a bad dream. Later, when she was alone with her aunt and out of earshot of her uncle, Lelia confided that a hand placed under her "drawers" had startled her. Confused and probably dazed by slumber, she assumed it to have been the hand of her bedmate. "I asked Addie what on earth she was doing." She then touched the hand that was probing her undergarments and discovered a large, rough hand obviously not belonging to her bedmate. Lelia screamed, and the intruder quickly jerked his hand away. She rolled over and through the ample light from the moon could see that it was "Old Uncle Patrick." He shook his fist at her threateningly, warning her to be quiet. When pressed by both family members and the court, Lelia positively identified Patrick as her assailant.[37]

Circumstances all but ensured a guilty verdict in the case of the Commonwealth against Patrick. Throughout the trial, the character of Patrick's accuser was never challenged. Lelia Wingfield's blood ties to Patrick's master no doubt lent her credibility and insulated her to a degree from scrutiny. Aside from Lelia's integrity and privileged social status, other factors seemed to warrant a guilty verdict. Above all, there was never any question about the identity of the perpetrator. Despite all this, however, the court decided on sale and transportation, not death, as the appropriate punishment.[38]

What would account for this leniency? The "usual" mitigating factors seem not to have played any role in this case. The defense offered no evidence undermining the credibility of Lelia Wingfield. Nor did the defense present testimony about any illicit sexual behavior by the complainant. Lelia's uncle's behavior, his complacency and his predisposition to doubt his niece, might have established the tenor of the trial, planting doubt in the minds of jurors. Vest, for whatever reasons, seemed quite reluctant to believe that Patrick would have made such an unwanted, salacious attack. Perhaps years of loyal service made Vest all too willing to view his niece's accusation as misguided and mistaken, though not malicious.

In contrast to the leniency shown in Henrico County, a jury in Henry County, convened in 1832 to hear testimony about the purported rape of a slaveholder's daughter, sentenced the twenty-year-old slave, George, to hang. The conviction rested heavily if not exclusively on the allegation of the slave's master, John Burgess. Shortly thereafter, however, the Commonwealth's own attorney filed a motion with the same court summoning John Burgess to address suspicions that he had perjured himself during testimony in the trial of George.

Burgess, it came to light, had falsely accused his slave of raping his daughter. It seems that Burgess had had George severely whipped, possibly excessively, for playing the fiddle and dancing. Someone, perhaps a neighbor, inquired about the reason for George's whipping. Burgess lied, saying that George was being whipped for the rape of his daughter. While the face-saving ploy may have made a severe beating of a slave palatable to neighbors, it set into motion a serious chain of events, creating additional problems for Burgess, who was forced to continue the lie and bring the matter before the authorities. But if he admitted lying while under oath, he risked prosecution for perjury. While the truth was eventually discovered and George spared from a wrongful execution, the conviction was not entirely set aside. Under the circumstances, George was transported instead of hanged. Perhaps this official action was intended to punish Burgess more than George. It is also important to note that the local court convicted George for the rape of Burgess's daughter on what had to have been flimsy evidence, suggesting that accusations of slave rape made by members of the slaveholding class were taken very seriously.[39]

Extralegal violence, though not the norm in antebellum cases of alleged black rape, did threaten occasionally, particularly when news of a slave's rape of his master's daughter percolated through the community. For instance, James Thornton's slave was believed responsible for the rape and murder in 1855 of Thornton's fourteen-year-old daughter. Alabama officials, fearing mob violence, granted a change of venue, but to no avail. A group of enraged citizens seized the alleged rapist from jail, chained him to a stake on the site where the murder was believed to have been committed, and burned him alive in full view of two to three thousand blacks and an untold number of whites.[40]

Of course, lynch mobs could also threaten when the children of nonslave-holders accused slaves of rape. U. B. Phillips cited an instance of a mob in Georgia in 1851 that seized a black man charged with sexually assaulting a white girl. The *Columbus Sentinel* reported that a "negro man" had attempted a rape upon a "little girl." After a "fair" trial, an "intelligent" jury rendered a guilty verdict. Despite the conviction, some community members continued to believe in the man's innocence and organized a pardon campaign, circulating a petition that was "very numerously signed." The petition was forwarded to the governor, who granted a full pardon. By the time news of the pardon reached the community, substantial crowds had already gathered to watch the execution. The mob refused to disperse and eventually overpowered the sheriff, seized the "unfortunate culprit," and hanged him.[41]

Mobs threatened in other slave-child rape cases as well. The mother of Lucy Dallas Beazley, aged twelve, who had charged a Virginia slave with rape in 1856, threatened to have him shot if he were not found guilty and hanged.[42] And in 1858 an Alabama slave was alleged to have committed a rape on a girl aged eleven or twelve. He was arrested but seized from the jail by a vengeful mob before he could be tried. The crowd intended to burn the slave at the stake and was in the act of "applying the torch" when some present objected, stating that such an action "would not be in keeping with the custom of an enlightened and civilized community." The slave was then promptly hanged from a nearby tree.[43]

By and large, however, the alleged rape of nonslaveholding children by slaves was far less likely to evoke either extralegal violence or swift, harsh official responses than similar allegations in slaveholding families. There was also another difference: accusations among the nonslaveholding were much more numerous. Moreover, the outcomes of those trials were much more ambiguous and unpredictable, suggesting that these female children were less likely than children of the privileged class to receive sympathy and support from communities and courts. To be sure, many of the accused were prosecuted to the fullest extent of the law. Typical is the case of a slave in Wood County, Virginia, in 1822 who was convicted and hanged for having carnal knowledge of a six-year-old white girl. The young accuser herself offered no testimony, as she was too young. James Rickman, the sole other eyewitness, happened upon the assault while he was hunting turkeys. He saw the head of Jack, the accused, at first mistaking him for a turkey. Realizing his mistake, Rickman then observed that the slave was lying on top of a young girl. When pressed, Rickman could not swear that actual penetration had taken place. Nor did he observe any evidence of semen on or near the girl's body. Proof of ejaculation, of course, aided in the corroboration of establishing rape. Evidence of seminal emission was not required under Virginia law, although some local judges could have operated under the incorrect assumption that is was.[44]

What Rickman did see, however, were the "privates of the prisoner exposed and his pantaloons unbuttoned." He also observed the accused "endeavor to open the private parts of the child" and said Jack was "spitting up on his penis apparently in the act of preparing it." The court found Jack guilty of carnally knowing and abusing Barbara Carpenter. Consequently, he hanged.[45]

Dinwiddie, a slave belonging to John Lamb of Sussex County, Virginia, suffered the same fate in 1826 for attempting an assault on Mary Jane Holloway, aged thirteen, who was walking home with her younger sister and cousin.[46] According to testimony, a black male followed the three, passed them, and feigned to be cutting brush with a knife. He then tried to catch Jane Judkins, Holloway's cousin, but she escaped. He caught Mary Jane Holloway instead. The other two girls escaped and ran for help. Holloway testified that Dinwiddie laid her down in the woods, "pulled up her clothes, pulled down his breaches and got upon her." He made her "kiss him twice and take hold of his black thing," all the while brandishing a knife near her throat. Dinwiddie was charged with attempting to rape Mary Jane Holloway, although it is not clear whether he actually consummated his assault.[47] Even so, Dinwiddie was executed, apparently without any interference from community or slaveholder.[48]

The circumstances of some alleged assaults shed light on why a disproportionate number of nonslaveholding girls brought forth charges of rape against slaves. Many of the nonslaveholding child victims of sexual assault were attacked while walking along public roads or in remote areas. Children in the nineteenth-century South, as in many rural cultures, typically provided invaluable service to their families by running errands that often required traveling unaccompanied or with other children to remote or distant places. Isolation then made these children likely prey for sex offenders of all races. Female members of the elite class were far less likely to be sent on such errands alone or accompanied by other children.

One such errand cost young Sally Hudgins of Cumberland County, Virginia, her life. The Hudgins family found their ten-year-old daughter dead in a pool of water near a spring one summer day in 1826. Sally Hudgins had been sent out to fetch a jar of milk. At first her father, William Hudgins, thought his daughter must have been struck by lightning. Further investigation revealed, however, that her clothes had been pulled over her head, a sign of sexual assault. Various witnesses testified that Sally Hudgins had been severely beaten; her shoulder, throat, and thighs were black from bruises, indicating that the child must have put up a struggle.[49]

For unstated reasons, suspicion quickly fell upon Charles, a slave owned by Robert Austin. One community member described him as "the vilest negro in the neighbourhood." Even Charles's mistress, Judith Austin, suspected him. He had been "roguish" and "frequently offended the neighbours." Likewise, her husband called Charles a rogue who would steal "any little thing." Charles's demeanor, his reputation for recalcitrance, and "his looks" had convinced Judith Austin that he murdered the Hudgins girl.[50] More substantive evidence was offered by Ginsey Hudgins, the deceased's sister, and a female slave of Hudgins, both of whom reported having been pelted by "clods" earlier in the day near the spring where Sally was murdered. Both believed that the clods had been hurled by Charles, who was lying close to the corner of the fence nearby.[51]

The most incriminating evidence, however, was the tracks left at the scene of the murder. Charles's feet purportedly matched the tracks near the spring. Eventually, Charles confessed to the crime, explaining that he had been "plaguing" Sally Hudgins and was afraid she would tell her parents, who would have him whipped. Charles made no mention of any sexual motives for the attack, which principals had deduced from the bruises on her inner thighs and from the position of the clothes that had been pulled above her head. Charles was found guilty of murder and hanged.[52]

An isolated locale was the site of an alleged attack on a white schoolgirl by a slave in Buckingham County, Virginia, in 1856. Late one September afternoon, Mary Harris had been on her way home from school when, she claimed, she and a younger sister encountered a black male driving a wagon near the local sawmill. He later reappeared about a quarter-mile from Mary's home, grabbed her, and dragged her into the woods, where he beat her about the head with a stick and attempted to rape her.[53] Her younger sister ran off to get some help.[54] The assailant, whom Mary identified as the slave Jesse, let the girl go and fled into the woods, but not before Mary had put up a good struggle against her attacker. Harris's mother described the numerous scratches on Mary's face, as well as bruises and cuts on her head. The girl's clothing was also torn in several places.[55] Testimony vouching for Jesse's politeness and general obedience to white people was unable to spare him from the gallows.[56]

One month to the day of Mary Harris's purported assault in 1856, Lucy Dallas Beazley of Spotsylvania County, aged twelve, also claimed to have been attacked by a slave known as Anderson while returning from a visit to her grandmother's one afternoon. Like Mary Harris, Lucy Beazley had been traveling on a road when attacked, about a mile from home. A younger sister accompanied her.[57]

Like most of the other young complainants, Lucy Beazley reported having been severely beaten, a factor that seems to have weighed heavily on jurors deciding this and other child rape cases. Proof of force by the assailant all but ruled out the accuser's consent, if it were in question. And as in other cases in which young girls claimed to have been attacked, Beazley struggled, resisting the assailant's advances "as long as she could stand." Her attacker threatened to kill her if she cried out, claiming to have a pistol in his pocket. In the end, help did not come in time: "He threw me down and pulled up my clothes and . . . he penetrated my body with his peanis." The court found Anderson guilty and sentenced him to hang.[58]

What followed was a bewildering whirlwind of activity that seems to have been orchestrated by Anderson's owner, William Goodwin, and spawned by post-trial disclosures that the purported attack had not played out exactly as Lucy Beazley claimed. Such confusion and contradictions were not uncommon when the accuser was young, as in Beasley's case. The new revelations cast doubt on the Beazley family's testimony that Anderson had completed the rape and that Lucy had been hurt in the attack. A man identified as Joseph Sanford signed a sworn statement that Lucy Beazley's uncle, Atwell Pleasant, had told him that the errant slave had not actually accomplished the rape.[59] This conversation, Sanford explained, took place after Anderson's conviction. Four days later, Sanford's wife, Agnes, appeared before the Spotsylvania County court clerk to make a sworn statement as well. She revealed that Clementina Beazley, the accuser's mother, told her before trial that the slave had unsuccessfully attempted to commit a rape upon her daughter. Lucy Beazley, present during this conversation, did not deny her mother's version of the attack, according to Sanford. Anderson's owner, William Goodwin, also swore out an affidavit stating that his father had requested that the girl be examined for evidence of a rape, but that none had been performed. And yet another citizen reported that Lucy's grandmother's husband, Isaac Cornwall (or Carndale?) claimed that there were no marks about Lucy's neck, as had been asserted in court.[60]

Confusion about whether the act of rape had been consummated permeated the proceedings as well as the discussion that followed. The confusion may have been due to the child's uncertainty over the nature of the assault, ignorance of sexuality, and reticence over publicly testifying about a sexual assault. Proof of seminal emission, evidence of penetration, as observed in this exchange, mattered in the eyes of the law because without it, the accused would be guilty of nothing more than an attempt.[61] Child rape cases tended to be characterized by much confusion about whether a man charged with rape was guilty of rape or merely attempted rape. No doubt, especially in the cases of children or young girls, much of this commotion stemmed from ignorance or from embarrassment about sexual relations. Elizabeth Smith's testimony against a slave who she claimed had raped her sheds some light on this state of confusion about what constituted rape. Though not a child, Smith was described by some as a "very simple weak woman." In the rape trial of Dennis in 1819, she offered contradictory testimony. Dennis was charged with rape, although Smith testified that he "did not enter her body." Dennis's attorney, unable to make headway in clarifying the matter, grew exasperated, finally demanding of Smith, "In plain english, did he fuck you[?]" Smith answered that he had, that he "done as he pleased, Rogered her and got off, after satisfying himself."[62]

There is another, equally important explanation for why much attention is paid in many nineteenth-century southern rape cases to the physical act of emission. In a patriarchal, racist society, a woman or girl who was raped constituted damaged goods. Evidence of consummation would have had profound and long-lasting social and personal consequences for a victim of rape. If ejaculation had taken place, she might have been seen as "polluted," especially when the assailant was a black man, and therefore tainted for the rest of her life. Anna Clark's study of rape in nineteenth-century England informs us about the lifelong burden that Lucy Beazley and her family would have been saddled with had it been established that the rape was successful. Clark observes that men "seemed to view ejaculation as a physical pollution or despoilation of a woman, rendering her damaged property forever." It is therefore understandable that family members might have urged their young daughters to deny that ejaculation had taken place. The conflicting and contradictory versions recounted by members of the Beazley family—Lucy's mother telling neighbors that the rape had not been consummated, but telling the court that it had—may reflect the family's mixed feelings about wanting justice for the sexual violation of Lucy while knowing that the cost was likely ostracism by the community and ultimately a low probability of marriage for Lucy.[63] Despite the obvious harm to Lucy's reputation, her mother, Clementina, testified to her certainty that her daughter had been raped and "very much wounded." Lucy buttressed her mother's testimony with unequivocal affirmation that the act had taken place. He "penetrated my body with his peanis. I was very much wounded."[64]

Whether or not Anderson actually consummated the act of rape upon Lucy Beazley made little practical difference in the eyes of Virginia's slave law. A slave convicted of either the rape or attempted rape of a white female faced a death penalty. Clearly, though, Anderson's master, William Goodwin, understood that if Anderson had any chance of a reprieve, doubt about the consummation of the rape would have to be cultivated.[65]

Accompanied only by a younger sister, Lucy Beazley, like many girls in the rural South, appeared to have been an easy target for a man bent on taking sex by force. Opportunity appears to have played an important role in shaping the circumstances of sexual assault of southern white women and girls. Lucy just happened to be on an isolated road and in the presence of a young child, an ineffective deterrent to her attacker. In all likelihood, Anderson, if he were guilty of the crime alleged, took advantage of the vulnerability of a young girl. Would he have attacked had Lucy been older? Did her youthfulness make her a more attractive target? Was she purposefully targeted because she was not an elite member of white society? Were some slaves, like other members of society, pedophiles who specifically targeted girls? Or were slave attacks of girls merely random acts? Trying to assess a rapist's motives and modus operandi is tricky business even in contemporary cases.[66] Looking back

150 years and imagining what a rapist might have been thinking seems all the more elusive and perhaps futile. Nonetheless, by exploring why some slaves seem to have targeted female children, most particularly those of the poorer and middling classes, we can learn something about what nineteenth-century southerners, black and white, thought of sexual violence, childhood, and sexuality as well as conventions of gender and class.

If slaves viewed young girls as easy prey—physically weak, easily manipulated—and less credible witnesses, the number of such girls who reported their crimes, bringing them to the attention of the courts, must have come as a surprise to their attackers. When threatened with death or physical violence, some girls remained quiet and compliant, but usually only for a short time. Eventually, they seem to have confided to someone close who often took the first step in lodging a formal complaint. Moreover, we know from court records that many if not most of these young girls, despite their youth, fought back, either physically or by reporting their assault to others.[67]

Youthfulness in an accuser, while likely to elicit sympathy from a jury, made a rape prosecution more difficult, as defense attorneys sometimes capitalized on a perception that young girls were less credible accusers than adult females.[68] Given the high stakes in a slave rape case, courts did seem vigilant about establishing the credibility of girl accusers, even when the alleged attacker was a black man. Rosanna Green, aged eleven, had a history of making mischief and "telling tales" that made her accusation of rape against the slave Gabriel seem less than truthful and was probably crucial in the slave's eventual pardon. Even the mother of the four-year-old Sally Briggs at one point asked her "if what she had said was not a story." Ultimately, the integrity of Lucy Dallas Beazley was also impeached, although not sufficiently or timely enough to spare the life of her alleged rapist. And recall the doubts of Lelia Wingfield's own uncle that "Old Uncle Patrick" had entered her bedroom as she claimed.[69] If these examples are any indication, white southerners were not necessarily inclined to take the word of a young accuser, given the serious nature of the assault and the grave consequences, without some sort of independent corroboration or interrogation of the veracity of the accuser.

The young age of some victims also jeopardized the successful prosecution of the sexual assault cases in another way. Law proscribed the sworn testimony of those too young to comprehend the concept of swearing an oath. The crime of rape, however, is often witnessed by no one other than the victim herself. Consequently, state attorneys frequently had to rely on the secondhand testimony of a mother or older sibling that may not have had the impact on a jury that the testimony of the victim herself would have had.[70] In addition, even if they were old enough to testify in court, child accusers typically made poor witnesses because their lack of experience and knowledge of sexual relations and anatomy often yielded vague, unspecific, even contradictory testimony about the assault and thus provided defense attorneys with ammunition for cross-examination.

Moreover, when girls accused black men of sexual assault, their reputations might be scrutinized for evidence of debauchery and deceit, just as readily as if they had been adults. Neither age nor race protected young girls from probing, intimate questions by a defense attorney or the larger white community. Indeed, mere blood ties to a promiscuous adult female might be enough to throw doubt on a child's claim of rape.[71] Although a court in Frederick County, Virginia, found Tasco Thompson, a free black man, guilty of an attempted rape on an eleven-year-old, Mary Jane Stevens, the jury appealed for leniency on the grounds that the girl's mother "had long entertained negroes." The jury reasoned that Thompson had "repaired to the house of Mrs. Stevens in the belief that she would cheerfully submit to his embraces, as she doubtless had often done before, but finding her absent he probably supposed his embraces would be equally agreeable to her daughter."[72]

It is difficult to estimate what proportion of purported slave rape victims were children. The age of an accuser in a rape case is not always stipulated in court papers (typically, court papers noted only that the child was under the age of ten). Still, data drawn from Virginia cases of slave rape or attempted rape from 1800 to 1860 reveal a relatively small number of white girls who brought forth charges of rape against slaves. Of the 123 instances in which white females swore out complaints against slaves for sex crimes, only 11 were identified as girls thirteen or younger, roughly 9 percent.[73] This figure seems low based on both regional and chronological comparisons, although of course the pool of black-on-white sexual assaults would differ in important ways from a larger pool that included white assailants. Rape trials of young girls frequently revealed that their attackers either threatened or bribed them into remaining silent, so a low level of reporting is not unexpected. We cannot know how many children actually came forward with experiences of sexual assault, but certainly many children kept their attacks secret out of fear. The low incidence of reported sexual assaults of white girl children also fails to speak to the frequency of child molestation by acquaintances and family members.[74]

Even so, when compared to sexual assaults in New York City from 1790 to

1820, the number of recorded child sexual assaults by black males in the antebellum South seems quite low. Marybeth Hamilton Arnold found that fully one-third of the 48 cases of sexual assault brought before the New York County Court of General Sessions involved girls under the age of fourteen. Similarly, Christine Stansell found that in a random sample of 101 rape cases in New York City between 1820 and 1860, 26, or roughly one-quarter, involved complainants under the age of 16 years. Of these, 19 were under 12 years of age. A very recent study of New York City in the early twentieth century yields similar results. Stephen Robertson, looking at select sexual assault cases from 1886 to 1921, found that about 26 percent of all rape cases involved children as the accusers.[75] What might account for such a wide disparity in the incidence of child rape between New York City and a single southern state? Arnold argues that children in the urban working class of New York City were saddled with tremendous adult responsibilities that at times blurred sexual boundaries as well.[76] Stansell too grounds part of her explanation in the burgeoning urban, commercial environment, namely the transition of the working-class man's understanding of class from an essentially masculine entity to a heterosexual one, an outgrowth of which was a new code of sexual behavior that was more sexually abusive and exploitative of all females, including young ones.[77]

Clearly the rural antebellum South did not reflect the urban, culture milieu of New York City of the same era. The same socioeconomic and ethnic factors that thrust countless young girls into the streets of New York did not exist in the South. Nonetheless, poor and middling children living in a rural culture performed essential chores that made them at times vulnerable to attacks. They were frequently called upon to fetch water, gather eggs, pick berries, or run a message to a neighbor, all of which potentially placed them alone or with other children in secluded spots. For example, a white fourteen-year-old girl in North Carolina was allegedly assaulted by a black male near Raleigh in 1834 while she was picking blackberries.[78] Juriah Young, a sixteen-year-old from Franklin County, Virginia, had been gathering "snaps" in her father's corn-field, about five hundred yards from her father's house, when she claimed to have been attacked by a neighbor's slave.[79] In short, young girls or children in rural areas may have been attacked only because they were accessible and unprotected. Children of the poorer to middling classes, moreover, would have been even more vulnerable, because elite children would not have been performing such mundane tasks. Slaves, not small children, would have been sent off on the kind of errands that poorer children performed routinely. But only additional studies will determine whether the low incidence of reported child rape in the antebellum South accurately reflected the extent of the crime.

Blacks in the antebellum south were of course aware that death was a likely outcome of an accusation of child rape, which could help account for the relatively low incidence of the crime. While most cases of slave rape of female children resulted in death sentences for the convicted rapists, occasionally leniency was extended to slaves charged with sexually assaulting white girls. Evidence suggests that white communities seriously deliberated such cases and did not routinely find accused slave rapists of children guilty. Sometimes, for example, juries settled on a lesser offense. A slave in Georgia went on trial in 1849 for the rape of a white four-year-old girl. The jury ultimately found insufficient evidence on the charge of assault with intent to rape, instead finding the defendant guilty of assault and battery, which when committed upon a white person was nonetheless a capital offense.[80]

Even slaves who were convicted of sexually assaulting girls might find themselves the recipients of rather lenient sentences (lenient that is, compared to death), suggesting that although southerners tended to come down hard on child rapists, there were exceptions. In Louisiana, a special tribunal found a slave named David guilty of assault with intent to commit rape of a white girl under ten years of age. He was ordered to receive 200 lashes and ten years of hard labor in prison, hardly a mild punishment, but a far cry from execution.[81] And as far back as 1724, a slave from Spotsylvania County, Virginia, was convicted of the attempted rape and buggery of a four-year-old white girl only to receive rather minimal corporal punishment: twenty-one lashes, one-half hour standing at the pillory, and having both ears severely cropped,[82] admittedly a horrendous and inhumane form of punishment.

Young girls also learned that like adult female accusers, they would not necessarily be shielded by their whiteness from official or community scrutiny. Despite the seriousness with which white officials and residents appear to have viewed child rape, youthfulness did not completely render a girl children immune from charges of improper sexual conduct. As with white women who accused slaves of sexual assault, low status in the community was inseparable from notions of depravity and debauchery.[83] The case of the servant girl Rosanna Green demonstrates that ample sympathy among certain whites for a slave charged with attempted rape of a white girl could be effectively mobilized to spare his life. In the process, interclass, intraracial antipathy was unleashed.

Rosanna Green complained to a slave woman on Good Friday in 1829 that Gabriel, a forty-year-old slave, had attempted to have his way with her. Rosanna had been sent by Mrs. Kincer, her mistress, to look for eggs in the hayloft of the barn. There, Green claimed, Gabriel grabbed her, covered her mouth, and carried her to the end of the barn, where he attempted to have sex with her.[84]

Few good things were said by anyone about the character and integrity of Rosanna Green, an eleven-year-old orphaned servant girl who lived in Wythe County, Virginia, with the family of Peter Kincer, Gabriel's owner. Neighbors, slaves, and Kincer rallied to defend Gabriel from Rosanna's charge. Rachel, the slave to whom Rosanna complained, testified that Rosanna had appeared angry at the time, but afterward was in a good humor. Rachel also reported having heard rumors that Green had "behaved badly with a black boy in the neighborhood." Another slave, Milly, swore that Green had a reputation for "telling stories" and "making mischief," which jeopardized the credibility of her testimony.[85]

White neighbors and Rosanna's own master and mistress, whom she had learned to call mother and father, also derided her character. Both Catharine and Peter Kincer claimed that Green was practically incapable of telling the truth. Joseph Atkins, a neighbor, considered Green a girl of "bad character on account of telling lies." He also reported as fact that she had had sex with a six-year-old "negro boy" from the neighborhood.[86]

The lone advocate for Rosanna Green was an uncle, William Mingle, who had taken out the warrant against Gabriel on Rosanna's behalf. Although his testimony contains no information about Green herself, Mingle did divulge that his actions had created a rift with his sister-in-law, Catharine Kincer. Kincer resented Mingle's interference in what Kincer no doubt regarded as a personal, not a community, matter.[87]

The court found Gabriel guilty, but extenuating circumstances led the court, probably persuaded by the barrage of defamatory testimony against the eleven-year-old girl, to recommend leniency. This decision provoked outrage in at least one white citizen of Wythe County, prompting him to complain to the governor and demonstrating that sympathy for the slave was by no means universal. In a letter to the governor one community member, Alexander Smith, urged him to disregard pleas for leniency: "I think it right to say, that I apprehend [Gabriel] a proper subject to be made an example, and that an example is required. It is not many years since a man suffered emasculation for an attempt on his mistress; and a few days since a youth received 120 lashes from his master for an attempt on a girl. This fellow seems to be 40, and is notorious as a thief."[88] Enclosed with the letter was a newspaper clipping that conveyed sympathy for the orphan girl. "Had her father been living, or, had she have had any natural protector, who had reaked the vengeance due to such an offence, in the blood of the perpetrator, we could never have consented to his punishment for the offence."[89] In other words, male kin would have sought personal justice through revenge and not left the girl to be publicly vilified in the local court. Likewise, we can infer that the author of the letter sensed class bias at work in the adjudication process. Had Rosanna Green not been a servant girl, the outcome might have been substantially different. In the end, Smyth's appeal went unheeded; the slave's life was spared, and he was sold and transported out of Virginia.[90] The Kincers had succeeded in saving their slave's life but had lost his services nonetheless. Based upon their testimony, we can imagine that they were quite perturbed at the loss of a good, sturdy, reliable slave merely on the say-so of a disreputable, troublesome child who was more expendable than her alleged assailant. The attempted sexual assault of a white child by a slave in the antebellum South, at least in this case, did not seem to some to warrant the death of the slave.

Neither race nor youthfulness afforded an eleven-year-old servant girl absolute protection from white scrutiny. Few members of the community regarded her as innately innocent. To the contrary, in spite of her youth, local whites and blacks maintained that she had knowingly acted improperly and had somehow invited Gabriel's advances. In fact, some members of the white community acted to shield the presumably vulnerable slave from the wiles of a child, tacitly recognizing the obligations of the paternalistic elites in a slaveholding society to protect their charges. Protection was forthcoming to a slave, not so for a child inhabiting the fringes of respectable society.[91]

Sometimes the mere association of girls with deviant female family members was enough to taint them as well. Victoria Bynum documents a white-on-white case of a fifteen-year-old North Carolina boy convicted of raping of a young girl. Over 120 residents of Guilford County signed a petition to the governor soliciting a pardon for the teenage boy on the grounds that the "mother of the victim was of bad character and her daughter . . . [was] completely under her domination."[92] Similar disdain was shown for the mother of Mary Jane Stevens, the eleven-year-old Virginian who in 1833 charged a free black man with attempted rape. Because her mother had consorted with blacks, both she and her mother "yielded their claims to the protection of the law."[93]

Sympathy displayed for the black assailants of Rosanna Green and Mary Jane Stevens, however striking, could not accurately be characterized as typical in the antebellum South. The rape of children and child molestation seem to have been perceived as especially heinous, in many circles, whether committed by black or white men. White men too were occasionally sentenced to die for raping children[94] (though not, importantly, in Virginia), as we learn from published appellate decisions. The earliest nineteenth-century case appeared in South Carolina in 1813. Francis LeBlanc was convicted of raping a seven-year-old girl in his barbershop one August afternoon. The child refrained from telling anyone for several days until her mother noticed blood on her underclothes. A medical examination not only confirmed the assault but also revealed that the young girl had contracted the "same disease" as the defendant had been suffering from, probably venereal. LeBlanc's appeal proved unsuccessful, the jurists refusing to "rescue him from the punishment he so justly deserves."[95] Quite possibly, the jury had believed LeBlanc to be especially depraved because he had been infected with a sexually transmitted disease and, worse, infected a young girl.

Two white residents of North Carolina were likewise convicted of raping children in the mid-nineteenth century, and both were sentenced to hang. A courtroom in Cumberland County was the stage for the rape trial of Alfred Terry, also known as Alfred Goings. Terry was charged with raping Mary M. Cook, aged seven.[96] Several years later, in 1844, Jesse Farmer, a laborer in Bertie County, was convicted of raping Mary Ann Taylor, a ten-year-old.[97] Both convictions were upheld; in both cases the death penalty was presumably carried out.

Many white southerners thus displayed the utmost abhorrence for perpetrators of child rape, regardless of the race of the accused, as manifested in the very harsh sentences handed down. Courts were especially tough on the accused when there was evidence of violence used to effect rape. In a highly paternalistic society, the question of whom to protect was usually, though not always, settled on the side of the white female child. Both black and white men convicted of raping white girls could and sometimes did suffer death for their purported offenses. Moreover, the rape trials of children were characterized by a higher degree of consensus about the accused's guilt than in other sexual assault cases. Still, slaves convicted of sexually assaulting female children faced death much more frequently than white men did.

While the sexual abuse or assault of white girls was viewed as especially reprehensible, there is some fragmentary evidence suggesting that whites also expressed disdain for the sexual assault of African American children. This is especially noteworthy because virtually all scholarship has suggested that females of color, especially slaves, were left unprotected by sexual assault statutes. Admittedly, there are very few cases in which slave children (or slave women, for that matter) officially brought charges of rape against either a black or white man. Most scholars have assumed that African American females were not protected by rape legislation.[98] Indeed, their unique status as both property and human beings problematized the issue of sexual assault. How could property be sexually violated?

Historians have been acutely aware that masters and their male kin represented the greatest sexual threat to their female slaves. A master's consent or intercession would have been necessary if rape charges were to be filed, and it would have been unthinkable for a master to seek redress for the violation of a slave committed by him himself or by a male family member. Moreover, unlike the rape of a female family member—an unmarried daughter, for example—which unquestionably damaged the girl's reputation and made her unmarriable, the rape of a slave child posed no similar social and economic burden to a white slaveowner, unless the rape was accompanied by significant violence. In fact, in older slave girls, rapes could result in pregnancies that would actually benefit the master. Finally, masters had no incentive to subject their own male slaves to trial for rape of female slaves, even if law allowed. The punishment of any slave would directly affect the condition and value of his property. So there was little inducement for a master to seek redress from the courts. In all probability, when made aware of sexual assault of slave girls, masters took matters into their own hands, if they acted at all.

Thus the conditions and circumstances of bondage virtually precluded slave females victimized by sexual assault from seeking the protection of the white courts. Nevertheless, most legal and southern historians have been inaccurate in stating that the rape of African American females was unacknowledged by the law and society. Invariably, they cite the case of the slave George, who was tried and convicted in Mississippi in 1859 for raping a slave girl. In fact it was George's defense attorney, not the prosecutor, who argued that the "crime of rape does not exist in this State between African slaves." He reasoned that the "regulations of law, as to the white race, on the subject of sexual intercourse, do not and cannot, for obvious reasons, apply to slaves; . . . the violation of a female slave by a male slave would be a mere assault and battery." The defendant's counsel went on to cite Mississippi statute law that made slave rape of white women a capital offense. In short, counsel asserted, there was no provision under common or statutory law that made the rape of slave women or girls an offense, let alone a capital one. The high court concurred.[99]

But the harsh, sterile tone of this one case should not be the only consideration shaping our understanding of rape law and female slaves. Several overlooked aspects of the case suggest that not all white Mississippians agreed with the high court's finding. First, someone, and someone white, had to have been motivated to bring the charge to the attention of local law officials in the first place: perhaps the master of the young victim, or an outraged neighbor (the published record is silent). Second, some justice of the peace or magistrate took the complaint seriously enough not to dismiss it out of hand and followed through with issuing a warrant. Third, and this is a fact that is often overlooked, an all-white Mississippi jury found the slave guilty of raping the slave girl. White neighbors who sat in judgment of George believed that the young slave child was capable of being raped, the law notwithstanding.[100]

Furthermore, the case appears to have prompted state lawmakers to action. Before the end of the year, the Mississippi legislature passed a law making the actual or attempted rape by a "negro or mulatto" on a female "negro or mulatto, under twelve years of age" punishable by death or whipping, as determined by the jury. Georgia soon followed suit by amending its rape law to embrace slave women. Punishment for a white man raping a white woman was two to twenty years in the penitentiary; for the rape of a woman of color, fine and imprisonment "at the discretion of the court."[101] The racial disparity in punishment is glaring and irrefutable. But in crafting the statute, Mississippi and Georgia were conceding that slave females were owed some element of legal protection from sexual violation.

A few antebellum southern communities interpreted rape statutes as encompassing nonwhite females. Though quite scarce, there are cases of white men charged with raping slave girls. The owner of one slave girl in Tennessee brought charges of rape against James Keyton, a white man. The grand jury handed up an indictment in the case, although Keyton was eventually acquitted. Still, it is instructive to recognize that some members of the white community—the girl's master, the magistrate or justice of the peace, a grand jury— responded to a charge of rape of a slave girl in the same way that they would have done had a white girl claimed to have been raped.[102] Perhaps some had been appalled at the blatant use of force in the attack. Or it is possible that enslaved children may have been considered, in a very loose sense, part of the paternalistic household and a master may have felt compelled to seek redress for reasons of personal honor. Only with more dogged research in the local court records will we be able to determine the extent to which slave children were accorded legal protection from white or black sexual predators.

One Virginia case of a rape of an African American child that aroused a tremendous amount of anger and emotion was that of Ned, the property of Walter Mills of Fredericksburg, Virginia. Ned was over sixty years of age and worked as sexton of a cemetery in Fredericksburg. He went on trial in the spring of 1859 for raping two children, a six-year-old African American girl, Betty Gordon, and her nine-year-old white friend, Eunice Thompson. According to Betty Gordon's testimony, Ned lured her into the cemetery with the promise of flowers. There he gave her something sweet to drink that he said would do her good. He then raped her. She told the court, "He pulled down his clothes. He hurt me. He put his paenis against me. He tried to put it in my body. I do not know whether he did get it in or not. It hurt me very badly." So young was this child that she could not even provide the court with the proper names of her own genitalia. She described the part of her body that had been abused by Ned as "the part of my body where I make water from."[103] Ned alternately held out threats and rewards in an attempt to secure Betty's silence. He threatened to dig a hole and put her in it. He said he would eat her, and that he would cut off her head with a nearby sickle. But he also promised to buy her some biscuits. The combination of threats and bribes proved very effective, and Betty kept their secret—for a time.[104]

No doubt a terrified Betty did her best to avoid Ned, a nearly impossible task since her aunt sent her to fetch water from a spring near the cemetery two or three times a day. A few days after the alleged rape, on a Saturday afternoon, Betty encountered Ned again. This time she was with her nine-year-old white friend, Eunice Thompson. Perhaps Betty had brought her friend with her purposefully, mistakenly thinking that Ned would dare not bother her if she were accompanied by a friend. But Ned was unfazed by the presence of a second child, a white one at that. He successfully lured the two children into the cemetery with the promise of flowers. Once in, he locked the gate behind them. He took the girls behind the vault, where he threw Betty down on the ground and began raping her. Eunice stood close by, afraid to move, for Ned had again threatened to kill the girls with the sickle. After assaulting Betty, he turned to Eunice and raped her. Eunice described her assault in much the same way that Betty had.[105]

Neither girl reported the attack to family members for several days. Betty Gordon's aunt, Virginia Gordon, became concerned when Betty spent most of Sunday lying down. It was not until Tuesday that Betty finally divulged to her aunt what Ned had done to her. Upon examination, Virginia Gordon found her niece's vagina very bruised and irritated. The next morning the outraged aunt went looking for Ned in the cemetery, demanding to know what he had done to "her little girl." Ned denied hurting Betty.[106]

At about the same time that Betty was divulging her horrible secret to her aunt, the Thompson household was also unraveling the story of the assault. Eunice had revealed the secret to an older sister, who in turn reported the incident to Jane Thompson, the child's mother. Like Betty's aunt, Thompson first had the impulse to confront Ned personally with the accusation. Unable to enter the locked gates of the cemetery, Jane Thompson swore out a warrant for Ned's arrest. Two arrest warrants were issued against Ned on May 19, 1856, one for the rape of Eunice Thompson, a white girl, and a second for the rape of Betty Gordon, "a negro female child." Ned was tried on June 9 and sentenced to die. The hanging was to take place on August 5, 1859, and would have been the first execution in Fredericksburg in fifty years.[107]

Neither the court records nor the local newspaper mention anything of the commotion that the crime incited in Fredericksburg. Only indirectly do we learn of the town's agitation. Governor Henry A. Wise received a letter from a P. F. Howard Wise praising the work of Richard Beach, whose title and occupation are unclear, but who may have been the sheriff. Acting in some official capacity, Beach had "returned with the convict Ned . . . in spite of the most violent opposition and threatening indications of personal violence." Beach found a mob gathered outside the jail, angrily declaring that "the negro should never be brought off alive" and that he deserved to be shot.[108]

Since Ned had been sentenced to hang, the mob's threat is on one level a bit curious. Community members may have been irked by a delay in meting out justice. The warrants for Ned's arrest had been sworn out in May. He was arraigned, tried, and found guilty in the first two weeks of June. But his execution was not scheduled until August 5. Perhaps the townspeople had grown weary of waiting. Nor is there evidence to suggest that anyone, Ned's owner included, was working to get Ned a reprieve, a circumstance that sometimes triggered mob intervention. In the end, however, the threat of vigilantism abated and Ned hanged.[109]

Fredericksburg's emotional vigilante response to the rape of two small children, one white, one black, is what some works have incorrectly characterized as the "usual" response to accusations of black rape of whites.[110] More often than not, however, charges of black rape, even of white children, made their way calmly through antebellum courts. Eugene Genovese has correctly observed that "the extent to which the law, rather than the mobs, dealt with slave criminals appeared nowhere so starkly as in the response to rape cases."[111] It was, however, cases involving alleged sexual assaults of children that most frequently brought a community to the brink of vigilante justice, as witnessed in Fredericksburg, Virginia, in 1859.

To summarize, the cases of slaves accused of raping or attempting to rape white girls have some of the same characteristics of those involving white adult female accusers.[112] Typically, the cases proceeded through the legal system without threat of vigilante violence, regardless of the social status of the accuser. In the trials, slaves were accorded certain rights: the right to interrogate an accuser, and the right to present defense witnesses, and the right to appeal. There are a few cases of lynch mobs that intervened when a slave was suspected of raping a white child, but these were relatively rare.

As when adult women accused slaves of rape, social standing mattered a great deal. For one, the absence of privilege in the lives of poorer white children exposed them to circumstances that made them more vulnerable to attack. Unable to rely on servants to perform chores, middling and poor folk frequently relied on young girls to run errands, either alone or with small children, thus providing attackers of both races with greater opportunities for assaults. Functioning as servants for their families, these girls came into frequent daily contact with slave males. In this regard, the sexual vulnerability of poor and middling young girls is not unlike that which prevailed in antebellum cities. Christine Stansell's study of antebellum New York City finds that girls of the working class were especially vulnerable to sexual affronts by grown men whose attraction to young girls was common enough to be characterized as a "practice that existed on the fringes of 'normal' male sexuality."[113]

Second, like female adult rape cases, child rape cases sometimes served as loci for class and gender prejudices. White girls, especially those of the poorer classes, risked having their lives scrutinized for evidence of illicit behavior, sexual or otherwise. White girls, like adult white women, were judged within a culture steeped in grave suspicion of women. Misogyny was not blinded by some romantic notions of youthful innocence. The combination of young age and lower-class status seems to have weakened any taboos against sexual activity with girls, if such taboos ever existed.

The behavior of white southerners in these cases also lays bare a gap between an ideology that idealized children and the means by which children were actually protected. Elite white southerners romanticized children; yet the statutory law recognized only girls under ten as incapable of consenting to sex. Local courts would rigorously interrogate the testimony of young girls in a manner that belies the sentimentalization of children. Poor and middling families sent their young children off on errands for great distances—and of great danger. The halting protection accorded to some children who brought forth charges of sexual assault seems to reflect the limitations of sentimental notions about childhood. The ideology simply had not evenly permeated all aspects of southern antebellum society, and specifically had failed to permeate the law.[114]

The ideology that sentimentalized children left out not only nonelites but more pointedly African Americans. Social and economic institutions built on racial slavery could not have survived if white southerners had been forced to reconcile bonded slavery with notions of treating slave children delicately and with great affection, as demanded by the condition of childhood. Moreover, slave children performed many of the same chores as poor whites did, thus exposing them to sexual danger. Predisposed to believe that African American females were innately promiscuous and thus that raping them was a logical impossibility, local authorities in the antebellum South confronted by the rape of black girls would look the other way. Slave recollections and reminiscences remind us that the rape of slave females by whites, especially masters, was rampant. That much is indisputable. However, the courts did hear isolated cases in which black girls charged rape. Occasionally, sectors of the white community made clear their revulsion and established limits for sexual outrages committed against slave children, at least when committed by men of color.

Race figured most conspicuously in the treatment of the accused in child rape cases. African American men were more likely to be sentenced to death for the sexual assault of white girls, though a few white men also hanged for child rape. Convicted slaves ran a much higher chance of dying for their alleged offense than when charged with raping women. This disparity apparently reflects a more general trend in the antebellum South to punish rapists of girls more harshly than rapists of women. This book focuses exclusively on the South, but an initial comparison with studies of antebellum New York suggests that southern communities dealt more harshly with child rapists, black and white. This can only be a tentative, qualified assertion, however. The recent work of Mary Block, for example, which looks primarily at appellate law (only some of which I have referenced here), finds that southern appellate judges frequently overturned the convictions of child rapists, both black and white, in effect negating community decisions. She describes a very unchivalrous record among southern appellate courts, calling into question the umbrella of protection white men claimed to have held up for women and children.[115] There is an intriguing manifestation of paternalism in the high court decisions. If we think of the paternalism of appellate judges as a form of humanitarianism, we see that it does not apply equally to (male) slaves, whom we (rightly) think of as the most oppressed people in southern society, and poor (female) children. In fact, the decisions underscore just how powerless and neglected these female children must have been.

Importantly, the relatively harsh sentences handed down to slaves convicted of sexually assaulting white girls should not diminish the importance of the deliberations that courts and other legal officers entered into during these cases. In this highly paternalistic society, judges were ever mindful of the need to utilize the law as a social arm of protection. But whom to protect, slaves or young white girls? White men, individually and through the institutions that they created and represented, took seriously their responsibility to manage their charges and to fairly adjudicate conflicts that emerged, including sexual transgressions. At times the balance between protecting slaves (from unfounded accusations of rape) and white children (from black sexual predators) proved difficult, yielding some apparent ambivalence and even contradictions in court decisions and community debates. The courts—judges and juries— seem to have understood that the stakes were too high to take the word of a mere child at face value without interrogation. A vengeful, manipulative mother could too easily instigate charges of rape by a daughter to exact compensation from a wealthy slaveholder. Or less nefariously, a child could have simply misinterpreted or been confused by an innocuous display of affection. Either way, the scrutiny and sometimes ill treatment of white children who leveled charges of black rape reflects, not contradicts, the paternalistic ethos of the South.

HE SHALL SUFFER DEATH
Black-on-White Rape Law in
the Early South

3

Slaveholding states, to the one, prescribed the severest punishments conceivable for blacks convicted of sexually assaulting white females: death and castration. For some historians, these draconian rape statutes have served as a social barometer with which to gauge the level of white anxiety about black sexual aggression, suggesting that castration and death sentences for black rape, in stark contrast to less stringent punishments for white offenders, signaled near unconditional intolerance and revulsion among whites for sexual affronts to white women by black men. But such an interpretation fails to account for the implementation of the law, which could be much more relaxed than the written code would allow. Each colonial or state government had at its disposal the means to ameliorate the harsh rape law and to fashion a response that enabled officials to consider a multiplicity of factors, not merely the law itself. As Joshua Rothman observes, "Maintaining social stability, rather than enforcing draconian implementation of the law, dictated the strategy of governing officials when they confronted such potentially explosive matters" as sexual criminality.[1] Despite extremely rigid and harsh punishments for black rape, governments had at their disposal the means to skirt the severe sentences when warranted by compelling considerations. Death or castration for blacks convicted of sexual assault was hardly a guaranteed outcome.

Judging white attitudes about black-on-white rape on the basis of the law alone leaves the impression that the white South took an unequivocally hard line on black rapists. Yet as previously cited cases indicate, such an approach fails to account for the behavior of southern whites who, for many reasons, took issue with the harshly crafted laws and at times worked to forestall the severe punishments and negotiate the outcome of black rape cases. Most notably, slaveowners had plenty of incentive to keep slaves—their property—

healthy and alive. Other factors, for example the deep-seated prejudices about poorer women who did not conform to societal conventions of appropriate sexual behavior, help to explain why some whites lent their support to black men accused of sexually assaulting white females. White women, or even girls, who behaved badly in the eyes of a community were thought to deserve the rough treatment they received when the community sat in judgment. Inelastic statutes of course made no accommodation for mitigating circumstances. Yet juries and judges in the early slave South frequently made distinctions outside the strictures of the written law and fashioned their decisions accordingly. A closer look at the cases therefore enables us to gauge more accurately the values of a community in a way that slave criminal statutes alone cannot.

The findings in the first two chapters of this book reveal the need to evaluate black rape statutes in the larger lived world of white and black southerners. In their hands, the law was molded to conform to custom. This chapter explores the evolution of those rigid statutes from the colonial era through the antebellum period. It surveys the origins of prescribed punishments for black rape in historical context, suggesting that utilitarian concerns emanating from the unique condition of slavery, as well as racism, guided lawmakers in crafting black rape statutes. Contrary to the conclusions that some historians have drawn about the causal link between black rape laws and white sexual anxiety, I argue that the harsh punishments reserved for slave rapists, like harsh punishments for other serious slave offenses, derived from the system of slavery generally and cannot be explained solely on the basis of anxiety about black rape. Moreover, the outcome of numerous slave rape trials was not death or castration, as mandated by law, but rather transportation, signaling deference to competing interests and values within the slave South. The financial value of a slave weighed heavily in determining the outcome of a slave rape trial.

In some scholarly renderings castration especially stokes images of white men seeking bloody vengeance for the rape of a white female by a black man. On one level, it is easy to imagine a white community, consumed by racism and wedded to the exalted view of its female members, exacting retribution for an assault upon a white woman through the physical emasculation—and hence the annihilation of sexual agency—of the perpetrator. But officially sanctioned castration in slave rape cannot fully be understood without first examining its origins and its historical context.

Castration of black sex offenders, like hanging, stemmed not from white rape fears directed at black men but rather from the peculiar circumstances of slavery. Shaped on the one hand by the need to maintain strict control over the region's bondsmen and to deter future infractions, and on the other hand by the need to protect the financial investments of slaveholders and to prop up the region's political and economic elite, the two considerations seem hopelessly irreconcilable. This tension played out when local communities tried slaves for rape and, at times, attempted to shield them from the unforgiving and unequivocal language of the written law.

A very influential body of work premised on statutory evidence has argued that widespread sexual anxiety among whites pervaded slaveholding America. Some historians have cited statutory law as proof, specifically laws that singled out slaves and free blacks accused of rape for harsher punishment than whites. Sentences of death and castration typically followed convictions of slave rape and have been held out as evidence of virulent white fears of black rape. These laws, to some, are a monument to white concerns about black sexual assault of white women, and no better example exists than the statutes that called for the castration of convicted black rapists.[2]

The occasional colonial statute that imposed castration on black males convicted of sexually assaulting white females is frequently advanced as evidence of sexual anxiety among whites about black male sexuality.[3] Winthrop Jordan wrote that the "white man's fears of Negro sexual aggression were . . . apparent in the use of castration as a punishment in the colonies."[4] One historian even asserted that the castration of slaves who made sexual advances on white women was virtually automatic: "It almost goes without saying that the penalty for a slave who dared lust after white women's flesh was castration, first by the law of the slave code, later by community justice alone."[5] More recently, Peter Bardaglio has argued that "anxieties of southern white males about black sexual aggression found their most morbid expression" in the castration of black males for the rape or attempted rape of white females.[6]

While it is true that both slaveholders and local officials at times utilized castration as a means to control errant slaves, the punishment was never exclusively used in cases of alleged sexual affronts and seems to have been limited to four southern jurisdictions: Virginia, North and South Carolina, and later Missouri.[7] And anxiety about black rape was not the chief motive. Initially at least, castration was not even reserved for black rapists. In South Carolina, it was the punishment for slaves who ran away for a fourth time;[8] in Virginia, for troublesome "outlying" slaves.[9] North Carolina excepted black rapists outright, reserving castration for first-time offenders of serious crimes *other than rape* and murder.[10]

Nor was castration reserved solely for African American slaves. A measure passed in colonial New Jersey in the first decade of the eighteenth century directed that "if any Negro, Indian or Mallatto Slave shall attempt by force or perswasion to Ravish or have carnal Knowledge of any White Woman, Maid, or Child . . . [he] shall be Castrated."[11] The wording of the statute suggests that slaves, whether Indian or African descendants, were the object of this directive. Importantly, free blacks do not appear to have been encompassed by this law. Pennsylvania's statute permitted the castration of white men, although there is no evidence that the punishment was ever carried out on white men.[12] That some colonies legally sanctioned castration for Indians and even whites calls into question the claim that the castration penalty for sex crimes has its colonial roots primarily in white stereotypes about black lasciviousness.

Reliance on southern rape statutes to gauge white sexual anxiety about blacks has led some historians to claim that whites were preoccupied with black rape in colonial and early America. Indeed, judging by colonial rape statutes, it would appear that southern legislative bodies took sexual assault very seriously, regardless of the race of the perpetrator. Several southern colonies, and later states, held out the death penalty for both black and white rapists. In Virginia, for example, before 1796 the law was equally harsh to rapists free and unfree, European- and African-descended; death could be prescribed for all.[13] Likewise, colonial South Carolina sentenced black and white rapists to death.[14] Among the southern colonies that did in fact treat black and white sex offenders differently were Georgia, Maryland, and North Carolina.[15] The norm for British America, however, was to hold out capital punishment for all rapists regardless of color.

The castration of slaves as a form of punishment emerged and continued not so much because black male sexual ardor was feared but rather because slaves were property. In the colonial South, numerous crimes when committed by slaves or African Americans were considered capital.[16] Since the colonial treasuries were required to compensate slaveowners for executed slave criminals, some colonies looked to sexual dismemberment as a means not only to punish and deter but to do so at minimal cost.[17] The punishment was serious, yet it spared colonial governments the costly burden of compensating slave masters for the loss of slave lives. One North Carolinian in 1737 complained bitterly about the high cost of reimbursing masters for executed slaves: "The Planters suffer little or nothing by it, for the Province is obliged to pay the full value they judge them worth to the Owner; this is the common Custom or Law in this Province, to prevent the Planters being ruined by the loss of their Slaves, whom they have purchased at so dear a rate."[18]

The policy of reimbursing masters for condemned slaves came under closer scrutiny during the French and Indian War when the cost of the war strained colonial coffers even further. In an attempt to reduce the huge sums paid in compensation for executed slaves, the North Carolina legislature in 1758 passed a law that substituted castration for execution in all but cases of murder and rape.[19] During the years in which the law was in place, 1759–64, officials castrated sixteen slaves.[20] Once the war was over and dire economic conditions eased, the castration clause was removed, and executions of convicted slave criminals resumed.[21]

By the end of the eighteenth century official use of castration to punish slaves diminished substantially.[22] In 1769 the Virginia legislature severely circumscribed the use of castration as punishment, reasoning that "dismemberment is often disproportionate to the offense." Thereafter, the castration of slaves was forbidden, except in cases of attempts to ravish a white woman.[23] Even so, Philip Schwarz, in his survey of crime among Virginia slaves, could locate only four instances of officially sanctioned castration after passage of the law.[24] Among these, a slave in Northampton County, Virginia, was castrated in 1782 after a court was convinced that he had attempted to rape a white woman.[25] Six months later another Virginia slave, Bob of Southampton County, was castrated for the rape of his owner's mother.[26]

While the state virtually abandoned castration as a remedy for black rape by the late eighteenth century, masters at times utilized castration as a private means of retribution and punishment or as a way to curtail "high spirits."[27] In a dispute over damages arising from the sale of three slaves in 1818 that found its way before the South Carolina supreme court, we learn of a belligerent slave who had been castrated, presumably by private individuals, not officials. Evidently the slave was castrated not for any sexual improprieties but because of a "malicious and vindictive" temper that had manifested itself as thievery and running away.[28] But here too, the motivation appears not to have been white alarm about black rape.

Not all white southerners approved of castrating slaves. At least one colony, Georgia, passed a law *outlawing* the castration of slaves as a form of punishment. Violators risked a stiff fine of ten pounds sterling.[29] Charles Janson reported that in his travels through North Carolina, probably in the late 1790s, he came across a planter-doctor who had been pressed into service by a slaveowner plagued by his slave's repeated "attempts on the chastity of his female neighbors." The doctor reluctantly performed the castration on the slave but refused to accept payment, apparently a reflection of the doctor's uneasiness about the procedure.[30]

Other white southerners shared the doctor's apprehensions and misgivings about the propriety of castration as an acceptable form of slave control, and the procedure seems to have been perceived by some eighteenth-century southerners as cruel and inhumane. An anonymously written contribution to the *Virginia Gazette* in December 1773 publicly chastised a Virginia slaveowner known for the inhumane treatment of his slaves, including the castration of one runaway slave.[31] In 1784 officials in Mecklenburg County, Virginia, outraged that a local slaveowner had directed one of his slaves to castrate another, slapped him with a warrant. Henry Delong appeared before the county court, charged with "cutting and destroying the testicles of the Negro man Will." While Delong confessed to having ordered his slave Ned to castrate Will, the court held that the crime was not a felony and thus discharged Delong. Although in the end Delong escaped punishment for his action, even his being ordered to appear before the court to account for the castration demonstrates that certain officials felt he had exceeded his authority.[32]

As late as 1850, authorities in Tennessee prosecuted a slave master who castrated one of his slaves, Josiah, again not for any sexual infractions but because of a "turbulent, insolent" disposition. Gabriel Worley, described as a yeoman "somewhat advanced in life" who was "remarkable for his kindness and humanity toward his slaves," had apparently grown weary of Josiah's repeated escapes as well as his harassment of other slaves. Worley banished all the female family members from the premises, and with the assistance of his son and a "certain razor" "did strike, cut off, and disable the organs of generation" of Josiah.[33] Worley then summoned a physician to dress the wound, with the court noting that Josiah recovered quickly. Local officials nonetheless charged Worley with mayhem, an act outlawed by Tennessee statute.[34] The Tennessee supreme court justices were repulsed by the owner's actions. They upheld his two-year jail term.[35]

The individual use of castration at the hands of slave masters, as in these several instances, most likely represented attempts to curb more general turbulent behavior in male slaves, much like a farmer's neutering of a bull or horse. That masters would borrow from the pages of basic husbandry manuals that recommended castrating unruly male livestock and apply these same principles to their slaves should surprise no one. Simply put, castration of slaves as a means to modify behavior and curtail unruliness was an entirely logical extension of some of the most basic elements of agrarian culture.

These anecdotes do not imply that alleged black sex offenders escaped castration entirely. The fact remains that many slaves—and no known whites— were castrated for the crime of rape or attempted rape. Moreover, many more errant slaves in colonial early America were executed as prescribed by their sentences. In 1738, for instance, Jemmy, a slave owned by James Holman of

Goochland County, Virginia, was tried and convicted for raping Elizabeth Weaver, daughter of Samuel Weaver. The court sentenced him to hang.[36] Two years earlier one of Richard Bradford's slaves, Andrew, had been sentenced to die for raping Elizabeth Williams, the wife of Joseph Williams of Caroline County, Virginia.[37] When the alleged victim of a rape was a member of the slaveowner's family, retribution was no doubt swifter than usual. In 1775 Natt, a slave in Lancaster County, was sentenced to die for raping Sarah James, the daughter-in-law of his owner, Walter James.[38] Extreme official reprisal for black rape was within the spectrum of community responses.

Sometimes death alone was deemed an inadequate deterrent to other would-be slave rapists, especially in the early eighteenth century. In 1701 one Virginia slave was hanged for the rape of a married white woman. His severed head was then placed on a pole as a warning to "Negroes and other Slaves from Committing the Like Crymes and Offences."[39] In 1777 the body of Titus, a North Carolina slave, was burned after he was hanged for the crime of rape.[40]

Clearly some blacks received the full force of the law after their rape convictions. The larger point, however, is that despite the harsh tenor of Virginia's colonial rape statutes and the frequent executions of convicted black rapists, some convicted slave rapists actually got off relatively lightly. In 1724 Caesar, a slave owned by Gawen Corbin of Spotsylvania County, was charged with the attempted rape and buggery of a four-year-old white girl. Recall that although Caesar was convicted, he nonetheless was sentenced only to corporal punishment: twenty-one lashes, one half-hour standing at the pillory, and the severe cropping of both ears.[41] A similar account was recorded in 1737 in the *Virginia Gazette* involving a free black man in Isle of Wight County who was convicted of the attempted rape of a seven-year-old white girl. The man was condemned not to die but to receive twenty-nine lashes and an hour in the pillory, and then to be sold to pay court costs and fees. The paper reported that he was pilloried, then "much pelted by the Populace; and afterwards smartly whipp'd."[42] And in the same Virginia county where in 1775 a slave had hanged for raping his master's daughter-in-law, the same court roughly one week later heard testimony in a similar case involving Tom, a slave owned by Nancy Dameron of Northumberland County. Tom purportedly attempted to rape a white woman, Chloe Carter. But rather than execute Tom the court decided that he should have "each of his Ears nailed to the Pillory, & then cut out, to be branded on the Cheek with a hot Iron & to receive thirty nine Lashes well laid upon his bare Back at the publick Whipping Post."[43] The gruesome fate of some convicted black rapists in the eighteenth-century South has to be juxtaposed with the slap on the wrist that some black men received for their alleged sexual crimes.

While occasionally black men convicted of sexually assaulting white females received relatively lenient sentences, those who escaped death more often than not had colonial or state executives to thank. Daniel, a slave belonging to John Brummall of Chesterfield County, Virginia, cheated the executioner by appealing to governor. Having stood trial in the fall of 1753 for raping Mary Danfork (spelling of surname uncertain), Daniel received the death penalty but then escaped from jail. Officials soon recaptured him and wasted no time in reinstating the original guilty verdict; however, this time the court attached an addendum recommending that the governor reprieve Daniel. It seems that since Daniel's flight, the court had obtained information leading it to "suspect the veracity of the witness upon whom his testimony he was convicted." The governor acceded to the court's wishes.[44] A slave owner in Maryland also proved successful in receiving a pardon for his slave, Abraham, who had been convicted of breaking and entering, stealing, and attempting to ravish a white woman. Petitioners, including Abraham's accuser, requested the pardon, in large part because Abraham's master had elicited a confession under the duress of a whipping. The pardon was granted conditionally upon the slave's departure from Maryland within ten days.[45]

Colonial and state legislatures conferred liberal powers of review and commutation on governors and executive bodies. In Virginia, all slaves convicted of capital crimes—and rape-related offenses were indeed capital crimes—had their trial records forwarded to the governor, who then determined whether grounds existed to extend mercy. The governor, after his executive council had reviewed the trial summary and any attached appeals or recommendations, might find no compelling reason to intervene, in which case the council advised the governor to allow the execution to take place. The council, on the other hand, could be persuaded that extenuating circumstances merited leniency. The governor might then respond by reprieving the convicted slave from the sentence of death and selling him to a buyer who would then agree to transport the slave out of the state. Transportation, as this latter procedure was called, allowed the state to offset some of the cost of reimbursing slaveowners for the loss of condemned slaves. But it was also believed by some that the action was a form of humanitarian intercession, something that the statutory law did not allow. Finally, transportation proved to be a good substitute for execution, which some Virginians had come to believe was no longer an effective deterrent to slave crime.[46] So while the legislature had implemented stringent rape laws for black men, it also opened the door to case-by-case intervention by state officials through the check of commutation.

Execution and castration, the draconian punishments prescribed for black rapists, were thus anything but a guaranteed outcome. Lenient treatment of slave rape and reprieves by the governor demonstrate that despite the harshness of colonial rape statutes, officials may not have vigorously enforced them, which is one of the major contentions of this book. Race unquestionably played a conspicuous role in determining whether to prosecute alleged rapists, as well as what sentences were deemed appropriate. Certainly African American men in the colonial South accused of rape or attempted rape were treated more harshly than white men who stood accused of the same crimes. Indeed, numerous black men convicted of sexually assaulting white women or girls in the eighteenth century did die for their alleged crimes. Nonetheless, the cases of colonial African Americans convicted of rape or attempted rape of white females who escaped execution or castration demonstrate that justice meted out to convicted black rapists was not universally harsh, although decidedly harsher than that meted out to white men similarly convicted.[47] Even though the statutes dealt with rapists, black and white, in a severe manner, the result was not routinely a death or castration sentence. Eugene Genovese's consideration of the hegemonic function of the law is valuable in understanding this contradiction. Genovese has argued that slaveholders, in fashioning strict slave codes, never intended rigorous enforcement. Instead, severe legislation was meant to be used at the government's discretion during times of crisis and emergency, such as a slave insurrection.[48] Another historian has put it more forthrightly: "When the crime of the slave threatened the institution of slavery or otherwise encroached on the economic welfare of the slaveholder, the punishment meted out was as harsh as the law allowed; but if, in contrast, the crime was of no economic consequence, or, if severe punishment would have been contrary to the economic interest of the slaveholder, mitigation was the rule."[49]

The treatment of black males in early southern rape statutes reflects not white anxiety about black rape but rather the broader codified conviction that blacks, and more pointedly slaves, had to abide by a different, stricter set of legal standards to ensure greater control of the region's bonded labor force. Moreover, the punishment of castration enabled colonial and state governments to spare their treasuries the exorbitant costs of compensating slaveowners whose slaves were convicted of serious crimes, among which were rape and attempted rape. Castration served the dual purposes of saving money while maintaining control over the slave population; it allowed colonial authorities to punish felonious slave behavior and deter future slave crime while minimizing the financial losses to individual slaveowners and the colonial or state governments.[50] Like slaveowners, state and colonial governments, out of practical considerations of which the most important were financial, balked at exacting the strict punishments called for in cases of black-on-white sexual assault.

Eighteenth-century executive and legislative largess toward convicted black rapists had its limits. Arguing that pardons and light sentences for convicted African American sex offenders were common in the early South does not insinuate that such men were treated "fairly."[51] In fact, black males accused of sexually assaulting white females did experience a high conviction rate, demonstrating some measure of restraint or reluctance by government officials to intervene and possibly overturn a death sentence. Philip Schwarz, in his comprehensive study of slave crime in Virginia, has found that between 1706 and 1785, fifty-nine slaves were accused of rape and attempted rape. Of those, fifty, or 84.7 percent, were convicted. Still, a high conviction rate of black rapists does not prove that white colonials were obsessed with black rapists. Slaves charged with hog stealing, for example, experienced a higher conviction rate than those charged with rape and attempted rape.[52] Slaves brought before the courts in the South in general were dealt with more harshly than the white population. Slave rapists were no exception.

The era of the American Revolution, the swell of Enlightenment ideals, and the subsequent founding of the new nation mitigated some of the more severe features of colonial law, for both blacks and whites. Legal reform, as well as the overhaul of judicial systems, became the focus of many Americans during this era, including Virginians. Virginia lawmakers, for example, restricted official use of castration in 1769 to only one slave offense, the attempted rape of a white woman.[53] In 1772 the Virginia legislature passed two major reforms regarding slave justice. First, it extended the benefit of clergy to slaves convicted of breaking and entering at nighttime. Second, a majority vote of justices deciding the fate of an accused slave criminal was necessary to condemn the slave to death.[54] But as Philip Schwarz rightly points out, one can read too much into these reforms. For one thing, they did not necessarily translate into action. As well, they were bound to be limited when applied to the bonded population. Nonetheless, post-revolutionary humanitarianism did bring about some amelioration in the law of slavery, albeit a temporary one.[55] Importantly, the number of crimes considered capital when committed by slaves diminished, as did the rigorous enforcement of harsh slave codes in the nineteenth-century South.[56]

By the mid-nineteenth century, virtually all southern states had fine-tuned their rape statutes along the very specific lines of race, slave status, or both. With few exceptions, black men, usually slaves, who raped or attempted to rape white females were singled out for harsher punishment than white men who raped or attempted to rape white females, in part because the rape of white women when committed by men of color was perceived by southern white society as a worse crime than white-on-white rape. This was true, however, of virtually all criminal acts against person and property when committed by a slaves or free blacks, and was institutionalized in the earliest colonial laws. Slave attacks on white persons and their property challenged the social and economic underpinnings of the slaveholding South. For that reason, southern lawmakers early on devised laws, usually in the form of a slave code, for their bonded population that by definition had to be race specific.[57] A British legal adviser assigned to review Barbadian slave laws in 1679 justified separate codes for slaves by asserting, "Negros in that Island are punishable in a different and more severe manner than other Subjects are for Offences of the like nature; yet I humbly conceive that the Laws there concerning Negros are reasonable Laws, for by reason of their numbers they become dangerous, and being a brutish sort of People and reckoned as goods and chattels in that island, it is of necessity or at least convenient to have Laws for the Government of them different than the Laws of England, to prevent the great mischief that otherwise may happen to the Planters and Inhabitants in that Island."[58]

Legislating harsher punishments for slave sex offenders, therefore, is no accurate indication of white sexual anxiety about black male sexual aggression. There was an implicit understanding that slaves and non-slaves needed to be governed by different systems of law.[59] Sexual assault, like all other forms of assault, was treated more seriously when committed by a slave on a white person than by a white person.[60]

The other racial component of the black rape statutes was the race of the victim. Universally, black rape was defined as forced sex with a white female. But rape statutes intended to apply to white men generally did not specify the race of the victim. For example, a compilation of South Carolina statutes published in 1814 defined rape in rather race-neutral language. "Where a man ravisheth a woman married, lady, damosel, or other, with force" was how the

South Carolina lawmakers defined rape. Class connotations notwithstanding, black females were not excluded from this definition. Similarly, a Virginia law in 1792 defined a rapist as "whatsoever person shall take a woman against her will."[61] Only Kentucky crafted white rape laws spelling out the race of the victim as white.[62] Most southern states operated under the unstated racial assumption that a person's race was presumed to be white unless explicitly stated to the contrary.

Slaveholding states appeared to operate under two sets of codes, one for their black population, the other for their white population. For example, two separate Alabama laws in 1840 addressed rape and race. African Americans, regardless of bondage status, committed a capital offense when raping a white woman: "Every slave, free negro, or mulatto, who shall commit, or attempt to commit the crime of rape on any white female . . . shall suffer death."[63] The statute intended for whites did not even mention race: "Any person who shall commit the crime of rape and be convicted thereof, shall be punished in the penitentiary for life."[64] With a single exception, southern legislatures did not feel it necessary to specify race; it was implicitly understood.[65]

At first glance it would appear that southern states in the nineteenth century, as in the colonial period, considered the sexual assault of a white female a heinous crime whether committed by a black or a white male. Nine slaveholding states at various times before the Civil War prescribed death for white rapists.[66] Of these, four retained the death penalty for white rapists through the Civil War.[67] Conviction of white men for particularly abominable sex crimes, for example, rape of children, made a death sentence for whites more likely but not inevitable.[68] The more prevalent punishment for white offenders after the Revolution was imprisonment. Of the southern states that punished white rapists with prison terms, the least harsh were Georgia (two to twenty years), Missouri (not less than five years), and Texas (not less than one year at hard labor, later changed to five to fifteen years). Alabama, Louisiana, and Mississippi at one time or another sentenced white rapists to life imprisonment.[69] Virginia for most of the nineteenth century sentenced convicted white rapists to ten to twenty or twenty-one years in the penitentiary, as did Kentucky. Prison registers from that state reveal that white men serving time for rape or attempted rape were sentenced to anywhere from three to twenty years, although most served from ten to seventeen years.[70]

On the whole, sentences for white rapists diminished in severity as the nineteenth century progressed, reflecting a trend toward the restricted use of the death penalty.[71] Some states that at first punished white rapists with the death penalty and later prescribed a penitentiary sentence were probably responding to the emergence of penitentiaries built, in part, to spare some convicted criminals from execution. Before the construction of a state prison in the 1830s, for example, Georgia statutes contained an astonishing 160 offenses for which the death penalty could be invoked.[72] Most states regarded rape as a serious crime and had few options, other than the death penalty, at their disposal. When states built penitentiaries, they often modified their penal codes accordingly. What might have been a capital offense before the building of a state penitentiary later became a noncapital offense. This was the case in Arkansas, Alabama, and Texas.[73] Thus the lessening of penalties for convicted white rapists should not be interpreted as reflecting increasing indifference toward sexual assault by lawmakers or their constituents. Rather, states continued to view rape as a serious offense, but generally not one deserving of execution, at least when committed by white males. The opening of penitentiaries gave officials greater flexibility in sentencing as well as the opportunity to incorporate less severe punishments, for rape as well as other violent and criminal acts.

Apart from the trend toward ameliorating punishment in response to the opening of penitentiaries, the majority of southern states made no major revisions of their statutes governing white rape before the Civil War. A few states inexplicably modified rape laws to make punishment for white rape harsher.[74] While variations make it difficult to generalize about uniform statutory punishments for convicted white rapists, all slaveholding states, save one, held out death for men of color convicted of rape, attempted rape, or assault with intent to rape.[75] The most glaring disparity in southern rape law was that for the most part, attempted rape or assault with intent to rape by a white man was only rarely a capital offense. Men of color faced the death penalty almost universally for unconsummated rape. This same disparity, it should be noted, was mirrored in nonsexual assault statutes. In most slaveholding states black-on-white assault was a capital crime; for whites, a misdemeanor.

The literalness of statutory southern rape law—black men who raped white women shall suffer the most severe punishment—leaves the misleading impression that statutes reflected a fundamental anxiety about black rape. Closer examination of those statutes, specifically their application and historical context, reveals a more complex picture, one that challenges the use of rape laws alone as an accurate measure of sexual anxiety about black men. In practice, convicted slave rapists frequently eluded the severe punishments of capital punishment and castration provided for by law. Yes, the law unequivocally stated that death or castration was the appropriate penalty for black rapists. But we must look beyond the legal texts themselves and not take them at face value if we are to arrive at a better understanding of the racial, class, and gender dynamics that were at work in the antebellum South.

Southern executive, legislative, and judicial processes provided a level of flexibility that allowed interested community members and their elected officials to withhold the most draconian punishments for condemned black sex offenders. Governors, supported by their executive support staffs, could exercise their powers of review and clemency and spare any condemned black man a trip to the gallows. Petitioners frequently besieged governors' offices with pleas for leniency on behalf of condemned slave rapists. Some of these petitions came from the self-interested owners of the ill-fated slaves, who most likely were making their case to a sympathetic fellow member of the slaveholding elite. Governors were often persuaded that extenuating circumstances—a hapless, naïve slave caught up in the web of a designing woman, for instance—merited a reprieve from the death sentence. In this way, governors proved that they shared the gender and class biases of some southern communities. Moreover, governors were also acting as guardians of their own state treasuries. Reprieves, followed by transportation, allowed states to offset some of their financial losses incurred by compensating owners for executed slaves.

For various reasons white southerners—community members, lawyers, jurors, slaveowners, governors—found ways to circumvent the ostensibly mandated penalty of execution or castration for slave rapists, revealing that the law did not function in a vacuum: community customs and standards played an important role. Moreover, lay and official efforts to thwart the letter of the law in rape statutes demonstrate that whites in the early South were not convulsed by sexual fears of black men. Had they been, far more alleged black rapists would have died at the hands of the executioner.

THE VERY HELPLESSNESS
OF THE ACCUSED APPEALS
TO OUR SYMPATHY
Rape, Race, and Southern
Appellate Law

4

White southerners of the Old South, animated by myriad motives, found numerous ways to sidestep harshly worded slave rape laws and spare the lives of convicted rapists. White community members responded in a variety of ways to charges of black rape, sometimes lining up with others of their race to support the accuser, sometimes to endorse the case of the accused, but only rarely to deny the accused a formal hearing in court. And even when a jury found a black man guilty of sexual assault and no pardoning campaign ensued, one additional route remained for some accused black rapists: the state appellate courts. Condemned slaves, including black rapists, routinely made their way through the appellate process for further adjudication, another avenue through which an accused slave rapist could plead his case and hope for a favorable outcome.[1] The decisions of state supreme courts often reflected a reading of the law and the record that betrayed a fundamental contempt or disregard for the white female complainants who claimed to have been sexually assaulted by black men.

Appellate decisions in black-on-white rape cases throughout the Old South do not lend themselves to tidy generalizations. Yet it is clear that state supreme court justices, like the local judges who originally heard the cases, the white neighbors who took stock of them, and the governors who received pardoning petitions, responded to cases of black-on-white rape rationally and methodically, unencumbered by worries about the threat of black sexual aggression. In fact, decisions in black rape cases are noteworthy particularly for the absence of rhetoric about the bestial proclivities of black men. Rather, high courts in the antebellum South took seriously their charge to adjudicate claims of legal missteps, and the nature of the crime—sexual assault of white females—appears not to have held any special distinction for the jurists. There is no evidence to suggest that high court judges overlooked or minimized minor procedural irregularities or errors in black rape cases to better protect white communities from a perceived black sexual threat. More to the point, by overturning black rape convictions, appellate judges surely understood that they risked returning a black rapist to the community, possibly to sexually assault another white female.

Paternalism figures prominently in jurists' decision making in black rape cases. Appellate judges boasted of their role as watchdogs over slaves charged with serious criminal offenses. Fully aware that local prejudices, inept lawyering, and parochial judging could derail justice for accused slaves, they understood the importance of checking faulty decisions, even when black men had been convicted of sexually assaulting white females. In numerous cases, appellate courts in the Old South scrutinized and sometimes overturned rape convictions of African Americans or remanded their cases for various reasons, among them faultily worded indictments, coerced confessions, and improperly impaneled juries. Appellate judges, most of whom were slaveholders themselves, behaved like supreme paternalists who decided rape cases with an eye toward shielding defenseless, lesser charges.

Scholars of slave law have ably demonstrated that the legal reasoning of southern justices was shaped by several factors, chief among them commitments to legal formalism, humanitarianism, and, importantly, protecting slaveholders' property. Slave rape appears to have been regarded no differently from other slave crimes that the courts heard. Rape was not considered especially heinous, at least judging by the many times that slave rape convictions were overturned or remanded for retrial. Southern justices took seriously the appeals of convicted black rapists whose counsel charged lower courts with legal missteps and botched decisions.

The legal elites of the antebellum South tended to view themselves in slave cases as the guardians of last resort, protectors of slaves, the weakest and most vulnerable members of society. Yet black-on-white rape cases that made it to the highest courts in southern states also exposed the vulnerability of another group of lesser charges: poor, sometimes unattached white females. Black rape appeals were sites that invoked the notions of white womanhood, honor, and chivalry, all of which required the extension of protection to women. Cases in which African American men stood convicted of sexually assaulting white females pulled judges in opposite directions: they wished to ensure that convicted African American rapists were treated fairly in the eyes of the high court, while also displaying sensitivity to the sexual violation of white females who would be forever tainted as damaged goods in white society. The tension between these two interests often broke in favor of the condemned black rapist, revealing heavily misogynistic assumptions and stereotypes as well as a gendered identification with black men accused of sexual assault. The judges well understood the power of a woman who accused a man of rape and therefore subjected her charges—and her character—to rigorous scrutiny. Their decisions demonstrate that southern high court judges often fell back on traditionally gendered evidentiary assumptions and practices of the law when evaluating the cases in which white women accused African American men, slave or free, of rape. Misogyny thus shaped appellate slave law every bit as much as racism did. Judging from black rape appeals, elite southern judges were often more troubled by the possibility of false accusations of rape by designing white women than they were by the sexual threat of African American men.

L ower courts frequently committed technical and procedural errors in slave criminal cases.[2] Again and again, the appellate system scrupulously worked to correct these legal blunders. Slave rape cases were no different. That slaves were accorded considerable procedural fairness is something that has been well documented.[3] Among the legal rights staked out for many slaves was the right to appeal, though the appeals process varied from state to state.[4] In 1812 the North Carolina Supreme Court held that a slave had the right to appeal a verdict rendered by a county court.[5] South Carolina had a very limited appeal system for blacks until 1833.[6] Georgia had no supreme court until 1845, and not until 1850 were any appeals heard from slaves.[7] Kentucky slaves had the right to a jury trial, but its high court heard no appeals from slaves until 1859.[8] Louisiana entertained no appeals from slaves or free blacks until 1847, when a new constitution permitted them.[9] The Maryland appellate court accepted no slave appeals in the antebellum years. And Virginia offered no appellate provisions for its slaves, although free African Americans could and did appeal decisions.[10] Instead, Virginia relied on its executive branch to review capital slave cases.

Convicted slave criminals, through their counsel and with the backing of their owners, frequently availed themselves of these appeals processes, spotty as they were. Appellants included slaves, and less frequently free men of color, found guilty of sexual assault. For the years 1800 to 1865, sixty-one cases of African American males from southern states appealing sex-related crimes can be found in the published reports of state appellate courts.[11]

Despite the musings of one judge in Georgia—"Will the age of technicalities never pass away?"—southern high courts took seriously the numerous appeals of slave rape on what often appear to have been rather trivial, nonsubstantive aspects of the cases.[12] Juridical blunders by lower courts were somewhat common, especially given the informal and inadequate legal training of some lower court judges, and high court judges at times grew perturbed by the incompetent and sloppy legal maneuvers and decisions that characterized numerous black rape trials in inferior courts.

For southern appellate judges, evidence that local courts had permitted or countenanced breaches of juridical procedure in black rape trials was no minor matter. Southern judges functioned as advocates for a slaveholding society and the institutions that undergirded it, underscoring their role as advocates of last resort for aggrieved slaves. Their guardianship of convicted slave rapists helped to legitimize the slave system.[13] Legal abuses and mistreatment of slaves, allowed to go unchecked, provided fodder for the antislavery forces. It was incumbent upon them, therefore, as overseers of the appeals process, to effect judicial correctives in cases where black men had been convicted of sexually assaulting white females.[14]

One of the more common grounds on which southern high courts reversed slave rape convictions was faultily worded indictments. Within a span of two years the Tennessee Supreme Court threw out the convictions of two slaves condemned as rapists because the original indictments failed to state the race of the victim. The significance of such oversights cannot be overstated. Rape of a nonwhite female was not a capital crime. Failure to specify the race of the accuser was therefore a serious, indefensible omission. As pointed out by Judge Nathan Green, "Such an act committed upon a black woman, would not be punished with death . . . this fact [that the person assaulted was white], which gives to the offense its enormity . . . must be charged in the indictment and proved in the trial."[15]

The Virginia Supreme Court likewise overturned the conviction of a free black man for attempted rape, "because it is no where in the Indictment stated, that Mary M'Causland was a white woman."[16] A Florida circuit court judge grappled unsuccessfully with this same issue in 1847. A slave stood charged with assault with intent to commit a rape. Once again, the race of the accuser was omitted from the indictment. Reluctant to rule, the judge himself in an unusual step appealed directly to Florida's high court.[17]

Omission of the race of the accused from an indictment, unlike omission of the race of the accuser, generally did not constitute grounds for an appeal. Typically the alleged rapist was identified as a slave and of course the presumption was that he was black. As Judge Thomas R. R. Cobb of Georgia observed, "the black color of the race raises the presumption of race."[18] Inserting the alleged slave rapist's race into an indictment would have been superfluous. In the case of the Mississippi slave Dick, however, the indictment included the inadvertent description "negro." Although the mention of race was unnecessary, once it was made the prosecution was compelled to *prove* it. This posed quite a dilemma for the prosecution because according to the statutory definition Dick was in fact a mulatto. But because the word "negro" had been placed in the indictment, "it became a part of his identity." The high court had no choice but to order a new trial.[19]

Confusion over racial identity also proved problematic for the Alabama high court, which chided its legislature in 1856 for a sloppily constructed rape statute aimed at nonwhites. The case involved Thurman, a free man of color condemned to die for the rape of a white woman. Alabama law made rape a capital offense when committed by a "slave, free negro, or mulatto."[20] The state legally defined mulatto as "a person that is the offspring of a negress by a white man, or of a white woman by a negro." Thurman's racial mix fell outside these categories, as he was born to a white mother and a mulatto father. The high court, reflecting the conservative predisposition of southern state courts generally, adopted a strict interpretive posture with relation to the statute.[21] The court's hands were tied by the legislature's precisely clear definition of mulatto, and it insisted that any change would have to come from that body, not the court. Expounding a bit on racial ideology and eerily anticipating the "one drop rule" developed in the twentieth century, the court noted: "If the statute against mulattoes is by construction to include quadroons, then where are we to stop? If we take the first step by construction, are we not bound to pursue the line of descendants so long as there is a drop of negro blood remaining?"[22]

Ill-crafted indictments led to reprieves for two slaves charged with rape-related offenses in North Carolina in the 1830s. One indictment incorrectly charged that Martin did "feloniously attempt to ravish" a white woman when it should have referred to his "intent to commit a rape." The eminent Judge Thomas Ruffin wrote in a scolding opinion that precise language in the indictment was a requisite, "not only to denote the disposition of the accused, but also to describe and identify the crime as that for which the particular punishment is prescribed."[23] Five years later Ruffin again overturned the conviction of a thirteen-year-old slave that had been based on an incorrectly worded indictment.[24] One North Carolina slave pushed this logic too far, however, and his appeal was denied. Legal counsel for Tom of Mecklenburg County argued that the improperly worded indictment charged felonious assault with an "intention," not an "intent," to commit a rape. The court, staking out its limits for tolerating technical challenges to criminal convictions, dismissed the exception as an "absurdity"[25]

New trials were also awarded to some condemned African American rapists because of errors such as improperly impaneled juries. The case of Everett Day, a free mulatto from Virginia, came before the state's high court on two occasions. In both instances Day's counsel alleged that impaneled jurors had failed to meet residency requirements and thus had been improperly seated. The court ordered new trials both times.[26]

Southern appellate courts remanded numerous rape cases to the lower courts for other procedural errors. The Arkansas high court, for instance, faulted a lower court judge for hamstringing defense counsel's right to question the accuser about an alleged scheme to extort money from the slave's master in exchange for not bringing charges of attempted rape against the slave. The same slave received a second hearing before the high court two years later, at which time the court again addressed similar issues. The lower court had erred again, this time in disallowing questions about the accuser's character and in denying permission to the slave's owner to testify on his behalf.[27]

In 1827 the Alabama Supreme Court overturned the conviction of Phil, a slave accused of assault with intent to commit a rape, because he had been denied a speedy trial. Unable to muster a full jury for the first available court session, the local sheriff was forced to hold the case over until the following court term, at which time the presiding judge begged leave for a family emergency. In response, defense counsel filed a motion for dismissal, which was promptly denied, and the case was again held over until the next term, when Phil was found guilty and sentenced to die. One year and nine months had elapsed since the defendant first appeared before the court. Judge John Gayle held that this constituted a violation of the prisoner's rights and ordered him released.[28] The law required that when an accused is "not tried at or before the second stated term of the Court, and the delay is not on his application or with his consent, he must be discharged, although the trial has been prevented by the unavoidable adjournment of the Court."[29] With that, the court set Phil free—free, that is, to return to his master.

Not all reversals of slave rape convictions emanated from purely technical aspects of the law. One of the most common errors cited by southern supreme courts in the conviction of black males for rape or attempted rape related to the substantive issue of force. Successful prosecution of rapists hinged on proof of coercion in the perpetration of the act. An accuser had to prove that her attacker used force in the assault. The only exceptions to this requirement involved children, usually under the age of ten or twelve, in which case consent was irrelevant, although some questions arose occasionally about "feeble minded" females and their inability to give consent.[30] But in all other cases evidence of force was essential, or else there could be no felony. Without documented use of force, the most that a slave or free black man could be charged with was illicit sexual relations between the races, decidedly serious but not a capital offense. Appellate courts, informed that lower courts convicted black rapists without sufficient proof of force, frequently ruled in favor of the appellant. For example, an indictment that had failed to include the word "force" as part of the charge against a black male was likely to be thrown out. Without the words "forcibly and against the will" on an indictment, a North Carolina slave could be found guilty of no more than a misdemeanor.[31]

Although in Arkansas in 1850 an indictment of a slave for assault with intent to rape did allege force, the prosecution failed to prove it. Almyra Combs, aged fourteen, had spent the night at a friend's house with three other girls. The four friends all slept in the same bed, with Combs lying on the outside. She was awakened around four o'clock in the morning by someone trying to roll her over in a "rude manner." Combs screamed and the intruder ran off. Charles, a hired slave working for Michael Summerton, in whose home the girls slept, was found guilty. Upon conviction, Charles's attorney filed a number of exceptions with the appellate court, one of which proved successful. The high court reversed the conviction because, it ruled, the prosecution had failed to show that force had been used as alleged in the indictment. The judges conceded that there was little doubt of Charles's intent to have sexual relations with the young girl, especially given the hour of the intrusion. However, there was no proof whatsoever that he intended to accomplish his means through the use of force. On the contrary, he planned to have sex with her while she slept. The accused used no force, and therefore there was no felony and no capital offense.[32]

In a similar case, Letitia Boltze testified that a man rubbing his face against hers awakened her. She supposed it to be her husband, but discovered that it was a "Negro," the slave Lewis, and ordered him to "clear out". The imposter quickly complied. The Alabama high court reversed the judgment against Lewis, asserting that "force . . . is a necessary ingredient in the crime of rape." Consent "procured by fraudulent personation of the female's husband" did not constitute force. Fraudulent impersonation of a husband was not even against the law, let alone a felony. This logic was reiterated in the case of a Tennessee slave who had also unsuccessfully impersonated the victim's husband in bed. The high court awarded a new trial ruling that "fraud cannot be substituted for force, as an element of this offense."[33]

The "impersonation" defense likewise confounded a Virginia jury that heard the case of Tom Fields, a free African American of Rockbridge County who stood accused of the attempted rape of a white female. The jury reached a "special" verdict, reasoning that Fields had not planned to have carnal knowledge of his intended victim by forceful means. Rather, the attempt was made while she slept. Truly stymied by the obvious legal loophole, the jury sidestepped a decision and deferred to the appellate court, which curtly ruled that the prisoner should be acquitted.[34]

In these slave rape cases high court judges ruled strictly and narrowly according to the letter of the law, reflecting adherence to a legal philosophy that scholars refer to as legal formalism.[35] Rape law, as written, required proof of force to establish rape, even when committed by slaves on white women. Some judges were not happy about the "fraud" loophole in rape law that allowed slaves who attempted to have sexual relations with white women by deceit to go unpunished. In 1853 the Arkansas high court prodded the state legislature to correct the oversight. "We are bound to declare that this is the law applicable to negroes; but whether there should not be an amendment of the statute so as to punish, as a distinct offence, and more severely that it can be, under existing laws, the carnal knowledge of a white woman by a slave, or the attempt of it by fraud, and without force . . . is in our opinion, worthy of the serious consideration of the legislature."[36]

An Alabama judge also displayed his irritation with the statutory loophole, comparing the act of impersonation for the purpose of having sexual relations to fraud and likening a woman's body to stolen property, reasoning that "one who obtains goods under false pretenses is guilty as if he had stolen them."[37] Some state legislatures, perhaps acting in response to these cases, eventually enacted provisions that encompassed rape by fraud.[38]

In addition to legal loopholes, southern appellate judges also considered putative confessions of black prisoners when reviewing rape convictions. They scrutinized confessions as evidence, ever mindful of the unequal power relationship between an accused black prisoner and any white interrogator. Mark Tushnet argues that southern courts operated under the assumption that the "subordination inherent in the slave's position would make involuntary any statement . . . made to a white."[39] Prosecutors were well aware of this concern and at times seemed to have coached state witnesses, many of whom made unprompted disclaimers denying that confessions were made under influence or duress.[40]

An appellate court justice in antebellum Louisiana was outraged at the admission of an accused slave rapist's confession, made while he was subjected corporal punishment: "A conviction upon such evidence is abhorrent to the principles of that humane system of laws from which we derive most of our rules of criminal proceedings, and cannot be countenanced." The appellate court ordered a new trial.[41] An appeals court in Georgia demonstrated similar concerns over the case of a convicted slave rapist, Stephen. "A confession, whether made upon an official examination or in discourse with private persons, which is obtained from a defendant, either by the flattery of hope, or by the impressions of fear, *however slightly the emotion may be implanted*, IS NOT ADMISSIBLE IN EVIDENCE." The Court further remarked that "the cases are probably rare, in which unfounded self-accusations occur" and that "confessions are the weakest of all evidence and should always be received with suspicion."[42] By interrogating and frequently rejecting the confessions of black rapists as evidence, southern jurists reflected a paternalistic commitment to extending legal protection to the most vulnerable members of antebellum southern society.

Judges seated on the highest courts of southern states also advocated for masters, who attempted to testify for their own slaves when they were accused of rape. Southern appellate courts grappled with the matter of bias and self-interest when slaveholders testified on behalf of their property, and frequently their testimony failed to pass muster at the trial level.[43] Masters or other slaves were sometimes presented as defense witnesses, to supply alibis or other testimony on behalf of an accused rapist. Some lower courts disallowed such testimony on the grounds that it was prejudiced. Dubious inferior court judges suspected that masters would go to extraordinary lengths to protect their chief form of investment from the gallows, even lying under oath. As a result, many judges refused to accept masters as defense witnesses.

The defense team for Peter, a Louisiana slave convicted of raping a thirteen-year-old white girl in 1859, was thwarted in its efforts to substantiate its client's innocence through an alibi corroborated by the slave's owners. Peter's mistress claimed to have seen Peter plowing at the time of the alleged assault. The state objected to the testimony on the grounds of "interest in the witnesses" and the court sustained the objection. The Supreme Court of Louisiana staunchly disagreed, chiding the local court that "slaves are prosecuted as persons, and they ought not to be deprived of the testimony of their owners, because the verdict may injure them in a pecuniary view. The point is not their value, but their guilt or innocence. The rights of a slave to have all the testimony that may establish his innocence are superior to the principle which would exclude his owners on the ground of interest, and their testimony ought to be received."[44] The North Carolina high court was every bit as insistent that the accused slave's life weighed more heavily than the possibility that a master might offer biased or even dishonest testimony in order to win his slave's acquittal. The court shuddered to think that "when a prisoner calls a witness to prove his innocence, who, it may be, is the only person on earth to whom a fact is known that will save his life, that he must be repulsed by the cold announcement, 'he is your master—he has an interest in saving your life, . . . and therefore, has a pecuniary interest which makes him incompetent, so he cannot be heard in your behalf,' shocks all the best feelings of our nature. . . . Frail as human nature may be, dollars and cents should not be weighed in the balance with life. It cannot be presumed that the 'almighty dollar' is so controlling in its influence, as to overcome all other considerations."[45]

The judicial reasoning here demonstrates the difficulty of regarding slavery as merely an economic institution and slaves as mere investments in the legal arena. Clearly Judge Ruffin, the author of the passage, grappled with the slave's dual status as both property and person.[46] In this case, he came down on the side of slave as a human being. Judge Ruffin ordered a new trial that would include Jim's master's testimony.

Appellate courts were also called upon to determine whether lower courts had erred in refusing to allow testimony on behalf of accused slave rapists by other slaves. Nat, a slave in North Carolina owned by a Mr. Edwards, was charged with the attempted rape of a white woman. Another of Edwards's slaves, Lucy, and her husband, Sam, a slave from a neighboring farm, testified, providing an alibi for Nat. The judge charged the jury to assess the credibility of the evidence in light of the "relation in which [the witnesses] stand to the parties and to the cause," noting that Sam and Lucy "showed much feeling and partiality for the prisoner." The jury did not believe the slaves' testimony and found Nat guilty. In this case, however, the high court ruled that the judge had not erred in his charge to the jury. One of the justices likened the situation to that of a mother testifying on behalf of her son in a capital case and ruled that the relationship did affect the credibility of the witnesses and their testimony.[47]

Questions surrounding the motives and credibility of female accusers proved to be among the few nonprocedural, evidentiary issues that southern appellate judges were willing to consider in cases of black-on-white rape.[48] In one instance, the Tennessee Supreme Court intervened in the case of Major, a slave found guilty of assault and battery on a white girl with intent to commit a rape. The justices were not satisfied that the identity of the prisoner had been satisfactorily established, so a new trial was ordered, with the case eventually finding its way back to the high court three years later. The case was a quagmire of contradictory testimony and botched investigation. Three credible witnesses contradicted the accuser who had admitted under oath that she harbored ill feelings toward the prisoner. We know that the relationship between the girl and Major, whatever its nature, had been a long one. At one time, the girl and her mother shared sleeping quarters with the slave. Once again, the court reaffirmed its role as a watchdog in the judicial process for bondspeople. "This case strongly admonishes us," the appellate court wrote, "of the necessity of a watchful vigilance and an unyielding firmness on the part of the judicial officers to see that the invaluable right of fair trial by an 'impartial jury' should not be disregarded."[49] The court then took the unusual step of aborting the guilty verdict.[50]

Appellate courts, like lesser courts, also addressed gender issues head on, specifically the question of what constituted appropriate behavior by the accuser. Legal elites were not immune to society's assumptions about proper conduct by women. Unchaste women were not entitled to the same protections at law as chaste women. Southern high courts, in highly misogynistic fashion, sustained the view that a documented history of illicit sexuality by a rape accuser bore a causal relationship to consent and credibility, the cornerstones of a successful rape prosecution. The predilection of southern elites to view women's accusations of rape warily allowed many appellate judges to decide rape cases in favor of the convicted African American rapists. Justices understood that even blacks, who were believed intellectually inferior by nature, had to be protected from the machinations of conniving and treacherous temptresses. In fact, the judges reasoned, because of their innate mental inferiority blacks were easy targets for designing women, a vulnerability that mandated diligence from the appellate system.

No better case illustrates this point than that of Cato, a slave in Florida who stood accused of raping Susan Leonard, a white woman described by twelve defense witnesses as a "common prostitute." Antebellum appellate courts, like inferior courts, rigorously scrutinized the motives of the female accusers in slave rape cases.[51] The accusers' whiteness did not insulate them from queries about their character and motives.[52] Such was the case with Susan Leonard, who in recounting the details of the assault testified that her attacker wielded a knife and threatened her life, compelling her to give up her fight. The lower court judge had instructed the jury that even if a woman yielded her consent to carnal relations to avoid assault or death, as Leonard claimed she had, the crime was rape nonetheless. Furthermore, despite convincing testimony that Leonard and her housemate and corroborating witness, Sarah Alsobrook, were prostitutes, the judge instructed the jurors that "if a man have carnal knowledge of a woman against her will, although she be a common strumpet or a common prostitute, it will be rape, just as much as if the offence had been committed upon the purest and most virtuous woman in the world."[53] Anachronistically, the court acknowledged that a woman deemed sexually deviant by her neighbors had the right to protection from rape, something that many twentieth-century judges failed to concede.

On review, the Florida Supreme Court acknowledged its role in balancing the scales of justice, noting on the one hand "that a most foul offense" had been perpetrated and on the other that "the life of a human being" was dependent on the outcome; in essence, the court appreciated the delicate balance between a defenseless (but possibly savage) black slave and a dishonest (but maybe violated) white woman. Painfully aware of its commitment to overseeing justice for accused slaves, the court boasted of the "crowning glory of our 'peculiar institution,' that whenever life is involved, the slave stands upon as safe ground as the master." The court acknowledged the "abundant proof" that the alleged victim and her friend who testified for the state were "common prostitutes," and without corroborating testimony the court demurred from relying solely on the word of these two women. Refusing to turn its back on Cato, the high court vacated the execution and ordered a new trial.[54] In this case the word of two white women proved insufficient to sustain the rape conviction of a black man.

Justices on high court benches throughout the slave South repeatedly expressed sympathy for black defendants who might be wrongly accused of rape by white women with suspicious motives and of dubious backgrounds. In a protracted four-year legal battle that saw a slave convicted of attempted rape in Arkansas appeal to the state's high court twice, we see similar issues tackled by high-level jurists. Pleasant's attorney filed numerous exceptions that were carefully weighed by the appellate court. By far the most complicated of these involved the sexual history of the accuser and the possible relevance of her behavior to her credibility as a witness. The lower court judge had disallowed most questions pertaining to Sophia Fulmer's sexual history. The defense attorney had grilled Fulmer about sexual relations with men other than her husband, naming at least four. He also asked the accuser about a rape charge that she had allegedly filed five years earlier. Finally, Pleasant's attorney hinted at neighbors' reports of strained relations between Fulmer and her husband, presumably over her infidelity. But the state objected to this line of questioning and the presiding judge upheld the objection.[55]

The high court struggled with the issue of chastity and its relationship to credibility. The court halfheartedly acknowledged that the law protected "every class and condition of white females . . . regardless of their character or position in society" and that the "character of the female, however abandoned, furnishes no justification for the act [of rape]." Yet the court was persuaded that evidence of an accuser's chastity had a direct bearing on the issue of consent. Falling back on English case law, the court reached a somewhat murky compromise. The chastity of the accuser could be "impeached by general evidence" but a prisoner could not offer evidence of specific instances of illicit sexual behavior. The court drew the line at "inquisitorial" examinations of the accuser herself, fearing that eliciting such testimony was likely to "compel her to criminate and disgrace herself, or to commit perjury."[56] The decision by the Arkansas court represented what Thomas Morris has characterized as "an accommodation between sexism and racism within the legal presumptions used by Southern white males."[57] The court labored to secure some middle ground that would protect unwitting slaves from lustful, seductive Jezebels while continuing to cordon off respectable white women from black men sexually.

The Arkansas judges found precedent for their ruling in a case decided in North Carolina in 1846 in which the state supreme court mapped out rather peculiar distinctions between the types of evidence about behavior and character that could and could not be introduced. Although in *State v. Jefferson* the slave's appeal proved unsuccessful, the reasoning of the high court is nonetheless revealing. Jefferson was accused by Elizabeth C. Rogers of rape. Jefferson countered that his sexual relations with Rogers were consensual. One of Jefferson's fellow slaves buttressed these claims on the witness stand by claiming that he had seen Jefferson treat Rogers in a "free and familiar manner." The county court however refused to allow testimony regarding Rogers's purported behavior with other slaves. While the North Carolina supreme court permitted the evidence of "familiarities" between the prisoner and his accuser, particular instances of relations with other slaves would not be admissible, reasoning that the claim that "the woman was a strumpet" rested on more "general evidence" because it involved a question of character. In other words, the court believed that evidence of a sexual relationship between the accused and accuser was appropriate and relevant because it spoke to the issue of force. That the woman could have been a "strumpet" might also be admitted as evidence, but only if introduced as a general character issue.[58]

In some legal hair splitting, the North Carolina Supreme Court in 1857 rejected the relevance of testimony suggesting that a white woman who charged a slave with attempted rape had previously "made an indecent exposure of her person" to other slaves. The evidence had been barred at trial and the slave's attorney took exception. The state court agreed, reasoning that the defense had failed to establish whether the prisoner had known about the woman's behavior before the alleged assault. In other words, the mere fact that the accuser had acted in an aberrant, immoral fashion bore no relation to the guilt or innocence of the accused, unless it could be proved that he had been aware of her behavior at the time of the alleged assault. Had he been, the court would have been willing to entertain the accuser's behavior as a mitigating factor. Knowledge that a woman, even a white woman, had acted so indiscreetly could have induced the defendant to take liberties with her.[59]

Attacking the accuser's character, though, had its limits in the eyes of southern jurists. In *State v. Anderson*, the defense elicited information about the notorious reputation of Rebecca Ann Hewitt's family from an African American defense witness by asking, "Do you know what the girl's people did for a living?" and "Do you know what the girl's mother did for a living?" This tactic failed, however, when the appellate court denied the appeal, reasoning that a "child's teeth shall not be set on edge because its father has eaten sour grapes."[60]

We learn much about the elite legal community and its perceptions about race, sexuality, class, and gender by exploring appellate cases involving African American men accused of sex crimes.[61] For one, class weighs in as an important factor shaping the outcome of the black rapists' appeals. In numerous cases, state justices found fault with decisions at law by lower court judges. County court judges proved susceptible to the prevailing atmosphere in their communities, in particular local racial and class prejudices that might percolate to the surface in a black-on-white rape trial. Trial judges, for example, seem to have been much more reluctant than appellate judges to allow testimony about the background and character of the accuser, though to be sure, such evidence did surface in many black rape trials.[62] Assuming that the vast majority of the accusers in these cases were poor to middling females, their relatives and friends may have been able to mobilize support for them among common folk that translated into pressure on the court. Trial judges were not insulated from local pressures in the same way as appellate judges, who therefore had considerable freedom in exercising their decisions. Hence, elite jurists often ruled in a manner that subverted the popular will while upholding the interests of the convicted slave rapists' owners.

Appellate judges had no compunctions about ruling in favor of convicted black rapists when convinced that the defendants had received an unfair hearing. State supreme courts insisted that African Americans, even those accused of the heinous crime of sexually assaulting white females, be accorded procedural rights, suggesting that allegations of sexual assault seem not to have had any extraordinary onus attached to them. The judgment of the privileged legal establishment was not clouded by fears of black sexual aggression. Its members appear to have acted rationally and methodically in deciding black-on-white rape cases. Every indication is that these judges ruled as they would and did in many other cases of slave crime; rape was not singled out for zealous vigilance.

Moreover, as is clear from antebellum southern appellate cases in which slaves and free black men had their rape convictions overturned or returned for retrial, supreme court justices believed that white women could in fact be attracted to black men, and they appear not to have been threatened by this apparent social reality.[63] Southern appellate decisions in black-on-white rape cases betray a judicial concern that black men needed the intercession of white benefactors to shield them from wily white women who might fall back on their racially privileged status to seduce or entrap black men. The remarkable empathy that members of southern high courts exhibited for accused rapists across the color line was inextricably tied to their animus toward the white women claiming to have been sexually violated. Judge Joseph H. Lumpkin of Georgia revealed his identification with slave men accused of rape when he opined that the "very helplessness of the accused . . . like infancy and woman-hood, appeals to our sympathy."[64] The Florida Supreme Court invoked Lord Hale's famous characterization of rape as "an accusation easily to be made and hard to be proved and harder to be defended by the party accused, though never so innocent."[65]

Gender sympathy and suspicion about white women's sexuality merged with racist, paternalistic beliefs about the nature of black men and the role that men of legal and social standing had in protecting them. African Americans, believed to possess inferior intellectual and reasoning capacities and therefore more easily led astray, merited special attention from the region's judicial patriarchs. Constitutionally ill equipped to fend off lecherous women, black men were especially vulnerable to seductresses and thus required the oversight and protection of the judicial apparatus.

Quite possibly the fear of being falsely accused of rape was a personal worry that many elite white men harbored as well, allowing them to extend their code of masculinity to men not of their caste or race. Appellate judges demonstrated an understanding of the predicament facing these accused black sex offenders, in the process baring a profound suspicion of women, particularly poor women. In this regard, southern jurists appear not to have been very different than their northern counterparts. Judge Esek Cowen, of New York, for exam-ple, was a strong proponent of allowing alleged rapists to introduce evidence of a complainant's sexual history by explaining, "once a whore, always a whore."[66]

While a gentleman jurist from the South might not have been so indelicate in his choice of words, the sentiment was shared many learned legal scholars of the South. In short, the region that then, as later, trumpeted its eagerness to protect womanhood manifested considerable fear of the accusatory power of women and denied them the protection of the highest courts.

AGAINST ALL ODDS?
Free Blacks on Trial for Rape in the Antebellum South

S lave rape trials tell us much generally about the social dynamics among white southerners as well as perceptions of race and gender relations. More pointedly, such trials provide a case study of the master-slave relationship and the importance of economic motives in animating a master's defense of a slave accused of sexually assaulting a white female. A slave's value as property was a powerful incentive for a master to exonerate an accused slave rapist. If executed, the slave represented some degree of financial loss to a master. Heroic efforts to spare a slave—a master's chief form of investment—would make sense in this light.

In addition, there is something to be said for the relationship that may have developed between master and slave that also motivated a slaveowner to invest a substantial amount of money, time, and effort in getting his accused slave acquitted of a rape charge. Consider a master who may have known the accused slave rapist his whole life and with whom he developed congenial or even intimate ties; the slaveowner could have shared a childhood with him, or cultivated a paternalist image that embraced the accused as a sheltered family member, one who needed protection from more worldly, scheming, lower-class whites. In short, a master might have viewed the impending death of a condemned slave as the death of a "family" member, and therefore took some pains to save his "boy" from the gallows.[1] In this light, publicly taking the side of one's own slave charged with raping a poor white neighbor may not seem so remarkable after all.

Whatever a slaveowner's motives for supporting one of his slaves on trial for rape, we cannot get at broader issues of race relations in the Old South underlying such cases unless we also look at the rape trials of free men of color. Paternalism and financial interests combined to create powerful motives for masters to advocate reprieves for slaves convicted of rape. Accused slave rapists, indeed slaves charged with any capital crime, appear to have benefited enormously from their value as property as their cases played out.

Lacking value as property and presumably close ties with whites, free men of color charged with rape in the Old South at first blush would appear to have been at a far greater disadvantage. Cases of free blacks accused of rape thus ought to reveal even more about the importance—and the limits—of economic motives in efforts to spare accused or convicted rapists; one would expect free blacks to have had a tougher time than slaves in receiving leniency, for the very reason that they did not represent a financial interest for slaveholders.[2]

Free men of color accused of raping or attempting to rape white women and girls, like slaves accused of the same crimes, sometimes found allies in the white community. Some whites worked aggressively to secure pardons for free blacks convicted of rape and condemned to die. Although free blacks possessed no value as property, economic motives nonetheless appear to have influenced white support. Many free blacks, particularly those who had acquired reputations for industriousness and integrity in white circles, won the respect and patronage of whites in the community for whom free blacks performed valuable services. Not all whites, it should be understood, rallied around free blacks on trial for rape. To the contrary, these trials mirror the sometimes sharp divisions within white society itself.

Moreover, white women who brought rape charges against free black men, like those who made accusations of rape against slaves, were regarded suspiciously by court officials and community members. Frequently the burden of proof fell upon the accuser to prove she was neither lying about the assault nor had invited the rape, as some whites were apt to believe. The resulting rough treatment of some female accusers, especially those of the lower orders of society, occurred regardless of the race or status of the accused. Misogyny permeated the legal system, informing both courtroom principals and observers, and shaping the outcome of many antebellum rape trials whether the alleged rapist was white or black, free or enslaved.

Historical works focusing on free blacks in the early South have generally found their status to have been rather fluid and often ambiguous. Free blacks in revolutionary North Carolina, for instance, served in the militia and for a time could vote.[3] By some accounts, however, early fluidity gave way to worsening conditions for free African Americans by the time of the Civil War. One work suggests that the "free Negro caste [was pushed] to the edge of extinction."[4] Such claims usually have as their basis the harsh statutes that discriminated against free blacks.[5] It is important to reiterate that without understanding how these statutes actually were implemented we cannot accurately gauge their impact.[6] Recent scholarship has also made the point that vitriolic public rhetoric about free blacks in general, also used as evidence to suggest pervasive harsh treatment of free blacks, belied how many of the southern whites felt about individual free blacks, whom they knew and often respected.[7] The patronage of white citizens could be a valuable asset for free blacks maneuvering in a slave society.[8] Indeed, a patron-client relationship between whites and free blacks could prove mutually beneficial to both parties.

Thus despite repressive laws and discrimination, a number of free blacks managed to carve out a considerable degree of autonomy and agency as well as command some rights and privileges.[9] In addition, some free blacks seemed to have cultivated the respect of white community members.[10] Gary Mills's study of miscegenation in antebellum Alabama offers two possible explanations. First, free blacks "knew their place." They understood their condition to be contingent upon the good will of white neighbors. A free black was not foolish enough to demand "the full acceptance and equality that white America could have never given him in that era." Second, free blacks were so few in number that southern whites had no reason to fear them. The scurrilous white rhetoric against free blacks as a group, so often cited as evidence of their repressed, hated status in the Old South, frequently masked or overshadowed the more amiable attitudes of whites who dealt with free black neighbors daily one on one.[11]

The relationships between some whites and free blacks described by Mills appear to have played a central role in securing white support for accused black rapists. Like their enslaved counterparts, free black rapists also at times received leniency and backing from white officials and community members in their attempts to avoid execution. White southerners on occasion actively sided with accused or even convicted free black rapists in cases brought by white women or girls and intervened to save the lives of those accused.

In Southampton County, Virginia, the site of Nat Turner's revolt in 1831, a man of color was alleged to have committed a rape. Henry Hunt appeared in superior court twice, in 1826 and again in 1827, accused of raping a white woman named Sydney Jordan. Hunt, a twenty-two-year-old laborer from St. Luke's parish, was described by his jailer as six feet tall, "straight and well made," with "a considerable share of effrontery."[12] Hunt's defense rested on his assertion that his relations with Sydney Jordan were entirely consensual. Hunt claimed to have "long been in the habit of sexual intercourse" with Jordan. Furthermore, he maintained that on the night of the alleged sexual assault not he but another free black man had bedded Jordan.[13]

Hunt's protestations and the dubious sexual history of a marginal white woman notwithstanding, the jury found him guilty of rape and sentenced him to hang. Rape or attempted rape of a white female by a free black male was an offense mandating an automatic death sentence.[14] In an astonishing turn of events, though, a group of white citizens from Southampton County, including Hunt's jailer, the court clerk, and a member of the jury that had found him guilty, petitioned the governor and the executive council to extend clemency to Hunt.[15]

The petitioners cited the lack of credibility and illicit behavior of the accuser. Sydney Jordan, the petitioners explained, had lied to the court about her relationship with Hunt and others. Hunt steadfastly insisted throughout his defense that his and Jordan's relationship was based on mutual consent. This Jordan denied; in fact, she claimed she had never met Henry Hunt before the night of the alleged assault. The petitioners claimed to have exposed Jordan's ruse, asserting that Jordan had given birth to a "black child" over a year after the alleged rape. The birth of a nonwhite child betrayed Jordan's claims that she had maintained no intimate relations with black men, thus lending credibility to Hunt's account. Eventually, and no doubt under pressure, Jordan acknowledged the child's father to have been Nicholas Vick, the free black man who Hunt maintained he had found in bed with Jordan the night she claimed to have been raped by Hunt. With her lies no longer salvageable, Jordan confessed to having had "frequent criminal intercourse with . . . Henry Hunt and Nicholas Vick." The petitioners therefore concluded that Henry Hunt was not guilty of the alleged sexual assault and pleaded that "humanity requires the interposition of the Executive council to rescue him from an undeserved doom."[16] A sympathetic governor complied by granting Hunt a pardon.[17]

Official records yield two additional cases of attempted rape of young white girls by free black men in Virginia in 1833, a mere two years after Nat Turner's rebellion. In both instances, some whites advocated pardons for the free black men convicted of attempted rape. Caleb Watts, a free black man, met Jane Barber, aged eleven, one summer day at the local mill and offered to carry her ground corn part of the way. At the place where the two were to part, according to Barber, the assault took place. By his own admission, Watts had asked for some sort of compensation for his good deed. Barber replied that she was but a poor girl who had nothing to give but herself. "Give me yourself, then," Watts was said to have demanded. Barber screamed, prompting Watts to choke the girl and threaten her with a knife to quiet her.[18]

Watts was indicted and tried for attempted rape upon Jane Barber and the jury found him guilty. Defense counsel appealed the conviction on the grounds that the victim was, at the time of the assault, under the age of twelve and thus had not yet attained puberty; therefore, Jane Barber was not a woman according to the strict statutory definition. The Virginia high court found this argument specious and ordered that the death sentence be passed upon the prisoner.[19]

As a last resort, Watts's attorney, Edward Wood, launched a feverish correspondence campaign with the governor of Virginia, Littleton Waller Tazewell. Wood wrote two letters himself along with a preachy but emotional petition ostensibly signed by "almost every man of respectability," including one jury member. Although Wood never directly challenged the sexual morality of Barber, he alleged that she and her mother were of the "lowest order in society" and questioned the credibility of "a girl who has been raised with an aunt who has given birth to several bastard children."[20] In other words, Barber was guilty by association.

Watts's attorney was not the only party to intervene on his behalf. Even the disinterested attorney for the Commonwealth, W. Thurman, who prosecuted the case in county court, wrote to the governor conceding that he harbored doubts about the alleged victim and cited discrepancies in testimony of some witnesses who Thurman claimed possessed "prejudice against the defendant, and eagerness for his condemnation." He also insinuated that "strong popular prejudice and excitement against the prisoner" affected the jury's deliberation, preventing a fair hearing, a sure sign that whites did not unanimously support Watts's cause.[21]

If Watts's case had aroused "strong popular prejudice and excitement," he did seem to have cultivated the sympathy of several members of the local elite. Whether their patronage was sufficient to win a reprieve for Watts is not known, as no documentation of his fate has been found.[22] Nonetheless the case, outcome aside, demonstrates that the white community was far from unified in its response to the charge of black rape. Clearly, the alleged crime excited a segment of the community, and some citizens wished to see Watts hang. Still others, those not motivated by economic self-interest as a slaveholder might be, displayed great empathy for the free black man and his predicament, a man who "had borne a character of singular respectability for one of his own caste."[23] Presumably Watts's boosters were willing to defame an eleven-year-old white girl to save his life, though as we have seen, most southerners took the sexual assault of children seriously.

In another rape case mirroring that of Caleb Watts, Tasco Thompson, a free black blacksmith from Frederick County, Virginia, was found guilty in 1833 of the attempted rape of an eleven-year-old white girl, Mary Jane Stevens. The defense had however presented mitigating factors at trial that persuaded the jury foreman to formally recommend leniency, citing the "exceedingly disreputable character of the family of the said Stevens." "It was notorious," he stated, "that the mother had long entertained negroes, and that all her associations, with one or two exceptions were with blacks. . . . In a word she was below the level of the ordinary grade of free negroes. . . . There is no doubt that [Thompson] repaired to the house of Mrs. Stevens in the belief that she would cheerfully submit to his embraces, as she doubtless had done before, but finding her absent he probably supposed his embraces would be equally agreeable to her daughter."[24] The sins of the mother are the sins of the daughter. Furthermore, the foreman took a nasty swipe at the women in the Stevens kin network, arguing that had Mrs. Stevens been colored there would have been no case. The Stevenses "yielded their claims to the protection of the law by their voluntary associations with those whom the law distinguishes as their inferiors." In short, Mrs. Stevens acted "colored" and therefore deserved to be treated as "colored."[25] Because of her previous liaisons with black men, Mrs. Stevens had forfeited the privilege that her white skin might have accorded her, not only for herself but for her daughter.

Despite the jury foreman's condemnation of cross-racial sexual relations, Mrs. Stevens and Tasco Thompson were apparently not exceptional in their reported sexual transgressions across the color line. Other examples of illicit interracial sexual activity can be found in the court records of Frederick County, Virginia. Shortly after Thompson was alleged to have assaulted Mary Jane Stevens, for instance, three white men were officially charged with the crime of cohabiting with free women of color. The women appear not to have been cited.[26]

Thus the white community in this pocket of antebellum Virginia tolerated interracial sexual activity to a degree. Before the trial of Tasco Thompson, such an environment might have enabled Thompson and Mrs. Stevens to become acquainted or to travel in shared social circles. Thompson's actions toward the younger Stevens, whether an assault or consensual sex gone awry, seem to have occurred in a social setting where conventions forbidding sex across the color line were ignored. Such a tradition would help to explain why some whites in Frederick County came out in support of Thompson.

Nonetheless, some white citizens demonstrated revulsion at interracial relationships or at least recognized limits to any tacit toleration. Charges against Thompson appear to have been filed in the spring of 1833. Official action taken against the three white men for their illegal cohabitation with women of color took place in the months following. Possibly viewing the attempted rape charge as the inevitable consequences of an overly permissive and liberal community, concerned whites could have initiated the arrests as a warning not only to the three white male offenders, but also to the community at large, highlighting the danger of allowing interracial commingling. News of a black-on-white rape might have been regarded by some as a foreboding, the inevitable fallout of tolerating black-white sexual relations. The increased policing of the community coupled with Thompson's conviction suggests that toleration for illicit interracial behavior had reached its limits among some whites.[27]

For those who had come to Thompson's side the articulated reason for their support was the belief that Mary Jane Stevens's mother had demonstrated deviant behavior, and that this behavior had tainted her daughter. The opprobrium toward promiscuous women in the Old South was important in shaping the outcomes of the rape trials of free black men. A cautionary tale of what happens to white women who take free black lovers is reflected in the reporting of the *Richmond Daily Dispatch* in 1854. The author of the piece, as well as white residents, questioned the credibility of a white woman's claim that a free black man attempted to rape her because of her past involvement with free black men. The paper related that "if the charge be true, the black imp deserves to be hung, without judge or jury [but] when the characters of the parties are made known, and the court is informed that the complainant associates with none other than the lowest and most debased free negroes in the valley, it will be a difficult job to induce them to believe a simple sentence uttered by her. . . . The white woman may have told the truth, but very few who know her believe it."[28]

A consensual relationship across racial lines gone awry and culminating in an accusation of rape set the stage for the rape trial of John Holeman of Shenandoah County, Virginia. Susanna Boughman (or Baughman) charged that in June 1816, Holeman, a free black laborer, raped her. Holeman was convicted that fall but appealed on the grounds that the verdict was contrary to the evidence. The sitting judge granted a new trial, but on the grounds that jury deliberations had been compromised. Ordinarily, a retrial would have taken place in the following spring, but because the trial judge was indisposed, Holeman was held over for the fall term in 1817, sixteen months after the alleged assault. At trial Holeman was again found guilty. However, the defense presented new evidence to the court. Boughman had given birth to a child allegedly conceived "at the time of the rape committed." Recall that much debate over the North Carolina slave Jim's purported rape of the servant Polly Lane revolved around the popular medical belief that women could not be impregnated as the result of forced sex.[29] The same misconceptions about rape and conception appear to have permeated the rape trial of John Holeman. In addition, the accuser's testimony left the trial judge dubious about her truthfulness. He described her account of the event as "inconsistent and contradictory." The defense also presented evidence of a history of "familiarity" between Holeman and Boughman. The judge concluded that the alleged rape was in reality consensual sex.[30]

But the jury differed with the judge's finding about Holeman's and Boughman's relationship and returned a guilty verdict. A sympathetic judge attempted to check the jury's decision and offered Holeman a new trial. Holeman declined. Instead he appealed directly to the governor of Virginia for a pardon. Holeman's motives here elude us. Perhaps he was merely trying to avoid another six months in jail while awaiting the next term of superior court. More likely, Holeman had no reason to believe that a different jury would find him innocent. He had already been convicted twice.[31] The support of the judge in this case could have persuaded Holeman's attorney that his only hope was to avoid another jury trial and take his chances with the governor.

Holeman had no trouble enlisting the support of local whites to take his case to the governor. The trial judge, squarely in Holeman's camp, professed his belief that Holeman and Boughman had been having a consensual sexual relationship. Judge Hohnes also hinted that Holeman had more or less paid his dues for his indiscretion, having already spent a considerable amount of time incarcerated. Furthermore, Boughman had since left the area for Ohio and was now "beyond the reach of the court." Whether or not Boughman's accusation of rape was true, she was forever tainted in a way that probably made it impossible for her to resume a normal life in Shenandoah County.[32] The judge who presided over her rape case, however, chose to interpret Boughman's self-imposed exile as yet another reason why her alleged attacker should be pardoned and allowed to resume life in Shenandoah County.

In appealing through his attorney to Virginia's governor for intercession, Holeman, like many slaves charged with rape, appeared to be manipulating the paternalist inclinations and sensibilities of legal and elected officials. Though written in the third person, Holeman's letter is signed by him though in all probability his attorney wrote it. The tone is predictably deferential and strategically avoids recounting the risqué details of the case, a breach that might very well have offended the governor's sensibilities. Nor did the letter ever refer to Boughman by name or in any derogatory way. Holeman simply and cautiously referred to her as the principal witness who he claimed had "unquestionably sworn to that which was not true."[33] Holeman cast his plight as a familiar one: a naïve man ensnared by a dishonorable, lying temptress.

Holeman's plea is also situated in the nexus of paternalistic responsibilities and duties. He explained his reason for turning down the judge's offer for a new trial, believing that "justice would be found in the executive, where no prejudice could interpose to say its influence." Here he is appealing to the supreme political patriarch, casting himself as a weak charge imploring protection from the lower order of society, rife with racial prejudices. Holeman had lost faith in his ability to get a fair trial by any all-white jury in Shenandoah County. Racial animus seemed to ordain a guilty verdict. Few local residents appeared to share Judge Hohnes's concern for Holeman's predicament. Holeman asserted his innocence while deferentially acknowledging that he "has much erred, and for this error he has atoned by long imprisonment." What had his error been? Perhaps in a veiled or coded way he was expressing regret for crossing the lines of color for sex, by his own words an act of "impudence." Or maybe he was actually apologizing for the sexual assault although he clearly denied committing rape.[34] In any event, John Holeman, twice convicted by juries in Shenandoah County, took his chances with the governor rather than face a third jury trial.[35]

Unlike some rape trials of African American men, Holeman's trial appears to have prompted no significant mass movement to get him pardoned. Holeman's appeal revealed that much "prejudice" existed in the community, and we must assume that he meant race prejudice. Despite that, we know that at least the trial judge backed him in two ways. First, the judge sentenced him to ten years in the penitentiary either at hard labor or in solitary confinement,[36] the lightest possible sentence.[37] Second, the judge supported Holeman's effort to obtain a pardon and negate the conviction. Whether the governor was persuaded to pardon Holeman, we do not know.[38] But if Holeman did escape his sentence, the judge who presided over his rape trial played a major role in effecting that outcome.

From the cases cited above we can tease out enough pieces of information to suggest that the rifts emanating from Old South rape trials of free black men sometimes fell along class lines. None of the appeal campaigns was characterized by widespread popular backing. To the contrary, the petitions submitted on behalf of Watts and Holeman cited the "strong popular prejudice and excitement" that prevailed in the community throughout the trial.[39] Instead, the support that the men received in their attempts to procure reprieves appears to have stemmed from small groups of local notables in their communities, who took to heart their perceived paternalist responsibilities. The judge presiding in John Holeman's trial lent support to Holeman when few if any others did. Perhaps Judge Hohnes, trained in the law to administer "blind justice," attempted to counteract the unabashed racial bias of jury members. Ten community members wrote on Caleb Watts's behalf, but the two principal attorneys from the trial wrote most of the correspondence to the governor. Seventeen signatures appear on the community petition submitted on behalf of Henry Hunt, including a juror, the court clerk, and the jailer. At least two were prominent, well-known citizens. One signer, William A. Spark, went on to represent Southampton County in the state legislature in the 1830s and 1840s.[40] The court clerk, James Rochelle, descended from a Huguenot family that settled in Southampton County and rose to local prominence.[41] Few white supporters of these convicted free black rapists appear to have come from the lower ranks of white society.

The support that white elites and notables could afford to offer to free men of color charged with rape derived from two sources. First, accused free black rapists garnered the support of their respectable patrons by comporting themselves in a manner deemed honorable and orderly. Residents of Westmoreland County vouched for Caleb Watts's honesty, industry, and "upright deportment."[42] Moreover, Henry Hunt, Caleb Watts, and John Holeman were laborers, Tasco Thompson a blacksmith. They may have performed services for local whites that made them indispensable, in the process cultivating a personal, albeit unequal, relationship across racial lines. One study of Virginia's free black population documented numerous examples of petitions made by whites to keep free black workers from being legally and forcefully "removed" after passage of a law in 1806 requiring emancipated slaves to leave the state within twelve months. Many petitions stressed the need for the services that these free blacks provided.[43] On the other hand, free black laborers provoked jealousy and fears among working-class whites who struggled to compete in the same trades and occupations. A rival white working class had ample reason to resent its African American counterparts and bristle at the cozy relations between free blacks and local white elites.[44]

Second, white sponsors of convicted free black rapists adhered to an ideology that viewed poor white women as intrinsically licentious, immoral, and base, a belief that necessarily put them at odds with poor whites. Jane Barber, the eleven-year-old who accused Caleb Watts of raping her, was characterized as being from the "lowest order in society." Barber, despite her youth, personified the stereotypical "lying temptress." Had Barber been born into a wealthier class, such personal attacks on her character would have been inconceivable.[45]

Depictions of poor white girls and women as licentious and treacherous were not likely to have been shared by white men of the lower class, whose mothers, daughters, wives, and sisters would have been similarly depreciated. In this way, the rape trials of free men of color exposed the fault lines of class in the Old South. Elites hunkered down to protect their own interests or to uphold an imagined paternalistic obligation, at times at the expense of the common white folk, who sometimes struck back by using the power of the jury box.

Not all white juries hearing evidence against a free black defendant charged with rape found a guilty verdict easy to come by, another possible indication of class divisions. The jury summoned to hear testimony in the attempted rape case of Tom Fields struggled mightily before rendering a verdict. On New Year's Eve in 1831, it was alleged that Fields, a free black laborer hired by John Leech of Rockbridge County, tried to rape Leech's daughter, Sally. Sally testified that she was awakened in the middle of the night by someone who was removing her clothes and "laying violent hands on her." Sally screamed for her father. John Leech testified that he heard his daughter's cries and saw Fields run out of her bedroom.[46]

The jury heard the testimony from father and daughter, was convinced that Fields intended to have sexual relations with Leech, and yet was stymied by the letter of the law. Obviously Tom Fields had attempted to have sex with Sally Leech, probably against her will, but he had not used force. It seemed that Fields intended to have sex with Sally Leech while she slept. Virginia's rape statute, like nearly all rape statutes at the time, defined rape as sexual relations by force. This the jury understood. The jury's unusual solution was to find a "special verdict" that it appealed directly to the high court itself. "If the law be for the prisoner . . . , then we find him not guilty; but if against him, then we find him guilty; and, in that case, if the offence be not punishable by death, but by confinement in the public jail and penitentiary house, we ascertain the term of his imprisonment therein, to be six years."[47]

The truly remarkable thing about this case is that the jury, though convinced that Fields had had every intention of having nonconsensual sexual relations with Sally Leech, recognized the loophole in the law and was willing to free Fields in order to comply with its letter. If Fields was guilty, the jury was prepared to sentence him to six years' imprisonment. The Virginia supreme court ruled in Fields's favor. In an unusual step, it did not order a retrial but directed that an acquittal should be rendered.[48]

A divided, confused jury also deliberated the fate of Benjamin Smith, a free black man from Washington County, Virginia, who had been convicted of raping Margaret Trent, a white "girl." Through a published appellate decision we learn that Smith was found guilty but appealed his conviction, taking issue with the court's admission of his own confession as evidence. The high court elaborated at considerable length before finally concluding, in a divided ruling, that the circuit court had not erred in allowing the confession. Smith's conviction and judgment of death were affirmed.[49]

While the published appellate opinion reveals precious little about the specifics of the case, two tantalizing shards of information emerge. First, Smith's initial trial resulted in a hung jury.[50] Second, we learn that Margaret Trent, the accuser, had previously charged another black man by the name of Campbell with rape. Campbell had been convicted and executed. Had the first jury become dubious of Margaret Trent's accusation in light of this information? The jury might also have wondered in its deliberations whether Smith would have been foolish enough to become involved with a white female who had previously brought charges of rape against another black man and had him executed.[51]

Free men of color who were charged with rape or attempted rape had some noteworthy common ground with slaves in the same position. First, a disproportionate number of accusers were poor to middling females, many of whom appear not to have had male protectors in their immediate family. For example, in August 1863 Mary Boyd testified that Wesley McDaniel, a free black teen from North Carolina, broke into her sister-in-law's home with the intent to commit a rape. The two women apparently lived alone.[52]

The rape trials of free blacks, like those of slaves, also saw white communities divided over the guilt or innocence of the accused, and over whether a convicted black rapist deserved mercy or the full force of the law. Jurors in Johnston County, North Carolina, took but a few minutes to find Henry Carroll, "a free boy of color," guilty of an attempted rape. Carroll's execution, however, was repeatedly delayed by the efforts of North Carolinians, who vigorously solicited Governor Montfort Stokes for a reprieve for Carroll.[53]

A third similarity between slave and free black rape trials is that among those whites who worked on behalf of accused or convicted rapists, were many well respected, established leaders of the community who took seriously their charge to adjudicate and rectify perceived injustice toward disadvantaged African Americans in society. Cognizant of the handicaps that blacks, slave and free, faced in the slave South, white leaders extended financial and moral support in many cases. Likewise, those charged, or perhaps their attorneys, tapped into the paternalistic ethos espoused by many white social, judicial, and political patriarchs to effect commutation or exoneration. Frequently, however, siding with black rapists incited opposition from lower and middling whites: laying claim to racial privilege, these whites exerted their own influence —in the jury box, in letters to newspapers, in appeals of their own to governors —to check the influence and privilege of white elites.

While the rape trials of slaves and free blacks had much common ground, a look at the rape trials of white men also reveals important similarities between white-on-white rape trials and black-on-white rape trials. While the differences are glaring and substantial—foremost, white men generally did not face the death penalty—similarities in how the trials proceeded and how the communities responded to charges of rape are noteworthy.

In many respects, white-on-white rape cases reflect some of the same traits as black-on-white rape cases. Surprisingly, some white men accused of sexual assault, like their black counterparts, charged that community prejudice hindered justice for white accused rapists. In the early 1850s there were two rape cases in Virginia in which Irish immigrants were charged. Pervasive anti-Irish sentiments purportedly thwarted fair trials for both men.[54] As in some of the cases of free African Americans charged with rape, the ethnicity of the accused seemed to stir prejudices and excitement among a substantial number of whites. In 1851 John Conway went on trial for the rape of Susannah Shoulders, aged seventy-three. The age of Conway's accuser alone might have been sufficient to arouse community passions and outrage against him. Compounded by Conway's Irish heritage, this seemed to him to make a fair trial all but impossible.

Although few details are given in court records, there appears to have been some confusion about whether the rape was fully consummated. Shoulders's testimony left some courtroom observers unsure of whether Conway should have been charged with rape or attempted rape. Shoulders herself may have been confused; or perhaps genteel attorneys were reluctant to elicit graphic and explicit testimony from an elderly woman. In the end, the court tried Conway on the original count of rape.

Complicating matters for the prosecution was Shoulders's inability to positively identify Conway as her attacker. At one point during the trial Susannah Shoulders was asked to identify her attacker in the courtroom. She identified Conway's attorney![55]

The jury nonetheless found John Conway guilty of rape and sentenced him to serve ten years in the penitentiary. Perhaps jury members were swayed by Susannah Shoulder's advanced age. Petitioners, however, writing to the governor on Conway's behalf, cited ethnic prejudices. John Bennett wrote to Governor John Letcher that at the time Conway was convicted, "there existed in

Lewis [County] a great prejudice against the entire Irish population of which Conway is one." A second petition written nine years after the alleged attack recounted that in this area of Virginia, "Irishmen were dreaded by the citizens of this, then, backward portion of the country." The letter conceded that Conway may have entered the home of "the old woman," an infraction the petitioners attributed to Conway's being in a "state of inebriety." The rape conviction, the petition continues, could be blamed on, "the dred of the Wild Irish that the slightest attempt of any kind of freedom would then by such be construed into the worst meaning." The invocation of freedom certainly suggests that to some degree, as is evidenced from this case, Irish immigrants shared a degraded status with southern blacks.[56]

The following year, in Norfolk, Bartholomew Maloney, another Irishman, was found guilty of rape as well, and some observers believed that his conviction too emanated from anti-Irish sentiment in the city. Maloney received the maximum sentence for the rape, twenty years, as well as an additional twenty years for aiding and abetting others involved in the rape. The accuser was a white eighteen-year-old named Susan C. Bowers. Three petitions were received by the governor in 1861 on Maloney's behalf. One from the mayor of Norfolk touted Maloney as a "worthy citizen of Norfolk." A second petitioner, named Sheffey, claimed that Maloney "was convicted at a time when the excitement and prejudice against Irishmen was so intense, that honest Irish witnesses were either frightened from court or disbelieved." Like Mayor Lamb of Norfolk, Sheffey portrayed Maloney as a man of excellent character and of "industry and sobriety," an apparent attempt to disabuse the governor of prevalent nineteenth-century stereotypes about the Irish as heavy drinkers.[57] These personal traits were also reflected in a third petition that boasted of Maloney's "unimpeachable and exemplary character." The governor was persuaded and intervened.[58]

In white-on-white rape cases (more often when the accusers were not children), communities exhibited divisiveness, as factions, some allied with the accused and others with the accuser, vied for the acceptance of competing versions of "the truth." Factions of whites in Rockingham County, Virginia, squared off in 1860 after a jury convicted Abraham H. Showalter of raping Julia Ann Keesaer, seventeen, and sentenced him to twelve years' imprisonment, two years more than the minimum sentence. But other courtroom observers did not share the jury's sensitivity to the complainant's charge. According to one petition, Keesaer's performance on the witness stand prejudiced the jury. Her testimony was interrupted by frequent "feinting" spells. Each time Julia Keesaer was pressed for details about the assault, she fainted and had to be carried out of the courtroom for fresh air. Petitioners claimed that each episode incited deeper indignation and sympathy for the accuser, precluding a fair trial for Showalter. Eventually the court adjourned to give Keesaer time to recover, but to no avail. Her fainting resumed once the trial reconvened. Finally, defense counsel conceded that a cross-examination was impossible under the circumstances and excused Keesaer, who went unquestioned by the defense. Nonetheless, her presence and her actions, feigned or not, had a tremendous impact on the jury.[59]

The defense managed to present some incriminating evidence that cast doubt on Keesaer's truthfulness. Friends of the accuser testified that she had complained to them of "great pain and soreness in consequence of the fact." According to this testimony, Keesaer maintained that Showalter experienced great difficulty entering "her person," so he took a razor and "cut it" (presumably the hymen) "that he might accomplish his ends." These same friends swore in court, however, that when they examined Keesaer they found "no marks of violence whatever."[60] This contradictory evidence, it was asserted in the petition, was eclipsed by the visual image of Keesaer's repeated fainting episodes.

The fifty-three male petitioners concluded that Keesaer's actions were part of a "sham" to hamper a "fair and full investigation" of the alleged assault. The letter ended with a sentimental appeal to reunite Showalter with his family, "an interesting wife and three small children" who were suffering because of their father's incarceration. The governor, John Letcher, convinced that "excitement prevailed" throughout the trial, thus thwarting a fair and impartial hearing for Showalter, pardoned him, citing the petition signed by "the most respectable citizens."[61]

No allegations of sexual impropriety were ever made against Julia Keesaer, but the petitioners were convinced that her fainting spells were a ploy designed to evade cross-examination that might divulge exculpatory evidence. But given testimony that Showalter had tied up Keesaer and used a razor on her vagina, her concern may have been simply to avoid having to publicly relive a traumatic and humiliating experience, though the lack of corroborating evidence about the cutting makes this possibility less credible. The petition written on behalf of Abraham Showalter argued that Julia Keesaer had lied about being raped. Showalter's supporters winced at the thought of a man spending years of his life in prison merely on the word of one woman.

Residents in Bedford County, Virginia, in 1843 also challenged the veracity of a woman who claimed to have been raped. In July 1843 Mrs. Lucinda Dearing filed charges of rape against William B. O. "Otey" Franklin, aged eighteen; at the October term, he was found guilty and sentenced to ten years in the penitentiary, the most lenient sentence allowable. Friends and family members quickly rushed to Franklin's defense over the ensuing years. Petitions presented to the governor for Franklin's early release from incarceration cited technical reasons as well as past infidelities by Mrs. Dearing.[62]

Sexual indiscretions committed outside marriage—whether infidelity, as was alleged to have been at the root of Lucinda Dearing's rape charge, or premarital sex, or sex across the color line—exposed white women accusing white men of rape to the likelihood of a public challenge to their veracity and integrity. Neighbors maligned the woman who accused Edward Ledbetter of raping her in April 1859, calling her a "common strumpet" who had given birth to at least two children of color. One petitioner noted, "negroes were in the habit of visiting her house." Ledbetter, according to the petitioners, visited the home of two women, a mother and daughter. A companion testified that Ledbetter entered the home but emerged after an audible row inside the house. After obtaining fifty cents from his friend, saying the woman wanted to be paid, Ledbetter reentered the home and returned after about half an hour. Two days later, he and his companion were arrested for rape.[63]

During the trial the race of the accuser came under intense scrutiny. Because she had given birth to mulatto children, questions were raised about her own lineage. This might have been an ingenious defense ploy, because Virginia law did not allow people of color to testify against white defendants. Although the accuser's own mother swore that her daughter was white and that her father was a white man from Dinwiddie County, the judge called upon a black spectator from the courtroom to examine the accuser and to determine whether in fact she was black. The ad hoc "expert" on race told the court that if the accuser had any "Negro blood, to a certain degree, there would be no grisel or cartilage in the nose." After subjecting the accuser to a humiliating court-room "inspection," he announced the absence of cartilage in her nose, and thus judged her to be black. The judge accepted this determination.[64]

Accordingly the judge refused to admit the accuser's testimony into evidence. The prosecution's case was not lost, however. The accuser's mother, whose whiteness was not contested, was a material witness, and therefore her testimony was admissible. The jury, after hearing the mother's version of events, returned a guilty verdict and sentenced Edward Ledbetter to ten years in the penitentiary.[65]

Two aspects of this case merit further discussion. First, it is noteworthy that once the accuser's race was established to be mixed, the rape charges were not dropped. Even though the court viewed her as a woman of color, it did not dismiss the case. A woman of color could charge a white man with rape, provided that white witnesses could corroborate the charge. This requirement may account for why so few women of color brought charges of rape against white men, rather than the oft-repeated assertion that African American females could not be raped in the eyes of the law. If no white witnesses could independently confirm that the offense had occurred and testify to the rape, there was no case. Second, even though the court received "evidence" that the accuser was of mixed race, had given birth to mixed-race children out of wedlock, and had a reputation for cavorting with blacks, the jury nonetheless found the rape charge credible. Not only did the trial continue in light of the new information about the accuser, the jury found the offender guilty of rape[66]

Make no mistake, however. Hamstrung jury members were not happy about sending Ledbetter to prison for such a long term, probably because they believed that the sexual assault of a nonwhite woman was a minor matter, certainly not one warranting a lengthy prison term. But the law mandated ten years as the minimum sentence. Frustrated jurors therefore petitioned for Ledbetter's early release, arguing that "ten years is too long."[67]

It would be reading too much into the fragmentary sources to say that white men accused of rape were no better off than black men similarly accused. But it is clear that pockets of sympathy in white communities, in the courts, and in executive offices militated in favor of leniency and second chances for both black and white rapists in the Old South. Sometimes support came in a swell, other times in a trickle. The thread running through nearly all the accounts of official rape was a deep suspicion and mistrust of the female accuser. Women filing charges of sexual assault against black and white men had to surmount a number of obstacles before their charges would be believed. And even when juries and communities felt that the evidence supported claims of rape, a number of conditions and circumstances merited treating convicted rapists, black and white, with leniency, thus demonstrating, I think, a fair amount of gender sympathy even across the color line.

Arguably, white men only infrequently faced death for their sexual infractions against white women. But maybe the very fact that black men stood to die made white southerners more cautious and introspective about their decisions in black-on-white cases. Simply put, a human life weighed in the balance. And community members, courts, and elected officials, cognizant of grave consequences, at times interceded to spare the life of a convicted free black rapist.[68] Motives here are less apparent but could include any combination of humanitarianism, economic ties, personalism, misogyny, class prejudice, or paternalism. Those whites who opposed efforts to commute the death sentences of convicted black rapists more likely were motivated by personal grievance, fear of job competition, racial superiority, and a sense of entitlement to the benefits of being white in a slave society.[69] Political climate, demographics, and economic conditions also shaped the community reaction to charges of black rape. Woe to the accused black rapist in the wake of a slave insurrection or a recent death of a white victim at the hands of a black murderer.

The common denominator in sexual assault cases of both slave and free defendants seems to have been the notions of class and gender that animated white elites, permitting them to hold poor white women and girls in such low regard that they would ally with African American men against their white female accusers.[70] Moreover, whether slave or free, white patrons had strong self-interested, material reasons for not wanting black men charged with rape to die. This does not mean that every black man charged with raping a white female could with certainty expect white intervention and reprieve. That was, however, one possible outcome.

RARELY KNOWN TO VIOLATE A WHITE WOMAN
Slave Rape in Civil War–Era Virginia

6

In 1894 Frederick Douglass wrote an essay entitled "Why Is the Negro Lynched?" in which he explored white motives for lynching black men. His purpose was to expose as a sham the murder of black men by southern whites under the pretense that they had raped white women. Denouncing the racist caricature of black men as rapists, Douglass cited the southern home front during the Civil War, asking how slaveowners could have absented themselves from the plantations during the war, leaving wives, mothers, and daughters behind "in absolute custody" of their slaves if black men were innately predisposed to raping white women. "During all those long four years of terrible conflict," Douglass wrote, "when the Negro had every opportunity to commit the abominable crime now alleged against him, there was never a single instance of such crime reported or charged against him. He was never accused of assault, insult, or an attempt to commit an assault upon any white woman in the whole South"[1]

Like Douglass, Ida B. Wells-Barnett, tireless antilynching reformer, saw through the hypocrisy of white supremacists who sought to recast the black man as a sexual menace. In slavery, she wrote, no charge was ever made of slave rape, "not even during the dark days of the rebellion, when the white man, following the fortunes of war went to do battle for the maintenance of slavery. While the master was away fighting to forge the fetters upon the slave, he left his wife and children with no protectors save the Negroes themselves. And yet during those years of trust and peril, no Negro proved recreant to his trust and no white man returned to a home that had been despoiled."[2]

Paradoxically, the position of Douglass and Wells-Barnett was shared by turn-of-the-century white southern apologists, who for very different purposes similarly argued that the region's blacks had posed no sexual threat to white females left unprotected on the home front during the war. Attempting to advance the white supremacist agenda that accentuated the barbarity of black men since the end of slavery, Lost Cause enthusiasts fondly recalled slave times, when relations between slaves and masters were harmonious, even blissful. W. Cabell Bruce, for one, wrote that during the Civil War the black man, "was rarely known to violate a white woman."[3] Henry McHattan, who had grown up on a plantation in Louisiana, reminisced, "there was no lock between any Negro and my mother's bedroom. My father was often absent. During the war there were thousands of white women isolated on plantations alone under the care of slaves for months, and even years. Many women made trips through the country day and night alone in charge of Negro drivers. If this trust was ever betrayed, I have never heard of it."[4]

By envisioning family slaves as the ultimate protectors of white women during the war, southern whites could then argue that the "New Negro"—no longer schooled in civilization on the plantation—posed a real problem for the "New South." Nostalgic descendants of slaveholders reflected on an imagined era when white women, even under the strains of war and dislocation, needed not fear their male slaves because of "the natural trust and affection subsisting between the two races."[5] The transformation of the ex-slaves, from loyal protectors in proxy during the crisis of war into menacing brutes intent on ravishing white females after the war, helped to justify myriad measures, legal and extralegal, such as lynching and disfranchisement, to subjugate the region's black population.

The use of black rape by race reformers and Lost Cause apologists alike to advance a particular position on the state of race relations, decades after the demise of slavery, is but one example of how black-on-white rape has been highly politicized and in the process grossly distorted. Still, this turn-of-the-century debate evinces compelling concerns that surely confronted slaveholding whites during the Civil War, chief among them the vulnerability of white women left unattended and unprotected by men who abandoned them for the front. Nothing less than the edifice of paternalism was at stake.

Recent historical treatments of gender and the Civil War have fittingly characterized the period as a crisis in gender.[6] The paternalistic and patriarchal structure of both the antebellum southern household and society was grounded in a hierarchy of gender, race, and class premised on reciprocal obligations. The power and authority of white males was shored up by the deference and loyalty of household subordinates, white women and black slaves, who in turn expected protection and sustenance. Men's and women's roles were clearly delineated in this arrangement. White men managed the slaves and the crops, negotiated the public sphere of business and politics, and made all important decisions regarding the household. Women attended to the domestic realm, which included childrearing, supervising food preparation and managing the household, visiting neighbors, nursing the sick, and serving as moral guardians to their charges.[7]

The departure of thousands of white men to the front beginning in 1861 upset these traditional gender-defined roles, thrusting women into unfamiliar and unaccustomed responsibilities. Slaveholding women had no choice but to assume the reins of control over slaves, unsavory and unladylike though the task was.[8] Lacking male guidance, many mistresses were left to make important financial decisions on their own.[9] Others, out of necessity, ventured into professions and jobs heretofore the domain of men: nursing, spying, clerical work, teaching.[10] An antebellum code of feminine values that lauded docility, deference, dependence, and frailty provided few guideposts to women confronted with challenging new roles and responsibilities, once the purview of their husbands and fathers. The suffering and deprivation attendant to war only exacerbated the already destabilized gender hierarchy. The war wreaked havoc on the personal lives of women on the home front; they suffered from shortages and starvation, fear and uncertainty, loneliness and lawlessness. Abandoned by their men and betrayed by a cause, elite and nonelite women struggled to survive the tumultuous war years unprotected and abandoned.

The absence of husbands, fathers, and sons from white households throughout the South brings us back to the paradox exposed by Douglass and Wells: How could male slave masters in good conscience have abandoned their plantations, homes, and farms during the war, leaving wives, mothers, and daughters behind "in absolute custody" of their slaves, if they believed that black men posed a sexual threat to white women?

Apparently most southerners of the slaveholding class did not believe that slaves posed such a threat during wartime. The war, despite the anxiety and uncertainty that it engendered, appears not to have spawned or fanned white fears of black rape.

As is clear from letters and diaries penned during the Civil War, slaveholders clung tenaciously to the longstanding notion that slaves, especially their own, were trustworthy. Mary Chesnut for one boasted in the first year of the war that "a genuine slaveowner born and bred will not be afraid of negroes—*quand même*. Here we are as the moonbeams and as serene. Nothing but negroes around us—white men all gone to the army."[11] Eliza Frances Andrews recalled how at the outbreak of war her sister, Mrs. Troup Butler, lived alone with two small children on a plantation in southwest Georgia. Butler "lived there with no other protector, for a good part of the time, than the negroes themselves . . . they were faithful, and nobody ever thought of being afraid on their account."[12] Henry William Ravenal crowed of the steadfast loyalty demonstrated by the slaves throughout the war: "They have faithfully done their duty during this trying time. . . . In all this reign of disorder and anarchy I have not seen or heard of any violence or even rudeness or incivility from the plantation negroes. Docility and submissiveness still prevail."[13]

Letters from slaveholding fathers and husbands rarely betrayed apprehension about their own slaves. When Alexander Faulkner Fewell, a South Carolinian serving in the Confederate army, wrote to his wife, Martha Ann, he bade her "tell the negroes all howdy for me." Fewell had left his wife and children virtually alone—a few male relatives were to visit periodically—with nary a thought that the slaves might have posed a risk to his female family members. Instead he wrote sanguinely, "encourage the negroes to do the best they can."[14]

Of course not all white southerners were so blithe about their relations with their slaves during the war. Those who were less confident about slave fidelity and more apprehensive, however, tended to voice concerns about insurrection, not sexual assault. Keziah Goodwyn Hopkins Brevard, a wealthy widow living alone on her large plantation in South Carolina with her slaves, captured the ambivalence about slaves that seemed to bedevil most slaveholders during the war: "Why is it at times I feel safe as if no dangers were in the distance?—I wish I could feel as free from fear at all times as I do tonight—it is dreadful to dwell on insurrections—many an hour have I laid awake in my life thinking of our danger."[15]

Despite the occasional expression of concern about potential slave insurrection during the Civil War, few southern whites, as evidenced by their own recorded words, seemed gripped by sexual fears of slave men. As Martha Hodes has noted, "while whites feared slave uprisings during the Civil War, no great tide of sexual alarm engulfed white southerners as white men left white women at home with slave men."[16] Winthrop Jordan concurs. "One looks in vain [in diaries] for sustained allusions to the Negro as rapist."[17] White southerners for the most part did not regard their slaves as violent, or even potentially violent.[18] Long-held ideas about racial difference—the belief that blacks were childlike by nature—held considerable sway, even through the chaos of war. Slaveholders like Edmund Ruffin, who believed that they knew their slaves well, cited the "natural timidity of the negro race," leading them to discount the threat of slave revolt or violence.[19] Paternalistic hubris also shaped ideas about the docility of slaves. Many masters confidently held that "the attachment of slaves to their masters" would effectively thwart armed rebellion.[20]

Slave violence before and during the Civil War was never as rare as many contemporary white southerners would like to have believed or recalled. And despite postwar nostalgic reminiscences, there were in fact wartime reports of slave rape, though admittedly recorded cases were few. In Virginia, there are at least nine cases of slaves who were officially charged with and convicted of rape or attempted rape during the war years. By examining these nine cases we can learn a great deal about the impact of the Civil War on notions of sexuality, race, gender, and class.

The Civil War has been frequently described as a watershed in American history on many fronts. The war had tremendous social, legal, political, and economic consequences but also unequivocally settled vexatious issues like states' rights and the place of slavery in America that had plagued the country since its birth. Some historians of the South in particular have built their professional reputations on the claim that the Civil War was the most important catalyst for change in southern, if not American, history.[21]

To a large degree this chapter attempts to sort out the extent to which patterns and trends of behavior in antebellum black-on-white rape cases continued during the Civil War, a time of great uncertainty and chaos, of economic deprivation, when institutions were shaken to the core and faith in a slave-based, patriarchal system would be sorely tested. In essence, what follows is an attempt to measure the extent to which long-held ideas about sexuality, gender, race, and class were altered by the conditions of war. By continuing to trace the behavior of both white communities and officials in black rape trials through the war, we are in a position to discern important changes that will better inform our understanding of sexual and racial dynamics before and after the war, as well as the factors that shaped those changes.

One obvious example is the pattern of treating accused slave rapists rather leniently, especially compared to the postbellum years. Under slavery, it could be argued, white southerners had the luxury of being lenient to convicted black rapists. Doing so fit into their paternalist worldview. Leniency softened the blow to the pocketbooks of individual slaveholders and to the state coffers. With war, concerns about the welfare of women on the home front might trump the inclination to continue offering trials to black slaves accused of rape. There might be greater pressures to make examples out of miscreant slaves. Testing this hypothesis might afford greater insight into the early origins of white fears of black rape. These wartime slave rape cases, I argue, can be mined for evidence about the preoccupation—or, as I see it, the lack of preoccupation—of white southerners about slave rape during wartime.

Finally, the slave rape cases brought before local and state communities during the war provide a window through which to view class and gender dynamics and to determine the extent to which these were affected by the circumstances of war. The cases show, I assert, that war did not obliterate class divisions among white southerners. To the contrary, we observe in some cases that war intensified those divisions. These interclass feuds were often played out in black-on-white rape trials, as slaveowners' property interests, under greater assault with the onset of war, clashed with demands for legal and communal redress by poor women who charged slaves with sexual assault. As in the antebellum South, white women on the margins—the poor, the unmarried, the abandoned, those of diminished mental capacity—struggled to be encompassed under the umbrella of protection, which proved elusive on many occasions.

As sectional tensions worsened and the political debate over slavery heated up in the years preceding the outbreak of war, we might expect to find a concomitant increase in anxiety about black sexual assault. Abolitionists had brought the issue of white sexual assault of slave women to the forefront, making interracial sexuality a highly charged political subject.[22] Embarrassed and defensive slaveholders might have responded by deflecting attention onto an imaginary black sexual threat, thus perhaps rationalizing the necessity of keeping black men enslaved and their primitive libidos in check.

By looking at the trends in the transportation rates of convicted slaves out of the state of Virginia during this time, we can indirectly gauge the pulse of the white community for any fears of black rapists. Governors were in no position to antagonize large pools of voters by pardoning or commuting the sentences of convicted African American rapists if concerns over the "black-beast-rapist" were rampant.[23] In short, if heated sectional politics and the war itself breathed life into the myth of the black rapist, that should be discernible in the actions taken by governors, who continued to hear appeals on behalf of black rapists throughout the Civil War.

In fact, transportation patterns by Virginia executives reveal that as the Civil War approached, and in the early part of the war, a convicted black sex offender stood a reasonable chance of being transported out of Virginia or even conscripted to work on public works projects rather than being hanged (Table 6.1). This pattern marks a decided change from the early part of the century, when execution was the punishment of choice for slaves convicted of rape or

TABLE 6.1. Virginia Slaves Convicted of Rape or Attempted Rape and the Outcomes, 1860–1865

Year	Slave	County	Outcome
1860	George	Halifax	Transported
1860	Jim	Isle of Wight	Transported*
1860	Patrick	Henrico	Transported
1860	Sam	Berkeley	Transported*
1860	Bill	Jefferson	Transported*
1861	Sam	Halifax	Transported
1861	Albert	Henry	Unknown
1862	John	Chesterfield	Transported*
1862	Ben	Amherst	Unknown
1862	John	Pittsylvania	Transported*
1862	Bibb	Sussex	Executed
1862	Emmanuel	Lunenberg	Executed
1864	Nat	Pittsylvania	Executed
1865	Claiborne	Franklin	Executed

Sources: Data gathered from an array of sources at the Library of Virginia, including VEPLR, Pardon Papers, and transportation and execution records from the Auditor of Public Accounts, as well as bond documents; county court order and minute books; and Schwarz, *Twice Condemned*.
*Sentence was further commuted by the governor of Virginia to life on public works.

attempted rape (Table 6.2). As the Civil War neared, even as political and social tensions heightened in response to the politics of antislavery and sectionalism, state officials spared the lives of convicted slave rapists with much greater frequency that they had at the beginning of the nineteenth century. As civil war grew closer and the institution of slavery came under considerable and rather relentless attack, when one might have expected to observe more rigorous local and state control over errant slaves, convicted slave rapists routinely escaped the fate of the noose. In fact, when political and social anxieties should have increased the likelihood that convicted slave rapists would be vigorously prosecuted and executed, the opposite was true. No Virginia slave convicted of rape or attempted rape in 1860 was ever hanged. Of the nine slaves convicted of raping or attempting to rape white females during the war years themselves, only four can with certainty be documented as having been executed.[24] The tendency toward leniency for slaves charged with serious crimes, including the rape or attempted rape of white females, continued at least through the early years of war. In the final stages of war, however, this trend abruptly ended, with virtually all condemned slave rapists executed.

The pattern of extending leniency to slave rapists in legal proceedings is

TABLE 6.2. Virginia Slaves Convicted of Rape or Attempted Rape and the
Verifiable Outcomes, 1800–1865

Decade	Transported	Executed	Unknown Outcome	Total Known Outcome
1800–1809	7 (39%)	10 (56%)	0	18[a]
1810–19	0 (0%)	9 (82%)	0	11[ab]
1820–29	10 (37%)	17 (63%)	2	27
1830–39	8 (42%)	11[c] (58%)	0	19[c]
1840–49	14 (54%)	12 (46%)	0	26
1850–59	16 (55%)	13 (45%)	0	29
1860–65	8 (67%)	4 (33%)	2[d]	12

Sources: Data gathered from an array of sources at the Library of Virginia including
VEPLR, Pardon Papers, and transportation and execution records from the Auditor of
Public Accounts, as well as bond documents; county court order and minute books;
Schwarz, *Twice Condemned*; and James Hugo Johnston, *Race Relations in Virginia and
Miscegenation in the South, 1776–1860*.
Note: Percentages based on total number of known and verifiable outcomes.
[a] Includes one sentence of castration
[b] Includes one slave who escaped from jail
[c] Includes one case of rape-murder
[d] No records of financial compensation to the slaves' owners can be located among funds
dispersed by the Virginia treasury.

borne out not only in statistics, as seen above, but in communities' deliberations during slave rape trials, when white Confederates continued to find
reasons to ameliorate the harsh punishments prescribed for slave rapists, including the mental state of the accused. A slave with diminished intellectual
capacity required the protection of the white community, even in cases of
sexual assault, and even during the Civil War.

Barely two months after the firing on Fort Sumter, a court in Halifax County
was confounded by a local slave's aberrant behavior when he was charged with
assault with intent to rape a white woman. Dianna and Richard Boyd and their
family had moved into the neighborhood six months earlier, although they
had lived in the vicinity for at least two years. The Boyd household comprised
ten white and three black members, including Susan Boyd, a daughter. So
while the family owned slaves, its wealth as defined by slave property was
modest. We can also deduce the middling status of the Boyds by work assign-
ments. The Boyd children attended to barnyard chores, as they did the morning of June 17, 1861. Susan, accompanied by her five-year-old sister and a nine-
year-old slave, was sent by her mother to the cow pen to perform chores.[25]
Typically Susan's mother had done most of the household and farm chores,
but for about the previous five to six months illness forced her daughter to
assume most of those responsibilities. Susan Boyd was tending the cows when

Sam, a seventeen-year-old slave belonging to Thomas Whitworth, a neighbor who lived about half a mile from the Boyd home, approached her. He claimed to have been sent by his young mistress to fetch her. Susan, with her little sister in tow, began making her way "through the gap" toward the Whitworth residence when she noticed Sam standing suspiciously behind a bush. He asked Susan whether she had seen any of his cows. Wary, Susan turned to "go back" to her home, which was still in full view. Perhaps sensing that his ruse was about to unravel, Sam seized Susan Boyd, dragging her about fifty yards toward a wooded area. Boyd screamed and struggled. She managed to grab hold of a tree and stubbornly refused to release her grip. Boyd later told of Sam's attempt to raise her clothes, a fact legally necessary to substantiate the accused's intent to commit a rape. By this time the slave boy accompanying Boyd had run to get her father, who had already been alerted by the hollering and screaming of his daughter.[26]

Since Sam's actions were incontrovertible, his motive apparent, much of the trial testimony focused on his state of mind, suggesting that the white community was struggling to comprehend how a slave could possibly commit such an egregious act as assaulting a white female in broad daylight within earshot of family members. Most whites who knew Sam agreed that he did not have "good sense." Susan's father, for one, testified that he had known Sam for two or three years and believed that he did not possess "as good sense as some other negroes." Asked by the prosecutor whether he thought Sam had enough sense to know right from wrong, Richard Boyd replied, "He may not know it in every case but he does in many cases. I would not consider him a smart negro." Further queried by the commonwealth's attorney, "Do you think he has sense enough to keep his hands off of a white woman?" Boyd responded with a bit of an understatement, "It appears that he did not at that time."[27]

Attempting to cast his slave's actions in a more sympathetic light, Thomas Whitworth, Sam's master of ten years, described Sam as "childish," not a person of good mind, although Whitworth testified that generally Sam's character was good and described him as a very obedient servant. Whitworth could not entrust Sam with "complicated" orders, but he would not go so far as to call Sam an "idiot," although he had observed signs of "laziness." Sam's owner denied that his slave had ever shown any "forwardness or impertinence" to the white females in the Whitworth family.[28]

As in earlier slave rape cases, the defense was falling back on a carefully crafted strategy that depicted Sam as mentally deficient, suggesting that he had been incapable of distinguishing between appropriate and inappropriate behavior. And that strategy proved at least partially successful. Although Sam was convicted, the jury appears to have been swayed enough to sentence him to transportation and thus spare him a death sentence.[29]

The Civil War in this case appears not to have altered the well-established practice of providing accused slave rapists with a trial. Similarly, white notions about the nature of slaves' temperament and character appear to have remained intact. Whites, left with little male protection on the home front and worried about the control of their slaves, might have manifested increased anxiety about the "true" nature of their slaves. Instead, the white community's willingness to regard Sam's mental frailty as grounds for mercy, even against a backdrop of war, reveals a continued confidence in slaves as individuals and slavery as a system. The ideological underpinnings of slavery would not be dislodged quickly, even by war.

Material factors merge with ideological convictions to offer a plausible explanation for continued leniency during the war. As has been well documented for the antebellum period, a slave's value as property surely figured prominently.[30] Obviously Sam's owner, Whitworth, was attempting to spare his slave, his property, a trip to the gallows. That endeavor was made difficult, however, because given the eyewitness testimony of the Boyds, there was no denying Sam's actions. Challenging the integrity of the accuser, a tactic widely utilized throughout the nineteenth century, seems not to have been an option either, presumably because there was no evidence of illicit or dubious sexual history in Susan Boyd's past.[31] We have to assume that the Boyds were sufficiently well respected in the neighborhood to have forestalled a challenge to the accuser's character, one of the more successful strategies employed in slave rape trials. It was left, then, to assert mental incapacity of the accused.

The defense asked the jury to use common sense in its consideration: what slave in his right mind would ever, in broad daylight no less, accost a white woman? The argument, as framed by the defense and considered by the jury, reveals that the criminal and aggressive behavior of Sam stymied local whites. They struggled to comprehend how a slave, with any sense at all, could have been so foolhardy as to risk his life in an attempt to force a white woman to have sex with him. Sam's affront fell outside their experience, and they struggled for an explanation. The answer that most whites, even the father of the accused, seem to have come up with is mental deficiency. The resulting discussion that centered on "sense"—Did Sam have any? How much did he have? Enough to know right from wrong?—might be viewed as a white community's self-affirming humane intervention in the court of law. By blunting the draconian slave code that held out death for such an infraction, this Halifax County community, in the throes of a war over the future over slavery, might very well have been puffing out its chest, admiring its own paternalistic largess. Sam was not responsible for his actions, heinous as they might have been, because he was weak-minded. Mercy, not harshness, was required.[32] However, such reasoning might also have been a psychological requirement in a time of great instability and uncertainty. Lacking male caretakers on the home front, white southerners may have found great comfort in reaffirming their collective belief in the natural docility of their slaves. To have believed otherwise might have compromised the war effort. Believing that slaves were a dangerous menace, Confederate women might not have been quite so eager to let their husbands, sons, and fathers go to the front; and their men may not have gone at all.

The decision of the Halifax County court to take into account a slave's feeble mental state when deliberating his alleged attack on a white woman highlights the continuity of ideas about slaves' nature and the relative leniency that convicted slave rapists often received in the nineteenth-century South. Another case, ironically one that also involved mental capacity, demonstrates the continued marginalization of poor white women, even during the Civil War. The case involved a white female who charged a slave with rape in the following year, 1862, in Pittsylvania County, Virginia, and her treatment contrasts sharply with the relative sympathy shown toward Sam. Curiously, while white Virginians had been willing to consider the mental state of male slaves in their deliberations of rape trials, residents of Pittsylvania County resisted granting the same consideration to a white teenaged accuser who was, by their admission, severely mentally handicapped.[33] Whereas the court in Sam's case was persuaded that a slave rapist's weakened mental state was a mitigating condition demanding leniency, the Pittsylvania court seemed convinced that the same condition worked against the female accuser.

Neither the court nor the white eyewitnesses to the rape seemed particularly sympathetic to a young white woman made more vulnerable to sexual assault because of not only her developmental handicap but the additional handicap of being unable to speak. Regarded by most in the neighborhood as an "idiot," the mute Tabitha Reynolds was forced to rely on family and neighbors to advance her case against a slave alleged to have raped her. And not all appeared to have Reynolds's best interest in mind when they testified.[34]

William Walker, a local miller, was the chief eyewitness to the assault. He narrated for the court how one day in March he left his mill briefly, leaving instructions for his hired slave, John, to remain at the mill.[35] Upon his return, Walker found John missing. Walker's attentions quickly turned to a noise coming from the nearby creek bed. Accompanied by his uncle, Walker investigated the commotion and reported observing John, the prisoner, on top of Reynolds near the creek. Walker testified that John "had her clothes all up, he had his left arm around the girl's neck and was in the act of kissing her. . . . I spoke [to] the prisoner. He just rolled off of the girl and put his penis back in his britches. I saw his penis distinctly. It was out of his pantaloons."[36]

Walker's reaction to witnessing the sexual violation of a young white woman by a slave could hardly be characterized as outrage. By his own admission, approximately one to one and a half minutes elapsed from the time he first observed the assault until John "rolled off of her." That may not seem like much time, but considering that Walker stood only five or six steps away, one has to wonder why his response was not more immediate.[37]

Walker's testimony is replete with contempt and derision for Reynolds. He informed the court that she had ceased making noise before he spotted her and John, implying that she had thus made herself a consenting partner.[38] Pressed, Walker doubted that Reynolds's noisemaking was evidence of initial resistance. He explained that Reynolds "was in the habit of making the same kind of noise whether in distress or not and [is] the only kind of noise she can make." Furthermore, Walker asserted that Reynolds did not appear at all disturbed by the incident, noting nothing "unusual" about her appearance: "I do not think she had sense enough to be alarmed or distressed." Walker's testimony exudes irritation with and disdain for Tabitha Reynolds, demonstrating that he belittled the seriousness of the rape charge because the accuser was mentally and physically impaired, in stark contrast to the inquiry into the issue of "sense" in the case of Sam.[39]

Walker may have had a personal stake in John's fate, and thus the motivation to minimize the assault, but his uncle, A. L. H. Muse, managed to convey measured concern for Tabitha Reynolds. Muse's interpretation of the events differed markedly from that of Walker, for example, on the question of penetration and emission. Walker doubted that penetration had occurred. Muse, though, was convinced that it had. He testified that when John rolled off of Tabitha Reynolds, "his penis looked wet and greasy to me as though he had just gotten through with his operation." This issue was of the utmost importance to the state's case, since the chief prosecution witness, the mute accuser, could not speak and testify to the assault. With evidence of seminal emission and therefore penetration, John would have been found guilty only of an attempted rape.[40]

Muse also interpreted Tabitha Reynolds's reaction after the assault differently from Walker. "I thought she looked distressed," he said, "wild," "scared." Another area of disagreement was over signs of a struggle at the scene. Walker, when asked about evidence of a "scuffle," replied that he had not noticed any sign of a struggle. His uncle, in contrast, told the court that he observed "right smart signs of scuffling." Compassion nonetheless had its limits. Muse reported that he shook his head at Reynolds and pointed to her father's house, signaling not only disapproval but that Reynolds was to some degree responsible for the rape.[41]

The starkly different renderings of events by the two white male witnesses is significant. Walker, though not John's owner, could have been troubled at the prospect of losing John's labor and therefore shaped his testimony to be helpful to the accused. More importantly, it seems, Walker's posturing during the trial was designed to thwart criticism about his slipshod supervision of a slave with whom he had been entrusted.[42] Whatever the history of the three principals, Walker's sympathies clearly lay with the accused slave, signaling some sort of gender identification across the color line or antipathy for the accuser or both.

William Walker was not John's only advocate. Several character witnesses attested to John's good conduct and demeanor. Nancy Wray, John's owner, swore that he had always conducted himself well. Wray's neighbors knew of no other incidents of misbehavior. Community members as well as the court were convinced that John's youthfulness was an extenuating circumstance in the case. (Wray estimated John's age to have been about twelve or thirteen at the time of the alleged rape.) Juries in antebellum rape cases were frequently persuaded by defense arguments that the sex act could not be physically committed by young males under fourteen and as a result were reluctant to convict a young sex offender, black or white.[43]

John's youthfulness may have helped save his life, for he was found guilty of rape but sentenced to transportation rather than death. This relatively light sentence was further commuted, if not in John's eyes then certainly in the eyes of Virginia officials and of the governor of Virginia, who assigned John to public works for life.[44]

Importantly, the trial reveals the continued marginalization of nonelite white women as well as a willingness to treat convicted slave rapists with leniency, even under the strains of war, when white Virginians might have been inclined to act more harshly to keep miscreant slaves in line. Not even war, it seems, could immediately dislodge pervasively held misogynistic ideas about the depravity of poor white women. Class and gender hierarchies that framed antebellum southern society held up during the war, though Confederate wartime policies, profiteering, and the sacrifices required of the war sharply accentuated class divisions among white southerners, as poorer and middling whites at times vehemently demonstrated their discontent. As Paul Escott has noted, the crisis of North Carolina's "internal war" "destroyed interclass unity and revealed a fissure that had run beneath the surface of the antebellum social system."[45] Some of the wartime slave rape cases from Virginia were a lightning rod for such class tensions.

The most unabashed social clash among principals in a slave rape case occurred in Lunenberg County in 1862. Elizabeth Bowen, wife of an overseer who had gone off to war, charged that Emmanuel, property of Mary Bagby, had broken into her home with the intention of raping her. H. L. Bowen had worked as the overseer for Mary Bagby for about three years until the outbreak of war, when he enlisted in the "army of Winchester." His wife, Elizabeth, remained on the Bagby plantation along with her unmarried sister, Jane Dodd, and Dodd's child.[46]

On the Sunday before the alleged attack, according to court testimony, Emmanuel came to the Bowen house contending that H. L. Bowen, his overseer, owed him money. Elizabeth Bowen was not at home at the time, but her sister subsequently informed her of Emmanuel's visit. The accused slave, it was alleged, returned on the night of November 16, 1862, around ten o'clock and forcibly entered the Bowen home by breaking a window. One of the women struck the intruder with a chair and he then retreated, but only temporarily. When he returned fifteen minutes later he broke down the door, sending the two sisters dashing upstairs to escape. Bowen jumped out a window, leaving her sister and three young children behind. She told the court that she sought refuge at a neighbor's place but lost her way in the dark. Consequently, she remained outside for virtually the entire rest of the night. She returned later that morning with two male neighbors to find the door broken down, the window broken, and her bed torn to pieces. Among the missing items were a blanket and a sheet. Her sister was not there, also having fled the intruder, thus leaving alone in the house her child and Bowen's three children, the youngest of whom was seven months old. Bowen complained that the children, particularly the baby, were in a "suffering condition."[47]

During the trial much was made of the two women's inability to identify the intruder. According to their own testimony, there had been no light in the room. Bowen's claim that she had somehow managed to recognize him out of doors, where there was more light, seems untenable and contradictory in view of her testimony about having been lost for most of the night because of darkness. Bowen reconciled the discrepancy by saying that it had been dark only until the moon came out. Even so, the only feature of her attacker that she could describe with any certainty was the hat he had worn during the attack.

Apparently during the intruder's first forced entry into the house he had inadvertently left his cap behind. Both women swore that they got a good look at the green cap and thus were able to identify their attacker as Emmanuel. This was problematic because Bowen had told the Wilson family members, in whose home she sought help the next morning, that she did not know who broke into her house and was able to describe him only as a "low chunky bushy headed negro."[48]

The women's testimony was dotted with other discrepancies, some minor, others not. For instance, Bowen told the court that her sister had struck the intruder with a chair. Jane Dodd, however, swore that it was Bowen who had picked up the chair and hit the attacker. So many inconsistencies were elicited by the defense that at the close of testimony the Commonwealth's attorney, in a chivalric display of lawyering, demanded to know whether defense counsel meant to impeach the testimony of Bowen and Dodd. The defense refused to respond. The prosecution then requested permission to hear testimony attesting to the women's "general character for veracity." The court refused.[49]

Despite the defense's obvious campaign to depict the testimony of Bowen and her sister as unreliable, and despite their presentation of an alibi—several Bagby slaves testified that Emmanuel never left the cabin the night of the attack—Emmanuel was found guilty and sentenced to hang. In response, Emmanuel's owner, Mary Bagby, launched an energetic campaign to have him pardoned by the governor. The application for pardon, written by her attorney, challenged Emmanuel's conviction on several grounds. The first was technical. Bagby asserted that one of the magistrates who had served on the jury that found her slave guilty had been improperly seated, which would have left the panel one short of the required number. In her view, an unlawfully constituted court had tried Emmanuel. Since slaves had no right to appeal in Virginia, arguing this legal challenge before the governor was Bagby's only avenue for rectifying the procedural irregularity.[50]

Bagby's second tactic was to impeach the testimony of Elizabeth Bowen, the accuser, which she characterized as "confused and deficient in proving any other offense than a burglary" and even more deficient in establishing the identity of the perpetrator with absolute certainty. Bagby cited the specific instances in which the sisters' testimony contradicted one another. Bagby also insinuated that the prisoner had been to Bowen's bed previously. How else could the intruder, in the dark, have gone "straight to the bed where Mrs. Bowen was lying"? On these matters, Bagby bore in. "Mrs. Bowen is entirely silent!"[51]

The governor, unswayed by the appeal, denied Mrs. Bagby's first application. But Bagby, undaunted, petitioned for a thirty-day reprieve to regroup for a second application. The second appeal was no more effective than the first, and Emmanuel hanged.[52]

The final disposition of the case, however, is of less importance than its demonstration that war gave rise to increased class dissension among white southerners and that class tensions often played out in black-on-white rape cases. Mary Bagby, callous in her response to a female tenant's claim to having been assaulted by one of her slaves, wasted no time in aligning with her slave. The standoff between Bowen and Bagby is, by all appearances, an example of how the Civil War bared intraracial, interclass splits among southern whites. Had Elizabeth Bowen's husband not been off fighting the war, perhaps Mary Bagby would not have been so aggressive in her efforts to exonerate her slave. With her overseer gone, Mary Bagby had no reason to keep his family on. It is also noteworthy that Mary Bagby did not appear alarmed when her male slave willfully broke into the home of white women, a fact that she readily conceded. Bagby's efforts to exculpate her convicted slave transcended any larger concerns that his criminal and violent actions threatened patriarchal authority, already taxed because of the war. Bagby's financial stake in saving Emmanuel's life was obviously bolstered by his worth as a laborer during a time when loss of manpower due to the war made him even more valuable. In staking out a position in support of a slave convicted of attempted rape, Bagby alienated herself from the accuser, a white woman of an inferior class, and quite possibly others of that class as well. That the court ruled in Bowen's favor may suggest that the local officials who convicted Emmanuel and the governor who refused to intercede came to view their role as male protectors in absentia.

The case of Emmanuel and others similar to it raise more questions than they answer. If in fact Emmanuel had broken into the Bowen home as the court found, had he been encouraged by the absence of a male head of household? Was he attempting to exploit the crisis of war that left women alone and vulnerable? Were more slaves, sensing the pending social and racial disarray promised by a northern victory, encouraged to challenge the institution of slavery by committing crimes, including the sexual assault of white women? Court records indicate that a spate of slave crime during the war plagued Lunenberg County, most notably breaking and entering and theft. Emmanuel's actions, viewed in this context, seem part of a more general response by the slave population to the unsettled conditions wrought by civil war. Note also that Emmanuel made no attempt on his mistress although she too was left without male protection; rather, again assuming his guilt, he turned his attentions to a woman, also unprotected, of an inferior social class.[53]

Whether Mary Bagby's insinuation about a consensual relationship between Elizabeth Bowen and her slave Emmanuel was based in truth or rather served up in a self-interested courtroom ploy to win exoneration for him is not clear. But had Bowen turned to a male slave for sexual intimacy, as Bagby hinted, she would not have been alone. Interracial contact, especially between white women and men of color, increased as a result of the war. In the antebellum world, poverty blurred the boundaries between races. With increased deprivation and scarcity during the war, more white women, many of them poor and struggling for the first time, relied on the black community to meet many of their needs. Some of the wartime slave rape cases suggest that increased interracial contact, including sexual contact, resulted in official charges of rape.[54] The case of the slave Albert in April 1861 holds out such a possibility.

At first blush the case of the rape and murder by a slave of Susan Stuart, an unmarried thirty-year-old, reads like a turn-of-the-century "black-beast-rapist" narrative. Stuart lived with her mother and her father, who was the overseer to Colonel Peter P. Penn. The woman's body was discovered about 350 yards from the Stuart home in Henry County, Virginia. She had been brutally beaten. Her skull had been smashed in, the eyeball protruding from its socket. Bruises covered her throat, neck, genitals, and legs. Pieces of skin had been torn from her neck. Her arm was broken. Her body lay with legs apart and her clothing pulled above her waist. For undisclosed reasons, suspicions immediately fell upon one of Penn's slaves, Albert, who had run away. A posse of neighborhood men gathered, some on foot, some on horseback, and searched for the slave. A few hours later, Albert was discovered hiding in nearby woods. According to witnesses, he "confessed" almost immediately. Albert was put on trial and convicted of raping and murdering Susan Stuart.[55]

The court transcript of Albert's trial leaves much unanswered, but it does disclose a murky subtext of a possible interracial liaison between the victim and her accused murderer. Those early on the scene of Albert's capture asked him to explain his motive for killing Susan. According to Jesse Giles, Albert admitted killing Susan because she "threatened to tell her father about seeing him." A second witness, Samuel H. Franklin, offered a somewhat different and possibly sanitized version of the "confession." Franklin explained that Albert had killed Susan after he had raped her and she had threatened to tell her father. A few other testimonial clues imply that Giles's account might have been the one closer to the truth. For one thing, Samuel Franklin testified that Stuart dispatched a slave to summon Penn with the news that "Al had killed Miss Susan." Stuart, in this account, was predisposed to believe that Albert had murdered his daughter. Why Albert? If Stuart had been aware that his daughter had been "seeing" Albert, such suspicion would not seem so unreasonable. Still another clue: Susan had excused herself after the noon meal to "hunt for the nest of some turkeys." Had this been a ruse concocted by Susan Stuart herself to conceal a rendezvous with Albert? If we entertain the idea that Susan had in fact been "seeing" Albert, might she have provoked him by attempting to end their relationship, then threatening to tell her father? Recalling the case of Polly Lane, we might also wonder whether Susan could have been pregnant. There is no evidence to support this, but the birth of a racially mixed child would certainly raise questions that eventually might have got Albert into a lot of trouble with his overseer, and murdering Susan might have seemed one way out. Facts, however, simply elude us, and we are left to speculate about the nature of Susan's and Albert's relationship.[56]

Of course had Susan Stuart been romantically involved with one of her father's slave charges, that would have been nothing new for the slave South. A spate of historical works in recent years has established unequivocally that intimate relations across racial boundaries in the Old South were more common and more widely tolerated than previously believed.[57] The onset of war in some ways increased the opportunities for these illicit relationships to continue. Indeed, the fallout of war may have pushed white women into relationships with slave men who often would have been the only available source of labor, goods, and even companionship.

Such motives seem to have undergirded the relationship between Mrs. Arlenia Jenkins of Franklin County, Virginia, and a slave named Claiborne, who she claimed raped her in the final months of the war. According to the testimony of Jenkins, the defendant, calling himself Wiley Meese, and a black woman named Cynthia came to her house on Tuesday evening, January 10, 1865, to barter some food for a dress.[58] For reasons that Jenkins did not disclose, she chose not to make the trade, and the two left. When Claiborne departed he told Jenkins that he was going to "watch her." A few days later, on a Friday evening, Claiborne returned to Jenkins's home and, according to her testimony, broke down the locked door of her home, seized her, struggled with her, and threw her onto a bed where her three children lay. She resisted "until her strength gave out," and then he ravished her. The attack took about fifteen minutes. She hollered but no one responded, her nearest neighbor living about a quarter-mile away. Jenkins reported the assault the next morning to her uncle, John Perdue, and his wife.[59]

On cross-examination, Jenkins admitted that on Tuesday evening, when

Claiborne and Cynthia came to her home they stayed "a rite smart while," suggesting a rather convivial visit. Although she did not ask them to have a seat, Jenkins reported that the woman sat down and commenced talking about trading butter and potatoes for a dress. During that time Claiborne neither said nor did nothing improper.[60]

The defense attorney interrogated Jenkins further about the nature of her relationship with Claiborne, insinuating that Jenkins had had some intimate connection with him. Claiborne's attorney had plenty of ammunition, most likely provided by the defendant himself, and came at Jenkins with rapid-fire accusations. For one, he asked whether Claiborne "did not whisper to her" or she to him during their meeting before the alleged attack. Jenkins also denied a defense allegation that she had seen Claiborne the night following the purported assault. Claiborne, according to the justice of the peace, had admitted to having visited Jenkins three nights that week. Claiborne's attorney also attacked Jenkins on inconsistencies between the details of the complaint she made with the justice of the peace and her own testimony. The justice of the peace asserted that Jenkins claimed to have been raped two or three times. On the witness stand she could not recollect whether she had told anyone that. She also denied a defense suggestion that Claiborne had brought apples for her children, which if true might have signaled familiarity. Finally, in what must have been a courtroom bombshell, she rejected as untrue a defense allegation that she was pregnant.[61]

The defense team could not have been more transparent. Repeatedly, Claiborne's attorney ostensibly questioned Jenkins, in the process disclosing important gems of indirect evidence to the jury that in toto suggest that Jenkins and Claiborne had been involved in an ongoing consensual, sexual relationship. Her motive in crying rape, he intimated, was that she was pregnant and her relationship was about to become public knowledge. In a preemptive measure, she charged Claiborne with rape. This scenario seems all the likelier in light of a conversation that Jenkins admitted having with Claiborne about the hanging of the Pittsylvania slave, Nat, for the rape of Susan Corbin. She testified that on the night of the purported assault Claiborne told her that a "negro man had been hung in Pittsylvania County for the same thing and the woman cryed out against him." Claiborne had heard about "Mayhan's negro" who had been hung for "keeping a soldier's wife and feeding her." Jenkins denied telling Claiborne that she would not "cry out" against him because she had seen a man hanged in Missouri and presumably found it distasteful.[62]

Jenkins's credibility was further eroded by the testimony of her own aunt, A.

Ann Perdue, to whom Jenkins first reported the rape on the morning of January 14. Although Perdue confirmed that the upper hinge of the door to Jenkins's home had indeed been broken as if by forced entry, as Jenkins had reported, Perdue told the court that she observed no "marks of violence on the said Jenkins" or on Jenkins's clothing. More damaging to the prosecution's case was Perdue's claim that Jenkins was "a very weak minded woman [who] does not know when to say yes or no." Perdue's reference was to Jenkins's poor bartering skills, but the defense seemed to be raising the specter of sexual bartering as well. Perdue impeached Jenkins's credibility further by stating outright that she "would not believe every thing which the said Arlenia Jenkins would state to her." Coming from kin, this testimony had to have had a powerful impact on the jury. The magistrate who arrested Claiborne, also a neighbor of Jenkins, confirmed this characterization of Jenkins by saying that she was "an idiot woman" who "has no mind." Although possessing a "general character that is good," she was "easily embarrassed and confused."[63]

We lack the direct voice of the accused, Claiborne, but we receive his version of the events as relayed by the arresting justice of the peace, W. C. Bennett, and the questions posed by his defense attorney. Claiborne told Bennett that he had been to visit Jenkins at her home three times that week. On Friday night, the night when Jenkins claimed that Claiborne raped her, he ended up spending nearly the entire night. Claiborne also told Bennett that Jenkins agreed to have intercourse with him and that they had sexual relations as many as four times.[64]

Given the well-established antebellum pattern of leniency in similar situations, a conviction, or at least an execution, would seem unlikely. Arlenia Jenkins, after all, was characterized as an "idiot woman," and her veracity had been called into question by her own aunt. The defense garnered testimony alluding to a consensual relationship that may have resulted in pregnancy. The defense also managed to plant doubt about the identity of attacker. Jenkins originally testified that her attacker identified himself as Wiley Meese. A witness testified that a slave of that name belonged to the "widow" Meese and bore a striking resemblance to Claiborne.[65]

The jury in Claiborne's trial thus was presented with an abundance of mitigating circumstances should it have been inclined to believe the defense's case. Overall, the prosecution's case was weak. Despite the handicap of not having Claiborne testify, the defense managed to communicate his version of the events to the jury through witnesses and his own lawyer. His rather convincing explication implicated Arlenia Jenkins as a willing sex partner of a black man. Jenkins was also a woman of the lower orders of antebellum Virginia society. This we can infer from her bartering with slaves, a type of economic exchange not practiced by women of more comfortable means. One or all of these factors would have typically saved the life of a convicted slave rapist in Virginia until this time. But in Claiborne's case, his life was not spared. He hanged on March 17, 1865, just weeks before the war's end.[66]

The failure of Virginia's governor to pardon a convicted slave rapist so late in the war, especially when mitigating circumstances prevailed, breaks with the general antebellum trend of executive intervention and reprieve, possibly suggesting that the imminent end of the war and the Confederacy (and with it, slavery) may have affected the outcome of slave rape cases, especially those that arose late in the war years. Another slave rape case in Virginia occurred late in the war with the same results. In November 1864, an eighteen-year-old slave in Pittsylvania County, Nat (the slave referred to in the trial of Claiborne), was charged with the rape of Susan J. Corbin, the daughter of his master, Abner Mahan, who lived on her father's property while her husband was off fighting in the war. Although Corbin lived alone, on the night of the attack several siblings and slaves were present. Staying with Jane Corbin were her brother and younger twelve-year-old sister, two slave youngsters (John, belonging to her father-in-law, and a ten-year-old girl), and two of her own children. Corbin testified that during the night of October 7, 1864, a "negro man" broke down the door of her home, which was about one-half to three-quarters of a mile from her father's place. She called for her brother and the boy slave to bring a gun and make up a light. The intruder, whom Corbin could only identify as a "black, heavy built negro," shoved the young slave into the corner and doused the fire with water. According to Corbin, the assailant then grabbed her and carried her out of the house into the yard, where he raped her. She named one of her father's slaves, Nat, as her attacker.[67]

Testimony offered up by another slave, Jim, owned by Joseph Wright, indirectly gave Nat's account of that night's events. Jim, Nat, and a handful of slaves from surrounding plantations gathered at Abner Mahan's around nine o'clock at night. Jim and Nat negotiated the barter of a bed. Soon thereafter, around ten, Nat departed. Upon his return about an hour later, Nat reported to the other slaves that he had heard a "mighty fuss" near Jane Corbin's place. Three slaves debated the best course of action. Nat wanted to "tell the white people." In a comment that casts suspicion on Jack himself as the possible rapist, Jack testified that he admonished Nat, warning him "not to be disturbing the white people." In the end, Nat did get involved and told his owner about the ruckus he had heard near his daughter's house, specifically that he had heard Jane

Corbin calling for help. In fact, Mahan brought Nat to Corbin's house. Mahan admitted that Nat did not appear at all suspicious.[68]

Why, then, did suspicion eventually settle on Nat? William A. J. Finney, probably the justice of the peace, was charged by Abner Mahan with finding the man responsible for raping his daughter. Finney first examined the ground outside Corbin's home for tracks but found none. He then shifted his attention to the site of the assault, where he observed signs of a "scuffling." In addition, he found the area to have been very muddy, causing Finney to conclude that the attacker's clothing would be covered with mud. Searching for clues among Mahan's slaves, Finney inspected the slave quarters, where he discovered mud on the knees of Nat's trousers and on the elbows of his coat. Moreover, the coat matched a description provided by Corbin. Nat accounted for the mud on his clothing by explaining that he had soiled his clothing in a "rassel" with slaves owned by William Smith, a neighbor, the Sunday previous. Another slave, Alick, corroborated Nat's explanation of a brawl but testified that Nat had no coat on during the fight.[69]

When asked to account for his whereabouts during the time of the alleged rape, Nat explained that on the night in question he had headed out for a visit with his wife, a slave owned by William Smith, a neighbor of Mahan. Those investigating the case told Nat to recount his route, and after following that path Smith found no tracks, leaving him skeptical about Nat's alibi.[70]

As in other antebellum and Civil War cases in which slaves were charged with the rape or attempted rape of white females, a good deal of court testimony in Nat's trial was devoted to determining motive. White southerners' repeated bewilderment at such purported behavior by slaves suggests that slaveholders truly did not believe their slaves capable of such violent, offensive conduct, absent extraordinary circumstances. Having ruled out a weakened mental state, the principals in Nat's rape case debated whether alcohol was to blame. One of the slaves who testified in the trial was asked whether there had been any "brandy or whiskey" about the cabin that night. He replied that he saw no such evidence. Nat's owner, Abner Mahan, also speculated about Nat's drinking, stating, "I make brandy. Saw a jug at my house. It was said to be Nat's. . . . Do not know whether there was any brandy in it or not." William Smith testified that Mahan had indeed made brandy but heard nothing about liquor in relation to the accused.[71]

Propping up an accused rapist as the victim of "demon rum" was not an uncommon rape defense in the Old South. In this case, however, the defense attempt to present drinking as a mitigating factor failed. They jury returned a guilty verdict and valued Nat at a whopping $4,000. Nat was executed by year's end.[72]

White southerners and their descendants who reminisced about the "docility and submissiveness" of their slaves during the war overstated their case by a long shot. Historical records are replete with evidence of increased slave unruliness and defiance during the war. Masters, especially in the war's later stages, complained bitterly about slave discipline. Sensing the direction of the war and observing the loosening of the reins of control, slaves might very well have broached the boundaries of proper behavior with white women and taken advantage of the more vulnerable. In Amherst County, Virginia, Elizabeth Rowsey, a thirty-nine-year-old white woman living only with her seven-year-old son, claimed that around midnight on March 14, 1862, she was awakened by a knock at the door. A man who identified himself as P. Gibson from Lexington, on his way to Lynchburg, explained that he was in search of a black man named Henderson and needed some fire. Rowsey was apprehensive about opening the door for a stranger in the dead of night and demurred, saying she was sick and could not get out of bed. The visitor persisted and insisted that Rowsey give him fire. Rowsey, still reluctant to allow him entrance, placed some hot coals on a shovel and pushed it under the door. The visitor then demanded to know if the man he was searching for was inside. Rowsey assured him that he was not, but the man demanded to be let in to search for himself. Finally Rowsey complied, opening the door and allowing the man to look around. He seemed to be satisfied and according to Rowsey pretended to leave, but soon came back. Rowsey again let him in, allowing him to warm his feet by the fire. The unwanted guest then seized Rowsey, threw her on the floor, and raped her. Rowsey testified that she resisted and managed to scratch him during the struggle. It was to no avail, however, as the intruder succeeded in accomplishing "his purpose as fully as he could."[73]

The assailant had concealed his identity with some sort of cloth covering. Rowsey testified that she did not even know he was black at first. During the struggle, however, his disguise was pulled off and Rowsey was able to identify him as the slave Ben. Ben had been hired out to Isaac Pryor by James Metcalf of Bedford, Virginia, and it was to Pryor's slave cabin that the rapist was traced. In addition to matching tracks in the muddy ground to Ben's shoes, the search party found fresh scratches about his face. Initially Ben refused to confess to the rape, but according to one witness, while on the way to jail the prisoner made a "voluntary" confession without "threats or any promise."[74]

Despite having a child without ever having been married, Elizabeth Rowsey proved not to be a particularly good target for defense attorneys, who seemed

unable to make much headway in attacking her character. One witness, probably the justice of the peace, testified only that he knew nothing of her character
except that she had a "bastard child": "In her deportment and statement she
seemed modest." Isaac Pryor told the court that Miss Rowsey "since the birth
of her child has conducted herself well so far as I know." Rowsey lived in a
cabin on the property of her sister's husband, R. C. Burks.[75]

Of the prisoner, Isaac Pryor stated that he had been obedient and submissive. In this case, however, the court found that Ben had not been obedient and
submissive; they found him guilty and sentenced him to hang.[76]

The war compelled many white women to go it alone without a male
protector, perhaps for the first time in their lives. Not only were
women left to manage farmsteads, plantations, businesses, and families unas-
sisted for extended periods, they also were forced to travel about unchaperoned or underchaperoned and unaccompanied by male protectors, thus exposing them to more attacks than before the war. In July 1862, Mrs. Permalia
Cosby (or Cosly or Costly) of Chesterfield County charged that she had been
attacked by a slave while she and her sister, Frances Cole, were making their
way home from the "Clover Hill pits." On their return they came across John, a
local slave owned by L. L. Lester, and another black male. The slaves asked the
women if they were interested in purchasing some "meal." The women were
not. The two women stopped at a spring for a drink where they saw the two
slaves run past them. About three hundred yards from their home, John
grabbed Cosby by the neck and told her that if she did not let him have his way
with her he would kill her. Cosby screamed, and John again threatened to kill
her if she did not quiet down. "I told him to kill me then as I would resist as
long as I had breath," she testified. John then choked her, and in what seemed
like an attempt to physically disable her, put his fingers in her ears. He then
pulled up her clothes and put his hands on her "in such a position as to cause"
her to know what his "purpose" was. Cosby's sister meanwhile picked up a
nearby fence rail and threatened the assailant. The threat appears to have been
ineffective, for the assault continued until Frances Cole pretended to see her
father coming. John fled, but not before grabbing a pair of new shoes that
Cosby had just purchased, as well as some postage stamps.[77]

Although John was convicted of an attempted rape, the court seems not to
have been convinced that rape was the actual motive since a robbery was also
committed. The jailer offered that the slave's design had been to steal Cosby's
shoes and money, not to ravish her. John was convicted and sentenced to

transportation. The governor then commuted the sentence to labor on the public works for life.[78]

Robbery or breaking and entering were acts associated with a number of the slave rape and attempted rape accusations in wartime Virginia, suggesting that perhaps slaves were, like many other southerners, resorting to whatever means available to survive. The attendant assault charges might have been raised by hysterical women making assumptions about the real motives of a slave assailant. Or, quite possibly, sexual assault occurred to some slave burglars as an afterthought. Or perhaps some slaves had sexual assault of white women in mind all along. Mrs. Alice Spiers of Sussex County, married but living alone, claimed that her home had been broken into in the early morning hours of July 4, 1862. She testified that about three o'clock in the morning she was awakened by the prisoner, a slave named Bibb, putting his hands on her "private parts." Spiers jumped up and made for the door. The two scuffled and in doing so fell out into the yard, where Spiers remarked to her attacker that she recognized him. Bibb was found guilty and hanged.[79]

At least four slaves, at most five or six, convicted of rape or attempted rape during the war years hanged for their purported crimes. The alleged offenses of these condemned slaves tended to occur in the latter half of the war, the last two executions taking place in the final six months. If it can be said that leniency was routinely offered to convicted slave rapists just before and right after the outbreak of hostilities, the same does not hold true for later cases. Throughout the war white southerners did continue to respect the custom and law of providing accused slave rapists with a trial. Only one case of a lynching of a suspected slave rapist in all of wartime Virginia can be documented.[80] These recorded rape trials, and the single extralegal execution of a black man alleged to have raped a white woman during the war, underscore the willingness of white Virginians throughout the Civil War to allow local officials to handle cases of purported slave rape through proper legal channels. Furthermore, they were not so unnerved by the exigencies and turbulence of war as to have reacted harshly and decisively to any sexual threats, real or perceived, that their slaves may have posed to their women. The cases presented here, I argue, show that Confederates were not convulsed with fears of slave rape. The leniency accorded to accused black rapists—whether by friendly white witnesses, court judges, or governors all too willing to commute death sentences—indicates that white southerners felt little compulsion to make examples of convicted slave rapists. Even under the extraordinary circumstances of war, white Virginians appear not to have been pressured to forgo the custom of giving accused slaves at least the appearance of a fair public hearing, a trend that has been well documented for the antebellum period. (I cannot help wondering whether early in the war an even higher value was placed on slave labor, as Confederate Virginia had to allocate vast resources to war preparations and fortifications while sending able-bodied white men to the front.) A discernible change of heart seems evident in later slave rape cases, perhaps portending developments arising with the end of slavery.

Yet as Virginia court records show, and contrary to Lost Cause propaganda, slaves were indeed charged with rape and attempted rape during the Civil War. One plausible explanation may lie in the increased rate of crime by both blacks and whites that plagued the war-torn Confederate South. Rape was simply one of many crimes that increased in the wake of war. Although virtually impossible to reliably quantify, a number of historians suggest that slave resistance and violence increased during the war years.[81]

Another possible reason for wartime slave rapes may lie in the grim circumstances that white women faced as a result of war. Such women, desperate to provide for their families, may for the first time have become involved in exchange or bartering networks with slaves or free blacks. Such contact may have blurred the boundaries that previously segregated the two groups. Greater familiarity with white women may have enticed slaves to see these women as possible bedmates, to be taken forcefully or otherwise. Moreover, some of the women who brought charges of rape or attempted rape against slaves may indeed have been trying to conceal consensual affairs. Alone and bored, perhaps they took the only intimate companions available to them—slaves. Victoria Bynum has documented a number of adultery cases in North Carolina of former soldiers claiming that their wives had been unfaithful during their absence.[82] Likewise, Drew Faust has found evidence that some elite Confederate women whose husbands were gone for long periods took up with slaves.[83] It is even possible that a number of the accusers engaged in prostitution in response to the massive deprivations and shortages of the war, trying to make a living from what few resources they had available to them.

Early in the war southern white communities continued to balance two weighty considerations in slave rape cases: the value of slave rapists as property and the need to address aberrant slave behavior and protect the larger community, especially women. In this sense, little had changed from the antebellum period. As Laura Edwards finds in her study of a North Carolina slave rape case from 1864, "rape did not seem to be as great a threat as it would be after emancipation and the Confederacy's defeat."[84] But as the war progressed, especially in its latter stages, conditions changed and priorities shifted. With the imminent Confederate defeat came the end of slavery. Executing a convicted slave rapist who in all probability would soon achieve his freedom anyway became not only more palatable but more prudent.

OUR JUDICIARY SYSTEM IS A FARCE
Remapping the Legal Landscape of Rape in the Post-Emancipation South

7

The end of civil war and the dismantling of slavery ushered in unprecedented institutional and legal changes in the South that fundamentally altered the way rape and race would be defined, regarded, and perceived. In some states rape of a nonwhite female, which had not been against the law or at least not a capital offence, had become a criminal act. Rape and attempted rape by a black man, for the most part, were no longer capital offences, at least temporarily. Legislators, local and appellate courts, and individual citizens grappled with the consequences of Reconstruction revisions in the rape statutes. White men were now liable to be jailed for rape of a black female. Black men too could be arrested for sexually assaulting black women. Conversely, women of color were empowered to bring charges, not only in cases of rape but for other criminal acts as well. Consequently, African American women virtually flooded the courts in the years after emancipation charging men, mostly black, with sexual assault.

A discussion of rape and race after the Civil War would not be complete without being plumbed against the larger legal and political terrain that characterized the postbellum South. Southern whites fashioned their responses to black rape amid great social and political turmoil. By and large, native whites no longer controlled the legal and political apparatuses. Perceptions of widespread corruption, cronyism, partisanship, and fraud gradually unleashed resentment toward an institution long respected and upheld in the Old South: the law. Thus the stage was set for a challenge to the law on multiple fronts, of which black rape was one. Stereotypes about black men and sexuality, vague and inchoate during slavery days, were beginning to take hold, later to spread like a noxious weed.

Arguably the most dramatic change that took place in rape law after the Civil War was that women and girls of color obtained the legal right to accuse a man, black or white, of rape. With freedom black women acquired both the right to bring charges of rape and a forum in which to air their complaints. Emancipation and federal policies forced former slaveholding states to purge their laws, including those pertaining to rape, of racial categories and to include black females as among those who could now be raped in the eyes of the law. A Tennessee law passed in Reconstruction, for instance, came to define rape as "the unlawful carnal knowledge of a woman forcibly and against her will." Previously, the Tennessee law, as well as those in most other slaveholding states, had singled out white women for this protection from black men. The rape statute meant to apply to white men did not specifically refer to white women; that was an implicit assumption.[1] A few states steadfastly resisted the move to remove racial distinctions in rape statutes, at least in the early years of Reconstruction. In 1867 Kentucky, for example, defined a rapist as one who shall "unlawfully and carnally know any white woman, against her will or consent." Likewise, South Carolina continued to make use of racial categories when crafting its rape law in 1865. Both states later amended the rape statutes with race-neutral language.[2]

Just as important in allowing African American females to charge men with rape were new laws that allowed nonwhites to testify in court against whites. In slavery, slaves could not offer sworn testimony against a white defendant. After the Civil War, "colored persons" were permitted to testify in both civil and criminal cases to which they were a party.[3] The ability of African Americans to testify against white defendants removed a formidable obstacle for black rape victims seeking justice.

The change in rape laws and the ability of African American females to charge men with rape certainly did not deter men from sexually assaulting these women. As Laura Edwards has found in her study of Granville County, North Carolina, African American women, always especially vulnerable to sexual assault in the antebellum era, became more sexually exposed in a different way after emancipation.[4] White men began to use rape as a weapon of terror against black women in the Reconstruction South to intimidate them and their families. Federal authorities were made aware of many such assaults, frequently committed by local Ku Klux Klan members. For example, officials of the Freedmen's Bureau reported in 1866 that Klan members robbed, assaulted, and shot a black preacher from Bath County, Kentucky, then ravished his wife.[5] Two freedwomen in South Carolina were allegedly raped by men dressed in disguise under cover of night.[6] Hannah Tutson, a middle-aged woman of color residing in Clay County, Florida, was targeted by local whites who tried to force her off land she claimed she had purchased. Members of the KKK stormed into her home, carried Tutson about a quarter-mile away, whipped her repeatedly, then raped her. One attacker "talked all kind of nasty talk to her." Of another, Tutson testified, "[he] pulled my womb down so that sometimes now I can hardly walk."[7] Three white Kentuckians from Nicholas County took turns raping the fifty-year-old wife of a black man on New Year's Day in 1866. Two months later a white male sexually assaulted a young black girl, not yet twelve years old, on a public highway.[8] Governor Rufus B. Bullock of Georgia announced a reward of $5,000 for information related to several gruesome Klan attacks in 1870–71 near Rome, Georgia, including one by a band of nearly forty men who "visited" the plantation of a Colonel Waltemire, a former colonel in the Union army, whipped and beat two black hands, and raped two or three young black girls.[9]

Federal records are replete with instances of African American females sexually assaulted by white men during Reconstruction. In Memphis, black women who had relationships with black Union soldiers found themselves the target of white rape. Hannah Rosen in her study of the Memphis Riot of 1866 makes clear that these white rapists intended to reassert their sexual and racial power over the female relatives of black soldiers as a way to demasculinize them and reestablish their own superiority and domination over the city's freed slaves.[10] After raping an African American woman in Georgia, white attackers vowed revenge against family members of those who served in the "God damned Yankee army."[11] It is quite clear that the white rape of freedwomen during Reconstruction was used as an instrument of terror to intimidate and exercise control over the entire black community, with the larger goal of reestablishing the privilege and status of whiteness.

Freedwomen who associated with politically active freedmen often found themselves the object of sexual attacks that were obviously intended to intimidate their male relatives. Elias Hill, a freedman from South Carolina, testified that the Klan paid him and his brother a midnight visit. Hill was whipped for preaching political sermons, and his sister-in-law was raped.[12] Klansmen beat a freedman in Alabama, George Moore, in 1869 for voting "the radical ticket" and raped a young girl who was visiting his wife at the time.[13]

While it is possible that white men who raped black women in the aftermath of emancipation may have been trying to reassert sexual ownership over their former slaves and concubines, it seems more plausible that their assaults merely represented part of the more general violence and intimidation that many, if not most, freedmen and women underwent in the throes of Reconstruction. Women of color in the postwar years underwent all sorts of white abuse, including sexual abuse.

Some of these terror-rapes were reported to local authorities, but more often the rape of a woman of color by a white man went unreported.[14] For obvious reasons freedwomen walked a tightrope, providing for themselves and their families by working in white homes or providing services to whites in the community and not wanting to antagonize their white employers and benefactors. Moreover, white officials did their best to discourage females of color from pursuing formal charges of rape against white men. That failing, they sometimes manipulated the judicial system to coerce black women into dropping charges.[15] So the number of white-on-black cases officially filed and heard was quite small. Nonetheless, the effect of statutory revisions during Reconstruction was that women and girls of color could now officially charge men, black and white, with rape and attempted rape, a remarkable departure from slave times.[16]

This newfound right was not lost on former slave women, many of whom seized upon the opportunity to seek redress for sexual violations, primarily those alleged to have been committed by black men. This unprecedented practice—the filing of rape charges by women of color against men of color— probably represents the single most notable distinction between the nature of rape in the South before the war and after. Freedwomen, refusing to tolerate sexual violence, took advantage of the legal right to bring charges of rape and attempted rape, and frequently did, though much more often against men of color than white men. And at times, these cases of reported black-on-black rapes were played out against the backdrop of Reconstruction politics.

In July 1863, even before the war's end, Mrs. Sarah B. Millan (the spelling is uncertain), an African American woman, filed rape charges against William Hunter, a thirty-one-year-old African American, in occupied Fairfax County, Virginia. Hunter was tried, convicted, and sentenced to five years in the state penitentiary, where he was received on August 30, 1865, only a few short months after the war's end. In the fall of 1868 Hunter petitioned the governor of Virginia for a pardon. The provisional governor of Virginia at that time was Henry Horatio Wells, a New Yorker who served in that capacity from April 1868 through September 1869. Perhaps given the volatile political climate of the time, Hunter was buoyed by the presence of a northern Republican in the state's highest office. Curiously, in his statement Hunter recounted that he had been arrested on July 31, 1863, in Alexandria charged with having committed a rape on a woman of color. He was brought before the provost judge, none other than H. H. Wells, who, Hunter claimed, upon hearing the evidence dismissed the complaint. By Hunter's account, he fell victim to the political tug-of-war between federal and local authorities vying for jurisdiction in the case. Only a few hours after federal authorities dismissed the case Hunter claimed to have been rearrested by civil authorities, who in the end convicted him of rape.[17]

The likely reason why white civil authorities may have been eager to prosecute Hunter emerges in Hunter's appeal for a pardon. Hunter claimed that he had been cohabiting for about a year with Sarah Millan, the black woman who accused him of rape. A vindictive Millan was seeking to avenge Hunter's attempts on her son's life, he explained. Hunter confessed to having lain in ambush on several occasions waiting for Millan's son, who had been a "bushwacker" commissioned by "Mosbey" to "prey upon union people." Hunter was referring to John Singleton Mosby, a Confederate famous for his daring guerilla exploits in western and northern Virginia during the war. Whether or not this was true, Hunter surely used the information to curry favor with the pro-Union governor and perhaps win an appeal. Governor Wells was not won over so easily, however. Despite Hunter's declaration of innocence and his plea that the governor allow him to return to his wife and five children, Wells rejected Hunter's petition for freedom. In fact, Wells denied ever having heard Hunter's case. Hunter, it seemed, had lied, or at least stretched the truth in an attempt to secure his early release. Hunter was eventually pardoned, however, only to be rearrested again for the rape of another woman of color.[18]

Former Confederate civil authorities sometimes vigorously pursued alleged black rapists, though more for their pro-Republican actions and sympathies than because of outrage at the rape of a female of color. For example, Thomas Young, a twenty-three year-old African American man from Halifax County, Virginia, was imprisoned for ten years for the rape of a twelve-year-old girl of color. D. A. Claiborne, a sympathetic petitioner seeking a gubernatorial pardon on Young's behalf, was appalled at his conviction. The girl had consented but cried rape when the white family with which she resided began to question the girl after seeing her walk "as if she had been injured." If Young had been a white man, Claiborne speculated, he never would have been tried for the offense. His arrest and conviction were the result of "prejudice in the minds of a certain class of men against his race and color." Claiborne, who in former times had owned the plantation adjacent to the one owned by Young's previous master, further stated that he knew of only one "infamous thing" Young committed, which was to have voted "for [H. H.] Wells [the Republican governor] and the Underwood Constitution."[19] Young's political association with the Republican Party appears to have contributed to his arrest for the rape of an African American girl.

As the petition of D. A. Claiborne shows, white southerners at times intervened to lend support to convicted black rapists after the Civil War, just as they had done before. Many white male petitioners expressed considerable sympathy for freedmen charged with raping females of color, often claiming that former male slaves were being unfairly held accountable under alien rules of sexual and moral conduct. More to the point, the sweep of a pen had empowered black women with an important new protection, one criminalizing male behavior that before emancipation had been either regarded as acceptable or at least tolerated by most. As slaves, some argued, these men could never have faced the gallows for raping a female slave. After William Hunter's second conviction and incarceration in 1868 for raping an African American woman, a crime which under ordinary circumstances his benefactors felt warranted "the utmost severity," conditions after emancipation demanded clemency. The petition called the governor's attention to "the social conditions of these people, who having lived, and been raised together without any of the [indecipherable] and checks thrown about the promiscuous intercourse of the sexes, have not yet acquired any knowledge of virtue or virtuous conduct."[20]

A group of "the most respectable citizens," white citizens from Nottoway County, Virginia, expressed similar sentiments in the fall of 1866 when they urged the governor to reprieve Manuel Marshall, an eighteen-year-old man of color, from a death sentence resulting from a rape conviction of a "little colored girl." After the governor commuted the sentence to a prison term correspondence continued unabated, this time asking the governor to go further and issue a pardon. Virtually all the petitioners acknowledged that the act of coitus had occurred between Marshall and the ten-year-old girl when she had been visiting Marshall's family. However, the letters claimed that the child had consented. The governor apparently concurred, noting that the "evidence showed that the girl was willing, consenting and helping."[21]

Moreover, those appealing on Marshall's behalf cited the peculiar conditions of emancipation as mitigating circumstances. Marshall's former counsel complained that "the law making such an act as he was charged with by one of his race previously in slavery was entirely new and was not known to him and he had no idea that he was committing any crime against the penal laws of the state. There was really no harm done."[22] A minister from Nottoway County also cited the accused's "ignorance of the laws," and the "almost universally degraded condition of that unfortunate race to which he belongs."[23] Numerous "respectable" whites were quite willing to countenance black-on-black rape, even when the victim was a child, excusing it as a byproduct of slavery.

"The previous education of these people had taught them to regard with little . . . concern the virtue which is so dear to us." One petitioner chalked the act up to the "childish ignorance on the part of both the boy and the girl."[24]

Marshall commanded significant support from whites in Nottoway in his bid for a reprieve. Not so for Frank Smith of Princess Anne County, Virginia, who stood accused of the rape of Agnes Ruffin, a fourteen-year-old African American girl. Jurors appear to have been so incensed that they sentenced Smith to die for his purported crime, this despite at least one party's claim that Ruffin was a prostitute and had been cohabiting with Smith, a local fisherman, before the alleged assault. In deciding for death, the jury may have been swayed by evidence that Smith had been convicted previously of raping an eleven-year-old African American girl.[25]

African American girls and women like Agnes Ruffin who alleged rape underwent the same close scrutiny as poor white accusers. Questions arose about the integrity of Lucy Jane Higginbotham, an eleven-year-old from Campbell County, Virginia, who initially accused a black man, Blair Graves, of raping her but later amended the charge to attempted rape. According to the testimony of Higginbotham, she and Graves were walking home together toward her father's home after dark on April 17, 1867. Higginbotham told the court that Graves suggested they stop and rest. Graves pulled her down, pulled up her clothes, "got upon her and drew blood." The accuser's father, Andrew Higginbotham, exercised one of the paternalistic prerogatives that he inherited with his freedom and filed rape charges against Graves on behalf of his young daughter.[26] J. B. Crenshaw, the justice of the peace, arrived at the Higginbothams' residence with a surgeon to examine the girl for evidence of rape, as was the custom. However, the family refused to consent to the examination, maintaining that the attack had been only an "attempt" at rape. Perhaps the Higginbothams, wishing to spare their daughter the embarrassment of a gynecological examination, settled on the lesser charge. Or perhaps the child was unclear about what had occurred during the attack. Or, despite initial reports, maybe the rape was not completed. Whatever the reason, Graves was charged with the lesser charge of attempted rape.

At trial, Graves admitted to taking "indecent liberties" with the girl. His defense counsel nonetheless asserted that the charges emanated from a "spirit of malice" between the Higginbotham and Graves families. To bolster his client's reputation as an upright citizen, Graves's counsel had his employer testify that Graves was his "number one hand, industrious, obedient, honest and well behaved," "a hardworking negro." By contrast, Lucy Higginbotham was a "mischievous, storytelling girl" whom he would not believe. The governor, Francis H. Pierpont, acquiesced and granted a pardon two months into Graves's one-year sentence.[27]

In 1867 Susan Burroughs, a woman of color and mother of three, underwent the same kind of scrutiny when she swore out a complaint against Edward Powell, aged eighteen, of Mecklenburg County, Virginia, for rape.[28] The court found the evidence persuasive and handed down a sentence of twenty years in the state penitentiary. In a bid for early release, Edward Powell himself employed the "lying temptress" defense in a petition to Governor William Cameron in 1882. Powell never denied raping Susan Burroughs. Nevertheless, he implied that her credibility was questionable and her accusation baseless. He explained that Burroughs was the mother of three children "*and had never been married.*" According to Powell, she was also "proven to be a woman of *loose, depraved character.*"[29] Such reasoning, that a depraved woman could not be raped, was employed again and again throughout the nineteenth century in the rape trials of females, regardless of race or age. In this respect, African American women who brought charges of rape after slavery bore the same burden as white women of low status had: needing to demonstrate evidence of good character.

Governor William Cameron, to whom Powell pleaded his case, proved receptive and sought independent corroboration of Powell's account. He ordered a judge in Mecklenburg County to look into and report back to him on the particulars of the case[30]—the judge who had presided over Powell's case, as well as some jurors, having since died. Judge C. Alexander reported that Susan Burroughs's reputation was far from stellar. Citing the statement of the justice of the peace who had presumably received the initial complaint from Burroughs, the judge reported considerable doubt from the outset about the legitimacy of her claim of rape. The judge also noted Powell's youth, as well as Burroughs's physical stature, which he characterized as "being of equal strength [to Powell]." Burroughs, he claimed, had "tamely submitted to the outrage," leading him to believe that in the absence of evidence of resistance, Burroughs might not have been raped after all. Moreover, in his estimation Burroughs was a "prostitute" and Powell a "bad boy." Judge Alexander closed his report by stating that most in the community had forgotten about the case. The judge concluded that Powell, who at this time was suffering from asthma and consumption, had already suffered plenty. (No mention was made of the well-being of his alleged victim.) The governor acceded and ordered Powell discharged from prison, five years early.[31]

As in the rape trials of slaves, Reconstruction-era jurors had little leeway when handing down sentences after convictions of rapists. The newly revised rape laws tied the hands of jurors who might have wished to hand down mild sentences for the rape of women and girls of color. Regardless of mitigating circumstances—the youth or "ignorance" of the perpetrator, the reputation of the accuser, the belief that former slaves did not comprehend the illegality and immorality of raping African American females—Virginia jurors could hand down sentences of no less than ten years for men convicted of rape. It would therefore be misleading to deduce that because convicted black rapists of black females typically received stiff sentences—death or lengthy prison terms—white juries willingly extended protection to African American complainants.[32]

To the contrary, some southerners, black and white, simply did not take the sexual assault of African American females very seriously. Generations of nearly universal white sexual access to black females, coupled with long held beliefs about the innate licentiousness of black women, bred a reluctance to include black women into the new rape statutes. A case in point is the black-on-black rape trial of Jacob Holmes Jr. of Nelson County, Virginia. Holmes was charged in 1873 with the rape of Emma Coleman, a ten-year-old African American girl. Holmes himself was not much older. One account puts him at thirteen, while another estimates his age at the time of the alleged attack to have been about fourteen or fifteen. Although Holmes was convicted of rape, there was some doubt whether penetration had occurred.[33] Evidence suggests that early on local white officials did not take Coleman's accusation seriously. One local official, when informed of the charge, initially told the boy's father to give him a "good whipping," a "punishment sufficient for the offense committed." Even after complying and administering corporal punishment to his son, Holmes's father sent him away to Albemarle County, the site of the family's former residence, evidently sensing trouble were he to remain. Trouble did indeed continue to plague the boy. Emma Coleman's mother, acting on her daughter's behalf, demonstrated considerable agency and tenacity by refusing to accept the indifferent treatment that her daughter received. She finally persuaded the sheriff of Nelson County to sign out a warrant for Holmes's arrest. The sheriff of Albemarle County, where Holmes had since relocated, refused to act on the warrant, possibly believing that such a fuss over the rape of an African American girl was unjustified. Holmes therefore went untouched until his voluntary, if imprudent, return to Nelson County a little over two years later, when he was arrested and promptly put on trial for the rape of Emma Coleman.

The jury found Holmes guilty of rape, although an array of mitigating circumstances filled their deliberations.[34] For one, there had been some question regarding penile penetration, which if not proved would have dictated a charge of attempted rape at most. There was also the issue of the boy's young age, which may have been under thirteen. This raised a legal red flag, as ample legal precedent, based on medical expertise, held that young boys were physically incapable of committing a rape.[35] Finally, advocates for Holmes's early release challenged the veracity of the accuser. Despite Emma Coleman's extreme youthfulness (she was variously described as a girl between the ages of five and six and as ten at the time of the purported assault), she nonetheless was denounced as the "daughter of a notorious woman or a woman of notorious bad character" who may have carried a grudge against the Holmes family.[36]

Once it had rendered a verdict, the court turned its attention to settling on a punishment for Holmes. Although plenty of ameliorating circumstances dictated leniency, leniency was not forthcoming. The law fixed a rapist's punishment as death, at the jury's discretion, or ten to twenty years in the state penitentiary.[37] A jury thus had no leeway to hand down anything less than a ten-year prison term. But the jury in this case opted for the middle of the road and sent Holmes to the penitentiary for fifteen years. It would seem that jurors were sufficiently appalled by the crime to send the convicted Holmes to prison for more than the minimum prescribed by law. The jury's sentence reflected disdain for the crime of rape, particularly when children were the victims and even when the child was African American. The jurors' sentence mirrored community sentiment, which "was very much aroused against the perpetators of such offenses as this."[38]

Thus one consequence of the revised postbellum rape laws, purged of references to race, was that if a jury believed a man of color to be guilty of raping an African American woman or girl, it had no choice but to levy a severe punishment. Even the Commonwealth's attorney in a black-on-black rape case in Virginia in 1870 felt the imposed minimum sentence of ten years too harsh. Urging executive clemency for Benjamin Johnson, James M. Love believed that had the jury been given an option to fix a shorter sentence, it certainly would have done so. He too balanced the severity of the crime of rape with the former condition of slavery and a presumed laxness in sexual morals: "Whilst I consider this the most heinous crime known to law, yet such has been the morals of these people . . . I always feel the greatest leniency towards them."[39] Harsh sentences for black men and boys convicted of raping black females do not reflect compassion for the African American victims of sexual assault but rather were the result of rigid postwar rape laws that gave juries little flexibility in determining prison sentences.

Cases of African American females charging black males with sexual assault raise another important issue pertaining to the families of freedmen and women. The frequency with which African American females filed sexual assault charges against African American suggests considerable rancor and discord among emancipated black families and communities. Historians such as Herbert Gutman and John Blassingame have described the slave family and marriage as healthy, positive, thriving male-dominated institutions. That characterization has come under attack in the last ten or so years, primarily by feminist historians writing about gender and race.[40] As Brenda Stevenson has recently argued, all classes in Virginia before the Civil War placed a high value on a stable family. But for the slave family, poverty and discrimination made such an ideal elusive. Periodic violence by slaves aimed at their children and their partners, documented by Stevenson and Deborah Gray White, underscores the tensions and stress endemic to slave families.[41] Seen in this light, former slaves who continued to live under adverse conditions in freedom, as has been documented, might very well have allowed discord to spill into the sexual arena.

Yet another factor to consider is that in slavery a black male's sexual assault of a slave female was likely to be ignored. Slave-on-slave rape almost certainly occurred. But slave females who claimed to have been raped by slaves were not likely to have been encouraged to seek redress through their masters, let alone the courts. The frequency with which women and girls of color charged black men officially with rape or attempted rape after the Civil War may have reflected common practice during slavery, except that in freedom these women had obtained the right to pursue legal action against their assailants. It is entirely possible that widespread racist assumptions among white southerners about the innate promiscuity and licentiousness of black women may have been internalized by some black males as well. We know, for example, that southern black men accused of raping black females at times employed the "Jezebel" defense: that is, they invoked the allegedly immoral character of black females to excuse their own sexual conduct.[42] Since many antebellum white courts and masters had not regarded the rape of slave females as a crime, perhaps some slave men also came to view sexual access to slave women as a kind of male privilege, one available to both blacks and whites. The many black-on-black rape cases that made their way to the Reconstruction courts may have resulted from some black males' sense of entitlement to the sexuality of emancipated slave women. African American women, however, newly empowered with revised rape statutes, were resolute in defining their freedom as freedom from coerced or nonconsensual sex and often sought protection from the courts.[43]

The inclusion of women and girls of color into the newly revised Reconstruction rape statutes, and the resulting expansion of who could be raped in the eyes of the law, was only one of the ways in which postbellum rape laws in the South were adjusted along racial lines. Southern rape statutes could no longer single out men of color for more severe punishments than whites convicted of rape.[44] Southern lawmakers, under the watchful eye of rights-minded Republicans, were precluded from differentiating criminal punishments along racial lines. Race-neutral rape statutes created a disagreeable conundrum for southern lawmakers that became readily apparent. Because race could no longer serve as a category for either the assailant or the victim, no distinction could be made between the punishments meted out to black and white sex offenders. Since a majority of slaveholding states before 1865 made rape or attempted rape of white females by black men a capital offense, how were legislatures to craft their laws in such a way as to continue to punish black males more harshly than white males? Mandating blanket death sentences exposed white males convicted of raping white and black females (not to mention African American males convicted of raping African American females) to an unprecedentedly harsh punishment. Most southern white conservatives were probably reluctant to jeopardize the lives of white men convicted of raping women or girls of color, an act that was not even a crime a few years earlier. A practical challenge for white southern lawmakers remained: how to construct rape statutes that would allow harsh sentences for black men charged with raping white women while at the same time sparing the lives of white men convicted of raping black women.

Initially, and for the most part provisionally, some southern states simply eliminated capital punishment for the crime of rape. Kentucky, Mississippi, Missouri, and Tennessee abolished the death penalty in cases of rape, leaving instead prison terms ranging anywhere from five years to life. Eliminating capital punishment from the rape statutes yielded an important and historic change in southern rape law. Black men could rape white women and escape a death sentence. Probably in recognition of this fact, eventually each of these states appended capital punishment to their rape statutes, thus giving jurors in rape cases broad discretion in levying sentences. Only South Carolina seems to have completely divested its rape statute of the death penalty.[45]

Southern lawmakers during Reconstruction in some cases took years to settle on whether rape should be made a capital crime or not. The uncertainty about how to proceed is best demonstrated in the evolution of Texas rape law in the postbellum years. The case of Texas, which was surely typical of southern states, suggests that lawmakers were not really sure how changes in rape law would play out racially. Their first attempt at revision in 1866, setting five years to life as the proper sentence for rape, appears to have been unsatisfactory because within four years the maximum sentence had been pared back to fifteen years. But by 1873 convicted rapists could receive a prison term as short as five years, or be put to death.[46] These statutory maneuverings during Reconstruction suggest that southern lawmakers were confounded by the new status of former slaves as citizens and found it difficult to accommodate black men's "equal" status in rape statutes. Clearly, these lawmakers did not have it all worked out racially, not knowing whether, or how, rape should or could be made a capital offence in the wake of emancipation.

In due time southern legislatures, like that in Texas, hit upon a scheme that would allow their rape statutes to remain race neutral, while still accommodating a double standard along racial lines. They empowered local courts with a wide range of sentencing options. Juries or judges were permitted to sentence convicted rapists to either death or a prison sentence, which generally ranged from a few years to life. Of course it took some experimenting and grappling with consequences, intended or otherwise, to work things out. An Alabama law from 1866 contained no reference to race whatsoever, but prescribed death or "imprisonment in the penitentiary for life, or by hard labor for the county for life." Such ample discretion was eventually accorded to courts hearing rape trials in Florida (death or life in prison), Maryland (death or eighteen months to twenty-one years), and Virginia (death or ten to twenty years). In Georgia defendants faced death unless the jury recommended mercy, in which case the punishment would be a prison sentence of one to twenty years.[47] Only Arkansas, Louisiana, and North Carolina retained the death penalty for all rapists after the Civil War.[48] When the dust had settled, southern lawmakers hit upon the most efficacious way to maintain dual racial standards in rape statutes without explicitly referring to race in the letter of the law. Armed with a broad spectrum of penalties for sexual assault, white-dominated courts could mete out prison sentences to white rapists while reserving the death penalty for blacks.[49] White southern lawmakers had found a way to circumvent federal laws prohibiting racial discrimination in criminal statutes while implementing racial distinctions in the sentencing of rapists.

After some fits and starts, southern states found a way to provisionally keep rape a capital crime. The case for attempted rape, though, was very different as it was virtually eliminated as a capital offense. Nearly all slaveholding states had reserved death exclusively for blacks convicted of attempted rape, a crime for which white males rarely faced the death penalty.[50] After the Civil War most southern states no longer retained the death penalty in cases of attempted rape.

The same held true for cases of assault with intent to commit a rape. Before the war, blacks in nearly all southern states found guilty of assaulting white women with intent to commit a rape faced death. With freedom and the subsequent revision of the statutes governing attempted rape, black men no longer faced hanging for the crime of attempted rape or assault with intent to rape.[51] Any act short of forced intercourse, therefore, was no longer a capital crime when committed by a black man on a white woman.

The diminution of punishment for sexual assault after the Civil War as applied to freedmen was not lost on native white southerners. During Reconstruction in most former slaveholding states a black man could conceivably attempt forced intercourse on a white woman or girl and serve only a prison sentence, a stark contrast to the antebellum period. The region's deposed and disfranchised whites took note of the change and saw it as portending a larger trend of ill-advised liberal treatment of black criminals.

Revised rape laws in the Reconstruction South constituted only one of numerous changes that affected the judicial process and conditions in which black men alleged to have committed rape or attempted rape were tried. Any study of rape and race in the Reconstruction period, as well as the white community's views on the subject, must take into account the myriad material changes as well as the precarious and constantly evolving political and legal circumstances of the Reconstruction period. Moreover, any analysis of black rape must be viewed in the larger context of black-white relations.

Ironically, nothing heightened the vulnerability of black southerners charged with capital crimes after emancipation more than losing the status of valuable property. In the Old South, slaves, as property, had represented the greatest source of personal wealth. Masters made monumental efforts to exonerate their convicted slaves, sometimes broke the law, or employed trickery and deception to keep slave criminals from the gallows.[52] This was one of the few times that being a slave actually worked to a slave's advantage. But once the ties of bondage were severed, there was no longer a financial incentive for former slave owners to work for the exoneration of African Americans charged with serious crimes. A white lawyer from Mississippi explained in 1871: "As a slave, the negro was protected on account of his value; humanity went hand in hand with the interest of the owner to secure his protection. . . . But as a free man, he was deprived of all the protection which had been given to him by his value as property; he was reduced to something like the condition of a stray dog."[53] J. T. Trowbridge reported a conversation he had with a white farmer in Tennessee in the months following the war about a white man who murdered a freedman that "sassed him": "Befo'e the wa' the owner of the nigger'd have had the man arrested. He was so much property. It was as if you should kill or maim my horse. But now the nigger had no protection."[54] No longer property, freedmen on trial for rape or attempted rape lost their most motivated boosters: their masters.

Although ex-slaves lost the support of ex-masters, in many places in the former Confederacy that void was filled by the Bureau of Refugees, Freedmen, and Abandoned Lands, more commonly known as the Freedmen's Bureau. Control over the judicial structure and process was temporarily wrested from local white southerners and assumed by federal and military authorities, chiefly under the commission of the Freedmen's Bureau, which also functioned variously as guardian, enforcer, and arbiter. In Virginia former Confederates were frequently elected county officers, but by August 1865 Governor Francis Harrison Pierpont had stripped former rebels of their elected offices. Competing with indigenous courts were Freedmen's Bureau courts, consisting of specially appointed panels that regularly heard cases involving freedpeople. These courts sat until May 1866, when civil authority was restored. As Congressional Reconstruction was ushered in with the passage of the Reconstruction Acts in March 1867, military authorities again assumed control over the region's legal apparatus.[55]

Although conditions varied widely by time and place, throughout the South the Freedmen's Bureau generally set out to ensure that freedmen and women were treated fairly in the courts. As Eric Foner has pointed out, however, blacks often received "less than equal justice." Moreover, the goal of the bureau was never to replace the southern court system, but rather to induce white southerners to treat freedmen more equitably within the existing judicial structure. As early as late 1866 native white southerners in many areas had complied with federal requirements, such as permitting blacks to testify, and had largely regained control of their judiciary. Nonetheless, local bureau agents continued to monitor local court proceedings involving freedpeople, and promptly intervened when they observed or suspected discrimination. Presumably even the most hostile southern courts dealt with freedmen with an eye toward a vigilante bureau agent.[56]

Despite the eventual return of the judicial and legal institutions to local control, many white southerners claimed that key political offices remained unfairly filled by Republicans, who used their positions to secure and shore up political control of the region. The men who presided over the criminal trials of some freedmen may very well have been native northerners or Union sympathizers and therefore inclined to deal less harshly with African American defendants (or more harshly with white defendants). At least that was a perception widely shared among many native white southerners during Reconstruction.[57]

In general, perceptions of ineptitude and corruption of the judicial and political structures abounded among native white southerners. One white Georgian complained: "The truth is, for three years our people have not had confidence in the execution of the laws of the State in such a manner as to protect person and property. It is their conviction that those who have had the administration of our laws have been more intent upon making a good thing for themselves than protecting the people."[58] In the eyes of former Confederates, the newly constituted governments lacked legitimacy.[59]

Resentment centered on the freedmen, Union loyalists, and northerners who now held most positions of political importance and influence. In the eyes of many white southerners, justice was now unfairly skewed in favor of the freedpeople. A partisan judge, for example, would "not inflict any punishment, or adequate punishment upon members of his own party convicted of crime."[60] Whites, according to native white southerners, simply could not get their due hearing. As a result, more and more southern whites became "disgusted" and "despaired" and therefore disinclined to seek redress from the courts.[61]

By usurping local judicial authority, federal Reconstruction policies jeopardized the long-standing, revered ties between the law and the traditional power sources that had long prevailed in antebellum communities, instead planting seeds of distrust.[62] Discontent with perceived slow or unjust legal proceedings at times manifested itself in mob violence, but generally white citizens allowed the wheels of justice to turn without interference. Nowhere was this more evident than in antebellum cases in which slaves were accused of capital offenses. The combination of faith in the judicial system and the value that slaves represented gave assurances that accused slaves would have their day in court, albeit a flawed court and one steeped in racial discrimination. During Reconstruction, however, many whites came to see the increase in vigilantism in the occupied South as an inevitable result of the current flux in political affairs—corruption, ineptitude, political favoritism—"there was no protection of person or property in the State."[63] That whites would take matters into their own hands seemed logical and justifiable to some observers. "A man will seek his own defense if he cannot get it any other way."[64] A strong military presence was a constant reminder that white native southerners were not in control, and even when the civil courts were reconstituted and began hearing criminal cases of freedmen and women, they were not free to exercise complete autonomy. Freedmen's Bureau officials were ever present, keeping a vigilant eye on the proceedings.[65] This combination of political impotence and the usurpation of local justice by outsiders, the former enemy, fomented considerable resentment and distrust among white southerners who increasingly felt that entrusting the fate of black criminals, including alleged rapists, to the legal system was now futile. Hence they grew increasingly reliant on vigilante justice.

The loss of faith in the southern system of justice was exacerbated by the presence of northern and Unionist sympathizers as provisional governors, and later as elected Republican governors. Gubernatorial pardons of convicted black criminals, though exercised fairly liberally before the Civil War, took on greater political importance during Reconstruction and was a point of bitter contention, "a source of great dissatisfaction," among white conservatives.[66] The governors doing the pardoning for the most part were either transplanted northerners or "scalawags," pro-Union natives appointed as provisional governors when ex-Confederate officeholders were disfranchised. Pardons by these "governors," as some southerners were loath to call them, thus became especially odious. Second, the granting of pardons to freedmen was very nearly intolerable to some whites. From their perspective, pardons by the governor were motivated purely by political patronage. The pardoned black criminal, in a political quid pro quo, would repay the governor and his (Republican) party with political allegiance. The timing of such pardons was hardly coincidental, one judge in South Carolina complained. The governor's pardons suspiciously became "much more frequent at the approach of the elections."[67] There were complaints that pardoned black criminals were often "active and energetic" at the polls.[68] And suspiciously, the governor's pardons always seemed to be confined to "his own party friends."[69] Yet some southerners denied that partisanship was the sole motive. A few witnesses testified that Democrats and Republicans signed pardon petitions so that released convicts would work on the plantations, at least suggesting class as opposed to political resentment.[70]

Charges proliferated that southern governors on good terms with Union authorities pardoned convicted criminals indiscriminately. By one partisan estimate, Governor Robert K. Scott of South Carolina pardoned nearly half the 480 inmates in the state penitentiary. Among these, freedmen predominated.[71] A judge and former congressman from Georgia estimated that Governor Rufus Bullock issued between three and four hundred pardons in his two and a half years as governor, and of those perhaps eighteen to twenty were murderers, but only one was a convicted rapist.[72]

According to white conservatives, the charitable pardoning of convicted black criminals fostered considerable anxiety and insecurity among white communities that began to fear for their own safety.[73] Moreover, such a liberal policy only served to demonstrate that if "men can commit crimes with impunity, of course no one will be afraid to do so." A conservative in Georgia believed that a liberal policy of granting pardons to freedmen convicted of crimes would only "encourage people who are disposed to commit crime."[74] A fellow Georgian concurred: "I think this, that in this country, since the war, if a man violates the law, and the people are satisfied the courts will not punish him, there are men—I do not believe the generality of them would do it—who would go out and lynch him."[75]

A case in point is the story received in testimony before the Joint Select Committee of the U.S. Congress investigating conditions in the former Confederacy. Plato Durham, a white lawyer from North Carolina, recounted how a black man had been convicted in Gaston County for the rape of a fourteen-year-old white girl and sentenced to hang. "But about the time the sentence should have been executed Governor Caldwell respited him, and it is believed he will finally be pardoned."[76] A white resident of Tennessee complained that blacks sentenced to the penitentiary for ravishing some ladies were "turned out in a few days afterward."[77] In response to the several hundred pardons issued by Governor Bullock of Georgia, it was claimed, white Georgians turned to lynching to ensure justice. "I have heard it said again and again," a witness testified, " 'hang him,' or 'kill him, for if you don't Bullock will pardon him after you have sent him to the penitentiary.' "[78]

The forces of war and emancipation had indeed transformed the southern legal and political landscape in the former Confederacy in dramatic fashion. For some it surely must have seemed a world turned upside down. Rape laws now encompassed females of color, who in slave days had no official recourse after being raped. White men who in the past were immune from charges of sexually assaulting African American females would now face prison or even death. Black men who in slavery would have risked death for the conviction of attempted rape of white women no longer did.

In addition to these significant changes in rape law, white southerners navigated the unfamiliar and hostile conditions established by the victors: loss of political control and the imposition of measures designed to enforce racial equity. African American witnesses, negated verdicts, pardons of convicted blacks, "carpetbagger" governors, and allegations of corruption and patronage animated an increasingly jaded and alienated white populace.

Perhaps no case better illustrates the unfolding of these numerous Reconstruction developments than the assault trial of John Burns, formerly a slave owned by a Colonel Burke from Lexington, Virginia. On April 15, 1868, Burns went on trial in Lexington for the attempted sexual assault of a white sixteen-year-old, daughter of a pillar of the community.[79] It was alleged that Burns had sneaked into the bedroom of Lizzie Echols that she shared with her stepsister, Jenny, with the intention of immobilizing her with chloroform, then raping her. Instead, the family charged, Burns inadvertently succumbed to fumes himself, passed out, and lay with Echols until he was discovered by family members. Burns, however, presented a vastly different account of events. His story, buttressed by testimony of other African Americans, was that he had been having a consensual relationship with Lizzie Echols.

The case quickly became a showdown between conservative southern whites, who sought to use the case to mobilize support for the reassertion of white political and social control through the legal and judicial apparatus, and officials of the Freedmen's Bureau, whose job it was to ensure that freedpeople received justice once control of the courts had been returned to local whites. White Lexingtonians had no choice but to play by the "new rules" forced upon them by virtue of defeat. They saw to it that Burns obtained counsel and received a hearing and a jury trial, albeit not exactly by a jury of his peers. Having played by the rules, many in the white community were incredulous when federal officials, advocates for the freedman, intervened and effectively negated the court's conviction of Burns. The bureau's involvement in the case, as in other cases, fostered considerable disaffection among whites, many of whom were coming to believe that the South's judicial and political processes had become irretrievably poisoned by the self-serving machinations of the Republican Party.

In addition to representing a contest for political and judicial autonomy between native white southerners on one side and freedpeople and federal officials on the other, Burns's trial also makes plain the impact of war's end and the demise of slavery on rape law and judicial procedures for African Americans. This single black-on-white sexual assault case, albeit a very unusual one, illustrates how the changing legal culture in the postbellum South gave rise to conditions that would eventually encourage and sanction extralegal violence against the region's African American people, including black men accused of raping white women.

I make no claims for the representativeness of this singular case. To the contrary, it stands as one of the least representative of black-on-white Reconstruction rape cases, almost all of which involved white women of low social and economic status. The trial of John Burns stands out precisely because the accuser is from a white family of means. Despite this exceptionalism, it reveals much about southern society in the wake of defeat and emancipation. Native whites, freedmen and women, and the agents of the Freedmen's Bureau who were their advocates all contested the racial and gender boundaries within the framework of an inchoate, reconstituted legal system. Local whites who resented federal intrusion sought autonomy in their legal and political worlds and fought to wrest control from federal representatives and to resist granting legal rights and political equality to freedmen. Frustrated with what they viewed as the thwarting of justice and the usurpation of power, native whites in Lexington, like those throughout the Reconstruction South, began to lose faith in the judicial process. Along the way, interracial sexual violence became politically charged with an intensity not witnessed in the antebellum South.

The scenic beauty of the picturesque Shenandoah Valley, where Lexington, Virginia, lies nestled and where the trial of John Burns unfolded, provides a stark contrast to the ugly scenes of violent interracial clashes that were all too common there in the immediate postwar period. In the fall of 1866 a white law student from Lexington had been charged with killing a freedman.[80] Soon after, another white resident of Rockbridge County, Dr. James Watson, "one of the most respectable gentlemen of Rockbridge County," murdered a freedman for merely passing the carriage that was carrying Watson and his family to church. White-controlled civil courts acquitted both of these white men.[81] Conditions for the county's blacks so disturbed one agent for the Freedmen's Bureau that he despaired, "no Justice will be given the Freedmen in cases of any importance where white persons are interested."[82] Given this grim assessment of race relations so soon after war's end, the emergence of Ku Klux Klan activity in Rockbridge County, one of the areas in Virginia where the Klan made its first appearance, should not be surprising.[83] On April 1, 1868, the local newspaper reported that Klan notices had been secretly posted nearby. Two weeks later the issue of "mixed schools" was debated at the state constitutional convention, prompting a diatribe about the proper place of the newly emancipated slaves and predictions of the freedmen's "relapse into barbarism."[84]

Tense race relations and outbreaks of interracial violence thus served as the backdrop to the trial of John Burns. For conservative whites, nothing less than the future of traditional white society waited in abeyance until the trial's outcome. The closing arguments by the Commonwealth's attorney encapsulate the apprehension evident among white Lexingtonians and laid bare the very high stakes of the trial's outcome. He forewarned the jury, "If you clear this Negro you will never have order or quiet again. No family amongst us will be safe. Remember that he is of a lower race and now placed over us. If you have any respect for the little constitutional and civil liberties that are left us you will convict this prisoner."[85] High stakes indeed.

The prosecution's version of the attack was presented first. Lizzie's stepmother, the state's first witness, told the court how on the stormy night of November 28, 1867, her fifteen-year-old daughter, Jenny, awakened her claiming to have seen an intruder in the room she shared with her stepsister, Lizzie. Mrs. Echols's first impulse was to shoo Jenny back to bed, but Jenny persisted. To appease her daughter, Mrs. Echols sent for her son to fetch a pistol and investigate. To the mother's surprise, they discovered Burns lying together with Lizzie on a pallet on the floor, where both appeared fast asleep. Mrs. Echols explained to the court that Lizzie had been in the habit of sleeping on the floor because Lizzie's bedmate, her stepsister, was a poor sleeper and had once kicked Lizzie out of bed.[86]

Lizzie's stepsister, Jenny, took the stand next and recounted how she had followed Lizzie to bed that night. Soon thereafter she was startled by a rattling at the window and observed the "glimmer of the panes of glass" as someone removed the lower window sash from the outside and placed it on the floor. After she noticed a "dark figure" in the room, Jenny crept out of bed to report the intrusion to her mother.[87]

Lizzie's stepbrother, John London Echols, testified next, describing how he found Lizzie and John Burns as they lay facing each other in a near embrace. Echols kicked Burns a few times in the head to awaken him, ordering him out lest he would kill him. The Echols brother also remarked that he observed a handkerchief in the accused's hand, a crucial piece of evidence in the prosecution's case, as will be shown. He described Burns as "stupid and drowsy [and] hard to wake up." After Burns departed, John carried his sister to another room. He then called on a neighbor to assist him in the arrest of Burns who (inexplicably for someone who had just allegedly attempted a rape) had returned to the kitchen and gone to sleep.[88]

The narrative elicited on the stand from members of the Echols family reveals the Commonwealth's strategy in explaining away the compromising predicament in which Lizzie Echols found herself, and its strong suggestion that she had engaged in consensual sex with Burns. The star witness, the accuser herself, offered no testimony whatsoever incriminating John Burns. Lizzie seemed to have amnesia, recalling only waking up to find her mother, brother, and stepsister in the room. She denied any recollection of events before that. As a way of explaining Lizzie's "amnesia," the prosecution called upon several "experts" who testified to the effects of chloroform. They told courtroom observers how, when administered to a patient, the drug induces a stuporous or unconscious state. These so-called experts added that someone who administered chloroform could also inadvertently be overcome by the substance, neatly accounting for why John Burns was found asleep with Lizzie Echols.[89] In this version of the "attack," Lizzie Echols was quite literally divested of all agency and rendered incapable of resisting her attacker.[90]

This recounting of events also allowed the family to maintain that Burns had been unable to consummate rape, which importantly spared their daughter its social stigma. A physician who claimed to have examined Lizzie Echols for signs of coitus confirmed that Lizzie was still a virgin. The assertion that Echols remained sexually pure, and presumably not deflowered by a black man, enabled the Echols family, including Lizzie, to maintain its respectability in the community. Whether Lizzie had been defiled through a rape or consensual sex mattered not; a young, unmarried woman known to have had any sexual experience was damaged goods in middle-class nineteenth-century society. The prosecution's strategic maneuver came with a tradeoff, however. By conceding that no rape occurred, the prosecution forfeited a possible death penalty.[91]

The prosecution, in apparent close collaboration with the Echols family, had carefully constructed a scenario that it presented as the truth. John Burns had feloniously entered the Echols mansion for the purpose of raping Lizzie Echols. He entered through a bedroom window with a handkerchief doused in chloroform that he administered to Lizzie, which would explain how she knew nothing of the assault. But unexpectedly Burns too was taken in by the effects of the chloroform and fell fast asleep. Burns was unable to consummate his sexual designs upon Lizzie as was his intent. Instead, he and Lizzie were discovered by family members in a chloroform stupor.

This version of the facts did not go unchallenged. Freedmen and women who worked with Burns testified that he and Lizzie Echols had been having intimate relations before the alleged attack. The Echols family's cook, Edith, told the court how on one evening she had seen Burns put his arm around Lizzie's neck on the porch after dinner and kiss her. Chapman Johnson gave a more graphic account of his observations. He maintained that once Burns bragged to him of going off to have sex with Lizzie Echols. Indeed, later that night Johnson saw Burns sitting on a fence smoking a cigar, heard him whistle, and then saw Lizzie Echols emerge from the house and walk to the garden for an apparent secret rendezvous. Burns followed. Johnson, no doubt very curious, also followed and claimed that he saw the couple having sex in a clump of bushes only a few feet away. Johnson quickly retreated but shortly thereafter saw the couple emerge from their tryst, walking together, talking and whispering. Startled by Johnson, a frightened Burns "dropped on all fours and scampered away through the brush." Lizzie Echols came to Johnson crying. He recalled for the jury how he reprimanded her: "It is no use to cry now Miss Lizzie." The next morning she came to Johnson again and he repeated his admonition. Another former slave, Jim Cary, told the court how he had seen Lizzie Echols writing a letter to John Burns, snatched it away and "commenced plaguing the prisoner by reading it." The implication was that Cary had confiscated a love letter from Lizzie Echols, the contents of which not only embarrassed Burns but exposed him to great danger.[92]

The defendant himself testified to his consensual affair with Lizzie. Burns told the court that he had been to Lizzie Echols's room frequently and that he had had "connection" with her over twenty times. He also acknowledged a fear of getting caught. He shared this fear with Lizzie, but she quieted him, telling him there was no danger.[93]

Formally, of course, Lizzie Echols was not the one on trial. But the testimony of these freedpeople did impeach the integrity, not to mention dispute the chastity, of the young woman and had to have been a source of great embarrassment to Lizzie and her family. Given widespread white hostility to the very notion of black testimony, however, the white jurymen seem likely to have discounted the claims of the former slaves that Burns and Echols had been intimate. The jury, consisting of twelve white men, found John Burns guilty. In dismissing the exculpatory evidence presented by the freedmen and women, the jurors instead opted to believe the prosecution's version of events, as implausible as it was.

Through its decision, the jury not only found Burns guilty but ostensibly rescued the reputation of a white teenager and her family from rumors about an affair between Echols and Burns that probably existed before the alleged attack. Even if some on the jury doubted the Echolses' claim that their daughter was entirely innocent, they seemed to be sending a message that the guardians of the white community, while forced to accept emancipation, would not idly permit a black man to have unhampered sexual access to a white female in good standing with the community.[94] (This latter qualification is important because during Reconstruction, as in the antebellum period, white women *not* in good standing were accorded a lesser measure of support by the white community, as we shall see in the next chapter.)

A guilty verdict, nonetheless, would send a man to prison for many years for a crime that seems likely he did not commit. This miscarriage of justice was not lost on local agents and officials from the Freedmen's Bureau, one of whom characterized the trial as a "virtual conspiracy to subvert justice so as to screen one of the participators," meaning of course Lizzie Echols.[95] No single person played a greater role in challenging the perceived injustice than General Douglas Frazar, the bureau agent who had been monitoring the proceedings.

After the verdict Frazar compiled a report summarizing the trial and describing egregious acts of injustice. To begin with, Frazar doubted that fair legal representation of Burns was even possible. Not a single member of the bar in Lexington initially agreed to take Burns as a client. While in the Old South many states guaranteed that slaves charged with capital crimes would receive counsel, an emancipated slave could no longer expect this legal protection. Most freedmen and women accused of crimes were probably too poor to hire a lawyer, and even if they had been able to, as the defendant here was able to do, few white lawyers willingly defended former slaves.[96] In this instance, perhaps because of the vigilant watch of the Freedmen's Bureau, the court appointed counsel for John Burns. The judge assigned the unenviable task to two Lexington notables, General Samuel McDowell Moore and W. W. Scott. Moore was an accomplished, well-respected attorney with twenty-two years of experience who took on the assignment "with the greatest reluctance." Frazar once overheard Moore declare that he did not even know the names of his own defense witnesses. Moore was seventy-two years old and quite frail. Most troubling to Frazar was his relationship with the Commonwealth's attorney, Captain David E. Moore. The two Moores were related.[97]

If senior defense counsel was hostile to his own client, old, and compromised by a conflict of interest, the junior attorney for Burns, who possessed virtually no courtroom experience, was no better. The scrupulous Frazar scoured the court docket for the April term, and although 145 cases were entered, the name of W. W. Scott failed to appear even once as counsel of record. Frazar also questioned Scott's objectivity given that he happened to be the editor of the *Lexington Gazette and Banner*, the local newspaper, which ran inflammatory articles about the case, portraying his own client as "a bold, black Negro."[98]

Frazar's misgivings about the bias and competence of the accused's own defense team appear to have been well founded. He discovered, for instance, that the defense neglected to interview witnesses before trial, and neither were they given even rudimentary instructions. "Dazed, ignorant, and frightened they fell easy prey to the insinuating or blustering cross examinations." In contrast, witnesses for the Commonwealth were interviewed by Robert Echols, the accused's father, or one of the prosecuting attorneys before and after testifying, and were, in Frazar's estimation, coached in the delivery of their testimony. Frazar also decried the cross-examination of the Echols family members by the defense as too soft, leaving numerous important questions unasked and therefore unanswered.[99]

In conducting their ostensible defense of Burns, attorneys failed to capitalize on numerous glaring inconsistencies that Frazar outlined for his superiors. First, why would a freedman be so "fool hardy (especially a Negro in a southern State)" to venture an attack upon a white woman with another person present in the very room? And how did the defendant know that the young women sleeping in the same room would not be in bed together? Surely, had he intended to rape one of the Echols teens, would the other not have awakened if in the same bed? How would he have known that one of them would be sleeping on a floor pallet had he not been told? And why was Lizzie not sleeping with her sister? Recall that Mrs. Echols attributed Lizzie's self-imposed banishment to the floor to her sister Jenny's rambunctious sleeping habits. A dubious Frazar insinuated that the story of the floor pallet was more likely a ruse to facilitate a nocturnal tryst with Lizzie's lover.[100]

There were other conspicuous holes in the prosecution's story. Frazar reasoned that a partially clad man, underneath the bedclothes, asleep, and "almost in the arms of the prosecutrix" proves "beyond the shadow of a doubt that he was expected and received." And if he had been in the process of committing a rape, would he not have been alarmed by Jenny Echols's departure from the room? And is it not puzzling, Frazar continued, that a man alleged to have just attempted a rape was allowed to retire to the kitchen of the same house and go to sleep, strongly suggesting that family members themselves suspected Burns had been invited to Lizzie Echols's bed? One of the defense attorneys in closing did ask the jury why Lizzie Echols's brother "did not kill the prisoner at once, if there was not some knowledge that she the prosecutrix was to blame?" The father's testimony also seems to lend credence to Frazar's suspicions. Robert Echols, who had not been home when the alleged assault took place, testified that upon his return he "heard rumors" prompting him to "find out the truth" about any "suspicious" conduct between his daughter and the accused by interrogating other servants in the household.[101]

Douglas Frazar took seriously his commission to safeguard the civil rights of Virginia's emancipated slaves. From the evidence presented and from his own observations, he became persuaded of Burns's innocence and considered it his duty to intercede.[102] Frazar monitored the proceedings diligently, but he also investigated the backgrounds of the principals, scrutinized the credibility of the testimony, and eventually reported his findings to his superiors with a recommendation that a military commission retry the case, thus removing it from civil jurisdiction. He prevailed upon his superiors with a poignant, heartfelt plea: "Much as I pity her I ask as does the prisoner Burns through me for *justice, justice.*" It should be noted too that Frazar's advocacy of Burns was not taken up without some personal sacrifice. He predicted that his position would alienate him "from many friends."[103] It was just the sort of Yankee "interference" that white southerners had grown to detest.

Frazar confirmed what other federal officials seeking to reconstruct the former Confederacy sensed as well, that considerable racial animus existed in white southern communities and that without federal vigilance, the lives and welfare of the thousands of emancipated slaves in the region were imperiled. He wrote, "no Negro in a case similar to the above can receive justice from the courts of this county. Prejudice is too great and strong."[104] Another bureau official wrote, "experience has convinced me that it would be extremely difficult to select a jury of native Virginians who would acquit a colored man, under similar circumstances, where the good name of a daughter of one their 'first families' is in so great a degree involved."[105]

In this regard, bureau agents provided an invaluable service to freedmen who found themselves in a hostile white community charged with raping a white female. Moreover, the zealous activism of military representatives like Douglas Frazar was not isolated. Lieutenant Josiah Chance attended the rape trial of John Price in Franklin County, Virginia, then reported to the governor that after hearing all the evidence he believed Price innocent, contrary to the jury's guilty verdict. The jury's finding, along with its ten-year prison sentence, was "unjust, and resulted more from a popular prejudice rather than from the proof of his guilt."[106] The presence of federal military officials was often the last line of defense for accused black rapists seeking justice in the early Reconstruction South.

The "popular prejudice" exhibited in black-on-white Reconstruction rape trials in Franklin and Rockbridge Counties was palpable. A newspaper report of the Burns trial epitomizes how an incident of alleged black sexual assault had become injected with the politics of race and occupation. The article, hysterical in tone, presented the case as foreboding others if decisive action were not taken: "The case of John Burns might as well have happened in the household of any citizen of the county, as in that of the esteemed and respected family in which it occurred, the sanctity of a daughter or wife's chamber invaded by some daring perpetrator of outrage, and the character and feelings of a virtuous and refined female blackened and polluted by the foul and perjured oaths of degraded witnesses."[107] Calling for racial solidarity, the author warned that no class of whites was safe from the threat. The article invoked the chivalric tenet of protecting womanhood by any means necessary, including extralegal violence: "Swift, sudden and certain death should be meted out to the offender, whether white or black, on the instant. Any one so acting will be fully justified in taking summary vengeance on the offender in the eyes of God and man."[108]

The shrill, stirring, racist rhetoric of this passage, and the racially constructed images, so common in later years, of black brutes lying in wait for white women, should not obscure important differences with the rape scenarios later in the century. Above all, Burns was not lynched. The local white community seemed resigned to allowing the court to oversee the case and deliver a verdict. True enough, the key players—jurymen, judge, even defense attorneys—were white conservatives likely to facilitate a guilty verdict, in essence nearly a fait accompli. But by law the harshest sentence a court could hand down was a lengthy prison term, not death—all the more motivation to incite a lynching.[109]

But Burns was not lynched. Nor did he even serve out his sixteen-year sentence. Governor Henry Horatio Wells, Virginia's provisional governor from New York, pardoned Burns just a few months later at the request of none other than General O. O. Howard, commissioner of the Freedmen's Bureau.[110] Governor Wells's pardon of Burns prompted a vitriolic denunciation by the Lexington newspaper. An editorial vehemently denounced "Governor" Wells's action as an abrogation of justice, likening it to granting Burns a "passport for the commission of similar outrages."[111] Although gubernatorial pardons of convicted blacks had been granted fairly regularly in the antebellum South, such actions took on greater political importance during Reconstruction and were a point of bitter contention, "a source of great dissatisfaction," among native white southerners.[112]

The trial of John Burns underscores other important material conditions and circumstances that had substantially altered the postbellum legal culture in which cases of black rape were considered. Ironically, nothing amplified the vulnerability of black southerners charged with serious crimes after emancipation than their having ceased to be the valuable property of their masters. Under slavery, masters and the state had been financially motivated to insure that slaves charged with rape received some measure of procedural fairness. After all, a hanged slave represented a loss of property. Once they were no longer property, freedmen on trial for rape or attempted rape presumably lost their most motivated boosters: their masters. As a white southerner observed shortly after war's end, "nigger life's cheap now."[113]

Moreover, while nominally the criminal trial of a freedman, the case of John Burns also represented a trial of federal authority and actions that threatened the very social and political fabric of the traditional white South. First, the case affirms the central role that the Freedmen's Bureau played in monitoring and intervening in the judicial proceedings of freedpeople. Frazar, and others like him, were crucial advocates for freedmen accused of serious crimes and tried in courtrooms run by native white southerners. After being sentenced to a lengthy prison term, Burns had only Frazar to take his case to higher authorities for review. Many white Lexingtonians saw things very differently, of course, and expressed resentment toward this intrusion into their affairs.

Second, numerous white residents of Lexington protested against actions by pro-Union officials, believing that these actions effectively subverted justice by pardoning a black man whom they, through their own courts, had found guilty of a heinous crime. In this view, with the mere sweep of the (Republican) governor's pen federal authorities nullified democratic and legally sanctioned judicial proceedings. As a result, many white southerners, like those in Lexington, Virginia, began to lose faith in a judicial process that in their estimation had been derailed and corrupted. Their disillusionment and resentment intensified throughout Reconstruction and may very well explain, at least in part, the eruption of widespread extralegal violence in much of the region after the war.

Nothing less than the region's future lay at stake for the white community of Lexington, as it worked to reestablish racial and social boundaries in a new world without slavery. The responses of local whites to the news of a black man attempting to sexually assault an elite white woman reveal a determination in the community to delineate acceptable roles for blacks and whites, specifically black men and white elite women. The case also prompted warnings intended for nonelite whites whose wives and daughters were also presumably at risk in the wake of emancipation. This sort of foreboding became rather common later in the century, yet in the 1860s it was rather new. So in a sense, what we see unfolding in the case of John Burns are the nascent elements of the "rape myth" that will emerge full blown in later decades. While Reconstruction may very well have been the incubator for white fears of black sexual aggression, as some historians have claimed, the turn-of-the-century conflation of black political agency with black sexual agency was not evident because it had not yet crystallized in the Reconstruction South.[114] Had it done so, Burns's case would likely have had a very different outcome. Restrained white Lexingtonians after all allowed the case to proceed calmly through proper legal channels without incident.

The trial of John Burns brings to the fore significant changes that began to emerge in the South as a result of war, emancipation, and federal occupation. Federal Reconstruction policies that enforced the civil and political rights of freedmen helped to erode the long-standing, revered ties between the law and the traditional power sources that had long prevailed in antebellum communities, planting seeds of distrust instead. As Bertram Wyatt-Brown has asserted, for all its faults and shortcomings the Old South judicial system seems to have been respected.[115] With changes ushered in by Reconstruction, white southerners came to regard their legal and political worlds as irretrievably tainted by corruption, ineptitude, and political favoritism. Former Confederates testified to the percolating distrust and lack of faith in the judicial system. One North Carolinian complained, "I am pained to say that in our state our judiciary system is a farce; it is little more than nominal."[116] Any number of white residents of Lexington, Virginia, in 1868 would have concurred.

FOUL DAUGHTER OF
RECONSTRUCTION?
Black Rape in the
Reconstruction South

White southerners at the turn of the century were fond of blaming the "negro problem"—the perceived increase in the irascibility, impudence, and criminality of the region's African American population—on the misguided policies and ill-fated efforts of the Republican Party to expand the citizenry to include freedmen. Myrta Lockett Avary, looking back, squarely blamed northern interlopers for the perceptible change in African Americans' demeanor and the coeval rise in cases of black-on-white rape, which she claimed was "a development of a period when the negro was dominated by political, religious and social advisors from the North, and by the attitude of the Northern press and pulpit."[1]

Avary's voice was merely one in a chorus assailing federal policies that some saw as releasing uncivil, uneducated, and ill-prepared ex-slaves into southern society, with the vote to boot.[2] An entire genre of fiction emerged out of this fondness for blaming the region's race "problems" on reviled Reconstruction policies and found a very receptive audience both within and outside the region. The popular Reconstruction novels helped perpetuate the stereotype of the naïve freedman duped by northern interlopers into believing that "social equality" was a well-deserved fruit of newfound political equality. Sympathetic to the white South, hopelessly didactic, steeped in racial stereotypes, and casting scalawags and carpetbaggers as despicable and carnivorous, the novels portrayed freedmen as lustful, gullible, and easily manipulated. In these tales, well-meaning but disillusioned northerners regularly fell victim to their own misguided racial good will. And nary a Reconstruction novel failed to have a climactic scene in which a savage, beastlike freedman raped a young, virtuous, white maiden, who if she survived would suffer "a fate worse than death."[3]

One of the first of these novels was *Smoking Flax* (1897), by Hallie Erminie Rives, a Kentucky woman. In the story Elliott Harding, a southerner by birth relocated to the North as a child, returns to his family homestead after the war and is deeply disturbed by the deplorable state of race relations in the region, particularly the outbreak of lynching. Only the rape and murder of his fiancée at the hands of a local no-good Negro, and the delayed judicial process and eventual gubernatorial stay of execution, convince him that personal, extra-legal violence is the only solution. Racing to the train that is whisking away the accused rapist-murderer, Harding avenges the honor of his deflowered dead fiancée by shooting her assailant through the heart.[4]

Red Rock, written by Thomas Nelson Page the following year, similarly de-picted the nefarious and inept political leadership of scalawags and carpetbag-gers whose ill-conceived policies allowed the likes of Moses, a freedman turned preacher, to menace and threaten local white women with impunity. Justice is served—and the threat of rape removed—only when Moses is lynched.[5]

The best-known work of this genre was by Thomas Dixon, who wrote several novels purportedly chronicling the federal occupation of the South after the war. The first of these was *The Leopard's Spots* (1903), but the more famous was *The Clansman* (1905), which became the basis of D. W. Griffith's popular film *Birth of a Nation* ten years later. Both novels condemned the unwanted intrusion of northern carpetbaggers and treasonous scalawags. Both portrayed freedmen as lustful savages lurking about in the shadows for un-protected, unsuspecting white women. And both featured inflammatory black-on-white rape scenes as tragic dénouements that justified the "birth of a nation," the Ku Klux Klan, and its deadly tactics.[6]

The grossly distorted and racist version of Reconstruction invented by Lost Cause boosters and white southern novelists became virtually indistinguish-able from the contemporary scholarly treatments of professional historians. The best-known and influential of these Reconstruction historians from the turn of the century was William Archibald Dunning, who taught at Columbia University from 1886 to 1922. Dunning and his students, collectively dubbed the "Dunning school," incorporated these popular misperceptions about Re-construction into historical treatments of the period, writing, for example, that the era was characterized by misrule and corruption. Partisan and self-interested scalawags and carpetbaggers manipulated childlike freedmen by holding out the plums of suffrage and political equality. Dunning himself wrote, "With civil rights and political power, not won, but almost forced upon him, [the southern black man] came gradually to understand and crave those more elusive privileges that constitute social equality. . . . It played a part . . . in the hideous crime against white womanhood which now assumed new mean-ing in the annals of outrage."[7]

Black-on-white rape figured prominently in these historical treatments of Reconstruction. Portraying freedmen as intoxicated with new political power, historians like Claude Bowers described how "an awful fear rested upon the [white] women of the communities." Denying that as slaves black men had ever posed a threat to white women, he continued, "throughout the war, when men were far away on the battlefields, and the women were alone on far plantations with the slaves, hardly a woman was attacked. Then came the scum of northern society, emissaries of the politicians, soldiers of fortune, and not a few degenerates, inflaming the negroes egotism, and soon the lustful assaults began. Rape is the foul daughter of Reconstruction."[8] Black rape, these historians charged, grew out of the peculiarities of occupation, including naïve Northerners, self-interested politicians, and political equality dangled before former slaves.

Both fin de siècle historians and defenders of the white South thus asserted that the perceived black rape threat had its origins in Reconstruction. More recent historical accounts, recognizing of course that such rape fears among whites were imagined not real, likewise have sensed that Reconstruction logically was the incubator for "the rape myth." Some scholars hold that once masters lost control of their bonded property, especially slave women, they naturally began to fear retribution from black men.[9] Suzanne Lebsock has speculated that the ravages of war and its aftermath left white men poor, wounded, and divested of political power, in effect losers, and "losers are not inclined to be generous." And what more effective way to regain power and control in the family and in the political arena than to convince women that they need the constant protection of their men from an imaginary black "bogey-man-rapist"? "In the myth of rape, the suppression of blacks and the suppression of women came together with new and sickening clarity."[10]

Most recently, Martha Hodes has described how an uneasy toleration of interracial sexual relations during the colonial and antebellum eras was supplanted after the Civil War with an increasingly anxious and guarded view, somewhat approaching a cultural taboo. Arguing that sex between black men and white women became irretrievably politicized—demands for political equality for black men gave rise to concerns about "social equality"—Hodes claims that "white anxiety and alarm about black male sexuality reached an unprecedented level of intensity." She notes that the end of slavery threatened the racial hierarchy of the slave South and the categories it engendered: "Intertwining these unfamiliar dangers—the possibility of blurring the categories of 'black' and 'white' in a world without racial slavery, and the alarm of diminishing white supremacy—white people fastened on the taboo of sex between black men and white women with newfound urgency."[11]

Undeniably, the circumstances of Reconstruction dramatically affected the dynamics of race, class, and sexuality in the South. Incidents of violent responses to allegations of miscegenation or black-on-white sexual assault increased.[12] Unreconstructed southern legislatures attempted to enact new anti-miscegenation statutes or to increase the penalties under existing ones.[13] Racist rhetoric of southern whites became more commonly infused with fears of race mixing.[14]

Despite these well-known and documented changes, not all toleration for interracial sex, coerced or consensual, was swept away. Those conditions that had lain the foundation for toleration—paternalism, personalism, misogyny, class bias, racism—remained stubbornly rooted in southern postwar society and persisted throughout. Jettisoning such deeply held convictions would take much longer. In fact, local rape cases in southern communities after the Civil War display significant continuities with the antebellum period. Whites in the postemancipation South, like their forerunners, at times continued to treat African American men convicted of raping white women and girls with leniency by handing down light prison sentences and appealing for pardons. The lynching of black rapists, so common later in the century, did not supplant the legal process once slaves attained their freedom. Furthermore, white communities, as in the Old South, continued to view poor white female accusers, and with the abolition of slavery black female accusers, with considerable suspicion, causing some to root around for evidence of immoral behavior by the women who brought forth charges of rape against black men. Ideas on the danger of impure women, even white women, were not immediately dispelled by emancipation.[15] Nor did the forces effecting so much dramatic social and political change in a reconstituted South cause white observers and participants in black-on-white rape cases to close ranks along race lines. Indeed, although war and emancipation precipitated seismic political, cultural, and social changes in the South, they nonetheless failed to shatter long-standing ideas about the depravity of poorer white women, or for that matter the docility of black men. In a number of cases, white Southerners extended paternalist protections to black men, even those accused of rape. Evidence culled from local courts records in the decade or so after the war continues to show that "respectable" whites sometimes lined up squarely with freedmen accused of sexually assaulting white women. Class differences continued to shape the contours of black-on-white rape trials even after the Civil War.

But along with white toleration of interracial sex—coerced or consensual—local records reveal contrary examples of intolerance. White southerners during Reconstruction did occasionally lynch black men who they believed raped or in some way insulted white women. African American men convicted of rape were sometimes executed. In addition, legislatures tightened controls over sexual mixing and local authorities more actively thwarted interracial marriages. There is no question that in the face of emancipation and defeat, white southerners expressed greater concerns about black male sexuality than they ever had in the past.

But the point is that emancipation is not the definitive marker for the emergence of white fears of black rape. A greater level of discomfort about interracial sexual activity, less toleration for racial mixing on an intimate level, can be documented in the years immediately following the end of the Civil War. Gauging white anxiety about black rape in the Reconstruction South, however, yields contradictory findings. This chapter documents these ambiguous and complicated developments. Within the South there were varied white responses to news of a black man raping a white woman or girl. In one time and place, a white court could in essence slap a convicted black rapist on the wrist. White southerners also could and did exact death, with the sanction of the court or without. While it is tempting for the historian to throw up her hands, the actions of the participants make sense when viewed more broadly in the larger context of race and class relations in the same era. White southerners simply failed to act as a cohesive block and to respond in a "white" way. Instead, they responded in myriad ways that reflected their own personal experiences and made sense given local conditions. They were "trying on" new ideas about how race—and gender and class—would be played out in a world without slavery. Not quite so befuddling after all.

Perhaps one of the most astonishing observations about official black-on-white Reconstruction rape cases is the rather mild punishments that convicted black rapists sometimes received, an obvious continuity from the antebellum period.[16] Of course to a large extent the hands of jurors were tied by the new statutory revisions regarding race and rape. A attorney in an attempted black rape case in 1868 pointed out to the jury in his closing argument that before emancipation such a crime could have been punishable by hanging, but after the war the law provided that black offenders could be sentenced to a maximum of two years in prison.[17]

Even taking into account the less severe sexual assault statutes, some all-white juries handed down rather lenient prison sentences for convicted black rapists, less than the maximum staked out by statute. In July 1869, for example, a jury in Franklin County, Virginia, found a freedman, John Price, guilty of raping Martha Ann Stump, aged thirty-five, and sentenced him to only ten years in the state penitentiary. Perhaps the jury was responding to rather flimsy evidence identifying Price as the man who broke into the accuser's darkened home at night and raped her three times. Stump claimed to identify Price by his voice alone (which, by the way, she had heard on only one occasion, several months before the alleged attack). Or perhaps Price's attorneys were able to persuade jury members that Stump had been a "woman of notoriously abandoned character, totally destitute of chastity" since she had "been delivered of several bastard children since the death of her late husband," as they asserted in an appeal to the state's governor. Or maybe in the end the court became sympathetic to Price after hearing witnesses testify on his behalf. Peter Saunderson of Rocky Mount, Virginia, whose relationship with Price had endured for some twenty years, offered that Price was a good worker and a "gentleman to be relied upon." Accolades such as these were not lost on the jury, which, recognizing that John Price was a man of "good character and there being some conflict in the testimony," recommended executive clemency, in addition to sentencing him to a mere ten years in prison.[18]

The court's decision to convict John Price on the basis of rather weak evidence, however, coupled with the dubious reputation of the accuser, Martha Stump, signified some measure of disapproval of Price's actions. If Price was innocent, a ten-year prison sentence was indeed a stiff price to pay. Yet the jury, presented with the option of sentencing Price to hang for the rape of a white woman, demonstrated restraint and opted for a prison term instead. On some level it would appear that the white community's disapproval of and disdain for a white woman who carried with her the baggage of illicit sexual relations continued unabated in the postemancipation South.[19]

The rather relaxed sentences handed down to black men convicted of rape or attempted rape of white females were not limited to Virginia. In 1866 Bryant Oakes, a black man from Sampson County, North Carolina, was convicted of assault upon a white woman when evidence failed to sustain the original charge, assault with an intent to rape. His sentence consisted of two whippings of thirty-nine lashes each, and after the first whipping the chairman of the county court petitioned the governor of North Carolina to remit the second.[20] Again in North Carolina, in roughly the same period, two blacks in Rowan County were tried for assault with intent to commit a rape on a white woman. The jury acquitted one defendant and after finding the second guilty sentenced him to a month in jail and a ten-dollar fine.[21]

Laura Edwards found records of two convictions of black men for the attempted rapes of white females in Granville County, North Carolina. In 1869 William Somerville went on trial for the rape of Temple Cass, a white woman. The jury, unable to muster a unanimous guilty verdict, compromised and agreed to the lesser charge of attempted rape. In response, sixty men, including prominent Republican leaders of the county, petitioned the governor for a pardon. They argued that Cass, the mother of an illegitimate child, had prostituted herself and agreed to have sex with Somerville, but then reneged. Demonstrating considerable sympathy for Somerville, they concurred that he had every right to expect "the promised services." Six years later, another black man went on trial for assault with intent to rape a white child. Though found guilty, Alexander Chavis was sentenced to only seven and a half years in the state prison. Edwards observes that not only did this case fail to garner enough attention to be noted in the local newspaper, it shows that "even the rape of a white woman by a black man did not always provoke public outrage. Often, it did not receive much attention at all."[22]

Although one former slave, David Crawford of Lynchburg, Virginia, was sentenced by the jury to die for the rape of a nine-year-old white child, Caroline Schmidt, jurors were among the petitioners who later requested that Crawford's sentence be commuted. The letter cited as mitigating circumstances Crawford's lack of education and ignorance of the law, as well as what petitioners believed had been "too much familiarity" with the Schmidt family, in whose home Crawford lived. The jurors seemed to be implying that Crawford's white employer bore a certain degree of responsibility for the assault.[23]

Regardless of whether less-than-harsh sentences for African Americans convicted of raping white women reflected a degree of continued class prejudices or misogyny or were products of inflexible new rape statutes, or a combination of factors, it is important to note that white communities in these instances allowed the legal proceedings to continue without disruption by mob violence. Southern whites throughout Reconstruction routinely allowed accused black rapists to receive jury trials. And even when the results may not have been palatable to many, extralegal intervention was not the norm.

Nor did postbellum whites immediately relinquish their stereotypes about poor white women whose sexual behavior had earned them reputations as depraved.[24] Those women, in the minds of some whites, still did not deserve the same level of protection from the law and society that wealthier, better behaved women did. Granting freedom to slaves did little to alter that conception, as Sallie F. Nay (also Ney) of Albemarle County, Virginia, discovered. Her alleged attacker received substantial sympathy from white citizens and the court after Nay complained that Squire Lewis, a black man, had broken into her home at nighttime and attempted to rape her. The grand jury summoned to hear evidence of her charge, initially failed to indict Lewis. Some of the grand jurors, it seems, were aware of Mrs. Nay's "bad reputation" in the neighborhood and convinced other jurors that given her sullied reputation, it was unnecessary to hear all the evidence. Undaunted, Sallie Nay returned the next day with additional witnesses. Upon hearing the new testimony, the grand jury indicted Squire Lewis for the attempted rape of Nay.[25] Importantly, though, this white woman had to fight to have her charge of attempted rape taken seriously.

Once the case made its way to trial, jury members seemed inclined to accept Nay's story despite her dubious standing in the neighborhood. The prosecution's case rested on very weak evidence; Nay had great difficulty making a positive identification since the attack occurred at night. Instead, Nay relied on the sound of her attacker's voice to identify him. The jury evidently found her testimony credible, proclaimed Squire Lewis guilty, and sentenced him to nine years in the state penitentiary. John B. Spice, Lewis's attorney, wasted no time launching a campaign to pardon Lewis. He enlisted some of the community's most "respectable" and "very prominent citizens," nearly a hundred in all, in his endeavor. Lewis's master before the war, John M. Herndon, affixed his name to the petition, as did some jury members and a county constable. Micajah Woods, the Commonwealth's attorney in the case, believed that the "adulterous character and bad reputation of Mrs. Nay have excited sympathy for Lewis." In a letter to the governor Woods wrote, "Mrs. Nay bears a bad reputation in her neighborhood for chastity. It is well known that she was criminally intimate while [Mr.] Nay was living with her, with the man she has since married."[26]

Community animus toward deviant white women was not the only factor that persuaded white southerners to urge pardons for convicted black rapists. A black man's history of industriousness and a strong work ethic were sometimes offered up as grounds for leniency. Probably no question preoccupied southern whites in the wake of emancipation more than "Will the negro work?"[27] Whites, so accustomed to coercing blacks to work through bondage, could hardly imagine a free labor system in which blacks would work voluntarily. That assumption about the region's ex-slaves, coupled with acute shortages of labor in certain areas, influenced the responses of some whites to rape convictions of black men.[28] In several instances white citizens petitioning on behalf of black rapists noted the high value of reliable, hard-working African American laborers. Walter Mead, for one, enlisted legal counsel for the defense of one of his employees, Charles Abner, from the charge of rape. Abner's conduct and habits in the two years he had worked for Mead were excellent, "scarcely ever losing one day from his employment."[29]

Both white and black citizens lauded the work habits of Ned Lewis, a black man from Louisa County, Virginia, convicted in 1876 for raping Nicie Morris, a woman of color, and petitioned for his early release. Semple Goodwin, Lewis's former master and then employer, described him as a "faithful and dutiful employee." Lewis "[is of] good character, is peaceable and quiet and is good, [a] faithful and useful laborer." His value as an industrious, reliable worker was inestimable since "such laborers as he are always in demand in the community."[30] Material considerations, not just racial prejudices and animus, help to explain why white southerners at times advocated leniency for black men found guilty of rape. In the antebellum South, masters had been motivated to exonerate their own slaves from the charge of rape because they risked financial loss if the slaves were executed. After emancipation, self-interested employers, sometimes former masters, had similar reasons to help black men accused of rape escape harsh punishment.

Members of the white community throughout Reconstruction, just as before the Civil War, sometimes spurned women, even girls, of the poorer class who charged black men with sexual assault. Two sets of standards for white women persisted. Shabby treatment of poor white women during Reconstruction rape trials testifies to the resiliency and longevity of Old South ideas about the depravity of poor white women whose sexual behavior was believed to have deviated from accepted practice. The periodic voluntary unions of white women with black men, and the tacit toleration of the practice by others in the white community, are further evidence of the continued marginalization of women outside the planter class. Some of the black-on-white rape cases that made it to the courts in Virginia during Reconstruction suggest that consensual sexual relations between black males and white females were at the root of allegations of rape. This was almost certainly the case when John Burns of Lexington, Virginia, was charged with attempted rape in 1868.[31] How common such interracial affairs were in the years following the Civil War was debated by contemporaries and by later scholars.

Historians have of late documented numerous instances of white women who took black lovers beginning in the colonial period.[32] Once thought to have been quite rare, such relationships have been shown definitively by recent historical treatments of the colonial and antebellum periods to have been far from exceptional. Joshua Rothman claims that "interracial sex was ubiquitous in urban, town, and plantation communities throughout" Virginia, the subject

of his study.[33] Even more surprising to some is the relative if measured toleration of cross-racial sexual relationships. Only rarely did white southerners
before the Civil War ever take action, legal or otherwise, to express their
disapproval.[34] It is to be expected, however, that in the antebellum South
attitudes about miscegenation varied widely from one region to the next.
Some historians have attributed liberal attitudes toward miscegenation to
proximity to the frontier or to a shortage of white women.[35] Still others believe
that miscegenation was tolerated because under slavery it posed no threat to
existing social and racial hierarchies.[36] Whatever their reasons for coming
together, black men and white women continued to form connections during
the Reconstruction years, and their relationships were often tolerated by white
neighbors.

Whether sexual relations between the races increased or decreased in frequency as a result of the war is one that has occupied the attention of historians, as it did of both contemporary northerners and southerners.[37] Some
southerners, black and white, felt that with the abolition of slavery miscegenation would decrease. This belief was predicated upon the erroneous assumption that cross-racial relationships always involved white men and black
women, all but ignoring the possibility of black men cohabiting with or courting white women. And since white men, slaveowners and their sons, no longer
had free sexual access to their former slaves, the practice, some observers
predicted, would diminish. Charles Wallace Howard, a white editor of an
agricultural newspaper in Georgia, believed that miscegenation would decline
markedly for a very practical reason: With the end of slavery, white fathers
could now be forced by law to recognize the paternity of children conceived
out of wedlock and to support them.[38] T. G. Campbell, a black minister reared
in New Jersey who came to the South Carolina sea islands before the end of the
war, concurred: "In slavery the proprietor of slaves had two motives—his lust
and his avarice." With the end of slavery, slave masters no longer possessed an
incentive to impregnate their female slaves. Furthermore, Campbell testified,
in freedom former slaves were anxious to "discountenance any disreputable
acts, because they now want to be respected." Freedmen and women embraced
the Victorian, bourgeois notion of chastity.[39] Peter M. Dox, a congressman
from Huntsville, Alabama, confirmed that whites, taken in by these explanations, had little concern about miscegenation.[40]

In some quarters, however, considerable debate surrounded the issue of
interracial sex in the aftermath of emancipation. Richard R. Hill, a twenty-
four-year-old black Virginian, responded to queries by General O. O. Howard,
head of the Freedmen's Bureau, about a possible increase in amalgamation

now that slavery was abolished: "I do not think there is any more danger now than there was when slavery existed. At that time there was a good deal of amalgamation. There was no actual marrying, but there was an intermixture to a great extent." Surprised, General Howard asked, "But you do not think that a Virginia white man would have connexion with a black woman?" Hill replied, "I know it from past experience. It was nothing but the stringent laws of the south that kept many a white man from marrying a black woman." Howard assumed that such a relationship would be viewed as "a very wicked state of things." Hill was not so sure: "I will state to you as a white lady stated to a gentleman down in Hampton, that if she felt disposed to fall in love with or marry a black man, it was nobody's business but hers."[41]

Some observers in the South, perhaps reflecting their own racial prejudices, were convinced that relationships between black men and white women were uncommon. John William DeForest, a former official of the Freedmen's Bureau in Greenville, South Carolina, believed that unions of black men and white women were rare. What he really meant was that "respectable" women would not take black men as intimate companions. However, among the "low-down females" of Greenville, he knew of a few mulatto births, and of some white women who cohabited with black men, even one who took a black husband. This state of affairs DeForest blamed on the deaths of white men resulting from the war. Many white women were widows or orphans who had been "robbed of their natural protectors. There was no fastidious Uncle Joe to save or avenge."[42]

There are numerous instances in which cross-racial couples cohabited rather peaceably during Reconstruction, suggesting some level of community acceptance or toleration. Those couples that seem to have been tolerated nonetheless took great pains to be discreet about their arrangement. For example, R. T. Coleman was a respectable man of color living in Cumberland County, Virginia. Throughout his lifetime, he had taken three white wives. Perhaps Coleman was aided by his stature in the community, which was enhanced by his wealth. More importantly, he escaped local contempt and interference by discreetly marrying in the North and by maintaining his wives in homes separate from his own, in short, giving the appearance that they were not cohabiting.[43]

In those instances when local officials or neighbors did object, often the punishments seemed rather mild compared to those that would be inflicted later. Many whites viewed interracial unions as distasteful and expressed their disapproval in nonviolent but nonetheless effective ways, such as refusing legal endorsement. John B. Spice, a white lawyer in Albemarle County, Virginia, told of a young white woman and her mother who sought his help in 1874 in securing a marriage license for the daughter and James Carr, a man Spice described as "black a negro as I have ever seen." Spice refused, but the undaunted couple, with the help of family members who had obviously given their blessing, simply fixed up a small house on the mother's property and set up house. Shortly after the daughter gave birth to Carr's child, the two went off to Staunton, Virginia, where he claimed to have obtained a marriage license, and were married. "No one believed him" and eventually a magistrate arrested the couple.[44] Similarly, in February 1867 Jackson Hayley, a black man from Northampton County, Virginia, applied for a marriage so that he could marry Susan Fly, a woman "with a white skin." The clerk refused to issue the license and the "couple showed unusual anger."[45] Another cross-racial couple from Virginia fled after the black man's arrest for attempting to marry a white woman. The newspaper reported that he absconded with his "dulcinea" to parts unknown.[46]

Whether because of indifference or class bias, some interracial couples after the Civil War escaped the ire of disapproving whites. Not all who crossed racial lines sexually were so lucky, however. In some parts of the South, increased anxiety about miscegenation began to manifest itself in greater intolerance. A number men of color who had been cohabiting with white women for years suddenly found themselves singled out for castigation. A band of Ku Klux Klan members administered two hundred lashes to Joe Coulter of Chattanooga, Tennessee, for marrying a white woman. Remarkably, he had married the woman two to five years earlier but had been unmolested by the locals in the community until early 1871.[47] Other black men faced similar rebuke. A black man in Georgia was shot five times by Klan members for living in adultery with a white woman, whom they whipped severely.[48] Another man of color in Georgia and his white mistress were "paddled" by Klan members, who then burned down their cabin.[49] An African American man living in Kentucky was sentenced to nine years' imprisonment for the accidental death of his white wife, with whom he had been living for several years. By all accounts, the charge was merely a ploy to punish the man for becoming involved so intimately with a white woman.[50] A black man living with not one but two white women in South Carolina was shot to death on the steps of his home.[51] When a "saddle colored" member of the Mississippi legislature married a young white girl in 1874, there was "a good deal of talk" among local whites. One white contemporary recounted, "I think the more sensible people of the community concurred in the idea, that if she wanted to marry him it was her business; but among the riffraff of the population there was a great deal of talk about injuring him in some way."[52] Obviously the interracial marriage had not ruffled all within the white community but it did excite the poorer whites, perhaps because the woman was of their class.[53]

White women suspected of illicit sexual behavior, including sexual relations with African American men, also became targets of southern white ire. It was during Reconstruction that the gradual policing of white women and their morality became more noticeable, not exclusively but frequently focused on their sexual relationships with African American men. The practice suggests that whites were becoming aware of the growing importance of maintaining separation between the races, something that would become even more clear as the century came to a close. Forty to fifty members of the North Carolina Klan entered the house belonging to Mrs. Frances Gilmore, a white woman, and found two black males sleeping on a pallet. There were also four other women in the house, suggesting that it may have been a house of prostitution. The women were described as being of "rather bad character." The raiding party whipped the women and one of the black men. They shot the other as he tried to escape. The Klan singled out one of the women they had whipped, a young woman in her late teens, burned off part of her hair, then forced her to cut off the hair that remained.[54] These sorts of women, after the war as well as before, clearly fell outside the protection of chivalric ideology.

Women and girls of the elite class who occasionally transgressed into sexual relationships with black men, as in the case of John Burns and Lizzie Echols of Lexington, Virginia, elicited a far different response from fellow whites. "Respectable" white families, those held in esteem in their communities, could not afford the scandal of an interracial affair. So frequently the family marshaled its resources to exonerate the errant daughter, allowing her to continue living in the community without lingering questions about her character. Charges of rape appear to have been filed at times to mask a consensual relationship between an African American male and a white female. Members of one family in Virginia reacted swiftly and deliberately when they charged that Monroe Toler, a married man of color, had kidnapped and raped their thirteen-year-old daughter. Two widely differing versions of this episode emerge from the related court documents. The Wood family of Campbell County claimed that on January 6, 1869, Toler's wife lured the daughter, Martha, away from her yard into the woods. Monroe Toler soon appeared with pistol in hand, made threats against the girl's life, and forced her to steal away with him across the Staunton River. A man of color named William Arnold, it was charged, abetted the kidnapper by ferrying the two across the river and providing them with some food.[55]

The white community's reaction to this account of the events was one of "greatest bitterness and indignation." A band of white men quickly mustered "with arms and scoured the country for the parties, and offered violence to any person supposed to be friendly to Toler." Six days after the purported abduction, the couple was found about forty-two miles away in neighboring Pittsylvania County. The Wood family members claimed that Toler raped their daughter during the six-day escape.[56]

By contrast, friends of Toler offered a vastly different account of the alleged abduction. Toler's wife, for instance, testified that for months she had suspected "improper intercourse between Toler and Miss Wood" and finally caught the two "in criminal embrace" before the "elopement." The defense also challenged the prosecution's account of the so-called kidnapping. During the entire six-day flight, for instance, Martha Wood never attempted an escape or tried to alert anyone to her predicament, strongly intimating that Martha Wood was a willing participant in the flight and was coached into perjury to save face for the family.[57]

By all accounts the Woods, like the Echols family of Lexington, appear to have been a family of some means. They were wealthy enough to employ servants in their household and hire their own prosecuting attorney, an unorthodox action in a criminal case. In addition, they also put up a $50 reward for the apprehension of Toler and their daughter. Clearly these people had money and did not hesitate to use it to secure a conviction of Toler as well as the exoneration of the daughter who appears to have been carrying on a clandestine relationship with a married black man.

There are also indications that the family took advantage of political connections to insure a favorable decision from the courts. William Arnold, who testified in a preliminary hearing in May that he had ferried Toler and the thirteen-year-old Wood girl across the river, could corroborate Toler's testimony that the girl went along willingly. Consequently, Arnold found himself jailed as an accessory before the fact. Word of Arnold's arrest spread quickly, and by the trial date of August nearly twenty defense witnesses who had been set to substantiate Toler's version of the story failed to appear in court for fear that they too would be charged as accessories.[58] For good reason, it seems. William Arnold was found guilty of being an accessory before the fact to the rape of Martha Wood and sentenced to twelve years' imprisonment, a rather stiff sentence considering the limited extent of his involvement. Arnold's attorney appealed to the governor of Virginia for a pardon that was denied pending judicial review.[59] Toler's fate is unclear.[60]

Just as middling or elite families rallied around their daughters who they claimed were assaulted by black men, some whites too sought swift and sure retribution for perceived slights against "respectable" white women. In Georgia the Ku Klux Klan claimed responsibility for whipping a black man whom they charged with merely propositioning a white woman. Augustus Wright, the former congressman from Georgia who relayed this story to the Joint Committee in 1871, assumed the character of the woman in question to be "fair" because "if she had been a common whore or strumpet, I do not suppose they would have paid attention to it."[61] A purported insult by Jourdan Ware, a freedman from Georgia, had deadly consequences. Ostensibly he "insulted" a "white lady," perhaps by remarking "How d'ye, sis," as a lawyer and former Confederate officer testified to Congress.[62]

White southerners after emancipation continued to respond to allegations of black-on-white sexual infractions with an eye toward class, which still mattered to a considerable degree in determining whether a white woman deserved the protection of white society. The black Georgian whipped by the Klan had propositioned not just a white woman, but a white woman of good upbringing. And it was the poorer whites, or the "riffraff" as was described, who were so outraged by the marriage of a black man and a white woman in their community. The significance of class in shaping white reactions to interracial sexual relations, by consent or not, did not disappear with the end of slavery.

Class weighed heavily in the rape case of Coleman Davis, a man of color from Pittsylvania County, Virginia, in 1866. A little over a year after Lee's surrender at Appomattox, Davis was convicted of raping a poor white girl under the age of twelve. He was sentenced to ten years in the penitentiary, surprisingly the minimum punishment prescribed by law. The Virginia General Assembly had amended its rape law in February 1866, just a few months before Davis went on trial for the rape.[63] So it is possible that the court officials were not yet aware that such an offense was now punishable by death, or ten to twenty years in the penitentiary.[64] Before emancipation, if a white man had been convicted of raping a child he would have only faced ten to twenty years in the penitentiary.[65] So even if the jury sentenced Davis along the guidelines established for white rapists, it still gave him the mildest punishment permitted by law.

Perhaps the jury accepted, at least in part, the mitigating circumstances presented by D. H. Pannell, Davis's defense attorney. There was no question as to the fact of sexual intercourse, Pennell claimed. Nor was there any doubt as to the girl's consent. In fact, the girl's mother had allowed her to "associate freely" with Davis in the fields. The two had been discovered in the act of sexual intercourse in the tobacco barn. Davis's conviction, Pannell protested, rested upon a technicality. The accuser, presented to the court as having been under the age of twelve, was considered unable to give consent, although Pannell had reason to believe that the accuser's mother lied and that the child was actually twelve when she had sex with Coleman Davis.[66]

More revealing about class and race conditions in Pittsylvania County, Virginia, however, was a comment that Pannell made about the prejudice of the jury that convicted Coleman Davis. In his bid to win Davis a pardon Pannell wrote to the governor that "juries are comprised of low class white people who have bitter prejudice against the negro and [are] catching at the least thing to convict one especially for sexual intercourse with one of their own colour."[67] By this account, poor whites in a position to police the intimate relations between black men and poor white females did so emphatically and with considerable vigor. Just as poorer whites in the antebellum period were sometimes the most outspoken critics of leniency toward convicted black rapists, so too were many poor whites during Reconstruction. In postbellum society, however, the elimination of servitude and the concomitant erosion of racial and class barriers more directly threatened the social position of poor whites. Poor whites, who in slavery were guaranteed a social rung above that of slaves, were now being asked to make way for a new class, freed slaves. If Davis's case is a representative one in the former slaveholding states, poorer whites were seizing upon the time-honored ideology of honor to lay claims to their right to "protect" their women, just as elite whites had always done.

As in the Old South, bringing charges of rape was one way to salvage the honor of a young white girl and her family in the face of pregnancy. Such appears to have been done in Russell County, Virginia, in the summer of 1873. Rececca Meade, a fifteen-year-old white girl, charged Stephen West, a seventeen-year-old young man of color living and working in her family's home, with rape. The timing of her accusation strains credulity. It was not made until after she had given birth to a child, allegedly West's. Witnesses testified that the two had been having sexual relations for some time, allegedly with the knowledge of the girl's father. The couple reportedly had a rendezvous in the fields and in the kitchen at night. Meade was also observed sitting on West's lap. Despite this evidence—even the presiding judge doubted West's guilt—the jury convicted West, but only sentenced him to twelve years in the penitentiary. The guilty verdict signified disapproval of the cross-racial sexual relations, but the twelve-year prison term, far short of a death sentence, probably represented a compromise due to the mitigating circumstances. The girl was a willing sex partner with a former slave. The child's father also bore some responsibility and was chastised for failing to "guard against" his daughter's actions.[68]

If the case of Stephen West can be used to demonstrate the lenient treatment of black rapists in the postbellum South, it also suggests nonetheless that the outcome was shaped by vigorous racial prejudice, since the jury convicted although the judge doubted that West was guilty. In a similar case, the court clerk in the rape trial of John Spilman of Kentucky noted that the jury handed down its guilty verdict amid great "popular clamor" and the physical presence of Ku Klux Klan members during the trial.[69] "Race prejudice" was likewise cited as an important factor in the conviction of John Wilkins of Nansemond County, Virginia, for raping a six-year-old girl in 1875.[70] According to one petitioner in the case of Thomas Young, an African American from Halifax County, Virginia, convicted in the rape of a twelve-year-old girl of color, the conviction and ten-year sentence were based on "prejudice in the minds of a certain class of men against his race and color." If Young had been white, the petitioner continued, he would never have been tried.[71] After Washington Williams, not yet fourteen, was sentenced to seventeen years in the penitentiary for attempted rape, a petition, including the signatures of justices of the peace and jurors from the case, blamed the court's "hasty" conclusion on the "great excitement [that] prevailed" during the trial. There was even reason to fear for the boy's safety.[72]

Racial prejudice was similarly cited as the impetus for the conviction of an eighteen-year-old man of color from Greenville County, Virginia, who nonetheless received a mere two-year prison term in 1868 for the attempted rape of, his former employer, Mrs. Emiline Chambliss, renowned widow of a Confederate general. Chambliss testified that she has been awakened by "a touch" of some unknown person who then hurried out of her bedroom. Chambliss assumed Hall to have been the perpetrator, but she had some doubts. The staging and histrionics of Chambliss's testimony undoubtedly swayed the jurors. Mrs. Chambliss, whose husband had died in battle, was escorted into the courthouse on the arm of her brother-in-law, in a scene that was a living, poignant emblem of her vulnerability. To further emphasize her fragility Mrs. Chambliss wore a veil over her face that she never removed throughout her testimony. Her interrogation on the witness stand proved even more theatrical. Three minutes of silence passed between the first question posed by the prosecuting attorney and Chambliss's response. Hall stood no chance: in addition to lacking legal representation, according to one observer "the jury beyond all doubt was prejudiced against him on account of his color." The jury needed only twenty-five minutes to return a guilty verdict along with a two-year term in the penitentiary. Eventually, however, the interposition of a local

Republican leader and official of the Freedmen's Bureau secured an early release from prison by Governor Wells.[73]

While the lower status of a female accuser was likely to have been considered a mitigating factor—and likewise, the elite status of an accuser was viewed as an aggravating factor—notable exceptions dot the court records. Moreover, by no means was support for the exoneration or lenient treatment of convicted black rapists universal among white southerners during Reconstruction. Lengthy prison terms in addition to death sentences were frequently handed down to former freedmen convicted of sexually assaulting white females, some of whom were middling or poor. John Spilman of Garrard County, Kentucky, was sentenced to twenty years in prison after he was convicted in 1866 of raping Elizabeth Preston, a white woman. About ten years later, however, nine of the original twelve jurors who heard the case, as well as other "leading citizens," petitioned the governor to pardon Spilman, citing the influence of "popular clamor" and the powerful Ku Klux Klan, whose members monitored the trial. Spilman was indeed pardoned, but not before serving thirteen years of the twenty originally imposed for a crime it would appear he did not commit.[74]

For blacks to receive the death sentence for the rape of white females was not at all uncommon. David Crawford, a teenaged freedman, was sentenced to hang for the rape of a nine-year-old white girl from Lynchburg, Virginia, though he was pardoned.[75] An African American from Gaston County, North Carolina, also was sentenced to hang for the rape of a fourteen-year-old white girl.[76] In 1866, after an Alabama freedman allegedly assaulted a young white child with intent to ravish, a court found him guilty and sentenced him to die. An appeal to the state's high court failed to save him.[77]

Death also came to some alleged black rapists of white women at the hands of white mobs, certainly more frequently than before the Civil War. Of course, extralegal violence in general increased dramatically during Reconstruction.[78] For example, a superior court judge from Georgia reported an outrage alleged to have been committed by a black man in Dooly County, Georgia. Two poor white girls, aged seven and twelve, had begun their daily three-mile trek to school when they were "waylaid" by a black man. He murdered the youngest child, nearly severing her head with a razor. The assailant dragged the older girl into the woods, raped her, and then bound her arms and legs, raping her repeatedly throughout the day. She later told officials that her attacker tied a rope around her waist, believing that in pulling tightly and compressing a young girl's body, "it causes the body to protrude in such a manner that a rape could be more easily committed." While the attacker was digging a grave in which to hide the body of the murdered girl, the twelve-year-old escaped and reported the attack. The alleged rapist-murderer was quickly apprehended. The arresting party, made up of "orderly, quiet, good citizens," swiftly escorted the accused to the jail for safekeeping, fearing retribution from the girls' family. Two days later, fifteen to twenty men, purportedly including some blacks, descended upon the jailer's house, tied him up, took the keys to the jail, and made off with the accused black rapist-murderer. They hanged him about a mile from the jail.[79] The presence of blacks in the mob suggests that what fueled community outrage was not merely the sexual assault of white females by a black male but rather the heinous nature of the crime—the attack on girls so young, including the murder of the younger one.

Attacks on young, white girls in particular spawned vigilante justice. After a judge in Georgia found insufficient evidence to hold over an African American man, Charles Clarke, for the rape of a white school girl, a mob of about fifty men stormed the jail and murdered him.[80] Similarly, Archie Beevee (or Beebee), a freedman from Fayetteville, North Carolina, was murdered in 1867 while in custody for the assault on Elmira Massey, daughter of a Confederate veteran who died at the Battle of Gettysburg.[81] And one thousand spectators reportedly watched an African American burned at the stake in Jefferson County, Georgia, after it was alleged that he had raped a sixteen-year-old white girl.[82]

George Wright, in his study of racial violence in postbellum Kentucky, found that lynchings of black men for sexual assault occurred most often when the accuser was a child or teenaged girl. In 1866 a young black man allegedly attempted to rape the six-year-old daughter of his Frankfort employer. The accused was seized from the jail and hanged after the jailer offered no resistance. The local paper commended the vigilante action, believing it was the only way to "stop such outrages, the Freedmen's Bureau, Civil Rights bill, etc., etc." That very month another African American was shot dead near Louisville after it was alleged that he had raped a little girl.[83] The lynching of yet another African American jailed in Kentucky for the purported rape of a white woman came on the heels of a race riot in Frankfort that followed an election in August 1871.[84]

Lethal violence was not reserved for black men accused of forcing white females to have sex. Black men during Reconstruction were at times severely beaten, mutilated, or even killed for engaging in consensual intimate relations with white females. A black man by the name of Williams living in North

Carolina was reportedly murdered for "living in adultery with two old maids—two white women."[85]

Undeniably, violence against black men for purported infractions against white women increased in the years after the Civil War. Some of it was horrendously brutal and savage. But it is nonetheless important to view the lynching of alleged black rapists of white women in the larger context of racial violence that came in the wake of war and emancipation. Rape was not the only "crime" for which whites sought personal retribution from freedmen. Postemancipation racial violence, as numerous scholarly works document, was endemic throughout many areas of former slaveholding states.[86] Black rape was merely one of many alleged infractions to which white mobs responded with violence, often under the direction of organized groups such as the Ku Klux Klan. Scores of African Americans were beaten, intimidated, and killed in the Reconstruction South for myriad "crimes" and transgressions, many of which were simply challenges to the racial etiquette grounded in the slave South. Among the more popular "crimes" for which black southerners were punished were arson, voting or attempting to vote, voting the Republican ticket, belonging to the Union League, vagrancy, theft, threatening to leave a white employer, teaching in a "colored" school, and more generally "putting on airs" or "impudence." One white employer in North Carolina killed a black worker for using "offensive language" and singing "lewd songs."[87] A black youth in Georgia was seized from jail and hanged by a mob for allegedly killing a farm animal.[88] In 1865 a white hotel clerk in South Carolina beat a very light-skinned man of color for merely asking him to hold his bag.[89] Primarily, however, as George Wright has observed, during Reconstruction African Americans were lynched for their efforts to participate in the political process.[90]

In other words, just because whites sometimes lynched alleged black rapists during Reconstruction does not prove that rape took on the heightened importance that it did much later in the century; it does not mean that white southerners were consumed with anxiety about black rape.[91] Rather, in the years after the Civil War, charges of rape or attempted rape were among many charges for which a number of former African American slaves died or were viciously assaulted.

Without a doubt, more and more southerners began to express concerns about how freedom and equality would be defined in the most intimate of arenas, sex. The political and civil rights that black men acquired after the Civil War gave rise to questions about their proper place in the social sphere. Some of this dialogue began to crystallize around ideas of black male sexuality. Some whites became nervous about the potential sexual threat that black men posed in the reconfigured South. Dr. Pride Jones from Orange County, North Carolina, who had been pressed into service by Governor William Holden in 1870 to help rid the state of Ku Klux Klan activity, testified to the "pervasive" fear among poorer white women of menacing blacks. In Orange County "the poorer classes in the community, women who carry blackberries, cherries, eggs, butter, and things of that sort to town to sell, were afraid to go to town by themselves; they would only go when they could form large companies for mutual protection." They hesitated "for fear of being insulted or ravished by the negroes."[92] One Alabamian believed rape of white women to be among the most frequent crimes committed by blacks, right after adultery, petty larceny, and mule stealing.[93] Augustus Wright, former judge and congressman from Georgia, claimed that rape was "a very common crime with the black man; . . . it is vastly more frequent now than it was when he was in a state of slavery. I think we have had more rapes by negroes upon white women than almost in the whole history of the country before." When pressed about the number of black rapes in his own county, Wright conceded that he could not recall a single instance.[94]

Another white citizen of Alabama pointed to the raucous behavior of freedmen as the cause of white women's apprehension of black rapists: "When men who constitute a large majority of the population ride about night and day in a menacing manner, shouting and screaming, it is very natural for a female to have apprehensions of some sort of outrage."[95] Another white resident of Alabama observed, "There is not a respectable white woman in the negro belt of Alabama who will trust herself hardly outside of her house without some protector."[96]

How pervasive these rape fears were we cannot know for certain. But there seems to have been no vast preoccupation with black rape, as there would be in later years. White southerners certainly feared what slaves, unshackled and seeking freedom, might do to them out of retribution. But as Joel Williamson points out, the real fear was of black insurrection, "a massive and horrendous upheaval in which vast numbers of whites—men, women, and children—would suffer and die from the black rage."[97] Fear of black rape would take center stage later.

Debates about interracial marriage do seem to have been much more prevalent, however, and references to "social equality" are scattered in the newspapers and political discourse of the period. Politics at times became infused with sexual imagery as well as preoccupied with questions about whether black men, now equipped with political rights, would demand equal access to white women as well. White racists also feared that interracial mixing would result in "amalgamation" and the eventual obliteration of whites. Of course it did not occur to most that racial mixing in slave times—that vast majority of which resulted from white men's sexual exploitation of slave women—had already created a significant mixed-race population.[98]

The black newspaper *Colored American* called it "the great bugbear of the Southern white man": the preoccupation of white men that black men longed to marry white women. "He cannot sleep for dreaming of it; he cannot eat for thinking of it; and it would seem almost an impossibility for him to do business for arguing and speechifying against it."[99] Indeed it would seem that a great deal of the white South was consumed with the question of interracial marriage and its place in the new South, more so than black rape. Some whites saw only the direst consequences should black men be permitted to take white wives: "The states and people that favor this equality and amalgamation of the white and black races, God *will exterminate*. . . . A man cannot commit so great an offense against his race, against his country, against his God . . . as to give his daughter in marriage to a negro—a *beast*."[100] What does the black man want of the white man, James Pike reported a white South Carolina man asking rhetorically. To "introduce his white daughters."[101]

In granting black men political equality through suffrage, many southern whites feared a descent down a slippery slope, with eventual demands for social equality and the "right" of black men to marry white women. As a delegate to the Arkansas Constitutional Convention in 1868 saw it, black suffrage was the "stepping stone to miscegenation."[102] This line of reasoning, as Jane Dailey has recently pointed out, was not entirely illogical. The debate about political equality and suffrage for African American men had been framed in ideas about masculinity. It made sense on some level to wonder or worry whether "once the black man has been admitted to the republic, is there any way to limit his rights in private?"[103]

Most southern state legislatures responded to the expressed concerns of whites about social equality and quickly outlawed marriage between the races.[104] South Carolina banned intermarriage for the first time in its Black Codes of 1865. Alabama and Mississippi shored up their antebellum prohibitions on cross-racial marrying. Georgia, Virginia, Florida, Arkansas, Mississippi, North Carolina, Tennessee, and Missouri all banned interracial marriage. Prison sentences were common for those convicted under these statutes.[105]

The new or enhanced statutory bans on interracial marriage did little to stem white fears. Some whites, attempting to stir the passions of lower-class whites, predicted, "it is in the poor man's house that the negro will attempt to enforce his equality."[106] The proslavery physician John H. Van Evrie of New York made clear the fate of a white woman who partnered with an African American man: "We sometimes see the disgusting spectacle of a white woman mated with a negro, and instinctively regard her as vastly more repulsive than the negress."[107]

Nearly all the political rhetoric against social equality took aim at the marital unions of black men and white women. Efforts were made—legal and extralegal—to thwart such unions, which were deemed antithetical to a (white) democratic republic. In general, southern whites feared consensual sexual relations between black men and white women, not rape. Even though African American men were in the process of acquiring political authority and power, southern whites appear not to have leapt to conclusions about black men transforming into lecherous beasts. Southern whites had not yet equated black male political dominance with sexual dominance; rather they anticipated that black men with civil and political equality would want the next step—in the minds of white southerners, sexual equality. There is a marked distinction between the voiced fears of southern whites about black men who might marry their white daughters and black men who might rape them. While much of the white South was gripped by concerns about amalgamation, these concerns are distinct from rape fears that would become pervasive by the turn of the century.

For all the increased talk of black rape during Reconstruction, white communities were not convulsed with fears about black sexual aggression as they would be later. In numerous cases, accusations of black rape of a white woman or girl in the Reconstruction South did not elicit the hysterical, violent response that might be expected a few decades later. The conflation of black political agency with black sexual agency had not yet crystallized in the Reconstruction South, though importantly much of the ideological, legal, and social groundwork had been laid during this era. Importantly, white southerners throughout Reconstruction appear to have been more preoccupied with interracial marriage than black-on-white rape. Blacks in general were still regarded as docile and innocuous, though more innately lascivious than whites.[108] A related point is that while southern whites unquestionably became more sensitive to black men's sexuality and perhaps a little jittery about it, they had not yet become wedded to the stereotype of the black-beast rapist. Evidence divined from the many rape cases that made it to the courts suggests that black male sexuality, specifically fear of black rape among whites, never became a "major theme" in the politics of the Reconstruction South, as much

fictional and early historical literature would have us believe.[109] The rape of
white females, broadly defined, real and imagined, as well as interracial sex and
marriage, was indeed becoming increasingly political in some venues. Charges
of black-on-white rape did necessarily become enmeshed in the political im-
broglios of the day, but then so too did many other acts of "impudence"
committed by freedpeople. It is important to see fears of black rape in the
context of so many other concerns about black crime and "insolence."

Before the image of the "black rapist" could emerge full blown in the minds
of southern whites, they had to divest themselves of older, deeply entrenched
stereotypes of slaves as docile and childlike. The two images—one of a fiendish,
lascivious rapist-brute, the other of "Sambo," ignorant, weak, dependent—
were incompatible. Over and over in antebellum rape trials white principals
struggled to understand how slaves could deviate from their expected docile
behavior and rape a white woman. Alcohol, feeblemindedness, the wanton-
ness of the accuser—all aided whites in coming to terms with slave behavior
that did not comport with their stereotypes. For generations slaveholders had
(conveniently) become convinced of the innocuousness of slaves. Thousands
of white men would have been unable to leave their farms and plantations with
defenseless wives and mothers to fight in the Civil War had they believed their
slaves posed a serious danger, sexual or otherwise, to white family members. It
would take a dramatic ideological transformation, prompted by important
changes in the social and political terrain, to dislodge the "Sambo" stereotype
and replace it with one of black men as menacing sexual predator.

The Reconstruction period had not yet given birth to the rape myth. It
would be more accurate to say that the myth was still in gestation, though
perhaps vaguely recognizable. Many of the conditions necessary for its rise
later in the century did occur in the ten years following the end of the Civil
War: changes in rape law, a restructuring of the legal and judicial institutions
of the South, the severance of ownership ties to black men that made their lives
more expendable, fears that social equality would follow black political equality. Yet for all that had changed after war and emancipation, much remained
the same. Some whites, whether animated by paternalism, class bias, or self-
interest, continued to serve as advocates for freedmen despite the loss of a
vested financial interest. Established and respected whites remained deeply
suspicious about lower-class white females who charged freedmen with rape.
Class continued to matter a great deal in the disposition of black-on-white
rape cases.

THE OLD THREAD-BARE LIE
The Rape Myth and Alternatives to Lynching

9

In August 1888, Nash Griffin, an African American from Ocheeshee, Florida, was alleged to have written an insulting note to a white woman who in turn shared the note with other whites. A white masked mob of about forty paid Nash a visit, administered one hundred lashes, and ordered him to leave the county. When he refused, the mob shot him dead.[1]

Police in Alexandria, Virginia, engaged in a shootout with angry whites in the spring of 1897 after police refused to turn over Joe Walton, a black man, who it was alleged had raped his employer's daughters. Eventually the mob overcame police resistance and captured Walton, whom they lynched from a downtown lamppost.[2]

A mob of eighty of the "best people in the parish" in October 1886 seized Reeves Smith, an African American, from a jail in DeSoto Parish, Louisiana, where he was being held for the attempted rape of a well-respected white woman from the area. He was hanged from a tree in front of the local store. The local newspaper decried extralegal violence but rationalized it in this case since the penalty for attempted rape "would only have been two years in the Penitentiary, which is worse than farce."[3]

These stories of white mobs lynching alleged black rapists are familiar ones to both popular and scholarly audiences. They constitute the "usual" response to allegations of black-on-white rape at the turn of the century. The subject of lynching has long held the interests of historians and sociologists, not to mention novelists, with some of the most important and insightful work on lynching having been compiled in the last decade. Studies on lynching have aided our understanding of the psyches of whites, the virulent strain of racism that pervaded the South, and the complicated nexus of interracial relationships. Perhaps most importantly, in the words of the historian Fitzhugh Brun-

200

dage, the recent works on lynching have fostered "a degree of hope that the demise of lynching has emancipated African Americans from a gnawing fear and demonstrates that lapses into barbarism are not irreversible."[4] The lapse into barbarism to which Brundage refers is of course the spasm of extralegal violence that gripped the South between 1882 and 1930, taking the lives of 2,805 Americans, including 2,500 African Americans, 94 percent of whom died at the hands of whites.[5]

Allegations of rape or sexual impropriety figured prominently in many of the racial lynchings. Figures vary widely, but according to Brundage's study, alleged sexual violations account for more than 60 percent of lynchings in Georgia between 1880 and 1889. In Virginia, accusations of rape or attempted rape accounted for about half of all lynchings.[6] But as other historians and sociologists and some contemporaries have noted, statistically rape was not always the most common reason given for lynching black men.[7] The anti-lynching activist Ida B. Wells-Barnett offered that rape surfaced in only about one-third of the region's lynchings in the late nineteenth century.[8] Terrence Finnegan's study of lynching in Mississippi and South Carolina reveals that depending on the decade, between 20.8 percent and 46.7 percent of all lynchings were allegedly prompted by charges of rape or attempted rape.[9] The sociological study by Tolnay and Beck closely mirrors the statistics marshaled by Finnegan. Between 1882 and 1930, the proportion of black victims lynched ostensibly for rape-related offenses fluctuated between 26.7 percent and 40.6 percent.[10]

Thus the vitriolic clamor about black rape belied the extent to which black-on-white rape ostensibly precipitated lynchings. Regardless, rape rhetoric heated up considerably near the end of the nineteenth century. The excuse of black rape was offered up by defensive white apologists and politicians trying to win (white) support in the national debate over lynching. "If it needs lynching to protect woman's dearest possession from drunken, ravening human beasts," roared Rebecca Latimer Felton of Georgia in 1897, "then I say lynch a thousand times a week if necessary."[11] Falling back on chivalric axioms like the need to protect pure and defenseless (white) women, turn-of-the-century southern whites, both men and women like Felton, fanned racism with diatribes about the rape menace of black men. Cole Blease of South Carolina liberally employed similar rape rhetoric as the state's governor in the early twentieth century. "Whenever the constitution of my state steps between me and the defense of the virtue of the white woman, then I say to hell with the Constitution!"[12] "Pitchfork" Ben Tillman, who served as both governor and senator from South Carolina, also tapped into the rape hysteria to garner widespread political support. Tillman justified everything from stuffing ballot boxes to lynching to protect white women, declaring at one point that he would "lead a mob to lynch the negro who ravishes a white woman."[13] The confluence of race, rape, and politics had never before been so shrill, so pervasive, and so deadly.

Given the high-pitched and volatile rhetoric that surrounded black rape and its cousin, lynching, at the turn of the century, and the solid scholarship that has documented racial violence during those years, it may come as a surprise that not all accusations of black rape against white females resulted in lynchings. Few historical studies of the post-Reconstruction South have conceded anything other than swift and harsh extralegal or legal execution of African American men who stood charged with sexual infractions against white women. Given the horrific nature and deadly consequences of the lynching wave, and the outrage shared by both contemporaries and scholars, the focus on lynching is understandable. The story of lynching was and is a compelling one that needs to be told. But just as surely as scholars have focused on lynching, they have missed an alternative story, one that does not always end in the murder or emasculation of a black man charged with rape.

One compelling case that makes this point occurred in September 1881 in Rowan County, North Carolina, after an eight-year-old white girl, Charlotte Ann Klutz, cried to family members that she could not pick any more cotton because her sixteen-year-old African American neighbor, Morris Locke, had "hurt her." Klutz's mother examined her daughter and found her legs and vagina bloodied. The girl explained that she had gone with Morris "from the cotton patch" to fetch water from a nearby spring when, she recounted, "he caught me by the arm and threw me down, pulled up my clothes, pulled my legs open, layed down on me between my legs and I felt him force something into me and it hurt me."[14] A medical examination performed by a local physician corroborated the girl's claim of sexual violation. The doctor's testimony at trial graphically described the bloody tears to the girl's vagina and perineum.[15]

Locke was charged with rape, arrested, and placed in jail, where he remained as his case proceeded through the courts. Despite the complaint of Charlotte Anne Klutz identifying Morris Locke as her attacker and the corroborating testimony of both her mother and the doctor, the first jury that heard the case could not reach a unanimous decision and the judge was forced to declare a mistrial. Locke's attorney took advantage of the mistrial to press for dismissal. That attempt failed and Locke found himself on trial for a second time. The second jury, like the first, proved unable to reach unanimity on Locke's guilt, so the court, rather than declare a second mistrial, convicted on the lesser charge of assault with intent to commit a rape, for which Locke was sentenced to fifteen years of hard labor at the state penitentiary.[16]

This particular black-on-white rape case may strike us as quite extraordinary for the post-Reconstruction period, a time when gruesome lynchings over alleged black-on-white sexual infractions became, in some parts of the South, all too routine. Indeed, some of the hallmark ingredients of late-nineteenth-century lynchings characterized the Locke case, notably the sexual violation of an "innocent," "pure," white female, in this case a child. Conspicuous for its absence, however, is the abrogation of legal proceedings in favor of vigilante justice.[17] Even more astounding is the inability of the juries in the two trials to reach a guilty verdict and the willingness of the second jury to compromise on a lesser charge. The racial composition of the jury, in this case not forthcoming, would go a long way toward explaining the deadlocks. The presence of even a single black juror could account for anything short of a guilty rape verdict.[18] On the other hand, perhaps it was an all-white jury that was unconvinced of Locke's guilt. Given the mountain of scholarship that has carefully documented the wave of lynchings that accompanied the virulent racism at the end of the nineteenth century, how are we to view this case of restraint and deference to legal institutions and procedures? And what does it suggest about the patterns that had emerged and evolved from slavery through emancipation?

The case in some ways reflects many of the trials that took place before, during, and right after the Civil War. First, like most black-on-white rape cases, it ran its course without interference. No lynch mob of frenzied whites stormed the jail. Second, two juries sat through the trial, heard testimony describing a heinous sexual assault on a white child, allegedly by a black teenager, and neither was able to agree that Locke was guilty of rape. As in a number of earlier trials, the juries seem not to have been predisposed to finding an African American male guilty of rape simply on the say-so of a white female. Or if they had been, they could be at least have been persuaded by the evidence to overcome their prejudice. It would seem that these jurors were not yet consumed by the dread of the "black-beast-rapist" that in just a few short years would convulse much of the region.

The outcome of the Locke rape case punctuates other aspects of the black-on-white rape cases that took place throughout much of the South's history. A white female alleging sexual assault by a black male did not universally evoke absolute or unconditional white support. The evidence in this case is fragmentary at best, so our conclusions have to be circumspect. The social standing of the accuser, Charlotte Ann Klutz, was at best middling. She had been sent on an errand by one of her parents; had the Klutz family been one of some means, there probably would have been a servant to perform the chore. We also know that she was a child, but that despite her youth she did swear an oath and offer testimony. While children who testified at their own rape trials, when permitted, could conceivably elicit sympathy from a jury, they risked being seen as rather unreliable witnesses. In this case, it is entirely possible that the court attempted to determine whether penetration had occurred during the attack, a requirement to find for the act of rape; there was a greater possibility that the child accuser might have furnished confused, vague, or even contradictory testimony about the assault. The physician who examined Charlotte Ann testified that in addition to soreness and a tear near the perineum, he discovered that her hymen was gone, seemingly proof that vaginal penetration had occurred as a result of the attack. A sharp defense lawyer, on the other hand, could have argued that the child's hymen had been broken beforehand.[19] An unswayed or dubious jury might have found for the lesser offense simply because evidence on penetration was not conclusive. This was the case in 1877 when a jury in Nelson County, Virginia, failed to find the African American defendant Horace Givens guilty of raping an eleven-year-old girl (race unknown), instead finding him guilty of an attempt to commit a rape.[20] A jury in Hanover County, Virginia, found the African American teen Charles Bolling guilty of raping a white child in 1880, but apparently not without considerable difficulty in deliberations.[21] So while we are not privy to the reasons that gave these juries pause to convict, or to find for a lesser offense when a child charged rape, we do know that Morris Locke's life was spared. We simply do not know why. We can assume, however, that the representations of lecherous and predatory black sexuality had not yet fastened obstinately on the white North Carolina community that heard his case.

The absence of any discussion about the accuser's character or behavior, or that of her female relatives, suggests that Klotz's reputation was not at issue during Locke's trial. Nonetheless, the character and reputation of a number of white female accusers in the post-Reconstruction period were in fact scrutinized, just as they had been earlier in the century. For example, a white female resident of Campbell County, Virginia, filed rape charges against Josh Tanner in October 1892.[22] He had been sentenced to prison for ten years, and after about three years a group of citizens, including jurors and the prosecuting attorney from the case, implored the governor to release him early. Their petition cited "extenuating circumstances," namely that the accuser had been an inmate of the city poor house and that she was deaf, dumb, and uneducated. And although she was white, she had given birth to mixed-race children.[23]

Interrogating the character of a young white Virginia girl later in the century, in 1893, also proved an effective strategy in securing the early prison release of William Watson, a black sixteen-year-old who had been tried and convicted of the attempted rape of a twelve-year-old, Cora McGann. According to Watson's petitioners, the two had argued and Watson had slapped the girl. While McGann's testimony had been persuasive and credible enough to convince the jury of Watson's guilt, subsequent revelations cast doubt on her veracity. One petition to the governor revealed, "Cora has proved herself a degraded creature." McGann, orphaned at a young age, had been adopted by Rebecca Kilby, with whom she lived at the time of the incident. Kilby, some time after the trial, kicked McGann out of her home and rescinded her endorsement of McGann's character, after learning "personally" that she was a "desperate character, perfectly unreliable." Writing just two years after the alleged assault, Kilby doubted "whether the boy made any attempt at anything more than simply a fight."[24]

Some members of the white community continued to scrutinize the reputations of white accusers in black rape cases well into the twentieth century. In 1909 the governor of Virginia granted Daniel Johnson of Albemarle County a conditional pardon six years after his conviction for the attempted rape of a white woman. According to a petitioner writing on Johnson's behalf, the accuser was "one of a notorious Shiflett class from Shiflett Hollow in the Blue Ridge and this colored boy was received and treated in the family as though he was their social equal and while perhaps he made some improper advances to this woman, I have never considered that his conduct warranted such a severe sentence." The only thing Johnson was guilty of, according to the writer, was "a mere fondling of her—without force." As in the antebellum era, the behavior of the white accuser implied an improper familiarity across racial lines, thus warranting mitigation of the twelve-year sentence. White southern women in the twentieth century, it seems, were mistaken if they believed that their whiteness shielded them from questions about character. To quote Lisa L. Dorr, in whose study of black rape this case appears, "A woman's character was never fixed permanently, and a white woman's status as innocent victim was never wholly accepted, even after the jury rendered its verdict."[25]

In a trial over the alleged attempted rape of Martha Hartsock her character was not impugned, but her lowly station in life, that of widow and hired cook, seems to have played a role in the light sentence received by the African American defendant, Mance Cunningham. According to Hartsock's testimony in 1890, shortly after Cunningham was hired to work in the same household kitchen as an assistant cook, he propositioned her: "I like your look mighty well; let's you and me live together and be as one." According to Hartsock, she rebuffed Cunningham, saying that "she had not got low enough yet to live that way with white men, let alone with negroes." A few days later Hartsock was awakened by a "cold hand upon her leg." It was Cunningham, who she claimed told her "he came there to do something with her, and he was going to do what he came to do." The subsequent commotion and hollering scared Cunningham off.[26]

The jury, apparently persuaded that Cunningham had attempted to take liberties with Martha Hartsock, could have sentenced him to up to eighteen years in prison. Instead, they handed down the lightest sentence allowable by law, a mere three years. In spite of the relatively short sentence, Cunningham's lawyer tried to convince the appellate court that the jury had been "actuated by prejudice against the negro because he assaulted a white woman." The defense seems to have suggested that had Cunningham been white, the charge might not have been brought at all.[27]

Southern whites, of course, did at times line up on the side of white accusers in rape cases, closing ranks along racial lines. Scores of lynching cases offer evidence that black men accused of white sex crimes in the late nineteenth century fared poorly, especially when contrasted to black men earlier in the century. Just as importantly, "legal" lynchings, or state-sanctioned executions for black rape related crimes, became much more common in the last two decades of the century. One African American teenager, Charles Bolling of Hanover County, Virginia, hanged in 1880 for the rape of his white employer's five-year-old daughter.[28] And despite one gubernatorial stay of execution pending review of an appeal for clemency, Robert Jordan of Hampton, Virginia, was hanged for the rape of Mrs. E. H. Moore, presumably white, who allegedly "went mad" as a result of the assault.[29] Although Jordan hanged, he seemed to have garnered considerable support from a number of Hampton residents, including two jurors, an ex-mayor, and a justice of the peace, who unsuccessfully lobbied for his release on the grounds of mental instability.[30]

It would be erroneous, however, to deduce from Dorr's work and from the cases presented here that white perceptions about black-on-white rape remained static over the years. While the edifice of segregation was malleable enough to allow many accused black rapists to receive a trial and sometimes to escape death when convicted, anxiety about the black rape threat undoubtedly increased in certain areas and at certain times in the South. Much of this has been ably covered in earlier historical works that focus more generally on race relations and racism, such as George Fredrickson's *The Black Image in the White Mind* and Joel Williamson's *The Crucible of Race*. These works document the stereotype of the "Negro as beast" that seemed ubiquitous at the turn of the century, as well as the chief purveyors of that myth.[31] Familiar to all is the lurking black beast manufactured in the mind and inhabiting the fiction of Thomas Dixon; the image of the black menace threatening pure, chaste, white women summoned by Ben Tillman in his racist rants; the "scholarly" musings of Philip Alexander Bruce, who first addressed the "problem" of the "black rapist" in 1889 and blamed his emergence on the "degeneracy" of a new generation of blacks who had grown up not knowing slavery. What is less well understood is how southern whites, living and working with African Americans day to day, responded to these cultural depictions. Did the images and discourses of the "black-beast-rapist," so pervasive in the southern cultural landscape, resonate with all white Southerners? In other words, how did the image of the black sexual predator play out in communities? The cultural and intellectual studies that have examined the development of white fears and anxiety about black rape, long the definitive authority on the rape myth, need to be buttressed by analysis on the community level. Without an understanding of how individuals in the Jim Crow South responded to accusations of black rape, we cannot know for sure to what extent the constructed stereotype of the black rapist held sway.

It would risk reading too much into fragmentary sources to conclude from the cases discussed above that whites routinely accorded lenient treatment to blacks accused of sexually assaulting white females in the Jim Crow South. But it is clear that there were enough exceptions of leniency to warrant reflection. Nor should it be inferred that white perceptions about the black sexual threat remained constant and fixed well into the Jim Crow era. The sharp rise in lynching for alleged sexual infractions, precipitous in some regions in certain times, presages a dramatic change in the way most southern whites began to view black rape.

That extralegal violence supplanted the legal process in black rape cases with much greater frequency in the last two decades of the nineteenth century indicates a fundamental break with the antebellum period, when mob violence against purported black rapists was rare.[32] The antebellum pattern of deferring to the judicial process in cases of black rape gradually but decidedly gave way to extralegal violence after the Civil War. Whites had chafed under the occupation and control of northerners, blacks, and Union sympathizers who came to monopolize the legal and political structures in southern communities. During Reconstruction, white southerners had grown dissatisfied and disaffected with the criminal justice process, especially when the alleged offenders were black, and began to see "justice" as elusive under the conditions of occupation. Evidence suggests that disgruntled whites retained these sentiments through the Jim Crow era.[33] Increasingly, white southerners were reluctant to allow the courts to handle allegations of black rape, and the threat of mob action regularly accompanied charges of black rape, whether lynching actually ensued or not. In just one of many such instances, when it was reported that Bill Jefferson, an African American from Charleston, West Virginia, was wanted for an assault committed on a white girl in 1887, the local paper speculated that "public feeling against the negro is very bitter, and the probabilities are that he will not be allowed a trial."[34] By contrast, in the antebellum period only infrequently did records reveal local unrest when charges of black rape were leveled. In a marked change, accusations of black-on-white rape in the last two decades of the century often precipitated community disquiet, even when the cases eventually proceeded to trial. Petitioners appealing for a pardon on behalf of William Jefferson, convicted of rape in 1888, cited "considerable public excitement" and "intense excitement" as the likely reason why the jury convicted on the basis of flimsy evidence.[35] An appellant pleading for the early release of William Watson attributed the guilty verdict to local unrest: "There was a good deal of feeling about Gordonsville at the time against the boy."[36] It should be noted, however, that southern communities could clamp down just as hard on accused white rapists for their alleged sex crimes. The attorneys for Thomas Aikens and Robert Cooper of Montgomery County complained that there was "great excitement" surrounding their rape trial. C. A. Heermans complained that "no crime charged against man is so hard to defend [as rape] when the people are excited."[37] He allowed for no distinction on the basis of race. Likewise, George Dodson, a white man from Lewisburg, West Virginia, was held in connection with the assault of Mary Pierson near Buchanon, Virginia, in 1894. Eventually he was released after proving that he could not have been the woman's rapist, but only after considerable talk circulated about seizing him from his jail cell in Fincastle and lynching him.[38]

Southern whites at times grew very impatient if they believed that a black rape trial dragged on unreasonably, or if an accused black rapist appeared likely to have a conviction set aside on appeal. Residents of Wakefield, Virginia, grew restless when an accused black rapist, Reuben Cole, elected to be tried in circuit court rather than county court in 1887, thus delaying the start of his trial from summer until November. According to some witnesses, Cole taunted the locals, saying, "My lawyers can keep me from trial for two years at least." Cole was seized from the jail and hanged.[39] A party of Georgia "White Caps," indignant that an accused black rapist had been released on bond, hunted him down, murdered him, and then disposed of his body in a nearby river.[40] Jesse Mitchell of Amelia County, Virginia, met a similar end, having been convicted twice for an assault on a sixteen-year-old white teenager, Jane Thraves, in 1891. Both times appellate judges reversed the conviction and ordered a new trial. When two years—and two convictions—had passed without a legal execution, locals took matters into their own hands.[41]

Southern whites seem to have grown especially irritated when law officers sought to remove accused black rapists to a less hostile locale for their protection. Willie Leaphat was shot and killed in 1890 while awaiting execution after his conviction for raping a young white girl, presumably because of apprehensions that he might be pardoned. Whites from Lexington, South Carolina, were angered when after his conviction he was removed to Columbia for safekeeping. Public pressure forced the governor to return Leaphat to Lexington. Lending credence to white Lexingtonians' concerns, however, the governor eventually issued a reprieve, citing an affidavit by the accuser admitting that a white man, not Leaphat, had raped her. The very white man named in the affidavit purportedly responded to the reprieve by riling local whites into the lynching frenzy that took Leaphat's life.[42] For many whites in the new South, executive and judicial "interference" after a black rape conviction was anathema to a civilized society. Meddling by the courts and governors "would invite a disregard for law that unfortunately is too common in our state," in the words of one petitioner in 1891.[43] Lynching thus satiated the need for some southern whites to secure fair and swift "justice" in cases of black-on-white rape. In eschewing the criminal justice system, which was deemed flawed by many for its insistence on procedural fairness to blacks, southern whites abandoned a long-standing tradition of allowing accused black rapists to appear before judge and jury. This was unquestionably the most salient change in the way communities received news of a black-on-white sexual assault case.

There were other perceptible and revealing changes in the way black rape was regarded by the white communities in the late nineteenth century, and some of these can be deduced from descriptive inmate registers of the North Carolina State Prison for the years 1885 through 1899. The descriptive registers contain a trove of personal information about all inmates, including their place of birth, age, education level, "color", crime, and dates of admission and discharge. The logs thus list all African Americans in North Carolina convicted of sexual assault. Importantly, though, the registers do not include those men waiting to be executed (presumably a large number of black men convicted of raping white women would be sentenced to die). Nor do the registers disclose any information about accusers, including their race. Nevertheless, the logs

TABLE 9.1. African American Men Entering the North Carolina Penitentiary for Rape-Related Crimes, 1885–1899

Year	Number of Men Entering Penitentiary	Median Age (in Years)	Average Age (in Years)
1885	16	18.5	21.5
1886	10	20	23.5
1887	12	18	23.92
1888	16	26	26.06
1889	11	21	25
1890	15	19	21.47
1891	7	36	30.14
1892	15	20	22
1893	12	18	18.25
1894	17	18	23
1895	14*	20	25.92
1896	15	22	26.73
1897	11	28	31.73
1898	14	23	23.29
1899	16	21.5	22.44

Source: North Carolina State Prison Descriptive Registers, 1869–1917, North Carolina Department of Archives and History.
*One inmate's age not listed

reveal changes in the characteristics of African American men who served prison time for sexual assault, as well as changes in the nature of the sexual crimes themselves.

Morris Locke, the sixteen-year-old African American from Rowan County, North Carolina, whose indictment for rape of a white girl resulted in conviction of a lesser offense, would have been one of the youngest African American males serving time for sexual assault in North Carolina. Throughout the last five years of the 1880s, the average age for black sex offenders was 24.2 while the median age was 20.7 (see Table 9.1). Occasionally even younger convicts were admitted. In the late 1880s there were eight African Americans under the age of sixteen admitted to prison for sex crimes: four were thirteen, one fourteen, and three fifteen. The youngest to serve in the period under study was Harvie Carpenter of Gaston County, who was admitted to the prison in March 1894 at the age of eleven![44] The average age of the black sex offender housed in the North Carolina prison from 1890 to 1895 dipped just a bit, to 22.9, although the median age rose to 22. In the final half decade of the nineteenth century, the average age of the convicted black sex offender rose to over 26 while the median age remain virtually unchanged at about 22.[45]

TABLE 9.2. Literacy Rate of African American Men Convicted of Rape-Related Crimes Entering North Carolina Penitentiary, 1885–1899

Year	Number of Inmates	Literate		Illiterate	
		Number	Percentage	Number	Percentage
1885	16	6	38	10	63
1886	10	3	30	7	70
1887	12	3	25	9	75
1888	16	4	25	12	75
1889	11	3	27	8	73
1890	15	7	47	8	53
1891	7	3	43	4	57
1892	15	7	47	8	53
1893	12	6	50	6	50
1894	17	8	47	9	53
1895	14*	6	46	7	54
1896	15	8	53	7	47
1897	11	4	36	7	64
1898	14	4	29	10	71
1899	16	5	31	11	69

Source: North Carolina State Prison Descriptive Registers, 1869–1917. North Carolina Department of Archives and History.
Note: "Literate" is defined as having some ability either to read or to read and write, as determined by penitentiary officials. Illiteracy is defined as lacking the skills either to read or to write.
*No literacy information provided for one inmate in 1895

While the age of the typical black inmate serving time for sexual offenses edged up by the end of the century, the more telling change in the disposition of those serving was in the literacy rate. From 1885 to 1889, only one-quarter to one-third of African American males convicted of rape or attempted rape who entered prison could read even minimally. For example, of those who entered prison in 1885, 62.5 percent could neither read nor write, and the figure rose to 73 percent in 1889. By contrast, in the next seven years, from 1890 to 1896, nearly half of all sex offenders were considered able to read, write, or both (see Table 9.2). But that trend abruptly reversed in 1897, after which primarily illiterate black men were again being sent to prison for rape-related offenses.

The shift toward the imprisonment of better-educated blacks on rape or attempted rape charges in the first half of the 1890s appears significant in tracking the development of white rape fears, and mirrors larger trends in race relations at this time. In the 1880s the issue of educating the South's African American population had precipitated heated debate. Some white southerners who had their eyes on industrial and economic expansion, not to mention the pocketbooks of northern investors, believed that "Negro uplift," progress for African Americans, would translate into progress for the region as a whole. The race "liberal" and Methodist minister Atticus Greene Haygood, for one, advocated education of the South's blacks under the guidance and direction of southern whites. J. L. M. Curry, antebellum congressman from Alabama, similarly advocated black education and was an agent for the Peabody Fund, which like the Slater Fund that Haygood oversaw represented a northern philanthropic effort to educate the region's blacks. Curry feared widespread black illiteracy, declaring, "Such a mass of illiteracy as we have is worse than a foreign invasion, incites domestic violence, gives supremacy to bad appetites, and is a perpetual menace to the life and well-being of Republican institutions."[46] E. W. Gilliam conceded that black crime was on the rise in the 1880s, but posited a correlation between crime and ignorance: "In the acquisition of wealth and education, the negro, on the whole, gives promise of moderate advancement." Gilliam also imputed greater sexual impulses to *poorer* blacks: "In the contracted circle of enjoyments open to the poor and ignorant, sexual pleasures became prominent." With greater advances in education, however, blacks' "pleasures decline."[47] In other words, promiscuity and sensuality were linked not merely to race, but to class. Not all blacks were hypersexual, only those lacking a proper education. Only the class of poor, uneducated blacks posed a threat to southern society.

Not all whites shared this sanguine view of education and southern blacks. Some white southerners attacked the paternalistic racial benevolence of Haygood and others as ill conceived and dangerous. A few of these "race radicals," as Joel Williamson called them, denied that education would improve the lot of blacks. The "New Negro," symbolizing a generation of black men coming into manhood outside the institution of slavery, posed a serious new threat to the white South. Having come of age without having experienced the moral strictures of slavery, the New Negro, in the view of the race radicals, was reverting to his natural, bestial state. Educating the young blacks only stimulated this primal, evil tendency by holding up false hopes and cultivating a sense of superiority.[48] (No doubt some white southerners realized that educated blacks would be difficult to maintain as domestic servants or field hands. To quote "Uncle Remus," "Put a spellin-book in a nigger's han's, en right den en dar' you loozes a plow hand.")[49] In an apparent turnaround, Dr. E. W. Gilliam of Baltimore came to fear that black education would precipitate a race war: "This dark, swelling, muttering mass along the social horizon, gathering strength with education, and ambitions to rise, will grow increasingly restless

. . . it will assert that power destructively, and, bursting forth like an angry, furious cloud, avenge, in tumult and disorder."[50] John Roach Straton, professor at Mercer University in Macon, Georgia, reasoned that "prior to the war, the negro was not educated . . . prior to the war, the negro was not more criminal than other men. . . . After the war, the education of the negro began and advanced rapidly; but side by side with it has gone his increase in crime."[51]

What had happened since the early 1880s is that the image of the "bad Negro"—illiterate, transient, single, criminal—had dramatically expanded to encompass all blacks, not merely those of lower status. Most southern whites and a number of middle-class blacks alike allowed, as W. E. B. Du Bois had, that "a class of black criminals, loafers, and ne'er-do-wells" had emerged since the Civil War.[52] But as the decade wore on, most southern whites came to view all blacks, not just a small group, as possessing these traits. Thus in the past a certain type of black man would have been inclined to steal, destroy property, and attack, insult, or even rape white women. By the end of the nineteenth century, the moniker "black-beast-rapist" applied universally to all black men, whether educated or not. As Glenda Gilmore has argued, "By positing lust for white women as a universal trait in black men, whites explained away black Best Men's good behavior by arguing that they sought success simply to get close to white women."[53]

The statistics in the North Carolina prison records bear out this transformation. In 1887, three-quarters of all black males incarcerated for sex assault were described as illiterate. But over half of the fifteen African American men who entered prison in 1896 could read and write. The black rapist could now just as easily come from the ranks of the middle-class as from the underclass. For black men living in the turn-of-the-century South, race and class had been collapsed into a single category, race.

Coeval with emergence of an expanded number of black rapists at century's end, as imagined by many white southerners, was the expansion of the definition of rape.[54] The North Carolina prison records show that from 1885 through 1895 only eight black men entered as convicted rapists.[55] In that period 94 percent of African American males incarcerated for sex crimes had been convicted of either attempted rape or assault with intent to rape (there were two other charges: carnal knowledge and the sex through fraudulent means). And 105 men of color entered the North Carolina prison convicted of attempted rape.[56] This is not to suggest that black men were not accused of actual rape as well. Many could have been lynched or executed. They simply do not show up in the documents. Convicted black and white rapists faced execution, as the North Carolina statute on rape continued to be harsh and did not provide amelioration in the form of prison terms as in other southern states.[57] Lynching was the other likely fate of accused black rapists. Glenda Gilmore found eight accounts of black-on-white rape in North Carolina between 1897 and 1898 alone. Four of the men were sentenced to death. Three others were lynched.[58] Disclaimers aside, whites, compared to blacks, only infrequently served prison terms for attempted rape or assault with intent to rape. Between 1885 and 1895 only sixteen North Carolina whites entered prison for having attempted rape or committed assault with intent to rape. One way to interpret the widely differing figures for black and white sex offenders in these categories is that black behavior was more broadly construed as sexually menacing.

A case near the end of Reconstruction demonstrates how some white assumptions about the innate sexually predatory nature of black men had begun to take hold. Alexander Neely, a black man from Cabarrus County, North Carolina, was charged with assault with intent to commit rape. His white accuser testified that while she had been walking along the railroad tracks and then through the woods home to her brother-in-law's house, Neely hollered for her "to stop" and then chased her. She ran, pursued by Neely, until she reached her home, at which point he fled. The jury found Neely guilty of assault with intent to commit rape and he appealed, arguing that the court had mistakenly assumed his intent to rape. The Supreme Court of North Carolina was not sympathetic to Neely's exception. Chief Justice C. J. Pearson wrote for the majority: "I see a chicken-cock drop his wings and take after a hen: my experience and observation assure me that his purpose is sexual intercourse; no other evidence is needed. Whether the cock supposes that the hen is running by female instinct to increase the estimate of her favor and excite passion, or whether the cock intends to carry his purpose by force and against her will, is a question about which there may be some doubt. . . . Upon this case of the cock and the hen, can anyone seriously insist that a jury has no right to call to their assistance their own experience and observation of the nature of animals and of male and female *instincts*?" In the absence of evidence showing intent to kill the accuser, or rob her, "the intent must have been to have sexual intercourse."[59]

While Pearson's racist logic surely resonated with many unreconstructed white southerners, the dissenting opinion signified a lack of consensus on the issue of black men's sexual nature. Judge J. Rodman denounced the majority reasoning as both misleading and offensive: "It assumes that the prisoner is a brute, or so like a brute that it is safe to reason from the one to the other; that he is governed by brutish and, in his case, vicious passions unrestrained by reason and a moral sense. This assumption is unreasonable and unjust. The prisoner is a man, and, until conviction at least, he must be presumed to have the passions of a man, and also the reason and moral sense of a man, to act as a restraint on their unlawful gratification." Indignant at the unrestrained racism of the court, he continued to chastise his fellow justices: "Assume, as the opinion of the Court does, that the inquiry as to his intent is to be conducted upon an analogy from the intents of brutes, you treat him worse than a brute, because what would not be vicious or criminal in a brute, is vicious and criminal in him, being a man. When you assume him to be a brute, you assume him to be one of vicious propensities. If that be true, what need of court and jury?"[60]

The sexual nature of black men, as evidenced by this minority opinion, was still being contested in 1876. Further evidence that whites were divided on the sexual nature of black men can be deduced from the way the white community in Cabarrus County comported itself upon hearing news of the purported attack. The case proceeded to court without incident and through the appeals process without extralegal intervention. Had a substantial number of North Carolina whites shared Justice Pearson's assumptions about black sexual aggression and the threat that black men posed to white women, it is unlikely that Neely would have lived to see his day in court.

As the century progressed, though, fewer whites seem to have been inclined to resist ascribing sexual designs to black actions. Such assumptions seem to have propelled an eighteen-year-old Georgia woman in 1894 to impute sexual motives to a twenty-one-year-old black man, William Denham, when he stopped at her home asking for something to eat. Promising to go inside and get him something, she instead locked the door. Angered at being duped, Denham purportedly broke into the woman's home, from which she fled. Denham escaped, but a posse quickly organized to retrieve him. Allegedly he fled to another white woman's home, where he raped her and injured the six-week old infant she was nursing. Locals seized him from the jail and lynched him.[61] Whether or not Denham actually committed the assault on the second woman, the first woman he encountered assumed that a young black man approaching a white woman for something to eat was really angling for an opportunity to rape her. She broadly interpreted his behavior—a request for food—as a sexual infraction.

Whites in Loudon County, Virginia, in 1889 likewise interpreted the shenanigans of Orion Anderson, a black youth, as an attempted sexual assault. He merely sported a sack over his head to frighten a fifteen-year-old white girl on her way to school. He paid for his prank with his life.[62] An African American male was murdered in 1890 when he merely touched a white female lightly with a switch.[63] As testimony to how pervasive white southerners believed the sexual threat to white women to be, the Methodist bishop Warren A. Candler in 1926 warned that "possible danger to women is inherent in every offense against white women."[64]

By century's end, the black rape threat had been universalized and the definition of black rape expanded, signifying a dramatic transformation in the way whites perceived and responded to allegations of black-on-white rape over the nineteenth century. And as the white South expanded its definition of sexual threats to white women, southern courts increasingly loosened their stringent requirements for the definition of black-on-white rape by backing away from the long-held prerequisite of force as proof of a lack of consent.[65] In the process, the courts withdrew sexual agency from white women. In a number of cases in which white females alleged rape or attempted rape, judges assumed that no white woman would willingly consent to having sex with a black man. Following this legal logic, all acts of sex between black men and white women would be classified as nonconsensual and therefore as rape. The Georgia Supreme Court in 1899 asserted that no black man could assume that "a white woman would consent to his lustful embraces."[66] Senator John T. Morgan of Alabama, a former Confederate general, believed white women to be so revolted by the thought of sex with black men that "the snows will fall from heaven in sooty blackness, sooner than the white women of the United States will consent to the maternity of negro families."[67]

By century's end, few whites entertained the possibility that a white woman could desire a black man sexually. Before the Civil War, they had no such difficulty, especially regarding poor women, although an antebellum white woman motivated by lust, love, or money who partnered with a man of color would be vilified and stigmatized as deviant: there would be a price to pay, some measure of ostracism, for flouting society's conventions. But by the turn of the century race lines had been drawn more emphatically and clearly within the context of segregation. White women, especially poor women, had less middle ground to occupy. Although their whiteness had increased their status, there was a price as well. Poor white women, newly embraced in the racial politics of the turn of the century, had been divested of agency when it came to sexual relations outside their race. The boundaries between black men and white woman, which had been constructed in colonial times to keep the two groups apart, had always been ephemeral, the policing of sex across the color line to some degree futile and ineffective. In recognition of the failed efforts at maintaining racial separation on an intimate level, white southern society fell back on a different tack: deny white women the latitude to seek black sexual mates, not by defining interracial behavior as deviant, as in the past, but rather by classifying all sexual acts between black males and white females as rape. This development was made clear by the presiding judge in one of the Scottsboro trials in the 1930s: "Where the woman charged to have been raped, as in this case is a white woman there is a very strong presumption under the law that she would not and did not yield voluntarily to intercourse with the defendant, a Negro; and this is true, whatever the station in life the prosecutrix may occupy, whether she be the most despised, ignorant and abandoned woman of the community, or the spotless virgin and daughter of a prominent home of luxury and learning."[68]

This rendering of interracial rape differed substantially from that of the antebellum period. A white woman's character or reputation became less of a mitigating factor in the defense of a southern black man on trial for rape or attempted rape than it had in the past. There were exceptions to be sure; the racial boundaries that grew out of Jim Crow were no more impenetrable than those erected in the days of slavery. Still, the judge's observation at the Scottsboro trial reveals an unmistakable conflation of race and class, less recognizable in the Old South where protection was not bestowed unconditionally upon white women simply because of their race. Evidence suggests that poor white females, especially those who flouted sexual and racial mores, may have been stripped of protection when they claimed to have been sexually violated by black men—if in fact protection had ever been accorded them in the first place. Sometime after emancipation, however, poor white women began to receive some of the privileges and honor that had previously been the sole domain of their wealthier, well-behaved cousins. As Jacqueyln Dowd Hall has noted, "the connotations of wealth and family background attached to the position of the lady in the antebellum South faded in the twentieth century, but the power of 'ladyhood' as a value construct remained."[69]

EPILOGUE

In Harper Lee's *To Kill a Mockingbird*, lawyer Atticus Finch attempts to explain how elusive "justice" was for a black man charged with raping a white woman in the Depression-era South, saying: "Those are twelve reasonable men in everyday life, Tom's jury, but you saw something come between them and reason. . . . In our courts, when it's a white man's word against a black man's, the white man always wins. They're ugly, but those are the facts of life."[1]

Finch's South, like Lee's, was starkly divided along racial lines. Whites monopolized power; blacks were victims of those whites who utilized the power capriciously or spitefully. In Lee's rendering of race relations there is no accounting for class divisions among whites, though Finch's liberal stance on race places him at odds with most members of his community, many of them poor or middling whites. For Lee, the white men called upon to sit in judgment of an accused black rapist could not be expected to act reasonably, to listen to evidence and then render a reasonable decision. Their rabid racism would distort their response to an accusation that a black man sexually assaulted a white woman.

For decades a similar perception has dogged cultural understanding of southern justice for black men accused of raping white women. In this view whites, consumed by fanatical racism and believing the white race innately superior to the black, acted irrationally. In truth, for much of the nineteenth century whites were not unified in the ways they responded to accusations of black rape. Unlike the jurors whom Atticus Finch faced, many acted quite "reasonably." Whites, by and large, did not forsake financial self-interest for some vague ideological allegiance. White men, who themselves might have been the victims of some scheming seductress or knew men who had, did not reject their masculine world view and withhold their identification with men outside their race who had been victimized by devious, no-good women. White men who had worked side by side with black men did not reflexively put aside relationships—whether as neighbors, employers, patrons—cultivated over years merely on the say-so of a woman merely because she was white. Contrary to Finch's jeremiad, whites in many times and places in the pre- and postemancipation South did act rationally by lining up with black men accused by white women of rape.

The white slaveholders who crafted letters to governors asking for pardons for their slaves; the whites who interrogated white female accusers about their sexual history; the white jurymen who recommended leniency after convicting black men of rape; white judges who overturned convictions of black rape—these whites were not familiar to Harper Lee, yet they were the nineteenth-century southerners who took part in hundreds of black-on-white rape cases in the nineteenth-century South. They remind us that stubborn subscription to something called white supremacy, as entrenched and lethal as it could sometimes be, was not universal and not timeless in the American South.

Nor would Harper Lee recognize some of the black men who stood trial for rape in the nineteenth century, for not all were so guileless, not all so innocent as Tom Robinson. Black men, it would seem, at times coerced or forced sex from white women and girls. While a fair share of black-on-white rape cases resulted from white women like Mayella Ewall, who "cried rape," some number—how can we know how many?—emanated from genuine claims of sexual assault. And plenty of black men, when approached by white women interested in romance or sex, did not, like Tom Robinson, resist the advances. Despite the danger if discovered, many black men became willing partners in love or lust with white women.

What, then, are the lessons that can be drawn from this study of rape and race in the American South? For one, much recent scholarship of the last generation has unequivocally discredited the dichotomy of race, an analytical framework that purported to explain and interpret the behavior of white southerners in the colonial and early South. Race and little else was assumed to be at the core of people's actions and beliefs. So focused on race, many important works on southern history failed to consider that other factors were instrumental in determining and influencing behavior. Importantly, by embracing a "monolithic perception of race," many historians have neglected the explanatory power of nonracial factors, not the least of which was class.[2]

Nineteenth-century black-on-white cases lay bare vigorous, visceral class divisions, always taut but especially so when white women accused black men, notably slaves, of rape. Class tensions in any southern community may have been submerged beneath the façade of everyday life, but an accusation of black rape always threatened to expose fractious social differences. Rape trials of black men thus had the potential to polarize southern communities along class lines.

Law proved to be a site of great contest and struggle for principals in black-on-white rape trials, a flashpoint for class discord. Poor women, or their male protectors, laid claim to the statutory law to charge black men with rape-related crimes. Thus poor white women, though marginalized in the nineteenth-century South, wielded sufficient power to demand an official airing of their accusations, something women and girls of color, by and large, could and did not do. That power, however, often proved insufficient to secure the execution of an accused black rapist, as prescribed by statute. Instead, competing interests might utilize the judicial process to check or thwart the efforts of a female accuser. A trial aired testimony by white witnesses, sometimes yielding exculpatory evidence that was marshaled by a defense attorney, often at the behest of an interested master. Hence slaveholders were able to curb the power of a poor white woman who charged a black rape. While perhaps unable to secure an acquittal, masters could utilize other legal instruments to obtain a reprieve for their convicted slave rapists. Poor to middling white southerners thus could engage the legal apparatus to secure a conviction for black rape, but elite whites could, in essence, "appeal" such a conviction and circumvent the harsh letter of the law. It was a delicate balancing act and no single class could be assured that the case would ultimately be decided in its favor.

The balancing act of black rape trials faltered somewhat after emancipation. In the absence of slavery, class interests became confused and conflated. More frequently, accusations of black rape elicited a hysterical response often resulting in the extralegal killing of black men alleged to have been guilty of some sexual infraction with a white woman, poor or not. Nonetheless, significant exceptions to the "rape-lynch" scenario dotted the late-nineteenth-century South (and even the early-twentieth-century South), in no small measure because well-entrenched ideas about gender, class, and race stubbornly persisted well into the twentieth century.

While recent historical scholarship has recast the early South as complex and rife with divisions, and has acknowledged the multiplicity of concerns that shaped the everyday life of southerners, relatively few works have challenged the racial solidarity of the Jim Crow South. There the racial boundaries appear so much more formidable, impassable, and delineated. Segregation was the law and the custom of the region; the races were officially separated, the worlds of black and white distinct. But were the worlds of black and white so neatly divided? Or were the newly erected boundaries of the postemancipation South just as fluid and penetrable as those constructed in the antebellum South? Blacks and whites lived in separated worlds, yes, but they continued, much as they had during slave days, to work alongside whites and for whites. Without denying that racial injustice was rampant and racial violence spasmodic and brutal, there were times and places where everyday encounters between black and white southerners were amiable, where black men and white women engaged in sexual congress, whether out of lust or love, and were ignored by white and black neighbors alike. Class divisiveness, and the assumptions that underlay it, did not disappear in the Jim Crow South. They may have been eclipsed at times by racial rhetoric, but white southerners in the new South as in the old were never as unified in race as some have supposed. Perhaps Atticus Finch was less exceptional than we have imagined.

APPENDIX
RAPE, RACE, AND RHETORIC
The Rape Myth in Historiographical Perspective

The American South's hysterical fear of black men as rapists, often referred to as the "rape myth" or "rape complex," is well documented and has been memorialized in the pages of fiction and nonfiction alike for over a hundred years. Two works of fiction illustrate the dichotomy of characterizations that have attempted to encapsulate the rape myth. Thomas Dixon's *The Clansman*, sympathetic to the plight of white southerners after the Civil War, accepted the view that black men were innately barbaric and libidinous. Unable to restrain their animalistic passions, these black brutes gratified their lust by raping young (always young, always virginal) white women whose only recourse after such a heinous outrage was suicide.

This stereotype predominated in the first half of the twentieth century, but was eventually challenged. Authors, scholars, and contemporaries, sickened by the swelling numbers of black men lynched each year, ostensibly for raping white women, launched searing criticisms of the white South in an effort to expose the stereotype as sham, the "cry rape" a ruse. Harper Lee's *To Kill a Mockingbird* was written in this vein and remains one of the most enduring and familiar monuments to the lethal consequences of accusing a black man of raping a white woman in the South. It chronicles the plight of a black man, Tom Robinson, wrongly accused by a poor, disreputable white woman whose rebuffed sexual advances were observed by her irate, reprobate father. Tom's tragic death is inevitable from the start, no matter the exculpatory evidence, the unimpeachability of his character, or the questionable character of his accuser. Because he was a black man on trial for rape in a southern town, justice eluded him.[1] Despite the contrasting messages of each of these novels, implicit in both is the assumption that most white southerners believed black men predisposed to raping white women.

Fictional accounts of black rape could not rival the unimaginable atrocities committed in the American South in the name of avenging the rape of white women. The South witnessed numerous lynchings, many ostensibly of black men who had raped white women, whose only real crime may have been an inadvertent glance at a white woman that extended for a moment too long to be deemed appropriate. As portrayed in both *The Clansman* and *To Kill a Mockingbird*, threats to white women by black men in the South, real or perceived, were often capital offenses. More than likely, an accused black rapist did not even make it to trial. If he did make it to trial against all odds, as Tom did, the outcome was all but foreordained. Either before his arrest or after, a mob, often abetted by local law officials, would seize the alleged black rapist and murder him. The most notorious demonstration of the "rape complex" at its ugliest and most extreme was of course the trial of the "Scottsboro boys" in the 1930s. The nation, indeed the world, was mesmerized by the egregious injustice and naked racial discrimination that Alabama authorities were trying to pawn off as justice. Scores of other alleged black-on-white rape cases that never approached the Scottsboro trial in notoriety dotted the southern landscape.[2]

Americans over the years have shaped their conceptions of the "black-beast-rapist" from this hybrid of popular and historical presentations of the "rape myth." In recent times, two seemingly incontrovertible maxims have emerged. One, underlying Lee's novel, is that all a southern white woman had to do was "cry rape" and the white community would unconditionally unite behind her, demanding revenge. Both Lee and Dixon would concur on the second assumption: retribution was swift and fatal. To be a black man accused of raping or attempting to rape a white woman in the American South was to face certain death, at the hands of either the executioner or an angry mob. The historical and popular consensus has been that these two facets of the rape myth have been a constant throughout southern history.[3]

The rape myth has long been fodder for intellectual and scholarly consumption. For much of the twentieth century, sociologists, psychologists, physicians, and historians have analyzed and scrutinized the white South's preoccupation with black male sexuality, frequently referred to as the "southern rape complex."[4] Regardless of the discipline, these scholars have reached many of the same conclusions about the rape myth, but a good number have been predicated on untested assumptions. Also problematic is that historical studies of the rape myth have typically relied on the same sources, tracts written by well-educated white southerners, whose theories about race and rape have been accepted as applicable to all white southerners, including poorer whites. As a result, almost all that we know about the rape myth is divined from prolific and very racist elite southerners. A final consideration is that the road that maps the historiography of the rape myth has sharp bends and switchbacks that have confounded many unwitting travelers. Historians writing about the rape myth have been understandably influenced by the political and social circumstances of their own times. As a result, what has been presented as historical fact about the rape myth is not always borne out by the evidence.

In his seminal work *Mind of the South* (1941), Wilbur J. Cash is generally credited with invoking the term "rape complex" in characterizing white fears of black rape. Cash, a native southerner, denied contemporary racist claims about the prevalence of black sexual assault, laying greater odds that a white woman would be struck by lightning before she would be raped by a black man.[5] Cash was the first to link the twentieth-century rape fear to the antebellum period. The origins of the "rape complex," he explained, lay squarely in antebellum slave society, which placed the white woman on a pedestal and worshipped her as the symbol of virtue, honor, and chastity: "She was the South's Palladium, this Southern woman—the shield bearing Athena gleaming whitely in the clouds, the standard for its rallying, the mystic symbol of its nationality in the face of the foe. She was the lily pure maid . . . and Mother of God. Merely to mention her was to send strong men into tears—or shouts. There was hardly a sermon that did not begin and end with tributes in her honor."[6] Southern white men, Cash claimed, deified their women, a practice he termed "gyneolatry," which purged white women of their sexuality and made them sexually inaccessible. These same men, Cash wrote, turned instead to slave women to satisfy their lust. Over time, white southerners came to identify white womanhood with the South itself: "What southerners felt, therefore, was that any assertion of any kind on the part of the Negro constituted in a perfectly real manner an attack on the Southern woman."[7]

A work that preceded *Mind of the South* by several years, John Dollard's *Caste and Class in a Southern Town* (1937), was actually the earliest scholarly work to make a connection between sex and race in southern culture. Dollard, a northern white sociologist, spent five months living in Indianola, Mississippi, which he referred to by the pseudonym "Southerntown." He lived among the townspeople, observed, conversed, interviewed, and recorded. His findings were thus based largely on impressions, and despite his intentions he often unwittingly accepted white assertions at face value. Although his purview was southern race relations, Dollard also scrutinized sexual motives, which he saw as underlying the relationships between class and caste.[8]

Dollard's analysis of southern white rape fears, like Cash's, was heavily influenced by the psychoanalytic theories of Sigmund Freud. Dollard studied under Freud's disciples including Karen Horney, and he spent a year studying at the Berlin Psychoanalytic Institute. His work is so heavily indebted to Freud and his theories that Dollard confessed, "The writings and views of Freud have become so thoroughly worked through my thinking that I had rather ascribe to him a major orientation of my thought than cite him as frequently as I would otherwise have to."[9]

Dollard's analysis of the southern rape complex relied extensively on psychoanalytic theories about repression, projection, and the subconscious. For example, in holding white men responsible for perpetuating fears of black rape, Dollard suspected that the white men of Indianola possessed a subconscious "fear of reprisal for the things they do to Negro women." He also posited jealousy as an animating force among white men. White men viewed black men, believed to be virile and especially "capable" in the sexual sphere, as sexual competitors: "The idea seems to be that [black males] are more like savages, nearer to animal, and that their sexual appetites are more vigorous and ungoverned."[10] This perception, in conjunction with the widespread belief in the "dangerous size of the genitalia" of Negro males, magnified white notions of black male sexual prowess while underscoring white male sexual inadequacy. Dollard suggested that white men, unconsciously jealous of virile black men, assuaged their jealousy by projecting on to black males extraordinary sexual potency.[11]

Paradoxically, while Dollard intellectually acknowledged base motives for white anxiety about black sexuality, he nonetheless devoted considerable discussion to black motives for raping white women, thus validating in part the white belief in blacks' propensity to rape. Dollard believed that the rape of white women was not the *conscious* intention of most blacks ("there is no widespread overt prevalence of such wishes"). But, he continued, if the "unconscious, repressed and seldom realized wishes of Negroes are taken into account, it may be that the white caste is correct in this assumption." Citing the "superior prestige position of the white woman and her categorical inaccessibility," Dollard took for granted that black men would find the allure of white women irresistible.[12] Dollard appears to have projected onto black men his own feelings about masculinity; rape as retaliation seemed an entirely logical consequence to him. Revenge, he surmised, seemed the most likely motive for black rape of white women. Black men who could not protect their own women from the sexual forays of white men sought retribution through rape. The "Negro is wreaking on a symbolic member of the white caste the impotent rage which he so frequently feels at the seduction of his own women by white men." Black men experienced constant jealousy and hatred because of the sexual affronts to their women. Dollard undermined his own conclusion that preoccupation with black rape was an irrational fear when he speculated about black motives for raping white women, the fundamental premise of which was that black men did indeed rape white women.[13]

Lillian Smith, a white southern liberal like Cash, expanded on the rape myth in a searing criticism of the South, an autobiographical work entitled called *Killers of the Dream* (1949).[14] Smith had grown up in the segregated South and as an adult became horrified by the injustice and degradation heaped upon the region's blacks. Like Cash, she blamed the exaltation of sacred womanhood for poisoning white minds with the unfounded fear of black sexual assault. White men, she wrote, warned of the "'menace' of Negro men hiding behind every cypress waiting to rape 'our' women."[15] Also like Cash, Smith laid the origins of the rape myth at the doorstep of antebellum slave society. Because of the deified, desexualized status of white women, white men had turned to slave women to satisfy their sexual urges: "The more trails the white man made to backyard cabins, the higher he raised his white wife on her pedestal when he returned to the big house. The higher the pedestal, the less he enjoyed her whom he had put there."[16]

Thus the earliest analysts of the southern "rape complex" diagnosed the phenomenon as the consequence of large-scale sexual and psychological dysfunction, a direct legacy of slavery. Central to their arguments was the adulation of white womanhood as well as white male jealousy of black sexual virility. What became obvious for a generation steeped in Freudian psychoanalytic theory was that the white South had been plagued by a "rape complex." Analysts of the South, utilizing the psychoanalytic tools and methodology of Freud, put both black and white southerners on the couch. The first historical treatment of the southern rape complex borrowed heavily from these earlier studies of Cash and Dollard.[17]

The relationship between sex and race was at long last examined anew in a major historical work in 1968. Winthrop D. Jordan, through his massive and much revered work *White over Black*, offered the first real intellectual and historical insight into the complex relationship between whites' sexual anxiety and race. Jordan expanded upon the work of the "Cash school" by grafting its ideas onto the historical treatments of slavery and race. Cash's ideas on white womanhood, for example, were developed and elaborated upon by Jordan, who traced the glorification of white women to early English efforts to populate and colonize New World settlements. Jordan wrote that "white women were, quite literally, the repositories of white civilization. White men tended to place them protectively upon a pedestal and then run off to gratify their passions elsewhere."[18] Jordan theorized that guilt-ridden white men who sexually exploited slave women and who were jealous of presumed black male potency projected their own sexual desires onto slave men, in the process creating an irrational fear of black male sexuality. "It is not we, but others, who are guilty. It is not we who lust, but they."[19] The white image of black males as sexual beasts was further enhanced, Jordan argued, by the association of the black male with superhuman sexual potency, a perception that had its origins long before the colonization of the New World. The earliest English encounters with Africa and Africans firmly implanted racist notions about bestiality and licentiousness onto the minds of Englishmen. By coincidence, the discovery of the African and the ape simultaneously sparked the imaginations of curious Europeans. Englishmen wedded these early impressions of Africans to the particulars of slavery. In the slave South, partial nudity resulting from ill-fitting clothing, gossip about penis size, and divergent codes of sexuality between white southerners and their African slaves further fueled white beliefs about black licentiousness.[20]

Jordan's conjectures on the ties between race and sex have had an enormous influence on studies of southern and race history. Later historians took their Freudian cue from *White over Black* and expanded upon projection as the cornerstone of the rape complex. Furthermore, they built upon Jordan's contention that white views about black male sexual potency existed during slavery, perpetuating the assumption that white fears of black ravishment pervaded southern society before the Civil War. The fear, Earl Thorpe argued, was "not of the slave's barbarism, but of his revenge." Thorpe continued, "The slave was feared as an apparition lurking outside the white man's door, or peeping and leering at the keyhole or window, ready to wreak havoc and destruction."[21] Lawrence Friedman hypothesized that as white slaveholders recalled how they "craved interracial affairs, many of them probably projected their desires upon black bondsmen: as they desired Negro females, black males could seek revenge by assaulting white women."[22] Peter Wood saw broad societal implications of the rape myth in colonial South Carolina. "The increasing white obsession with physical violation . . . must be taken as an integral part of the white minority's struggle for social control. . . . Slaves were becoming a more numerous and distinctive group, and their very real efforts toward social and economic self assertion prompted the anxious white minority to fantasies of ravishment."[23]

Attesting to the staying power of Jordan's theories on white perceptions about black male sexuality is the more recent work by Peter Bardaglio in which he claims that antebellum white southerners, "both inside and outside the legal system, widely shared the belief that black men were obsessed with the desire to rape white women."[24]

A number of historians have also perpetuated the idea that black rape of white women in the antebellum South, as in the period after the war, was perceived as especially heinous and precipitated the same vitriolic response in retribution: lynching. "It goes almost without saying," wrote Bertram Wyatt-Brown, "that the penalty for a slave who dared lust after white women's flesh was castration, first by the law of the slave code, later by community justice alone."[25] Generalizations such as this one presume that nineteenth-century southerners were animated purely, if not solely, by race, that all white citizens, acting in response to their own whiteness, automatically rallied around a white woman accusing a black man of rape. Such an approach minimizes the complexities in the lives of these people and reduces them to one-dimensional caricatures.

The powerful and long-lasting influence of Cash, Jordan, and their followers on race and sex cannot be overstated. Later scholars from the field of history, as well as in other disciplines, have deferred to these figures as the definitive authorities on race and sex in the American South. As important as their groundbreaking works have been to students of race, however, some aspects merit critical reassessment.

Most fundamentally, these scholars have projected postbellum assumptions into colonial and antebellum southern culture, in the process finding widespread sexual anxiety where in fact it did not exist.[26] Observers of a South steeped in fears of black men as sexual aggressors, they found it nearly impossible to imagine a time in the region's history when whites did not fear the "black beast."

A spate of recent works specifically on sexuality and race in the Old South has done much to discredit assertions that the antebellum South was rife with white anxiety about black rape. Martha Hodes's *White Women, Black Men* disputes claims that white fear of rape was universal among southern whites. By examining various contexts in which black men and white women were intimate, whether through marriage, adultery, or premarital sex, Hodes persuasively challenges claims by Jordan and others that such encounters would likely have resulted in retribution by a unified white community. Rather than find that white communities were repulsed by interracial sexual relationships and intolerant of them, Hodes documents numerous instances when white citizens tolerated illicit acts that would have precipitated a harsh and swift response by whites had they occurred in the early twentieth century.

Writing elsewhere about black-on-white rape in the antebellum period, my work has shored up Hodes's claims. I traced the reaction of southern whites to charges of black rape and found that the typical response was restrained and deferential to the judicial process; lynching of accused black rapists in the antebellum era was in fact rare in contrast to the late nineteenth century, when fears of black sexual aggression were rampant. In many cases I demonstrated that whites were quite divided, often along class lines, by accusations of black rape. White elites frequently sided with their slaves who stood accused of rape, denigrated the character of poor white accusers, and utilized the legal apparatus to exonerate their slaves. Failing that, they often mounted aggressive petition campaigns to appeal for gubernatorial pardons, in the process smearing the reputation of the white female accusers. The work of Hodes and others on similar topics, as well as my own, lays bare the fluidity and diversity of white attitudes about sexual relations between white women and black men. This diversity was not taken into account in the analysis of Jordan and many who followed his lead, or was perhaps dismissed as consisting of pesky but insignificant exceptions. Antebellum white southerners tolerated sexual congress between black men and white women as long it was not flaunted. More recent research, focusing specifically on race and sexuality in the South, has definitively debunked two long-held assumptions about sex and race in the Old South. First, the rigid taboo against interracial sex (specifically sex between black men and white women) was not present with the introduction of slavery, as Jordan claimed, but rather evolved over time in response to the emancipation of slaves and the granting of political agency to black men. And second, sex between women and black men, despite harsh statutes prohibiting it, was not so remarkable, not so extraordinary after all. Indeed, recent scholarship documents widespread examples of interracial sexual relationships that belie white fears of black male sexuality.[27]

Another implicit assumption embraced by Jordan and others was that white females in southern society were passionless. Because southern elites deified their women, they effectively cordoned them off from sex, psychologically forcing white men to bed their slaves. And because white men could not freely enjoy sex with white women, they imagined that these white women were lusted after by black men. But this presumed frigidity of southern elite women has come under considerable challenge in recent years. Letters and diaries written by southern women suggest that southern elite women certainly embraced sexuality, or at least did not shy away from it. Elizabeth Fox-Genovese, for one, clarifies an important point. She claims that neither the conventions of ladyhood nor the male code of honor, frequently offered up to explain southern women's aversion to sex, denied female sexuality: "Slaveholding culture emphasized control of female sexuality; it did not deny its existence." To the contrary, the diaries and letters of slaveholding elite women convey the passion and joy that these women experienced and longed for in loving relationships with their husbands.[28] Jacquelyn Dowd Hall also has assailed those historians who have accepted as fact the presumed lack of passion among women of the Old South. Such a position, she argues, assumes that "white women were bad lovers and white southerners had bad sex."[29]

If we look at the arguments of Jordan and Cash anew, equipped with the findings of recent scholarship, they lose their plausibility. If white women were sexually active, there was no compelling reason for white men to turn to slaves for sex (though certainly many did), no reason to project their own sexual desires onto black men. Furthermore, knowledge that sexual relations between white women and black men were far more common in the antebellum South than previously thought, and that those relationships (or dalliances) were frequently tolerated by white neighbors, casts suspicion on claims that whites were overwhelmed with worry about black sexual aggression.

It is curious that twentieth-century historians have found sexual anxiety about black rape among antebellum white southerners when white southerners themselves writing after the war did not. The late-nineteenth-century radical racists who argued against educating and enfranchising blacks, so as not to exacerbate the "race problem," tended to romanticize the relations between slave and master. Turn-of-the-century men and women of letters often denied that slaves of the Old South had posed any sexual threat to white women. Animated by perceived changes in the "New Negro," increases in the black population, and a growing political threat, many authorities of the late nineteenth century and the early twentieth waxed nostalgic about the cross-racial plantation family.[30]

Central to the reasoning of turn-of-the century race commentators was the denial that slaves of the Old South had posed a sexual threat to white women. White mistresses did not fear slave men then because of "the natural trust and affection subsisting between the two races."[31] During the antebellum era, these southern apologists argued, illiterate, unschooled blacks rarely raped white women. Even during the Civil War, when white male protectors were away from the plantation, women had nothing to fear when left alone with their male slaves. Henry McHattan had grown up on a Louisiana plantation where, he reminisced, "there was no lock between any Negro and my mother's bedroom. My father was often absent. During the war there were thousands of white women on isolated plantations alone under the care of the slaves for months, and even years. Many women made trips through the country day and night alone in charge of Negro drivers. If this trust was ever betrayed, I have never heard of it."[32] Dr. Hunter McGuire of Richmond prefaced his remarks about blacks' "sexual perversion" with his belief that before "the late War between the States, a rape by a Negro of a white woman was almost unknown."[33] Atticus Haygood could recall but a single case of such a crime before the war, and that offender was burned.[34] W. Cabell Bruce proffered that during the Civil War, "and for many years after the war, unsettled as some of these years were, [the black man] was rarely known to violate a white woman."[35]

Even early-twentieth-century historians were seduced by this romanticizing of the Old South Negro. Walter Fleming recorded it as historical fact: "In no known instance was the trust [by the slave's master] misplaced. There was no insubordination among the negroes, no threat of violence. . . . Women and children felt safer then, when nearly all the white men were away, than they have ever felt since among free negroes."[36]

If slavery was not the cradle of the "black-beast-rapist," as these contemporaries claimed, then when did the myth emerge, according to white southerners? If male slaves who had lived in familial and spatial intimacy with white women, at times in the absence of white men, posed no sexual threat, what accounts for their transformation into ravishers? Many of the radical racists from the turn of the century placed the origins of the black "rape problem" in Reconstruction. Myrta Lockett Avary, for one, squarely blamed northern interlopers for the perceptible change in African Americans' demeanor and for the rise in cases of black-on-white rape, which was "a development of a period when the negro was dominated by political, religious and social advisors from the North, and by the attitude of the northern press and pulpit. It was practically unknown in wartime, when negroes were left on plantations as protectors and guardians of white women and children."[37]

Avary's was not a lone voice in blaming the South's race "problems" on hated Reconstruction policies. Fiction too began to mimic such contemporary reminiscences, and finding a very receptive audience, helped perpetuate the stereotype of the naïve freedman duped by northern interlopers into believing that "social equality" was a well-deserved complement to political equality.

The Reconstruction novel became a popular new genre in American fiction at the turn of the century outside as well as within the South. Sympathetic to the white South, hopelessly didactic, steeped in racial stereotypes, and casting scalawags and carpetbaggers as despicable and carnivorous, the novels portrayed freedmen as lustful, gullible, and easily manipulated. Well-meaning but disillusioned northerners fell victim to their own misguided racial good will. And nary a Reconstruction novel failed to have a climactic scene in which a savage, beastlike freedman raped a young, virtuous, white maiden, who if she survived would suffer "a fate worse than death."

One of the first of these novels was *Smoking Flax* (1897), by Hallie Erminie Rives of Kentucky. In the story Elliott Harding, a southerner by birth relocated to the North as a child, returns to his family homestead after the war and is deeply disturbed by the deplorable state of race relations in the region, particularly the outbreak of lynching. At one point he finds himself engaged in a debate about lynching with a native who chides, "When the sanctity of woman is violated, man, if he be, cannot but choose to avenge it."[38] Southern masculinity was thus contingent upon a man's willingness to defend womanly virtue and honor by taking the life of the black offender. Women's roles are carefully scripted throughout the work. Women are repeatedly urged to exercise caution and rely on their men for protection. Only foolhardy women flout convention and local custom. One such reckless woman in *Smoking Flax*, described as having a "spirit of independence," fails to heed the locals' warnings against unchaperoned visits and is later found murdered.[39]

In keeping with contemporary reminiscences of slavery that idealized relations between master and servant, one member of the local elite in *Smoking Flax* lauded the slaves' loyalty during the war: "Mid the stormy scenes a quarter of a century ago, when the bugle called the sons of the south to war, they went, leaving their wives, mothers, children and homes in the hands of slaves who, though their personal interests were on the other side, were true to their trust, protected the helpless women and children . . . and never one raised an arm to molest the helpless."[40] The description further served to highlight the change in the "New Negro" since emancipation.

Despite the sage advice of native white southerners, Elliott continues to reject traditional race and gender conventions. He finds himself enamored with a young southern maiden whom he sets out to make his bride. Three weeks before their wedding, Elliott travels north to seek support for a school that he proposes to build for southern blacks. Elliott arrives back in town to hear news of a mob forming to lynch a local no-good Negro, Ephraim Cooley. Unaware of Cooley's crime and true to his misguided humanitarianism, Elliott rushes off to the jail to foil the mob's plans. Not until he gets there does he learn that the black man sought by the mob was the one accused of raping and murdering his beloved Dorothy, whom Elliott had left behind alone and unprotected. Distraught and in shock, Elliott nonetheless sticks to his principles and allows official justice to take its course. Justice, however, is cruelly delayed by a defense request for a continuance, which is granted. When the trial resumes a guilty verdict is returned, only to be thwarted again by a dramatic, last-minute stay by the governor. Anxious and conflicted, Elliott can no longer restrain his masculine impulse to avenge the honor of his deflowered, dead fiancée: he races to the train that is about to whisk Ephraim Cooley to a safe haven and shoots him through the heart. The reader is left to conclude that justice has indeed been served, and Elliott's misplaced humanitarianism is remedied.

The year after *Smoking Flax* was published, *Red Rock*, another Reconstruction novel, appeared. The author, Thomas Nelson Page, borrowed heavily from contemporary accounts of Reconstruction. In *Red Rock*, nefarious scalawags and carpetbaggers seize control of the political apparatus and use their positions to confiscate property of loyal white southerners who cannot afford the high taxes they are now required to pay by the illegitimately elected officials. Honorable white men who served in the war are forced to flee or risk being jailed on trumped-up charges. The "black-beast-rapist" in the novel is Moses, a freedman turned preacher whose repulsive appearance is likened to that of a "reptile" and "beast." He happens upon Ruth, a young northern woman, who like Elliott in *Smoking Flax* disapproves of white southern vigilante justice, is aghast at reports of the Ku Klux Klan, and ignores local advice not to go off alone. Flouting the wise advice of southern whites, Ruth predictably encounters a menacing, lurking Moses; he runs off, frightened by the approach of Steve, a southern man of honor who comes to the rescue before the unthinkable can happen. Although Moses eludes the authorities he is lynched several years later, and once again, justice is served.[41]

Perhaps no author was more successful in writing Reconstruction novels than Thomas Dixon.[42] One prominent historian has claimed that Dixon "probably did more to shape the lives of modern Americans than have some Presidents."[43] Like other authors of the genre, Dixon used literature to document what he saw as the retrogression of southern blacks and the danger of northern benevolence toward them. As in the work of Rives and Page, a black-on-white rape scene is a staple in Dixon's postwar fiction.

Dixon's first novel, *The Leopard's Spots*, appeared in 1903, but *The Clansman* (1905) is better known, in large part because D. W. Griffith transformed it into the popular film, *Birth of a Nation* ten years later. The books have similar themes and caricatures. Both novels laud a proud past when slaves and master cared for each other, and decry the shattering of familial ties by the unwanted intrusion of northern carpetbaggers and treasonous scalawags. Both portray freedmen as lustful savages lurking in the shadows and threatening unprotected, unsuspecting white women and children. And both include inflammatory black-on-white rape scenes as tragic denouements justifying the "birth of a nation," the birth of the Ku Klux Klan.

In *The Clansman*, for example, Gus is a former slave who attacks Marion, a sweet, young, white, southern woman. "Gus stepped closer, with an ugly leer, his flat nose dilated, his sinister bead eyes wide apart, gleaming apelike, as he laughed. . . . The girl uttered a cry, long, tremulous, heart-rending, piteous. A single tiger spring, and the black claws of the beast sank into the soft white throat and she was still."[44] Forever tainted, Marion and her mother, tarnished by association, resolve to commit suicide together. What other choice is there? "The thought of life is torture. Only those who hate me would wish that I live."[45] In melodramatic fashion, characteristic of the Reconstruction novel, the pair, hand in hand, throw themselves off a steep cliff to escape a life of ignominy.

Although casting his work as fiction, Dixon relied heavily on the political culture of North Carolina for his inspiration. In *The Leopard's Spots* an eleven-year-old white child, Flora Camp, is found ravaged and beaten by a "brute," left for dead. "Flora lay on the ground with her clothes torn to shreds and stained with blood. Her beautiful yellow curls were matted across her forehead in a dark red lump beside a wound where her skull had been crushed."[46] The incendiary scene, according to Glenda Gilmore, historian of the Jim Crow South, came directly from the pages of North Carolina's Democratic newspapers, which reported a similar scene in 1898 in Concord. Gilmore asserts that it was virtually impossible to extricate racist propaganda, fiction in its own right, from fact at the turn of the century. White supremacist campaigns for disfranchisement and segregation carried the day. The press bombarded the South with stories about black criminality, including black-on-white-rape. The typical literate southerner, even if he or she read few books, could not escape daily accounts of black crime in the newspapers.[47]

This curious melding of fiction and political propaganda soon received validation as historical fact by professional historians. The best-known and influential of these Reconstruction historians was William Archibald Dunning, who taught at Columbia University from 1886 to 1922. Dunning and his students, collectively called the "Dunning school," incorporated popular perceptions about Reconstruction into the history books. The period, they wrote, was characterized by misrule and corruption at the hands of fiendish scalawags and carpetbaggers who manipulated childlike freedmen by holding out the plums of suffrage and political equality. Self-serving radical Republicans from the North, lacking firsthand experience with large numbers of blacks, committed a grave mistake in granting political rights to southern freedmen, because their doing so gave blacks unrealistic expectations about their future and ultimately led to aspirations for social equality with whites.[48]

In *Reconstruction, Political and Economic, 1865–1877* (1907), Dunning traced the tragic path from freedom to social chaos for "the mass of barbarous freedmen." The cruel promise of political equality gave blacks delusions about social equality: "With civil rights and political power, not won, but almost forced upon him, [the southern Negro] came gradually to understand and crave those more elusive privileges that constitute social equality. . . . It played a part . . . in the hideous crime against white womanhood which now assumed new meaning in the annals of outrage."[49]

Dunning's most influential student was Walter L. Fleming, who like his mentor portrayed the Reconstruction South as lawless and governed by ne'er-do-well whites and inept or nefarious blacks. Negroes were "poisoned against their former masters by listening to lying whites" from the North. After the war, Fleming wrote, "the worst class of negroes . . . [became] insolent and violent in their newfound freedom. Murders were frequent, and outrages upon women were beginning to be heard of."[50] Fleming explained that as the restraints of slavery had been removed, blacks fell into criminality. "The crime of rape became common, caused largely, the whites believed, by the social equality theories of the reconstructionists."[51]

Two decades later historical treatments of Reconstruction continued to follow the lead of William Dunning. In *The Tragic Era* (1929) Claude G. Bowers reiterated these themes and representations, including the freedman as a new, menacing sexual threat. Freedom for the slaves, he wrote, meant the freedom to indulge in sexual promiscuity. With these newly freed slaves, "armed and in easy reach of liquor, the shadow of an awful fear rested upon the women of the communities where they were stationed."[52]

Bowers, like the historians, novelists, and race commentators who preceded him, denied that enslaved African American males had ever posed a sexual threat to white women: "Throughout the war, when men were far away on the battlefields, and the women were alone on far plantations with the slaves, hardly a woman was attacked. Then came the scum of northern society, emissaries of the politicians, soldiers of fortune, and not a few degenerates, inflaming the negroes' egotism, and soon the lustful assaults began. Rape is the foul daughter of Reconstruction."[53]

Thus the myth of the black rapist was validated as historical fact by members of the historical profession.[54] Thomas Dixon's *The Clansman*, the North Carolina white supremacy campaign of the late 1890s, and William Dunning's *Reconstruction* all essentially told the same story: the black threat of rape was unprecedented and it was real.

It was not until 1918 that Ulrich B. Phillips, himself a student of William Dunning, would challenge this sanguine portrait of the sexually nonthreatening male slave. In his classic work, *American Negro Slavery*, Phillips documented 105 cases of slave rape or attempted rape in Virginia from 1780 to 1864, as well as a smattering of similar cases in five other southern states. In doing so, Phillips debunked the myth of the innocuous slave, discrediting the "oft asserted Southern tradition that negroes never violated white women before slavery was abolished."[55] This stance might strike an informed reader as inconsistent with Phillips's well-known portrayal of slaves as docile and content with their bonded status. But in discussing "abundant crime" by slaves, including rape, Phillips meant to demonstrate the benevolence of the southern judicial system as well as the paternalism and humanitarianism of slaveowners. Not coincidentally, Phillips documented numerous acquittals of slaves for serious offenses, as well as a pattern of lenient punishment. Furthermore, he asserted that the felonies with which slaves were charged were generally viewed as "criminal regardless of the status of the perpetrators." By implication, southern jurisprudence was colorblind, with "considerable impartiality to malefactors of both races and conditions."[56]

Phillips's contemporaries conveniently disregarded his important qualification about black rape and slavery. They chose instead to construct a nostalgic, but flawed, myth about congenial relations under slavery that was a useful prop in seeking to prove black retrogression in the late nineteenth century. Denying that black men had ever posed a sexual threat before emancipation became an important tenet of those who argued that a "race problem" was facing the region. Analysts reported that the black population had begun to "relapse" into barbarism. Black rape, implicitly black-on-white rape, was discussed in print in the larger context of increased black crime or as an example of Negro "degeneracy."

The literary piece usually credited with inaugurating the debate about the black male propensity to rape white women was a book written by Philip Alexander Bruce in 1889 entitled the *Plantation Negro White as a Freeman*.

Bruce's discussion of rape was limited to a few paragraphs in which he assessed the current race problem. Like many to follow, he traced what he perceived to be changes in the freedman since emancipation and observed a pattern of deterioration. He cited as evidence an increase in black crime and sexual immorality, coupled with a notable decline in respect for whites, as well as an increasingly "aggressive disposition."[57] Though rape was not the most frequent crime committed by blacks, according to Bruce, it certainly was the "most frightful crime." The black man's tendency toward raping white women stemmed from his innate attraction to women of the white race. "There is something strangely alluring and seductive to them in the appearance of a white woman; they are aroused and stimulated by its foreignness to their experience of sexual pleasures, and it moves them to gratify their lust at any cost and in spite of every obstacle."[58] White women of all classes, aware of this unnatural attraction, "are afraid to venture out to any distance alone."[59] In addition, Bruce continued, blacks saw the rape of white women as a means of exacting vengeance for years of white domination.

There followed a veritable flood of racist diatribes in the 1890s, many of which focused on black rape of white women. The common thread through all the literary pieces is the acceptance as fact that black rape was on the rise. "Why is it that the Negro has become such an habitual offender against female virtue in the South?"[60] "The crime of a Negro assaulting a white woman or female child seems to be growing in frequency."[61] The "alarming frequency of the most brutal outrages upon white women and children have excited the serious apprehension of every good citizen."[62] Atticus Haygood acknowledged the "unmistakable increase of this crime—the assaulting of white women by Negro men." And Walter Hine Page assured his readers that "competent observers in almost every part of the South agree that crimes against white women by Negroes are becoming very much more frequent." These incendiary missives, in many cases written by well-known authors, appeared in print frequently, lending authority and credibility to "the rape myth" among most white southerners—and many outside the South—as the nineteenth century waned.[63]

Popular musings about black rape were seemingly bolstered by scientific studies that set out to examine and quantify the "Negro rape problem" methodically and in the context of a more general trend of regression or decline. In 1896 Frederick L. Hoffman, a statistician employed by the Prudential Insurance Company, published a demographic study tracking racial trends in mortality, disease, miscegenation, crime, and economic conditions. Hoffman claimed that statistics proved blacks to be an inferior and deteriorating race. He compared white and black crime statistics and found that 40.88 percent of all rapists convicted in 1890 were black, a figure wildly disproportionate to the number of blacks in society. Criminal statistics marshaled for Charleston, South Carolina, from 1889 to 1894 produced even more dramatic results: seventeen of eighteen arrests for rape were of black males. Innate sexual immorality, a propensity for crime, and a tendency for the Negro to "misconstrue personal freedom into personal license" were at the heart of the latest wave of black rape, according to Hoffman.[64]

Medical professionals entered the debate about the "new crime." Two prominent physicians debated the nature of the Negro's "sexual peculiarities." A letter from G. Frank Lydston of Chicago to Hunter McGuire of Charleston, South Carolina, no doubt was a fairly liberal piece for its time. Lydston qualified many of his remarks and alluded to the sexual crimes of white men as well as black men. Nonetheless, he cited numerous factors that he believed accounted for the predisposition of black men to rape white women. One such factor was "hereditary influences descending from the uncivilized ancestors." For example, "When the Ashantee warrior knocks down his prospective bride with a club and drags her off into the woods, he presents an excellent prototype illustration of the criminal acts of the Negro in the United States."[65] Despite centuries of civilizing influences, Lydston asserted, such savage ancestral traits were bound to "crop out occasionally." Furthermore, African Americans were imbued with a "defective development . . . of psychological inhibition." Such an intellectual defect, "characteristic of a low grade of civilization," precluded more restrained responses to biologic impulses. The good doctor reminded his correspondent that slavery "merely bottled up the primitive instincts of the Negro race; it did not destroy those instincts."[66]

Before the late 1880s white southerners had certainly deliberated racial issues, but they had not yet identified black rape as a "problem."[67] Southerners had for years ruminated about the nature of relations between the two races. They speculated on general traits of black southerners, which did indeed include sexual stereotypes, but few, if any, of their accounts characterized African American men as sexually aggressive and a threat to white females. Amalgamation and concerns about black aspirations to "social equality" were discussed by southern theorists, yet the black man was rarely portrayed as a sexual beast, as he would be later.

Paradoxically, discussions of "amalgamation" during the 1880s were steeped in denials that interracial sexual relations were prevalent. Nathaniel Southgate Shaler in 1884 noted the "very rapid reduction in the number of half-breed mulattoes." Shaler did not even consider that such mulattoes could have a black father and a white mother. "It is now rare indeed to see a child under fifteen that the practiced eye will recognize as from a white father."[68] "The illicit commingling of white and black blood is now practically over," wrote another observer the same year.[69] Senator John T. Morgan of Alabama concurred: "Amalgamation is impossible, because it is forbidden by the instincts of both [races]."[70]

Whether these learned white southerners were accurately reporting post-Reconstruction social conditions, or merely whistling in the dark, eludes us. But certainly there is no evidence that through much of the 1880s they feared black men as rapists. What, then, changed by the 1890s to persuade much of the region that its white female inhabitants were under siege?

By most historical accounts, relations between blacks and whites in the South during the first half or so of the 1880s was characterized by a relative state of racial calm. The occupation of the former Confederacy had ended in the previous decade, allowing many white southern elites and officials to return to the political scene and vie for power. Political developments on the national scene buoyed white southerners' expectations that friends, not foes, would occupy the White House, the Congress, and the U.S. Supreme Court. In 1883 the Court ruled unconstitutional a portion of the odious Civil Rights Act of 1875. In the following year Grover Cleveland, a Democrat, was elected president. Such encouraging national political events, coupled with promising economic hopes for the "New South," proved fertile ground for liberal race ideologies. Racial accommodation and cooperation fed the creed of "New Paternalism," thus enabling white southerners to lapse momentarily into racial neutrality.[71]

The circumstances that had afforded white southerners the luxury of racial good will quickly dissipated, however, and the temporary truce in the race war was shattered. Shortly after Cleveland took office, he shocked southern whites by appointing African American men to federal positions. More frightening still to the white South were the national elections of 1888, which returned the Republican Party, the party of Lincoln and of southern blacks, to power in Congress and the White House. The newly elected Republican Congress promptly horrified the white South by debating the so called Force Bill, a measure that would have appointed a federal supervisor to oversee elections and make the exclusion of black voters illegal. A white South collectively shuddered at the prospect of federal intervention yet again into its political activities.[72]

These political developments in and of themselves may have been sufficient to forge a bunker mentality among white southerners on the race issue. Economic dislocations as well as the urbanization and industrialization that characterized the period further exacerbated the strain between the races and effectively muted the interracial good will that had been touted by racial moderates in the 1880s. White southerners of all classes began to see the region's blacks as scapegoats for their problems.

Such was the scene when Philip Alexander Bruce in 1889 addressed the "problem" of the "black rapist." Bruce and countless others identified a "Negro problem" emerging in the South. An increase in black crime and effrontery was blamed on the "New Negro," who by the 1890s had grown up outside the watchful eye of a master, unfamiliar with proper race etiquette and lacking the restraining features of slavery. Disorderly, reckless, wanton, barbaric, disrespectful—emancipated slaves had reverted to their original state of incivility and savagery, their natural state, which had been so successfully suppressed by their masters' strict control during slavery. This "degeneracy" or "regression" theory brought forth a deluge of racist polemics that continued unabated through the early twentieth century. As evidence that the "New Negro" posed a credible threat to all white southerners, but especially to women, radical racists repeatedly cited instances of black men assaulting white women. White southern politicians, even suffragists, were quick to maximize the political capital of the rape fear by using it as the cornerstone of white supremacist campaigns. Rebecca Latimer Felton, Benjamin Tillman, Coleman Blease, Frances Willard, and James K. Vardaman were just a few who effectively exploited and inflamed white fears of black men to advance their causes, their careers, or both.[73]

For many white southerners in the late nineteenth century and the early twentieth, the image of the "black-beast-rapist" was reality. Confronted with attacks on the region for its failure to halt lynching, the myth provided the white South with a convenient justification for extralegal violence. If any white southerners doubted the existence of the "black-beast-rapist" they kept quiet. A number of prominent African Americans who recognized the sham of the rape myth did, however, speak out. In 1894 Frederick Douglass countered white musings on the "Negro Problem" by offering up "a colored man's view." In "Why is the Negro Lynched?" he exposed justifications of lynching as a charade: "Now, what is the special charge by which this ferocity is justified, and by which mob law is excused and defended even by good men North and South? It is a charge of recent origin; a charge never brought before; a charge never heard in the time of slavery or in any other time in our history. It is a charge of assaults by Negroes upon white women. This new charge, once fairly started on the wings of rumour, no matter by whom or in what manner originated, whether well or ill founded, whether true or false, is certain to raise a mob and to subject the accused to immediate torture and death."[74] Douglass knew all too well that in the South, any white woman, even "an abandoned woman," had only to cry rape and the wheels of the lynch mob would be set in motion.[75]

Perhaps no African American was more outspoken on the alleged "new crime" among black men than Ida B. Wells-Barnett, a journalist living in Memphis who edited the black newspaper *Free Speech*. In 1892, outraged by the lynching of three black grocery store owners, Wells infuriated the white community of Memphis by suggesting that white grocers, acting out of fear of economic competition, were responsible. Her editorializing on the real motives behind southern lynching eventually moved some white men to burn the office of *Free Speech* and threaten Wells's life should she ever return to Memphis. Wells moved to New York, where she continued to write and lecture passionately for the anti-lynching cause.[76]

Wells-Barnett referred to the increasing alarm about black rape in the South as a "racket." "Nobody in this section of the country believes the old thread bare lie that Negro men rape white women."[77] She cited the behavior of male slaves during war as evidence that black men were not predisposed to commit outrages upon white women: "The world knows that the crime of rape was unknown during four years of civil war when the white women of the South were at the mercy of the race which is all at once charged with being a bestial one."[78] Wells-Barnett cited case after case of black men betrayed by their white lovers, who for fear of vigilant neighbors, pregnancy, or venereal disease cried rape to avoid public scorn. In nearly all cases, the black men were lynched or barely escaped being lynched.[79]

Wells-Barnett worked tirelessly to educate the country and the world to the atrocities that were being committed against black men in the name of white womanhood.[80] She framed her searing critique of lynching in the larger context of white oppression of blacks in general. During Reconstruction, she railed, whites justified violence and intimidation of southern blacks as necessary to rid the region of "Negro domination." Once disfranchisement rendered black men politically impotent and hence negated the threat of "Negro domination," southern whites were forced to look for a new excuse to terrorize its black population. The new excuse became the purported new wave of Negro assaults on white women.[81]

Ida Wells-Barnett, along with other African American women, stood at the vanguard of the anti-lynching movement in the early 1890s. Mary Church Terrell also tried to combat lynching through the print medium. In an article in *North American Review* in 1904 Terrell wrote, "it is a great mistake to suppose that rape is the real cause of lynching in the South. . . . It is easy to prove that rape is simply the pretext and not the cause of lynching." She claimed that 75 to 85 percent of men lynched were not even accused of sexual crimes.[82] A study published in 1919 by the NAACP buttressed Terrell's claims. Among African American males lynched, only 28.4 percent were accused of rape or "attacks upon women."[83]

H istorians of the late-nineteenth-century South who wrote in the years following World War II, sensitized to racial oppression by the Holocaust and later by the struggles of the civil rights movement and the egregious racial injustices that precipitated it, fully discredited the last remnants of the Dunning school. Their work reflects the same critical stance as that of Wells, Douglass, and other contemporary critics who understood that white fears of black rape were both irrational and unfounded. Although no single published study focuses exclusively on the rape complex itself, numerous historians writing on related topics have attempted to offer up explanations for its emergence. These explanations have included the political, the economic, the psychosexual, and combinations of the three.

While contemporary historians do not agree on the causes of the rape complex, most nonetheless agree by and large on when it emerged. In a much-needed corrective to earlier treatments, George Fredrickson linked the emergence of black rape fears to the development of racist ideology, which he tied to important political and economic markers. First, white fears of black political power were exacerbated by fusionist politics, the threatened alliance of white Populists with black Republicans in the 1890s. Second, the New South boosterism that had preached the saving graces of industrialism failed to create an economic boom. White southerners, displaced or disoriented by dizzying economic spasms, projected their disappointment onto the region's black population. Third, a significant consequence of segregation and the isolation of blacks had been to arouse suspicion among whites—What were the blacks up to? Thus the black male became a scapegoat for the political and economic tensions of the period. White southerners resorted to violence, lynching, and Jim Crow laws, all of which aimed at greater control over the region's black population. In an intriguing twist, Fredrickson argued that lynching preceded widespread sexual fears. White southerners constructed the image of the black male as a mad rapist with an insatiable sexual appetite to justify their barbarous treatment of the region's blacks.[84] White southern men, appealing to a universal code of masculinity, rationalized lynching under the guise of defending their women and their honor.

Joel Williamson, like Fredrickson, situated the origins of the rape complex in the 1890s. Unlike Fredrickson, however, Williamson placed greater emphasis on psychosexual motivation. Williamson explained that in the 1890s the southern white male had painted himself into a "sexual corner." The postbellum South had inherited the antebellum deification of white womanhood, and as earlier analysts have pointed out this tended to neuter white women. Owing a theoretical debt to Cash and Jordan, Williamson accepted the gendered double standard for sexuality: southern white women were presumed to be frigid, white men libidinous. By pressing reluctant wives to perform their "duty," Williamson reasoned, white men were forcing themselves on their women. In fact, it was the white men who were the "beasts" and thus found themselves in a psychosexual double bind: if they denied and repressed their sexual urges, they felt tension; but if they acted on those urges, they felt guilty and conflicted. Moreover, southern white men in the late nineteenth century no longer had slave women at their immediate disposal as in the years before the Civil War. As a result, after emancipation white men found themselves shut off sexually from both white and black women. In psychically working through their pent-up sexual tension, white men projected "upon black men extravagant sexual behavior. . . . To paint the black man as ugly and then to destroy him was to destroy the evil within themselves."[85]

Methodologically, Williamson's study rests on many of the same sources as Fredrickson's: essays and speeches by well-read, often well-known, prolific white southerners, who spoke authoritatively on the threat of black rape, painted with broad but unsubstantiated strokes, and claimed, by virtue of their race, to speak for all white southerners. Much of what we have come to know about white fears of black rape is based on this relatively narrow source base. Historians have gauged white fears of black rape by relying on it almost exclusively, declaring that the region's entire white population was gripped with anxiety about black rape. Works like Williamson's and Fredrickson's have not interrogated those claims nor sought out alternative white voices on the matter of rape fears. We are left to assume that these elite politicians, social scientists, and writers of the postbellum era, a sliver of the region's white population, spoke for all.[86] And the impact of the racist literature that perpetuated the image of the "black-beast-rapist" on the uneducated and inarticulate remains unexplored.

In some way, the argument put forth in Jacquelyn Dowd Hall's *Revolt against Chivalry* (1974) is reminiscent of Williamson's work and therefore places her analysis of the rape myth in the psychosexual camp. Her book focuses on the attempts of Jessie Daniel Ames, a white southern woman, to challenge the region's control of both black males and white women through lynching. Like Williamson, Hall grounded the image of the black rapist in the conflicted Victorian age, a time when Americans were preoccupied with the contest between "civilization" and "savagery."[87] The myth played out against a backdrop of clashing values and sexual tensions. "Sexual strivings—rejected, feared, and projected onto others—beat like a 'distracting savage drum' beneath the genteel discourse of white middle class life. . . . No image so dramatically symbolized the most lurid of Victorian fantasies and fears as that of violent sexual congress between a black man and a white woman."[88]

Where Hall parts company with Williamson is in her observation that the threat of black rape not only gave white men a powerful tool with which to control the black population but also proved an effective means for keeping white women dependent on white men for protection, thereby shoring up white patriarchal control. "It may be no accident," she suggested, "that the vision of the Negro as threatening beast flourished during the first organizational phase of the women's rights movement in the South."[89] Hall hypothesized that the origins of the rape complex had ties to a budding feminist impulse. Caught off balance by the emergence of unmanageable and noncompliant blacks and white women, southern white men latched onto the rape myth as the most effective means of controlling the region's blacks as well as white women.

At Hall's insistence, for the first time historians were being asked to look to the conditions affecting white women in the late nineteenth century for clues to the emergence of the black rape fear. In essence, Hall demanded that women get equal play in the analysis of white rape fears in the South. On one level, it is hard to imagine how in a study of such a gendered experience as rape, females could get anything less than equal treatment. But because so many black males were unjustly accused of sexually assaulting white females in the late nineteenth century and the early twentieth, and because so many of them faced lynch mobs as a result, it is easy to see how historians might react empathetically to the accused and antagonistically (or at least indifferently) to the accuser.

Approaching the subject of white rape fears of blacks with such a sensibility, however, has the consequence, unintended I am sure, of ignoring the impact that rape fears had on white women and removes them as significant agents (other than as false accusers). It also imperils any attempt to investigate incidents of black-on-white rape, specifically to entertain the possibility that black men could and did rape white women and girls. In short, the theoretical foundation laid by Cash, Jordan, and Williamson makes it virtually impossible to consider as credible a white woman's accusation of black rape in the nineteenth-century South.

In Cash's and Jordan's accounts of the origins of the rape myth, white males are the dominant players: out in the slave quarters, having sex with their female slaves, then having nothing better to do than imagine their wives doing the same with the male slaves. White women are pathetic creatures who retreat into a world of passionlessness and remain sexually unfulfilled. Williamson's interpretation likewise evokes the image of sexually robust white men, busying themselves searching for no-fault, guilt-free sex. Again men, not women, are at center stage.

Jacquelyn Hall has called Williamson to task on this point and taken steps to distance her own gender war interpretation from that of Williamson on one important point. She has admonished Williamson for projecting his own masculine views onto his subjects and for positing a "universal male sex drive": "I saw rape not as sex but as violence. As a consequence, I read white men's identification with the so called black rapist as an expression of misogyny rather than as a projection of desire."[90]

What Hall discovered in much of the rape myth scholarship was a white male identification with black men as victims. The works assumed that the charge of black rape was fabricated. The black man was always wrongly accused of rape by a poor white woman who, in an attempt to hide her indiscretion, "cried rape" and sacrificed her black paramour to the mob. Scholars like Williamson and Jordan have unwittingly identified with the predicament of the alleged "black rapist." Given the history of black men in slavery and freedom, such an identification is understandable. Nonetheless, it obscures the possibility that black men could and did sexually assault white females. As Hall has observed, the approach of Williamson and Jordan is infused with masculine and possibly misogynist overtones.

What for Hall had become a gender issue was for Nell Irvin Painter one primarily of class. Painter contends that sex "was the whip that white supremacists used to reinforce white solidarity, probably the only whip that would cut deeply enough to keep poor whites in line." Appeals to the preservation of property and wealth were futile if made to white men who had neither. In all likelihood, however, white men of voting age considered their women a form of property and could thus identify with white supremacist rhetoric that called for a unified front in protecting all white women regardless of class.[91]

Glenda Gilmore's award-winning work *Gender and Jim Crow* (1996) builds on the analytical foundation laid by Hall and Painter and constitutes the first major work to consider how race, gender, and class converged with politics to contribute to the rise of white anxiety about black rape. Gilmore argues that poor white women for the first time became critical components of the white supremacy apparatus in North Carolina in the 1890s. She found that the effects of industrialization and urbanization, and the attendant upheaval in gender roles, created a receptive climate for the myth of the black rapist among the state's white population. She also makes a strong case linking the political and economic advances of the African American middle class in the 1880s and early 1890s to the rise of white fears of black sexual aggression. By suggesting that black success fed a desire for social equality, the Democratic Party hoped to drive a wedge through the fusionist alliance of disgruntled whites and blacks and reap political advantage.[92]

But Gilmore goes beyond racial politics to show that racial control was not the only benefit to be derived from Democrats' manipulation of rape fears. She confirms the speculation of Hall that white women also paid a price for buying into white fears of black sexuality. As Gilmore explains, the veneer of traditional gender conventions and roles had cracked under the effects of industrialization and urbanization and had given rise to working-class women who flouted prescribed modes of feminine behavior, a clear rejection of patriarchal dominance. In perpetuating the rape myth, the white South assured its women that only greater dependence on men and restricted mobility could ensure their safety and protection. The rape myth not only served the political ends of white supremacists but reined in wayward white women as well. The nadir of race relations in the South and the zenith of white fears of black rape coincided with challenges by the region's "respectable" women for more rights and greater voice in the public and private spheres, and with challenges by poorer white women whose behavior deviated from accepted norms.[93]

Ironically, the earliest scholarly attempts to explain the rise of white rape fears focused on men, black and white, with the role of women almost an afterthought. Women's historians have forced us to consider the role that white women played in creating the rape myth. Paradoxically, this much-needed corrective runs the risk of portraying white women as passive pawns, duped by white men of all classes into becoming increasingly dependent on their men. Recent studies on topics other than the rape myth itself shed light on how gender figures even more prominently in the development of white anxiety about black rape.

Jane Dailey's recent study of the Readjuster movement in Virginia, *Before Jim Crow*, is an important contribution to our understanding of the origins of the rape myth. For one thing, the subject of her study is the period after Reconstruction but before Jim Crow, a moment, albeit brief, in which blacks and whites worked together to craft "forgotten interracial political alternatives" that historians too often gloss over or dismiss, aware of the harsh and rigid racism to come.[94] By calling attention to a time in the postemancipation South when racial attitudes had not yet hardened, Dailey allows us to understand how it is possible to imagine a time when white anxiety about black rape had not yet taken root. In Dailey's Virginia "before Jim Crow" it is easier to imagine how a black man accused of raping a white woman could have escaped a lynch mob.

Dailey's exploration of interracial political cooperation in Virginia documents the emergence of heightened concern about miscegenation in 1883, after two prominent African Americans were appointed to the Richmond school board. Integration of the school board, Dailey argues, unequivocally established black male authority over white female teachers and students. This inversion of the racial hierarchy laid bare the fiction of the political paradigm carefully constructed by the Readjusters, a coalition of black and white Virginians who forged a formidable interracial political alliance. White Readjusters, in an effort to allay concerns of whites who conflated black political and sexual rights, floated a "separate spheres" doctrine that clearly delineated public and private spaces and rights. Black men, it was imagined, could participate equally as citizens by serving in the public sphere, on juries and town councils. Black men, however, would operate in a racially segregated private sphere.

With the integration of the Richmond school board in 1883, white Democrats, many of whom had expressed fears of "social equality" since Reconstruction, finally attracted the attention of a worried audience, now more receptive to racist rhetoric about miscegenation. Opportunistic Democrats quickly made the leap from black political authority to sexual authority in the setting of public schools. African American school administrators would conceivably interview, hire, and supervise white female teachers. African American men would head classrooms filled with little white girls. One especially provocative political cartoon depicted an African American male teacher spanking a white girl. The sexual implications were clear. Vague allusions to blacks' political and sexual power had been bandied about since after the Civil War but were now infused with potency and harnessed, in the minds of concerned whites, to the tangible issue of schools. As Dailey asserts, the "schools had become the site on which white anxiety about the relationship between political rights and sex rights had been displaced."[95]

Still, apprehension about miscegenation or improper physical contact between black men and white women or girls is not the same thing as alarm about black-on-white rape. Nonetheless, Dailey's periodization—rooting an increasing white preoccupation with interracial sexual contact in the mid-

1880s—coincides generally with the beginning of an increase in antiblack violence in the South, especially for perceived sexual transgressions.[96]

In an attempt to locate the origins of the rape myth more precisely, Martha Hodes builds a case for the gradual escalation of white rape fears through the 1890s, but sees emancipation and the ensuing conflict over the black man's proper political place as a watershed: "Black freedom brought a marked shift away from uneasy toleration for sex between black men and white women, and a move toward increasingly violent intolerance." Hodes roots this change in the "newfound autonomy of [black] men," largely because of the political power they acquired. "After emancipation, expressions of white anxiety about sex between black men and white women reached an unprecedented intensity."[97] Like others, Hodes notes the precipitous rise of white-on-black violence, much of it sexual in nature, leading her to conclude that politics during Reconstruction had become "sexualized."[98] Sex and race had become irretrievably political. Hodes offers evidence of testimony from a congressional investigation in 1871 into racial violence in the immediate postbellum years that is replete with accounts of white retribution for perceived sexual infractions by black men. The dialogue that emerged from this hearing, Hodes argues, "differed markedly from the neighborhood conversations about sex between black men and white women that had come to pass in antebellum communities."[99]

For Hodes, Reconstruction, specifically emancipation, abruptly ends a long-standing antebellum tradition of white toleration of interracial sex, and with it, moderate or even lenient treatment of blacks accused of white rape. But this conclusion is somewhat misleading, in large measure because Hodes has shifted her focus from local community records in the antebellum era to primarily government records after the Civil War. In a way, her conclusion is predetermined by the nature of her sources. The subject of the congressional investigation is the violence of the Ku Klux Klan, which of course was responsible for some of the most atrocious acts of racial terrorism in the postwar South. Accounts of ordinary or restrained white responses to allegations of black rape, decidedly not what the KKK was accused of, were not likely to be recounted for the committee. Unmolested interracial couples, for the most part, are not going to show up in these records. Hodes may be correct in arguing for pervasive white anxiety about black rape during Reconstruction, but her evidence does not allow us to make that leap.

Having situated the "newly alarmist set of ideas about sex between black men and white women" squarely in the postbellum South, Hodes demonstrates that white anxiety about black rape, which emerged explosively during Reconstruction, continued to increase until it reached hysterical proportions at century's end.[100] Here Hodes collapses the time between the end of Reconstruction and the beginning of Jim Crow, as if drawing a seamless line from Reconstruction through the lynching craze. In this regard Hodes departs from the periodization laid out by Williamson, who grounded the rape myth's origins in the 1890s, following a decade of relative calm in racial matters in the South, and overlooks the more racially tolerant era "before Jim Crow" described by Dailey. The evidence that Hodes marshals, though, buttresses her claim. The cases that she interrogates demonstrate that southern whites increasingly responded with violence and intolerance to allegations of black-on-white sex, including rape. Yet a disproportionate amount of attention is paid to the rhetoric of black rape and to the more notorious cases of lynching, leaving us still unsure how whites living in southern communities dealt with accusations of black rape.

The 1890s were one of the most tumultuous decades in American history on competing and overlapping fronts. Race politics reached a fever pitch in the South, as populism mounted a viable, biracial, lower-class challenge to white Democratic rule. Disfranchisement and segregation became institutionalized throughout the South as white race "liberals" were drowned out by radical racists. Economic dislocations wrought anxiety as farmers lost their land and then migrated to mill towns where for the first time they encountered wage labor. Cheaper black labor cultivated ire and jealousy among poor white laborers and farmers. Fathers suffered the loss of patriarchal authority as daughters moved into factory work. A cacophony of tensions over class, gender, and race roles emanating from severe economic dislocation resounded all over the country. Historians have long debated which of these factors was most directly responsible for the rise in the white South's rape fears.

In the context of a larger study on crime and punishment in the nineteenth-century South, Edward Ayers in his book *Vengeance and Justice* (1984) grappled with the causes of the rape fear and the outbreak of lynching and racial violence in the late 1880s and early 1890s. Ayers assessed various theories on the origins of the rape complex. He astutely pointed out that many of the ingredients often cited as causes of white rape fears had been present throughout much of the South's earlier history: racism, poverty, political conflict, irrational white fears. Contending that "whites had long associated blacks with sexuality," Ayers is right to suspect that something unique about the period was at the root of the rape complex. He first considered populism. The unparalleled political threat posed by the fusion of poor whites and blacks would seem a logical cause of vitriolic white supremacy, of which the rape myth became a critical component. Ayers did not see it this way. "Political passions may have helped fuel the lynching crisis of the nineties by creating racial animosity," he wrote, "but overt political motives apparently accounted for little of the bloodshed."[101]

If populism was not directly responsible for the rape and lynching crisis, then could it be that the onus for the rape fears lay, as Williamson and others have argued, in subconscious psychological tensions among whites about gender? Did blame lie, as Jacquelyn Hall suggested, with "masculine guilt over miscegenation, the veiled hostility toward women in a patriarchal society, the myths of black sexuality—a dense web of sexual violation and desperate rationalization"?[102] Ayers is unconvinced. "This cluster of fears stretched on for decades before and after the crisis of the early 1890s, though, and there seems little indication that any change in gender relationships in the rural South generated the largest wave of lynchings in American history. The mysterious recesses of sex and race provided much of the fuel for the conflagration of the nineties, but not the spark."[103]

Ayers offers several explanations that he believes are unique to the period and more likely to have ignited the rape and lynching crisis. He argued that a "widespread and multifaceted crisis rocked the South" in the late 1880s and 1890s. The market economy that had infiltrated even the mountainous recesses of the South by the late nineteenth century now subjected more of its inhabitants to the precarious whims of the business cycle.[104] The late 1880s saw the beginning of dire economic conditions that directly affected the lives of more southerners than ever before. One of the byproducts of the economic crisis was a crime wave precipitated by geographic and occupational dislocation that bred criminals of a new sort, whose crimes were more serious and whom W. E. B. Du Bois described as "bad niggers," "a class of black criminals, loafers, and ne'er-do-wells who are a menace to their fellows, both black and white."[105]

Exacerbating the bleak economic and unstable conditions, Ayers continued, was the chronological and geographical space that had settled between the white and black communities in the South as a result of segregation. "The 'best' whites and blacks seldom had contact with one another, as both races increasingly withdrew into their own neighborhoods and churches. Virtually no white man under fifty years old in 1890 would have once been master of a slave plantation. At the time the lynching crisis hit the South no man under thirty years old, white or black, would have any memory of slavery at all—only of racial distrust, conflict, and bloodshed. . . . These men, white and black, feared each other with the fear of ignorance. They saw each other dimly, at a distance."[106] This sea of mistrust and suspicion no doubt accounts for numerous allegations by women of sexual assault: conditioned to fear black men and having little or no regular contact with them, these women probably misinterpreted approaches and acts of insolence as sexual affronts. By the turn of the century those acts of real and imagined black sexual aggression described by Ayers and others were more often than not punished swiftly through extralegal means.[107]

The impact of industrialization and urbanization that Ayers, Gilmore, and others describe propelled poor white southern women into visibility and made them players in the racial politics of the region. Economic convulsions also ushered in revolutionary changes in sexual ideology that contributed to evolving ideas about rape and race in the South. Numerous young girls migrated, often unaccompanied, to cities and mill towns in search of employment. Exposed to new forms of sexual exploitation—by coworkers, supervisors, landlords, strangers—and temptation, these "women adrift" attracted the attention of moralistic reformers who sought to check male sexual prerogatives and challenge the double standard of morality that they saw at the root of sexual danger, and prompted a nationwide campaign for the moral protection of young women.

Moral reformers set out to purge society of illicit sexual conduct and to promote social purity. Eventually anti-prostitution campaigns gave way to other reforms, such as an attack on white slave traffic, prison reform, and sex education. In the 1880s moral crusaders turned their attention to state rape statutes. They lobbied state legislatures to raise the age of consent, generally from the age of ten in most states.[108] By the late 1880s the campaign had become a national movement. Aggressive crusades were launched in virtually every state and continued through the 1890s. While the reformers registered important victories in many states, the South as a region lagged behind. Several southern states—Alabama, South Carolina, and North Carolina—stubbornly refused to raise their statutory age of consent from ten. Mississippi even *lowered* its age of consent to ten from twelve![109]

The southern variant of the age-of-consent reform campaigns was of course inexorably infused with race. Southern legislators stubbornly resisted raising age-of-consent reforms out of fear that African American women and girls could then use the revised statutes to prosecute white offenders. Reviving age-old stereotypes about black women's innate lasciviousness, white southern lawmakers opposed efforts to raise the age of consent on the grounds that such a law placed the "negro female on the same plane as the white female." The Kentucky legislator A. A. Tompkins in 1895 went so far as to say that African

American females, because of their "natural complaisance," could not be raped.[110] Still another white southerner warned, "To raise the age of consent ... would enable loose young women, both white and black, to wreak a fearful vengeance on unsuspecting young men. . . . Who of us that has a boy sixteen years old would be willing to see him sent to the penitentiary on the accusation of a servant girl?"[111] White male opposition to rape reform in the South represented a thinly veiled reluctance to relinquish institutionalized sexual exploitation of black women, what Jacquelyn Hall has termed the "cornerstone of patriarchal power in the South."[112]

White women reformers understood that the unspoken source of resistance to raising the age of consent was unfettered white male sexual access to white, as well as nonwhite, women. Leslie Dunlap, in her work on age-of-consent campaigns in the South, asserts that white women, through their activism, sought to stop white men from having sex with African American women. In doing so, they challenged this white male privilege, thus putting white men on the defensive.[113]

African American activists had long challenged the sexual double standard that permitted white men to sexually exploit nonwhite females without molestation but harshly punished black men who assaulted white women (or more accurately, were perceived to have sexually abused white women). Ida B. Wells-Barnett, for one, exposed such hypocrisy when she published accounts of white men whose sexual assaults of African American girls and women went unnoticed by the press and white communities. She relayed the brutal lynching in Nashville of a black man, Ephraim Grizzard, who had allegedly dared merely visit a white woman. "At the very moment when these civilized whites were announcing their determination 'to protect their wives and daughters,' by murdering Grizzard, a white man was in the same jail for raping eight-year-old Maggie Reese, colored girl. He was not harmed."[114] Frances Ellen Watkins Harper and Nannie Burroughs were but two African American women who joined Wells-Barnett in challenging white men's sexual prerogative at the turn of the century.[115] Both black and white women had complained about sexual abuse of slaves, but usually privately and to other women. At the turn of the century, however, these women, however discreetly and obliquely, broached the taboo of white men's exploitation of sex with black women and girls.

The national and regional debate about such topics as rape and consensual sex was not welcomed in the South. For one thing, the sensibilities of many white southerners had been offended by such explicit talk of sexuality. An editorial in the *Atlanta Constitution* in 1886 denounced the effort to reform rape laws, decrying it a "public indecency": "There are some evils unfit for public discussion, and this is one of them. . . . Some reforms are not to be spoken of in mixed company or mentioned in print."[116] And the uncomfortable discussions threatened much more than one's sensibilities. As Mary Odem has observed, "To take on the double standard and male sexual license in the South could mean confronting the practice of interracial sex and the sexual vulnerability of black women and girls at the hands of white men."[117]

The rise of the rape myth and the contemporaneous discourse about sex, rape, and the proper boundaries of consensual sex are more than just coincidence. Greater sensitivity to sexual abuse and heightened concern about rape in general were an outgrowth of the purity crusade. For the first time southerners were introduced to a social lexicon that included rape, to a discourse that teemed with cautionary tales of sordid sexual license. Sexual assault was no longer something to be whispered about; it was being debated openly in the halls of the legislature and in the pages of the local newspapers. Rape—at the same time race relations were the most strained, and political and economic times most volatile—became part of the southern consciousness as never before.

Just as unsettling to many white southerners, indeed to many middle- and upper-class Americans, was the manifestation of transforming ideas about sexuality and gender, specifically as they related to women's sexual nature. The turn of the century marked the waning days of Victorian sexual ideology, a central tenet of which denied women a libido but granted men license to indulge uncontrollable biological urges. Men were naturally sexually aggressive; women, passionless.[118] An expressive sexuality would have been regarded as irreconcilable with the spiritual and moral superiority that a mother and wife supposedly possessed. But sweeping changes wrought by the expansion of industrial capitalism, including the migration of many young girls and women into the paid workforce, hastened a new era of sexuality. As young girls withdrew from families and paternal supervision into the public world of work, they achieved unprecedented autonomy and independence. Shunning "respectability," a new generation of young women sought out the company of men in public spaces like street corners and amusement parks, wore makeup and high heels, and danced provocatively. Women, it seemed after all, did possess sexual desire, a realization that proved disturbing and unsettling to many who responded with attempts to control and police women's sexuality.[119]

Played out against the backdrop of the Jim Crow South, white society now faced the startling possibility that (white) women possessed a healthy desire for sex. It followed then that if women desired men sexually, they might actually desire black men. So when Alexander Manly, editor of the only African American newspaper in North Carolina, in 1898 goaded his readers with the comment that "white girls of culture and refinement" might actually find black men "sufficiently attractive," he hit a raw nerve.[120] So did Ida B. Wells-Barnett when she publicly disclosed that a white woman in Memphis loved a black man.[121] The real source of the rape charges was white women attracted to black men, who cried rape to avoid social censure upon discovery of their consensual interracial relationship. In an attack on lynching in 1887, Jesse C. Duke, editor of the *Montgomery Herald*, flatly rejected white women's charges of rape against black men. Rather, he suspected "the growing appreciation of the white Juliet for the colored Romeo as he becomes more intelligent and refined."[122]

Yet another pillar holding up southern culture was disintegrating. Not just any pillar, but one of the chief weight-bearing pillars upon which so many axioms of white southern society had rested. The sanctity of white womanhood defined the South, old and new. Southern gentlemen fashioned themselves as protectors of the pure and chaste and justified their position at the apex of the gender, racial, and social hierarchies on the basis of white purity. It is no coincidence, as Martha Hodes has noted, that "just as white ideas about the dangers of black men intensified after emancipation so, too, did white ideology about the purity of white women."[123]

The late nineteenth century was not hospitable to white men of the South. Politically, white southern men felt under siege. Unprecedented interracial political alliances throughout much of the region posed formidable challenges to race and class hegemony. The market economy wreaked havoc on isolated southern enclaves, bringing with it the disruptive forces that threatened white patriarchal control. Long-standing features of the South—racism, honor, widespread poverty, a weak state[124]—were now joined by an array of other developments: changes in gender behavior and roles; renewed concerns about black contacts with white females; a new willingness to debate taboo subjects such as rape and sexual behavior. Together these made the South an incubator for unparalleled fear of the black rapist.

While historians may wrangle over the precise origins of the rape myth, or the extent to which antebellum white southerners were animated by stereotypes of black sexual aggression, all agree on one fundamental truth: there *was* a rape myth. That is to say, there was a time when white southerners were convinced that black men posed a unique sexual threat to white women. There was a time in the South when a black man who stood accused of raping a white woman would surely die, whether by legal execution or by lynching. Evidence abounds. The venomous political diatribes of Ben

Tillman, Rebecca Lattimer Felton, and Cole Blease testify to the widespread sexual alarm among whites about black rapists. Scores of black men dangled at the end of a rope, charged with "the usual offense." Surely this spoke to a people consumed by the irrational fear that white women needed to be protected from the savage, predatory beast, the black man. Or did it?

While much of the recent literature on race and rape has authoritatively established, in the words of Martha Hodes, that "white anxiety about sex between white women and black men is not a timeless phenomenon in the United States," it nonetheless posits that a fundamental change was effected in how southern whites came to view black male sexuality by the twentieth century.[125] The very latest scholarly consideration of the rape myth might lead some to wonder: What rape myth? Lisa Lundquist Dorr has examined black-on-white rape in Virginia in the twentieth century. The questions raised by her findings point to new directions in the discussion about the rape myth, not the least of which is whether there was ever a time when death for an accused black rapist was foreordained. The statistics that Dorr marshals give us reason to pause. Of the 288 men accused of black-on-white sexual assault whom she identified in Virginia between 1900 and 1960, only about one-fourth were either lynched or executed.[126]

Dorr's analysis of the black rape in the twentieth-century South makes a compelling case for the continuity camp of southern historiography. Like their nineteenth-century counterparts, white southerners in the twentieth century who encountered charges of black-on-white rape stubbornly resisted acting out of their common whiteness. "White men did not automatically leap to the defense of white women."[127] Instead, they sometimes aligned with a black neighbor they had known for years over a white accuser new to the area. A white employer might intercede on behalf of his black laborer. White Virginians might side with an accused black rapist when his accuser was known to have an especially sullied reputation. These cases show, Dorr argues, that "significant continuities existed between nineteenth and twentieth century treatment of black-on-white rape, as white legal elites incorporated attitudes about gender, sexuality, respectability, and class status in determining what constituted 'justice' for convicted black men."[128]

Dorr's findings raise another question. If, as she claims, white responses to black-on-white rape were not uniform in twentieth-century Virginia, how is it that we have come to expect the "usual" response to have been death, at the hands of either an executioner or a vengeful mob? For one, Dorr explains, our customary frame of reference for twentieth-century black rape has been the most notorious cases, such as Scottsboro, which did elicit a rabidly racist response from most white southerners. Historians have also focused a great deal on lynching, much of it purported to have been in response to black rape. Dorr suggests that our understanding of black-on-white rape in the twentieth century has been shaped by the most egregious white reactions to black rape, which have received a disproportionate share of historians' scholarly attention. Her examination of "less notorious cases" suggests that what we have seen as the usual response to black rape may actually have been the exception.

Finally, Dorr's work prompts us to ask *how* this was possible. Given what we know about the hardened race lines in the twentieth century, and about the well-established fears of black rape embedded in white southern culture, how could black men accused of raping white women receive due process, let alone leniency? The answer, Dorr explains, lies in the nature of segregation. Relying heavily on the recent cultural analysis of racial segregation by Grace Elizabeth Hale, Dorr argues for the malleability of segregation, specifically its "ability to allow local improvisation within the basic southern script." By this she means that in practice, segregation was never as rigid as the rhetoric might lead us to think it was. Rather, segregation "could mutate to fit and control the circumstances of any mixed race southern community."[129] Analogizing black-white relations to a play with a script, a "theater of racial difference," Hale and Dorr contend that the boundaries between black and white, though definitive, were hardly impenetrable.[130] "Though the rules of segregation seemed clear, the boundaries around cross racial interaction remained elastic," permitting southern whites to tolerate some cross-racial sexual affairs (and treating ones that went awry with some leniency) while holding the feet of some malefactors to the fire. Messy day-to-day living often blurred segregation's precise racial boundaries. Twentieth-century southerners knew this, and therefore made accommodations on the "stage" of racial performance.[131] Dorr's study reveals a disjuncture between the rhetoric of race and rape on the one hand and how twentieth-century southerners *lived* race and rape in the American South on the other. While the discourse about black male sexuality (and purity and female whiteness) crystallized in the twentieth century, Dorr questions whether practice followed suit, thus providing a fruitful line of inquiry for future scholars.

It is clear that the debate over race and rape in the American South has had a long and contested history. It is equally obvious that the historiography of the rape myth is a convoluted one, a morass of half-truths and untruths, steeped in a cauldron of myth and misconception. Unraveled and disentangled, what does the evolution of scholarship about rape and race reveal about the bigger picture of race relations in America?

One of the most important insights that this discussion has yielded is just how very complicated lived relations were in the nineteenth- and twentieth-century South. Much historical scholarship of the South has lulled us into thinking that race was foremost in shaping the behavior of nineteenth-century southerners and has anesthetized us to competing or even contradictory possibilities. Because readily identifiable boundaries are so tempting, it made sense to imagine a region in which categories of race were carefully delineated and respected. Nell Painter has been especially critical of historians of the South and has called on historians to go "beyond lazy characterizations in the singular" and to recognize "the complex and contradictory nature of southern society." "Though southern history must take race very seriously," she has cautioned, "southern history must not stop with race."[132]

Nor must southern historians use race as their starting point, a long-standing practice that has tended to mute the inherent contradictions of antebellum southern society. What a survey of the historical treatment of the rape myth demonstrates is that historians, equipped with the knowledge of black victimization in the Jim Crow era, including the venomous rhetoric of black rape, have made claims for widespread white anxiety about black rape in the antebellum era when it did not exist. Stripped of such preconceptions, we can see an Old South in which there was far greater fluidity in race relations—and less in class relations—than historians heretofore have been willing to recognize. The recent scholarship by Hodes, Bynum, and others, including my own, reveals that peculiar cross-racial alliances underscore the complex web of contested loyalties confronting antebellum southerners. An appreciation of the fissures in the mind of white southerners along the fault lines of gender, race, and class may lead to a more complete understanding of how various groups within southern society were configured in relation to each other. Simply stated, what we learn from exploring the historiography of the rape myth is that race represented only one of a number of competing interests, and frequently one of the other interests prevailed. As Painter has reminded us recently, "Knowing a person's race, whatever that is, does not automatically tell you much about that person's life history."[133]

The survey of rape myth historical literature sheds light on a second area in the history of the South: the ongoing debate about continuity and change. And on this score, there is no consensus. Relying on the traditional demarcation of the Civil War as a watershed, we find agreement between such disparate individuals as Myrta Lockett Avary and Martha Hodes. Separated by time, profession, and most importantly sensibilities, the two nonetheless view the emancipation of slaves as a critical development in how whites came to view black sexuality and the threat to white females. For Avary, and for her generation of white Lost Cause adherents, Reconstruction marked an abrupt and unwanted change, the end of slavery. With political power came demands for social equality for black men. In mapping out white attitudes toward interracial sex, Hodes views the emancipation of slaves as the seat of important changes in perceptions about black sexuality that only intensified by the end of the century. For others—Williamson, Hall, Fredrickson—the marker for significant change was not the Civil War and Reconstruction but rather the late nineteenth century, when a panoply of political, social, and economic changes resonated throughout the region, crystallizing along fears of black rape. And in the most singular departure of all, Lisa Dorr suggests that claims for discontinuity have in fact been overstated. Uncovering overlooked black-on-white rape cases, she finds evidence of significant continuity between white attitudes about black sexuality and rape in the nineteenth and twentieth centuries, a continuity which, as she notes, stands in "glaring contradiction to the accepted historical paradigm."[134]

In a peculiar way, Dorr's findings bring us back full circle to the work of Winthrop Jordan, who argued for the continuity of white anxiety about black rape beginning in the colonial era, offering it as evidence of a timeless continuum in the American South. Dorr, though, in contrast to Jordan, offers that the continuity is marked by *lack* of white anxiety about black rape. In addition, what Jordan took to be rigid racial boundaries—"black" over "white"—for Dorr were fluid, malleable categories that functioned loosely as guides. Perhaps race relations, in practice, had always existed on a continuum of tension with ideological dogma. But by focusing on the more notorious and highly publicized cases of black-on-white rape, including lynchings, perhaps we have jumped to erroneous conclusions about race and sex in the twentieth-century South. A courtroom observer in the Scottsboro rape trial in 1933 took exception to the defense attorney's attempt to discredit the accuser's testimony, claiming she was "a 'lewd woman' " and a " 'girl tramp.' " The observer countered, falling into step with white supremacy rhetoric, that she "might be a fallen woman, but by God she is a white woman."[135] Perhaps we have erred in assuming that this white man spoke for the majority of white southerners.

NOTES

Abbreviations

APA	Auditor of Public Accounts
Bonds	Bonds for Transportation of Condemned Slaves
CJ	Cash Journal
CS	Condemned Slaves, Condemned Blacks, Executed or Transported, Records, 1783–1865
EJ	Executive Journal
EP	Executive Papers
GLB	Governors' Letter Book
GP	Governors' Papers
HED	House Executive Documents, 39th Cong., 1st sess., 1865
KKK Report	U.S. Congress, *Report of the Joint Select Committee to Inquire into the Condition of Affairs in the Late Insurrectionary States*, 42d Cong., 2d sess., 1872, 13 vols., S. Rept. 41, part 1
List	"A List of Slaves and Free Persons of Color Received into the Penitentiary of Virginia for Sale and Transportation from the 25th June 1816 to 1st February 1842"
LVA	Library of Virginia, Richmond
NCDAH	North Carolina Department of Archives and History, Raleigh
PP	Pardon Papers
RG	Record Group
SC	Secretary of the Commonwealth
VEP	Virginia Executive Papers
VEPLR	Virginia Executive Papers, Letters Received
VHS	Virginia Historical Society, Richmond

Introduction

1. Phillips, *American Negro Slavery*, 461–62.

2. Shoup, "Uncle Tom's Cabin Forty Years After," 96.

3. Fredrickson, *The Black Image in the White Mind*, 204–9; Williamson, *Crucible of Race*, especially ch. 4, "The Rise of the Radicals."

4. Straton, "Will Education Solve the Race Problem?," 786.

5. Somerville, "Some Co-operating Causes of Negro Lynching," 509.

6. See, for example, Lillian Smith, *Killers of the Dream*, 18, 145; Cash, *Mind of the South*, 86, 115–16.

7. Cash, *Mind of the South*, 115.

8. For example, Herbert Aptheker, *American Negro Slave Revolts*.

9. Donat and D'Emilio, "A Feminist Redefinition of Rape and Sexual Assault," 912–13.

10. See Chapter 3.

11. Gross, *Double Character*, 5. It is also instructive to consider Laura Edwards's view of the law as she applies it to the nineteenth-century South. She sees law "as an imperfect, unwieldy tool whose application could produce results that were open to multiple meanings. The system proved difficult for any single group to control completely because it was a complicated ideology that was rooted in the past with its own logic and universalizing principles that could alter and impede as well as facilitate the interests of those who tried to use it." Laura F. Edwards, "Law, Domestic Violence, and the Limits of Patriarchal Authority in the Antebellum South," 741 n. 11.

12. Rothman, *Notorious in the Neighborhood*.

13. Jordan, *White over Black*.

14. Painter, "'Of *Lily*, Linda Brent, and Freud," 259; Hodes, *White Women, Black Men*; Hodes, "The Sexualization of Reconstruction Politics"; Hodes, "Wartime Dialogues on Illicit Sex"; Laura F. Edwards, "The Disappearance of Susan Daniel and Henderson Cooper"; Buckley, "Unfixing Race"; Rothman, *Notorious in the Neighborhood*; Rothman, "James Callender and Social Knowledge of Interracial Sex in Antebellum Virginia."

15. Donald, *Liberty and Union*, vii–viii.

16. Others to make this argument include Williamson, *Crucible of Race*, and Fredrickson, *Black Image in the White Mind*. For an extensive survey of the specific historical context of the emergence of white fears of black rape, see the Appendix.

17. Dailey, *Before Jim Crow*, 6.

18. Stansell, *City of Women*; Sharon Block, "Coerced Sex in British North America, 1700–1820."

19. Kathleen M. Brown, *Good Wives, Nasty Wenches, and Anxious Patriarchs*, makes this argument about colonial Virginia.

20. Jordan's work is heavily influenced by psychoanalytic theory embodied in such works as John Dollard's classic *Caste and Class in a Southern Town* (1937). Dollard, who studied under Freud's protégée Karen Horney at the Berlin Psychoanalytic Institute, grounded white male fears of black rape in their own subconscious "fear of reprisal for the things they do to Negro women." Dollard further surmised that white men, unconsciously jealous of virile black men, assuaged these jealousy pangs by projecting on to black men extraordinary sexual potency." Dollard, *Caste and Class in a Southern Town*, 163, 134, 170. Wilbur J. Cash, in his widely read *Mind of the South*, applied similar Freudian concepts to antebellum white southerners and especially their images of white ladies. Southern white men, he claimed, practiced "gyneolatry," or the deification of their women, which in effect left white women bereft of sexuality and made them sexually inaccessible to their own husbands. Cash, *Mind of the South*, 86, 116.

21. Jordan, *White over Black*, 148.

22. Ibid., 152.

23. Ibid., 28–39.

24. For example, refer to Thorpe, *The Old South*, 91, 113; Lawrence J. Friedman, *White Savage*, 11; Peter H. Wood, *Black Majority*, 237; Wyatt-Brown, *Southern Honor*, 50; Bardaglio, "Rape and the Law in the Old South," 752. Importantly, a number of scholarly works outside the history discipline have also accepted as fact that white fears of black rape originated in the slave South. The civil rights movement of the 1960s, which surely motivated historians like Jordan and others to examine American race relations, also spawned a number of sociological studies of race, a few of which tackled issues of black male sexuality, interracial sexual relations, and white fears of black sexual assault. Most of these rely heavily on the "Cash-Jordan" theses on sex and race, for example, in their rehashing and reworking of projection theory, Cash's concept of gyneolatry, and Cash's and Jordan's acceptance of widespread plantation miscegenation. Some works, written by black men in the 1960s, are predictably angry and polemic in tone. See, for example, Hernton, *Sex and Racism in America*. Another example of social scientists' reliance on the "Cash-Jordan" school in framing the historical foundations of their studies on race and sex is the work on the sexualization of racism by two criminologists: Coramae Richey Mann and Lance H. Selva grounded fears of the black rapist in the white man's sexual exploitation of slave women, which resulted in the "intensification of the sexual anxieties of the Southern white male" who projected his own "tendencies for sexual atrocities onto the Black man." "The Sexualization of Racism," 169–70.

25. Peter H. Wood, *Black Majority*, 237.

26. Bardaglio, "Rape and the Law in the Old South," 752, and *Reconstructing the Household*, 64.

27. Bardaglio, *Reconstructing the Household*, 64.

28. Hodes, *White Women, Black Men*; "The Sexualization of Reconstruction Politics"; and "Wartime Dialogues on Illicit Sex."

29. Obviously not all archival records have been thoroughly researched. Thus, the number of recorded cases is bound to be much higher. This number reflects merely the number that I have come across in both primary and secondary sources. With few exceptions, the cases cited here are those in which the defendant was charged officially with rape or attempted rape, sometimes referred to as ravishment or carnal knowledge. A woman, or her male kin, would swear out a complaint and a local official, usually a justice of the peace, issued a warrant for the arrest of a man for rape or attempted rape. This definition of rape, of course, leaves many instances of coerced sex ignored. In addition, two cases of murder-rape are included. I have made no attempt to scrutinize assault and battery cases which may contain evidence of sexual assault or may have involved females resisting sexual assault. It should also be noted that an overwhelmingly disproportionate number of extant documents dealing with black sexual assault involves those males actually convicted of rape or attempted rape. Transcripts, many of them rich in detail and often accompanied by judges' and juries' opinions, were routinely forwarded to the governor or his executive council for review and hence filed among state papers. A black man acquitted of rape or attempted rape would have no need for his court records to be sent to state officials. The result for the researcher is that a preponderance of material pertaining to convicted black rapists exists and is readily found in state archival repositories. Only dogged and systematic research in

county court minute and order books, however, will afford scholars the license to make more reliable generalizations about rape and race.

Throughout the study I employ some twentieth-century terms, such as sexual assault and child molestation. I do not mean to imply that these terms then carried the same social and legal connotations that they do today. But I feel it is constructive to engage the reader in terminology with which he or she is familiar. Moreover, occasionally I will make use of the term "victim." I am painfully aware that some will take issue with this description of a female who charges a male with rape or attempted rape. By employing this term I have no intention of characterizing a rape accuser as powerless or divested of agency. In fact, my research shows that most women and girls fought their attackers with considerable effort. The word "accuser," which I rely on most extensively, has its own negative connotations; some might infer, for example, that a woman who *accuses* a man of rape may not actually be a woman who was raped. I have made every attempt to employ "neutral" terminology that does not inadvertently imply that an accused rapist was guilty or that an accuser lied. For the sake of simplicity and fluidity of writing, I will at times use the terms "rape" and "rapist" broadly to encompass attempted rape, understanding full well that a rapist is not the same as one who attempts rape. I will make careful distinctions where appropriate, for example, in detailing the exact charge that a slave faced.

30. This study examines cases in all former Confederate states in addition to the slave-holding border states of Maryland, Kentucky, and Missouri, focusing, as stated in the text, more closely on those in Virginia and North Carolina. The primary sources yielding information about accused black rapists include local and appellate court records and documents, petitions and letters to state governors, and newspapers. My decision to look at these two states was shaped by a number of factors, primarily the availability and preservation of a large number of official documents and the extensive scholarship on these two states for both the antebellum and postbellum periods. For those readers who might take exception to my decision to concentrate on Virginia and North Carolina, citing their geographic proximity to "the North," I would beg two considerations. First, though the notion of "the South" encompasses the extensive diversity and complexities of that region's past, all the southern states, including North Carolina and Virginia, shared the institution of forced enslavement of African Americans through the Civil War. Second, one need only look to twentieth-century statistics on rape, race, and execution to discern how deeply the "rape complex" was embedded in the cultures of both Virginia and North Carolina. Virginia, for example, was one of only three states in the country that continued to punish attempted rape with death. Furthermore, in the years 1908 through 1962, fifty-four black Virginians were executed for either rape or attempted rape while not a single white man was sentenced to death for the same crimes. This trend is mirrored in North Carolina. From 1901 through 1961, sixty-three blacks were sentenced to die for rape; seven whites and two Indians were sentenced to death for the same crime. William J. Bowers, *Legal Homicide*, 514–19, 472–79; Partington, "The Incidence of the Death Penalty for Rape in Virginia", 43–75. Further research may demonstrate whether findings presented in this study apply to other former slaveholding states.

31. In all cases the alleged victim was a white woman or girl. On southern rape law and whether women and girls of color could bring charges of rape, see Chapter 2, n. 98.

Though rare, there are a few instances of African American men brought before southern courts and charged with sexually assaulting women of color; for instance, in 1797 a slave in Virginia was hanged for the rape of a mulatto woman. CS Executed, 1799, LVA. Three cases of rape of female slaves by male slaves appeared before the Virginia courts from 1850 through 1858. In 1856 Coleman was found guilty of raping a slave child, Harriet, and sentenced to transportation out of the country. CS Transported, 1857, and in December 1856 folder, VEPLR, LVA. Charges were brought and subsequently dropped against William, a slave in Loudoun County, for raping Annette, a female slave, in 1858. Schwarz, *Twice Condemned*, 293 n. 21. John was sentenced to transportation for the rape of a slave in Spotsylvania County. Bond dated January 21, 1850, Bonds for Transportation of Condemned Slaves, 1840–57, LVA, and Schwarz, *Twice Condemned*, 293 n. 21. Several cases of slaves raping free women of color have also been found. Tom, a slave in New Kent County, was sentenced to hang for raping Dolly Boasman, a married free mulatto woman. He was spared and transported instead. CS Transported, 1810, and January 11–20, 1810 folder, box 164, (January–February 20, 1810), LR, VEP, LVA. Charles, a slave in Halifax County, was sentenced to transportation for the rape of Ann Freeman. Halifax County Court Minute Book, July 1857, 341 (microfilm reel 73); CS Transported, 1857, and Bond dated September 18, 1857, Bonds 1840–57, LVA. In December 1864 Henry Robertson, a slave in Wythe County, was tried for the rape of Mary Jane Wilson, a twenty-eight-year-old free woman of color. PP, January–April 1865, PP, LR, VEP, LVA. The *Raleigh Register and North Carolina Gazette* noted on April 12, 1836, that Jones Kiff (no mention is made of his race) was tried but acquitted in the rape of an eighty-year-old free black woman. Rarer still were trials of white men accused of raping women of color. In 1858 Edward B. Ledbetter of Sussex County, Virginia, was sentenced to ten years in the state penitentiary for the assault and rape of a twenty-four-year-old "free negress." Relying on a jury's recommendation for clemency, however, the governor pardoned Ledbetter, who incidentally found himself imprisoned three years later for raping another free woman of color. August 1863 folder and document dated December 1861, PP, January–June 1862, and July–November 1863, LR, VEP, LVA. Also, Arthur Howington found a case of a white man in Tennessee officially charged with raping a young slave girl. The grand jury indicted him but he was acquitted. Howington, "The Treatment of Slaves and Free Blacks in the State and Local Courts of Tennessee", 114. Despite these instances of African American women bringing charges of rape before officials, their numbers are indeed few. While rape statutes pertaining to African American men specified the race of the victim in sexual assault as white, females of color usually found that those statutes did not protect them from rape. However, the instances of African American females bringing official rape charges cited here suggest that local officials at times did interpret rape statutes that did not specify race as applicable to women of color. These "exceptions" have been overshadowed by the frequently cited court case of *George v. State of Mississippi*, in which a male slave was found guilty of raping a female slave and sentenced to hang. That state's supreme court ruled in favor of the convicted rapist, finding that the statutory definition of rape was race-specific. In fact, one justice reasoned, "The crime of rape does not exist in this State between African slaves." *George v. State*, 37 Miss. 316. A Mississippi statute passed in 1859 did, however, outlaw the rape of a negro or mulatto child under the age of twelve. See Mississippi Statutes (1859), ch. 62, secs. 1–2, p. 102.

32. Genovese, *Roll, Jordan, Roll*, 461–62.

Chapter One

1. June 1848 folder, box 391 (May–July 1848), VEP, LVA. The enumeration of this group of boxes is sometimes erratic and confusing, with some boxes labeled several times. Wherever possible I have noted the box number currently intended for use. Also, the Virginia Executive Papers are sometimes labeled Virginia Executive Papers, Letters Received. These are essentially the same group of documents. The shorter title appears to have been utilized for documents in the early part of the nineteenth century, the expanded title for the later period. I will use the cataloging label as it appears on each separate box. When directly quoting from nineteenth-century documents I sometimes alter spelling, punctuation, and capitalization to make the passage or quote more readable and to avoid distracting the reader with editorial notations. In making such changes, however, I was careful not to change the meaning or intent of the quote.

2. Ibid.

3. Ibid.

4. May 1–12, 1848 folder, ibid.

5. Ibid.

6. 1846–54 folder, "Slaves sold and transported," box 1972, Item 756, CS, APA, LVA. The numbers formerly allocated to the boxes in this collection, and denoted in some earlier scholarly works, are no longer in use. Researchers should rely upon dates instead of box numbers. Careful records were kept by the state auditor so that disbursements to the owners of condemned slaves could be properly made. These documents generally list the slave's name, owner, county of residence or trial, the crime for which the slave was condemned, date transported or executed, and the purchaser of transported slaves. Without these invaluable sources, verifying the fate of slaves condemned to die would be almost impossible.

7. The historiographical debate among historians about the extent to which slaves received "justice" will be discussed in Chapter 4.

8. Virginia slaves could not appeal their convictions to that state's supreme court, although many, through white intermediaries, appealed to the governor for executive action. Free blacks, on the other hand, could appeal to higher courts.

9. On the pardoning practices of governors and executive councils see Wyatt-Brown, "Community, Class, and Snopesian Crime," 194–97; Ernest James Clark, "Aspects of the North Carolina Slave Code, 1715–1860," 153; Ayers, *Vengeance and Justice*, 63–64; Schwarz, *Twice Condemned*, 23; Phillips, *American Negro Slavery*, 461–62; Phillips, "Slave Crime in Virginia," 339; Hindus, *Prison and Plantation*, 104, 112–24, 155–56; Hodes, *White Women, Black Men*, 7, 37, 43, 56, 57–66; Flanigan, "Criminal Procedure in Slave Trials in the Antebellum South," 543–45; Howington, "The Treatment of Slaves and Free Blacks in the State and Local Courts of Tennessee," 162; Lawrence M. Friedman, *Crime and Punishment in American History*, 92; Arthur P. Scott, *Criminal Law in Colonial Virginia*, 116–21; Rothman, *Notorious in the Neighborhood*, 141–42.

10. There is evidence suggesting that even after the Civil War some black men accused of sexually assaulting white women or girls received a sympathetic hearing from certain quarters of various white communities. Laura Edwards recounts that sixty men petitioned Governor William Holden of North Carolina for the pardon of William Somerville, convicted in 1869 of the attempted rape of a white woman. See Laura F. Edwards, "Sexual

Violence, Gender, Reconstruction, and the Extension of Patriarchy in Granville County, North Carolina," 250, and *Gendered Strife and Confusion*, 201–2. Edwards also observes that most cases of black males on trial for the rape or attempted rape of white females during this highly volatile and violent period generally proceeded through the courts with little excitement.

11. The issue of presumed guilt in this study is indeed a tricky one for the historian, especially in light of the many trumped up charges in the late nineteenth century and the early twentieth. To assume that all these defendants were guilty seems just as unwarranted as assuming that none of them were guilty. In some cases the evidence is more forthcoming, allowing the researcher to venture an educated guess. Other times, the evidence is stingy, yielding little. And never are we privy to the voice of the black accused. Nevertheless, it seems reasonable to concede that sexual assault takes place in all cultural universes. So, too, we must assume that some of these cases did in fact represent coerced and unwanted sexual relations. That stated, the use of discretion and caution in assessing culpability is essential in these cases.

12. Six years before this case the Virginia legislature passed a law allowing the governor and his council to sell condemned slaves to persons who promised to carry them out of the country, never to return to Virginia. This allowed the state to recoup some of the loss resulting from compensation of slaveowners of condemned slaves. From 1801 to 1864, fifty-four Virginia slaves were transported after their conviction of rape or attempted rape. Schwarz, *Twice Condemned*, 27–28; Schwarz, "The Transportation of Slaves from Virginia, 1801–1865," 216–21; Schwarz, *Laws of Slavery*, ch. 4. According to Michael Hindus in his study of antebellum South Carolina, high rates of executions of slaves (six per year in the period 1800–1855) indicate that "banishment was clearly not a complete substitute for execution." Hindus, "Black Justice under White Law," 596–97.

13. June 1–18, 1807 folder, box 145 (May–June 1807), LR, VEP, LVA. It is worth noting that the same arguments presented in this case by the defense—a woman's past sexual history, no evidence of force—were typically used to defend men against the charge of rape well into the twentieth century. It has only been relatively recently that statutory reforms have been initiated to protect victims of sexual assault and empower prosecutors to disallow such evidence. See Brownmiller, *Against Our Will*, 371–74, 384–87; Tong, *Women, Sex, and the Law*, 90–123. On the statutory requisite of force in antebellum southern rape laws see Chapter 6, n. 33.

14. Mary Block, " 'An Accusation Easily to Be Made,' " 81–114. See also Dubinsky, *Improper Advances*, 23; Lindemann, " 'To Ravish and Carnally Know,' " 68.

15. June 1–18, 1807 folder, box 145 (May–June 1807), LR, VEP, and CS Transported, 1807, LVA.

16. D'Emilio and Freedman, *Intimate Matters*, 95; Bynum, *Unruly Women*, 41–42, 45, 69, 88–93, 97; Lockley, "Crossing the Race Divide," 165–67.

17. May 9, 1803, LR, VEP, as quoted in Johnston, *Race Relations in Virginia and Miscegenation in the South, 1776–1860*, 260.

18. Ibid.

19. On prostitution in the antebellum South, see Rothman, *Notorious in the Neighborhood*, ch. 3, "The Church and the Brothel Are Only Separated by a Pane of Glass."

20. Ibid. and CS Transported, 1803, LVA. While transportation was certainly preferable to

death, one shouldn't underrate the possible harshness of this punishment. Banishment most assuredly meant separation from one's family and friends. Furthermore, masters frequently threatened their slaves with sale to states in the Deep South. Slaves and masters alike seem to have believed that conditions were far worse there than in the upper tier of slaveholding states. My appreciation to Philip Schwarz for making this point.

21. See Chapter 3 of this book for a summary of slave rape laws and prescribed punishments.

22. Nine letters or petitions from Westmoreland County dated October 1800, folder marked executive pardons, October 1800, box 115 (October 21–December 1800), VEP, LVA. One of the petitioners was Baldwin Lee, owner of the two slaves. Other signatories include local magistrates and jurymen. The two slaves escaped from jail but were recaptured. In the end they were pardoned and transported out of Virginia. October 11–20, 1800 folder, box 114 (September–October 20, 1800), VEP, LVA. The appeals also cited the youth of the accused and the "contradictory circumstances" in Bacchus's testimony, and they questioned the accuser's honesty.

23. For more on castration in slave rape cases see Sommerville, "Rape, Race and Castration in Slave Law in the Colonial and Early South," 74–89; Morris, *Southern Slavery and the Law, 1619–1860*, 305.

24. October 1808 folder, box 157 (October–December 11, 1808), VEP, LVA.

25. May–August 1860, box 471, PP, LR, VEP; CJ, LVA. (These cash journals indicate itemized payments for a variety of goods and services, including compensation for transported and executed slaves.) See also Halifax County Court Minute Book, 1859–62 (microfilm reel 74), June 1860, 121, and July 1860, 151–53, LVA.

26. May–August 1860, box 471, PP, LR, VEP, LVA.

27. Philip J. Schwarz refers to this case also, although he depicts Baker as a free black (*Twice Condemned*, 207). Thomas Morris characterizes Baker as a "free mulatto woman" (*Southern Slavery and the Law*, 306). Schwarz bases this characterization upon testimony to the court by Baker herself in which she mentions having lost her "register." Neither the 1820 nor 1830 censuses lists Baker. The court documents repeatedly refer to her as a "free white woman," so if she were a woman of color, this court did not recognize her as such. Contradictory classifications on the basis of race were not at all out of the ordinary, exemplifying, according to Adele Logan Alexander's work on free Georgian women of color, "the shifting, questionable, and amorphous lines of both race and freedom." Adele Logan Alexander, *Ambiguous Lives*, 63. Hodes also examines this case in *White Women, Black Men*, 58.

28. June 1–20, 1829 folder, box 311 (May 1–July 20, 1829), LR VEP, LVA.

29. Ibid.

30. Drucilla Kirkland is repeatedly referred to as "Mrs. Kirkland," although she revealed during her testimony that she never married. More curious is the nature of her relationship with Baker, which was never addressed by court officials or the two principals themselves. Ibid. Neither woman appears in the federal decennial censuses of 1820 and 1830.

31. June 1–20, 1829 folder, box 311 (May 1–July 20, 1829), LR, VEP, LVA. Kirkland's insistence at having personally witnessed coitus echoes an extraordinary lack of privacy similar to that documented in eighteenth-century New England. See Cott, "Eighteenth-Century Family and Social Life as Revealed in Massachusetts Divorce Records," 20–43.

32. June 1–20, 1829 folder, box 311 (May 1–July 20, 1829), LR, VEP, LVA.

33. Ibid.

34. Ibid.

35. Ibid. Italics mine.

36. Ibid. Martha Hodes deciphers this portion of the text differently from me. She writes that Baker claimed Lewis "said he would stick his *dick* in her if she attempted to escape." Hodes, *White Women, Black Men*, 58.

37. According to Amy Baker's testimony, Lewis assaulted her with such "great violence" that after the assault she was "so weak that she could scarcely move her body." Drucilla Kirkland swore that after the assault and while the accused slept she had to bathe Baker's legs and feet and minister to her before Baker could even walk. Ibid. In another case in which the convicted slave rapist was executed, the court clerk cites "aggravating circumstances," quite possibly the use of considerable force or violence, as warranting death. Letter of George Hite of Jefferson County, Virginia, July 7, 1803, July 1–10 folder, box 126, May–July 1803, VEP, LVA.

38. Jack, a slave in Orange County, Virginia, was executed in 1818 for raping Elizabeth Wright, an unmarried "spinster" who had one child out of wedlock and was pregnant at the time of the alleged assault. September 1–11, 1818 folder, August–September 1818, box 248, VEP; CS 1818, Executed, LVA.

39. Lewis was executed on July 24, 1829. See CS Executed, 1829, LVA.

40. On the sexual history of a female accuser as evidence in rape trials in the twentieth century consult Estrich, *Real Rape*, 5, 47–53.

41. Rosemarie Tong speaks to this issue when she writes that traditional legal thought "continues to be tainted by two misogynistic images of woman: woman as temptress and woman as liar." *Woman, Sex, and the Law*, 90–91, 99–104.

42. For similar perceptions in eighteenth-century England, see Anna K. Clark, *Women's Silence, Men's Violence*.

43. June 12–19, 1827 folder, box 299 (June 1–July 31, 1827), VEP, LVA. Guilt by association, at least in this case, proved an ineffective defense. Buck was executed. See CS Executed, 1828, LVA.

44. On southern ladyhood, including ideas of purity, see Anne Firor Scott, *The Southern Lady*; Fox-Genovese, *Within the Plantation Household*, 192–241; Clinton, *The Plantation Mistress*, 16–35, 92–106; Lebsock, *The Free Women of Petersburg*, 148; Bynum, *Unruly Women*, 8–9; Carby, *Reconstructing Womanhood*, 30; D'Emilio and Freedman, *Intimate Matters*, 94; Dorothy Ann Gay, "The Tangled Skein of Romanticism and Violence in the Old South," 21–62; Wyatt-Brown, *Southern Honor*, 50–53. On the nineteenth-century conception of sexual passionlessness as a womanly ideal see Cott, "Passionlessness," 219–36; Ireland, "The Libertine Must Die," 28–29; Lewis, "The Republican Wife," 681–82; Freedman, "Sexuality in Nineteenth-Century America," 199–200, 202, 208. On the desexualization of southern white women, see D'Emilio and Freedman, *Intimate Matters*, 94–95; Clinton, *The Plantation Mistress*, 110–11, 209; Lillian Smith, *Killers of the Dream*, 141, 120–21; Adele Logan Alexander, *Ambiguous Lives*, 64; Jacquelyn Dowd Hall, " 'The Mind That Burns in Each Body,' " 328–49. Elizabeth Fox-Genovese questions this characterization of southern women and argues that slaveholding culture "emphasized control of female sexuality; it did not deny its existence." *Within the Plantation Household*, 235–36 (quotation on 236), 240. Similarly, Steven M. Stowe documents the "culture of romantic love" embraced by southern elites as well as the concern

espoused by moral advisors for "the latent power of female passion." In Stowe, *Intimacy and Power in the Old South*, 50–121 (first quotation on 96; second on 54). See also Wyatt-Brown, *Southern Honor*, 293; Dorothy Ann Gay, "The Tangled Skein of Romanticism and Violence in the Old South," 105–6.

45. Bynum, *Unruly Women*, 7, 89, 101. Ideology linking class and sexuality was not confined to the Old South. See Stansell, *City of Women*, 20–27; Arnold, " 'The Life of a Citizen in the Hands of a Woman,' " 35–56; Lindemann, " 'To Ravish and Carnally Know,' " 79–81.

46. Hodes, "Sex across the Color Line," 2, 41, 60–63. Also, Hodes, *White Women, Black Men*, 5, 65–66, 131. For the postbellum period see Bardaglio, *Reconstructing the Household*, 197–98.

47. Clinton, *The Plantation Mistress*, 204.

48. Trial of Jim, August 16, 1858, Prince Edward County Court Order Book (1853–62), 281, 283, 288, as quoted in Schwarz, *Twice Condemned*, 292; CS Transported, 1858, LVA; *Richmond Enquirer*, September 24, 1858, 2, and September 28, 1858, 3.

49. Letter of September 10, 1856, September 1856, LR, VEP, LVA.

50. As reported in the North Carolina *Weekly Standard*, December 7, 1859.

51. Schwarz, "The Transportation of Slaves from Virginia, 1801–1865," 215–16, 232 n. 1; and CS 1839, Transported, LVA.

52. September–December 1860, box 472, PP, LR, VEP, LVA.

53. It is unclear whether the accuser's name is Miller or Moler. Searches in the 1850 censuses revealed no Mathilda or Matilda with either surname. Her companions included her daughter, Mrs. Emily G. Strider, aged thirty-two, mother of five children, and married to Joseph Strider, a farmer whose personal estate was valued at $1,500 in 1860. Virginia Census (1860), Jefferson County, Bolivar, 751, and Margaret M. House. The 1850 census lists a woman by this name as married to William House, a forty-five-year-old hotel keeper. His wife's age is listed as thirty-six. In the next census, William is no longer listed as residing in the House dwelling, which is home to ten people, perhaps indicating continued status as a hotel or boarding house. Strangely, however, Margaret's recorded age is thirty-seven, not forty-seven, which would be the correct age were she the same Margaret House listed in the 1850 census. This would appear to be an error, as all her children save her daughter continued to live with her. Virginia Census (1850), Jefferson County, Bolivar, 401, and Virginia Census (1860), Jefferson County, Harpers Ferry, 847.

54. September–December 1860, box 472, PP, LR, VEP, LVA. Note however that Bill did not hang. He was transported out of the state.

55. Guion Griffis Johnson, *Antebellum North Carolina*, 508. On slaves accused of sexual assault and lynched or nearly lynched see Hodes, *White Women, Black Men*, 58–59.

56. Morris, *Southern Slavery and the Law*, 230.

57. Ibid.

58. October 1–10, 1833 folder, box 334 (August 1–October 31, 1833), VEP, LVA.

59. In 1840 the Virginia legislature modified its compensation policy so that the market value of the condemned slave would be adjusted to reflect the purchaser's knowledge of the slave's offence. Virginia *Acts*, 1839–40, 51–52. Compensation rates for executed slaves varied widely over time and from state to state. Georgia, for example, offered slaveowners no compensation whatsoever. John Edwards, "Slave Justice in Four Middle Georgia Counties,"

266. Slaveholders in Texas whose slaves were condemned to death by courts received half the assessed value of the executed slave, not to exceed $1,000. Randolph B. Campbell, *An Empire for Slavery*, 100–101. By most accounts colonial compensation rates appear to have been more liberal, but rates diminished as the nineteenth century advanced, perhaps because compensation grew so costly. For example, the Virginia legislature appropriated $265,500 from 1835 to 1863 for compensation of transported or executed slaves. Virginia *Acts*, 1835–63. It seems highly unlikely that slaveholders in the antebellum period would have been fully compensated for executed slaves and therefore would have been motivated to salvage their property. See Kay and Cary, " 'The Planters Suffer Little or Nothing,' " 288–306; R. H. Taylor, "Humanizing the Slave Code of North Carolina," 329; Hindus, "Black Justice under White Law," 595–96; Crow, *The Black Experience in Revolutionary North Carolina*, 25–26; Phillips, "Slave Crime in Virginia," 336–40; Peter H. Wood, *Black Majority*, 279–81; Morris, "Slaves and the Rules of Evidence in Criminal Trials," 1213; Morris, *Southern Slavery and the Law*, 253–56.

60. Kenneth Stampp makes this very point about capital slave crimes in general. *The Peculiar Institution*, 227–28.

61. July 1831 folder, box 320 (July–August 1831), LR, VEP, LVA.

62. Ibid.

63. Ibid.

64. Letter dated July 9, 1831, Leesburg (author's name illegible), ibid.

65. Letter dated July 11, 1831, Leesburg, ibid.

66. In an analysis of community, class, and crime in the Old South, Bertram Wyatt-Brown argues that non-elites chafed at the bias they observed in the judicial process. When "decisions seemed flagrantly generous toward those with powerful friends, money, and batteries of legal talent, feelings of class animosity could be aroused." Wyatt-Brown, "Community, Class, and Snopesian Crime," 189.

67. July 1831 folder, box 320 (July–August 1831), LR, VEP; CS 1831, Executed, LVA.

68. An undated letter received December 16, 1846, November–December 1846, LR, VEP; CS Transported, 1847; Bonds, 1840–57, LVA. On class conflicts in southern communities over the rape trials of free blacks or slaves see also Flanigan, "The Criminal Law of Slavery and Freedom, 1800–1868," 69.

69. Flanigan, "The Criminal Law of Slavery and Freedom," 69. Implicit here is the notion that elites employed extralegal remedies in response to the rape of a family member whereas poor white women lodging complaints of sexual assault relied on the legal process to pursue justice, just the opposite of Douglas Hay's claim for eighteenth-century England. Hay, "Property, Authority and the Criminal Law," 17–64.

70. Court transcript for *George v. Commonwealth*, August 11, 1856, Mathews County; letter from George E. Bibb [?] to Governor Henry A. Wise, September 10, 1826; letter from John T. Seanine [?] to Governor Henry A. Wise, August 22, 1856; all in September 1856, LR, VEP, LVA. For another example of a slaveowner paying a white woman not to bring rape charges against a slave see *Pleasant v. State*, 13 Ark. 360, January 1853. In this case, however, the accuser and her husband appear to have extorted the $125 from the slaveowner and then reneged.

71. Letter from Elizabeth F. Borum [?] to Governor Henry A. Wise, August 29, 1856, September 1856, LR, VEP, LVA.

72. Ibid.

73. Letter from George E. Bibb to Governor Henry A. Wise, September 10, 1856, September 1856, LR, VEP, LVA.

74. This case is recounted in Wyatt-Brown, *Southern Honor*, 317–18; Guion Griffis Johnson, *Antebellum North Carolina*, 71; Franklin, *The Free Negro in North Carolina, 1790–1860*, 37; Sommerville, "The Rape Myth in the Old South Reconsidered," 481–518; and most recently and with far greater detail and analysis by Hodes, ch. 3, "Bastardy: Polly Lane and Jim," in *White Women, Black Men*. Facts relating to this case are taken from these secondary sources as well as the subsequently cited primary sources.

75. As Joshua Rothman has argued, Virginians "only rarely took legal or extralegal action to try to eliminate sexual criminality in their midst." Only when circumstances, such as the birth of a mixed race child in which the interracial relationship is exposed, were whites pressed to show disapproval publicly. Rothman, *Notorious in the Neighborhood*, 4. A growing body of scholarship now questions traditional assumptions that consensual sexual relations across the color line were rare. Recent works have entertained the possibility that some interracial relationships, if comported with discretion, were tolerated in the slave South. For discussions of miscegenation in the Old South see Mills, "Miscegenation and the Free Negro in Antebellum 'Anglo' Alabama," 16–34; Buckley, "Unfixing Race," 349–80; Buckley, *The Great Catastrophe of My Life*, 121–52; Hodes, *White Women, Black Men*, 2–5, 10, 27–95; D'Emilio and Freedman, *Intimate Matters*, 104, 95; Crow, *The Black Experience in Revolutionary North Carolina*, 20–21, 30; Stampp, *The Peculiar Institution*, 350–52; Franklin and Moss, *From Slavery to Freedom*, 128–29; Adele Logan Alexander, *Ambiguous Lives*; Dorothy Ann Gay, "The Tangled Skein of Romanticism and Violence in the Old South," 103–4, 113–17, 159–60; Litwack, *Been in the Storm So Long*, 243; Forrest G. Wood, *Black Scare*, 153; Berry and Blassingame, *Long Memory*, 117–20; J. William Harris, *Plain Folk and Gentry in a Slave Society*, 56–57; Anne Firor Scott, *The Southern Lady*, 52–53; Clinton, *The Plantation Mistress*, 209–11; Lebsock, *The Free Women of Petersburg*, 95–96, 104; Deborah Gray White, *Ar'n't I a Woman?*, 34–35, 43–44, 61; Cashin, *A Family Venture*, 23, 27, 102, 105–6, 110, 119; Bynum, *Unruly Women*, 41–42, 45, 69, 88–93, 97; Lockley, "Crossing the Race Divide," 159–73; Finkelman, "Crimes of Love, Misdemeanors of Passion"; Fischer, " 'False, Feigned, and Scandalous Words' "; Bradley and Leslie, "White Pain Pollen."

76. Petition dated December 8, 1825, Papers of Governor Hutchins Gordon Burton, GP 55, NCDAH.

77. M. Henderson to Governor Burton, December 5, 1825, and Alexander Gray to Burton, December 8, 1825, and March 24, 1826, ibid. Considerable debate and correspondence were devoted to the suspected pregnancy, which as time passed was confirmed. One issue was the date of conception. During the trial in October Polly Lane denied that she was pregnant. If Jim's contention that she was one month to six weeks pregnant by the date of the alleged rape, August 16, were true, her pregnancy would have been difficult to conceal but not impossible. As the advanced pregnancy made her lie untenable, Lane changed her story and claimed that she had been impregnated on August 16, the date when she claimed that Jim had raped her. That version of the story would have meant a delivery date around May 16, according to those Davidson County residents who were keeping track. When, in late March, the birth appeared imminent, about five weeks before a due date that would have

corresponded to conception on August 16, Polly Lane again adjusted her account to say that if the child born to her were a mulatto, it was conceived at the time she claimed that Jim had raped her. But if the child were white, it was fathered by a Mr. Palmer, a white man. A second but related concern was whether a woman could conceive as the result of a rape. Conventional, as well as medical, wisdom of the time erroneously held that arousal of the woman was necessary for fertilization. Governor Burton even solicited the opinion of a physician who concluded that "if an absolute rape were to be perpetrated it is not likely she would become pregnant." Letter of March 27, 1826, ibid. Physicians continued to believe that women could not conceive as a result of rape. One doctor wrote in 1862 that it was "as impossible for a woman to conceive while under the influence of terror, shock, and nervous exhaustion, as it would be for a man to perform the act of intercourse while prostrated by similar agencies." See "Can Pregnancy Follow Defloration in Rape, When Force Simply Is Used?," 272.

78. Six petitioners to Burton, December 8, 1825, Papers of Governor Hutchins Gordon Burton, GP 55, NCDAH.

79. Alexander Gray to Burton, December 8, 1825, and March 24, 1826, ibid. On the governor's reprieve, see Wyatt-Brown, *Southern Honor*, 317.

80. James Martin of Lexington to Burton, March 24, 1826, Papers of Governor Hutchins Gordon Burton, GP 55, NCDAH.

81. A. W. Shepperd to Burton, March 24, 1826, ibid.

82. Alexander Gray to Burton, May 18, 1826, ibid.

83. Letters from John M. Smith to Burton, March 23, 1826, and May 6, 1826 (quotation from Smith), and letter from A. W. Sheppherd, March 24, 1826, ibid.

84. Wyatt-Brown, *Southern Honor*, 318; Hodes, *White Women, Black Men*, 56.

85. Hodes, *White Women, Black Men*, 40.

86. Hodes, "Across the Color Line," 49 n. 29. It is worth mentioning that Morehead's political career was not tarnished by his defense of an accused slave rapist. Also of note, the two lawyers had developed a greater stake in procuring Jim's pardon because Abraham Peppinger promised to turn Jim over to the two should their efforts prove successful. John M. Smith to Burton, March 23, 1826, and J. M. Morehead to Burton, May 20, 1826, GP 55, NCDAH.

87. Wyatt-Brown, *Southern Honor*, 317; James Martin to Governor Burton, March 24, 1826, and Jesse Hargrave to Burton, March 24, 1826, GP 55, NCDAH.

88. Dunn's association with Mrs. Hensen is not stated in the court records, but she may very well have been a servant much like Polly Lane.

89. Letter of March 24, 1825, Papers of Governor Hutchins Gordon Burton, GP 55, NCDAH. This case is also reported in Guion Griffis Johnson, *Antebellum North Carolina*, 589–90; Hodes, *White Women, Black Men*, 62–63; and Wyatt-Brown, *Southern Honor*, 316.

90. Testimony of Mrs. Giddy, letter of March 24, 1825, Papers of Governor Hutchins Gordon Burton, GP 55, NCDAH.

91. Ibid.

92. Letter of March 24, 1825, ibid.; and official notation, April 13, 1825, GLB, no. 26, NCDAH.

93. Archy of Botetourt County, tried in April 1805 and hanged for the rape of Rosanna

Switzer, wife of John Switzer, owner, CS Executed, 1805, LVA; Dick of Southampton County, tried in November 1808 and hanged for the rape of Sally Briggs, four-year-old daughter of his master, Charles Briggs, owner, box 157, VEP and CS Executed, 1808, LVA; Joshua of Monongalia County, tried in July 1827 and later executed for the rape of Zilpha Collins, daughter-in-law of James Collins, owner, box 299, June 1–July 31, 1827, LR, VEP, LVA. Henry of Mathews County was convicted in July 1827 for breaking and entering the home of Thomas Davis Jr., the son of Thomas Davis Sr., his master, and "ill-treating" Ledelia Davis, daughter-in-law of Davis Sr., with intent to kill. The charge was not rape, however, although Henry was reportedly naked when he entered the house. He was transported. July 19–31, 1827 folder, box 299 (June 1–July 31, 1827), LR, VEP, LVA; 1806–39 folder, Bonds for Transportation, CS, LVA; Beverly of Halifax County was executed for the rape of Mary Phelps, wife of his master, John Phelps, in April 1843. CS Executed, 1843, and Halifax County Court Order Book, April 1843, 141–43, LVA. In a few cases the relationship of the accuser to the accused's master is not explicit, but shared surnames indicate a high probability that owner and accuser were related. See the case of Stephen of Fauquier County in March 1811, property of Enoch Jeffries, convicted and hanged for the rape of Lucinda Jeffries, CS Executed, 1811, LVA; Isaac of Albemarle County, owned by William Callerton, who was condemned to die for the attempted rape of Sally Callerton, CS Executed, 1825, LVA; and John, owned by Jacob Sipe of Rockingham County, who was convicted of the rape of Mary Sipe, identified as a white unmarried woman over sixteen years of age. John was transported, not executed. CS 1841, Transported, LVA. Secondary sources reveal a few cases of elite females allegedly raped by black men. The fourteen-year-old daughter of a slaveholder in Alabama was raped and murdered in 1855. See Huntsville *Democrat*, May 24, 1855, as reported in Sellers, *Slavery in Alabama*, 253, and Phillips, *American Negro Slavery*, 462. Phillips reports that the slave was burned alive. In 1844 a slave in Tennessee allegedly attempted an assault on a pregnant woman who was en route to visit her mother, a slaveowner. In *Bill v. State*, 5 Humphreys 155 (December 1844). There are at least two cases of slaves in eighteenth-century Virginia accused of assaulting slaveholding family members. Trial of Tom, September 14, 1775, and trial of Nat, September 6, 1775, Lancaster County Court Order Book (1778–83), 8, 7, LVA; Trial of Bob, June 13, 1783, Southampton County Court Order Book (1778–84), 27, 8, 7, LVA. Of course, not all court documents are forthcoming with information tying the slave's owner to the accuser. There may also be cases in which the accuser's last name may have been different from the master's and the ties of kin therefore escape us.

94. John of Rockingham County was transported. CS Transported, 1841, LVA. Henry of Mathews County was not formally charged with sexual assault. His alleged crime was breaking and entering the home of Thomas Davis Jr. and ill-treating his wife with intent to kill. Although Henry was naked when he entered the Davises' home, Ledelia Davis testified that she did not believe Henry had "any other purpose" than to murder her. This testimony reveals that rape was as least considered a possible motive for the breaking and entering. In Henry's "confession" he purportedly admitted that his objective had been to rape Mrs. Davis but that she had been "too strong for him." July 19–31, 1827 folder, box 299 (June 1–July 31, 1827), VEP, LVA.

95. Sommerville, "The Rape Myth in the Old South Reconsidered," 509.

96. Brownmiller, *Against Our Will*, 349.

97. Brownmiller believes that rapists target vulnerable and available females. *Against Our Will*, 347–61. It is the argument of some scholars that women of the slaveholding class were too closely monitored and chaperoned to have been made vulnerable to attack, or for that matter to have engaged in proscribed sexual relations with blacks. See Clinton, *The Plantation Mistress*, 72–74, 102, 109; Fox-Genovese, *Within the Plantation Household*, 208, 241; Wolfe, *Daughters of Canaan*, 64; Hodes, *White Women, Black Men*, 5, 50; Wyatt-Brown, *Southern Honor*, 293–94, 298, 315–19. Wyatt-Brown further argues that white women who willingly engaged in sexual relationships with African American men were "women with defective notions of their social position" (315) and were quite probably "mentally retarded or else had a very poor self-image" (316).

98. This observation is made also in Schwarz, *Twice Condemned*, 207.

99. Alexander Gray to Governor Burton, December 8, 1825, March 24, 1825, GP 55 NCDAH.

100. Flanigan, "The Criminal Law of Slavery and Freedom, 1800–1868," 47–48.

101. Schwarz, *Twice Condemned*, 202–5.

102. Trial of Lipscomb, June 14, 1842, Halifax County Court Minutes Book (1838–45), 20 (microfilm reel 71), LVA; trial of Jackson, April 13, 1856, Halifax County Court Minutes Book (1856–59), 192 (microfilm reel 73), LVA. One cautionary note, however: the race of the victim in both cases was not indicated. Moreover, antebellum official court records can be notoriously vague and incomplete. Court clerks often denoted defendants charged with a "felony" and failed to specify the nature of the crime. Many slaves charged with "felonies" had their cases dismissed by grand juries for lack of evidence or by court officials for technical reasons. Plausibly, some of these could have been sexual assault charges.

103. Flanigan, "The Criminal Law of Slavery and Freedom, 1800–1868," 256, 257.

104. Coulter, "Four Slave Trials in Elbert County, Georgia," 244–45.

105. Hayneville *Watchman*, May 18, 1860.

106. Davidson County Criminal Court, Minutes, December 1852, 343; April 1853, 385; August 1853, 583, as cited by Howington, "The Treatment of Slaves and Free Blacks," 270.

107. *New Orleans Daily Delta*, November 14 and December 6, 1845.

108. Sellers, *Slavery in Alabama*, 255.

109. Morris, *Southern Slavery and the Law*, 315.

110. Hindus, "Black Justice under White Law," 592; Morris, *Southern Slavery and the Law*, 316.

111. Among the historical works suggesting or implying that antebellum white southerners, especially those of the elite class, were anxious about black male sexual aggression are Jordan, *White over Black*, 28–39, 148, 152; Thorpe, *The Old South*, 91, 113; Lawrence J. Friedman, *White Savage*, 11; Peter H. Wood, *Black Majority*, 237; Bardaglio, "Rape and the Law in the Old South," 752; Wyatt-Brown, *Southern Honor*, 50.

112. Victoria Bynum found this to be the case in antebellum North Carolina also. *Unruly Women*, 88–110.

113. As Kenneth Stampp has asserted, "The slave as property clearly had priority over the slave as a person." *The Peculiar Institution*, 204, 227–28. See also Hodes, *White Women, Black Men*, 60–65.

Chapter Two

1. No single study on childhood in the South exists. Most studies on childhood in the South focus more generally on the family. See Lewis, *The Pursuit of Happiness*; Censer, *North Carolina Planters and Their Children, 1800–1860*; Daniel Blake Smith, *Inside the Great House*. Peter Bardaglio touches upon child custody and adoption in the antebellum South in *Reconstructing the Household*, ch. 3. James Marten has looked at the impact of the Civil War on Confederate fathers in "Fatherhood and the Confederacy," and at the Civil War more generally in *The Children's Civil War*. Wilma King's work *Stolen Childhood* is an important addition to our understanding of childhood in slavery; however, no one has taken her lead to look at childhood outside of slavery in the early South.

2. Most of what we know about childhood and sexuality in the antebellum years, specifically sexual assault, comes from a few studies of one northern city. Stansell, *City of Women*; Arnold, " 'The Life of a Citizen in the Hands of a Woman.' "

3. For the legal definition of rape consult Morris, *Southern Slavery and the Law*, 304.

4. See Chapters 4 and 5; Sommerville, "The Rape Myth Reconsidered," 112–15; Bardaglio, *Reconstructing the Household*, 76, 199–200.

5. Sharon Block, "Coerced Sex in British North America, 1700–1820," 1–45.

6. *Stephen, a Slave v. State*, 11 Ga. 238 (1852). See also on this case Morris, *Southern Slavery and the Law*, 304; Bardaglio, *Reconstructing the Household*, 37–38.

7. On British law and the age of consent, consult Sir Matthew Hale, *The History of the Pleas of the Crown*, 2:627; Bienen, "Rape I," 45, 49. On early American law and its reliance on British common law, see Washburn, "Law and Authority in Colonial Virginia," 117–18; Kermit L. Hall, *The Magic Mirror*, 5–6, 31; and Lawrence M. Friedman, *A History of American Law*, 33–37, 102–15. For the postbellum period consult Bardaglio, *Reconstructing the Household*, 199. On the difference between rape and carnal knowledge in English common law, consult Mary Block, " 'An Accusation Easily to Be Made,' " 17–18. On colonial America's adaptation of British common law on rape and carnal knowledge, see also Mary Block, " 'An Accusation Easily to Be Made,' " 24–29. I concede that legal scholars and jurists alike may take issue with my interchangeable use of "carnal knowledge" and rape and would rightly point out the technical difference; however, even in nineteenth-century laws, the distinction was often blurred. I use the two here to mean essentially the same thing, largely to make a more readable text.

8. For states that established the age of consent at ten see Alabama, *Laws* (1840), ch. 3, sec. 17, p. 124; Bush, comp., *Digest of the Statute Law of Florida*, ch. 43, sec. 41, p. 217; Georgia, *Laws* (1811), sec. 61, p. 44; Mayer, Fischer, and Cross, comps., *Revised Code of Maryland*, tit. 27, art. 72, sec. 14, p. 787; Sharkey, Harris, and Ellett, comps., *Revised Code of the State of Mississippi*, sec. 46, art. 218, p. 608; Scott, Napton, Morrow, and Jones, comps., *Revised Statutes of the State of Missouri*, ch. 47, art. 2, sec. 26, p. 348; Nash, Iredell, and Battle, comps., *The Revised Statutes of the State of North Carolina*, vol. 1, ch. 34, art. 5, p. 192; James, comp., *A Digest of the Laws of South Carolina*, "Act of 1792," 87; Caruthers and Nicholson, comps., *A Compilation of the Statutes of Tennessee*, ch. 23, sec. 15, p. 29 (Act of 1829); Oldham and White, comps., *A Digest of the General Statute Laws of the State of Texas*, tit. 17, ch. 6, art. 523, p. 523 (Act of 1856). Virginia initially established ten as the age of consent, Tate, comp., *Digest of the Laws of Virginia* (Richmond, 1823), sec. 11, §3, p. 127, but later raised it to twelve,

Patton and Robinson, *Code of Virginia*, tit. 54, ch. 191, sec. 15, p. 725. Kentucky initially established the age of consent at ten years, Littell, comp., *Statute Law of the State of Kentucky*, 2:469, §8 (Act of 1801), then raised it to twelve in 1813, Littell, comp., *Statute Law of the State of Kentucky*, 5:50, ch. 73, §4. Missouri raised its age of consent from ten to twelve in 1856, Hardin, comp., *The Revised Statutes of the State of Missouri*, 1:564, secs. 27–28. Louisiana and Georgia relied upon common law to prosecute, which established ten as the age of discretion. In Louisiana's black codes, white girls as well as women were included in the rape statute. Statute of June 7, 1806, *Louisiana Acts*, "Black Code," ch. 33, sec. 7, p. 198.

9. Arkansas determined the age of consent to be "puberty," English, comp., *A Digest of the Statutes of Arkansas*, ch. 51, art. 4, sec. 4, p. 380, but changed the age to ten after the Civil War, Price and Barton, comps., *Chapters of the Digest of Arkansas, Approved November 17, 1868*, ch. 2, sec. 4, p. 217. A later statute digest, however, appears to reinstate "puberty." Gantt, comp., *Digest of the Statutes of Arkansas*, ch. 42, art. 8, sec. 1303, p. 333.

10. Mississippi *Laws* (June 1822), sec. 55, p. 198 (slaves, age twelve); Mississippi *Laws* (1839), tit. III, sec. 22, p. 116 ("every Person," presumably meaning whites, age ten); Meigs and Cooper, comps., *The Code of Tennessee*, art. III, sec. 4614, p. 830 (whites, age ten); Meigs and Cooper, comps., *The Code of Tennessee*, art. III, sec. 2625, part 7, p. 509 (slaves, age twelve).

11. Sharkey, Harris, and Ellett, comps., *Mississippi Revised Code*, ch. 33, sec. 11, art. 58, p. 248 (raised to age fourteen for slaves).

12. Arkansas *Statutes* (1838), sec. 4, p. 122 (five to twenty-one years for whites); Gould, comp., *A Digest of the Statutes of Arkansas*, ch. 51, art. IV, sec. 9 (death for slaves); Harris, Hartley, and Willie, comps., *Penal Code of Texas*, ch. VI, art. 529, p. 103 (whites, five to fifteen years); Harris, Hartley, and Willie, comps., *Penal Code of Texas*, tit. III, ch. II, art. 819, p. 163 (slaves, death); Harris, Hartley, and Willie, comps., *Penal Code of Texas*, tit. III, ch. II, art. 824, p. 164 (free blacks, death or one year to life); Meigs and Cooper, comps., *Code of Tennessee*, part IV, tit. I, ch. 2, art. III, sec. 4611, p. 830 (whites, ten to twenty-one years); Meigs and Cooper, comps., *Code of Tennessee*, ch. 3, art. III, sec. 2625 §7 (slaves, death for having sexual intercourse with a free white female under age of twelve); Leigh, comp., *The Revised Code of the Laws of Virginia*, vol. I, sec. 3, p. 585 (whites, one to ten years); Virginia General Assembly (1847–48), tit. II, ch. 13, sec. 1, p. 126 (free blacks and slaves, death or five to twenty years). Although Florida appears not to have made statutory rape criminal until after the Civil War, almost certainly it relied on common law to prosecute it. Rape of a white child resulted in the same sentence as that of a woman, death for slaves. Thompson, comp., *Manual or Digest of the Statute Law of the State of Florida*, tit. IV, ch. 1, sec. 1, §6. In 1872 Florida passed a statutory rape law setting the age of consent at ten and establishing death or life imprisonment as punishment. Bush, comp., *A Digest of the Statute Law of Florida*, ch. 43, sec. 41, p. 217.

13. Missouri included in its definition of rape having carnal knowledge of a female under the age of ten, punishable, like forcible rape, by five to ten years in prison. Scott, Napton, Morrow, and Jones, comps., *Revised Statutes of Missouri*, ch. 47, art. II, sec. 26, p. 348. For slaves, see King, comp., *Revised Statutes of Missouri*, art. II, §28, p. 171 (castration).

14. Moore, Biggs, and Rodman, comps., *Revised Code of North Carolina*, ch. 34, sec. 5, p. 203 (whites, death); Moore, Biggs, and Rodman, comps., *Revised Code of North Carolina*, ch. 107, sec. 44 (slaves, death); James, comp., *A Digest of the Laws of South Carolina*, 87

(whites, death without benefit of clergy); Cooper and McCord, eds., *The Statutes at Large of South Carolina*, vol. 9, no. 2893, p. 258 (slaves, death without benefit of clergy for assault and battery on a white woman with intent to commit a rape). There appears to be no specific slave code criminalizing sex with a child; however, the language in the statute intended for whites was so universal that it would appear to have applied to nonwhites as well.

15. Alabama Session Laws 24:1 (1830), General Assembly, 12th sess., 13, passed January 13, 1831; Ormond, Bagby, and Goldthwaite, comps., *Code of Alabama*, tit. 1, ch. 2, art. 10, §3307, p. 594 (slaves and free blacks, death for rape and attempted rape); Ormond, Bagby, and Goldthwaite, comps., *Code of Alabama*, tit. 1, ch. II, art. II, sec. 3091, p. 562 (whites, life imprisonment).

16. Georgia Session Laws (1811), "An act to ameliorate the criminal code . . ." [December 14, 1811], ch. 60, p. 44 (whites); Georgia Acts (1816), sec. 1, p. 15 (slaves).

17. Kentucky *Acts* (1801), ch. 67, secs. 7–8, p. 120 (age of consent at ten, ten to twenty-one years); Kentucky *Acts* (1802, Act of December 22, 1802, ch. 53, p. 116) (slaves, death for rape); Littell, comp., *The Statute Law of Kentucky*, 5:50, ch. 73 §4 (age of consent raised to twelve). On the transition of Kentucky from backwater frontier to settled state, see Aron, *How the West Was Lost*.

18. *Charles (a Slave) v. State*, 11 Ark. 410 (July term, 1850).

19. English, comp., *A Digest of the Statutes of Arkansas*, ch. 51, art. IV, sec. 4, p. 330.

20. Ibid., sec. 9, p. 331. Italics mine.

21. Arkansas law established the onset of puberty as the age of consent. Ball, Roane, and Pike, comps., *Revised Statutes of Arkansas*, sec. 4, p. 122.

22. *Charles (a Slave) v. State*, 11 Ark. 410 (July term, 1850). Inexplicably, the court did not consider Almyra Combs's underage status, not yet having attained puberty, in deciding the issue of force and lack of it in this case.

23. *The State (of Louisiana) v. Bill*, 8 Rob. 527 (February 1844). See also Schafer, *Slavery, the Civil Law, and the Supreme Court of Louisiana*, 85–86.

24. *Sydney v. The State*, 22 Tenn. (3 Hum.) 465 (1842). See also Howington, "The Treatment of Slaves and Free Blacks," 186.

25. *Wright v. State*, 4 Hum. 194, as cited in Quarles, *Criminal Code of Tennessee* (1874), 818.

26. *State (of North Carolina) v. Sam, a Slave*, 1 Winst. 300. On age requirements for rapists see Bienen, "Rape I," 46, 49–50; Mary Block, "'An Accusation Easily to Be Made,'" 29–30.

27. See Chapter 1, n. 93.

28. Trial of November 19, 1808, box 157 (October–December 1808), LR, VEP, LVA. Wyatt-Brown also discusses this case in *Southern Honor*, 387–88.

29. Ibid.

30. See Chapter 1, n. 59.

31. This appears to have been an accepted practice. There is no evidence of challenges to such secondhand testimony as hearsay.

32. Trial of November 19, 1808, box 157 (October–December 11, 1808), LR, VEP, LVA.

33. Ibid.

34. CS Executed, 1808, APA, LVA.

35. September–December 1860, box 472, PP, LR, VEP, LVA. (Research note: Virginia pardon papers continued to be housed with the other Executive Papers, located among the official records of the Office of the Governor, until about 1866, when the pardons were

segregated from other executive correspondence and were instead housed among the papers of the Secretary of the Commonwealth, Record Group 13, under the title Executive Papers.)

36. Ibid.

37. Ibid.

38. Official notation, ibid.

39. Henry County Court Minute Book (1820–49), July 9, 1832, August 14, 1832, 183, 187 (microfilm reel 23); CS Transported, 1832; Bonds for Transportation, 1806–39, LVA. No specific age of the daughter is given.

40. Sellers, *Slavery in Alabama*, 253.

41. *Columbus* (Ga.) *Sentinel*, reprinted in the *Augusta* (Ga.) *Chronicle*, August 17, 1851, as cited by Phillips, *American Negro Slavery*, 461–62. Although the quotation does not make explicit the "negro" man's status, I have to rely on Phillips's keen researching skills to assume he was a slave, since this account is included in Phillips's chapter on slave crime. Nor does the account yield any information about the status of the young girl.

42. October 1856, VEP, LVA.

43. *New Orleans Bee*, October 9, 1858.

44. November 1–30, 1822 folder, box 274, (October 1–December 11, 1822), LR, VEP, LVA. Virginia rape statutes appear not to have required proof of seminal emission. A footnote to a statute enacted in 1819 states that penetration, not emission, is evidence of rape and cites Virginia and British case law (*Commonwealth v. Thomas*, 1 Va. Cas. 307; *Rex v. Cox*, Moo. C.C.R. 337; *Rex v. Reckspear*, ib. 342; *Rex v. Cousins*, 6 C. & P. 351) and the British statute 9 Geo. IV, c. 31, sec. 18. "Act of February 8, 1819–January 1, 1820," Tate, comp., *Digest of the Laws of Virginia*, 212. A Virginia statute of 1861 explains the legal logic behind the modification: "The statute of 9 Geo.IV. ch.31, sex.17, after reciting that upon the trials for the crimes of buggery and of rape, and of carnally abusing girls under certain ages, offenders frequently escaped by reason of the difficulty of the proof required of the completion of those crimes, enacts that it shall not be necessary, in any of those cases, to prove the actual emission of seed in order to constitute a carnal knowledge, but that the carnal knowledge shall be deemed complete, upon proof of penetration only." Matthews, comp., *Digest of the Laws of Virginia of a Criminal Nature*, ch. XV, sec. 15, p. 118, n. 8. See also Mary Block, " 'An Accusation Easily to Be Made,' " 33.

Anna Clark explores the medical and legal origins of this requirement in eighteenth- and nineteenth-century England. She asserts that early jurists, such as Lord Hale, did not require proof of ejaculation in cases of rape; however, many subsequent English judges in the late eighteenth century did. This stipulation may have satisfied many jurists' desire to establish incidence of rape on the basis of "scientific criteria." Clark also suspects that the law's intent was to free judges from enforcing capital punishment of convicted rapists. The alternative, attempted rape, thus enabled a judge to punish the act, but not with death. Not until 1828 did Parliament abandon this onerous requirement. *Women's Silence, Men's Violence*, 60–63. See also Mary Block, " 'An Accusation Easily to Be Made,' " 19 n. 18, 33; Tong, *Women, Sex, and the Law*, 92–93. An important point of departure, though, between the English and American treatments of the seminal emission standard for rape is that England abandoned the requirement in 1828 while some American courts continued to demand proof of emission in rape cases, though rather infrequently. Mary Block, " 'An Accusation Easily to Be

Made,'" 33. Most states seem to have been guided by the first published American account, *Pennsylvania v. Sullivan*, 1 Addison (Pa.) 142 (1793), in which the state's high court asserted that proof of emission was not necessary. A later Pennsylvania statute reaffirms the appellate reasoning. Bienen, "Rape I," 50 n. 62. Gradually, southern states began to remove the emission requirement from rape statutes, some earlier than others. See Tennessee *Laws* (1829), ch. 23, sec. 13, p. 29; English, A *Digest of the Statutes of Arkansas*, ch. 52, sec. 173, p. 413; Maryland *Laws* (1854), ch. 89, p. 87. North Carolina did not remove this condition until 1861, and then only in cases of the rape of children and buggery. North Carolina *Laws* (1861), ch. 30, p. 61.

45. November 1–30, 1822 folder, box 274, (October 1–December 11, 1822), LR, VEP; CS Executed, 1823, LVA.

46. Since the accuser in this case was over the age of ten, the prosecution would have had to establish the use of force by the defendant.

47. There is no testimony explaining why Dinwiddie was charged only with attempted rape. Although there is no mention of a third party interrupting the assault, that might have occurred. There is also the possibility that Holloway might have been too embarrassed to testify about such details as penetration and ejaculation. Given strict Victorian taboos and sensibilities that forbade discussions about sexuality and sex acts, even privately among family members and friends, a reluctance to graphically describe an act of sexual violation publicly and before strangers seems reasonable. And without testimony acknowledging the requisite penetration, attempted rape was the only crime with which Dinwiddie could be charged. The prospect of publicly recounting explicit and lurid details about their assault, not to mention the shame and fear emanating from the rape itself, may have encouraged many victims of sexual assault to drop charges, not bring charges at all, or agree to the lesser charge of attempted rape, which would not have required the humiliation of answering questions about penile penetration and ejaculation. Later in the century this requirement became a major justification for lynching rather than proceeding legally with a trial.

48. Trial of July 6, 1826, box 294 (May 21–July 31, 1826), VEP; CS Executed, 1826, LVA.

49. Trial of July 15, 1826, box 294 (May 21–July 1826), VEP, LVA.

50. Ibid.

51. Ibid.

52. Official notation, ibid.

53. As in the case of Dinwiddie (1826), it is unclear why the charge was attempted rape. There is no mention of anyone or anything having scared off the accused slave, Jesse, before he could rape Mary. Nor is there any testimony pertaining to penetration or ejaculation, which often accompanied such trial records. It may very well be that the young girl was reluctant to testify about the details of her assault and settled on the attempted rape charge to avoid public embarrassment.

54. September 1856, LR, VEP, LVA.

55. Ibid.

56. Ibid.; CJ, LVA.

57. October 1856, LR, VEP, LVA.

58. Ibid.

59. The uncle's name appears in one letter as "Atwell P. Carndale" [or Cornwall?] and in another as "Atwell Pleasant." Letter from W. P. Goodwin (Anderson's owner) to Governor

Henry A. Wise, November 3, 1856; sworn statement of Joseph Sanford, n.d., both in October 1856, LR, VEP, LVA.

60. Sworn affidavits of Agnes Sanford November 1, 1856; Joseph Sanford, October 28, 1856; William M. B. Goodwin, November 3, 1856, all in October 1856, LR, VEP, LVA.

61. In Virginia only proof of penetration, not ejaculation, was required to substantiate consummated rape. See note 46.

62. June 24–30, 1819 folder, box 254 (June 1819), LR, VEP, LVA; and Schwarz, *Twice Condemned*, 206.

63. Anna K. Clark, *Women's Silence, Men's Violence.* On the importance of reputation and its relationship to marriage for white southern females, consult Fischer, " 'False, Feigned, and Scandalous Words.' "

64. Sworn testimony of Clementina Beazley and Lucy Dallas Beazley, October 6, 1856, Spotsylvania County Court, October 1856, LR, VEP, LVA.

65. Letters of October 28, 1856, and November 1, 1856, from Robert Dabney, clerk of court of Spotsylvania County, October 1856, LR, VEP, LVA.

66. By exploring rapists' motives, I realize that I run the risk of acknowledging the guilt of at least some of those African American men on trial for sexually assaulting young white girls. However I think it fair to say that such assaults did at times occur.

67. Violence by the attacker as well as resistance by the rape victim was established in Marybeth Hamilton Arnold's study of New York City as well. See " 'The Life of a Citizen in the Hands of a Woman,' " 45–47.

68. For later, turn-of-the century assessments of the credibility of children as witnesses, consult Wigmore, *The Principles of Judicial Proof*, 286–92.

69. June 1–20, 1829 folder, box 311 (May 1–July 20, 1829), LR, VEP; box 157, October–December 11, 1808, VEP; October 1856, LR, VEP; September–December 1860, box 472, PP, LR, VEP, LVA.

70. There seem to have been no challenges to the admission of hearsay evidence. On the legal weaknesses of such testimony, see Wigmore, *The Principles of Judicial Proof*, 376–80. Wigmore allows that "exceptional" circumstances can permit secondhand testimony.

71. This continued to be the case well into the twentieth century. See Stephen Murray Robertson, "Sexuality through the Prism of Age," 72.

72. October 18, 1833, LR, VEP, as quoted in Johnston, *Race Relations in Virginia and Miscegenation in the South, 1776–1860*, 263. (This document as cited by Johnston could not be located at the Library of Virginia.) At the age of eleven, Mary Jane Stevens would not have been considered a "child" according to the definition of rape. Also, see *Thompson v. Commonwealth of Virginia*, 4 Leigh 652 (1833); Frederick County Superior Court Order Book, 1831–35, entries for May 22, 23, June 10, 1833, 208, 210, and microfilm reel 100, LVA. No documentation that verifies the outcome of Thompson's appeal has been found. However, his name does not appear on lists of blacks executed or transported in the early 1830s.

73. Sommerville, "The Rape Myth Reconsidered," 185–86.

74. I have only come across three antebellum southern cases of white men raping their own daughters, in two cases stepdaughters. The third case involved a seventeen-year-old daughter. Sommerville, "The Rape Myth Reconsidered," 271–72.

75. Stephen Murray Robertson, "Sexuality through the Prism of Age," 50.

76. Arnold, " 'The Life of a Citizen in the Hands of a Woman,' " 42. It is important to note

that sexual assaults of slave girls would not have entered the record, hence offering at least a partial explanation for why recorded southern rapes of children were fewer in number than in New York City.

77. Stansell, *City of Women*, 278 n. 33, 101.

78. Raleigh (N.C.) *Star*, July 17, 1834, as quoted in Guion Griffis Johnson, *Antebellum North Carolina*, 509.

79. September 1–15, 1817 folder, box 241 (September–November 1817), VEP, LVA. See also *The State v. William Marshall*, 61 N.C. (June term, 1866), 62.

80. *Alfred, a Slave v. State of Georgia* (March 1849), 483–86.

81. Schafer, *Slavery, the Civil Law, and the Supreme Court of Louisiana*, 86.

82. Trial of Caesar, November 18, 1724, Spotsylvania County Court Order Book (1724–30), 37 (microfilm reel 43), LVA.

83. Bynum, *Unruly Women*, 88–110; Sommerville, "The Rape Myth in the Old South"; Hodes, *White Women, Black Men*, 61–63; Bardaglio, *Reconstructing the Household*, 74–75; Laura F. Edwards, *Gendered Strife and Confusion*, 200–202.

84. June 1–20, 1829 folder, box 311 (May 1–July 20, 1829), LR, VEP, LVA.

85. Ibid. Slaves were precluded from testifying only in cases in which whites stood accused of a crime. In the case of slave crime, where the accused was not white, slaves often testified.

86. Ibid.

87. Ibid.

88. June 21–30, 1829 folder, ibid.

89. Ibid.

90. September 1829 entry, 1806–39 folder, Bonds for Transportation; CS 1829 Transported; August 7, 1829, entry, List, in CS, LVA.

91. Bynum makes this point in *Unruly Women*.

92. Petition to Governor Clark, August 23, 1861, GP, Clark, and GLB, 80, NCDAH, as quoted in Bynum, *Unruly Women*, 118.

93. October 18, 1833, LR, VEP, as quoted in Johnston, *Race Relations in Virginia and Miscegenation in the South, 1776–1860*, 263.

94. There are several antebellum cases in which white men were officially charged with sexually assaulting young girls. In 1810, William Dick, a laborer from Monroe County, Virginia, and himself the father of three, was convicted of raping Nancy Maddy, a child between the ages of ten and twelve. Dick received a sentence of eighteen years in solitary confinement, nearly the most severe penalty allowed by law. Despite the stiff sentence, however, the governor pardoned Dick in January 1824, four years before the end of his sentence. Ironically, as despicable as this act must have been viewed, as is evidenced from the sentence, several petitioners expressed great sympathy for Dick's plight, including apparently members of the Maddy clan who acknowledged that although they "view this crime with the utmost horror," they were willing to forgive. September 11–20, 1810 folder, box 168 (August–September 1810), VEP, LVA. Petition with fifty signatures, n.d., ibid. The law under which Dick was prosecuted held that the term of imprisonment for a convicted (white) rapist was ten to twenty-one years. Shepherd, ed., *The Statutes at Large*, II, ch. 2, sec. 4, p. 6, "Act of December 15, 1796." Norment Querry of Richmond likewise faced a harsh sentence upon conviction of child rape in 1853. He received twenty years in prison for raping a child under the age of twelve, the harshest punishment allowable under the law. Querry

solicited the governor in 1864 for release, ostensibly to fight in the war. Not until 1866 did the governor pardon Querry. It is also likely that the twenty-year sentence takes into account a history of prior convictions for sexual assault. The Virginia prison register received into the penitentiary on April 26, 1851, for a fifteen-year term a Normant Querry, who was released on April 26, 1866. At least a partial discrepancy in the recording of some of this information seems likely. VEPLR Pardons, January–March 1864, November 1864 folder; Virginia Prison Registers, entry for April 26, 1851, p. 150, LVA. Also suspicious is an act passed by the Virginia legislature in 1845 releasing the Norment family from the responsibility of repaying prosecution costs of William Norment of Caroline County for the crime of rape. Of course it is possible that two Virginia sex offenders shared an unusual name. Virginia *Laws*, ch. 194, p. 150 (passed March 3, 1846). For another white man sentenced to prison for the rape of a white child, see *Wright v. State*, 4 Hum. 194, as cited in Quarles, *Criminal Code and Digest of Tennessee*, 818.

95. *State v. LeBlanc*, 1 Tread. Const. 354 (1813). South Carolina lacked a penitentiary until after the Civil War. As a result, many more antebellum crimes were capital, even for whites, than in any other southern state. Hindus, *Prison and Plantation*, 210–49.

96. *State v. Alfred Goings, alias Alfred Terry*, 20 N.C. 289 (1838).

97. March 19, 22, 23, September 16, 1844, Bertie County Superior Court Minutes, 1828–57, NCDAH; *State v. Farmer*, 26 N.C. 224 (1844). In 1867 Franklin Smith (no race given) was convicted and sentenced to die for raping a girl under ten years of age. *State v. Franklin Smith*, 61 N.C. (June term, 1867), 304–5. On the other end of the spectrum, a white Missouri man received a mere three years in prison for an attempted rape of a nine-year-old girl. *McComas v. State*, 11 Mo. 116 (1847).

98. Relying almost exclusively on statutory law and not on court records, most claim that the sexual assault of a black female was not a capital offense, let alone a crime in some states. Mary Block, " 'An Accusation Easily to Be Made,' " 37; Schafer, "The Long Arm of the Law," 1256, 1265; Schafer, *Slavery, the Civil Law, and the Supreme Court of Louisiana*, 85; Brownmiller, *Against Our Will*, 162; Clinton, "Bloody Terrain," 315; Clinton, " 'Southern Dishonor,' " 65; Deborah Gray White, *Ar'n't I a Woman?*, 152; Getman, "Sexual Control in the Slaveholding South," 135; Cobb, *An Inquiry Into the Law of Negro Slavery*, 99; D'Emilio and Freedman, *Intimate Matters*, 101; Laura F. Edwards, *Gendered Strife and Confusion*, 9.

99. *George v. State*, 37 Miss. 316 (1859). For historians' treatments of this particular case consult Bardaglio, *Reconstructing the Household*, 67–68; Morris, *Southern Slavery and the Law*, 51; White, *Ar'n't I a Woman?*, 152; Clinton, "Bloody Terrain," 315; Clinton, " 'Southern Dishonor,' " 66; Tushnet, "The American Law of Slavery, 1810–1860," 120, 133–34. More generally on rape and slave women see Kolchin, *American Slavery, 1619–1877*, 124–25; Burnham, "An Impossible Marriage," 199; Clinton, " 'Southern Dishonor,' " 57–58, 65–66; McLaurin, *Celia, a Slave*; Hine, "Rape and the Inner Lives of Black Women in the Middle West," 912–13; Jennings, " 'Us Colored Women Had to Go through a Plenty' "; Landers, " 'In Consideration of Her Enormous Crime' "; Lecaudey, "Behind the Mask: Ex-Slave Women and Interracial Sexual Relations"; Painter, "Soul Murder and Slavery"; Jacobs, *Incidents in the Life of a Slave Girl, Written by Herself*.

100. Other cases of slaves indicted for rape of female slaves include *Commonwealth v. Kitt*, May 29, 1778, and *Commonwealth v. Kitt*, July 29, 1783, Westmoreland County Order Book, 1776–86, LVA, as quoted in Morris, *Southern Slavery and the Law*, 306. In 1797 a slave was

hanged for the murder of a woman identified as a mulatto. Schwarz, *Twice Condemned*, 207; Morris, *Southern Slavery and the Law*, 306. A slave in Mecklenburg County, Coleman, was convicted of raping a female slave child under the age of twelve. CS 1857, Transported; Mecklenburg County Court Order Book (1853–58), November 17, 1856; December 1856 folder, December 9, 28, 1856, VEP, LR, CJ, LVA.

101. Bardaglio, *Reconstructing the Household*, 68; "An act to punish negroes, and mulattoes, for rape or an attempt to rape," December 13, 1859, ch. 62, sec. 1, p. 102 (Mississippi law); Clark, Cobb, and Irwin, comps., *Code of Georgia*, tit. I, div. IV, §§4248–49, p. 824 (Georgia law).

102. Shelby County, Circuit Court Minutes, January 1855, 400–401, 425–27, 428, as cited in Howington, "The Treatment of Slaves and Free Blacks in the State and Local Courts of Tennessee," 114.

103. Depositions of various witnesses, n.d., trial of Ned, June 9, 1859, City of Fredericksburg Court Records, Fredericksburg Circuit Court House, Fredericksburg, Virginia. My thanks to Barry L. McGhee for making these documents available to me. Mr. McGhee is involved in an inventory and indexing of all Fredericksburg courts records until 1914. Researchers in African American history will be delighted to learn that part of the catalog and index functions are descriptors of race.

104. Ibid.

105. Ibid.

106. Ibid.

107. Ibid. Arrest warrants made out for Ned for the rapes of Eunice Thompson and Betty Gordon, May 17, 1859, by order of Hugh Scott, justice of the peace, ibid. The arrest warrant sworn out for a "negro" girl seems to refute blanket assertions that females of color could not be raped in the eyes of the law. *Fredericksburg* (Va.) *News*, June 14, 1859, 2.

108. Undated letter received August 29, 1859, August 1859, VEP, LVA. The purpose of the letter was to request a commendation for Beach.

109. Schwarz, *Twice Condemned*, 292–93, and CJ, LVA.

110. Typical is the characterization by James B. Sellers. "Most heinous of all crimes a Negro might commit was rape or attempted rape. No other crime aroused as much passion and thirst for revenge." Sellers, *Slavery in Alabama*, 252–53. He later qualifies this statement by acknowledging that despite arousing such excitement, "usually the law took its course and citizens abided by its decision." Ibid., 253. See also Stampp, *The Peculiar Institution*, 190–91. Of course in this double child rape in Fredericksburg, blacks (as well as incensed whites) could very well have participated in the mob.

111. Genovese, *Roll, Jordan, Roll*, 33. See also Morris, "Slaves and the Rules of Evidence in Criminal Trials," 1210–11.

112. See, for example, Chapter 1; Sommerville, "The Rape Myth in the Old South Reconsidered"; Sommerville, "Rape, Race, and Castration in Slave Law in the Colonial South"; Hodes, *White Women, Black Men*.

113. Stansell, *City of Women*, 182–83.

114. The landmark work in the history of childhood is Ariès, *Centuries of Childhood*. A spate of works on family followed, including Fliegelman, *Prodigals and Pilgrims*; Daniel Blake Smith, *Inside the Great House*; Greven, *The Protestant Temperament*; Lewis, *The Pursuit of Happiness*; Censer, *North Carolina Planters and Their Children, 1800–1860*. For

review essays on Ariès's influence and developments in the field of family history since his work, consult Cunningham, "Histories of Childhood," and Hareven, "The History of the Family and the Complexity of Social Change." An excellent summary of important works that speak to the development of childhood ideas in colonial and early American is Hessinger, "Problems and Promises."

Among the contributions of these historical works on childhood and family is the notion that a dramatic reconceptualization of childhood unfolded in the wake of important social, religious, and economic transformations in America. In time, waves of evangelical fervor helped erode deeply entrenched ideas about the innate sinfulness of small children and allowed for a deeper appreciation of the condition of childhood. A greater sensitivity to children occurred in the context of an increasing sentimentalization of family after the American Revolution.

115. Mary Block, " 'An Accusation Easily to Be Made.' " Of course this disjuncture might be understood as a community coming down hard on an accused child rapist by rendering a death sentence, and the judiciary functioning as a paternalistic check on the prejudices of locals.

Chapter Three

1. Rothman, *Notorious in the Neighborhood*, 6.

2. Some works that espouse this explanation of race and rape law include Jordan, *White over Black;* Bardaglio, "Rape and the Law in the Old South," 749–72; Bardaglio, *Reconstructing the Household*, 64; Getman, "Sexual Control in the Slaveholding South," 115–52; Wyatt-Brown, *Southern Honor*, 50.

3. Experts in legal history have cautioned against making sweeping generalizations about society on the basis of statutes alone. William M. Wiecek, for one, asserts, "statutes are not evidence of actual societal conditions. When a statute prohibits a certain type of behavior . . . it is no more reasonable to infer from the enactment of the statute that such behavior was common than to infer that it was rare." Wiecek, "The Statutory Law of Slavery and Race in the Thirteen Mainland Colonies of British America," 279. Likewise, Winthrop Jordan, while relying heavily on laws as evidence, acknowledged the danger in "assuming that laws reflect actual practice." Jordan, *White over Black*, 587. Timothy H. Breen and Stephen Innes also counsel against scholarly use of statutes in making generalizations about "white society." "To what degree did a planter elite set the cultural standards for less affluent whites?" Breen and Innes, *"Myne Owne Ground,"* 119 n. 14, 23–26. We know from a plethora of works that southern society, from colonial times through the Civil War, was racked with social discontent and challenges to the elite. Breen, "A Changing Labor Force and Race Relations in Virginia, 1660–1710," 3–25; Bailyn, "Politics and Social Structure in Virginia," 90–115; Edmund S. Morgan, "Slavery and Freedom," 5–29; Isaac, "Evangelical Revolt"; Isaac, *The Transformation of Virginia, 1740–1790*; Klein, "Frontier Planters and the American Revolution," 37–69; Kay, "The North Carolina Regulation, 1766–1776," 71–123; Ronald Hoffman, "The 'Disaffected' in the Revolutionary South," 273–316; Escott, *Many Excellent People*, 3–84; J. William Harris, *Plain Folk and Gentry in a Slave Society*, 64–93. Breen and Innes further argue that the historiography of race, at least for the colonial South, and I would add the nineteenth-century South, has been dominated by a "monolithic perception of race," in

essence a "racially determinative interpretation of behavior." Works embracing this analytical framework see race as the sole or most powerful factor influencing behavior. *"Myne Owne Ground,"* 23, 27. Generalizations about rape and race on the basis of statutes are predicated on a unified white response to blacks that clearly did not exist.

4. Jordan, *White over Black*, 154. Castration of convicted rapists had some basis in medieval English law. See Mary Block, " 'An Accusation Easily to Be Made,' " 13–16; Jordan, *White over Black*, 156 n. 40.

5. Wyatt-Brown, *Southern Honor*, 50.

6. Bardaglio, "Rape and the Law in the Old South," 752; Bardaglio, *Reconstructing the Household*, 64. For a challenge to that claim see Sommerville, "Rape, Race, and Castration in Slave Law in the Colonial and Early South," 74–89.

7. Hening, ed., *The Statutes at Large*, 3:461 (Act of 1705); Clark, ed., *The State Records of North Carolina*, 23:489 (Act of 1758); Cooper and McCord, eds., *The Statutes at Large of South Carolina*, 7:359–60 (Act of 1696); Missouri *Revised Statutes* (1844–45), ch. 47, art. II, sec. 3, p. 349. See also Morris, *Southern Slavery and the Law*, 305.

8. Cooper and McCord, eds., *The Statutes at Large of South Carolina*, 7:360.

9. Hening, ed., *The Statutes at Large*, 3:461 (Act of 1705). See also Guild, *Black Laws of Virginia*, 51, 53, 57; Wiecek, "The Statutory Law of Slavery and Race in the Thirteen Mainland Colonies of British America," 271–72; Arthur P. Scott, *Criminal Law in Colonial Virginia*, 300–301.

10. Alan D. Watson, "North Carolina Slave Courts, 1715–1785," 34.

11. Bush, comp., *New Jersey Archives*, 3d ser., vol. II, *Laws of the Royal Colony of New Jersey, 1703–1745*, 30.

12. Mitchell et al., *Statutes of Pennsylvania*, 2:7–8, as cited by Jordan, *White over Black*, 155 n. 39, and Kay and Cary, *Slavery in North Carolina*, 84 n. 46. The Pennsylvania statute called for the castration of married men convicted of sodomy, bestiality, or of rape for the second time. The law was repealed shortly thereafter. See *Statutes of Pennsylvania*, 2:178, 183–84 (Act of 1706). On the punishment of castration in colonial Pennsylvania consult Getman, "Sexual Control in the Slaveholding South," 134–54, and Higginbotham, *In the Matter of Color*, 282.

13. Higginbotham and Kopytoff, "Racial Purity and Interracial Sex in the Law of Colonial and Antebellum Virginia," 2008.

14. Cooper and McCord, eds., *Statutes of South Carolina*, 2:422 (Act of 1712).

15. Marbury and Crawford, comps., *Digest of the Laws of Georgia*, 430 (Act of 1770); Clark, ed., *State Records of North Carolina*, 23:23, 489 (Act of 1758). Colonial Maryland regarded rape by whites as a capital offense, relying on the authority and precedence of English law. Its legislature, however, provided for the death penalty for slaves convicted of rape but did not enact similar legislation for white rapists. See Ellefson, *The County Courts and the Provincial Court in Maryland, 1733–1763*, 290.

16. Because South Carolina was sluggish in revising its harsh legal code and because it had no penitentiary until after the Civil War, numerous crimes were capital, even for whites. In 1813 there were 165 capital crimes. See Hindus, *Prison and Plantation*, 196. A perusal of antebellum Virginia criminal codes reveals sixty offenses for which blacks could receive the death sentence and free whites would not. Stroud, *A Sketch of Laws Relating to Slavery in the Several States of the United States of America*, 77–80. See also Candler et al., eds., *The*

Colonial Records of the State of Georgia, xix, 219–22; Browne, Hand, Hall, and Steiner, eds., *Archives of Maryland*, XL (Act of 1737), 92–93. It is important to keep in mind that colonial courts handed down death sentences to white offenders of crimes, too. In 1760 James Horner, white, was sentenced to hang for the crime of rape. Ellefson, *The County Courts and the Provincial Court in Maryland, 1733–1763*, 290. White men convicted of even far lesser crimes sometimes received the death penalty. In 1760 a white laborer from Baltimore County was sentenced to die for breaking and entering and for the theft of meats and other property. *Archives of Maryland*, 32:314.

17. On the practice by colonial and state governments of compensating slaveowners for executed slaves, see Wiecek, "The Statutory Law of Slavery and Race in the Thirteen Mainland Colonies of British America," 275; Flanigan, "The Criminal Law of Slavery and Freedom, 1800–1868," 66; Schwarz, *Twice Condemned*, 20, 52–53; Hindus, "Black Justice under White Law," 25–26; Bassett, *Slavery in the State of North Carolina*, 14; R. H. Taylor, "Humanizing the Slave Code of North Carolina," 329; John Edwards, "Slave Justice in Four Middle Georgia Counties," 266; Phillips, *American Negro Slavery*, 491–92; Spindel, *Crime and Society in North Carolina, 1663–1776*, 133–34; Clark, ed., *State Records of North Carolina*, 23:489; Schwarz, "The Transportation of Slaves from Virginia, 1801–1865" 224–26. While slaveholders were usually compensated for condemned slaves, rates generally did not always reflect fair market value; masters thus had financial motives to save the lives of their slaves despite the policy of compensation. See Sommerville, "The Rape Myth in the Old South Reconsidered," 496–97, 503–5, 510–11.

18. Brickell, *The Natural History of North Carolina*, 273.

19. Clark, ed., *State Records of North Carolina*, 23:488–89. On North Carolina's use of castration of slave criminals during the French and Indian War, see also Crow, *The Black Experience in Revolutionary North Carolina*, 25–26; R. H. Taylor, "Humanizing the Slave Code of North Carolina," 324; Spindel, *Crime and Society in North Carolina, 1663–1776*, 134; Jordan, *White over Black*, 157; Alan D. Watson, "North Carolina Slave Courts, 1715–1785," 32; Fischer, "Dangerous Acts," 262–64.

20. Kay and Cary, " 'The Planters Suffer Little or Nothing,' " 298; Kay and Cary, *Slavery in North Carolina, 1748–1775*, 84.

21. After the end of the war executions of slaves quadrupled, and only two castrations can be documented for the period 1765 to 1772. Kay and Cary, *Slavery in North Carolina, 1748–1775*, 90.

22. Genovese, *Roll, Jordan, Roll*, 67. There was renewed interest in castration of slaves, especially among the "western" slaveholding states later in the nineteenth century. In Missouri during the antebellum period men of color faced castration for rape and attempted rape of white females. See Scott, Napton, Morrow, and Jones, comps., *Revised Statutes of Missouri* (1844–45), ch. 47, art. 2, sec. 31, p. 349. Two Missouri slaves convicted of sex crimes appealed their castration sentences to the state supreme court. See *Nathan v. State*, 8 Mo. 631 (July 1844), and *State v. Anderson*, 19 Mo. 241 (October 1853). A law enacted in Kansas in 1855 called for the castration of any black or mulatto convicted of rape or attempted rape, to be paid for by the accused! Wriggins, "Rape, Racism, and the Law," 105 n. 8.

23. Hening, ed., *The Statutes at Large*, 8:358. A revision of the Virginia slave code in 1792 left the castration punishment for attempted rape intact. Shepherd, ed., *The Statutes at Large of Virginia*, I, ch. 41, sec. 18, p. 125 (Act of 1792). A law enacted in 1805 provided that "if

any slave shall hereafter attempt to ravish a white woman, and shall be thereof lawfully convicted, he shall be considered guilty of a felony, and shall be punished as heretofore." Shepherd, ed., *The Statutes at Large*, III, ch. 5, sec. 11, p. 119 (Act of 1805). Not until 1823, however, did the death sentence replace castration for the crime of attempted rape of a white female by a slave. *Acts*, ch. 34, sec. 3, p. 37 (Act of 1823). See also Schwarz, *Twice Condemned*, 206; Morris, *Southern Slavery and the Law*, 305; Bardaglio, "Rape and the Law in the Old South," 753 n. 13; Higginbotham and Kopytoff, "Racial Purity and Interracial Sex," 2010–11 n. 201. Winthrop Jordan apparently stated incorrectly that castration of slaves convicted of attempted rape ended with the legislation of 1805. See *White over Black*, 473.

24. Schwarz, *Twice Condemned*, 152.

25. Trial of Peter, January 5, 1782, Northampton County Court Minute Book (1777–83), 334–35 (microfilm reel 50), LVA.

26. Trial of Bob, June 13, 1783, Southampton County Court Order Book (1778–84), 336 (microfilm reel 27), LVA.

27. Genovese, *Roll, Jordan, Roll*, 67.

28. *Mathews v. Sims*, 2 Mill 103 (May 1818).

29. Candler, ed., *The Colonial Records of the State of Georgia*, xviii, 132–33.

30. Janson, *The Stranger in America, 1793–1806*, 386–87.

31. *Virginia Gazette*, December 23, 1773. Philip Schwarz in *Twice Condemned*, 137–39, examines the conditions under which the slaves of Robert Munford, the slaveowner rebuked in the article, lived. I could not, however, locate this reference as cited.

32. Trial of Henry Delong, April 9, 1784, Mecklenburg County Court Order Book, (1779–84), 530 (microfilm reel 35), LVA. Philip Schwarz also located the case of a slave master in York County, Virginia, who was examined for having castrated a slave. Trials, November 18, 1773, York County Court Order Book (1774–84), 411 (microfilm reel 33), LVA; Schwarz, *Twice Condemned*, 162–63.

33. *Worley v. State*, 30 Tenn. (11 Hum.) 171 (1850), 172–75.

34. Tennessee "Act of 1829," ch. 23, sec. 55, which reads: "no person shall unlawfully and maliciously, by cutting or otherwise, cut off or disable the organs of generation of another, or any part thereof." Tennessee was not alone in outlawing castration. See also Hotchkiss, comp., *A Codification of the Statute Law of Georgia*, tit. I, ch. 28, art. 3, sec. 6, pp. 708–9 (under penalty of death); Moore, Biggs, and Rodman, comps., *Revised Code of North Carolina*, ch. 34, sec. 5, p. 203 (under penalty of death); Oldham and White, comps., *A Digest of the General Statute Laws of the State of Texas*, ch. 4, arts. 505–6, p. 521 (sentence was five to fifteen years, unless committed on a slave or free person of color, in which case punishment would be "in the same manner as if committed upon a free white person"). Bertram Wyatt-Brown reports yet another case of local officials admonishing a slaveowner for castrating a slave. A poor North Carolina farmer was fined $20 in 1831 for castrating a seventeen-year-old slave, his only one. Wyatt-Brown, *Southern Honor*, 376.

35. *Worley v. State*, 30 Tenn. (11 Hum.) 171 (1850).

36. Trial of Jemmy, July 13, 1738, Goochland County Court Order Book (1735–41), 327 (microfilm reel 21), LVA.

37. Trial of Andrew, May 28, 1736, Caroline County Court Order Book (1732–40), 349 (microfilm reel 13), LVA.

38. Trial of Natt, September 6, 1775, Lancaster County Court Order Book (1778–83), 7, 8

(microfilm reel 30), LVA. This case is also related in Schwarz, *Twice Condemned*, 158–59. For other cases of slaves in colonial Virginia sentenced to die for rape or attempted rape of white women or girls see trial of Harry, February 25, 1723, Lancaster County Court Order Book (1713–21), 334–36 (1721–29), 136–37, 141–42 (microfilm reel 27), and trial of Jack, June 12, 1772, Mecklenburg County Court Order Book (1771–73), 257 (microfilm reel 34), LVA.

39. Trial of Daniel, property of Henry Hatcher, in 1701, quoted in Schwarz, *Twice Condemned*, 72. Similar fates befell two condemned slave rapists from North Carolina: George, of Duplin County, in 1770 and Ben, in 1775, both recounted in Spindel, *Crime and Society in North Carolina, 1663–1776*, 134–35. See also the fate of a runaway Virginia slave who, along with an another runaway, was found guilty of breaking and entering the home of a married white woman, where he purportedly beat the woman and, in the mind of the court, intended to kill or ravish her. Trial of Olan, June 12, 1744, and Trial of Tom, August 6, 1744, Westmoreland County Court Order Book (1737–43), 34a, 37a, LVA; Schwarz, *Twice Condemned*, 133.

40. Trial of Titus, August 25, 1777, Onslow County, Miscellaneous Records, NCDAH, as cited in Alan D. Watson, "North Carolina Slave Courts, 1715–1785," 33 n. 38. It should be pointed out that convicted rapists were not the only slave criminals to suffer such barbaric postmortem treatment. A North Carolina slave found guilty of murder in 1785 was decapitated and his impaled head placed upon a pole for public display. Also in Alan D. Watson, "North Carolina Slave Courts, 1715–1785," 33. For other accounts of African Americans convicted of rape or attempted rape of white females and put to death legally in the colonial era see Fischer, "Dangerous Acts," 243; Browne, Hand, Hall, and Steiner, eds., *Archives of Maryland*, 28:181 (1739), 31:30–31 (1754), 32:306, 312 (1769).

41. Trial of Caesar, November 18, 1724, Spotsylvania County Court Order Book (1724–30), 37 (microfilm reel 43), LVA. See Chapter 2.

42. *Virginia Gazette*, August 19–26, 1737, 4.

43. Trial of Tom, September 14, 1775, Lancaster CCOB (1778–83) (microfilm reel 30), LVA. The reluctance of courts to execute condemned slaves is noted in the diary of the Virginia planter Landon Carter. Carter complained that the grand jury, which met on May 6, 1772, failed to hold over an errant slave (his alleged crime is not stated), although "every presumption was as strong as could be." Carter further groused about a "New law," the impact of which was that "a Negro now cannot be hanged, for there must be four Judges to condemn him; And such a court I am persuaded will never be got." Carter's allusion was to a law passed in 1772 which required a majority of justices to vote for sentence of death in capital cases of slaves. Hening, *The Statutes at Large*, 8:522. Carter speculated that the reform had been motivated by fiscal concerns: "I understand the Public frugality occasioned this law that they might not have too many slaves to be paid for." Carter predicted dire consequences of the new law. "Frugality go on with your destruction; and prosper thou the country whom thou intendest to serve if thou canst. My word for it, this law will not stand long." Greene, ed., *The Diary of Colonel Landon Carter of Sabine Hall, 1752–1778*, 2:676. Sometimes slaves who were brought up on charges of rape found themselves, perhaps in cases of weak evidence or a divided jury, judged guilty of lesser crimes. In 1742 the Virginia slave Jack was put on trial for raping a white woman. Instead, he was convicted of assault and given thirty-nine lashes. Arthur P. Scott, *Criminal Law in Colonial Virginia*, 161.

44. Trial of Daniel, August 23, 1753, and November 28, 1753, Chesterfield County Court

Order Book (1767–71) (microfilm reel 39), LVA; *Journal of the House of Burgess*, 1752–55, 115, and 1756–58, 270, as quoted in Schwarz, *Twice Condemned*, 163 n. 55.

45. Re Negro Abraham, Browne, Hand, Hall, and Steiner, eds., *Archives of Maryland*, 32:368–70 (June 1770). Governors' pardons were granted to other convicted slave rapists in colonial Maryland: Harry of Baltimore County was spared his life in 1752 after being convicted of raping a white widow woman at whose home his wife resided. The court, in recommending mercy, sympathized that Harry "had been always an orderly Fellow." Ibid., 28:577. In 1769 the governor of Maryland also pardoned Ben of Talbot County after a court found him guilty of assault with intent to ravish. Jurors who attached a plea for a pardon complained that the "Attempt [was] but small, and the Evidence not so clear as we could wish." Ibid., 32:270–71. The governor of Maryland was requested to issue a death warrant in 1751 for Sharper, a slave from Dorchester County convicted of rape, but refused because he believed that the proceedings that found him guilty were "erroneous." Ibid., 28:501–2.

46. Governors could also pardon the condemned slave completely, though in practice this was rarely done. On the commuting practices of governors and executive councils see Wyatt-Brown, "Community, Class, and Snopesian Crime," 194–97; Ernest James Clark, "Aspects of the North Carolina Slave Code, 1715–1860," 153; Ayers, *Vengeance and Justice*, 63–64; Schwarz, *Twice Condemned*, 23; Schwarz, *Slave Laws in Virginia*, 97–119; Phillips, *American Negro Slavery*, 461–62; Phillips, "Slave Crime in Virginia," 339; Hindus, *Prison and Plantation*, 104, 112–24, 155–56; Hodes, *White Women, Black Men*, 7, 37, 43, 56, 57–66; Flanigan, "Criminal Procedure in Slave Trials in the Antebellum South," 543–45; Howington, "The Treatment of Slaves and Free Blacks in the State and Local Courts of Tennessee," 162; Lawrence M. Friedman, *Crime and Punishment in American History*, 92; Arthur P. Scott, *Criminal Law in Colonial Virginia*, 116–21; Rothman, *Notorious in the Neighborhood*, 184–85.

47. A more comprehensive study of rape and white offenders is necessary before definitive conclusions can be drawn. Other black men charged with rape or attempted rape in the colonial South include Robin, who was being sought by Virginia officials in 1677 for the ravishment of a white woman. Robin was captured, convicted, and sentenced to death; however, his master intervened on his behalf. Robin's life was spared. McIlwaine, ed., *Minutes of the Council and General Court of Colonial Virginia*, 520. Jack Kecatan, a black servant in Charles City County, Virginia, had a reputation in the neighborhood for seducing or raping English servants, including one or more of his own master's female servants. Kecatan appears never to have been brought to trial for his alleged infractions. Schwarz, *Twice Condemned*, 71. Harry, a North Carolina slave, was convicted of raping a sixteen-year-old white girl and sentenced to hang. Spindel, *Crime and Society in North Carolina*, 76, 109. And Wills, a slave and conjurer from Dobbs County, North Carolina, knowledgeable in herbs and concoctions was charged with using his potions to seduce and impregnate a white woman in 1769. The accusation may have been an attempt by the accuser to cover up her affair with the slave. Crow, *The Black Experience in Revolutionary North Carolina*, 38–39.

48. Genovese, *Roll, Jordan, Roll*, 40–41. Strict laws frequently went unenforced. See Reinders, "Slavery in New Orleans in the Decade before the Civil War," 374. Schwarz criticizes Genovese on this point. Schwarz, *Slave Laws in Virginia*, 9–10.

49. Phifer, "Slavery in Microcosm," 87.

50. Higginbotham, *In the Matter of Color*, 168.

51. On this historiographical debate, consult Sommerville, "The Rape Myth in the Old South Reconsidered," 483 n. 7.

52. Schwarz, *Twice Condemned*, 39.

53. Hening, ed., *The Statutes at Large*, 8:358.

54. Ibid., 8:522, as discussed in Schwarz, *Twice Condemned*, 22–23.

55. Schwarz, *Twice Condemned*, 23. On the impact of the American Revolution on criminal law in Virginia see Preyer, "Crime, the Criminal Law, and Reform in Post-Revolutionary Virginia," 53–85. For an assessment of the more general impact of the American Revolution on the new nation's black population see Higginbotham, *In the Matter of Color*, 371–89; Jordan, *White over Black*, 269–311; Ira Berlin, "The Revolution in Black Life," 349–82.

56. Genovese, *Roll, Jordan, Roll*, 32.

57. On the construction of southern laws with regard to race, as well as the justification for disparate legal treatment of the races, see Tushnet, "The American Law of Slavery, 1810–60," 169–74; Stampp, *The Peculiar Institution*, 210. On the compiling of colonial slave codes refer to Wiecek, "The Statutory Law of Slavery and Race in the Thirteen Mainland Colonies of British America," 259–60.

58. Quoted in Edmund S. Morgan, *American Slavery, American Freedom*, 314.

59. This conviction was echoed by Judge J. Harris of the Mississippi State Supreme Court in 1859 in the case of a slave accused of raping a slave girl: "Masters and slaves cannot be governed by the same common system of laws: so different are their positions, rights, and duties." *George v. State*, 37 Miss 319 (1859).

60. Most southern states treated free blacks and slaves similarly, as revealed in their rape statutes. Free blacks in the South generally faced the same fate as slaves. Kentucky and Virginia were the last two states to treat free blacks differently from slaves in their rape statutes. Not until 1850 did the Kentucky general assembly revise its slave rape code to encompass free blacks. Kentucky *Laws* (1850), ch. 15, art. 7, sec. 4, p. 301. Until then, free men presumably would have been tried under the rape statutes that defined the perpetrator as "any person" with no mention of race or status. For example, see Kentucky *Laws* (1801), ch. 67, sec. 7, p. 120. In Virginia, a free black convicted of rape or attempted rape of a white woman could be executed or imprisoned for five to twenty years, at the jury's discretion. Virginia *Acts* (1847), ch. 13, sec. 1, p. 126.

61. Brevard, comp., *An Alphabetical Digest of the Public Statute Law of South Carolina*, II, tit. 179, sec. 1, and Virginia *Acts* (1792), ch. 42.

62. Wickliffe, Turner, and Nicholas, comps., *Revised Statutes of Kentucky*, ch. 28, art. 4, sec. 4. One historian has suggested that the Kentucky legislature was moved to revise its rape code in response to the growing abolitionist assaults on the sexual exploitation of slave women by their masters. By inserting "white" in front "woman" in rape statutes and thus narrowly defining rape only as the rape of white women, legislators ensured that white men could not be recognized as rapists, in effect shielding slaveholders from accusations of rape from their female slaves. Mary Block, " 'An Accusation Easily to Be Made,' " 36–37.

63. Alabama *Laws* (1840), ch. 15, sec. 3, p. 188.

64. Ibid., ch. 3, sec. 14, p. 124.

65. The single exception is Kentucky, which specified that "whoever shall unlawfully and carnally know any white woman, against her will" shall be guilty of rape. See discussion in note 62.

66. Toulmin, comp., *Digest of the Laws of the State of Alabama*, 207; Arkansas *Laws* (1842), 19; Florida *Laws* (1828), sec. 19, p. 53, and *Laws* (1832), no. 55, sec. 2, p. 63; Louisiana *Laws* (1806), ch. 29, sec. 1, p. 122, and *Laws* (1855), no. 120, sec. 11, p. 130; Mississippi *Laws* (1822), sec. 6, p. 206; Moore and Biggs, comps., *Revised Code of North Carolina*, ch. 34, sec. 5, p. 203; Brevard, comp., *An Alphabetical Digest of the Public Statute Law of South Carolina*, vol. I, tit. 21, secs. 17–19, p. 77; Hartley, comp., A *Digest of the Laws of Texas* (Act of 1836), art. 361, p. 179; Shepherd, ed., *Statutes at Large of Virginia*, 1:178 (Act of 1792). On antebellum southern rape statutes and race see Getman, "Sexual Control in the Slaveholding South," 134–36; Wriggins, "Rape, Racism, and the Law," 105–6; Bardaglio, "Rape and the Law in the Old South."

67. Arkansas *Laws* (1842), 19, and Gould, comp., A *Digest of the Statutes of Arkansas*, ch. 51, art. iv, sec. 2, p. 334; Florida *Laws* (1828), sec. 19, p. 53; Florida *Laws* (1832), act no. 55, sec. 2. p. 63; Thompson, comp., A *Manual or Digest of the Statute Law of Florida*, ch. 3, sec. 1, p. 490; Louisiana *Laws* (1855), no. 120, sec. 4, p. 130; Moore and Biggs, comps., *Revised Code of North Carolina*, ch. 34, sec. 5, p. 203.

68. *State v. LeBlanc* (S.C.), 3 Brev. 339 (1813); *State v. Goings* (alias Terry), 20 N.C. 289 (1839); *State v. Farmer*, 26 N.C. 224 (1844), and Bertie County Superior Court Minutes, March 19, 22, and 23 and September 16, 1844, NCDAH. Death for white rapists of young girls, however, was not universally imposed. In 1810 William Dick, a white laborer from Monroe County, Virginia, allegedly raped Nancy Maddy, a girl between the ages of ten and twelve years. Dick was sentenced to eighteen years of solitary confinement in the state penitentiary but pardoned by the governor after fourteen years. LR, VEP, box 168, August–September 1810, September 11–20 folder, LVA. John Farrington, presumed white, of Ashe County, North Carolina, was found guilty of rape in April 1831 and sentenced to hang. The governor granted Farrington a reprieve of four and a half months, after which time he was to be "fully executed." GLB, no. 2, Montfort Stokes, May 4, 1831, NCDAH.

69. Alabama *Laws* (1840), ch. 3, sec. 14, p. 124 (life imprisonment); Arkansas *Laws* (1838), sec. 4, p. 122 (five to twenty-one years); Georgia *Laws* (1816), sec. 33, p. 151 (two to twenty years' hard labor); Kentucky *Laws* (1801), ch. 67, sec. 7 (ten to twenty-one years); Louisiana *Laws* (1804), ch. 50, sec. 2, p. 416 (life imprisonment); Mississippi *Laws* (1839), tit. III, sec. 22, p. 117 (not less than ten years); Scott, Napton, Morrow, and Jones, comps., *Revised Statutes of the State of Missouri*, ch. 47, art. II, sec. 26, p. 348 (not less than five years); Tennessee *Laws* (1819), sec. 4, p. 195 (five to fifteen years), and *Laws* (1829), ch. 23, sec. 13, p. 29 (ten to twenty-one years); Oldham and White, comps., A *Digest of the General Statute Laws of the State of Texas*, art. 529, p. 523 (five to fifteen years).

70. Virginia *Acts* (1819), ch. 120 (ten to twenty years), and Patton and Robinson, comps., *Code of Virginia*, tit. 54, ch. 191, p. 725 (ten to twenty years); Wickliffe, Turner, and Nicholas, comps., *Revised Statutes of Kentucky*, ch. 28, art. 4, sec. 4, p. 248 (ten to twenty years). Department of Corrections (Record Group 42), State Penitentiary Prisoner Registers, 1863–76, LVA.

71. Masur, *The Rites of Execution*; Higginbotham and Kopytoff, "Racial Purity and Interracial Sex," 2008–9.

72. Ayers, *Vengeance and Justice*, 43.

73. Arkansas *Laws* (1838), sec. 4, p. 122. Inexplicably, four years later the Arkansas legislature reinstated the death penalty for white rape, citing the need for "more effectual punish-

ment of the crime of rape." Arkansas *Laws* (1842), sec. 1, p. 19. North Carolina, which retained the white death penalty for rape through the Civil War, had no state penitentiary until 1882. McKelvey, *American Prisons*, 177–78. After the Texas legislature authorized the construction of a state penitentiary in 1848 it revised its death penalty for white rape. Convicted white rapists would receive a sentence of not less than five years at hard labor in the penitentiary. Harris, Hartley, and Willie, *Penal Code of the State of Texas*, ch. 6, art. 528, p. 103. Likewise, Alabama eliminated capital punishment for white rapists after the construction of a penitentiary. Alabama *Laws* (1840), ch. 3, sec. 14, p. 124. Virginia established its prison much earlier than most other southern states, opening its doors in 1800. Consult Keve, *The History of Corrections in Virginia*. For more on penitentiaries in the Old South see Ayers, *Vengeance and Justice*, 34–72.

74. Arkansas, for example, punished white rapists with prison sentences in 1838, but in 1842 it increased the penalty to death. Arkansas *Laws* (1838), sec. 4, p. 122 (five to twenty-one years); Arkansas *Laws* (1842), sec. 1, p. 19 (death). Likewise, Mississippi early on held out the death penalty for white rapists, then changed its rape punishments to "not less than 10 years," which it later increased to life imprisonment. Poindexter, comp., *Revised Code of the Laws of Mississippi*, ch. 54, sec. 11, p. 298 (death); Mississippi *Laws* (1839), tit. 3, sec. 22, p. 116 (not less than ten years); Sharkey, Harris, and Ellett, comps., *Revised Code of the Statute Laws of the State of Mississippi*, sec. 46, art. 219, p. 608 (life imprisonment).

75. Alabama *Laws* (1830), sec. 1, p. 13; Alabama *Laws* (1840), ch. 15, sec. 3, p. 188 (included attempted rape as well; applied to slaves and free men of color); Ball and Roame, comps., *Revised Statutes of the State of Arkansas*, ch. 44, art. 4, sec. 8 (death to any black or mulatto male who commits assault with intent to commit a rape), English, comp., *A Digest of the Statutes of Arkansas*, ch. 51, art. 4, sec. 9, p. 331, and Gould, comp., *A Digest of the Statutes of Arkansas*, ch. 51, art. 4, sec. 9, p. 335; Thompson, comp., *A Manual or Digest of the Statute Law of Florida*, tit. 4, ch. 1, sec. 1, §6, p. 538 (death to any slave, free black, or mulatto convicted of assault with intent to commit a rape); Georgia *Laws* (1816), sec. 1, p. 15 (slaves and free men of color; rape and attempted rape); Georgia *Laws* (1821), sec. 1, and Prince, comp., *Digest of the Laws of the State of Georgia*, 791; Kentucky *Laws* (1802), ch. 53, sec. 19, p. 116 (death to slaves convicted of rape); Kentucky *Laws* (1810), ch. 235, sec. 4, p. 59 (death to slaves convicted of attempted rape); Kentucky *Laws* (1850), ch. 15, art. 7, sec. 4, p. 301 (death to slaves or free blacks convicted of rape); Louisiana *Laws* (1806), ch. 33, sec. 7, p. 198 (death to any "free negro, slave, mulatto, Indian, Mustee" who commits or attempts to commit a rape); Peirce, Taylor, and King, comps., *The Consolidation and Revision of the Statutes of the State of Louisiana*, sec. 113, p. 544; Mississippi *Laws* (1813), sec. 6, p. 10 (slaves convicted of attempted rape and rape shall suffer death); Mississippi *Laws* (1852), ch. 6, sec. 1, p. 27 (any slave, free negro, or mulatto who commits a rape shall suffer death); Sharkey, Harris, and Ellett, comps., *Revised Code of the Statute Laws of the State of Mississippi*, ch. 33, art. 58, p. 248; Taylor, comp., *Revisal of the Laws of North Carolina*, ch. 1229, p. 131 (any person of color convicted of assault with intent to commit a rape); Tennessee *Acts* (1835), ch. 19, sec. 10, p. 92 (any slave who shall commit assault and battery with intent to commit murder . . . or rape); Tennessee *Acts* (1833), ch. 75, sec. 1, p. 94 (any negro or mulatto, whether bond or free, who shall make an assault upon any white woman with intent to commit a rape); Hartley, comp., *Digest of the Laws of Texas*, art. 2539, p. 777 (slave or free person of color; rape or attempted rape); Virginia *Acts* (1804), ch. 5, sec. 11, p. 7 (if any slave shall attempt to ravish a white

woman); Virginia *Acts* (1837), ch. 71, p. 49 (slave or free black who shall ravish or attempt to ravish). Virginia law gave juries leeway in assigning either the death penalty or a prison sentence to free blacks convicted of rape or attempted rape. Slaves, however, were to be executed. See Patton and Robinson, comps., *Code of Virginia*, ch. 200, arts. 1 and 4, p. 753. Missouri stands alone in the nineteenth century in prescribing castration for black males convicted of rape or attempted rape. See Scott, Napton, Morrow, and Jones, comps., *Revised Statutes of the State of Missouri*, ch. 47, art. II, sec. 31, p. 349.

Chapter Four

1. On the use of appellate cases as historical method consult Censer, " 'Smiling through Her Tears,' " 25; G. Edward White, "The Appellate Opinion as Historical Source Material," 491–509; Bardaglio, *Reconstructing the Household*, xvii. A number of scholarly articles focus on antebellum slave case law, among them several articles by A. E. Keir Nash, including "Fairness and Formalism in the Trials of Blacks in the State Supreme Courts of the Old South," "The Texas Supreme Court and Trial Rights of Blacks, 1845–1860," "Reason of Slavery," and "A More Equitable Past?"; Schafer, "The Long Arm of the Law"; Tushnet, "The American Law of Slavery, 1810–1860"; Flanigan, "Criminal Procedure in Slave Trials in the Antebellum South"; Bardaglio, "Rape and the Law in the Old South"; and Mary Block, " 'An Accusation Easily to Be Made,' " 49–52, 88, 90, 117, 126–35.

2. On the ineptitude and inadequacies of antebellum lower courts in the South see Hindus, "Black Justice under White Law," 591; Hindus, *Prison and Plantation*, 7. Wyatt-Brown takes issue with Hindus on this point, arguing that for all its imperfections, criminal justice in the Old South worked remarkably well. "Community, Class, and Snopesian Crime," 173–206. Bardaglio compares the southern legal system with rural communities in other parts of the nation and finds little evidence of southern distinctiveness on this point. *Reconstructing the Household*, 11–12.

3. The broader question, hotly contested among historians, of whether blacks, and particularly slaves, generally received fair trials is beyond the scope of this chapter, although a major argument here is that they were indeed accorded certain procedural rights that were routinely denied accused black rapists in the postbellum South. Among those historians who recognize that accused slave criminals were treated fairly, at least to a certain degree, are Flanigan, "Criminal Procedure in Slave Trials in the Antebellum South," 537–64; Nash, "Fairness and Formalism in the Trials of Blacks in the State Supreme Courts of the Old South," 64–100; Nash, "A More Equitable Past?," 197–242; Nash, "The Texas Supreme Court and Trial Rights of Blacks, 1845–1869," 622–42; Johnson, *Ante-bellum North Carolina*, 497–510; Ernest James Clark, "Aspects of the North Carolina Slave Code, 1715–1860," 148–64; R. H. Taylor, "Humanizing the Slave Code of North Carolina," 323–31; Ayers, *Vengeance and Justice*, 134–37; Shingleton, "The Trial and Punishment of Slaves in Baldwin County, Georgia, 1812–1826," 67–73; Coulter, "Four Slave Trials in Elbert County, Georgia," 237–46; John Edwards, "Slave Justice in Four Middle Georgia Counties," 265–73; Genovese, *Roll, Jordan, Roll*, 25–49; Phifer, "Slavery in Microcosm," 87; Richter, "Slavery in Baton Rouge, 1820–1860," 387, 394; Hodes, *White Women, Black Men*; Bardaglio, *Reconstructing the Household*, 22; Brady, "Slavery, Race, and the Criminal Law in Antebellum North Carolina," 248–60; Randolph B. Campbell, *An Empire for Slavery*, 98, 104, 107; Morris, *Southern Slavery and the*

Law, 223, 227. Those who draw less sanguine conclusions about "fairness" include Stampp, *The Peculiar Institution*, 224–28; Alan D. Watson, "North Carolina Slave Courts, 1715–1785," 24–36; Schafer, "The Long Arm of the Law," 1247–68; Wyatt-Brown, *Southern Honor*, 387–89; Wyatt-Brown, "Community, Class, and Snopesian Crime," 173–206; Slaughter, *Bloody Dawn*, 147; Hindus, "Black Justice under White Law," 596–99; Schwarz, *Twice Condemned*, 23. A. E. Keir Nash dissects some of these important works in an extensive historiographical analysis. See "Reason of Slavery," 7–218, and a response by Robert B. Jones, "Comment: Reason of Slavery." A potentially more instructive way to assess the apparent fairness accorded slaves in appellate cases is advanced by Judith Kelleher Schafer in her study of Louisiana slave law. She steers the debate away from the question of whether slaves were treated fairly in the legal system of the Old South by suggesting that we view slave "justice" as an eminent domain issue. Foremost, she reminds us, slaves were property. In condemning slaves to death, courts were actually condemning private property in the interest of public good. She argues that "although slaves accused of crimes were vulnerable to criminal prosecution as persons, the legal procedure to determine their fate was strikingly like compensated property condemnations." Schafer, *Slavery, the Civil Law, and the Supreme Court of Louisiana*, 58–59.

4. Thomas Morris provides a brief but informative summary of slaves' appeal procedures in *Southern Slavery and the Law*, 226–28.

5. Nash, "Fairness and Formalism in the Trials of Blacks in the State Supreme Courts of the Old South," 73.

6. Flanigan, "Criminal Procedure in Slave Trials," 540–42; Hindus, "Black Justice under White Law," 577. After 1839 slaves were permitted to appeal to a single judge of the state's highest court but could not present their cases before the full court. Morris, *Southern Slavery and the Law*, 226.

7. Nash, "Fairness and Formalism in the Trials of Blacks in the State Supreme Courts of the Old South," 67 n. 13; Flanigan, "Criminal Procedure in Slave Trials," 545.

8. Flanigan, "Criminal Procedure in Slave Trials," 545.

9. Schafer, "The Long Arm of the Law," 1250; Schafer, *Slavery, the Civil Law, and the State Supreme Court of Louisiana*, 61–62; Morris, *Southern Slavery and the Law*, 226.

10. Flanigan, "Criminal Procedure in Slave Trials," 543–45. Although Virginia did not allow slave appeals, it seems to have relied heavily on executive pardoning as a means of rectifying legal improprieties. Free blacks could avail themselves of the appeals process. The pardoning system for slaves is discussed in greater detail in the preceding chapter.

11. Southern slaveholding states that heard cases from African Americans included Alabama, Arkansas, Florida, Georgia, Louisiana, Mississippi, Missouri, North Carolina, South Carolina, Tennessee, and Virginia. African Americans from Texas could also challenge their convictions all the way to the state supreme court, though no such cases are discussed here.

12. *Stephen v. State*, 11 Ga. 225 (February 1852).

13. On the hegemonic function of the law consult Genovese, *Roll, Jordan, Roll*, 25–49. For a study of southern high courts and their advocacy of slavery through their lawmaking, refer to Wiethoff, *A Peculiar Humanism*.

14. Southern jurists seem to have fancied themselves paternalists of last resort. This tendency for judges to assume the role of judicial patriarchs appears to be part of a wider nineteenth-century trend in domestic relations observed by Michael Grossberg in *Govern-*

ing the Hearth. Peter Bardaglio uses the term "state paternalism" to describe the enhanced role of state governance after the Civil War. *Reconstructing the Household*, xv–xvi, 36.

15. *Henry v. State*, 23 Tenn. 270 (Dec. 1843); *Grandison v. State*, 21 Tenn. 451 (Dec. 1841).

16. *Commonwealth v. Mann*, 2 Va. Cas. 210 (June 1820). This case is further complicated by the murky status of Mann. Although a slave, Mann had initiated a freedom suit, so he was tried as a free man.

17. *State v. Charles*, I Fla. 298 (January 1847). The appellate ruling, however, dealt not with the indictment itself but the issue of jurisdiction, which the court did not believe it had. In *Pleasant v. State*, 13 Ark. 360 (January 1853), a slave convicted of attempted rape won a new trial on the grounds that the prosecution had failed to prove that his victim was indeed white. In none of these cases was the race of the accuser in question; rather, the high courts addressed the formality of including the accuser's race on the indictment.

18. T. R. R. Cobb, *An Inquiry into the Law of Negro Slavery*, 67, as quoted in Morris, *Southern Slavery and the Law, 1619–1860*, 22.

19. *Dick v. State*, 30 Miss. 631 (April 1856). See also Flanigan, "Criminal Procedure in Slave Trials," 550.

20. Alabama *Laws* (1840), ch. 15, sec. 3, p. 188.

21. Bardaglio, *Reconstructing the Household*, 22.

22. *Thurman v. The State*, 18 Ala. 276 (June 1850). For more on this case as well as a discussion of sexual relations between free blacks and whites in Alabama before the Civil War see Mills, "Miscegenation and the Free Negro in Antebellum 'Anglo' Alabama," 16–34. The reasoning demonstrated by this judge strikes one as remarkably "modern." On the evolution of colorblind racial ideology that emerged out of judges' scrutiny of socially constructed racial categories see Pascoe, "Miscegenation Law, Court Cases, and Ideologies of 'Race' in Twentieth-Century America," 44–69.

23. *State v. Martin*, 14 N.C. (3 Dev.) 329 (June 1832).

24. *State v. Jesse*, 19 N.C. (2 Dev. & Bat.) 297 (June 1837).

25. *State v. Tom*, 47 N.C. 414 (August 1855). Two additional frivolous exceptions were filed in this case. Defense counsel claimed a faulty indictment, because although it clearly stated that the accuser was a white female, nowhere did it state that she was of the "human species." Moreover, the indictment failed to state that the accused was a male. Needless to say, neither of these schemes proved successful. For other appeals of condemned rapists on grounds of incorrectly worded indictments consult *Sullivan v. State*, 8 Ark. 400 (January 1848), and *State v. Jim*, 12 N.C. 142 (December 1826).

26. *Day v. Commonwealth*, 2 Grattan 562 (December 1845), and 3 Grattan 629 (December 1846).

27. *Pleasant v. State*, 13 Ark. 360 (January 1853), and 15 Ark. 634 (January 1855). On the matter of masters testifying on behalf of their slaves see Flanigan, "Criminal Procedure in Slave Trials," 558. See also *Elijah v. State*, 20 Tenn. 99 (December 1839).

28. For more on the political career of Judge Gayle see Thornton, *Politics and Power in a Slave Society*, 26, 28–31, 34, 43, 55, 87, 110, 113, 126, 244. Fox-Genovese also looks at the Gayle family in *Within the Plantation Household*, 1–28, 207, 272, and 398.

29. *State v. Phil*, I Stewart 31 (January 1827).

30. Mary Block, " 'An Accusation Easily to Be Made,' " 21–22, 41–80; Morris, *Southern Slavery and the Law*, 304–5.

31. *State v. Jim*, I Devereau 142 (December 1826). For a discussion of this case see Nash, "Reason of Slavery," 85–86. On the issue of force and parallel issues of consent and resistance in nineteenth-century rape law consult Mary Block, "'An Accusation Easily to Be Made,'" 41–150; Morris, *Southern Slavery and the Law*, 304. For a general survey of the North Carolina high court's treatment of slavery consult Bryce R. Holt, *The Supreme Court of North Carolina and Slavery*.

32. *Charles v. State*, 11 Ark. 389 (July 1850).

33. *Wyatt v. State*, 2 Swan 394 (December 1852).

34. *Commonwealth v. Fields*, 4 Leigh 648 (December 1832). One has to wonder about the circumstances under which these black men came to be accused of rape. One possibility, certainly bolstered by the findings of Martha Hodes, is that these cases, or some of them, involved consensual relations with white female participants who, upon being discovered, may have cried rape to avoid ostracism or punishment. Hodes, *White Women, Black Men*, 43–67.

35. Nash, "Fairness and Formalism in the Trials of Blacks in the State Supreme Courts of the Old South," 64–100; Bardaglio, *Reconstructing the Household*, 22.

36. *Pleasant v. State*, 13 Ark. 373–74 (January 1853).

37. *Lewis v. State*, 30 Ala. 54 (January 1857).

38. The Alabama legislature must have taken the judge's remarks to heart. Shortly after this case, it revised its rape law to make impersonation of a husband by a slave or free person of color for the purpose of having carnal relations a felony punishable by death. See Alabama *Laws* (1857–58), no. 240, secs. 1–2, p. 266; Clay, comp., *Digest of the Laws of the State of Alabama*, penal code, ch. 3, sec. 15, p. 414; Howard and Hutchinson, comps., *Statutes of the State of Mississippi*, ch. 50, tit. 3, p. 697; Meigs and Cooper, comps., *The Code of Tennessee*, art. III, sec. 4612, p. 830; Harris, Hartley, and Willie, comps., *Penal Code of the State of Texas*, ch. 6, art. 526, p. 102. After emancipation, South Carolina made sex by fraudulent means a crime only when committed by a "person of color" on a white woman. See South Carolina *Acts* (1865), no. 4731, 35–36, "An Act to Amend the Criminal Law," part I. North Carolina passed a law after the Civil War that criminalized impersonation of one's husband for the purpose of having carnal knowledge. North Carolina *Statutes* (1881), ch. 89, p. 144.

39. Tushnet, *The American Law of Slavery, 1810–1860*, 129–34. See also Schafer, "The Long Arm of the Law," 1254–55; Schafer, *Slavery, the Civil Law, and the Supreme Court of Louisiana*, 66–74. On the admissibility of slave confessions, also see Flanigan, "Criminal Procedure in Slave Trials," 559–64; Morris, "Slaves and the Rules of Evidence in Criminal Trials," 1227–28, 1230–38. This judicial concern is in stark contrast to southern appellate decisions in the twentieth century. For example, the Mississippi Supreme Court allowed the confession of a black defendant on trial for a capital offense that had been obtained after a whipping over the course of three days. *Brown v. Miss.*, 297 U.S. 278 (1936), as cited in Nash, "Fairness and Formalism in the Trials of Blacks in the State Supreme Courts of the Old South," 65.

40. Nash, "Fairness and Formalism in the Trials of Blacks in the State Supreme Courts of the Old South," 84–89; Tushnet, *The American Law of Slavery, 1810–1860*, 134; Schwarz, *Twice Condemned*, 53–54; Schafer, "The Long Arm of the Law," 1254–56.

41. *State v. Gilbert*, 2 La. An. 244 (March 1847). See also the Louisiana case of *State v. Peter*,

14 La. Ann. 527 (June 1859), as well as Judith Schafer's analysis of these cases in *Slavery, the Civil Law, and the Supreme Court of Louisiana,* 66, 86–87.

42. *Stephen v. State,* II Ga. 225 (February 1852). See also Bardaglio, "Rape and the Law in the Old South," 749–51; Mary Block, " 'An Accusation Easily to Be Made,' " 48–52. The court, however, gave earnest consideration to the defense contention that the confession admitted as evidence should have been disallowed. The local constable had left the prisoner in the charge of one Mr. Johnson, who testified for the state that Stephen made an unprompted, uncoerced confession. The high court, nonetheless, was satisfied that no legal impropriety had been committed. The verdict stood.

43. On masters' self-interest in trials of their slaves accused of crimes see Morris, *Southern Slavery and the Law,* 249–61.

44. *State v. Peter,* 14 La. An. 527 (June 1859), 529.

45. *State v. Jim,* 3 Jones N.C. 348 (June 1856), 351.

46. On the dual nature of slaves as persons and property consult Schafer, *Slavery, the Civil Law, and the Supreme Court of Louisiana,* 1–27; Tushnet, *The American Law of Slavery, 1810– 1860,* 67, 74; Alan D. Watson, "North Carolina Slave Courts, 1715–1785," 24.

47. *State v. Nat,* 6 Jones N.C. 114 (December 1858), quotation at sec. 115. Slaves could never testify against whites, but they were called frequently as witnesses in trials of slaves.

48. Flanigan, "Criminal Procedure in Slave Trials," 552.

49. *Major v. State,* 34 Tenn. (2 Sneed) 11 (December 1854) and 36 Tenn. (4 Sneed) 597 (December 1857); Flanigan, "Criminal Procedure in Slave Trials," 552; Flanigan, "The Criminal Law of Slavery and Freedom, 1800–1869," 114–15; Bardaglio, "Rape and the Law in the Old South," 761–62.

50. See Flanigan, "Criminal Procedure in Slave Trials," 551–52, for a more detailed account of this confusing case.

51. On sexual ideology and the law in the nineteenth century see Ireland, "The Libertine Must Die," 27–44. On the question of character evidence brought forth in rape trials against the accuser, consult Mary Block, " 'An Accusation Easily to Be Made,' " 116–50; Nemeth, "Character Evidence in Rape Trials in Nineteenth-Century New York," 219.

52. Victoria Bynum argues that white women who were unmarried and propertyless served no useful purpose in antebellum elite culture. When these women transgressed the boundaries of acceptable behavior, particularly in the sexual realm, courts were quick to police and punish. *Unruly Women,* ch. 4, "Punishing Deviant Women: The State as Patriarch."

53. *Cato v. State,* 9 Fla. 163 (1860).

54. Ibid., 173, 174, 186.

55. *Pleasant v. State,* 15 Ark. 624 (January 1855).

56. Ibid. The first appeal appears in *Pleasant v. State,* 13 Ark. 360 (January 1853).

57. Morris, *Southern Slavery and the Law,* 314.

58. *State v. Jefferson,* 28 N.C. 305 (June 1846). Northern appeals judges seem to have resorted to the same kind of hair splitting on this issue of character and chastity in rape trials. See Nemeth, "Character Evidence in Rape Trials in Nineteenth-Century New York," 214–20.

59. *State v. Henry,* 50 N.C. 65 (December 1857). Henry did, however, win a new trial

because the trial judge had incorrectly charged the jury about the weight of the accused's good character.

60. *State v. Anderson*, 19. Mo. 241 (October 1853).

61. Jane Censer affirms the usefulness of looking at appellate opinions to determine "how educated, middle and upper class men viewed women." Although her article focuses on antebellum divorce law, I argue the utility of this approach for discerning the views of this same class of white men on rape, sex, gender, and race. Censer, " 'Smiling through Her Tears,' " 25.

62. For example, see the cases *Pleasant v. State*, 13 Ark. (January 1853), and 15 Ark. 634 (January 1855); *Cato v. State*, 9 Fla. (1860); *State v. Jefferson*, 28 N.C. 305 (June 1846); *State v. Henry*, 50 N.C. 65 (December 1857); *State v. Anderson*, 19 Mo. 241 (October 1853).

63. My thanks to Jane Dailey for sharing her thoughts with me on this point. She further speculates that white men's anxiety about the accusatory power of white women may have actually defused anxiety about miscegenation. See her forthcoming *Sex and Civil Rights*.

64. *Stephen v. State*, II Ga. 225 (February 1852).

65. *Cato v. State*, 9 Fla. 163 (1860).

66. Nemeth, "Character Evidence in Rape Trials in Nineteenth-Century New York," 219.

Chapter Five

1. On the motives and behavior of masters whose slaves had committed criminal offenses, see Morris, *Southern Slavery and the Law*, ch. 11.

2. Far fewer cases involving free men of color are readily found in state archives. Because slaves constituted investment property, execution orders for slaves convicted of capital offenses left a vast paper trail of immense importance to historians. Since masters received monetary compensation in such cases, the jurisdictions and functions of various state and local officials and departments intersected. Local sheriffs had to document executions that had been carried out. State treasury departments and legislative bodies had to approve and process disbursements to masters for slaves officially executed. If condemned slaves received executive reprieves, these transactions too were recorded in state ledgers and journals as cash receipts from slave traders who purchased the errant slaves for sale in another state. In contrast, free men of color left no such official records, thus presenting a formidable challenge for the researcher. Further complicating any attempt to compare the experience of slaves and free blacks accused of rape is the bifurcated process of criminal procedure; bondage, not race, determined which court would hear the case. Slaves in Virginia, for example, regardless of the severity of their crimes, were tried in courts of oyer and terminer, essentially county courts. Free blacks accused of serious offenses such as rape or attempted rape, by contrast, appeared before superior courts. Free blacks in Tennessee were tried in regular circuit and criminal courts, not in slave courts. Howington, "The Treatment of Slaves and Free Blacks in the State and Local Courts of Tennessee," 312. The result is that the researcher is left to pore over the minutes and related documents of two sets of court records, a daunting assignment. Moreover, there were simply far fewer free blacks in the South than slaves. For all these reasons, there are not nearly as many extant records of sexual assault cases in which free blacks were the accused. A study seeking to include both slaves

and free blacks accused of rape or attempted rape would be unavoidably lopsided, yielding considerably more slave cases and a dearth of free black cases that may not accurately reflect either the prevalence of the crime or the rate of prosecutions. The cases presented here, then, can purport neither to be representative nor to allow a reliable comparison.

3. Crow, *The Black Experience in Revolutionary North Carolina*, 31–33. On race and the status of free blacks in the colonial period see Breen and Innes, *"Myne Own Ground"*; Higginbotham, *In the Matter of Color*, 202–6; Sobel, *The World They Made Together*, 45; Edmund S. Morgan, *American Slavery, American Freedom*, 154–57, 331, 334, 335, 337; Jordan, *White over Black*, 74, 76–77, 122–28; John H. Russell, *The Free Negro in Virginia, 1619–1865*, 16–41; Spindel, *Crime and Society in North Carolina, 1663–1776*, 74–75; Sterkx, *The Free Negro in Ante-Bellum Louisiana*, 13–48.

4. Ira Berlin, *Slaves without Masters*, 343. On the condition and status of free blacks in the slave South see Franklin, *The Free Negro in North Carolina*; Guion Griffis Johnson, *Antebellum North Carolina*, 582–612; Roark and Johnson, "Strategies of Survival," 88–102; Fisher, "The Legal Status of Free Blacks in Texas, 1836–1861," 342–62; Ebert, "A Window on the Valley"; Stampp, *The Peculiar Institution*, 93, 215–17; Norrece T. Jones Jr., *Born a Child of Freedom, Yet a Slave*, 30, 35–36; Jordan, *White over Black*, 406–14, 577–79; Goldfield, "Black Life in Old South Cities," 123–53; Dickson D. Bruce Jr., *Violence and Culture in the Antebellum South*, 127–28, 129; Franklin and Moss, *From Slavery to Freedom*, 136–57; Phillips, *American Negro Slavery*, 425–53; Sellers, *Slavery in Alabama*, 361–98; Genovese, *Roll, Jordan, Roll*, 398–413; Randolph B. Campbell, *An Empire for Slavery*, 110–14; Bogger, *Free Blacks in Norfolk, Virginia, 1790 to 1860*. On free women of color see Lebsock, "Free Black Women and the Question of Matriarchy," 271–92, and *The Free Women of Petersburg*, 87–111; Whittington B. Johnson, "Free African American Women in Savannah, 1800–1860," 260–83.

5. For example, Maryland's legal restrictions on its free population are outlined in Fields, *Slavery and Freedom on the Middle Ground*, 35. See also Sterkx, *The Free Negro in Ante-Bellum Louisiana*, 161–65; Howington, "The Treatment of Slaves and Free Blacks," 291–94, 306; Jordan, *White over Black*, 406–12; Dorsett, "Slaveholding in Jackson County, Missouri," 155–56; Reinders, "Slavery in New Orleans in the Decade before the Civil War," 371–73; Bogger, *Free Blacks in Norfolk, Virginia, 1790 to 1860*, 7–31.

6. See Ira Berlin, *Slaves without Masters*, 182–216, for examples of harsh statutes and policies against free blacks, and Mills, "Miscegenation and the Free Negro in Antebellum 'Anglo' Alabama," 17–18, for the criticism of this approach.

7. Mills, "Miscegenation and the Free Negro in Antebellum 'Anglo' Alabama," 17–18; Johnson and Roark, *No Chariot Let Down*, 7–11. William L. Richter, in his study of antebellum Baton Rouge, found considerable tolerance of free blacks among that city's white population. In Richter's view, whites of Baton Rouge did not directly compete economically with free blacks, whose primary trades included labor and cigar making and, later, barbering. Richter, "Slavery in Baton Rouge, 1820–60," 384–85.

8. Fields, *Slavery and Freedom on the Middle Ground*, 36.

9. Sterkx, *The Free Negro in Ante-Bellum Louisiana*, 170–73, 176–80; Bogger, *Free Blacks in Norfolk, Virginia, 1790 to 1860*, 90–94.

10. The respect accorded to local free blacks by whites has been substantiated by Crow, *The Black Experience in Revolutionary North Carolina*, 32; Phillips, *American Negro Slavery*, 430–34, 437; Franklin, *The Free Negro in North Carolina*, 45–46, 59; Mills, "Miscegenation

and the Free Negro in Antebellum 'Anglo' Alabama," 27, 30–31; Adele Logan Alexander, *Ambiguous Lives*; Genovese, *Roll, Jordan, Roll*, 399–405; Johnson and Roark, *No Chariot Let Down*, 11–12; Bogger, *Free Blacks in Norfolk, Virginia, 1790 to 1860*, 64; and Buckley, "Unfixing Race."

11. Mills, "Miscegenation and the Free Negro in Antebellum 'Anglo' Alabama," 31–32. Eugene Genovese has asserted that as tax-paying, duty-performing citizens, free blacks were simply too valuable to expel. *Roll, Jordan, Roll*, 403. Edmund Ruffin, while advocating harsher restrictions on the region's growing "inferior class," recognized the valuable contributions made by the many "virtuous and industrious" free blacks in the South. See his essay "The Free Negro Nuisance and How to Abate It," which appeared in *The South*, July 2, 1858, reprinted in Scarborough, ed., *The Diary of Edmund Ruffin*, 1:621–26.

12. Box 294 (May 21–July 21, 1826), LR, VEP. See also entries for June 12, 1826, and November 20, 1827, Southampton County Court Minutes, 1824–1830 (microfilm reel 33), LVA.

13. June 15, 1827, folder, box 299 (June 1–July 31, 1827), LR, VEP, LVA.

14. Ibid. and October 22–31, 1833 folder, box 334 (August 1–October 31, 1833), LR, VEP, LVA. Sympathetic jurors finding a black man guilty of rape but with mitigating circumstances, however, could and did recommend pardoning to the governor. This procedure applied to free men of color as well as slaves. Virginia *Acts* (1824–25), ch. 23, p. 22.

15. June 15, 1827, folder, box 299 (June 1–July 31, 1827), LR, VEP, LVA. On the practices of governors and executive councils regarding pardons see Chapter 1, note 9. At least one secondary work has shown that free blacks, like slaves, utilized this legal prerogative, sometimes with positive results. Extant records indicate that free blacks from Louisiana frequently appealed to the governor for reprieves and pardons and quite often received them. Sterkx, *The Free Negro in Ante-Bellum Louisiana*, 195–96.

16. June 15, 1827, folder, box 299 (June 1–July 31, 1827), LR, VEP, LVA.

17. Letter dated July 11, 1827, from William I. Everitt, jailer of Southampton County, box 299 (June 1–July 31, 1827), LR, VEP, LVA. It would be imprudent, not to mention inaccurate, to conclude from this account that Southampton County was an oasis of racial harmony: the repressive actions that followed the Turner revolt several years later make that clear. The willingness of some white Southampton residents to assist a free black convicted of raping a white woman does not necessarily reflect a blissful, harmonious relationship between the county's white and free black populations. To the contrary, court records reveal strained, even volatile relations between whites and free blacks. Some actually came to blows with one another. In November 1826, for example, shortly after Henry Hunt was charged with rape, Edwin Gray was fined $200 for "beating a free negro." Entry for November 22, 1826, Southampton County Court Minutes, 1824–30 (microfilm reel 33), 141, LVA. Hunt's is not a lone example of purported black-on-white assault from this period in Southampton County to have reached the courts. On January 16, 1827, a slave named Nelly was charged with murdering her mistress. Nelly was found guilty and sentenced to hang later in the year. And in August 1827 Moses, the property of Peyton Mason of Petersburg, was found guilty of shooting John Browne (presumably white) in the eye. Browne lost his eye, but surprisingly Moses was sentenced to the rather lenient punishment of thirty-nine lashes. Entries for January 16, 1827, and August 1827, Southampton County Court Minutes, 1824–30 (microfilm reel 33), 146–47, 175. For local studies of antebellum Southampton County consult

Parramore, *Southampton County, Virginia*; Crofts, *Old Southampton*. While the Hunt case predates the period examined in Crofts's study, it does reveal a little about free blacks in Southampton County from 1840 to 1850. In 1840, 12.5 percent of the county's population was composed of free blacks. In 1850 there were 348 households headed by free blacks, of which only 6.6 percent held any property at all. Assuming that Hunt had resided in Southampton County at the time of the alleged assault, chances are good that he lived in economic dependency and owned no land of his own, although he may have practiced a trade. See Crofts, *Old Southampton*, 16–18, 293, 295.

18. July 1834 folder, box 267 (April–October 1834), LR, VEP; October 16, 1833, 163–65, and April 23, 1834, 183–4, Westmoreland County Superior Court Order Book, 1831–39 (microfilm reel 72), LVA.

19. *Commonwealth v. Watts*, 4 Leigh 672 (December 1833). Watts's objection and the high court's opinion are summarized in April 23, 1834, 183–84, Westmoreland County Superior Court Order Books, 1831–39 (microfilm reel 72), LVA.

20. Undated petition and two letters by Ed. Wood, June 26, 1834 (second quotation) and July 11, 1834 (first and third quotations), July 1834 folder, box 267, VEPLR, LVA.

21. Thurman to Governor Littleton Waller Tazewell, June 11, 1834, July 1834 folder, box 267, VEPLR, LVA.

22. Watts's name does not appear on transportation or execution records, indicating that he may very well have been pardoned. In general, verifying the fate of a condemned free black rapist is much more difficult than that of a slave since he would have represented no financial loss to an owner.

23. Thurman to Governor Littleton Waller Tazewell, June 11, 1834, July 1834 folder, box 267, VEPLR, LVA. Such support for free blacks in southern communities was not as rare as we might first suspect. Perhaps we should reexamine U. B. Phillips's claim that southern whites in some localities embraced and respected industrious and productive free African Americans among their numbers. Phillips, *American Negro Slavery*, 430–37. See also Crow, *The Black Experience in Revolutionary North Carolina*, 32; Franklin, *The Free Negro in North Carolina, 1790–1860*, 45–46; Mills, "Miscegenation and the Free Negro in Antebellum 'Anglo' Alabama," 16–17, 27, 31–32; Adele Logan Alexander, *Ambiguous Lives*, 120; Fisher, "The Legal Status of Free Blacks in Texas, 1836–1861," 342–62; Buckley, "Unfixing Race," 349–80. For a contrasting view see Hindus, "Black Justice under White Law," 584. His study of two South Carolina counties documents free blacks prosecuted at a rate six times that of slaves.

24. October 18, 1833, LR, VEP, as quoted in Johnston, *Race Relations in Virginia and Miscegenation in the South, 1776–1860*, 263. (This document could not be located at the Library of Virginia as cited by Johnston.) Also, see *Thompson v. Commonwealth*, 4 Leigh 652 (July 1833); and entries for May 22, 23, June 10, 1833, 208, 210, and 224, Frederick County Superior Court Order Book, 1831–35 (microfilm reel 100), LVA. On Thompson's occupation refer to Ebert, "A Window on the Valley," 48.

25. October 18, 1833, LR, VEP, as quoted in Johnston, *Race Relations in Virginia and Miscegenation in the South, 1776–1860*, 263. No documentation that verifies the outcome of Thompson's appeal has been found. However, his name does not appear on lists of blacks executed or transported in the early 1830s.

26. "Commonwealth v. Richard Garrett," "Commonwealth v. George A. Walters," and "Commonwealth v. David Stephens," July 1833, Frederick County Court Order Book, 1831–

35 (microfilm reel 100), 245, LVA. On interracial cases of cohabitation brought before officials, consult Howington, "The Treatment of Slaves and Free Blacks in the State and Local Courts of Tennessee," 306–7; J. William Harris, *Plain Folk and Gentry in a Slave Society*, 56–57.

27. Some accounts of race in the colonial period claim that in the early years societies may have been somewhat tolerant of interracial sexual relationships. See Higginbotham, *In the Matter of Color*, 158. Higginbotham suspected that later proscriptions against miscegenation were rooted in white fears that a union between poor whites and blacks could threaten the plantation aristocracy, or, at the very least, pose an economic threat. Higginbotham, *In the Matter of Color*, 9, 47. Higginbotham and others agree that interracial sexual relations were more prevalent in the eighteenth century than in subsequent years. Higginbotham, *In the Matter of Color*, 47; Jordan, *White over Black*, 137; Lebsock, *The Free Women of Petersburg*, 95–96. Also on the colonial period see Billings, "The Cases of Fernando and Elizabeth Key," 467–74; Crow, *The Black Experience in Revolutionary North Carolina*, 20–21, 30. More recent scholarship has argued for the existence of white tolerance for sex across the color line in the antebellum years. See Mills, "Miscegenation and the Free Negro in Antebellum 'Anglo' Alabama"; Rothman, *Notorious in the Neighborhood*; Hodes, *White Women, Black Men*; Buckley, "Unfixing Race" and *The Great Catastrophe of My Life*. William Harris cautions that while some southern communities were tolerant of interracial sexual relationships, others diligently policed such involvements. *Plain Folk and Gentry in a Slave Society*, 56–57. On miscegenation in the Old South see also Clinton, *The Plantation Mistress*, 209–22; Anne Firor Scott, *The Southern Lady*, 52–53; Lebsock, *The Free Women of Petersburg*, 104, 95–96; Deborah Gray White, *Ar'n't I a Woman?*, 34–35, 43–44, 61; Adele Logan Alexander, *Ambiguous Lives*; Cashin, *A Family Venture*, 23, 27, 102, 105–6, 110, 119, 191 n. 19; Stampp, *The Peculiar Institution*, 350–52; Franklin, *The Free Negro in North Carolina*, 35–39, 215, 217; Wyatt-Brown, *Southern Honor*, 307–24; Genovese, *Roll, Jordan, Roll*, 413–31; Dorothy Ann Gay, "The Tangled Skein of Romanticism and Violence in the Old South," 103–8, 113–17, 159–60; D'Emilio and Freedman, *Intimate Matters*, 95–96, 102–3; Litwack, *Been in the Storm So Long*, 243; Berry and Blassingame, *Long Memory*, 116–41.

28. *Richmond Daily Dispatch*, April 27, 1854, as cited by Hodes, *White Women, Black Men*, 64–65. For more cases of free black men involved sexually with white women, consensually or otherwise, see Hodes, *White Women, Black Men*, 49–50, 65, 73, 75, 84, 92, 106.

29. See Chapter 1.

30. October 1–30, 1817, folder, box 241 (September–November 1817), LR, VEP, LVA.

31. Ibid.

32. Letter dated October 23, 1817, signed H. Hohnes [?], Shenandoah, Virginia, ibid.

33. Letter dated October 23, 1817, John Holeman of Shenandoah, Virginia, to Governor James Preston, ibid.

34. Ibid.

35. October 1–30, 1817, folder, box 241 (September–November 1817), LR, VEP, LVA. It should be noted, however, that community outrage about a local rape was not restricted solely to cases involving a purported black assailant. Ella Gertrude Clanton Thomas, a member of Georgia genteel society, discussed a white-on-white rape case and recalled the "excitement" it aroused in the neighborhood. Burr, ed., *The Secret Eye*, 145.

36. October 1817 folder, box 241 (September–November 1817), LR, VEP, LVA.

37. Tate, comp., *Digest of the Laws of Virginia*, 127 (Act of February 8, 1819). Free persons convicted of rape faced ten to twenty-one years in the penitentiary. A slave, of course, faced death. The act postdates this case, but it was modeled on an earlier law passed in 1796. Shepherd, ed., *The Statutes at Large for Virginia*, ii, 6. Free blacks were not treated in the same harsh manner as slaves until 1823, when the Virginia legislature changed the rape statutes to include free blacks in the same code as slaves. After 1823 any free black convicted of even an attempt to rape a white woman would suffer death. See Virginia *Acts* (1823), ch. 34, sec. 3, p. 37.

38. There is no official endorsement on any of the pardon papers, and since free blacks were of no financial value there is in all likelihood no other way to cross-check other archival sources for executive action taken.

39. Letter of W. Thurman, June 11, 1834, box 267, LR, VEP, LVA.

40. Crofts, *Old Southampton*, 50.

41. Ibid., 15.

42. July 1834 folder, box 267, LR, VEP, LVA.

43. Jackson, *Free Negro Labor and Property Holding in Virginia, 1830–1860*, 83–86. For a sample of petitions written by whites asking state officials for the pardon of a convicted free black, see Petition of 1843 on behalf of George Ware (convicted of manslaughter) by citizens of Fredericksburg, Virginia, to Governor James McDowell, Papers of Peck, Wellford & Co., Fredericksburg, Virginia, Mss3P3375a, VHS; Petition of December 5, 1832, from residents of Davidson County, North Carolina, on behalf of Abednego Valentine (convicted of forcibly entering a dwelling house), to Governor Montfort Stokes, GLB No. 29, NCDAH.

44. Such were the racial and class lines drawn in antebellum Charleston as described by Michael Johnson and James Roark, although they are primarily looking at well-to-do free blacks. *No Chariot Let Down*, 13. White working-class antagonism toward free working-class blacks is also suggested by Franklin, *The Free Negro in North Carolina*, 136–39, and Bogger, *Free Blacks in Norfolk, Virginia, 1790 to 1860*, ch. 3. On Northern white working-class antagonism toward black laborers in the early nineteenth century consult Slaughter, *Bloody Dawn*, 38–40.

45. On the nineteenth-century belief that poor women were prone to promiscuity see Hodes, *White Women, Black Men*, 5, 49, 61–62; Bynum, *Unruly Women*, 7; Bardaglio, *Reconstructing the Household*, 74; Clinton, *The Plantation Mistress*, 204.

46. February 1832, Rockbridge County Court Minute Book, 1831–34 (microfilm reel 40), 59, LVA. Fields was brought before the February 1832 term of the county court and held over to the April term of the superior court. Unlike slaves, free blacks in Virginia were tried in superior court.

47. *Commonwealth v. Fields*, 4 Leigh 648 (December 1832). See also Chapter 4.

48. Ibid.

49. *Smith v. The Commonwealth*, 10 Grattan 734 (July 1853).

50. Ibid.

51. For another example of jury divisiveness in the rape trials of free black men see the case of a free black man named Elihu who was indicted in Knox County, Tennessee, in 1859 for the attempted rape of Charity C. Barry. After two mistrials the circuit court judge allowed a change of venue to Blount County, where Elihu was eventually acquitted. Cited in

Howington, "The Treatment of Slaves and Free Blacks in the State and Local Courts of Tennessee," 326.

52. *The State v. Wesley McDaniel*, 60 N.C. 249 (June 1864).

53. Raleigh (N.C.) *Register*, April 14, 1831, and May 12, 1831; Gov. Montfort Stokes, GLB, May 5, 1831, 22, 45, NCDAH.

54. Anna Clark found similar prejudices at work in English rape trials of the eighteenth century. Anna K. Clark, *Women's Silence, Men's Violence*, 144 n. 7.

55. Four petitions or letters and one official court document (John Bennett to Governor John Letcher, July 30, 1860; unsigned, undated letter; forty-three petitioners from Upshur County to Governor Letcher, n.d.; thirty-three petitioners from Upshur County to Governor Letcher, n.d.; court summary by Lewis County clerk of court John Talbott, November 14, 1851), September–December 1860, Pardon Papers, LR, VEP, LVA. Upshur County was organized March 27, 1851, in part out of Lewis County. Upshur County now lies in the present state of West Virginia.

56. Ibid. Conway was pardoned on September 13, 1860, with about one year left to serve on his original sentence.

57. On perceptions among nineteenth-century Americans about the prevalence of drinking among Irish immigrants refer to Diner, *Erin's Daughters in America*, 56, 62, 64, 66–7, 112–14.

58. Bartholomew Maloney was pardoned in May 1861, thirty-one years before the end of his sentence. June 22–30, 1861, 1862 PP, LR, VEP, LVA.

59. Petition with fifty-three signatures, n.d., April 1863 folder, box 457 (January–June 1863), PP, VEP, LVA.

60. Ibid.

61. Official notation, ibid.; see also February 6, 1862, entry, EJ, LVA.

62. One letter challenged the verdict on technical grounds, specifically the improper seating of several jurors, of whom one, it was argued, was not a freeholder, and another had admitted before trial that he "hated" Franklin and always had. Another petition claimed that one of the jurors, perhaps the same juror who admitted hating Franklin, was a relative of Lucinda Dearing's by marriage. Letter, n.d., four signatures; and letter from Margaret Franklin bearing thirty-seven other signatures, n.d., December 1846 folder, box 384 (November–December 1846), LR, VEP, LVA.

63. Various petitions, August 1863 folder, July–November, 1863, and [ ]–December 1861, January–June 1862, PP, VEP, LVA.

64. Letter, June 20, 1862, August C. Butts to Governor John Letcher, January–June 1862, PP, VEP, LVA. On how physical examinations were conducted to determine "marks of race," refer to Johnson, *Soul by Soul*, ch. 5, "Reading Bodies and Marking Race"; Gross, *Double Character*, 124–28.

65. Ibid. Of the twelve white men from Virginia convicted of rape or attempted rape from 1800 to 1865 whose appeals for clemency were filed with the state executive or whose names appear on the rolls of the state penitentiary, five received the minimum sentence of ten years: William B. O. Franklin (1843), John Conway (1851), Edward Ledbetter (1859), all detailed above. The other two were James W. Grubb, age forty-five, convicted of rape in Wirt County in November 1859, in Prison Register, 1859, 150, and EJ, July 25, 1866; Thomas

Newman, convicted of rape in Botetourt County in April 1859, in Prison Register, 1859, and EJ, May 29, 1827, 269. I offer no generalizations about how representative this group of white men convicted of rape may have been. To make that determination, systematic research of local and county criminal records needs to be done. Given the widespread support that many convicted white rapists had, my suspicions are that rape and attempted rape charges were frequently dismissed before they even went to trial, or that the accused were acquitted. Only three received the harshest penalty allowable, twenty years. Of these, one was an Irishman convicted of raping an eighteen-year-old white girl; another was convicted of raping a child. At least six of the convicted white rapists were discharged before completing their original sentences. Only one appeal was flatly rejected, as best one can tell from the records. Official notations are absent on the documents of the remaining applicants, Bartholomew Maloney (1852) and Norment Querry (1853). John H. Dioink was convicted in Alleghany County in 1864 for rape and received twenty years also. Prison Register, 1864. Other white-on-white rape convictions in Virginia noted but not discussed here were those of Thomas Newman, tried in Botetourt County in April 1859, sentenced to ten years, and pardoned in May 1867, Prison Register, 1859, and Executive Journal, May 29, 1867, LVA; George Morris, convicted in Marshall County in September 1859 of breaking and entering with intent to rape and sentenced to three years, pardon refused, January–April 1860, PP, LR, VEP, LVA; William Ball, sentenced to twelve years in the penitentiary for a rape committed while at Camp Abingdon during the first year of the Civil War and pardoned in 1865, October 1863 folder, July–November 1863 and January–April 1865, PP, LR, VEP, LVA; James W. Grubb, given a ten-year sentence in 1859 in Wirt County for rape and discharged from prison in July 1866, Prison Register, 1859, 150, and EJ, July 25, 1866, LVA; James Rush of Augusta County, sent to prison for a term of seventeen years and pardoned in 1861, Prison Register, 1854, LVA. Henry Robertson of Southampton County left the state after purportedly committing a rape in 1824. Virginia officials requested his extradition from North Carolina. November 1, 1825, GP 55, H. G. Burton, NCDAH. In North Carolina, Ephraim Daniels and Jesse Whitlow of Rowan County were each charged with rape in 1821. Their records are woefully incomplete, so an outcome cannot be documented here. April 1821, State Docket Superior Court, Rowan County, 1821–35; and April 1821, Rowan County Superior Court Minute Docket, 1820–27, NCDAH.

A more systematic study of sexual assault in general is essential to address fundamental questions such as the pervasiveness of rape. Admittedly, court records reveal only a portion of sexual assault cases that were likely perpetrated. In the nineteenth century, it was rather common for young women and girls to live and work in the homes of other whites. Sexual coercion at the hands of the male head of household seems probable. And given the subservient nature of such relationships, chances are good that official action would have been taken only rarely. See Sharon Block, "Coercing Sex within the Bonds of Servitude, 1720–1820," and "Lines of Color, Sex, and Service," 141–63. Furthermore, legal and extralegal actions were taken to discourage women from bringing charges of rape, or, once filed, pursuing the charge. For example, Hannah Jenson of Rowan County, North Carolina, was blackmailed into dropping rape charges that she had filed against Henry Walker. Walker, Jenson claimed, used his political influence to get *her* jailed! Jenson was a material witness, and as such the court could demand that she post bond to assure her appearance in court. Jenson was poor and unable to post the bond, so she was jailed. A friend of Walker's, John

Bone, made "threats and menaces" to persuade Jenson to drop the charges, which she ultimately did to escape "being confined in a loathsome jail." April 12, no year given, letter from Hannah Jenson, Rowan County Criminal Action Papers, NCDAH.

66. August 1863 folder, July–November 1863 and [ ]–December 1861, PP, VEP, LVA.

67. Letter dated April 28, 1858, to Governor Henry A. Wise from John R. Chamblis [?]; juror's letter to Governor Henry A. Wise, n.d., [ ]–December 1861, VEPLR, Pardon Papers, LVA.

68. Other sexual assault cases involving freedmen as defendants include *Thurman v. State*, 18 Ala. 276 (June 1856); *Commonwealth of Virginia v. Jerry Mann*, 2 Va. Cas. 210 (June 1820); *Commonwealth of Virginia v. Tyree*, 2 Va. Cas. 262 (November 1821); *Commonwealth of Virginia v. Fields*, 4 Leigh 648 (December 1832); *Day v. Commonwealth of Virginia*, 2 Grattan 562 (December 1845) and 3 Grattan 629 (December 1846); *Smith v. Commonwealth of Virginia*, 10 Grattan 734 (July 1853). In 1854 the Virginia *Daily Dispatch* reported that a free black man stood accused of attempting to rape a white woman whose credibility the paper seemed to doubt because of her associations with the "lowest and most debased free negroes in the valley," as cited in Hodes, *White Women, Black Men*, 64–65. The *Raleigh Register* also reported the case of Henry Carroll, a free African American convicted of raping a white woman. His death sentence was stayed, at least for a time, by the governor in response to a petition signed by "respectable portions of our citizens." *Raleigh Register*, April 14, 1831, and May 12, 1831. In 1845 a free man of color, a steamboat steward from Louisiana, was acquitted of raping a white female, as was a free black from Tennessee by the name of Elihu. *New Orleans Daily Delta*, November 8, 1845; Howington, "The Treatment of Slaves and Free Blacks in the State and Local Courts of Tennessee," 326. At the other extreme, a free black man believed to have raped a small child was lynched. *New Orleans Bee*, October 9, 1858. Both these incidents are cited in Sterkx, *The Free Negro in Antebellum Louisiana*, 189. Robert Hill, a free black man from Sussex County, Virginia, was found guilty of assaulting a white female with intent to ravish. He was sentenced to die, although his execution has not been verified. May 6, 1843, Circuit Court of Sussex County Common Law Order Book, 2 (1831–66), 171; "Commonwealth v. Robert Hill, free negro," loose court papers of Sussex County, Virginia, 1843, box 311 (1754–1870), Sussex County Court House, Sussex, Virginia. My thanks to the court clerk, Gary M. Williams, for making me aware of these documents.

69. This last motive would explain any fissures in the white community over freedmen along class lines. Working-class or middling whites may have had reason to worry that free black men might market their skills and wares for less money, a factor which would also account for elite patronage of free blacks. Phillips, *American Negro Slavery*, 453.

70. This observation is consistent with Joel Williamson's overarching characterization of southern race relations from 1850 to 1915. In 1850, Williamson writes, the white elite allied with the "black mass," enabling the elite to maintain control over society. But by 1915 the white elite had virtually abandoned the black connection and bonded instead with the "white mass." Williamson, *Crucible of Race*, 512, 519.

Chapter Six

1. Philip S. Foner, ed., *The Life and Writings of Frederick Douglass*, 4:498–99.
2. Wells-Barnett, "A Red Record," in *On Lynchings*, 63–64.

3. W. Cabell Bruce, "Lynch Law in the South," 381.

4. McHattan, "The Sexual Status of the Negro, Past and Present," 8. There are numerous examples of white southern turn-of-the-century writers attempting to cast male slaves as the white woman's protector during the wartime years. Among them: McGuire and Lydston, "Sexual Crimes among the Southern Negroes Scientifically Considered," 105; Haygood, "The Black Shadow in the South," 167–75; Frederick L. Hoffman, *Race Traits and Tendencies of the American Negro*, 217; Felton, as quoted in Williamson, *Crucible of Race*, 128; Randle, *Characteristics of the Southern Negro*, 74; Brann, *Brann, the Iconoclast*, 1:25; Somerville, "Some Co-operating Causes of Negro Lynching," 509; Shaler, "The Negro since the Civil War," 29; Straton, "Will Education Solve the Race Problem?," 786; Charles Henry Smith, "Have American Negroes Too Much Liberty?," 182; Elizabeth Saxon, *A Southern Woman's War Time Reminiscences* (1905), 33, as quoted in Faust, *Mothers of Invention*, 60.

5. Shoup, "Uncle Tom's Cabin Forty Years After," 96. Early-twentieth-century historians were taken in by this romanticization of the innocuous, loyal slave. See Fleming, *Civil War and Reconstruction in Alabama*, 209, for example. This is also discussed at great length in the Appendix.

6. See, for example, Faust, *Mothers of Invention*; Faust, " 'Altars of Sacrifice' "; Faust, " 'Trying to Do a Man's Business' "; Faust, " 'If I Were Once Released,' "; Clinton and Silber, *Divided Houses*; Whites, *The Civil War as a Crisis in Gender*; Bynum, *Unruly Women*; Rable, *Civil Wars*; Glade, "Private Lives and Public Myths." Gender and Civil War as part of larger studies is treated in the following: Jean E. Friedman, *The Enclosed Garden*, 92–109; Lebsock, *The Free Women of Petersburg*, 239–40; Anne Firor Scott, *The Southern Lady*, 79–102; Clinton, *The Plantation Mistress*, 196–98; Bardaglio, *Reconstructing the Household*, 129–31.

7. On gender roles of elite white southerners see Clinton, *The Plantation Mistress*; Jean E. Friedman, *The Enclosed Garden*; Censer, *North Carolina Planters and Their Children*; Daniel Blake Smith, *Inside the Great House*; Stowe, *Intimacy and Power in the Old South*; Anne Firor Scott, *The Southern Lady*; Fox-Genovese, *Within the Plantation Household*.

8. One illustration of this is depicted in Faust, " 'Trying to Do a Man's Business.' "

9. Cashin, " 'Since the War Broke Out.' "

10. Kristie Ross, "Arranging a Doll's House"; Sizer, "Acting Her Part."

11. Woodward, ed., *Mary Chesnut's Civil War*, 234 (November 12, 1861).

12. Eliza Frances Andrews, *The War-Time Journal of a Georgia Girl, 1864–1865*, 19.

13. Childs, ed., *The Private Journal of Henry William Ravenal, 1859–1887*, 211, 220–22. For numerous other examples of white southerners professing not to fear their slaves during war consult Sommerville, "The Rape Myth Reconsidered," ch. 5. Drew Faust has uncovered a number of letters from white southern women to Confederate officials petitioning for the early release of their male providers from military or government duty that do cite worries about lack of protection and fears of slaves, some of them fears of sexual assault. I wonder about the sincerity of these claims and am inclined to believe that they were employed as a device to capitalize on paternalistic sympathies, an early effort to exploit the ideology of paternalism for reasons of self-interest. I base my belief on the plethora of evidence to the contrary, other written media that do not convey the same concerns or anxiety about the sexual threat of male slaves. Faust, *Mothers of Invention*, 58.

14. MacKintosh, ed., *"Dear Martha,"* 14. See also 177 (December 18, 1864), 179 (December 22, 1864), and 146 (October 13, 1864). In addition, see the exchange between Louisa Quitman

Lovell and her husband Joseph, July 28, 1861, in Quitman Family Papers, University of North Carolina, Chapel Hill, as cited in Jordan, *Tumult and Silence at Second Creek*, 18; and an entry in Scarborough, ed., *The Diary of Edmund Ruffin*, 3:630–31 (October 30, 1864).

15. John Hammond Moore, ed., *A Plantation Mistress on the Eve of the Civil War*, 54 (November 1860). Other passages expressing worry about slave insurrection include Childs, ed., *The Private Journal of Henry William Ravenal, 1859–1887*, 130; Coxe, *Memories of a South Carolina Plantation during the War*, 5; and Edmund Ruffin, Scarborough, ed., *The Diary of Edmund Ruffin*, 2:38 (May 29, 1861). Historians are divided on the extent to which masters truly believed their slaves to be childlike. George Fredrickson surveys this historiographical question in *The Arrogance of Race*, 15–27, 206–15. "Negrophobia," as Fredrickson calls it, was more likely to emerge in areas where whites were a distinct minority, such as South Carolina, where there were rumors or documented cases of slave conspiracy or unrest, and where large plantations with many slaves precluded close personal contact between master and slave. See also Fredrickson's *The Black Image in the White Mind*. William Messner found Louisiana whites worried about black violence in the early part of the Civil War, in "Black Violence and White Response." Ariela Gross's recent work examines how whites struggled to interpret slave behavior when it failed to conform to their own understanding of slaves' character. Gross, *Double Character*, 72–97.

16. Hodes, "Wartime Dialogues on Illicit Sex," 239. Victoria Bynum likewise fails to find evidence of white fears of black rape in the three North Carolina counties that make up her study. Bynum, *Unruly Women*, 117.

17. Jordan, *Tumult and Silence at Second Creek*, 159.

18. Ayers, *Vengeance and Justice*, 131.

19. Scarborough, ed., *The Diary of Edmund Ruffin*, 3:631 (October 31, 1864).

20. Childs, ed., *The Private Journal of Henry William Ravenal, 1859–1887*, 34.

21. Such works are too numerous to list, but classic historical studies that make this claim include Keller, *Affairs of State*, though Keller is careful to state that the Civil War "worked no great revolution in American life" (1); Nevins, *The War for the Union*, v ("The war measurably transformed an inchoate nation . . . into a shaped and disciplined nation"); and Fredrickson's *The Inner Civil War*, which views the Civil War as a watershed in American intellectual history. More recently, see Bardaglio, *Reconstructing the Household*, 116–17. On the status of southern women and the Civil War see Lebsock, *The Free Women of Petersburg*, 239–41.

22. Walters, "The Erotic South," 177–201.

23. A Virginia law passed in 1850 required governors to publish the reasons for reprieves or pardons of all convicts, black or white. Schwarz, "The Transportation of Slaves from Virginia, 1801–1865," 227. Governor Joseph Johnston transported the slave Jordan Hatcher after his conviction for the murder of a Richmond factory foreman in 1852. The decision, quite unpopular among certain sectors, cost Johnston politically. Link, "The Jordan Hatcher Case."

24. The fate of two convicted slave rapists is uncertain. Owners of condemned slaves who were either executed or transported were compensated by the state for their financial loss. For these two condemned slaves there is no documentation of any cash disbursements from the state auditor to the owners as compensation for their executions. Albert's guilty verdict and valuation of $500 are recorded in Henry County Court Minute Book 6, 1859–64, 281.

No mention of Albert's execution is made in the court's June or July sessions. Related court documentation can also be found in VEP, PP, [ ]–December 1861, May 1861 folder, LVA. However, Albert is not listed under Condemned Slaves. That said, Peter P. Penn, Albert's owner, petitioned the Virginia House of Delegates for compensation for the loss of his slave, "convicted of murder and sentenced to be executed by the county court of said county, May term 1861." In none of the House Journal's entries, though, is Albert's execution confirmed. Nor is there any mention of transportation or pardoning. *Journal of the House of Delegates of the State of Virginia, 1861–62 Session*, 96–97 (January 22, 1862), 106 (January 25, 1862), and 119 (January 30, 1862). See also EJ, January–December 1861, 188, LVA. The records are even more inconclusive in the case of Ben. His name is not listed in the Cash Journal, even under unspecified felonies. There is no record of the trial of Ben in the Amherst County Order Book, 1859–64. See RG 3, Governor's Office, EP, January–June 1862, and EJ, January 1861–October 1862, 104, LVA. There is no record that Ben's master, James Metcalf, was compensated for Ben's loss.

25. Susan's age is not revealed in related court documents.

26. July 1861 folder, [ ]–December 1861, PP, LR, VEP; June 1861 entry, Halifax County Court Minute Books, 1859–62 (microfilm reel 74), 276–77, LVA.

27. Ibid. Virginia law made no ameliorative provisions for accused rapists or attempted rapists who were proven to be mentally handicapped. The only allowance that most southern states made for an accused rapist was for age. English common law, from which most colonies and then states borrowed, dictated that a boy under the age of fourteen, the normal age for the onset of puberty, was physiologically incapable of committing the act of rape. Mary Block, "'An Accusation Easily to Be Made,'" 13, 22, 30–31. The North Carolina high court, for example, threw out the conviction for rape of a slave in 1864 because he was under the age of fourteen. *State v. Sam*, 60 N.C. 293 (1864). Florida appellate rulings late in the nineteenth century, pointing to common law, asserted that a boy under the age of fourteen could be guilty of rape or assault with intent to commit a rape. *Williams v. State*, 20 Fla. 777 (1884); *McKinney v. State*, 29 Fla. 565 (1892). The Georgia Supreme Court held that the state bore the burden of proof in a case in which it claimed that a boy under the age of fourteen did have the physical capacity to commit rape. *Gordon v. State*, 93 Ga. 531 (1893). See also the statutory provision in Paschal, *A Digest of the Laws of Texas*, ch. 6, art. 2189, p. 447. Only Louisiana seems to have rejected the age stipulation in cases of rape. In 1887 its justices wrote that the English basis for such a requirement was rooted in the presumption that puberty typically began at fourteen and was "based entirely on the physiological fact that, under the climate and other conditions prevailing in England, puberty is very rarely attained under that age." Earlier onset of puberty, in contrast, was "unquestionably the fact in Louisiana." *State v. Jones*, 39 La. Ann. 935 (1887).

28. July 1861 folder, [ ]–December 1861, PP, LR, VEP; June 1861 entry, Halifax County Court Minute Books, 1859–62 (microfilm reel 74), 276–77, LVA. A few other locals testified on Sam's behalf. Dr. B. R. Fleming recounted that about ten years earlier, when Sam was seven years old, he had been offered up for sale. The doctor had been inclined to purchase him but had been dissuaded against the purchase because the boy lacked "sprightliness of appearance."

29. Ibid.

30. Sommerville, "The Rape Myth in the Old South Reconsidered," 502–5.

31. See, for example, Sommerville, "The Rape Myth in the Old South Reconsidered," 495–98; Bynum, *Unruly Women*; Hodes, *White Women, Black Men*, 61–63.

32. I should also add parenthetically that this response can be seen in other sexual assault cases involving slaves. In August 1860 a well-respected woman of some means was attacked by a slave in Jefferson County, Virginia. As in this case, the accuser's character seemed above reproach. Similarly, the court yielded testimony that the slave was of a disposition described as "stupid" and "childish" but that he "seemed to be fond of liquor," which occasionally resulted in "wild and reckless" behavior. As with Sam, the jury bought the defense argument that imbecility and liquor, or the volatile combination of both, was to blame. They sentenced Bill to transportation instead of death. September–December 1860, box 472, PP, LR, VEP, LVA.

33. First, a brief primer on nineteenth-century American rape law, the crux of which was the issue of consent. If a woman physically resisted her attacker, she was believed to be demonstrating her refusal to grant permission for sexual intercourse, and this requirement of force was in fact necessary to establish rape. But women and girls who were intellectually and developmentally disadvantaged were often incapable of comprehending the nature of a sexual attack or were unable to resist and thus fell outside the protection of this rather strict definition of rape. State lawmakers were slow, though, to make adjustments to their rape statutes to offer greater protection to these females. However, by mid-century state appellate courts began interpreting the rape statutes more broadly, ruling that a female who was over the age of consent, "but still a child in physical and mental development," would be regarded as a minor. Sommerville, " 'I Was Very Much Wounded,' " 137–38. On the case law refer to *Stephen v. State*, 11 Ga. 225 (1852); *Anschicks v. State*, 6 Tex. App. 524 (1879); *Caruth v. State of Texas* (Cr. App.) 25 S.W. 778 (1892). For cases outside the slaveholding South see *State v. Crow*, 1 Ohio Dec. 586 (1853); *State v. Tarr*, 28 Iowa 397 (1870); *Commonwealth v. Burke*, 105 Mass. 376 (1870). Kentucky appears unique in that its antebellum rape statute specifically gave protection to "idiots" in much the same way that it did to minor children. Wickliffe, Turner, and Nicholas, comps., *Revised Statutes of Kentucky*, ch. 28, art. 4, p. 248. Georgia lawmakers relegated the interpretation of appellate decisions regarding the rape of developmentally handicapped women to a footnote in its rape statutes. Irwin, Lester, and Hill, comps., *Code of the State of Georgia*, part IV, tit. I, div. IV, §4349, p. 788. Virginia lawmakers did not move to protect mentally challenged women until 1895, when they passed a law to protect "lunatics." Virginia *Acts of Assembly*, regular session 1885, ch. 374, §18, 417: "If any person carnally know a female of the age of twelve years or more, against her will, by force, or carnally know a female child under that age, or a female inmate of any lunatic asylum, who has been adjudged a lunatic, he shall be, at the discretion of the jury, punished by death, or confined in the penitentiary not less than ten nor more than twenty years."

34. January–June 1862, PP, LR, VEP, LVA.

35. Walker did not actually own John but had hired out the thirteen-year-old slave from his owner, Mrs. Nancy Wray.

36. January–June 1862, PP, LR, VEP, LVA.

37. Ibid.

38. Throughout many sectors in colonial and early America, there was a not a clear boundary between rape and illicit though consensual sex. Coercion or even violence was

roundly accepted as part of the ritual in pursuing sex. Sharon Block, "Coerced Sex in British North America, 1700–1820," 22.

39. January–June 1862, PP, LR, VEP, LVA.

40. Ibid.

41. Ibid.

42. There are other possible explanations for Walker's having sided with the slave rapist. Had Walker himself raped the girl, or at least imagined it, on a previous occasion or occasions? Or had Walker spoken so contemptuously of Reynolds in the past in John's presence that John inferred Walker's tacit approval of forcible sex with her?

43. January–June 1862, PP, LR, VEP, LVA. On the question of age and the capacity to rape see note 27 in this chapter. Most slaves grew up never knowing their actual age or birth date. See Quarles, ed., *Narrative of the Life of Frederick Douglass*, 23.

44. January–June 1862, PP, LR, VEP; CS Transported, 1862, LVA.

45. Escott's book is just one of many recent works documenting serious political, regional, and social fissures in the slaveholding states during the Civil War and debunking ideas of racial and regional solidarity in the South. Escott, *Many Excellent People*, 81, and 32–84. See also J. William Harris, *Plain Folk and Gentry in a Slave Society*, 149–60, 170, 177–79; Eric Foner, *Reconstruction*, 11–18; Inscoe and McKinney, *The Heart of Confederate Appalachia*; Inscoe and Kenzer, *Enemies of the Country*; Sutherland, ed., *Guerillas, Unionists, and Violence on the Confederate Homefront*; Durrill, *War of Another Kind*.

46. July and December 1862 folders, July–December 1862, PP, LR, VEP, LVA.

47. Ibid.

48. Ibid.

49. Ibid.

50. Ibid.

51. Ibid.

52. Ibid. Although there appear to be no cash disbursements recorded in the Cash Journal for Emmanuel, county records indicate that he was executed. July–December, 1862 bundle, Lunenberg County, County Court Decisions/Justice of the Peace Records, 1861–69, LVA.

53. In September 1862 Ned was convicted of breaking and entering into a storehouse and stealing brandy, for which he received eighty lashes. Earlier that year a female slave had been tried but acquitted of breaking and entering into a home and stealing clothes. And in June 1864 two slaves, Joe and Dabney, were charged with breaking and entering a smokehouse with intent to steal bacon. July–December, 1862 bundle, Lunenberg County, County Court Decisions/Justice of the Peace Records, 1861–69, LVA.

54. Laura F. Edwards, "The Disappearance of Susan Daniel and Henderson Cooper," 375–76; Bynum, *Unruly Women*, 122; Hodes, *White Women, Black Men*, 130–39.

55. May 1861 folder, [ ]–December 1861, PP, LR, VEP, LVA.

56. The jury found Albert guilty and sentenced him to hang. His fate, however, is uncertain. Henry County Court Minute Book 6, 1859–64, 281. No mention of Albert's execution is made in the court's June or July sessions. See expanded discussion in note 24 of this chapter.

57. See note 27 in chapter 5.

58. On trade between nonelite whites and blacks in the antebellum South see Lockley, "Trading Encounters between Nonelite Whites and African Americans in Savannah."

59. January–April 1865, PP, LR, VEP, LVA.

60. Ibid.

61. Ibid.

62. Ibid.

63. Ibid.

64. Ibid.

65. Ibid.

66. Ibid. Sources that cite examples of the hangings of African American men in other parts of the South during the Civil War for alleged sexual assaults on white females include *The True Issue* (La Grange, Texas) of January 1, 1863, which is in turn cited in Wiley, *Southern Negroes*, 81.

67. Although her name is presented in court documents as Susan J. Corbin, those in her family and neighborhood seem to have referred to her as Jane (presumably her middle name). News of Nat's rape trial made its way to neighboring Franklin County, as is evidenced in the subsequent rape trial of another Virginia slave a few months later. I base my conjecture that Jane Corbin's husband was off to war on the report about the alleged rape in which Nat, her accused black rapist, is said to have been hanged for "keeping a soldier's wife." January–April 1865, PP, LR, VEP; November 1864 folder, April–December, 1864, box 528, PP, LR, VEP, LVA.

68. November 1864 folder, April–December, 1864, box 528, PP, LR, VEP, LVA.

69. Ibid.

70. Ibid.

71. Ibid.

72. Ibid. Edmund Ruffin commented on the rising cost of slaves during the Civil War: "It is surprising that the prices of slaves continue so high, notwithstanding their now precareous tenure wherever the Yankee forces can extend their occupancy. . . . After a slight decline through the earlier times of the war, because of want of employment & profit of labor, more than the hazard of losing slaves, the demand in the market, & the prices, have rallied, & latterly have been increasing. The nominal market prices now are higher than before the war, or at any previous time. But the depreciation of our paper currency makes a large deduction from nominal to real prices—how much I do not know, but perhaps 40 to 50 percent should be thus abated. Even with this abatement, the present ready prices for slaves are higher than any available employment can return a profit upon now." Scarborough, ed., *The Diary of Edmund Ruffin*, 2:466.

73. January–June 1862, PP, LR, VEP, LVA.

74. Ibid.

75. Ibid.

76. He was valued at $800 and his owner, James Metcalf, was ordered to pay $25 toward the court-appointed defense attorney, and court costs. But again, it is not clear that Ben ever faced his scheduled day of execution. There is no record of disbursement made to James Metcalf as compensation either for a transported or executed slave. January–June 1862, PP, LR, VEP, LVA.

77. July 1862 folder, July–December 1862, PP, LR, VEP, LVA.

78. Ibid. and CS Transported, 1862.

79. August 1862 folder, July–December 1862, PP, LR, VEP and CJ, LVA.

80. Giles Buckner Cooke, twenty-five, while serving in the Confederate States Army of Western Virginia on the staff of Samuel Jones, recorded in his diary the hanging of a slave belonging to Stuart Buchanon in Saltville in Smyth County for raping a white woman. Diary of Giles Buckner Cooke, July 7, 1863, entry, June 28–August 8, 1863, bound volume, VHS. There are documented lynchings of black men believed to have raped or attempted to rape white women in other parts of the South. A slave in Georgia was proclaimed guilty by a justice of the peace of the assault (it is not certain whether the assault was sexual in nature) of an overseer's wife and ordered held over for trial in superior court in July 1862. An angry mob seized the jailed slave and hanged him. It was stated that the extralegal lynching was prompted by fears that the slave's master would spirit the accused away and sell him to an unknowing party. Merton Coulter states that the owner would not have received compensation for a legally executed slave. Coulter, "Slavery and Freedom in Athens, Georgia, 1860–1866," 352.

81. J. William Harris, *Plain Folk and Gentry*, 173–76.

82. Bynum, *Unruly Women*, 119.

83. Faust, *Mothers of Invention*, 126–27. See also Hodes, "Wartime Dialogues on Illicit Sex," 235.

84. Laura F. Edwards, "The Disappearance of Susan Daniel and Henderson Cooper," 370.

Chapter Seven

1. Thompson and Steger, comps., *A Compilation of the Statute Laws of the State of Tennessee*, vol. II, tit. xii, ch. 2, art. 3, sec. 4610, p. 48; Meigs and Cooper, comps., *The Code of Tennessee*, art. 3, sec. 2625, part 5, p. 509, and art. 3, sec. 4611, p. 830. See also Gantt, *A Digest of the Statutes of Arkansas*, ch. II, sec. 1, p. 217; Bush, comp., *A Digest of the Statute Law of Florida*, ch. 43, secs. 41–42, p. 217; *Revised Statute Laws of the State of Louisiana* (1870), sec. 787, p. 160; Mayer, Fischer, and Cross, comps., *Revised Code of the Public General Laws of the State of Maryland*, tit. 27, art. 72, secs. 13–14, p. 787; Campbell, Johnston, and Lovering, comps., *Revised Code of Statute Laws of Mississippi*, ch. 58, art. 27, secs. 2672–73, p. 584; Denny, comp., *The General Statutes of the State of Missouri*, part iv, tit. xlv, ch. 200, sec. 23, p. 780; *Acts of the General Assembly of North Carolina* (1868–69), ch. 167, pp. 406–7; Ferris, Bassett, and Wilson, comps., *The Revised Statutes of Texas*, tit. xv, ch. 7, art. 528, p. 73; Matthews, comp., *Digest of the Laws of Virginia of a Criminal Nature* (1871), ch. 12, §15, p. 166. Some unreconstructed state legislatures like that of North Carolina in its Black Code of 1865 maintained death for a black man convicted of intent to rape a white woman. This and five other provisions of the code that discriminated on the basis of race were amended in July 1866 and distinctions on the basis of race were purged. Roberta Sue Alexander, *North Carolina Faces the Freedmen*, 49.

2. Stanton, comp., *The Revised Statutes of Kentucky*, ch. 28, art. iv, sec. 4, pp. 379–80; *The Statutes at Large of South Carolina* (1865), no. 4731, pp. 35–36. See Bullitt and Feland, comps., *The General Statutes of Kentucky*, art. iv, sec. 5, p. 322; Corbin, comp., *The Revised Statutes of the State of South Carolina*, ch. 128, sec. 12, p. 711. The Georgia legislature, responding to a state supreme court ruling in favor of a slave condemned to die for the rape of a slave girl, expanded the definition of rape to include slave and free women as early as 1861. Clark,

Cobb, and Irwin, comps., *The Code of the State of Georgia*, tit. I, div. iv, sec. 4248, p. 824. The case caused considerable excitement among the slave community as well. The judge of the circuit court in Bibb County testified that he himself had to go to the jail to prevent other blacks from killing the convicted slave rapist. See *KKK Report*, vol. 7, Georgia, 1191. *George v. State*, 37 Miss. 316 (1859). See also Chapter 2.

3. For example, *Act of the General Assembly of the State of Virginia*, passed in 1865–66, ch. 24, p. 89 (February 28, 1866).

4. Laura F. Edwards, *Gendered Strife and Confusion*, 199, and "Sexual Violence, Gender, Reconstruction, and the Extension of Patriarchy," 252–54, 258–59. See also Bardaglio, *Reconstructing the Household*, 195; Hodes, *White Women, Black Men*, 147–75; Rosen, "'Not That Sort of Women.'"

5. HED, No. 70, *Freedmen's Bureau*, 204.

6. *KKK Report*, vol. 5, South Carolina, 1409, 1475.

7. *KKK Report*, vol. 13, Florida, 59–64.

8. HED, No. 70, *Freedmen's Bureau*, 207. See also *KKK Report*, vol. 8, Alabama, 548, 553; vol. 9, Alabama, 930; vol. 2, North Carolina, 148.

9. *KKK Report*, vol. 7, Georgia, 914, 949. White women were not immune from sexual attacks by Klan members. A white man from Fayette County, Alabama, was whipped by a party of Klansmen who then raped his wife. A seventeen-year-old white girl who was staying at the home of George Moore, a man of color, and his wife in the summer of 1869 was raped when a Ku Klux Klan band of intruders attacked the Moore home. Moore's wife went unmolested only because she told her attackers that she had just miscarried. A Klan raiding party whipped a white Alabama man and ravished his wife. *KKK Report*, vol. 8, Alabama, 549; vol. 9, Alabama, 1188–89. See also vol. 8, Alabama, 547.

10. Rosen, "'Not That Sort of Women,'" 267–93.

11. Litwack, *Been in the Storm So Long*, 280.

12. *KKK Report*, vol. 5, South Carolina, 1408–9.

13. Eric Foner, *Reconstruction*, 427.

14. I did not find any trials definitively involving white-on-black rape in Virginia during Reconstruction. With the end of slavery and the loss in value of African Americans as property, state officials had less motivation to track the fate of condemned black criminals, so the meticulous recordkeeping for black criminals ceased. Also, the tracking of the racial identity of accusers and the accused in rape cases became more cumbersome after slavery ended. Officials were inconsistent about their denotation of race.

15. For example, a justice of the peace in Virginia dismissed the charges made by a fourteen-year-old African American girl against a white man in 1866, ostensibly because her witnesses had failed to appear. Another popular tactic in discouraging African Americans from swearing out complaints against white persons was to demand that the complainant, as a key witness, post bond. Since most freedmen and women could not afford to do so, they faced a jail sentence. Blair, "Justice versus Law and Order," 170. When Hannah Tutson reported her abuse by Ku Klux Klan members to officials, both she and her husband were jailed. *KKK Report*, vol. 13, Florida, 59–64. On the difficulty that freedpersons faced in filing charges against whites during Reconstruction see Litwack, *Been in the Storm So Long*, 285. Laura Edwards documents one official case of white-on-black rape in Granville County, North Carolina, in 1878. The justice of the peace held the accused white man over for

superior court and denied him bail. Although he was eventually acquitted for lack of evidence, Edwards rightly points out the significance of a such postbellum case, for it "indicates that the African American community had forced whites to acknowledge that nonconsensual sex with a black woman was in fact a crime." Laura F. Edwards, "Sexual Violence, Gender, Reconstruction, and the Extension of Patriarchy," 248.

16. Laura Edwards also makes this point. *Gendered Strife and Confusion*, 200. For appellate cases involving black-on-black rape in the South after the Civil War see Bardaglio, *Reconstructing the Household*, 190–91.

17. Prison Register, 1868; entry October 7, 1868, EJ, 1868; December 23, 1870, packet, box 16 (December 16–31, 1870), EP, SC, LVA. Confusion over jurisdiction in criminal cases in this period was not unusual. Eric Foner described a "bewildering array of federal, state, and local authorities" that existed in the early Reconstruction period. Presumably this was the case in occupied northern Virginia Union, where military leaders established provost courts to hear criminal complaints of freedmen and women. Eric Foner, *Reconstruction*, 148–49.

18. Prison Register, 1868; entry October 7, 1868, EJ 1868; December 23, 1870, packet, box 16 (December 16–31, 1870) EP, SC, LVA. Under Mosby's command this small guerilla company operated in small parties of twenty to eighty and never totaled more than eight hundred. McPherson, *Battle Cry of Freedom*, 737–38. For recent studies of guerilla warfare between pro-Union and pro-Confederate southerners, consult Inscoe and McKinney, *The Heart of Confederate Appalachia*, 105–38; Sutherland, ed., *Guerillas, Unionists, and Violence on the Confederate Home Front*. Hunter's pardon came in December 1868. The second rape charge filed against Hunter was made by a twenty-five-year-old woman of color with three "bastard children." Hunter was sentenced to the penitentiary for eleven years. Letter to Governor Gilbert C. Walker from fourteen petitioners of Culpeper County, n.d., December 23, 1870, packet, box 16 (December 16–31, 1870), EP, SC; Prison Register, 1870, LVA.

19. Letter from D. A. Claiborne, Wolf Trap, Virginia, March 21, 1870, December 23, 1870, packet, box 16 (December 16–31, 1870), EP, SC, LVA. The Underwood Constitution to which Claiborne referred was adopted in 1869 after a state constitutional convention, headed by a federal judge and native New Yorker, John C. Underwood, and meeting from December 1867 to April 1868, ratified it. Among other things, the new constitution provided for universal manhood suffrage and established a statewide system of publicly supported schools. Many features were particularly odious to former Confederates, especially the disfranchisement of many their own. See for instance Salmon and Campbell, eds., *The Hornbook of Virginia History*, 52–53, 98; Dailey, *Before Jim Crow*, 10–21, 24–25, 27, 37, 162, 174 n. 5; Moger, *Virginia*, 6–11, 70, 77, 181, 239; Eckenrode, *The Political History of Virginia during the Reconstruction*, 87–103; Lowe, *Republicans and Reconstruction in Virginia, 1856–70*, 121–63; Smith, "Virginia during Reconstruction, 1865–1870," 63–116; Louis Moore, " 'The Elusive Center,' " 210–17; Salmon and Salmon, *Franklin County, Virginia, 1786–1986*, 314.

20. Letter to Governor Gilbert C. Walker from fourteen petitioners from Culpeper County, n.d., December 23, 1870, packet, box 16 (December 16–31, 1870), EP, SC; Prison Register, 1870, LVA. Edward Ayers observed a similar theoretical rationale among petitions written by white southerners trying to get black criminals pardoned. Ayers, *Vengeance and Justice*, 205.

21. January 8, 1867, packet, box 3 (January–March, 1867), EP, SC, LVA. Virginia law

protected only those girls "under" the age of twelve through its statutory rape laws. Chapter 2, note 8. Even though the accuser in this case was covered by the age-of-consent law and therefore in the eyes of the law deemed incapable of granting consent for sex, the petitioners treated her as a consenting female.

22. Letter from C. C. Blankenship of Nottoway, Virginia, February 15, 1869, March 23, 1869, packet, box 9 (January–April, 1869), EP, SC, LVA.

23. Letter from the Rev. G. H. Ray, Burkeville, Virginia, February 13, 1869, ibid. The argument fell on deaf ears, however, as there is no evidence that Marshall was ever pardoned. See also November 16, 1866, January 8, 1867, March 23, 1869, and June 17, 1869, EJ, LVA; letter from C. C. Blankenship and nine signatories of Nottoway, November 15, 1866, November 16 packet, box 2 (July–November, 1866); petition of forty-seven signatories, June 7, 1869, June packet, box 10 (May–August 14, 1869); petition of sixty-nine signatories from Nottoway County, n.d., and letter from W. C. Knight of Richmond, October 25, 1870, December 27, 1870 packet, box 16 (December 16–31, 1870), all in EP, SC, LVA.

24. Petition, n.d., "citizens of Nottoway" (thirty-six signatories), March 23, 1869, packet, box 9; and letter of October 25, 1870, from W. C. Knight, a manufacturer in Richmond, to governor, item 2, December 27, 1870, packet, box 16, December 16–31, 1870, both in EP, SC, LVA.

25. November 6, 1877, packet, box 40 (October–December 1877), EP, SC; July 11, September 15, and November 6, 1877, 130, 167, and 189 in EJ, LVA. Despite a temporary respite the governor does not appear to have pardoned Smith or commuted his sentence.

26. Laura Edwards offers that African American men filing charges of rape on behalf of their daughters and wives were exercising patriarchal prerogatives and establishing their own authority by playing the role of male protector. Laura F. Edwards, "Sexual Violence, Gender, Reconstruction, and the Extension of Patriarchy," 252–54.

27. June 25, 1867, packet, box 4 (April–August 1867), EP, SC, and June 25, 1867, entry, EJ, LVA. Francis Pierpont served as the provisional governor of Virginia from May 1865 to April 1868. Salmon and Campbell, eds., The Hornbook of Virginia History, 111.

28. Prison records indicate that Powell's age upon his receipt into the penitentiary was eighteen; however, in Powell's petition to the Virginia governor in 1882, he claimed that his age at arrest had been fourteen years and eight months. September 25, 1867, entry, Prison Register, and letter from Edward Powell to Governor William E. Cameron, May 1882, State Penitentiary, Richmond, June 26, 1882 packet, box 59 (April 18–June 1882), EP, SC, LVA.

29. Letter from Edward Powell to Governor William E. Cameron, Richmond, May 1882, ibid. Underlining is Powell's.

30. Cameron, a Readjuster from the city of Petersburg, served as governor of Virginia from January 1882 to January 1886. Dailey, Before Jim Crow, 66, 74–75, 81, 83–84, 96–100, 146, 150, 157, 158; Salmon and Campbell, eds., The Hornbook of Virginia History, 111.

31. Official notation from Judge C. Alexander of Mecklenburg County, Virginia, n.d., and letter from Edward Powell to Governor William E. Cameron, Richmond, May 1882, ibid.; June 28, 1882, 108, EJ, LVA.

32. Acts of the General Assembly of the State of Virginia, 1865–1866, ch. 25, sec. 1, p. 90; Matthews, comp., Digest of the Laws of Virginia of a Criminal Nature (1871), ch. 12, sec. 15. p. 166.

33. Virginia law required proof of penetration for the prosecution of rape. Without such

proof, the charge would stand as merely an attempt. Matthews, *Digest of the Laws of Virginia of a Criminal Nature* (1871), ch. 12, sec. 15, n. 8, pp. 166–67.

34. An undated petition received November 26, 1880, stated that although Holmes could not afford legal counsel, the court arranged with a member of the bar to represent him. The boy's father, Jacob Holmes Sr., in a petition to the governor, informed him that he had been too poor to hire a lawyer and "believes he had no counsel." Petition with fifty-five signatories, n.d., November 26, 1880, packet, box 53 (November 17, 1880–February 12, 1881), EP, SC, and letter from Jacob Holmes Sr., September 8, 1880, September 22–30, 1886 packet, box 76 (September 22–December 8, 1886), EP, SC, LVA. Lacking or substandard representation for accused blacks in legal proceedings after the war highlights an important distinction in the nature of criminal justice for African Americans. Both courts and slaveholders in the Old South generally saw to it that slaves accused of severe crimes had access to some level of legal counsel.

35. Letter from S. M. Page, n.d., September 22–30, 1886, packet, box 76 (September 22–December 8, 1886), EP, SC, LVA.

36. Letter from W. T. Smith of Lynchburg, Virginia, November 20, 1880, November 26, 1880, packet, box 53 (November 17, 1880–February 12, 1881), and letter from Jacob Holmes Sr., September 8, 1880, ibid. On the antebellum treatment of southern girls who charged sexual assault see Sommerville, " 'I Was Very Much Wounded.' "

37. *Acts of the General Assembly of the State of Virginia, Regular Session 1865, Code of Virginia*, ch. 14, sec. 15, p. 82 (February 9, 1866); Mathews, comp., *Digest of the Laws of a Criminal Nature of the State of Virginia* (1871), ch. 12, sec. 15, p. 166.

38. Petition with fifty-five signatories, n.d., November 26, 1880, packet, box 53 (November 17, 1880–February 12, 1881), EP, SC, and letter from George S. Stevens of Lovingston, Virginia, September 13, 1886, September 22–30, 1886, packet, box 76 (September 22–December 8, 1886), EP, SC. Jacob Holmes Jr. entered the Virginia state penitentiary on January 29, 1876. Prison Register, 1876, LVA. It is instructive, too, that outrage at sexual assault was not limited to cases in which it was believed that black men had raped white women.

39. Letter of December 19, 1872, from James M. Love, January 23, 1874, packet, box 27 (January–February 1874), EP, SC; January 23, 1874, 15, EJ; Prison Register, 1870, LVA.

40. Scholarly works questioning or denying that the black family was characterized by households headed by females were responding to the early work of the black sociologist E. Franklin Frazier's *The Negro Family in the United States* and later Daniel Patrick Moynihan's *The Negro Family*, commonly referred to as the "Moynihan Report." Works insisting that black families were "normal," male-dominated institutions include Gutman, *The Black Family in Slavery and Freedom, 1750–1925*, 432–60; Fogel and Engerman, *Time on the Cross*; Blassingame, *The Slave Community*, 167–91; Blassingame, *Black New Orleans, 1860–1880*, 79–105; and Genovese, *Roll, Jordan, Roll*, 490–94. Yet another revisionist body of literature emerged, embracing alternative models of the black family that were mother-centered or matrifocal: Deborah Gray White, *Ar'n't I a Woman?*, 157–67; Deborah Gray White, "Female Slaves," 248–61; Lebsock, "Free Black Women and the Question of Matriarchy," 271–92; and Lebsock, *The Free Women of Petersburg*, 87–111.

41. Stevenson, "Distress and Discord in Virginia Slave Families, 1830–1860," 103–24. On the African American family in slavery and freedom consult first and foremost Gutman,

The Black Family in Slavery and Freedom. See also Berry and Blassingame, *Long Memory*, 70–86. On the slave family see Litwack, *Been in the Storm So Long*, 7–8; Stampp, *The Peculiar Institution*, 340–49; Deborah Gray White, *Ar'n't I a Woman?*; Jacqueline Jones, *Labor of Love, Labor of Sorrow*, 31–38, 43; Blassingame, *The Slave Community*, 149–91; Fox-Genovese. *Within the Plantation Household*, 177–78, 297–98, 374; Genovese, *Roll, Jordan, Roll*, 450–514. On the African American family after emancipation refer to Litwack, *Been in the Storm So Long*, 230–46; Williamson, *After Slavery*, 306–12; Jacqueline Jones, *Labor of Love, Labor of Sorrow*, 48–51, 58, 64–68, 81–95, 102–9. For a discussion of the historiographical treatment of the black family as well as an analysis of free women of color in this context see Lebsock, *The Free Women of Petersburg*, 87–111. On free black families in the slave South consult Johnson and Roark, "Strategies of Survival," 88–102. On domestic violence among slave families see Stevenson, "Distress and Discord in Slave Families," 117, 122, 124; Deborah Gray White, *Ar'n't I a Woman?*, 151–53.

42. Deborah Gray White elaborates on the "Jezebel" stereotype at length in *Ar'n't I a Woman?*, 27–34, 46, 60–61, 105, 165–67.

43. Virtually all studies of African American women that discuss their sexual exploitation in slavery and freedom have overwhelmingly focused upon the white male as the primary sexual threat. For instance, Clinton, " 'Southern Dishonor,' " 52–68; Fox-Genovese, *Within the Plantation Household*, 189, 292, 299, 315, 323, 325–26, 374; Blassingame, *The Slave Community*, 153–54, 172–73. A few notable exceptions are White, *Ar'n't I a Woman?*, 152–53; and Hine, "Rape and the Inner Lives of Black Women in the Middle West," 914–15. The close physical quarters that slaves shared with kin and non-kin, let alone the futility of a complaint from a female slave to her master, accentuate the vulnerability of female slaves to sexual abuse by slave males. This is an area that demands far greater scholarly attention. For examples of North Carolina freedwomen bringing sexual assault charges against African American men see Laura F. Edwards, "Sexual Violence, Gender, Reconstruction, and the Extension of Patriarchy," 237–38, 246–48, 252–53.

44. To cite just one example, Tennessee in May 1866 passed a law stating "that persons of color shall not be subject to any other or different punishment, pains or penalties for the commission of any act or offense than such as are prescribed for white persons committing such like acts of offenses, and that all acts and parts of acts, or laws inconsistent herewith, are hereby repealed." Quarles, comp., *Criminal Code and Digest of Tennessee*, 820. See also Bardaglio, *Reconstructing the Household*, 189.

45. Stanton, *The Revised Statutes of Kentucky* (1867), art. iv, ch. 28, sec. iv, pp. 379–80, and Bullitt and Feland, *General Statutes of Kentucky* (1881), ch. 29, art. iv, sec. 5 (death or ten to twenty years); Campbell, Johnston, and Lovering, comps., *The Revised Code of the Statute Laws of the State of Mississippi*, ch. 58, art. 27, sec. 2672, and Campbell, *The Revised Code of the Statute Laws of the State of Mississippi*, ch. 77, sec. 2942, p. 768 (death or life imprisonment); Denny, *The General Statutes of the State of Missouri*, part iv, tit. xlv, ch. 200, sec. 23, p. 780, and Hockaday, Parrish, McDaniel, and McIntyre, comps., *The Revised Statutes of the State of Missouri*, vol. I, ch. 24, art. 2, sec. 1253, p. 221 (death or not less than five years); Thompson and Steger, comps., *Compilation of the Statute Laws of Tennessee*, vol. II, tit. xii, ch. 2, art. 3, sec. 4610, p. 48; Quarles, *Criminal Code of Tennessee*, 822; Thompson and Steger, comps., *A Compilation of the Statute Laws of the State of Tennessee*, 2:48–49; Milliken and Vertrees, comps., *The Code of Tennessee*, part 4, tit. 1, ch. 2, art. 3, sec. 5362 (death or ten

years to life); Corbin, comp., *Revised Statutes of the State of South Carolina*, ch. 128, sec. 12, p. 711 (hard labor for life or for not less than ten years). See also Bardaglio, *Reconstructing the Household*, 190.

46. Paschal, comp., A *Digest of the Laws of Texas* (1870), ch. vi, art. 2190, p. 447; Paschal, A *Digest of the Laws of Texas* (1873), vol. 2, ch. 3, art. 6539, p. 1329.

47. Stone and Shepherd, comps., *The Penal Code of Alabama*, tit. 1, ch. 8, sec. 119, pp. 44–45; Bush, comp., A *Digest of the Statute Law of Florida*, ch. 43, sec. 41, p. 217; McClellan, comp., A *Digest of the Laws of the State of Florida, 1822–1881*, ch. 55, sec. 36, p. 355; Mayer, Fischer, and Cross, comps., *Revised Code of Maryland*, tit. 27, art. 72, sec. 13, p. 787; Munford, comp., *Code of Virginia* (1873), tit. 54, ch. 187, sec. 18, pp. 1190–91; Virginia General Assembly, Regular Session (1865), ch. 14, sec. 1, p. 82; Clark, Cobb, and Irwin, *The Code of the State of Georgia*, part 4, tit. 1, sec. 4284, p. 841. During Reconstruction Tennessee revised its rape law and held out prison sentences of ten to twenty-one years for conviction of rape. Thompson and Steger, comps., *Compilation of the Statute Laws of Tennessee*, vol. 2, tit. 12, ch. 2, art. 3, sec. 4611, p. 48. But when the state's criminal code was revised and published twelve years later, the punishment for rape had been amended. Convicted rapists could "suffer death by hanging: Provided, The jury before whom the offender is tried and convicted, may, if they think proper, commute the punishment for the offense to imprisonment in the penitentiary for life, or for a period of not less than ten years." Milliken and Vertrees, comps., *The Code of Tennessee*, part 4, tit. 1, ch. 2, art. 3, sec. 5362, p. 1030.

48. Gantt, A *Digest of the Statutes of Arkansas*, ch. 42, sec. 1302, p. 333; *The Revised Statute Laws of the State of Louisiana*, sec. 787, p. 160; Seay and Young, comps., *The Revised Statutes of the State of Louisiana*, sec. 2633, p. 663; *Acts of the General Assembly of North Carolina* (1868–69), ch. 167, sec. 2, pp. 406–7; and Amis, *The North Carolina Criminal Code and Digest*, 240–41.

49. This trend is most salient in the twentieth century. The following statistics represent the number of African American men executed for the crime of rape, attempted rape, or assault with intent to rape, compared to the number of men of all races executed for one of the same crimes: Alabama, 1927–65 (twenty-five of twenty-eight); Arkansas, 1913–64 (nineteen of twenty-one); Florida, 1924–64 (forty of forty-two); Georgia, 1924–64 (sixty of sixty-six); Kentucky, 1911–62 (twenty of twenty-two); Louisiana, 1957–61 (three of three); Maryland, 1923–61 (twenty-one of twenty-seven); Mississippi, 1955–64 (nine of nine); Missouri, 1938–65 (four of six); North Carolina, 1901–61 (sixty-three of seventy-two); South Carolina, 1912–62 (fifty-eight of sixty); Tennessee, 1909–60 (twenty-four of thirty); Texas, 1924–64 (seventy-one of eighty-eight); Virginia, 1908–62 (fifty-three of fifty-three). Statistics taken from William J. Bowers, *Legal Homicide*, 399–523.

50. See Chapter 3.

51. Walker, comp., *Revised Code of Alabama*, tit. 1, part 4, sec. 3670, p. 700 (imprisonment in the penitentiary, or hard labor in the county for not less than two, nor more than twenty, years); Gantt, comp., *Digest of the Statutes of Arkansas*, ch. 42, sec. 1304, p. 333 (three to twenty-one years); Bush, comp., A *Digest of the Statute Law of Florida*, ch. 43, sec. 42, p. 217 (any term of years, or for life, or by fine not exceeding $1,000); Clark, Cobb, and Irwin, comps., *The Code of the State of Georgia*, part 4, tit. 1, sec. 4285, p. 841 (one to twenty years); *Revised Statute Laws of Louisiana* (1870), sec. 792, p. 161 (hard labor, not exceeding two years); Denny, comp., *The General Statutes of the State of Missouri*, part iv, tit. 45, ch. 200,

sec. 29, p. 780 (not exceeding ten years); *Acts of the General Assembly of North Carolina* (1868–69), ch. 167, sec. 2, pp. 406–7 (five to ten years); Clark, comp., *The Criminal Laws of Texas*, ch. 3, art. 503, p. 169 (two to seven years). See also Bardaglio, *Reconstructing the Household*, 190. Virginia reinstated the death penalty for attempted rape in the 1890s. Brundage, *Lynching in the New South*, 177.

52. A slaveholder in Mississippi by the name of John B. Owen, whose slave was believed to have committed a rape, spirited him away to a neighboring county to avoid arrest. He then sold the slave, a fugitive from justice, to a slaveholder named Joseph Doughty for a bargain price. Doughty, court records revealed, knew of the slave's offense. Owen's motive for breaking the law, to keep his slave from going to trial, is never spelled out, however. *Doughty v. Owen*, 24 Miss. 404 (1852). A number of slaveholding states enacted legislation to force masters to turn over slaves charged with capital offenses. Those not in compliance risked severe penalties and jail time. See, for example, O'Neall, *The Negro Law of South Carolina*, 47; South Carolina *Acts* (1843), no. 2893, p. 257 ($1,000 fine and imprisonment not to exceed twelve months); Alabama *Acts* (1840), ch. 5, sec. 21, p. 142 ($1,000 fine or two-year imprisonment).

53. *KKK Report*, vol. 11, Mississippi, 305.

54. Trowbridge, *The South: A Tour of Its Battlefields and Ruined Cities. . . .*, 314. On how emancipation and the loss of value of former slaves jeopardized freedmen after the war see Trelease, *White Terror*, xliii; Cash, *Mind of the South*, 119–20; George C. Wright, *Racial Violence in Kentucky, 1865–1940*, 2; Litwack, *Been in the Storm So Long*, 275, 282; Hodes, *White Women, Black Men*, 158.

55. Blair, "Justice versus Law and Order," 165–72. Blair argues that Virginia's minor judiciary during the early years of Reconstruction was characterized by outrages committed against the state's freed population. Joe M. Richardson draws the same conclusion about Florida's judiciary in the early years of Reconstruction. See *The Negro in the Reconstruction of Florida, 1865–1877*, 44–51. On Florida's judiciary during early Reconstruction consult Richardson, *The Negro in the Reconstruction of Florida, 1865–1877*, 44–51. On the Freedmen's Bureau and its early attempts to adjudicate in southern jurisdictions immediately after the end of the Civil War, see Richardson, *The Negro in the Reconstruction of Florida, 1865–1877*; McConnell, *Negroes and Their Treatment in Virginia from 1865 to 1867*, 24–26, 62–63; Eric Foner, *Reconstruction*, 149; Roberta Sue Alexander, *North Carolina Faces the Freedmen*, 138–51. The bureau's role in overseeing the fair judicial treatment of freedpeople is described in Salmon and Salmon, *Franklin County, Virginia, 1786–1986*, 303; Wharton, *The Negro in Mississippi, 1865–1890*, 76–77.

56. Eric Foner, *Reconstruction*, 149. See also Roberta Sue Alexander, *North Carolina Faces the Freedmen*, 138–51; Blair, "Justice versus Law and Order," 172. On the bureau's role of overseeing the fair judicial treatment of freedpeople see Salmon and Salmon, *Franklin County, Virginia, 1786–1986*, 303; Wharton, *The Negro in Mississippi, 1865–1890*, 76–77.

57. Testimony presented to the House Committee on Ku Klux Klan activity in 1871 is rife with charges of incompetence and partisanship in the judiciary of southern states.

58. *KKK Report*, vol. 7, Georgia, 766.

59. Bardaglio, *Reconstructing the Household*, 127.

60. *KKK Report*, vol. 2, North Carolina, 371.

61. *KKK Report*, vol. 3, South Carolina, 172.

62. As Bertram Wyatt-Brown has asserted, southerners before the war placed great value on a community's informal, innate sense of what was fair and just, frequently irrespective of the law and subject to wide local discretion, as evidenced by the relatively small amount of mob violence. In short, for all its faults and shortcomings, the Old South judicial system seems to have been respected. Wyatt-Brown, "Community, Class, and Snopesian Crime," 173–206.

63. *KKK Report*, vol. 3, South Carolina, 237.

64. *KKK Report*, vol. 2, North Carolina, 247.

65. See, for example, Blair, "Justice versus Law and Order," 168.

66. *KKK Report*, vol. 3, South Carolina, 125. On antebellum community reaction to gubernatorial pardons see Wyatt-Brown, "Community, Class, and Snopesian Crime," 195–97.

67. *KKK Report*, vol. 3, South Carolina, 209, 270–71.

68. Ibid., 262.

69. Ibid., 209. On the belief that gubernatorial pardons were politically motivated see *KKK Report*, vol. 2, North Carolina, 315.

70. *KKK Report*, vol. 6, Georgia, 40; vol. 3, South Carolina, 125.

71. *KKK Report*, vol. 3, South Carolina, 236–37, 154, 221. On the belief by some southern whites that the pardoning practices of southern governors during Reconstruction were liberal see ibid., 154, 209, 221, 125, 177; vol. 2, North Carolina, 315; vol. 6, Georgia, 31, 72, 101, 137–38, 153, 167; vol. 7, Georgia, 766–67, 780, 822–24, 832, 840, 1076–78, 1210.

72. *KKK Report*, vol. 6, Georgia, 101, 153. Governor Bullock requested a report and a breakdown of those criminals pardoned in the previous three years. His executive secretary compiled the information that showed Governor Bullock had pardoned 389 criminals either before or after they were convicted and he commuted the death sentences of 15 convicted murderers. Of the 389 criminals pardons, only 1 had been convicted of rape, 5 for assault with intent to rape. In addition, Bullock denied the pardon petitions of 60 others, including 2 convicted of rape. There is no racial breakdown of those pardoned. *KKK Report*, vol. 7, Georgia, 809–10.

73. *KKK Report*, vol. 3, South Carolina, 270, 237, 209. See also vol. 7, Georgia, 1077.

74. *KKK Report*, vol. 3, South Carolina, 237; vol. 6, Georgia, 168.

75. *KKK Report*, vol. 7, Georgia, 1210.

76. *KKK Report*, vol. 2, North Carolina, 314–15.

77. *KKK Report*, vol. 13, Tennessee, 7.

78. *KKK Report*, vol. 6, Georgia, 101. For additional accounts of southerners who believed that excessive pardoning of black convicts inevitably led to extralegal violence see vol. 6, Georgia, 234, 237, 286; vol. 7, Georgia, 1076. Southern Reconstruction governors did indeed pardon many freedmen, including convicted rapists, but sometimes at the prompting of whites. On white southerners petitioning for the pardons of convicted black criminals in the postbellum era see Ayers, *Vengeance and Justice*, 205–6. A court in Lynchburg, Virginia, sentenced one freedman, David Crawford, to death for the rape of Caroline Schmidt, a nine-year-old white girl with whose family Crawford had been living for some time. The governor did indeed commute the original sentence to twenty years in prison. He did so, however, only after he received two petitions on behalf of Crawford. One was purportedly signed by eleven of the jury members who found him guilty, and one came from the judge

in whose courtroom the trial was heard. Two petitions from Lynchburg, Virginia, one dated January 12, 1870, and signed by twelve citizens including eleven jurors and one from Judge Betts, in January 25, 1870, packet, box 12 (November 1869–February 1870), EP, SC, LVA.

79. According to a history of Rockbridge County, "Captain Edward Echols, who lived at the mouth of the North River, was a brother to General John Echols, of the Confederate army, and consequently an uncle to the late Edward Echols, of Staunton. He was a citizen of considerable local prominence, and died in 1874 at the age of fifty-seven." Morton, *A History of Rockbridge County, Virginia,* 251–52. General John Echols was Lizzie's uncle, brother to her father. Robert Echols, a merchant, and his family had been living in Richmond in 1860. While he listed no real estate or personal property for himself or his two children by a previous wife, he did note that his second wife and her three children owned property valued at $99,000. U.S. Census, Henrico County, 430. Echols is listed in the 1860 Richmond *Directory* (89) as being employed by "Gooch & E." Since no directories exist for Richmond from 1861 to 1870, it is difficult to ascertain when he and his family relocated to Lexington. LVA.

80. *Richmond Enquirer,* November 3, 1866, as quoted in Alrutheus A. Taylor, *The Negro in the Reconstruction of Virginia,* 83.

81. So outraged at Watson's acquittal was General John M. Schofield, the military officer in command of Virginia, that he ordered him retried by a military commission. Eventually the attorney general of the United States interceded and ruled that the military commission lacked jurisdiction in the matter and Watson was released. *Richmond Times,* November 24, 1866, as quoted in Alrutheus A. Taylor, *The Negro in the Reconstruction of Virginia,* 83. See also Bogue, "Violence and Oppression in North Carolina during Reconstruction, 1865–1873," 119–20; Alderson, "The Freedmen's Bureau in Virginia," 122; McConnell, *Negroes and Their Treatment in Virginia from 1865 to 1867,* 66–67, 71; Blair, "Justice versus Law and Order," 165–72; Eric Foner, *Reconstruction,* 149; Roberta Sue Alexander, *North Carolina Faces the Freedmen,* 138–51. For a discussion of Florida's judiciary during early Reconstruction consult Richardson, *The Negro in the Reconstruction of Florida, 1865–1877,* 44–51. Attempts by the Freedmen's Bureau to adjudicate in southern jurisdictions immediately after the end of the Civil War are discussed in Richardson, *The Negro in the Reconstruction of Florida, 1865–1877,* and McConnell, *Negroes and Their Treatment in Virginia from 1865 to 1867,* 24–26, 62–63. Additional discussion of the bureau's role in overseeing the fair judicial treatment of freedpeople is in Salmon and Salmon, *Franklin County, Virginia,* 303, and Wharton, *The Negro in Mississippi, 1865–1890,* 76–77.

82. Quoted in Blair, "Justice versus Law and Order," 171. For a description of conditions that were hostile to Freedmen's Bureau agents in Rockbridge County see Alderson, "The Freedmen's Bureau in Virginia," 57, 109–10, 122, 132.

83. Blair, "Justice versus Law and Order," 179 n. 51. On Klan activity in Virginia see Trelease, *White Terror,* 65–68, 114, 185.

84. *Lexington* (Va.) *Gazette and Banner,* April 1, 15, May 6, 1868. Articles later that summer denounced Negro suffrage and other civil rights. The newspaper also reported numerous instances of "Negro outrages" throughout the South, although there were no specific references to black rape. See entries from June through August, 1868.

85. Report of the case of the *Commonwealth of Virginia v. John Burns (Freedman),* April 19, 1868, from General Douglas Frazar, in July packet, box 6 (1868), EP, SC, LVA.

86. Ibid.

87. Ibid.

88. Ibid.

89. Ibid.

90. Ibid.

91. Ibid. The use of chloroform to effect sexual relations raised a tricky legal issue. Nearly all states in the early nineteenth century required proof of force in cases of rape where the victim was not a child. In cases in which the accused, usually a physician, had administered chloroform to sedate his intended victim, she was rendered incapable of offering resistance. Thus, there was no use of force according to the letter of the law. Moreover, the testimony of the accuser was subject to scrutiny because of the sedative effects of the chloroform. Medical experts in defense of physicians charged with such a crime often cited a phenomenon they called "anaesthetic illusion," common, they claimed, especially among women who were menstruating at the time anesthesia was administered. Legal experts seem to have concluded that the use of chloroform and similar types of anesthesia in rape cases robbed women of the ability to consent. However, they cautioned that other conditions must be supported by evidence to weed out accusations that were merely "fabrication" or "invention." See Walker, "The Law of Rape: Chloroform in Rape Cases," 289–309, and "Chloroform in Rape Cases," 592. By mid-century many states had revised their rape statutes to provide that sexual intercourse facilitated through the administration of chloroform or similar substances did indeed constitute rape. See Ormond, Bagby, Goldthwaite, and Semple, comps., *The Code of Alabama*, tit. 1, ch. 2, art. 2, sec. 3091, p. 562; Ball, Roane, and Pike, comps., *Revised Statutes of Arkansas*, ch. 44, sec. 4, p. 245; Sharkey, Harris, and Ellett, comps., *Revised Code of Mississippi*, sec. 46, art. 219, p. 608; *Revised Statutes of Missouri* (1844–45), art. 2, ch. 47, sec. 27, pp. 348–49; Meigs and Cooper, comps., *The Code of Tennessee*, art. 3, sec. 4613, p. 830; Oldham and White, comps., *A Digest of the General Statute Laws of the State of Texas*, tit. 17, ch. 6, art. 526, p. 523 (Act of 1856).

92. Report of the case of the *Commonwealth of Virginia v. John Burns (Freedman)*, April 19, 1868, from General Douglas Frazar, in July packet, box 6 (1868), EP, SC, LVA. As mentioned previously, the testimony of African Americans was not new during Reconstruction. In antebellum Virginia slaves and free blacks testified under oath at trials of other African Americans, though not of whites. In Virginia's first postwar attempt to accommodate freed people in the judicial system the legislature passed a law in 1866 allowing the testimony of persons of color, including Indians, in cases in which "the interest, direct or indirect, of a colored person was involved, or in which any crime had been done or attempted to be done or threatened to the person, property, or rights of a colored person." Thus initially Virginia still restricted the right of African Americans to testify against whites. Not until the passage of federal legislation, the Civil Rights Act of April 1866, did all freedmen acquire the political rights accorded whites, including the right to testify in trials of white defendants. McConnell, *Negroes and Their Treatment in Virginia, from 1865 to 1867*, 80–82. On the right of freedpeople to testify see also the reports in the *New York Times*, September 10, 1865, 2, and November 9, 1866, 1. This issue aroused considerable controversy throughout the former slave South and was considered an egregious affront to southern whites who resented the blacks' encroachment into a previously all-white privilege. On the virulent white response to blacks' right to testify against whites consult Wharton, *The Negro*

in *Mississippi, 1865–1890*, 134–36; Richardson, *The Negro in the Reconstruction of Florida, 1865–1877*, 42; Reid, *After the War*, 410. In part, whites feared that African Americans might attempt to capitalize on any opportunity to seek revenge on white southerners by leveling false accusations on the witness stand. Some whites felt that freedpeople, given to lying anyway, had little comprehension of swearing under oath. The bottom line was that few white southerners were willing to entrust the fate of a white defendant to a former slave whose veracity would not pass muster by white standards. So resistant to giving blacks the right to testify were the North Carolina legislators that they included restrictions on black testimony as only one of six racially discriminatory provisions of their Black Code, passed in 1866. Roberta Sue Alexander, *North Carolina Faces the Freedmen*, 49, 145–46. Although these restrictions were eventually repealed, judges throughout North Carolina consistently denied blacks the right to testify or severely restricted their ability to do so. In fact, a near-riot erupted in Wilmington, North Carolina, after some blacks attempted to prevent the public whipping of five men after a trial that had excluded black testimony. Litwack, *Been in the Storm So Long*, 289, see also 286–87. Kentucky managed to resist federal efforts to give African Americans the right to testify against whites until well into the 1870s. George C. Wright, *Racial Violence in Kentucky, 1865–1940*, 22–23. Even in instances where African American witnesses swore to tell the truth in criminal cases, many white southerners appear to have fallen back on age-old prejudices that put little stock in their testimony. Eliza Frances Andrews, the daughter of a prominent Georgia judge before the war, recounted how an old black woman had been brutally murdered in July 1865 and two white men were charged with the crime. Andrews's father, who served as legal counsel for the two, feared that one if not both would hang, even though "there is only Negro evidence for all these horrors, and nobody can tell how much of it is false." See Eliza Frances Andrews, *The Wartime Journal of a Georgia Girl, 1864–1865*, 341–42. Most Negroes, one white South Carolinian explained, "are very ignorant; are uneducated and depraved by political associations, and I do not believe they tell the truth much." *KKK Report*, vol. 5, South Carolina, 1336. No doubt speaking for many of his race, one white Virginian, indignant at the thought of freedmen testifying against whites, trumpeted, "Why, we'd never let a nigger give evidence against anybody but people of his own color." Quoted in Dennett, *The South as It Is*, 75, see also 111, 157, 168, 181.

93. Report of the case of *Commonwealth of Virginia v. John Burns (Freedman)*, April 19, 1868, from General Douglas Frazar, in July packet, box 6 (1868), EP, SC, LVA.

94. The status of the white female accuser was likely to have been central in white Lexington's decision to back the Echols family in this case. There are numerous instances in the Reconstruction years of elite and middle class white southerners who backed the accused black rapist when the accuser was a woman of dubious character or had a history of sexual relations outside marriage. See Sommerville, "The Rape Myth Reconsidered," ch. 6, "The Politicization of Rape in the Reconstruction South"; Laura F. Edwards, "Sexual Violence, Gender, Reconstruction, and the Extension of Patriarchy," 242–43; and Chapter 8 in this book.

95. Official notation by Orlando Brown, July 14, 1868, July packet, box 6 (1868), EP, SC, LVA.

96. Report of the case of *Commonwealth of Virginia v. John Burns (Freedman)*, April 19, 1868, from General Douglas Frazar, in July packet, box 6 (1868), EP, SC, LVA. Donald

Nieman finds a more sanguine situation in Washington County, Texas, where black defendants who received court-appointed counsel fared quite well, considering. Nieman, "Black Political Power and Criminal Justice," 411–12.

97. Frazar contended that Samuel McDowell Moore and David Moore were brothers when in fact they were probably cousins. Ibid. and Morton, *A History of Rockbridge County, Virginia*, 268. On the importance of the prosecutor in shaping the outcome of African Americans' trials during Reconstruction see Nieman, "Black Political Power and Criminal Justice," 412–13.

98. Report of the case of *Commonwealth of Virginia v. John Burns (Freedman)*, April 19, 1868, from General Douglas Frazar, in July packet, box 6 (1868), EP, SC, LVA; and *Lexington* (Va.) *Gazette and Banner*, April 22, 1868.

99. Ibid.

100. Ibid.

101. Ibid. The affront of either rape or consensual sex between a former slave and one's daughter was especially egregious in the patriarchal South and spoke volumes to the inability of Robert Echols to protect his household and uphold the family name. Bardaglio, *Reconstructing the Household*, 189.

102. Frazar's actions support the argument made by Richard Lowe that bureau officials in Virginia did not act in the best interests of the master class, contrary to considerable scholarship that asserts otherwise. "The Freedmen's Bureau and Local White Leaders in Virginia," 455–72.

103. Report of the case of the *Commonwealth of Virginia v. John Burns (Freedman)*, April 19, 1868, from General Douglas Frazar, in July packet, box 6 (1868), EP, SC, LVA.

104. Ibid.

105. Letter from Jacob Wagner to Governor H. H. Wells, May 7, 1868, Lexington, Virginia, July packet, box 6 (1868), EP, SC, LVA.

106. Official notation, July 10, 1869, Lieutenant Josiah Chance of Rocky Mount, Virginia, August 16, 1869, packet, box 11 (August–October 1869), EP, SC, LVA.

107. *Lexington* (Va.) *Gazette and Banner*, April 22, 1868.

108. Ibid.

109. White southerners were indeed capable of taking justice into their own hands in cases where black men improperly broached sexual boundaries with elite white women, as in a South Carolina town late in the war. See Cashin, "A Lynching in Wartime Carolina," 109–31. For general works on lynching in the South, consult the most recently published: Brundage, *Under Sentence of Death*; Brundage, *Lynching in the New South*; Tolnay and Beck, *A Festival of Violence*; Dray, *At the Hands of Persons Unknown*.

110. Initially Governor Wells declined to interfere in the case, stressing that the executive had authority to commute punishments only in cases of capital crimes or "by an absolute pardon." Wells returned the case to the military authorities that he believed had jurisdiction. Freedmen's Bureau agents eventually enlisted the help of General Orlando Brown, supervisor of Virginia, and General O. O. Howard, who headed up the entire bureau. Howard wrote Wells a letter on July 17, 1868, and Wells complied by issuing a complete pardon on July 20. See related documents in July packet, box 6 (1868), EP, SC, and EJ, 1868, LVA.

111. *Lexington* (Va.) *Gazette and Banner*, July 19, 1868. The quotation marks are original, a defiant challenge to the validity of his office.

112. *KKK Report*, vol. 3, South Carolina, 125. On antebellum community reaction to gubernatorial pardons see Wyatt-Brown, "Community, Class, and Snopesian Crime," 173–206. On gubernatorial pardons during Reconstruction see the *KKK Report*, vol. 3, South Carolina, 125, 154, 177, 209, 221, 236–37, 262, 270–71; vol. 2, North Carolina, 314–15; vol. 6, Georgia, 31, 40, 72, 101, 137–38, 153, 167–68, 234, 237, 286; vol. 7, Georgia, 766–67, 780, 809–10, 822–24, 832, 840, 1076–78, 1210; vol. 13, Tennessee, 7.

113. Reid, *After the War*, 352.

114. Historians of the "Dunning school" were among the first and most adamant to claim that black rape of white women emerged out of federal policies, misrule, and corrupt officials courting favor with black Republicans. These historians accepted as fact the claims of white southerners immersed in the Lost Cause ideology that black criminality was directly attributable to granting to black men civic and political rights. See, for example, Dunning, *Reconstruction*; Fleming, *Civil War and Reconstruction in Alabama*; Claude Bowers, *The Tragic Era*. More recently historians of Reconstruction have challenged white assertions that black rape increased after the war and have focused on why white southerners became so anxious about black rape. See for instance Lebsock, *The Free Women of Petersburg*, 247–48. More recently still, Martha Hodes argues that in fact white anxiety about black rape, usually referred to as the "rape myth," did emanate from political conditions during Reconstruction. Hodes, "The Sexualization of Reconstruction Politics." On the conflation of black male sexuality with black political equality see Gilmore, *Gender and Jim Crow*, 91–118.

115. Wyatt-Brown, "Community, Class, and Snopesian Crime."

116. *KKK Report*, vol. 2, North Carolina, 247.

Chapter Eight

1. Avary, *Dixie after the War*, 384.

2. For other examples, consult Olds, "The Rape Complex in the Postbellum South," 125–28.

3. The harsh and racist treatment of blacks in turn-of-the-century fiction stands in contrast to their cultural depiction in the late 1860s and early 1870s, reflective of what Nina Silber calls "romantic racialism." Silber, *Romance and Reunion*, 124–25.

4. Rives, *Smoking Flax*.

5. Thomas Nelson Page, *Red Rock*. On Page and his fiction, see Silber, *Romance of Reunion*, 113–15, 117, 140, 147, 186; Olds, "The Rape Complex in the Postbellum South," 166–68, 186.

6. Dixon, *The Leopard's Spots* and *The Clansman*. For more detailed summaries and greater analysis, see Sommerville, "The Rape Myth Reconsidered," 32–38. On Dixon, consult Williamson, *Crucible of Race*, 140–79; Silber, *Romance of Reunion*, 181, 185–86; Olds, "The Rape Complex in the Postbellum South," 187–88.

7. Dunning, *Reconstruction*, 212–14. For historiographical essays on Reconstruction consult Eric Foner, "Slavery, the Civil War, and Reconstruction," 73–92; Weisberger, "The Dark and Bloody Ground of Reconstruction Historiography."

8. Claude Bowers, *The Tragic Era*, 53. For a similar rendition see Fleming, *Civil War and Reconstruction in Alabama*.

9. See, for instance, Jacqueline Jones, *Labor of Love, Labor of Sorrow*, 149; D'Emilio and Freedman, *Intimate Matters*, 195; Bardaglio, *Reconstructing the Household*, 176–201; Laura F. Edwards, "The Disappearance of Susan Daniel and Henderson Cooper."

10. Lebsock, *The Free Women of Petersburg*, 247–48.

11. Hodes, "The Sexualization of Reconstruction Politics," 403, and *White Women, Black Men*, ch. 7, 147, 157. While I agree with Hodes that Reconstruction ushered in unprecedented concerns about black sexuality emanating primarily from black men's acquisition of political rights, I nonetheless am uneasy with her characterization of those concerns. Her use of words like "taboo" and "unprecedented intensity" when describing how white ideas about black sexuality developed after the war seem to preclude the many exceptions that I will document in this chapter. Hodes, in her work on Reconstruction, relies primarily on testimony before Congressional hearings in 1871 about the racial violence spearheaded by the Ku Klux Klan in the former Confederate states. While this chapter relies on some of those very same sources, I also incorporate records generated from local court proceedings. Hodes's conclusions about race and sex in Reconstruction may very well aptly apply to Klan members, but are not interchangeable regarding the masses of white Southerners who lived out their day-to-day experiences with black neighbors and who may not have embraced the venomous racism or terrorist tactics of the Klan. A differing source base then may, in part, explain why Hodes and I differ not only on the degree to which whites became anxious over black male sexuality during this period but also the degree to which race and sex became politicized. The "rape myth," as I will argue, was not a foregone conclusion, even during Reconstruction. Hodes's assertion that "following the war, white anxiety and alarm about black male sexuality reached an unprecedented level of intensity" is overstated and in need of qualification. Hodes, "The Sexualization of Reconstruction Politics," 403. In fairness, it should be noted that Hodes somewhat modifies her earlier conclusions about the origins of white fears of black rape in her later, completed study, to some extent moderating her previous claims as I have quoted them here (*White Women, Black Men*, 147–75). Though the language is somewhat tempered in her book, implicit in her chapter on Reconstruction and race, indeed an essential part of her argument, is that emancipation and blacks' acquisition of political rights were critical developments that gave rise to white fears of black rape and subsequently an end to the tradition of white toleration of sex between black men and white women. (She writes that "black freedom brought a marked shift away from uneasy toleration for sex between black men and white women, and a move toward increasingly violent intolerance" and that "the threat of rape, though persistent in some measure in wartime and Reconstruction white rhetoric, would be much more blatantly emphasized and much more violently acted on in the last decades of the century." *White Women, Black Men*, 146. See also pages 175–78, 198–201.) Hodes roots this change in the "newfound autonomy of [black] men" largely because of the political power they acquired. "After emancipation, expressions of white anxiety about sex between black men and white women reached an unprecedented intensity" (147).This argument frames her larger one: that interracial sex, including black rape of white women, became highly politicized on a regional and national level, coming to "matter beyond local boundaries" (*White Women, Black Men*, 148). I will argue that in fact sex and race in numerous cases remained a local issue devoid of the kinds of ideological and political connotations that Hodes described in her work.

I harbor similar reservations regarding Peter Bardaglio's characterization of black rape during Reconstruction, specifically his charge that "white anxiety about black male sexuality rose to a fever pitch" (*Reconstructing the Household*, 189). Nor am I convinced, as Bardaglio claims, that emancipation ushered in an "obsession with racial purity" ("'Shamefull Matches,'" 122). These descriptions more aptly apply to a later period. The local cases I marshal here do not support Bardaglio's assertions. Once again, the evidentiary base may help to explain our differing views on race and sex in the period. Bardaglio looks almost exclusively at statutes and case law.

12. Hodes, *White Women, Black Men*, 147–75; Trelease, *White Terror*, xx, xxxviii, 84, 94, 196, 322, 324–36; George C. Wright, *Racial Violence in Kentucky, 1865–1940*, 43–46; Williams, *The Great South Carolina Ku Klux Klan Trials, 1871–1872*, 32–35.

13. Kennedy, "The Enforcement of Anti-Miscegenation Laws," 145; Bardaglio, "'Shamefull Matches,'" 122.

14. Litwack, *Been in the Storm So Long*, 265, 267; Fredrickson, *The Black Image in the White Mind*, 171–74.

15. Bardaglio, *Reconstructing the Household*, 197–98; Hodes, *White Women, Black Men*, 161–64.

16. Astonishing, in light of the tradition of historical accounts that have well documented the brutality with which white southerners were capable of treating blacks for innumerable offenses, sexual assault among them. To name just one example, Trelease, *White Terror*. Bardaglio finds ample evidence of procedural fairness and leniency accorded well into the late 1890s to convicted black rapists who appealed their cases. *Reconstructing the Household*, 193–95. See also Laura F. Edwards, "Sexual Violence, Gender, Reconstruction, and the Extension of Patriarchy," 250–51.

17. Letter from P. K. Jones to Lieutenant F. M. Kimball, Hicksford, Virginia, December 7, 1868, letters, July 6 packet, box 10 (May–August 14, 1869), SC, EP, LVA.

18. Box 11 (August–October 1869), EP, SC, LVA. On the continuing disdain for poor white women of dubious character in postbellum cases see Hodes, *White Women, Black Men*, 161–63; Bardaglio, *Reconstructing the Household*, 197–98. Bardaglio, though, finds no postbellum appellate cases in which a history of illicit sexual behavior by a white accuser succeeded in overturning a black-on-white rape conviction: "Before the Civil War, evidence of a white woman's lack of chastity sometimes persuaded the courts to treat black defendants with relative leniency. But not so after the war." (194–95) The Alabama black-on-white rape case that he cites, indeed the only such case he examines, was heard in 1887, years after the end of Reconstruction.

19. Letter from Hughes Dillard, Edmund Irvine, and William T. Taliaferro, July 8, 1869, court transcript, and letter from Peter Saunderson, Rocky Mount, Virginia, July 27, 1869, in August 16, 1869, packet, box 11 (August–October 1869), EP, SC; August 16, 1869, 227, EJ, LVA. Governor H. H. Wells acceded and pardoned Price almost immediately. See also the case of Charles (Abner) Harris of Henrico County, Virginia. Harris was convicted in the spring of 1869 for raping a female identified in executive papers only as Miss Shepherdson. In all probability the accuser was a white female. Rarely if ever did white southerners accord to females of color such polite status as to refer to unmarried women and girls as "Miss." Harris was sentenced to a twenty-year prison term. September 14, 1869, packet, box 11 (August–October 1869), EP, SC, and Prison Register, 1869, LVA. Nonetheless, I am reluctant to present this as a black-on-white rape case because of the slim chance that the accuser was

actually a female of color. After the Civil War recordkeepers noted race rather inconsistently. This is problematic for the researcher investigating rape in postbellum legal records. Usually the race of the offender can be quickly verified, if not in the court documents themselves then in prison registers, which meticulously noted not only race but shades of color and other identifying features such as scars, physical build, and deformities. Such descriptions were necessary in the event of prisoner escapes. Thus, establishing with absolute certainty the race of the accuser is a much more cumbersome and difficult task. On this methodological dilemma see Alexander, *North Carolina Meets the Freedmen*, 144. Similarly frustrating is determining the racial composition of juries. Occasionally records will indicate that a jury was all white, usually to emphasize the unfairness of a decision. It is possible that in other cases the presence of nonwhite jury members accounts for lenient sentences. Donald Nieman finds that in one county in Texas, freedmen played an important role on postwar juries. Nieman, "Black Political Power and Criminal Justice," 398–401. One judge in South Carolina told congressmen that in a number of trials in which African Americans were convicted of crimes, the juries consisted of a majority of nonwhites. *KKK Report*, vol. 6, Georgia, 3. See also Bardaglio, *Reconstructing the Household*, 128–29. In all the postwar court records I have looked at I have never once encountered a reference to anything but an all-white jury.

20. Bogue, "Violence and Oppression in North Carolina during Reconstruction, 1865–1873," 151–52.

21. Roberta Sue Alexander, *North Caroline Faces the Freedmen*, 144.

22. Laura F. Edwards, "Sexual Violence, Gender, Reconstruction, and the Extension of Patriarchy in Granville County, North Carolina," 250–51 (quote on 250). Edwards cites five additional black-on-white rape cases that also "went quietly to trial" (250 n. 32).

23. Prison register 1879; court transcript, October 15, 1869; undated letter of eleven jury members to Governor Gilbert C. Walker; letter dated January 12, 1870, from Judge [?] to Governor Gilbert C. Walker, all found in January 25 packet, Box 12 (November 1869–February 1870), SC, EP; Prison Register, 1870, LVA.

24. Martha Hodes's analysis of Reconstruction and sex leads her to conclude that "ideas about the sexual depravity and agency of poor white women no longer overshadowed ideas about the dangers of black male sexuality; the twin ideologies now bore more equal weight." "The Sexualization of Reconstruction Politics," 417. I would argue that these cases refute that claim. Hodes tempers this assertion in her book, pointing out that "white women of the lower classes . . . could not count on ideology about female purity to absolve them of alleged illicit sexual activity." *White Women, Black Men*, 161.

25. September 30 packet, box 32 (June–October 1875), SC, EP, LVA.

26. Ibid. and Prison Register, 1874. The governor refused to pardon Lewis. See EJ, September 30, 1875, 125, LVA.

27. On ex-slaves and labor after the Civil War consult Litwack, *Been in the Storm So Long*, ch. 7.

28. On labor shortages during Reconstruction refer to Eric Foner, *Reconstruction*, 138–40, 402, 595.

29. Letter to B. Wardell from Walter Mead, August 13, 1869, August 16 packet, box 11 (August–October 1869), EP, SC, LVA.

30. Petition of twenty-seven white and thirty-four "colored" citizens, Fredericks Hall,

Virginia, December 6, 1877, December 29, 1877, packet, box 40 (October–December 1877), EP, SC. On the shortage of labor in the Reconstruction South see Wharton, *The Negro in Mississippi, 1865–1890*, 118. Many whites held the belief that most freedmen were "worthless," incompetent, or unreliable laborers. See Wharton, *The Negro in Mississippi, 1865–1890*, 118–21; Richardson, *The Negro in the Reconstruction of Florida, 1865–1877*, 63.

31. What makes this particular case so compelling and unique is that Echols was from a well-respected white family. Although such liaisons were reported far less frequently, the relationship between Echols and Burns was not an exception. In October 1866 an official from the Freedmen's Bureau in Franklin County, Virginia, noted the case of a white woman property-holder and slaveowner who had been living with a black man for twenty years. She reportedly had several children by him. The case prompted the agent, William F. DeKnight, to remark, "amalgamation here, between the two races must be far greater than even it is in the North." Cited by Salmon and Salmon, *Franklin County, Virginia 1786–1986*, 304, 497 n. 19. See also Litwack, *Been in the Storm So Long*, 243.

32. Clinton, " 'Southern Dishonor,' " 60. For works that discuss cross-racial sexual relations in the early and antebellum South, see Blassingame, "The Planter on the Couch," 325–29; Johnston, *Race Relations in Virginia and Miscegenation in the South, 1776–1869*; Adele Logan Alexander, *Ambiguous Lives*; Mills, "Miscegenation and the Free Negro," 16–34; Franklin, *From Slavery to Freedom*, 215, 217; Bynum, "Misshapen Identity"; Hodes, *White Women, Black Men*, 19–38; Kathleen M. Brown, *Good Wives, Nasty Wenches, and Anxious Patriarchs*, 126, 188–89, 195–201; Richter, "Slavery in Baton Rouge, 1820–1860," 390; Rothman, *Notorious in the Neighborhood*; Buckley, "Unfixing Race"; Buckley, *The Great Catastrophe of My Life*, ch. 4.

33. Rothman, *Notorious in the Neighborhood*, 4.

34. Ibid., 5.

35. Mills, "Miscegenation and the Free Negro," 26.

36. Hodes, *White Women, Black Men*, 6.

37. See, for example, Clinton, *The Plantation Mistress*, 210; Ayers, *Promise of the New South*, 152–53; Berry and Blassingame, *Long Memory*, 120–22; Bardaglio, *Reconstructing the Household*, 178; Hodes, *White Women, Black Men*, 139–40.

38. *KKK Report*, vol. 7, Georgia, 842. On the maximization of slave reproduction and sexual control within the patriarchal system consult Clinton, " 'Southern Dishonor,' " 55–68.

39. *KKK Report*, vol. 7, Georgia, 862.

40. *KKK Report*, vol. 8, Alabama, 446.

41. *Report of the Joint Committee on Reconstruction*, 39th Congress, 1st sess., part II, p. 56. On the legendary interracial marriages among the children of a former slave woman and a white Civil War deserter from Mississippi see Bynum, "Misshapen Identity." Bynum makes the point that twentieth-century descendants, looking back, imposed invective about sex and race on those dubious relationships, intimating that there may have been more tacit acceptance of such relationships in the nineteenth century than the racial conditions of the mid-twentieth century would allow.

42. DeForest, *A Union Officer in the Reconstruction*, 138. A few scholarly works have surmised that marriages or relationships between white women, frequently poor white women, and black men increased in the early years of Reconstruction because of the large

number of white men killed in the war. See Clinton, *The Plantation Mistress*, 210; Berry and Blassingame, *Long Memory*, 120–21; Olds, "The Rape Complex in the Postbellum South," 46; Hodes, *White Women, Black Men*, 265 n. 4.

43. Alrutheus A. Taylor, *The Negro in the Reconstruction of Virginia*, 62. As Joshua Rothman has shown for the eighteenth century, white southerners often silently ignored illicit interracial sexual behavior, responding only when such behavior was made public and thus harder to overlook. Rothman, "James Callender and Social Knowledge of Interracial Sex in Antebellum Virginia."

44. Letter from John B. Spice from Albemarle County, July 14, 1875, September 30, 1875, packet, box 37 (June–October 1875), EP, SC, LVA.

45. *Richmond Enquirer*, February 15, 1867, as cited in Alrutheus A. Taylor, *The Negro in the Reconstruction of Virginia*, 57.

46. Ibid. Taylor recounted numerous other instances of black Virginians marrying or cohabiting with white women from 1866 to 1878. See pp. 57–62. For other examples see Hodes, *White Women, Black Men*, 149–51.

47. *KKK Report*, vol. 13, Tennessee, 46–47. Bynum found cases of harassment of previously tolerated interracial marriages in Montgomery County, North Carolina, during the Civil War. *Unruly Women*, 124–25.

48. *KKK Report*, vol. 6, Georgia, 1096.

49. *KKK Report*, vol. 6, Georgia, 94. Augustus Wright, whose testimony this case comes from, may have been referring to the account of Joe Kennedy, a black man who had married a light-skinned mulatto woman. Many in the white community presumed that she was white. On Kennedy see also 45, 75, 274, 286.

50. George C. Wright, *Racial Violence in Kentucky, 1865–1940*, 55.

51. *KKK Report*, vol. 3, South Carolina, 212.

52. Fleming, ed., *Documentary History of Reconstruction in Alabama*, 291.

53. For more citations regarding the unions of white women and black men as well as a discussion about white perceptions of sexual deviancy and class during Reconstruction, consult Hodes, "The Sexualization of Reconstruction Politics," 410–12.

54. *KKK Report*, vol. 2, North Carolina, 37. In an attack on a woman of color in the same area of North Carolina, a band of Klan members burned the woman's pubic hair and sexually mutilated her. Ibid., 37, 49. Sometimes white women from the lower order of society were terrorized for "disorderly behavior," a term that encompassed an array of behavior. Ann Warren, reputedly a woman of "very bad character" from North Carolina, was whipped by the Klan, although there is no evidence that she consorted with black men. *KKK Report*, vol. 2, North Carolina, 28. A white "woman of low character" in South Carolina was tarred and feathered for reportedly keeping "a sort of low house." *KKK Report*, vol. 3, South Carolina, 44. Moreover, women of color increasingly were punished in southern communities for illicit relationships with white men. A woman of color and the white man in Georgia with whom she dwelled received a visit from neighbors who gave them a good "thrashing" after both escaped punishment by the local court. *KKK Report*, vol. 6, Georgia, 274. A former house servant in North Carolina was told that she would not be whipped by the Klan if she kept secret the name of her baby's father, a wealthy and respected "gentleman." *KKK Report*, vol. 2, North Carolina, 134. For other examples of Klan attacks on white women see *KKK Report*, vol. 2, North Carolina, 106.

55. September 14, 1869, box 11 (August–October 1869), SC, EP, LVA.

56. Ibid.

57. Ibid.

58. Ibid.

59. Ibid.; September 14, 1869, 246, EJ, LVA. Arnold is not listed in the prison register, which, if accurate, suggests one of two things. Either Arnold won his judicial appeal or he was pardoned by the governor before he even entered prison. The case against Monroe Toler is represented only in the appeal of William Arnold.

60. Prison Register, 1869, 1870, LVA. There are no records of any petitions made by or on behalf of Monroe Toler among the governors' papers, so his fate cannot be determined there. Nor are there any extant birth or death records from that period from Campbell County. Toler's name does not appear on any prison registers, suggesting that he may have died, escaped, or been executed.

61. *KKK Report*, vol. 6, Georgia, 125.

62. Ibid., 74–75. For more on this particular case consult Trelease, *White Terror*, 325; Hodes, *White Women, Black Men*, 153–54.

63. Letter from D. H. Pannell, Pittsylvania Court House, April 25, 1868, April 1868 packet, box 6 (1868), EP, SC, LVA.

64. Virginia *Acts* (1865–66), ch. 14, sec. 1, p. 82.

65. Matthews, comp., *Digest of Laws of a Criminal Nature of the State of Virginia* (1861), ch. 15, p. 118.

66. Letter from D. H. Pannell, Pittsylvania Court House, April 25, 1868, April 1868 packet, box 6 (1868), EP, SC, LVA.

67. Ibid. Coleman Davis, nineteen years old, was received into the state penitentiary on June 13, 1866. His attorney claimed that his prison sentence was for a period of ten years, but the prison register indicated that he was to serve for fourteen. Davis was "transferred" from the penitentiary in Richmond, although it is not clear when or to where he was transferred. The governor rejected his attorney's plea for a pardon. See April 28, 1868, EJ, and 1866 Prison Register, LVA.

68. January 1882 packet, box 61 (October–December 1882), EP, SC; Prison Register, 1873, LVA. Campbell J. Trigg, West's lawyer, spearheaded an unsuccessful bid to win an early release for West. Governor Frederick William M. Holliday, a conservative, turned down the request on November 19, 1881.

69. George C. Wright, *Racial Violence in Kentucky, 1865–1940*, 54–55.

70. The race of the girl is not specified, but I am assuming her to have been white given the nature of the comments about race prejudice at trial. January 27, 1877, EJ; letter dated January 19, 1877, January 27 packet, Box 36, November 5, 1876–February 10, 1877, box 36, SC, EP, LVA.

71. December 23 packet, box 16, December 16–31, 1870, SC, EP, LVA.

72. July packet, June–September 21, 1886, box 75, SC, EP; January 25 packet, November 17–February 12, 1881, box 53, SC, EP, LVA. Again, the race of the accused is not provided.

73. Letter from P. K. Jones to Lieutenant F. M. Kimball, Hicksford, Virginia, December 7, 1868, ibid. See also Prison Register, 1868; EJ, July 6, 1869. Virginia prison registers show that before the war no man, white or black, served time for attempted rape. That changed in

1865. In that year two Irishmen entered prison, one for attempted rape (one-year sentence) and the other for assault with attempt to commit a rape (two years). A thirteen-year-old boy of color was imprisoned for attempted rape, a crime for which he received three years. The only prisoner serving considerably more time that year for attempted rape was a black man named George Washington. He received a twenty-year sentence. Throughout the 1860s no other man, black or white, served more than two years for attempted rape or assault with attempt to rape. Beginning in 1870 the terms of incarceration for attempted rape increased. From 1870 through January 1876, the period for which prison registers exist, only one white man was admitted to prison for an attempted rape, suggesting that African American men received harsher punishments for this crime than white men. It may also suggest that women were more inclined to interpret a wide array of actions by black men as sexually motivated. Moreover, beginning in the early 1870s, sentences for attempted rape rose incrementally. Five- and eight-year terms grew more common, reflecting a change in legislation. Gradually, even longer sentences can be noted, the longest of which was eighteen years. Seven letters, July 6 packet, box 10 (May–August 14, 1869), SC, EP, LVA.

74. George C. Wright, *Racial Violence in Kentucky, 1865–1940*, 54–55.

75. Crawford's death sentence was eventually commuted to twenty years in prison. January 25, 1870, packet, box 12 (November 1869–February 1870), EP, SC, and Prison Register, 1870, LVA.

76. *KKK Report*, vol. 2, North Carolina, 315. Governor Caldwell issued at least a temporary reprieve although this source testifying before Congress believed that the convicted rapist would be pardoned.

77. *Witherby v. State*, 39 Ala. 702 (1866). It is important to note that white men were also being sentenced to die for rape, especially in North Carolina where the death penalty applied to both black and white rapists. John Allen Ketchet, aged thirty-one, was condemned to die for the rape of Milly Besehever, age sixteen or seventeen. 1873–74 folder, Criminal Action Papers, Rowan County, 1846–88; Rowan County Minute Docket, Superior Court, 1879–83, 280–82, 317, NCDAH.

78. For general treatments of racial violence during Reconstruction look to Trelease, *White Terror*; Eric Foner, *Reconstruction*, 119–23, 342–43, 425–44, 454–59, 590; Litwack, *Been in the Storm So Long*, 193, 231, 274–80, 286, 289, 303, 373, 416, 417; Williamson, *Crucible of Race*, 183; Hogue, "The Battle of Colfax." On lynching during Reconstruction see also George C. Wright, *Racial Violence in Kentucky, 1865–1940*, 3; Cutler, *Lynch-Law*; McGovern, *Anatomy of a Lynching*; Hofstadter, "Reflections on Violence in the U.S."

79. *KKK Report*, vol. 7, Georgia, 1190. For other cases of black men lynched for the alleged sexual violation of a white female during Reconstruction see Richardson, *The Negro in the Reconstruction of Florida, 1865–1877*, 164; George C. Wright, *Racial Violence in Kentucky, 1865–1940*, 43–46, 49–50; Trelease, *White Terror*, 33, 196, 317, 319; *Louisville Daily Courier*, May 9, 1866.

80. *KKK Report*, vol. 7, Georgia, 653, 655–62, 664–65, 723, 1060–61.

81. Bogue, "Violence and Oppression in North Carolina during Reconstruction, 1865–1873," 108.

82. *KKK Report*, vol. 6, Georgia, 214.

83. George C. Wright, *Racial Violence in Kentucky, 1865–1940*, 43–46.

84. *New York Times*, August 9, 1871, 1. Wright estimates that 16.2 percent of the lynchings in Kentucky during Reconstruction were linked to accusations or rape or attempted rape. Nineteen men were lynched for such offences; of these, seventeen were African American. George C. Wright, *Racial Violence in Kentucky, 1865–1940*, 43–46.

85. *KKK Report*, vol. 3, South Carolina, 212. For additional examples of lynchings or near-lynchings of accused black rapists, see Hodes, *White Women, Black Men*, 269 n. 26.

86. Eric Foner, *Reconstruction*, 119. On lynching during Reconstruction see John Raymond Ross, "At the Bar of Judge Lynch," 113–16. See also notes 78–79 above.

87. Roberta Sue Alexander, *North Carolina Faces the Freedmen*, 133.

88. Litwack, *Been in the Storm So Long*, 289.

89. Williamson, *After Slavery*, 257.

90. George C. Wright, *Racial Violence in Kentucky, 1865–1940*, 48.

91. For similar conclusions see Olds, "The Rape Complex in the Postbellum South," 124; Williamson, *Crucible of Race*, 183.

92. *KKK Report*, vol. 2, North Carolina, 8–9.

93. Ibid., vol. 8, Alabama, 242.

94. Ibid., vol. 6, Georgia, 124.

95. Ibid., vol. 8, Alabama, 446.

96. Testimony by General J. H. Clanton, *KKK Report*, Alabama testimony (volume number not indicated), as quoted in Fleming, *Documentary History of Reconstruction in Alabama*, II, 331.

97. Williamson, *Crucible of Race*, 183.

98. For a thoughtful analysis of white views on interracial marriage and "amalgamation," consult Fredrickson, *The Black Image in the White Mind*, 171–74, 187–93. It is worth noting that the politics surrounding the presidential election of 1864 are generally credited with injecting interracial sex into political discourse. Thus, miscegenation concerns seem to have been implanted in the North. Fredrickson, *The Black Image in the White Mind*, 171; Hodes, *White Women, Black Men*, 6, 144–45.

99. *Colored American* (Augusta, Ga.), January 6, 1866.

100. Quoted in Fredrickson, *The Black Image in the White Mind*, 188–89.

101. Pike, *The Prostrate State*, 44.

102. Quoted in Bardaglio, *Reconstructing the Household*, 177.

103. Dailey, *Before Jim Crow*, 87.

104. Fleming, *Documentary History of Reconstruction in Alabama*, 1:274, 294, 288–89.

105. Bardaglio, " 'Shameful Matches,' " 122; Stone and Shepherd, comps., *Penal Code of Alabama*, ch. 5, sec. 61, p. 31; Walker, comp., *Revised Code of Alabama*, part 4, ch. 5, sec. 3602, p. 690; Berry, "Judging Morality," 839; Hockaday, *Revised Statutes of Missouri*, ch. 50, sec. 3265, pp. 553–54; Dailey, *Before Jim Crow*, 88.

106. Cited in Escott, *Many Excellent People*, 151.

107. Van Evrie, *Negroes and Negro "Slavery,"* 18.

108. Olds, "The Rape Complex in the Post-bellum South," 112; Fredrickson, *The Black Image in the White Mind*, 168–69.

109. Hodes, "The Sexualization of Reconstruction Politics," 403. See also notes 1–11 in this chapter and the Appendix.

Chapter Nine

1. Tolnay and Beck, *A Festival of Violence*, 63.

2. Brundage, *Lynching in the New South*, 155.

3. Tolnay and Beck, *A Festival of Violence*, 88.

4. Brundage, *Lynching in the New South*, 259.

5. Tolnay and Beck, *A Festival of Violence*, ix.

6. Brundage, *Lynching in the New South*, 68. The most recent addition to this weighty collection of literature is Dray, *At the Hands of Persons Unknown*.

7. Hodes, *White Women, Black Men*, 176; Tolnay and Beck, *A Festival of Violence*, 48; Brundage, *Lynching in the New South*, 264.

8. Wells-Barnett, "Southern Horrors," in *On Lynchings*, 30.

9. Finnegan, "At the Hands of Parties Unknown," 167–68.

10. Tolnay and Beck, *Festival of Violence*, 48–49.

11. Quoted in Williamson, *Crucible of Race*, 128.

12. Quoted in Bryant Simon, "The Appeal of Cole Blease of South Carolina," 387. On Blease see also Williamson, *Crucible of Race*, 428–29.

13. Quoted in Williamson, *Crucible of Race*, 133. See also Kantrowitz, "Ben Tillman and Hendrix McLane, Agrarian Rebels," and *Ben Tillman and the Reconstruction of White Supremacy*.

14. 1881 and 1882 folders, Rowan County Criminal Action Papers, 1846–83; Rowan County Superior Court Minute Docket, 1879–83, 332, 337, 346, 369, 370, 429, 446; federal censuses of 1870, 1880, Rowan County, North Carolina, NCDAH.

15. Ibid.

16. Ibid.

17. In 1883 William Staton, an eighteen-year-old black man from Union County, North Carolina, was convicted of assault with intent to commit rape. The victim, Julia Edwards, was identified only as being under the age of ten. While court records do not reveal her race, they do identify the appellant, Staton, as a colored man. The absence of such a marker for Edwards leads me to believe that she was white. Staton, like Locke, was sentenced to a prison term, in this case twelve years. He was pardoned in 1891. North Carolina State Prison Descriptive Register, December 1884–May 1896, 5602–11500 (vol. 2), NCDAH; *State v. Staton*, 88 N.C. (February term, 1883), 631–32.

18. Black jurors in the post-Reconstruction era were not that uncommon. Laura Edwards documents a black-on-white rape case in North Carolina in 1887 that was tried by a jury including at least eight black jurors, which incidentally found the black defendant, Albert Taborn, guilty. Laura F. Edwards, *Gendered Strife and Confusion*, 251.

19. For such cross-examination, see the North Carolina case of *State v. Parish* (September 1889), in which an eleven-year-old charged her father with repeated rape. The physician who examined the child was forced, under cross-examination, to consider acts or conditions other than sexual intercourse that might have accounted for a ruptured hymen. *State v. Parish* (September 1889), 684–85.

20. *Givens v. Commonwealth*, 29 Gratt. 830 (January Term 1878).

21. May 7 packet, box 51, May–August 1880, SC, EP; EJ, May 7, 1880, 80, LVA.

22. Tanner's race is unknown.

23. May 1895 packet, box 113 (April 16–June 15, 1895), SC, EP, LVA.

24. Box 115, August–November 15, 1895, September packet, SC, EP, LVA. On the character of accusers in postbellum appellate decisions, consult *State of North Carolina v. Wright Daniel* (October 1882), 507.

25. Cited in Dorr, "Black-and-White Rape and Retribution in Twentieth-Century Virginia," 729. Also in Dorr, "Men, Even Negroes, Must Have Some Protection," 730–33.

26. *Cunningham v. Commonwealth* (July 1891), 37–44.

27. Ibid., 44.

28. EJ, May 7, 1880, 80; box 51, May–August 1880, May 7 packet, SC, EP, LVA.

29. I surmise that Moore was white based on court documents referring to her as "Mrs.," a title of respect generally not accorded to nonwhite women.

30. Box 98, September 22, 1891–January 1892, September 22–30, and October packets, SC, EP, LVA. A database of Virginia executions performed under civil authority lists ten black men executed for rape, two for attempted rape (one black, the other not listed), and two for rape-murder, both black, for the years 1877–99. Espy and Smykla, comps., *Executions in the United States, 1608–1991*. This database should not be considered a complete list. Some of the black rapists I have documented as having been executed do not appear on the "Espy" list.

31. Fredrickson, *The Black Image in the White Mind*; Williamson, *Crucible of Race*.

32. This development presents a methodological obstacle for the continued analysis of court cases of black rape. Many cases are simply not making their way through the court system any longer. While I attempt to remain loyal to the court-generated sources of black rape trials and therefore consistent in methodology, I must, by necessity, move into other sources to compensate, including prison records and newspaper accounts of lynchings. Moreover, identifying the race of the principals is more and more difficult to discern in turn-of-the-century records, since clerks and other officials are less likely to have denoted race in legal documents. Determining the race of the accused, especially if he is sentenced to prison, is relatively easy, as penitentiary logs continue to carefully register the race of the inmates. (Recall, however, that the Virginia penitentiary ledgers are incomplete.) More elusive, frustratingly so, is the race of the accuser. I have been far less successful in verifying the race of women and girls who file charges of sexual assault. As a result, I am left with quite a few interesting cases of black rape, but am unable to say with assurance that the accuser was white.

33. On the distrust of the post-Reconstruction legal system see Hodes, *White Women, Black Men*, 204; Brundage, *Lynching in the New South*, 96–102.

34. *Richmond Dispatch*, September 27, 1887, 4.

35. Letter of George Junkin and others to Governor P. W. McKinney, n.d., and letter of George Wilson, July 14, 1894, July packet, box 104, June 11–September 1893, SC, EP, LVA. I am deducing that the accuser in this case was white on the indirect testimony offered in these petitions, specifically the accuser's claim that "she had been raped by a negro."

36. Letter to Governor Charles O'Ferrall, July 15, 1895, box 115, August–November 15, 1895, September packet, SC, EP, LVA.

37. Letter from Thomas L. Moore to Governor P. W. McKinney, March 14, 1893, and letter from C. A. Heermans, October 9, 189[?], March 11–June 10, 1893, packet, SC, EP, LVA.

38. *Richmond Dispatch*, May 8, 1894, 2; May 10, 1894, 3.

39. Ibid., September 27, 1887, 1; Johnson, "The Fever Breaks," 35–36.

40. *Macon Telegraph*, June 10, 1890.

41. *Richmond Dispatch*, August 8, 1891; Brundage, *Lynching in the New South*, 282.

42. *Richmond Planet*, May 17, 1890.

43. Letter from James McMenamin to Governor P. W. McKinney, October 20, 1891, box 98, October packet, SC, EP, LVA.

44. Recall that in the antebellum period alleged rapists so young, even black youth, were believed physically incapable of rape. See Chapter 2, n. 25.

45. North Carolina State Prison Descriptive Register, December 1884–May 1896, 5602–11500 (vol. 2) and (vol. 3), NCDAH.

46. Fredrickson, *The Black Image in the White Mind*, 204–16, quote on page 214. See also Williamson, *Crucible of Race*, 88–93. On black elevation consult Olds, "The Rape Complex in the Postbellum South," 115–23.

47. Gilliam, "The African Problem," 420, 423, 422.

48. Williamson, *Crucible of Race*, 111–16.

49. Quoted in Olds, "The Rape Complex in the Postbellum South," 119.

50. Ibid., 122.

51. Straton, "Will Education Solve the Race Problem?," 786.

52. W. E. B. Du Bois, *Some Notes on Negro Crime* (1904), as quoted in Ayers, *Vengeance and Justice*, 252.

53. Gilmore, *Gender and Jim Crow*, 83.

54. On the broadening of the definition of black rape see Hodes, *White Women, Black Men*, 203; Brundage, *Lynching in the New South*, 58.

55. Actually, only five accusers were involved in these eight rape cases.

56. North Carolina State Prison Descriptive Register, December 1884–May 1896, 5602–11500 (vol. 2) and (vol. 3), NCDAH.

57. Amis, comp., *The North Carolina Criminal Code and Digest*, 241; Pemberton and Jerome, comps., *The North Carolina Criminal Code and Digest*, 419. While prison terms were not an option for convicted rapists, "rape" could also mean statutory rape or fraudulently impersonating a husband, which allowed for imprisonment. Ibid., 421–22.

58. Gilmore, *Gender and Jim Crow*, 83–84.

59. *State v. Neely*, 74 N.C. 425 (January 1876). On this case see also Berry, *The Pig Farmer's Daughter*, 209.

60. Ibid.

61. Ayers, *Vengeance and Justice*, 253–54.

62. Brundage, *Lynching in the New South*, 61.

63. *Richmond Planet*, August 30, 1890.

64. Bishop Warren A. Candler, in *Forum* 76 (December 1926): 813, as quoted in Brundage, *Lynching in the New South*, 58.

65. The relaxation of the legal requirement of force in sexual assault cases occurred in a larger context of heightened sensitivity to sexual assault as a crime against a person and not against property (trespass). Beginning in the 1880s, moral reformers targeted heinously low ages of consent, predominantly in the South, for statutory revisions. An important by-product of these age-of-consent campaigns was the development of greater appreciation for the seriousness of rape and attempted rape on females. On rape reform and the movement

to protect the sexuality of young women see Pivar, *Purity Crusade*; Odem, *Delinquent Daughters*; Larson, " 'Even a Worm Will Turn at Last' "; Parker, " 'To Protect the Chastity of Children under Sixteen' "; Dunlap, "The Reform of Rape Law and the Problem of White Men."

66. *Dorsey v. State*, 108 Ga. 477 (July 1899).

67. Quoted in Hodes, *White Women, Black Men*, 179.

68. Carter, *Scottsboro*, 297; Goodman, *Stories of Scottsboro*, 227.

69. Jacquelyn Dowd Hall, " 'The Mind That Burns in Each Body,' " 335–36.

Epilogue

1. Lee, *To Kill a Mockingbird*, 220.

2. Innes and Breen, *"Myne Owne Ground,"* 23, 27.

Appendix

1. Dixon, *The Clansman*; Lee, *To Kill a Mockingbird*.

2. On the Scottsboro trial consult Carter, *Scottsboro*; Goodman, *Stories of Scottsboro*.

3. For a discussion of the rape myth in the later nineteenth century see Fredrickson, *The Black Image in the White Mind*, especially ch. 9, "The Negro as Beast: Southern Negrophobia at the Turn of the Century"; Williamson, *Crucible of Race*, 111–39, 306–9; Olds, "The Rape Complex in the Postbellum South." For works dealing with the rape complex in the twentieth century see Myrdal, *An American Dilemma*, 561–62, 587–92, 1355–56 n. 41; Davis, Gardner, and Gardner, *Deep South*, 25–28; Jacquelyn Dowd Hall, *Revolt against Chivalry*; MacLean, *Behind the Mask of Chivalry*, 128–57. A number of black rape cases in the 1930s received considerable contemporary attention and have been the subject of recent analysis, especially those previously cited about the Scottsboro trial. Also consult McGovern, *Anatomy of a Lynching*; Martin, "Oklahoma's 'Scottsboro' Affair," 175–88; Crabb, "May 1930," 29–40. For cases after World War II of black southerners accused of raping or making improper sexual advances toward white women see Whitfield, *A Death in the Delta*; Rise, "Race, Rape, and Radicalism," 461–90; Rise, *The Martinsville Seven*; Martin, "The Civil Rights Congress and Southern Black Defendants," 25–52; Lawson, Colburn, and Paulson, "Groveland," 1–26; Davies, *White Lies*.

4. The use of this terminology more strongly conveys the belief that such an anxiety—again, based in the illogical—was a form of mass psychosis. Lawrence J. Friedman defined the "southern rape complex" as "a hypothesis invoked by several analysts of the region to explain certain hostilities of whites toward blacks." Lawrence M. Friedman, "The Southern Rape Complex," 1029.

5. Cash, *Mind of the South*, 115.

6. Ibid., 86.

7. Ibid., 116.

8. Dollard, *Caste and Class in a Southern Town*, 134, 135.

9. Ibid., 37 n. 5.

10. Ibid., 163.

11. Ibid., 170.

12. Ibid.

13. Ibid., 170, 297, 163, 164. The psychologist Helene Deutsch, also a Freudian, in an ambitious, authoritative, multivolume work, *The Psychology of Women* (1944), likewise addressed white rape fears. Unlike Dollard, who believed that culpability for the rape myth rested with white men, Deutsch claimed that white women were responsible: "My own experience of accounts by white women of rape by Negroes . . . has convinced me that many fantastic stories are produced by the masochistic yearnings of these women." Deutsch, *The Psychology of Women*, 1:256.

14. For a fascinating comparison of the divergent fictional representations of the South and race, consult Grace Elizabeth Hale, *Making Whiteness*, 241–96.

15. Lillian Smith, *Killers of the Dream*, 145.

16. Ibid., 18.

17. Actually, one earlier historical treatise, misleadingly entitled *Southern Rape Complex*, purported to examine the phenomenon. In reality, the work was little more than a rambling synopsis of southern history with only passing reference to the subject in its title. The author, Lawrence Baughman, relied extensively on the theories first put forth by Dollard and Cash, and his views on the Reconstruction era borrow from the "Dunning school". He characterized southern Reconstruction legislators as "freedmen, carpetbaggers and scalawags: a fantastic assemblage of ignoramuses, opportunists and crooked-as-hells." Baughman, *Southern Rape Complex*, 14.

18. Jordan, *White over Black*, 148.

19. Ibid., 152.

20. Ibid., 28–39.

21. Thorpe, *The Old South*, 91, 113.

22. Lawrence J. Friedman, *White Savage*, 11.

23. Peter H. Wood, *Black Majority*, 237.

24. Bardaglio, "Rape and the Law in the Old South," 752. See also Bardaglio in *Reconstructing the Household*, 64–65, 69. A number of scholars outside the discipline of history have also accepted as fact that white fears of black rape originated in the slave South. The civil rights movement of the 1960s, which motivated many historians to examine American race relations, also spawned a number of sociological studies of race, a few of which tackled issues of black male sexuality, interracial sexual relations, and white fears of black sexual assault. Most of these rely heavily on the "Cash-Jordan" theses on sex and race, for example, by rehashing and reworking projection theory, Cash's concept of gyneolatry, and Cash's and Jordan's acceptance of the notion that miscegenation on plantations was widespread. Some works, written by black men in the 1960s, are predictably angry and polemical in tone. See, for example, Hernton, *Sex and Racism in America*. Another example of social scientists' reliance on the "Cash-Jordan school" in framing the historical foundations of their studies on race and sex is the work on the sexualization of racism by two criminologists, Coramae Richey Mann and Lance H. Selva. Mann and Selva grounded fears of the black rapist in the white man's sexual exploitation of slave women, which resulted in the "intensification of the sexual anxieties of the Southern white male" who projected his own "tendencies for sexual atrocities onto the Black man." Mann and Selva, "The Sexualization of Racism," 169–70.

25. Wyatt-Brown, *Southern Honor*, 50.

26. This is not to deny the existence of white beliefs about the innate promiscuity and licentiousness of both black men and women, a belief that Winthrop Jordan has rooted in

early English contacts with Africa. However, making the leap from assumptions about black men as libidinous to those about black men as rapists is misguided. Though related, these two conceptions are not one and the same. For a discussion on white perceptions about African American female sexuality in the Old South see Deborah Gray White, *Ar'n't I a Woman?*, 29–46, 60–61; D'Emilio and Freedman, *Intimate Matters*, 97, 101; McLaurin, *Celia, a Slave*, 22–23; Adele Logan Alexander, *Ambiguous Lives*, 64, 144; Clinton, *The Plantation Mistress*, 222; Angela Davis, "Rape, Racism, and the Myth of the Black Rapist," 174, 182; Fox-Genovese, *Within the Plantation Household*, 292, 325–26; Genovese, *Roll, Jordan, Roll*, 427–28; Glatthaar, *Forged in Battle*, 91; Berry and Blassingame, *Long Memory*, 115–16; Hodes, *White Women, Black Men*, 5, 65; Carby, *Reconstructing Womanhood*, 20–39.

Slaveholders assuredly feared acts of violence by their slaves—arson, poisonings, assault, murder, and perhaps most of all, armed rebellion. There is little evidence, however, to suggest that white southerners were apprehensive or anxious about slaves raping white women. On white fears of slave violence consult Herbert Aptheker, *American Negro Slave Revolts*; Phillips, *American Negro Slavery*, 473–76, 481–88; Stampp, *The Peculiar Institution*, 127–28, 136–38; Blassingame, *The Slave Community*, 230–38; Williamson, *Crucible of Race*, 117; Guion Griffis Johnson, *Antebellum North Carolina*, 510–21; Crow, *The Black Experience in Revolutionary North Carolina*, 40, 56–61, 85–95; Fredrickson, *The Black Image in White Mind*, 8–9. Fears of slave conspiracy and uprising during the Civil War are explored and ingeniously reconstructed in Jordan, *Tumult and Silence at Second Creek*.

A few notable works have in fact expressed skepticism about the existence of antebellum white rape fears, but their remarks on this subject seem to have been all but ignored. "On the whole," wrote Eugene Genovese, "the racist fantasy so familiar after emancipation did not grip the South in slavery times." Genovese, *Roll, Jordan, Roll*, 33. Elizabeth Fox-Genovese concurs: "The presumed threat of black male sexuality never provoked the wild hysteria and violence in the Old South that it did in the new." Fox-Genovese, *Within the Plantation Household*, 291. While acknowledging that the roots of the rape myth lay deep in racist white society, the race historian George Fredrickson notes that "this image came to the surface in a new and spectacular way around the turn of the century." Fredrickson, *The Black Image in the White Mind*, 276–77. Most recently the work of Martha Hodes suggests that white fears of black sexual threats did not pervade the antebellum or even war years. Hodes writes that "while whites feared slave uprisings during the Civil War, no great tide of sexual alarm engulfed white southerners as white men left white women at home with slave men." Hodes, "Wartime Dialogues," 239; Hodes, *White Women, Black Men*, 26–27.

27. Hodes, *White Women, Black Men*; Hodes, "The Sexualization of Reconstruction Politics"; Hodes, "Wartime Dialogues"; Sommerville, "The Rape Myth in the Old South Reconsidered"; Sommerville, "Rape, Race, and Castration in Slave Law in the Colonial and Early South"; Sommerville, " 'I Was Very Much Wounded.' " Other works that substantiate a general toleration for the sexual congress between white women and black men in the Old South include Bynum, *Unruly Women*; Rothman, *Notorious in the Neighborhood*; Buckley, "Unfixing Race"; Buckley, *The Great Catastrophe of My Life*; Lockley, "Crossing the Race Divide"; Mills, "Miscegenation and the Free Negro in Antebellum 'Anglo' Alabama."

28. Fox-Genovese, *Within the Plantation Household*, 235, 240. See also Stowe, *Intimacy and Power in the Old South*, 50–121; Censer, *North Carolina Planters and Their Families*, 72–74.

29. Jacquelyn Dowd Hall, *Revolt against Chivalry*, xxxiv–xxxv.

30. Fredrickson, *The Black Image in the White Mind*, 204–9; Williamson, *Crucible of Race*, especially ch. 4, "The Rise of the Radicals."

31. Shoup, "Uncle Tom's Cabin Forty Years After," 96.

32. McHattan, "The Sexual Status of the Negro, Past and Present," 8.

33. McGuire and Lydston, "Sexual Crimes among the Southern Negroes Scientifically Considered," 105.

34. Haygood, "The Black Shadow in the South," 167–75.

35. W. Cabell Bruce, "Lynch Law in the South," 381. For other late-nineteenth-century and early-twentieth-century reminiscences denying that African American men posed a threat, especially of a sexual nature, to white women see Frederick L. Hoffman, *Race Traits and Tendencies of the American Negro*, 217; Rebecca Lattimore Felton, as quoted in Williamson, *Crucible of Race*, 128; Randle, *Characteristics of the Southern Negro*, 74; Brann, *Brann, the Iconoclast*, 1:25; Somerville, "Some Co-operating Causes of Negro Lynching," 509; Shaler, "The Negro since the Civil War," 29; Avary, *Dixie after the War*, 384; Straton, "Will Education Solve the Race Problem?," 786; Charles Henry Smith, "Have American Negroes Too Much Liberty?," 182; Shoup, "Uncle Tom's Cabin Forty Years After," 95–96.

36. Fleming, *Civil War and Reconstruction in Alabama*, 209.

37. Avary, *Dixie after the War*, 384.

38. Rives, *Smoking Flax*, 79.

39. Ibid., 122.

40. Ibid., 81.

41. Thomas Nelson Page, *Red Rock*.

42. For accounts of Dixon, his literary works, and their impact see Williamson, *Crucible of Race*, 140–76, 296, 312–15, 336, 461, 466–67; Gilmore, *Gender and Jim Crow*, 66–70, 135–38; Gunning, *Race, Rape, and Lynching*, 19–47; Fredrickson, *The Black Image in the White Mind*, 280–81, 283, 307. Williamson's treatment of Dixon relies heavily on psychosexual analysis. He explains much of Dixon's rabid racism and his obsessions with black sexual aggression as rooted in Dixon's own "psychic needs" that stemmed from an unhappy childhood. Dixon believed that his mother, whom Williamson characterizes as "extremely anxious" and "apprehensive," had been forced into an early marriage (she was thirteen when she married Dixon's father). This preoccupation with his own fragile mother's sexual violation was manifest as a theme repeated throughout Dixon's work: the need to save white southern women from the clutches of the Negro beast. In fact, Williamson writes, "Dixon became a Radical and wrote *The Leopard's Spots* because he had a very deep emotional problem" (151–52, 170, 159–60, 158). Gilmore, while acknowledging the importance of psychosexual motives for Dixon's fiction, argues that North Carolina, Dixon's home state, was ripe to receive his racist message, in light of the white supremacy and disfranchisement campaigns which were ongoing when Dixon's books were released (281).

43. Williamson, *Crucible of Race*, 140.

44. Dixon, *The Clansman*, 304.

45. Ibid., 306.

46. Dixon, *The Leopard's Spots*, 375.

47. Gilmore, *Gender and Jim Crow*, 135–36.

48. For historiographical essays on Reconstruction consult Eric Foner, "Slavery, The Civil

War, and Reconstruction," 73–92; Weisberger, "The Dark and Bloody Ground of Recon-struction Historiography," 427–47.

49. Dunning, *Reconstruction*, 212–14.

50. Fleming, *Civil War and Reconstruction in Alabama*, 275, 383, 654.

51. Ibid., 762.

52. Claude Bowers, *The Tragic Era*, 53.

53. Ibid., 307–8.

54. For a historiographical discussion of the Dunning school with particular emphasis on its treatment of blacks and the rape myth consult Newby, *Jim Crow's Defense*, 65–66; Olds, "The Rape Complex in the Postbellum South," 3, 114. James Goodman testifies to the pervasive popular influence of the "Dunning school," the work of Claude Bowers in particular, in providing a historical frame of reference during the trials of the "Scottsboro boys" in the 1930s. *Stories of Scottsboro*, 159–60.

55. Phillips, *American Negro Slavery*, 459.

56. Ibid., 456.

57. Olds, "The Rape Complex in the Postbellum South," 139; Philip Alexander Bruce, *The Plantation Negro as a Freeman*, 248–49, 51 (quotation), 59.

58. Philip Alexander Bruce, *The Plantation Negro as a Freeman*, 83–85. The most frequent crime, according to Bruce, was petit larceny (87).

59. Ibid.

60. W. Cabell Bruce, "Lynch Law in the South," 380.

61. McGuire and Lydston, "Sexual Crimes among the Southern Negroes, Scientifically Considered," 105.

62. Charles Henry Smith, "Have American Negroes Too Much Liberty?," 176.

63. Haygood, "The Black Shadow in the South," 172; Walter Hines Page, "The Last Hold of the Southern Bully," 303.

64. Frederick L. Hoffman, *Race Traits and Tendencies of the American Negro*, 220, 227, 229–35, 329. See also Williamson, *Crucible of Race*, 122–23; Fredrickson, *The Black Image in the White Mind*, 249–51, for more on Hoffman and his study.

65. McGuire and Lydston, "Sexual Crimes among the Southern Negroes, Scientifically Considered," 110.

66. Ibid., 112.

67. Olds, "The Rape Complex in the Postbellum South," 112.

68. Shaler, "The Negro Problem," 706. Shaler was a Harvard professor whose status as a scientific expert lent credibility to the "retrogression theory." Wiener, "The 'Black Beast Rapist': White Racial Attitudes in the Postwar South," 223.

69. Gilliam, "The African Problem," 418.

70. John T. Morgan, "Shall Negro Majorities Rule?," 587.

71. Williamson, *Crucible of Race*, 182, 112; Fredrickson, *The Black Image in the White Mind*, 198–216.

72. Williamson, *Crucible of Race*, 113.

73. Ibid., 124–39; Fredrickson, *The Black Image in the White Mind*, 257, 276; Newby, *Jim Crow's Defense*, 137; Bordin, *Frances Willard*, 216–18; Holmes, *The White Chief*, ix, xi, 37–38, 88–89; Whites, "Rebecca Latimer Felton and the Wife's Farm," 368–72; Jacquelyn Dowd Hall, *Revolt against Chivalry*, 146, 194–95.

74. Philip S. Foner, ed. *The Life and Writings of Frederick Douglass*, vol. 4, *Reconstruction and After*, 493.

75. Ibid., 494.

76. Jacquelyn Dowd Hall, *Revolt against Chivalry*, 78–79. On the life of Wells-Barnett see Schechter, *Ida B. Wells-Barnett and American Reform, 1880–1930*. For a literary treatment, consult Gunning, *Race, Rape, and Lynching*, 81–89.

77. Wells, *Southern Horrors*, reprinted in *On Lynchings*, 4.

78. Ibid., 5.

79. Ibid., 7–12.

80. On Wells's campaign to bring lynching to the forefront of the American conscience see Bederman, "'Civilization,' the Decline of Middle-Class Manliness, and Ida B. Wells's Antilynching Campaign (1892–94)," 5–30; Jacquelyn Dowd Hall, *Revolt against Chivalry*, 78–80, 146, 149, 165.

81. Wells, *A Red Record*, in On *Lynchings*, 8.

82. Terrell, "Lynching from a Negro's Point of View," 853–54.

83. National Association for the Advancement of Colored People, *Thirty Years of Lynching in the United States, 1889–1918*. White reformers slowly came on board the antilynching campaign and began to challenge the chivalric rhetoric that tenaciously defended lynchers of alleged black rapists. In 1930, for example, Jessie Daniel Ames helped found the Association of Southern Women for the Prevention of Lynching (ASWPL). Jacquelyn Dowd Hall, *Revolt against Chivalry*. Other white liberals followed suit. In the 1930s and 1940s whites, among them some native southerners, began a broader assault on radical racist ideology and criticism of southern culture, including the depiction of the black man as rapist or "beast," which for so long had been the linchpin in the white South's scheme for racial control.

84. See ch. 9, "The Negro as Beast: Southern Negrophobia at the Turn of the Century," in Fredrickson, *The Black Image in the White Mind*.

85. Williamson, *Rage for Order*, 186–90. For a strident rebuke of Williamson's analysis of the causes of lynching, see Kousser, "Revisiting a Festival of Violence."

86. The only dissertation on the rape complex continues this historiographical trend. Madelin Joan Olds traced the changes in the image of the black rapists as depicted in southern literature from Reconstruction through the early twentieth century. She established a most helpful chronological framework to periodize white anxiety about black male sexual aggression. From 1877 through the late 1880s, literary evidence of widespread sexual fear was rare, though some element of black retaliation was anticipated by whites. Many white southerners were dedicated to "black elevation," the process of educating blacks and making them productive. Most argued that blacks, though immoral, harbored no sexual designs on white women. By the 1890s, however, the southern rape complex had emerged, and it quickly became a preoccupation among whites. Authors of this period argued that black sexual assault of white women resulted from lack of adequate white controls, which had effectively kept blacks in check during slavery. They further contended that attempts to uplift blacks, by education or the vote, aroused black lust and passions. These authors distinguished black aggression from black sexuality. Olds, "The Rape Complex in the Postbellum South," 138.

87. For an overview of this cultural transition, see Singal, *The War Within*. Gail Bederman's work likewise situates the white rape fears in the turn-of-the-century discourse about

"civilization," which turned on male dominance and white supremacy. White men were civilized; black men were savage and barbaric. Bederman's purview is the nation at large, not merely the South. Bederman, *Manliness and Civilization*.

88. Jacquelyn Dowd Hall, *Revolt against Chivalry*, 147–48.

89. Ibid., 153.

90. Ibid., xxxiv–xxxv.

91. Painter, " 'Social Equality,' Miscegenation, Labor, and Power," 47–67.

92. Gilmore, *Gender and Jim Crow*.

93. Fitzhugh Brundage seems to be in agreement with Gilmore on this point. He asserts that "because sexual relations, let alone sexual attacks on white women, could not be separated from contemporary attitudes that bound sexuality, gender, and power, violations of the racial barrier in sexual relations were blows against the very foundations of society and, in the eyes of whites, were the most abhorrent of all crimes." Brundage, *Lynching in the New South*, 59.

94. Dailey, *Before Jim Crow*, 7.

95. Ibid., 98–99, 102.

96. See, for example, Brundage, *Lynching in the New South*, 70–71; Finnegan, "At the Hands of Parties Unknown"; Tolnay and Beck, *A Festival of Violence*.

97. Hodes, *White Women, Black Men*, 146–47.

98. Ibid., 165; Hodes, "The Sexualization of Reconstruction Politics." Others who regard race and sex in the context of Reconstruction as an important break with the antebellum period include Edwards, *Gendered Strife and Confusion*, 1–23; Bardaglio, *Reconstructing the Household*, 117, 176–201. For a literary study that situates the origins of the rape myth in Reconstruction, consult Gunning, *Race, Rape, and Lynching*, 6–7, 19–47.

99. Hodes, *White Women, Black Men*, 148.

100. Ibid., 174.

101. Ayers, *Vengeance and Justice*, 239. The sociologists Tolnay and Beck concur with Ayers on this point. *A Festival of Violence*, 66–69. Ayers utilized crime statistics throughout most of his work, but backed off the social history sources when discussing rape fears. Instead, he mostly relied upon secondary sources and contemporary accounts in considering the motives behind rape fears.

102. Jacquelyn Dowd Hall, *Revolt against Chivalry*, 156. Other adherents to this theory include Trudier Harris, *Exorcising Blackness*. See also Brundage's point about fictional support for this explanation in his discussion of Faulkner's novel *Light in August*. Brundage, *Lynching in the New South*, 11.

103. Ayers, *Vengeance and Justice*, 243. J. Morgan Kousser is similarly skeptical, basing his doubt on statistics that show only a third of the lynchings of blacks by whites in the South to have been attributable to alleged sexual infractions. I am not convinced, however, that the stated reasons for lynching are always the real reasons and therefore the best measure of determining motive. A defender of Williamson and his allies might counter that lynchers could very well be unaware of the unconscious "psychosexual" reasons underlying their violent behavior. Kousser, "Revisiting a Festival of Violence," 171–73.

104. For a discussion of the impact of industrialization of the Piedmont and Appalachian South see Jacquelyn Dowd Hall et al., *Like a Family*; Eller, *Miners, Millhands, and Mountaineers*.

105. W. E. B. Du Bois, *Some Notes on Negro Crime* (1904), as quoted in Ayers, *Vengeance and Justice*, 252. The increase in crime in general in the late 1880s across the color line has been documented by Ayers and others.

106. Ayers, *Vengeance and Justice*, 241.

107. Greater attention has been devoted to the subject of lynching and its prominent but ugly place in postbellum southern society. Gunnar Myrdal, in his masterly study of race relations, *An American Dilemma*, asserted that lynching became common in the South in part because of the boredom of rural life and lack of recreational activities. Myrdal quoted H. L. Mencken's explanation that "lynching often takes the place of the merry-go-round, the theatre, the symphony orchestra, and other diversions common to larger communities." Myrdal gave significantly more weight to the fear of economic and political competition of blacks. Violence, or the threat of violence, kept blacks from reaching, or even striving for, parity in these areas. Myrdal, *An American Dilemma*, 560–66. In a fascinating recent work on the culture of racial segregation, Grace Elizabeth Hale attributes what she terms "spectacle lynching" to the way in which white southerners became enmeshed in the consumer culture of the early twentieth century. See Grace Elizabeth Hale, *Making Whiteness*, ch. 5, "Deadly Amusements."

108. See, for example, Pivar, *Purity Crusade*; Odem, *Delinquent Daughters*; Stephen Murray Robertson, "Signs, Marks, and Private Parts," 359–60; Larson, " 'Even a Worm Will Turn at Last,' " 1–71; Parker, " 'To Protect the Chastity of Children under Sixteen,' " 49–79.

109. Pivar, *Purity Crusade*, 141–43.

110. A. A. Tompkins, "The Age of Consent from a Physio-Psychological Standpoint" (1895), as cited in Odem, *Delinquent Daughters*, 32.

111. *Nashville Banner*, March 11, 1893, 4, col. 3, as cited in Dunlap, "The Reform of Rape Law and the Problem of White Men," 360.

112. Jacquelyn Dowd Hall, " 'The Mind That Burns in Each Body,' " 332. For white-on-black sexual assault in the late nineteenth century, see *State of North Carolina v. John Powell* (February 1890), 635–39.

113. Dunlap, "The Reform of Rape Law and the Problem of White Men."

114. Wells-Barnett, *Red Record*, in *On Lynchings*, 148–49.

115. Dunlap, "The Reform of Rape Law and the Problem of White Men," 354–55.

116. *Atlanta Constitution*, September 17, 1866, 4, quoted in Dunlap, "The Reform of Rape Law and the Problem of White Men," 352.

117. Odem, *Delinquent Daughters*, 35.

118. Cott, "Passionlessness."

119. Odem, *Delinquent Daughters*; Peiss, *Cheap Amusements*.

120. Prather, *We Have Taken a City*, 68–75; Gilmore, *Gender and Jim Crow*, 105–6; Hodes, *White Women, Black Men*, 193–95.

121. Wells-Barnett, *Southern Horrors*, in *On Lynchings*, 19.

122. Harlan, ed., *The Booker T. Washington Papers*, 2:326. The vitriolic and highly defensive white response to Manly, Duke, and Wells is encapsulated in Hodes, *White Women, Black Men*, 188–97.

123. Hodes, *White Women, Black Men*, 201. Here I somewhat differ from Hodes on this point. What she situates "after emancipation" I see unwrapping in the 1880s, some years later.

124. Ayers, *Vengeance and Justice*, 238.

125. Hodes, *White Women, Black Men*, 1.

126. Dorr, "Black-on-White Rape and Retribution in Twentieth-Century Virginia," 714–15. On the years after World War II, consult Dorr, "Another Negro-Did-It Crime," 249–50, and her book-length treatment, *White Women, Rape, and the Power of Race in Virginia, 1900–1960*.

127. Dorr, "Black-on-White Rape and Retribution in Twentieth-Century Virginia," 724.

128. Ibid., 721–22.

129. Ibid., 718.

130. Grace Elizabeth Hale, *Making Whiteness*, 284.

131. Dorr, "Black-on-White Rape and Retribution in Twentieth-Century Virginia," 746.

132. Painter, "Of *Lily*, Linda Brent, and Freud," 259.

133. Painter, "What People Just Don't Understand about Academic Fields," B4, B6.

134. Dorr, "Black-on-White Rape and Retribution in Twentieth-Century Virginia," 748.

135. Carter, *Scottsboro*, 295.

BIBLIOGRAPHY

Primary Sources

Manuscripts and Archival Records

Durham, North Carolina
Special Collections, William R. Perkins Library, Manuscript Collection, Duke University
    Lucy Muse (Walton) Papers
        Lucy Muse Diary

Fredericksburg, Virginia
Fredericksburg Court House
    Circuit Court Records

Raleigh, North Carolina
North Carolina Cultural Resources, Department of Archives and History
    Albemarle County
        Commonwealth Causes, 1886–87
    Alexander County
        Criminal Action Papers, 1861–1909
    Bertie County
        Criminal Actions Papers, 1790–1844
        Slave Papers, 1744–1840
        Superior Court Appearance and Trial Dockets, 1807–13
        Superior Court Minutes, 1807–1915
        Superior Court Trial Dockets, 1845–68
        Tax List, 1836
    Cabarrus County
        Superior Court Minute Docket, 1819–67
    County Court Minutes
    Criminal Action Papers
    Federal Censuses
        North Carolina (1820), Rowan County
        North Carolina (1840), Bertie County
        North Carolina (1850), Bertie County, Cabarrus County

North Carolina (1860) Cabarrus County, Rowan County
North Carolina (1870), Rowan County
Governors' Letter Books
Governor's Office
Governors' Papers
Elizabeth Moore Collection
Democratic Circular, 1898
Prison Documents
Descriptive Registers of Prisoners, 1869–1917
Rowan County
Court Minutes
Criminal Action Papers, 1756–1845, 1846–88
Miscellaneous Records
Slaves and Persons of Color, 1822–34
State Docket Superior Court, 1821–35, 1857–69
Superior Court Execution Docket
Superior Court Minute Docket, 1820–32, 1850–66, 1879–83
Superior Court Trial Docket, 1815–69
Slave Papers
State Dockets for Superior Courts
Superior Court Minute Dockets
Superior Court Minutes

Richmond, Virginia
Library of Virginia
Accomack County
Court Minute Book, 1871–72
Court Order Book, 1870–73
Albemarle County
Court Law Order Book, 1865–70
Court Minute Book, 1854–56, 1866–68
Commonwealth Causes, 1867, 1880, 1886, 1887
Amherst County
Common Law Order Book, vol. 7 (1860–68), vol. 8 (1868–75)
Court Minute Book 6 (1859–64)
Auditor of Public Accounts
Condemned Blacks, Executed or Transported, 1783–1865 (Condemned Slaves)
A List of Slaves and Free Persons of Color Received into the Penitentiary of Virginia for Sale and Transportation from the 25th June 1816 to the 1st February 1842
Reports of Free Negroes
Augusta County
Court Order Book 60 (1865–67)
Botetourt County
Common Law Order Book, 1867–73, 1873–78
Court Order Book, 1857–67

Chesterfield County
    Circuit Court Records
        Criminal Causes, 1874–75
      Court Order Book, 1845–57
County and City Records
    County Court Loose Records
    Court Minute Books
    Court Order Books
    Death Registers
Culpeper County
    Court Order Book 29 (1887–92)
Department of Corrections
    Register of Convicts (prison registers), 1865–84 (Acc 30770)
Executive Journals
Federal Censuses
    Virginia (1810), Shenandoah County
    Virginia (1820), Caroline County, Frederick County, Isle of Wight County,
        Mecklenburg County, Southampton County
    Virginia (1830), Chesterfield County, Frederick County, Grayson County, Halifax
        County, Loudoun County, Rowan County, Westmoreland County, Wythe County
    Virginia (1840), Dinwiddie County and Index
    Virginia (1850) Grayson County, Ohio County, Spotsylvania County, Washington
        County
    Virginia (1860) Botetourt County, Dinwiddie County, Mathews County, Montgomery
        County, Jefferson County , City of Richmond, Rockingham County
    Virginia (1870), Accomack County, Albemarle County, Botetourt County,
        Chesterfield County, Elizabeth City County, Grayson County, Greensville County,
        Isle of Wight County, Lunenberg County, Pulaski County, City of Richmond, and
        Index.
    Virginia (1880) (Soundex S536), Franklin County
Franklin County
    Chancery Papers
        Insolvents and Reports of the Overseers of the Poor, 1822–1904
    Index of Births, Deaths, and Marriages, 1853–98
    Marriage Bonds, 1786–1905
    Register of Births, 1853–79
    Register of Deaths, 1853–71
Frederick County
    Superior Court Order Book, 1831–35
Grayson County
    Court Minute Book, 1835–70
    Court Order Book, 1865–67
    Register of Births, 1853–70
    Register of Deaths, 1853–70
Greensville County

Court Minute Book, 1852–66

Halifax County

County Court Minute Book, 1821–66

County Court Order Books, 1830–58

Henrico County

Court Minute Book, 1860–61

Henry County

Circuit Court Law Order Book

Court Minute Books, 1820–49, 1859–64

Court Records

Determined Papers, no. 147, 1874–77

Register of Persons Convicted of a Felony, 1883–1914

Isle of Wight County

Court Records

Court Papers, 1871–73

Journals of the House of Delegates of the Commonwealth of Virginia, 1861–63

Journals of the Senate of the Commonwealth of Virginia, 1861–63

King and Queen County

Court Minute Book, 1866–71

Superior Court Order Book, 1854–67

King George County

Court Order Book, 1839–47

Lunenberg County

County Court Decisions, 1822–83

Justice of the Peace Records, 1861–69, 1870–79

Mathews County

Dead Papers and Official Judgments, 1867

Mecklenburg County

Court Order Books, 1853–58

Court Records

Court Papers, 1854–1904

Orange County

Court Judgments, March–May 1870

Superior Court Minute Book, 1841–85

Pittsylvania County

Court Order Book, 1860–63

Powhatan County

Court Order Book, 1851–56

Prince Edward County

Court Order Book, 1853–62

Pulaski County

Circuit Court Order Book, 1857–76

Court Order Book, 1839–50

List of Felons, 1872–1926

Rappahannock County

Court Minute Book, 1866–71

Richmond City

Hustings Court Minutes, no. 29, 1863–66

List of All Persons Convicted of a Felony, 1870–96

Richmond *Directory*, 1860

Roanoke County

List of Persons Convicted of a Felony, 1870–1966

Rockbridge County

Court Minute Book, 1831–34

Register of Free Negroes, 1831–60

Secretary of the Commonwealth, Pardon Papers

Shenandoah County

Superior Court Minute Book

Southampton County

Court Minute Books, 1824–30

Smyth County

Register of Births, 1857–85

Register of Deaths, 1857–96

Tazewell County

Circuit Court

Criminal Presentments and Prosecutions, 1852–1913

Treasury Cash Journal

Virginia Executive Papers, Letters Received

Pardon Papers

Washington County

Court Minute Book

Westmoreland County

Register of Free Negroes

Superior Court Order Books, 1831–39

Virginia Historical Society

Robert Augustus Armistead Papers

Justice of the Peace Execution Book, 1852–61

Aylett Family Papers, 1776–1945

George William Bagby Papers, 1828–1917

"The Old Virginia Negro" (1875)

Frances (Norton) Baylor Papers, 1759–1815

Byrd Family Papers

Correspondence, 1834–63

George Llewelyn Christian Papers

Daniel W. Cobb Diary, 1843–72

Giles B. Cooke Diary, 1838–1937

Robert V. Davis Papers

Harrison Family Papers

Correspondence of Burr Williams Harrison

Hollday Family Papers

Peachy R. Gilmer Letters
William Huntington Diary, 1839–41
Keith Family Papers, 1830–1979
Thomas Eugene Massie Papers, 1822–63
Charles Stephen Morgan, 1799–1859
    Account Book, 1799–1859
Peck, Welford & Co., Fredericksburg, Virginia, Papers, 1834–44
Marie Gordon (Pryor) Rice Reminiscences, ca. 1855–85
Smith Family Papers
Spragins Family Papers
Virginia Governor, 1808–11 (John Tyler)

Sussex, Virginia
Sussex County Court House
    Circuit Court of Sussex County Common Law Order Book
    Loose Court Papers

Newspapers and Periodicals

Carolina Watchman
Charleston Mercury
Colored American (Augusta, Ga.)
Columbus Daily Sun
Fredericksburg (Va.) *News*, 1853–61
Greensboro Patriot
Hayneville (Ala.) *Watchman*, May 18, 1860
Lexington (Va.) *Gazette and Banner*
Louisiana Bulletin
Louisville Courier Journal
Louisville Daily Courier
Macon Telegraph
Meriwether County Vindicator
Nashville Banner
New Orleans Bee, October 9, 1858
New Orleans Daily Delta November 14 and December 6, 1845
New Orleans Republican Courier
New Orleans Tribune
New York Times
North Carolina Weekly Standard
Pulaski (Tenn.) *Citizen*
Raleigh Gazette
Raleigh Register and North Carolina Gazette
Raleigh Register, April 14, 1831, and May 12, 1831
Raleigh Star
Richmond Dispatch
Richmond Enquirer

Richmond Planet
Richmond Times
Roanoke Times
Savannah Republican
Southern Banner
Oxford (N.C.) *Torchlight*
Virginia Gazette, December 23, 1773
Virginia Herald, 1799–1800, 1802–5, 1806–9
Watchman
Waycross (Ga.) *Herald*
Weekly Advertiser
Weekly Standard (N.C.)
Western Carolinian
Wilmington (N.C.) *Journal*
Wytheville (Va.) *Dispatch*

Select State Supreme Court Reports, ca. 1800–1899

Alabama, 1827–93
Arkansas, 1843–91
Florida, 1847–95
Georgia, 1847–93
Kentucky, 1860–96
Louisiana, 1844–94
Maryland, 1858–87
Mississippi, 1850–95
Missouri, 1844–95
North Carolina, 1812–99
South Carolina, 1813–99
Tennessee, 1839–80
Texas ?–1896
Virginia, 1820–99

Published State Statutes from Legislative Sessions (microfiche),
ca. 1800–1899

Alabama, 1818–65
Arkansas, 1838–64
Florida, 1822–65
Georgia, 1810–65
Kentucky, 1800–51
Louisiana, 1806–65
Maryland, select years, 1818–57
Mississippi, 1813–59
North Carolina, 1820–95
South Carolina, select years, 1823–65
Tennessee, 1801–29, 1831–36, 1847–55, 1857–59

Texas, 1850–59

Virginia, 1819–99

Primary Sources: Published Legal and Official Sources

Acts of the General Assembly of the State of Virginia, Passed in 1865–1866 in the 89th year of the Commonwealth. Richmond: Allegre and Goode, 1866.

Aikin, John, comp. *Digest of the Laws of Alabama*. Philadelphia: Alexander Tower, 1833

Amis, M. N., comp. *The North Carolina Criminal Code and Digest*. Raleigh: Edwards, Broughton, 1886.

Ball, William McK., Samuel C. Roane, and Albert Pike, comps. *Revised Statutes of the State of Arkansas*. Boston: Weeks, Jordan, 1838.

Brevard, Joseph, comp. *An Alphabetical Digest of the Public Statute Law of South Carolina*. 2 vols. Charleston: John Hoff, 1810.

Browne, William Hand, Clayton Colman Hall, and Bernard Christian Steiner, eds. *Archives of Maryland*. 72 vols. Baltimore: Maryland Historical Society, 1883–1908.

Bullitt, J. F., and John Feland, comps. *The General Statutes of Kentucky*. Frankfort: Major, Johnston and Barrett, 1881.

Bullock, Edward I., James M. Nesbit, and George W. Craddock, comps. *The General Statutes of the Commonwealth of Kentucky*. Frankfort: S. I. M. Major, 1873.

Bush, Allen H., comp. *A Digest of the Statute Law of Florida*. Tallahassee: Charles H. Walton, 1872.

Bush, Bernard, comp. *New Jersey Archives*. 3d ser., vol. 2. *Laws of the Royal Colony of New Jersey, 1703–1745*. Trenton: New Jersey State Library, 1977.

Campbell, J. A. P., comp. *The Revised Code of the Statute Laws of the State of Mississippi*. Jackson: J. L. Power, 1880.

Campbell, J. A. P., Amos R. Johnston, and Amos Lovering, comps. *The Revised Code of the Statute Laws of the State of Mississippi*. Jackson: Alcorn and Fisher, 1871.

Candler, Allen D., et al., eds. *The Colonial Records of the State of Georgia*. 28 vols. Atlanta: Franklin Printing and Publishing, 1904–19.

Caruthers, R. L., and A. O. P. Nicholson, comps., *A Compilation of the Statutes of Tennessee*. Nashville: J. G. Shepard, 1836.

Catterall, Helen T., ed. *Judicial Cases Concerning American Slavery and the Negro*. 5 vols. Washington: Carnegie Institute, 1924–26.

Chapters of the Digest Approved by the General Assembly of the State of Arkansas, November 17, 1868. Little Rock: Price and Barton, 1869.

Clark, George, comp. *The Criminal Laws of Texas*. Waco: W. C. Watkins, 1881.

Clark, R. H., T. R. R. Cobb, and D. Irwin, comps. *The Code of the State of Georgia*. Atlanta: John H. Seals, 1861. Atlanta: Franklin Steam, 1867. 2d rev. ed., Macon: J. W. Burke, 1873.

———. *The Code of the State of Georgia*. Atlanta: Franklin Steam Printing House, 1867.

Clark, Walter, ed. *The State Records of North Carolina*. 16 vols. Winston and Goldsboro: State of North Carolina, 1895–1906.

Clay, C. C., comp. *Digest of the Laws of the State of Alabama*. Tuscaloosa: Marmaduke J. Slade, 1843.

Cobb, Howell, comp. *A Compilation of the Penal Code of the State of Georgia*. Macon: Joseph M. Boardman, 1850.

Cooper, Thomas A., and David J. McCord, eds. *The Statutes at Large of South Carolina.* 10 vols. Columbia: A. S. Johnson, 1836–1841.

Corbin, D. T., comp. *The Revised Statutes of the State of South Carolina.* Columbia: Republican Printing, 1873.

Dallam, James Wilmer, comp. *Digest of the Laws of Texas.* Baltimore: John D. Toy, 1845.

Denny, A. F., comp. *The General Statutes of the State of Missouri.* Jefferson: Emory S. Foster, 1866.

English, E. H., comp. *A Digest of the Statutes of Arkansas.* Little Rock: Reardon and Garritt, 1848.

Ferris, J. W., B. H. Bassett, S. A. Wilson, George Clark, and C. S. West, comps. *The Revised Statutes of Texas.* Galveston: A. H. Belo, 1879.

Gantt, Edward W., comp. *A Digest of the Statutes of Arkansas.* Little Rock: Little Rock Printing, 1874.

Gould, Josiah, comp. *A Digest of the Statutes of Arkansas.* Little Rock: Johnson and Yerkes, 1858.

Hardin, Charles H., comp. *The Revised Statutes of the State of Missouri.* 2 vols. Jefferson City: James Lusk, 1856.

Harris, John W., O. C. Hartley, and James Willie, comps. *Penal Code of the State of Texas.* Galveston: News Office, 1857.

Hartley, Oliver C., comp. *A Digest of the Laws of Texas.* Philadelphia: Thomas Cowperthwait, 1850.

Hening, William W., ed. *The Statutes at Large, Being a Collection of All the Laws of Virginia.* 13 vols. Richmond: Samuel Pleasants, 1809–23.

Herty, Thomas, comp. *A Digest of Laws of Maryland, 1798–1803.* 2 vols. Washington: O'Reilly, 1804.

Hockaday, John A., Thomas H. Parrish, Benjamin F. McDaniel, and Daniel H. McIntyre, comps. *The Revised Statutes of the State of Missouri.* 2 vols. Jefferson City: Carter and Regan, State Printers and Binders, 1879.

Hotchkiss, William A., comp. *A Codification of the Statute Law of Georgia.* 2d ed. Augusta: Charles E. Grenville, 1848.

Howard, V. E., and A. Hutchinson, comps. *Statutes of the State of Mississippi.* New Orleans: E. Johns, 1840.

Irwin, David, George N. Lester, and W. B. Hill, comps. *The Code of the State of Georgia.* 2d ed. Macon: J. W. Burke, 1873.

James, Benjamin, comp. *A Digest of the Laws of South Carolina.* Columbia: D. & J. J. Faust, 1822.

Johnson, M. C., James Harlan, and J. W. Stevenson, comps. *Code of Practice in Civil and Criminal Cases for the State of Kentucky.* Frankfort: A. G. Hodges, 1854.

Journal of the House of Delegates of the State of Virginia, 1852 Session. Richmond: William F. Ritchie, 1852.

Journal of the House of Delegates of the State of Virginia, for the Session of 1861–62. Richmond: William F. Ritchie, Public Printer, 1862.

Keyes, Wade, Fern M. Wood, and John Roquemore, comps. *The Code of Alabama.* Montgomery: Barrett and Brown, 1877.

King, A. A., comp. *The Revised Statutes of the State of Missouri.* St. Louis: Argus, 1835.

Leigh, B. W., comp. *The Revised Code of the Laws of Virginia*. 2 vols. Richmond: Thomas Ritchie, 1819.

Littell, William, comp. *Statute Law of the State of Kentucky*. Frankfort: Johnston and Pleasants, 1810.

——. *Statute Law of the State of Kentucky*. Frankfort: Kendall and Russell, 1819.

Major, Samuel C., Norton B. Anderson, Francis L. Marchand, et al., comps. *The Revised Statutes of the State of Missouri*. Jefferson City: Tribune Printing, 1889.

Marbury, Horatio, and W. H. Crawford, comps. *Digest of the Laws of Georgia*. Savannah: Seymour, Woolhapter, Stebbins, 1802.

Matthews, James M., comp. *Digest of the Laws of Virginia of a Criminal Nature*. Richmond: West and Johnson, 1861. 2d ed., Richmond: J. W. Randolph and English, 1871.

Mayer, Lewis, Louis C. Fisher, and E. J. D. Cross, comps. *Revised Code of the Public General Laws of the State of Maryland*. Baltimore: John Murphy, 1879.

McClellan, James F., comp. *A Digest of the Laws of the State of Florida, 1822–1881*. Tallahassee: Floridian Book and Job, 1881.

McIlwaine, H. R., ed. *Journals of the Council of the State of Virginia*. 5 vols. Richmond: Division of Purchase and Printing, 1931–52.

——. *Legislative Journals of the Council of Colonial Virginia*. 3 vols. Richmond: Colonial Press, Everett Waddey, 1918–19.

——. *Minutes of the Council and General Court of Colonial Virginia*. 2d ed. Richmond: Virginia State Library, 1979.

McIlwaine, H. R., et al., eds. *Executive Journals of the Council of Colonial Virginia*. 6 vols. Richmond: Virginia State Library, 1925–66.

Meigs, Return J., and William F. Cooper, comps. *The Code of Tennessee*. Nashville: E. G. Eastman, 1858.

Milliken, W. A., and John J. Vertrees, comps. *The Code of Tennessee, Being a Compilation of the Statute Laws of the State of Tennessee*. Nashville: Marshall and Bruce, 1884.

Mitchell, James T., and Henry Flanders, Commissioners. *The Statues at Large of Pennsylvania from 1682 to 1801, Compiled under the Authority of the Act of May 19, 1887*. [Harrisburg:] C. M. Busch, State Printer of Pennsylvania, 1896–1915.

Moore, Bartholomew, and Asa Biggs, comps. *Revised Code of North Carolina*. Boston: Little, Brown, 1855.

Munford, George W., comp. *The Code of Virginia*. 3d ed. Richmond: James E. Goode, 1873.

Nash, Frederick, James Iredell, and William H. Battle, comps. The *Revised Statutes of the State of North Carolina*. 2 vols. Raleigh: Turner and Hughes, 1837.

Oldham, Williamson S., and George W. White, comps. *A Digest of the General Statute Laws of the State of Texas*. Austin: John Marshall, 1859.

Ormond, John J., Arthur P. Bagby, George Goldthwaite, and Henry C. Semple, comps. *The Code of Alabama*. Montgomery: Brittan and DeWolf, 1852.

Paschal, George W., comp. *A Digest of the Laws of Texas*. Washington: W. H. and O. H. Morrison, 1866, 1870, 1873.

Patton, John M., and Conway Robinson, comps. *Code of Virginia*. Richmond: W. F. Ritchie, 1849.

Peirce, Levi, Miles Taylor, and William W. King, comps. *The Consolidation and Revision of the Statutes of the State of Louisiana*. New Orleans: Bee Office, 1852.

Pemberton, Samuel J., and Thomas J. Jerome, comps. *The North Carolina Criminal Code and Digest*. Raleigh: Edwards and Broughton, 1892.

Petigru, James L., comp. *Portion of the Code of Statute Law of South Carolina*. Charleston: Evans and Cogswell, 1860–62.

Phillips, U. B., comp. *The Revised Statutes of Louisiana*. New Orleans: John Claiborne, 1856.

Poindexter, George, comp. *Revised Code of the Laws of Mississippi*. Natchez: Francis Baker, 1824.

Prince, Oliver H., comp. *A Digest of the Laws of the State of Georgia*. Milledgeville: Grantland and Orme, 1822. Athens: Published by the Author, 1837.

Quarles, James M., comp. *Criminal Code of Tennessee and Digest of Criminal Cases*. Nashville: Tavel, Eastman and Howell, 1874.

Revised Statute Laws of the State of Louisiana. New Orleans: Republican Office, 1870.

Rice, B. F., John N. Sarber, M. L. Rice, John Whytock, and N. W. Cox, comps. *Code of Practice in Civil and Criminal Cases for the State of Arkansas*. Little Rock: John G. Price, 1869.

Robinson, M. M., comp. *Digest of the Penal Law of the State of Louisiana*. New Orleans: M. M. Robinson, 1841.

Seay, William A., and John S. Young, comps. *The Revised Statutes of the State of Louisiana*. Baton Rouge: Leon Jastremski, 1886.

Scott, William, William B. Napton, James W. Morrow, and William C. Jones, comps. *Revised Statutes of the State of Missouri*. St. Louis: J. W. Dougherty, 1844–45.

Sharkey, William L., William L. Harris, and Henry T. Ellett, comps. *Revised Code of the Statute Laws of the State of Mississippi*. Jackson: E. Barksdale, 1857.

Shepherd, Samuel, ed. *The Statutes at Large for Virginia from October Session 1792, to December Session 1806, Inclusive*. 3 vols. 1835–36. Reprint, New York: AMS, 1970.

Stanton, Richard H., comp. *The Revised Statutes of Kentucky*. 2 vols. Cincinnati: Robert Clarke, 1860, 1867.

Stone, George W., and J. W. Shepherd, comps. *The Penal Code of Alabama*. Montgomery: Reid and Screws, 1866.

Stroud, George M. *A Sketch of Laws Relating to Slavery in the Several States of the United States of America*. Philadelphia: H. Longstreth, 1856. Reprint, New York: Negro Universities Press, 1968.

Tate, Joseph, comp. *Digest of the Laws of Virginia*. Richmond: Shepherd & Pollard, 1823.

———. *Digest of the Laws of Virginia*. Richmond: Smith and Palmer, 1841.

Taylor, John L., comp. *Revisal of the Laws of North Carolina, 1821–25*. Raleigh: J. Gales and Son, 1827.

Thompson, Leslie A., comp. *A Manual or Digest of the Statute Law of the State of Florida*. Boston: Charles C. Little and James Brown, 1847.

Thompson, R. H., George G. Dillard, and R. B. Campbell, comps. *The Annotated Code of the General Statute Laws of the State of Mississippi*. Nashville: Marshall and Bruce, 1892.

Thompson, Seymour D., and Thomas M. Steger, comps. *A Compilation of the Statute Laws of the State of Tennessee*. 2 vols. St. Louis: W. J. Gilbert, 1873.

Toulmin, Harry, comp. *Digest of the Laws of the State of Alabama*. Cahawba: Ginn and Curtis, 1823.

U.S. Bureau of the Census. Federal censuses.

U.S. Congress. House Executive Document 70. Freedmen's Bureau. *Letter from the Secretary of War in Answer to a Resolution of the House of March 8, Transmitting a Report by the Commissioner of the Freedmen's Bureau, of All Orders Issued by Him or Any Assistant Commissioner.* 39th Cong., 1st sess. 1866.

———. *Report of the Joint Committee on Reconstruction.* 39th Cong., 1st sess. 1866.

———. *Report of the Joint Select Committee to Inquire into the Condition of Affairs in the Late Insurrectionary States.* No. 22, 13 vols. 42d Cong., 2d sess. 1872.

U.S. War Department. *The War of the Rebellion: A Compilation of the Official Records of the Union and Confederate Armies.* Washington: Government Printing Office, 1886.

Voorhies, Albert, comp. *The Revised Statute Laws of the State of Louisiana.* New Orleans: B. Bloomfield, 1876.

Wagner, David, comp. *The Statutes of the State of Missouri.* 2 vols. St. Louis: W. J. Gilbert, 1870.

Walker, A. J., comp. *Revised Code of Alabama.* Montgomery, 1867.

Wickliffe, C. A., S. Turner, and S. S. Nicholas, comps. *Revised Statutes of Kentucky.* Frankfort: A. G. Hodges, 1852.

Primary Sources: Published

Allan, Elizabeth Preston. *The Life and Letters of Margaret Junkin Preston.* Boston: Houghton Mifflin, 1903.

Anderson, Lucy London. *North Carolina Women of the Confederacy.* Fayetteville, N.C.: North Carolina Division, United Daughters of the Confederacy, 1926.

Andrews, Eliza Frances. *The War-Time Journal of a Georgia Girl, 1864–1865.* Edited by Spencer Bidwell King Jr. New York: D. Appleton, 1908. Reprint, Macon, Ga.: Ardivan, 1960.

Andrews, Miss E. F. "Grant Allen on the Woman Question." *Popular Science Monthly* 36 (1889–90): 552–53.

Andrews, Sidney. *The South since the War: As Shown by Fourteen Weeks of Travel and Observation in Georgia and the Carolinas.* Boston: Ticknor and Fields, 1866.

Atkinson, Edward. "The Negro a Beast." *North American Review* 181 (1905): 202–15.

Avary, Myrta Lockett. *Dixie after the War.* New York: Doubleday, 1906. Reprint, Boston: Houghton Mifflin, 1937.

Baker, S. C. "Recent Erotic Tendency of the Southern Negro." *Carolina Medical Journal,* March 1900, 89–94.

Bellanger, J. "The Sexual Purity and the Double Standard." *Arena* 2 (1895): 370–77.

Berlin, Ira, et al. *Freedom: A Documentary History of Emancipation, 1861–67.* Ser. 1, vols. 1–2; ser. 2, vol. 2. Cambridge: Cambridge University Press, 1982.

Berlin, Jean V., ed. *A Confederate Nurse: The Diary of Ada W. Bacot, 1860–63.* Women's Diaries and Letters of the Nineteenth-Century South. Columbia: University of South Carolina Press, 1994.

Bittinger, J. B. "Crimes of Passion and Crimes of Reflection." *Princeton Review,* n.s. 2 (April 1873): 219–40.

Blassingame, John, ed. *Slave Testimony: Two Centuries of Letters, Speeches, Interviews, and Autobiographies*. Baton Rouge: Louisiana State University Press, 1977.

Bleckley, L. E. "Negro Outrage No Excuse for Lynching." *Forum* 16 (November 1893): 300–302.

Boggs, Marion Alexander. *The Alexander Letters, 1787–1900*. Savannah: Privately printed for George J. Baldwin, 1910.

Boney, F. N., ed. *A Union Soldier in the Land of the Vanquished: The Diary of Sergeant Mathew Woodruff, June–December, 1865*. University: University of Alabama Press, 1969.

Botkin, B. A., ed. *Lay My Burden Down: A Folk History of Slavery*. Chicago: University of Chicago Press, 1945.

Boughton, Willis. "The Negro's Place in History." *Arena* 16 (1896): 612–21.

Brann, William C. *Brann, the Iconoclast: A Collection of the Writings of W. C. Brann in Two Volumes*. New York: Brann, 1898.

Brickell, John. *The Natural History of North Carolina*. Dublin, 1737. Reprint, Murfreesboro, N.C.: Johnson, 1968.

Broden, George. "Ku Klux Klan: An Apology." *Southern Bivouac* 4 (1885): 103–9.

Bruce, Philip Alexander. "The Negro Population of the South." *Conservative Review* 2 (1899): 262–80.

——. *The Plantation Negro as a Freeman: Observations on His Character, Condition, and Prospects in Virginia*. New York: Putnam's, 1889. Reprint, Williamstown, Mass.: Corner House, 1970.

Bruce, W. Cabell. "Lynch Law in the South." *North America Review* 155 (1892): 379–81.

Burr, Virginia Ingraham, ed. *The Secret Eye: The Journal of Ella Gertrude Clanton Thomas, 1848–1889*. Chapel Hill: University of North Carolina Press, 1990.

Cable, George Washington. *The Silent South*. New York: Charles Scribner's Sons, 1889. Reprint, Montclair, N.J.: Patterson Smith, 1969.

Campbell, Robert Bond. *The Status of Women under the Laws of the State of Mississippi*. 1891.

"Can Pregnancy Follow Defloration in Rape, When Force Simply Is Used?" *American Journal of the Medical Sciences* 45 (January 1863): 272.

"Capital Punishment." *Southern Quarterly Review* 4 (1843): 81–97.

Carroll, Charles. *"The Negro a Beast," or "In the Image of God . . ."* St. Louis, 1900. Reprint, Miami: Mnemosyne, 1969.

Cartwright, Samuel A. "Negro Freedom an Impossibility under Nature's Laws." *DeBow's Review* 30 (May–June 1861): 648–59.

Childs, Arney Robinson, ed. *The Private Journal of Henry William Ravenal, 1859–1887*. Columbia: University of South Carolina Press, 1947.

"Chloroform in Rape Cases." *Central Law Journal* 1 (November 27, 1874): 592.

Clagett, Sue Harry. "Miscegenation." *Nation* 40 (1885): 139.

Clift, G. Glenn, ed. *The Private War of Lizzie Hardin: A Kentucky Confederate Girl's Diary of the Civil War in Kentucky, Virginia, Tennessee, Alabama, and Georgia*. Frankfort: Kentucky Historical Society, 1963.

Cobb, Thomas R. R. *An Inquiry into the Law of Negro Slavery in the United States of America to Which Is Prefixed an Historical Sketch of Slavery*. 1858. Reprint, New York: Negro Universities Press, 1968.

Coffin, Joshua, ed. *An Account of the Principal Slave Insurrections.* [1822–60.] In *Slave Insurrections, Selected Documents.* Westport, Conn.: Negro Universities Press, 1970.

Coleman, Kenneth, and Milton Ready, eds. *The Colonial Records of the State of Georgia: Original Papers, Correspondence to the Trustees, James Oglethorpe, and Others, 1732–1735.* Athens: University of Georgia Press, in cooperation with the Georgia Commission for the National Bicentennial Celebration and the Georgia Department of Archives and History, 1982.

Coxe, Elizabeth Allen. *Memories of a South Carolina Plantation during the War.* 1912.

Crabtree, Beth G., and James W. Patton, eds. *The Journal of a Secesh Lady: The Diary of Catherine Ann Devereux Edmondston.* Raleigh: North Carolina Division of Archives and History, 1979.

[Croly, David, and George Wakeman.] *Miscegenation: The Theory of the Blending of the Races Applied to the American White Man and Negro.* New York: H. Dexter, Hamilton, 1863. Reprint, Upper Saddle River, N.J.: Literature House, 1970.

Crowsom, E. T. *Life as Revealed through Early American Court Records . . .* Easley, S.C.: Southern Historical Press, 1981.

Crump, F. O. "Seduction." *County Courts Chronicle* 21 (May 1, 1868): 121–22.

Davis, Adwan Adams. *Plantation Life in the Florida Parishes of Louisiana, 1836–1846, as Reflected in the Diary of Bennett H. Barrow.* New York: Columbia University Press, 1943.

Dawson, Marion L. "The South and the Negro." *North American Review* 172 (February 1901): 279–84.

Dawson, Sarah Morgan. *A Confederate Girl's Diary.* Edited by James I. Robertson. Bloomington: Indiana University Press, 1960.

Defense of Southern Slavery and Other Pamphlets. Reprint, New York: Negro Universities Press, 1969.

DeForest, John William. *A Union Officer in the Reconstruction.* Edited by James H. Croushore and David M. Potter. New Haven: Yale University Press, 1948.

Dennett, John Richard. *The South as It Is, 1865–1866.* Edited by Henry M. Christman. New York: Viking, 1965.

Dixon, Thomas, Jr. *The Clansman: An Historical Romance of the Ku Klux Klan.* New York: Grosset and Dunlap, 1905.

——. *The Leopard's Spots: A Romance of the White Man's Burden, 1865–1900.* New York: Doubleday, Page, 1902. Reprint, Ridgewood, N.J.: Gregg, 1967.

Douglass, Frederick. "Why Is the Negro Lynched?" Bridgewater, England: John Whitby and Sons, 1895. Reprinted in *The Life and Writings of Frederick Douglass,* edited by Philip S. Foner, vol. 4. New York: International, 1955.

Elliot, E. N., ed. *Cotton Is King and Pro-Slavery Arguments.* Augusta, Ga.: Pritchard, Abbott and Loomis, 1860.

Escott, Paul D., ed. *Slavery Remembered: A Record of Twentieth-Century Slave Narratives.* Chapel Hill: University of North Carolina Press, 1979.

Espy, M. Watt, and John Ortiz Smykla, comps. *Executions in the United States, 1608–1991: The Espy File.* Computer file, University of Alabama. 3d ed., Ann Arbor: Inter-university Consortium for Political and Social Research, 1994.

"Experiences of the Race Problem." *Independent* 56 (1904): 590–94.

Fleming, Walter L. *Documentary History of Reconstruction in Alabama: Political, Military,*

Social, Religious, Education and Industrial, 1865 to 1906. 2 vols. Cleveland: Arthur H. Clark Co., 1906–7. Reprint, New York: McGraw Hill, 1966.

Foner, Philip S., ed. *The Life and Writings of Frederick Douglass.* 4 vols. New York: International Publishers, 1955.

Ford, Worthington Chauncey, ed. *War Letters, 1862–65, of John Chipman Gray and John Codman Ropes.* Cambridge, Mass.: Riverside Press for the Massachusetts Historical Society, 1927.

Gay, Mary Ann Harris. *Life in Dixie during the War.* Atlanta: Charles P. Byrd, 1897.

Gayarre, Charles. "The Southern Question." *North American Review* 125 (1877): 472–98.

Gibbes, James G., ed. *Who Burnt Columbia?* Newberry, S.C.: Elbert H. Aull, 1902.

Gilliam, E. W. "The African Problem." *North American Review* 139 (1884): 417–30.

Gilman, Caroline. *Recollections of a Southern Matron.* New York: Harper and Bros., 1838.

Goodell, William. *The American Slave Code in Theory and Practice: Its Distinctive Features Shown by Its Statutes, Judicial Decisions, and Illustrative Facts.* New York: American and Foreign Anti-Slavery Society, 1853. Reprint, New York: Negro Universities Press, 1968.

Grady, Henry. *The Complete Orations and Speeches of Henry W. Grady.* Edited by Edwin DuBois Shurter. Norwood, Mass.: Norwood Press, 1910.

Greene, Jack P., ed. *The Diary of Colonel Landon Carter of Sabine Hall, 1752–1778.* 2 vols. Charlottesville: University Press of Virginia for the Virginia Historical Society, 1965.

Gregorie, Anne King, ed. *Records of the Court of Chancery of South Carolina, 1671–1779.* Washington: American Historical Association, 1950.

Guild, Jane Purcell. *Black Laws of Virginia: A Summary for the Legislative Acts Concerning Negroes from Earliest Times to the Present.* Richmond: Whittet and Shepperson, 1936.

Hale, Sir Matthew. *The History of the Pleas of the Crown.* Edited by George Wilson. London: E. Rider, Little-Britain, 1800.

Halsey, Ashley, ed. *A Yankee Private's Civil War by Robert Hale Strong.* Chicago: Henry Regnery, 1961.

Hampton, Ann Fripp, ed. *A Divided Heart: Letters of Sally Baxter Hampton, 1853–1862.* Spartanburg, S.C.: Reprint Company, 1980.

Harlan, Louis R., ed. *The Booker T. Washington Papers.* Urbana: University of Illinois Press, 1972.

Harris, Mrs. L. H. "A Southern Woman's View" [letter to the editor]. *Independent* 51 (May 18, 1899): 1354–55.

Haygood, Atticus G. "The Black Shadow in the South." *Forum* 41 (October 1893): 167–75.

——. *Our Brother in Black.* Nashville: S. Methodist Publishing House, 1881. Reprint, Freeport, N.Y.: Books for Libraries, 1970.

Hoffer, Peter Charles, and William B. Scott, eds. *Criminal Proceedings in Colonial Virginia: [Records of] Fines, Examination of Criminals, Trials of Slaves, etc., from March 1710 [1711] to [1754].* In *American Legal Records*, vol. 10. Athens: University of Georgia Press for the American Historical Association, 1984.

Hoffman, Frederick L. *Race Traits and Tendencies of the American Negro.* Publications of the American Economic Association. New York: Macmillan, 1896.

Holland, Rupert Sargent, ed. *Letters and Diary of Laura M. Towne, Written from the Sea Islands of South Carolina, 1862–1884.* 1912. Reprint, New York: Negro Universities Press, 1969.

Horsmanden, Daniel. *The New York Conspiracy: A Journal of the Proceedings in the Detection of the Conspiracy Formed by Some White People . . .* New York, 1744. Reprint, New York: Negro Universities Press, 1969.

Howard, William Lee. "The Negro as a Distinct Ethnic Factor." *Medicine* 9 (May 1903): 423–26.

Hummel, Ray O. *More Virginia Broadsides before 1877*. Richmond: Virginia State Library and Archives, 1975.

Jacobs, Harriet A. *Incidents in the Life of a Slave Girl, Written by Herself*. 1861. Annotated ed., edited by Jean Fagan Yellin, Cambridge, Mass.: Harvard University Press, 1987.

Janson, Charles, William. *The Stranger in America, 1793–1806: Containing Observations Made during a Long Residence in That Country, on the Genius, Manners and Customs of the People of the United States . . .* London: J. Cundee, 1807. Reprint, New York: Press of the Pioneers, 1935.

Jervey, Susan R., and Charlotte St. J. Ravenal. *Two Diaries: From Middle St. John's, Berkeley, South Carolina, February–May, 1865. Journals Kept by Miss Susan R. Jervey and Miss Charlotte St. J. Ravenal, at Northampton and Poshee Plantations, and Reminiscences of Mrs. (Waring) Henagan with Two Contemporary Reports from Federal Officials*. St. John's Hunting Club, 1921.

Jones, Katharine M., ed. *Heroines of Dixie: Confederate Women Tell Their Story of the War*. Indianapolis: Bobbs-Merrill, 1955. Reprint, Westport, Conn.: Greenwood, 1973.

Kearney, Belle. *A Slaveholder's Daughter*. New York: Abbey, 1900. Reprint, New York: Negro Universities Press, 1969.

Kemble, Frances Anne. *Journal of a Residence on a Georgian Plantation*. Edited by John A. Scott. New York: Alfred A. Knopf, 1961.

Kidd, Randy, and Jeanne Stinson, comps. *Lost Marriages of Buck County, Virginia; Drawn from a Newly Recovered Marriage Register, 1854–1868 and from Federal Manuscript, Newspapers and Printed Sources*. Athens, Ga.: Iberian Publishers, 1992.

King, Spencer Bidwell, ed. *Ebb Tide, as Seen through the Diary of Josephine Gray Habersham, 1863*. Athens: University of Georgia Press, 1958.

King, Wilma, ed. *A Northern Woman in the Plantation South: Letters of Tryphena Blanche Holder Fox, 1856–1876*. Women's Diaries and Letters of the Nineteenth-Century South. Columbia: University of South Carolina Press, 1993.

LeConte, Emma. *When the World Ended: The Diary of Emma LeConte*. Edited by Earl S. Miers. New York: Oxford University Press, 1957.

LeGrand, Julia. *The Journal of Julia LeGrand, New Orleans 1862–1863*. Edited by Kate Mason Rowland and Mrs. Morris L. Croxall. Richmond: Everett Waddy, 1911.

Leigh, Frances Butler. *Ten Years on a Georgia Plantation since the War*. London: Richard Bentley and Sons, 1883. Reprint, New York: Negro Universities Press, 1969.

Leland, Isabella Middleton, ed. "Middleton Correspondence, 1861–65." *South Carolina Historical Magazine* 65 (January 1964): 33–44; 65 (April 1964): 98–109.

Life and Dying Speech of Arthur, a Negro Man Who Was Executed at Worcester, October 20, 1786, for a Rape Committed on the Body of One Deborah Metcalfe. Boston, 1768. [broadside]

Lovejoy, W. P. "Georgia's Record of Blood." *Independent* 51 (1899): 1297–1300.

Lucy, J. M., et al. *Confederate Women of Arkansas in the Civil War, 1861–65: Memorial*

Reminiscences. Little Rock: H. G. Pugh for the United Confederate Veterans of Arkansas, 1907.

Lumpkin, Katharine DuPre. *The Making of a Southerner*. New York: Alfred A. Knopf, 1947.

MacKintosh, Robert Harley, Jr., ed. *"Dear Martha": The Confederate War Letters of a South Carolina Soldier, Alexander Faulkner Fewell*. Columbia, S.C.: R. L. Bryan, 1976.

Martineau, Harriet. *Society in America*. 3 vols. London: Saunders and Otley, 1837.

McGuire, Hunter, and G. Frank Lydston. "Sexual Crimes among the Southern Negroes, Scientifically Considered: An Open Correspondence." *Virginia Medical Monthly* 20 (May 1893): 105–25.

McHattan, Henry. "The Sexual Status of the Negro, Past and Present." *American Journal of Dermatology and Genito-urinary Disease* 10 (January 1906): 6–9.

McKelway, A. J. "The North Carolina Suffrage Amendment." *Independent* 52 (1900): 1955–57.

Minor, John B. *A Synopsis of the Law of Crimes and Punishments of Virginia*. 2d ed. Richmond: M. W. Hazelwood, 1869.

Moore, John Hammond, ed. *A Plantation Mistress on the Eve of the Civil War: The Diary of Keziah Goodwyn Hopkins Brevard, 1860–1861*. Women's Diaries and Letters of the Nineteenth-Century South. Columbia: University of South Carolina Press, 1993.

Moore, Raymond S., ed. *A Man of Letters in the Nineteenth-Century South: Selected Letters of Paul Hamilton Hayne*. Baton Rouge: Louisiana State University Press, 1982.

Morgan, John T. "Shall Negro Majorities Rule?" *Forum* 6 (1988): 586–99.

"The Negro Problem." *Independent* 54 (1902): 2224–28.

Nottingham, Stratton, comp. *Marriage License Bonds of Westmoreland County, Virginia, 1786 to 1850*. Oranock, Va.: Stratton Nottingham, 1928.

O'Neall, John Belton. *The Negro Law of South Carolina*. Columbia, S.C.: John G. Bowman, 1848.

Owens, William. "Folk-Lore of the Southern Negroes." *Lippincott's Magazine* 20 (1877): 748–55.

Page, Thomas Nelson. "The Lynching of Negroes: Its Cause and Its Prevention." *North American Review* 178 (January 1904): 33–48.

——. *The Negro: The Southerner's Problem*. New York: Charles Scribner's Sons for the Young People's Missionary Movement of the United States and Canada, 1904. Reprint, New York: Johnson Reprint, 1970.

——. *Red Rock: A Chronicle of Reconstruction*. New York: Charles Scribner's Sons, 1898.

Page, Walter Hines. "The Last Hold of the Southern Bully." *Forum* 16 (November 1893): 303–14.

Parks, Willis B. *A Solution to the Negro Problem Psychologically Considered: The Possibilities of the Negro in Symposium*. Atlanta: Franklin, 1904. Reprint, New York: Negro Universities Press, 1969.

Pearson, Elizabeth Ware, ed. *Letters from Port Royal: Written at the Time of the Civil War*. Boston: W. B. Clarke, 1906. Reprint, New York: Arno, 1969.

Pike, James S. *The Prostrate State: South Carolina under Negro Government*. Reprint, New York: Loring and Mussey, 1935.

[Priest, Rev. Josiah.] *Slavery, As It Relates to the Negro or African Race*. Albany, 1843. Reprint, New York: Arno, 1977.

Quarles, Benjamin., ed. *Narrative of the Life of Frederick Douglass, an American Slave, Written by Himself*. 1960. Reprint, Cambridge, Mass.: Harvard University Press, 1988.

Rainwater, Percy L., ed. "The Civil War Letters of Cordelia Scales." *Journal of Mississippi History* 1 (July 1939): 169–81.

Randle, E. H. *Characteristics of the Southern Negro*. New York: Neak, 1910.

Reid, Whitelaw. *After the War: A Southern Tour, May 1, 1865 to May 1, 1866*. Cincinnati: Moore, Wilstach, and Baldwin, 1866.

Rives, Hallie Erminie. *Smoking Flax*. New York, 1897. Reprint, Freeport, N.Y.: Books for Libraries, 1972.

Robertson, James I. *The Diary of Dolly Lunt Burge*. Athens: University of Georgia Press, 1962.

Robertson, Mary D., ed. *Lucy Breckinridge of Grove Hill: The Journal of a Virginia Girl, 1862–1864*. Columbia: University of South Carolina Press, 1994.

Rosengarten, Theodore. *All God's Dangers: The Life of Nate Shaw*. New York: Alfred A. Knopf, 1974.

Ruffin, Edmund. *The Diary of Edmund Ruffin*. 3 vols. Edited by William K. Scarborough. Baton Rouge: Louisiana State University Press, 1972.

Scomp, Henry A. "Can the Race Problem Be Solved?" *Forum* 8 (1889): 365–76.

Shaler, Nathaniel. "The Negro Problem." *Atlantic Monthly* 54 (November 1884): 703.

——. "The Negro since the Civil War." *Popular Science Monthly* 57 (May 1900): 29–39.

Shoup, Francis A. "Uncle Tom's Cabin Forty Years After." *Sewanee Review* 2 (November 1893): 88–104.

Smith, Charles Henry. "Have American Negroes Too Much Liberty?" *Forum* 41 (October 1893): 176–83.

"Some Fresh Suggestions about the New Negro Crime." *Harper's Weekly* 48 (January 23, 1904): 120–21.

Somerville, Henderson N. "Some Co-operating Causes of Negro Lynching." *North American Review* 177 (October 1903): 506–12.

"South Carolina Idea, The." *Nation* 49 (1889): 4–5.

Spencer, Cordelia Phillips. *The Last Ninety Days of the War in North Carolina*. New York: Watchman, 1866.

Stevens, Michael E., ed. *Journals of the House of Representatives, 1787–88. The State Records of South Carolina*. Columbia: University of South Carolina Press for the South Carolina Department of Archives and History, 1981.

Stirling, James, ed. *Letters from the Slave States*. London: John W. Parker and Son, 1857.

Straton, John Roach. "Will Education Solve the Race Problem?" *North American Review* 170 (June 1900): 785–801.

"Studies in the South, X." *Atlantic Monthly* 50 (1882): 750–63.

"Studies in the South, II." *Atlantic Monthly* 49 (1882): 179–95.

Terrell, Mary Church. "Lynching from a Negro's Point of View." *North American Review* 177 (June 1904): 853–68.

Thompson, Maurice. "The Voodoo Prophecy." *Independent* 44 (1892): 1.

Thorne, Jack [pseud.]. *Hanover*. Reprint, New York: Arno, 1969.

Trowbridge, J. T. *The South: A Tour of Its Battlefields and Ruined Cities, a Journey through the Desolated States, and Talks with the People*. Hartford: L. Stebbins, 1866.

Van Evrie, John H. *Negroes and Negro "Slavery": The First an Inferior Race, the Latter Its Normal Condition*. New York: Van Evrie, Horton, 1861.

"Vivid War Experiences at Ripley, Mississippi." *Confederate Veteran* 13 (June 1905): 262–65.

Walker, M. B. "The Law of Rape: Chloroform in Rape Cases." *Monthly Western Jurist* 1 (November 1874): 289–309.

Weisiger, Benjamin B., comp. *Chesterfield County, Virginia: 1850 Census*. Richmond: B. B. Weisiger, 1988.

Wells-Barnett, Ida B. *On Lynchings: Southern Horrors; A Red Record; Mob Rule in New Orleans*. [1892–1900.] Reprint, New York: Arno, 1969.

White, John E. "Prohibition: The New Task and Opportunity of the South." *South Atlantic Quarterly* 7 (1908): 130–42.

Woodward, C. Vann, ed. *Mary Chesnut's Civil War*. New Haven: Yale University Press, 1981.

Secondary Sources

Abbott, Martin. *The Freedmen's Bureau in South Carolina, 1865–1872*. Chapel Hill: University of North Carolina Press, 1967.

Abrams, Ray H. "Copperhead Newspapers and the Negro." *Journal of Negro History* 20 (April 1935): 131–52.

Alderson, William T., Jr. "The Freedmen's Bureau in Virginia." Master's thesis, Vanderbilt University, 1951.

Alexander, Adele Logan. *Ambiguous Lives: Free Women of Color in Rural Georgia, 1789–1879*. Fayetteville: University of Arkansas Press, 1991.

Alexander, Ann Field. " 'Like an Evil Wind': The Roanoke Riot of 1893 and the Lynching of Thomas Smith." *Virginia Magazine of History and Biography* 100, no. 2 (April 1992): 173–206.

Alexander, Roberta Sue. *North Carolina Faces the Freedmen: Race Relations during Presidential Reconstruction*. Durham: Duke University Press, 1985.

Ames, Jessie Daniel. *The Changing Character of Lynching: Review of Lynching, 1931–1941*. Atlanta: Commission on Interracial Cooperation, 1942.

Anderson, Eric. *Race and Politics in North Carolina, 1872–1901: The Black Second*. Baton Rouge: Louisiana State University Press, 1981.

Anderson, Eric, and Alfred A. Moss Jr., eds. *The Facts of Reconstruction: Essays in Honor of John Hope Franklin*. Baton Rouge: Louisiana State University Press, 1981.

Aptheker, Bethina, ed. *Lynching and Rape: An Exchange of Views*. New York: American Institute for Marxist Studies, 1977.

Aptheker, Herbert. *American Negro Slave Revolts*. 5th ed. New York: International, 1943.

Ariès, Philippe. *Centuries of Childhood: A Social History of Family Life*. New York: Random House, 1965.

Arnold, Marybeth Hamilton. " 'The Life of a Citizen in the Hands of a Woman': Sexual Assault in New York City, 1790–1820." In *Passion and Power: Sexuality in History*, edited by Kathy Peiss and Christina Simmons, 35–56. Philadelphia: Temple University Press, 1989.

Aron, Stephen. *How the West Was Lost: The Transformation of Kentucky from Daniel Boone to Henry Clay*. Baltimore: Johns Hopkins University Press, 1996.

Avins, Alfred. "Anti-Miscegenation Laws and the Fourteenth Amendment: The Original Intent." *Virginia Law Review* 52 (November 1966): 1224–55.

Ayers, Edward L. *Vengeance and Justice: Crime and Punishment in the Nineteenth-Century American South.* New York: Oxford University Press, 1984.

Bailyn, Bernard. "Politics and Social Structure in Virginia." In *Seventeenth-Century America: Essays in Colonial History*, edited by James Morton Smith, 90–115. Chapel Hill: University of North Carolina Press, 1959. Reprinted in *Colonial America: Essays in Politics and Social Development*, edited by Stanley N. Katz and John M. Murrin, 207–30. New York: Alfred A. Knopf, 1983.

Bardaglio, Peter. " 'An Outrage upon Nature': Incest and the Law in the Nineteenth-Century South." In *In Joy and Sorrow: Women, Family, and Marriage in the Victorian South*, edited by Carol Bleser, 32–51. New York: Oxford University Press, 1988.

——. "Rape and the Law in the Old South: 'Calculated to Excite Indignation in Every Heart.' " *Journal of Southern History* 60 (November 1994): 749–72.

——. *Reconstructing the Household: Families, Sex, and the Law in the Nineteenth-Century South.* Chapel Hill: University of North Carolina Press, 1995.

——. " 'Shamefull Matches': The Regulation of Interracial Sex and Marriage in the South before 1900." In *Sex, Love, Race: Crossing Boundaries in North American History*, edited by Martha Hodes, 112–38. New York: New York University Press, 1999.

Bartlett, Irving H., and C. Glenn Cambor. "The History and Psychodynamics of Southern Womanhood." *Women's Studies* 2 (1974): 9–24.

Bartlett, Irving H., and Richard L. Schoenwald. "The Psychodynamics of Slavery." *Journal of Interdisciplinary History* 4 (1974): 627–33.

Bassett, John Spencer. *Slavery in the State of North Carolina.* Johns Hopkins University Studies in Historical and Political Science, series 17. Baltimore: Johns Hopkins University Press, 1899.

Baughman, Laurence E. *Southern Rape Complex: One Hundred Year Psychosis.* Atlanta: Pendulum, 1966.

Bedau, Hugo Adam, and Michael L. Radelet. "Miscarriages of Justice in Potentially Capital Cases." *Stanford Law Review* 40 (November 1987): 91–172.

Bederman, Gail. " 'Civilization,' the Decline of Middle-Class Manliness, and Ida B. Wells's Antilynching Campaign (1892–1894)." *Radical History Review* 52 (Winter 1992): 5–30.

——. *Manliness and Civilization: A Cultural History of Gender and Race in the United States, 1880–1917.* Chicago: University of Chicago Press, 1995.

Berlin, Ira. "The Revolution in Black Life." In *The American Revolution: Explorations in the History of American Radicalism*, edited by Alfred F. Young, 349–82. DeKalb: Northern Illinois University Press, 1976.

——. *Slaves without Masters: The Free Negro in the Antebellum South.* New York: Oxford University Press, 1981.

Berry, Mary Frances. "Judging Morality: Sexual Behavior and Legal Consequences in the Late Nineteenth-Century South." *Journal of American History* 78 (December 1991): 835–56.

——. *The Pig Farmer's Daughter and Other Tales of American Justice.* New York: Alfred A. Knopf, 1999.

Berry, Mary Frances, and John W. Blassingame. *Long Memory: The Black Experience in America.* New York: Oxford University Press, 1982.

Bienen, Leigh. "Rape I." *Women's Rights Law Reporter* 3 (December 1976): 45–57.

Billings, Warren. "The Cases of Fernando and Elizabeth Key: A Note on the Status of Blacks in Seventeenth-Century Virginia." *William and Mary Quarterly*, 3d ser., 30 (1973): 467–74.

Blair, William A. "Justice versus Law and Order: The Battles over the Reconstruction of Virginia's Minor Judiciary, 1865–1870." *Virginia Magazine of History and Biography* 103 (April 1995): 157–80.

Blassingame, John W. *Black New Orleans, 1860–1880*. Chicago: University of Chicago Press, 1973.

——. "The Planter on the Couch: Earl Thorpe and the Psychodynamics of Slavery." *Journal of Negro History* 60 (1975): 230–31.

——. *The Slave Community: Plantation Life in the Antebellum South*. 2d ed., rev. and enlarged. New York: Oxford University Press, 1979.

Bleser, Carol, ed. *In Joy and Sorrow: Women, Family and Marriage in the Victorian South, 1830–1900*. New York: Oxford University Press, 1991.

——. *Secret and Sacred: The Diaries of James Henry Hammond, a Southern Slaveholder*. New York: Oxford University Press, 1988.

Blight, David W. " 'For Something beyond the Battlefield': Frederick Douglass and the Struggle for the Memory of the Civil War." *Journal of American History* 74 (March 1989): 1156–78.

Block, Mary. " 'An Accusation Easily to Be Made': A History of Rape Law in Nineteenth-Century America." Ph.D. diss., University of Kentucky, 2001.

Block, Sharon. "Coerced Sex in British North America, 1700–1820." Ph.D. diss., Princeton University, 1995.

——. "Coercing Sex within the Bonds of Servitude, 1720–1820." Paper presented to the annual meeting of the American Historical Association, Chicago, January 6, 1995.

——. "Lines of Color, Sex, and Service: Comparative Sexual Coercion in Early America." In *Sex, Love, Race: Crossing Boundaries in North American History*, edited by Martha Hodes, 141–63. New York: New York University Press, 1999.

Bloomfield, Maxwell H. "The Texas Bar in the Nineteenth Century." *Vanderbilt Law Review* 32 (January 1979): 261–76.

Boatwright, Eleanor M. "The Political and Civil Status of Women in Georgia, 1783–1860." *Georgia Historical Quarterly* 25 (December 1941): 301–24.

Bogger, Tommy L. *Free Blacks in Norfolk, Virginia, 1790 to 1860: The Darker Side of Freedom*. Charlottesville: University Press of Virginia, 1997.

Bogue, Jesse Parker, Jr. "Violence and Oppression in North Carolina during Reconstruction, 1865–1873." Ph.D. diss., University of Maryland, 1973.

Boles, John B. *Black Southerners, 1619–1869*. Lexington: University Press of Kentucky, 1983.

Bonner, James C. *Milledgeville, Georgia's Antebellum Capital*. Athens: University of Georgia Press, 1978.

Bordin, Ruth. *Frances Willard: A Biography*. Chapel Hill: University of North Carolina Press, 1986.

Bowers, Claude. *The Tragic Era: The Revolution after Lincoln*. Cambridge, Mass.: Literary Guild of America, 1929. Reprint, Cambridge, Mass.: Houghton Mifflin, 1957.

Bowers, William J. *Executions in America*. Lexington, Mass.: Lexington Books, 1974.

——. *Legal Homicide: Death as Punishment in America, 1864–1982*. Boston: Northeastern

University Press, 1974. Boyett, Gene W. "The Black Experience in the First Decade of Reconstruction in Pope City, Arkansas." *Arkansas Historical Quarterly* 51 (Summer 1992): 119–34.

Bradley, Josephine Boyd, and Kent Anderson Leslie. "White Pain Pollen: An Elite Biracial Daughter's Quandary." In *Sex, Love, Race: Crossing Boundaries in North American History*, edited by Martha Hodes, 213–34. New York: New York University Press, 1999.

Brady, Patrick. "Slavery, Race, and the Criminal Law in Antebellum North Carolina: A Reconsideration of the Thomas Ruffin Court." *North Carolina Central Law Journal* 10 (Spring 1979): 248–60.

Braxton, Bernard. *Women, Sex and Race: A Realistic View of Sexism and Racism*. Washington: Verta, 1973.

Breen, Timothy H. "A Changing Labor Force and Race Relations in Virginia, 1660–1710." *Journal of Social History* 7 (1973): 3–25.

Breen, Timothy H., and Stephen Innes. *"Myne Owne Ground": Race and Freedom on Virginia's Eastern Shore, 1640–1676*. New York: Oxford University Press, 1980.

Brown, Elsa Barkley. "Womanist Consciousness: Maggie Lena Walker and the Independent Order of Saint Luke." *Signs* 14 (Spring 1989): 173–95.

Brown, Kathleen M. *Good Wives, Nasty Wenches, and Anxious Patriarchs: Gender, Race, and Power in Colonial Virginia*. Chapel Hill: University of North Carolina Press, 1996.

Brown, Richard. *Strains of Violence: Historic Studies of American Violence and Vigilantism*. New York: Oxford University Press, 1975.

Brown, Steven. "Sexuality and the Slave Community." *Phylon* 42 (Spring 1981): 1–10.

Brownmiller, Susan. *Against Our Will: Men, Women and Rape*. New York: Simon and Schuster, 1975.

Bruce, Dickson D., Jr. *Violence and Culture in the Antebellum South*. Austin: University of Texas Press, 1979.

Brundage, W. Fitzhugh. *Lynching in the New South: Georgia and Virginia, 1880–1930*. Urbana: University of Illinois Press, 1993.

———, ed. *Under Sentence of Death: Lynching in the New South*. Chapel Hill: University of North Carolina Press, 1997.

Bryant, Jonathan M. " 'We Have No Chance of Justice before the Courts': The Freedmen's Struggle for Power in Greene County, Georgia, 1865 to 1874." In *Georgia in Black and White: Explorations in the Race Relations of a Southern State, 1865 to 1950*, edited by John C. Inscoe, 13–37. Athens: University of Georgia Press, 1994.

Bryant, Keith. "The Role and Status of the Female Yeomanry in the Antebellum South: The Literary View." *Southern Quarterly* 18 (Winter 1980): 73–88.

Buckley, Thomas E. *The Great Catastrophe of My Life: Divorce in the Old Dominion*. Chapel Hill: University of North Carolina Press, 2002.

———. "Unfixing Race: Class, Power, and Identity in an Interracial Family." *Virginia Magazine of History and Biography* 102 (July 1994): 349–80.

Bumiller, Kristen. "Rape as a Legal Symbol: Essay on Sexual Violence and Racism." *University of Miami Law Review* 42 (September 1987): 75–91.

Burnham, Margaret A. "An Impossible Marriage: Slave Law and Family Law." *Law and Inequality* 5 (July 1987): 187–225.

Burt, Martha R. "Rape Myths." In *Confronting Rape and Sexual Assault*, edited by Mary E. Odem and Jody Clay-Warner, 129–41. Wilmington, Del.: Scholarly Resources, 1997.

Bynum, Victoria E. "Misshapen Identity: Memory, Folklore, and the Legend of Rachel Knight." In *Sex, Love, Race: Crossing Boundaries in North American History*, edited by Martha Hodes, 237–53. New York: New York University Press, 1999.

——. *Unruly Women: The Politics of Social and Sexual Control in the Old South*. Chapel Hill: University of North Carolina Press, 1992.

——. " 'White Negroes' in Segregated Mississippi: Miscegenation, Racial Identity, and the Law." *Journal of Southern History* 64 (May 1998): 247–76.

Campbell, Randolph B. *An Empire for Slavery: The Peculiar Institution in Texas, 1821–1865*. Baton Rouge: Louisiana State University Press, 1989.

Carby, Hazel V. *Reconstructing Womanhood: The Emergence of the Afro-American Woman Novelist*. New York: Oxford University Press, 1987.

Carpenter, John A. "Atrocities during the Reconstruction Period." *Journal of Negro History* 47 (1962): 234–47.

Carr, Lois Green, and Lorena S. Walsh. "The Planter's Wife: The Experience of White Women in Seventeenth-Century Maryland." *William and Mary Quarterly*, 3d ser., 34 (October 1977): 542–71.

Carter, Dan T. "The Anatomy of Fear." *Journal of Southern History* 42 (August 1976): 345–64.

——. *Scottsboro: A Tragedy of the American South*. rev. ed. Baton Rouge: Louisiana State University Press, 1979.

Cash, W. J. *Mind of the South*. New York: Alfred A. Knopf, 1941. Reprint, New York: Vintage, 1991.

Cashin, Joan. *A Family Venture: Men and Women on the Southern Frontier*. New York: Oxford University Press, 1991.

——. "A Lynching in Wartime Carolina: The Death of Saxe Joiner." In *Under Sentence of Death: Lynching in the South*, edited by W. Fitzhugh Brundage, 109–31. Chapel Hill: University of North Carolina Press, 1997.

——. " 'Since the War Broke Out': The Marriage of Kate and William McClure." In *Divided Houses: Gender and the Civil War*, edited by Catherine Clinton and Nina Silber, 200–212. New York: Oxford University Press, 1992.

Cell, John W. *The Highest State of White Supremacy*. 1982. Reprint, Cambridge: Cambridge University Press, 1989.

Censer, Jane Turner. *North Carolina Planters and Their Children, 1800–1860*. Baton Rouge: Louisiana State University Press, 1984.

——. " 'Smiling through Her Tears': Antebellum Southern Women and Divorce." *American Journal of Legal History* 25 (January 1981): 24–47.

Chafe, William H. *The American Woman: Her Changing Social, Economic, and Political Roles, 1920–1970*. New York: Oxford University Press, 1972.

——. *Women and Equality: Changing Patterns in American Culture*. New York: Oxford University Press, 1977.

Clark, Anna K. *Women's Silence, Men's Violence: Sexual Assault in England, 1770–1845*. New York: Pandora, 1987.

Clark, Cornelia Anne. "Justice on the Tennessee Frontier: The Williamson County Circuit, 1810–1820." *Vanderbilt Law Review* 32 (1979): 413–45.

Clark, Ernest James. "Aspects of the North Carolina Slave Code, 1715–1860." *North Carolina Historical Review* 39 (1962): 148–64.

Cleaver, Eldridge. *Soul on Ice*. New York: McGraw-Hill, 1968.

Clinton, Catherine. "Bloody Terrain: Freedwomen, Sexuality and Violence during Reconstruction." *Georgia Historical Quarterly* 76 (Summer 1992): 313–32.

——. *The Plantation Mistress: Woman's World in the Old South*. New York: Pantheon, 1982.

——. " 'Southern Dishonor': Flesh, Blood, Race and Bondage." In *In Joy and Sorrow: Women, Family, and Marriage in the Victorian South, 1830–1900*, edited by Carol Bleser, 52–68. New York: Oxford University Press, 1991.

——, ed. *Half-Sisters of History: Southern Women and the American Past*. Durham: Duke University Press, 1994.

Clinton, Catherine, and Michele Gillespie, eds. *The Devil's Lane: Sex and Race in the Early South*. New York: Oxford University Press, 1997.

Clinton, Catherine, and Nina Silber, eds. *Divided Houses: Gender and the Civil War*. New York: Oxford University Press, 1992.

Collins, Winfield H. *The Truth about Lynching and the Negro in the South*. New York: Neale, 1918.

Cortner, Richard C. *A "Scottsboro" Case in Mississippi: The Supreme Court and Brown v. Mississippi*. Jackson: University Press of Mississippi, 1986.

Cott, Nancy F. "Eighteenth-Century Family and Social Life Revealed in Massachusetts Divorce Records." *Journal of Social History* 10 (1976): 20–43.

——. *The Grounding of Modern Feminism*. New Haven: Yale University Press, 1987.

——. "Passionlessness: An Interpretation of Victorian Sexual Ideology, 1790–1850." *Signs* 4 (Winter 1978): 219–36.

Coulter, E. Merton. "Slavery and Freedom in Athens, Georgia, 1860–1866." In *Plantation, Town, and County: Essays on the Local History of American Slave Society*. Edited by Elinor Miller and Eugene D. Genovese, 337–64. Urbana: University of Illinois Press, 1974.

——, ed. "Four Slave Trials in Elbert County, Georgia." *Georgia Historical Quarterly* 41 (September 1957): 237–38.

Cox, Oliver C. *Caste, Class and Race: A Study in Social Dynamics*. New York: Doubleday, 1948.

Crabb, Beth. "May 1930: White Man's Justice for a Black Man's Crime." *Journal of Negro History* 75 (Winter–Spring 1990): 29–40.

Crofts, Daniel W. *Old Southampton: Politics and Society in a Virginia County*. Charlottesville: University Press of Virginia, 1992.

Crow, Jeffrey. *The Black Experience in Revolutionary North Carolina*. Raleigh: Division of Archives and History, 1983.

Cunningham, Hugh. "Histories of Childhood." *American Historical Review* 103, no. 4 (October 1998): 1195–1208.

Curtin, Mary Ellen. *Black Prisoners and Their World: Alabama, 1865–1900*. Charlottesville: University Press of Virginia, 2000.

Cutler, James E. *Lynch-Law: An Investigation into the History of Lynching in the United States*. New York: Longmans, Greene, 1905.

Dailey, Jane. *Before Jim Crow: The Politics of Race in Postemancipation Virginia*. Chapel Hill: University of North Carolina, 2000.

———. *Sex and Civil Rights*. New York: Harcourt, forthcoming.

Dargan, Marion. "Crime and the *Virginia Gazette*, 1736–1775." *University of New Mexico Bulletin*, Sociological Series, 2 no. 1 (1934): 1–61.

Davies, Nick. *White Lies: Rape, Murder, and Justice Texas Style*. New York: Pantheon, 1991.

Davis, Allison, Burleigh B. Gardner, and Mary R. Gardner. *Deep South: A Social Anthropological Study of Caste and Class*. Chicago: University of Chicago Press, 1941. Reprint, Los Angeles: University of California for the Center for Afro-American Studies, 1988.

Davis, Angela. "Rape, Racism, and the Myth of the Black Rapist." In *Women, Race and Class*, edited by Angela Davis, 172–201. New York: Vintage, 1983.

Davis, David Brion. "Terror in Mississippi." Review of *Tumult and Silence at Second Creek: An Inquiry into a Civil War Conspiracy*, by Winthrop Jordan. *New York Review of Books* 40, no. 18 (November 4, 1993): 6–11.

Day, Beth. *Sexual Life between Blacks and Whites: The Roots of Racism*. New York: World, 1972.

Dayton, Cornelia Hughes. *Women before the Bar: Gender, Law, and Society in Connecticut, 1710–1790*. Chapel Hill: University of North Carolina Press, 1995.

Degler, Carl N. *Neither Black nor White: Slavery and Race Relations in Brazil and the United States*. New York: Macmillan, 1971.

———. *Place over Time: The Continuity of Southern Distinctiveness*. Baton Rouge: Louisiana State University Press, 1977.

———. "What Ought to Be and What Was: Women's Sexuality in the Nineteenth Century." In *The American Family in Social-Historical Perspective*. 2d ed., edited by Michael Gordon, 403–25. New York: St. Martin's, 1973.

D'Emilio, John, and Estelle B. Freedman. *Intimate Matters: A History of Sexuality in America*. New York: Harper and Row, 1988.

Deutsch, Helene. *The Psychology of Women: A Psychoanalytic Interpretation*. 2 vols. New York: Grunne and Stratton, 1944.

Diner, Hasia R. *Erin's Daughters in America: Irish Immigrant Women in the Nineteenth Century*. Baltimore: Johns Hopkins University Press, 1983.

Dollard, John. *Caste and Class in a Southern Town*. Garden City, N.Y.: Doubleday, 1937.

Donald, David Herbert. *Liberty and Union*. Boston: Little, Brown, 1978.

Donat, Patricia L. N., and John D'Emilio. "A Feminist Redefinition of Rape and Sexual Assault: Historical Foundations and Change." *Journal of Social Issues* 48, no. 1 (1992): 9–22. Reprinted in *Confronting Rape and Sexual Assault*, edited by Mary E. Odem and Jody Clay-Warner, 35–49. Wilmington, Del.: Scholarly Resources, 1997.

Dorr, Lisa Lundquist. " 'Another Negro-Did-It Crime': Black-on-White Rape and Protest in Virginia, 1945–1960." In *Sex without Consent: Rape and Sexual Coercion in America*, edited by Merril D. Smith, 247–64. New York: New York University Press, 2001.

———. "Black-on-White Rape and Retribution in Twentieth-Century Virginia: 'Men, Even Negroes, Must Have Some Protection.' " *Journal of Southern History* 66 (November 2000): 711–48.

———. " 'Messin' White Women': White Women, Black Men, and Rape in Virginia, 1900–1960." Ph.D. diss., University of Virginia, 2002.

——. *White Women, Rape, and the Power of Race in Virginia, 1900–1960*. Chapel Hill: University of North Carolina Press, 2004.

Dorsett, Lyle Wesley. "Slaveholding in Jackson County, Missouri." In *Plantation, Town, and County: Essays on the Local History of American Slave Society*, edited by Elinor Miller and Eugene D. Genovese, 146–60. Urbana: University of Illinois Press, 1974.

Dray, Philip. *At the Hands of Persons Unknown: The Lynching of Black America*. New York: Random House, 2002.

Dubinsky, Karen. *Improper Advances: Rape and Heterosexual Conflict in Ontario, 1880–1929*. Chicago: University of Chicago Press, 1993.

——. "Sex and Shame: Some Thoughts on the Social and Historical Meaning of Rape." *Resources for Feminist Research/Documentation sur la Recherche Féministe* 19 (1990): 81–85.

DuBois, Ellen Carol, and Linda Gordon. "Seeking Ecstasy on the Battlefield: Danger and Pleasure in Nineteenth-Century Feminist Sexual Thought." In *Pleasure and Danger: Exploring Female Sexuality*, edited by Carole S. Vance. Boston: Routledge and Kegan Paul, 1984.

Du Bois, W. E. B. *Black Reconstruction in America: An Essay toward a History of the Part Which Black Folk Played in the Attempt to Reconstruct Democracy in America, 1860–1880*. New York, 1935. Reprint, New York: Russell and Russell, 1963.

Dunlap, Leslie. "The Reform of Rape Law and the Problem of White Men: Age-of-Consent Campaigns in the South, 1885–1910." In *Sex, Love, Race: Crossing Boundaries in North American History*, edited by Martha Hodes, 352–72. New York: New York University Press, 1999.

Dunning, William A. *Reconstruction: Political and Economic, 1865–1877*. New York: Harper and Bros., 1907.

Durr, Virginia Foster. "The Emancipation of Southern, Pure, White Womanhood." *New South* 26 (1971): 46–54.

Durrill, Wayne. *War of Another Kind: A Southern Community in the Great Rebellion*. New York: Oxford University Press, 1990.

Eaton, Clement. *Freedom-of-Thought Struggle in the Old South*. 1940. Reprint, New York: Harper and Row, 1964.

——. "Mob Violence in the Old South." *Mississippi Valley Historical Review* 19 (December 1942): 351–70.

Ebert, Rebecca A. "A Window on the Valley: A Study of the Free Black Community of Winchester and Frederick County, Virginia, 1785–1860." Master's thesis, University of Maryland, 1986.

Eckenrode, Hamilton J. *The Political History of Virginia during Reconstruction*. 1904. Reprint, Gloucester, Mass.: P. Smith, 1966.

Edwards, John. "Slave Justice in Four Middle Georgia Counties." *Georgia Historical Quarterly* 57 (Summer 1973): 265–73.

Edwards, Laura F. "The Disappearance of Susan Daniel and Henderson Cooper: Gender and Narratives of Political Conflict in the Reconstruction-era U.S. South." *Feminist Studies* 22 (1996): 363–86.

——. *Gendered Strife and Confusion: The Political Culture of Reconstruction*. Urbana: University of Illinois Press, 1997.

——. "Law, Domestic Violence, and the Limits of Patriarchal Authority in the Antebellum South." *Journal of Southern History* 65 (November 1999): 733–70.

——. "Sexual Violence, Gender, Reconstruction, and the Extension of Patriarchy in Granville County, North Carolina." *North Carolina Historical Review* 68 (July 1991): 237–60.

Edwards, Susan S. M. "Sex Crimes in the Nineteenth Century." *New Society* 49 (September 13, 1979): 562–63.

Elkins, Stanley M. *Slavery: A Problem in American Institutional and Intellectual Life*. 3d ed., rev. Chicago: University of Chicago Press, 1962.

Ellefson, Ashley. *The County Courts and the Provincial Court in Maryland, 1733–1763*. New York: Garland, 1990.

Eller, Ronald D. *Miners, Millhands, and Mountaineers: Industrialization of the Appalachian South*. Knoxville: University of Tennessee Press, 1982.

Erno, Richard B. "Dominant Images of the Negro in the Antebellum South." Ph.D. diss., University of Minneapolis, 1961.

Escott, Paul D. *Many Excellent People: Power and Privilege in North Carolina, 1850–1900*. Chapel Hill: University of North Carolina Press, 1985.

Estrich, Susan. *Real Rape*. Cambridge, Mass.: Harvard University Press, 1987.

Etherton, Norman. "Natal's Black Rape Scare of the 1870's." *Journal of Southern African Studies* 15, no. 1 (October 1, 1988): 36–53.

Evans, Patricia. "Rape, Race, and Research." In *Blacks and Criminal Justice*, edited by Charles E. Owens and Jimmy Bell, 75–84. Lexington, Mass.: Lexington Books, 1977.

Faust, Drew Gilpin. "'Altars of Sacrifice': Confederate Women and the Narratives of War." *Journal of American History* 76 (March 1990): 1200–1228.

——. "'If I Were Once Released': The Garb of Gender." Paper presented at Rutgers Center for Historical Analysis, Rutgers University, November 30, 1993.

——. *James Henry Hammond and the Old South: A Design for Mastery*. Baton Rouge: Louisiana State University Press, 1982.

——. *Mothers of Invention: Women of the Slaveholding South in the American Civil War*. Chapel Hill: University of North Carolina Press, 1996.

——. *A Sacred Circle: The Dilemma of the Intellectual in the Old South*. Baltimore: Johns Hopkins University Press, 1977.

——. "'Trying to Do a Man's Business': Slavery, Violence and Gender in the American Civil War." *Gender and Theory* 4 (Summer 1992): 197–214.

Fellman, Michael. *Inside War: The Guerilla Conflict in Missouri during the American Civil War*. New York: Oxford University Press, 1989.

Fields, Barbara Jeanne. "Slavery, Race and Ideology in the United States." *New Left Review* 181 (May–June 1990): 95–118.

——. *Slavery and Freedom on the Middle Ground: Maryland during the Nineteenth Century*. New Haven: Yale University Press, 1985.

Finkelhar, David. *Sexually Victimized Children*. New York: Free Press, 1979.

Finkelman, Paul. "Crimes of Love, Misdemeanors of Passion: The Regulation of Race and Sex in the Colonial South." In *The Devil's Lane: Sex and Race in the Early South*, edited by Catherine Clinton and Michele Gillespie, 124–35. New York: Oxford University Press, 1997.

Finnegan, Terence. "'At the Hands of Parties Unknown': Lynching in Mississippi and South Carolina, 1881–1940." Ph.D. diss., University of Illinois, 1993.

Fischer, Kirsten. "'False, Feigned, and Scandalous Words': Sexual Slander and Racial Ideology among Whites in Colonial North Carolina." In *The Devil's Lane: Sex and Race in the Early South*, edited by Catherine Clinton and Michele Gillespie, 139–53. New York: Oxford University Press, 1997.

Fisher, John E. "The Legal Status of Free Blacks in Texas, 1836–1861." *Texas Law Review* 4 (Summer 1977): 342–62.

Flanders, Ralph B. *Plantation Slavery in Georgia*. 1933. Reprint, Cos Cob, Conn.: John E. Edwards, 1967.

Flanigan, Daniel J. "The Criminal Law of Slavery and Freedom, 1800–1868." Ph.D. diss., Rice University, 1973.

——. "Criminal Procedure in Slave Trials in the Antebellum South." *Journal of Southern History* 40 (1974): 537–64.

Fleming, Walter L. *Civil War and Reconstruction in Alabama*. New York: Macmillan, 1905. Reprint, Cleveland: Arthur H. Clark, 1911.

Fliegelman, Jay. *Prodigals and Pilgrims: The American Revolution against Patriarchal Authority, 1750–1800*. New York: Cambridge University Press, 1982.

Fogel, Robert W., and Stanley L. Engerman. *Time on the Cross: The Economics of American Negro Slavery*. Boston: Little, Brown, 1974.

Foner, Eric. *Emancipation and Its Legacy*. Baton Rouge: Louisiana State University Press, 1983.

——. *Reconstruction, 1863–1877: America's Unfinished Revolution*. New York: Harper and Row, 1988.

——. "Slavery, the Civil War, and Reconstruction." In *The New American History*, edited by Eric Foner, 73–92. Philadelphia: Temple University Press, 1990.

Fox, Greer Litton. "'Nice Girl': Social Control of Women through a Value Construct." *Signs* 2 (1977): 805–17.

Fox-Genovese, Elizabeth. *Within the Plantation Household: Black and White Women of the Old South*. Chapel Hill: University of North Carolina Press, 1988.

Fox-Genovese, Elizabeth, and Eugene Genovese. "Yeomen Farmers in a Slaveholders' Democracy." In *Fruits of Merchant Capital, Slavery and Bourgeois Property in the Rise and Expansion of Capitalism*, by Elizabeth Fox-Genovese and Eugene D. Genovese, 249–64. New York: Oxford University Press, 1983.

Frankel, Noralee. *Freedom's Women: Black Women and Families in Civil War Era Mississippi*. Bloomington: Indiana University Press, 1999.

Franklin, John Hope. *The Free Negro in North Carolina, 1790–1860*. Chapel Hill: University of North Carolina Press, 1943. Reprint, New York: Russell and Russell, 1969.

——. *The Militant South, 1800–1861*. Cambridge, Mass.: Belknap, 1956. Franklin, John Hope, and Alfred A. Moss Jr. *From Slavery to Freedom: A History of Negro Americans*. 6th ed. New York: McGraw-Hill, 1988.

Frazier, E. Franklin. *The Negro Family in the United States*. Chicago: University of Chicago Press, 1939.

Fredrickson, George M. *The Arrogance of Race: Historical Perspectives on Slavery, Racism, and Social Inequality*. Middletown, Conn.: Wesleyan University Press, 1988.

——. *The Black Image in the White Mind: The Debate on Afro-American Character and Destiny, 1817–1914*. Middletown, Conn.: Wesleyan University Press, 1971.

——. *The Inner Civil War: Northern Intellectuals and the Crisis of the Union*. New York: Harper and Row, 1965.

——. *White Supremacy: A Comparative Study in American and South African History*. New York: Oxford University Press, 1981.

Freedman, Estelle B. "Sexuality in Nineteenth-Century America: Behavior, Ideology and Politics." *Reviews in American History* 10 (December 1982): 196–215.

Friedman, Jean E. *The Enclosed Garden: Women and Community in the Evangelical South, 1830–1900*. Chapel Hill: University of North Carolina Press, 1985.

Friedman, Lawrence J. *White Savage: Racial Fantasies in the Postbellum South*. Englewood Cliffs, N.J.: Prentice-Hall, 1970.

Friedman, Lawrence M. *Crime and Punishment in American History*. New York: Basic Books, 1993.

——. *A History of American Law*. 2d ed. New York: Oxford University Press, 1989.

——. "The Southern Rape Complex." In *Encyclopedia of Southern History*, edited by David C. Roller and Robert W. Twyman, 1029. Baton Rouge: Louisiana State University Press, 1979.

Gay, Dorothy Ann. "The Tangled Skein of Romanticism and Violence in the Old South: The Southern Response to Abolitionism and Feminism, 1830–1861." Ph.D. diss., University of North Carolina, 1992.

Genovese, Eugene D. *The Political Economy of Slavery: Studies in the Economy and Society of the Slave South*. New York: Pantheon, 1965.

——. *Roll, Jordan, Roll: The World the Slaves Made*. New York: Random House, 1974.

——. *The World the Slaveholders Made: Two Interpretive Essays*. New York: Pantheon, 1969.

Getman, Karen A. "Sexual Control in the Slaveholding South: The Implementation and Maintenance of a Racial Caste System." *Harvard Women's Law Journal* 7 (Spring 1984): 115–52.

Gilmore, Glenda Elizabeth. *Gender and Jim Crow: Women and the Politics of White Supremacy in North Carolina, 1896–1920*. Chapel Hill: University of North Carolina Press, 1996.

Glade, Elizabeth. "Private Lives and Public Myths: The Bagbys of Virginia." Ph.D. diss., University of Colorado, 1996.

Gladwin, Lee A. "Sexual Mores in Colonial Virginia." *Virginia Social Science Journal* 9, no. 2 (November 1974): 21–30.

Glatthaar, Joseph T. *Forged in Battle: Civil War Alliance of Black Soldiers and White Officers*. New York: Free Press, 1990.

Goldfield, David R. "Black Life in Old South Cities." In *Before Freedom Came: African-American Life in the Antebellum South*, edited by Edward D. C. Campbell Jr. and Kym S. Rice, 123–53. Charlottesville: University Press of Virginia, 1991.

——. *Black, White, and Southern: Race Relations and Southern Culture, 1940 to the Present*. Baton Rouge: Louisiana State University Press, 1990.

Goodman, James. *Stories of Scottsboro: The Rape Case That Shocked 1930s America and Revived the Struggle for Equality*. New York: Pantheon, 1994.

Grantham, Dewey. *Southern Progressivism: The Reconciliation of Progress and Tradition*. Knoxville: University of Tennessee Press, 1983.

Greven, Philip. *The Protestant Temperament: Patterns of Childrearing, Religious Experience and the Self in Early America*. New York: Alfred A. Knopf, 1977.

———. *Spare the Child: The Religious Roots of Punishment and the Psychological Impact of Physical Abuse*. New York: Alfred A. Knopf, 1991.

Griffin, Susan. *Rape: The Power of Consciousness*. New York: Harper and Row, 1979.

Gross, Ariela J. *Double Character: Slavery and Mastery in the Antebellum Southern Courtroom*. Princeton: Princeton University Press, 2000.

———. "Litigating Whiteness: Trials of Racial Determination in the Nineteenth-Century South." *Yale Law Journal* 108 (October 1998): 109–88.

———. "Pandora's Box: Slave Character on Trial in the Antebellum Deep South." *Yale Journal of Law and the Humanities* 7 (Summer 1995): 267–316.

Grossberg, Michael. *Governing the Hearth: Law and Family in Nineteenth-Century America*. Chapel Hill: University of North Carolina Press, 1985.

Gunning, Sandra. *Race, Rape, and Lynching: The Red Record of American Literature, 1890–1912*. New York: Oxford University Press, 1996.

Gutman, Herbert. *The Black Family in Slavery and Freedom, 1750–1925*. New York: Vintage, 1976.

Gutman, Herbert, and Richard Sutch. "Victorians All?: The Sexual Mores and Conduct of Slaves and Their Masters." In *Reckoning with Slavery: A Critical Study in the Quantitative History of American Negro Slavery*, edited by Paul David, 134–62. New York: Oxford University Press, 1976.

Hagood, Margaret Jarman. *Mothers of the South: Portraiture of the White Tenant Farm Woman*. 1939. Reprint, Charlottesville: University Press of Virginia, 1996.

Hale, Grace Elizabeth. *Making Whiteness: The Culture of Segregation in the South, 1890–1940*. New York: Pantheon, 1998.

Hall, Jacquelyn Dowd. " 'The Mind That Burns in Each Body': Women, Rape, and Racial Violence." In *Powers of Desire: The Politics of Sexuality*, edited by Ann Snitnow, Christine Stansell, and Sharon Thompson, 328–49. New York: Monthly Review, 1983.

———. *Revolt against Chivalry: Jessie Daniel Ames and the Women's Campaign against Lynching*. New York: Columbia University Press, 1974. Rev. ed. 1993.

Hall, Jacquelyn Dowd, et al. *Like a Family: The Making of a Southern Cotton Mill World*. Chapel Hill: University of North Carolina Press, 1987.

Hall, Kermit L. "Essays on Problems and Prospects in Southern Legal History: The Promises and Perils of Prosopography—Southern Style." *Vanderbilt Law Review* 32 (January 1979): 331–39.

———. *The Magic Mirror: Law in American History*. New York: Oxford University Press, 1989.

Haller, John S., and Robin M. Haller. *The Physician and Sexuality in Victorian America*. Urbana: University of Illinois Press, 1974.

Halsell, Grace. *Black/White Sex*. New York: William Morrow, 1972.

Hareven, Tamara K. "The History of the Family and the Complexity of Social Change." *American Historical Review* 103, no. 4 (October 1998): 95–124.

Harris, Cheryl I. "Whiteness as Property." *Harvard Law Review* 106 (1993): 1707–91.

Harris, J. William. *Plain Folk and Gentry in a Slave Society: White Liberty and Black Slavery in Augusta's Hinterlands*. Middletown, Conn.: Wesleyan University Press, 1985.

Harris, Trudier. *Exorcising Blackness: Historical and Literary Lynching and Burning Rituals.* Bloomington: Indiana University Press, 1984.

Harris, W. Stuart. "Rowdyism, Public Drunkenness and Bloody Encounters in Early Perry County." *Alabama Review* 33, no. 1 (January 1980): 15–24.

Hay, Douglas. "Property, Authority and the Criminal Law." In *Albion's Fatal Tree: Crime and Society in Eighteenth-Century England*, edited by Douglas Hay et al., 17–63. New York: Pantheon, 1975.

Helg, Aline. "Black Men, Racial Stereotyping, and Violence in the U.S. South and Cuba at the Turn of the Century." *Comparative Studies in Society and History* 42 (2000): 576–604.

Henry, Howell M. *The Police Control of the Slave in South Carolina.* 1914. New York: Negro Universities Press, 1968.

Hernton, Calvin C. *Sex and Racism in America.* New York: Grove, 1965.

Hessinger, Rodney. "Problems and Promises: Colonial American Child Rearing and Modernization Theory." *Journal of Family History* 21 (April 1996): 125–43.

Higginbotham, A. Leon, Jr. *In the Matter of Color: Race and the American Legal Process.* New York: Oxford University Press, 1978.

Higginbotham, A. Leon, Jr., and Barbara K. Kopytoff. "Racial Purity and Interracial Sex in the Law of Colonial and Antebellum Virginia." *Georgetown Law Journal* 77 (August 1, 1989): 1967–2027.

Hindus, Michael S. "Black Justice under White Law: Criminal Prosecutions of Blacks in Antebellum South Carolina." *Journal of American History* 63 (December 1976): 575–99.

——. *Prison and Plantation: Crime, Justice, and Authority in Massachusetts and South Carolina, 1767–1878.* Chapel Hill: University of North Carolina Press, 1980.

Hine, Darlene Clark. "Rape and the Inner Lives of Black Women in the Middle West: Preliminary Thoughts on the Culture of Dissemblance." *Signs* 14 (Summer 1989): 912–20.

Hodes, Martha. "Sex across the Color Line: White Women and Black Men in the Nineteenth-Century American South," Ph.D. diss., Princeton University, 1991.

——. "The Sexualization of Reconstruction Politics: White Women and Black Men in the South after the Civil War." *Journal of the History of Sexuality* 3, no. 3 (1993): 402–17.

——. "Wartime Dialogues on Illicit Sex: White Women and Black Men." In *Divided Houses: Gender and the Civil War*, edited by Catherine Clinton and Nina Silber, 230–42. New York: Oxford University Press, 1992.

——. *White Women, Black Men: Illicit Sex in the Nineteenth-Century South.* New Haven: Yale University Press, 1997.

——, ed. *Sex, Love, Race: Crossing Boundaries in North American History.* New York: New York University Press, 1999.

Hoff, Joan. *Law, Gender, and Injustice: A Legal History of U.S. Women.* New York: New York University Press, 1991.

Hoffman, Ronald. "The 'Disaffected' in the Revolutionary South." In *American Revolution: Explorations in the History of American Radicalism*, edited by Alfred F. Young, 273–316. DeKalb: Northern Illinois University Press, 1984.

Hoffman, Ronald, Thad W. Tate, and Peter J. Albert, eds. *An Uncivil War: The Southern Backcountry during the American Revolution.* Charlottesville: University Press of Virginia for the United States Capitol Historical Society, 1985.

Hofstadter, Richard. "Reflections on Violence in the United States." In *American Violence: A Documentary History*, edited by Hofstadter, 3–43. New York: Alfred A. Knopf, 1970.

Hogue, James. "The Battle of Colfax: Paramilitarism and the Advent of Counterrevolution in Louisiana." Paper given at the Southern Historical Association Conference, Atlanta, November 6, 1997.

Holmes, William F. *The White Chief: James Kimble Vardaman*. Baton Rouge: Louisiana State University Press, 1970.

Holt, Bryce R. *The Supreme Court of North Carolina and Slavery*. Durham: Duke University Press, 1927.

Holt, Michael F. *The Political Crisis of the 1850s*. New York: John Wiley and Sons, 1978.

Horton, James Oliver. "Gender Conventions among Antebellum Free Blacks." *Feminist Studies* 12 (Spring 1986): 51–76.

Howington, Arthur F. "Not in the Condition of a Horse or an Ox." *Tennessee Historical Quarterly* 34 (Fall 1975): 249–63.

——. "The Treatment of Slaves and Free Blacks in the State and Local Courts of Tennessee." Ph.D. diss., Vanderbilt University, 1982.

Hudson, Janet G. "Ben Bess and the Dictates of White Supremacy: The Unpardonable Crime?" *Proceedings of the South Carolina Historical Association* (1999): 15–27.

Inscoe, John C., ed. *Georgia in Black and White: Explorations in the Race Relations of a Southern State, 1865–1950*. Athens: University of Georgia Press, 1994.

Inscoe, John C., and Robert C. Kenzer, eds. *Enemies of the Country: New Perspectives on Unionists in the Civil War South*. Athens: University of Georgia Press, 2001.

Inscoe, John C., and Gordon B. McKinney. *The Heart of Confederate Appalachia: Western North Carolina in the Civil War*. Chapel Hill: University of North Carolina Press, 2000.

Ireland, Robert M. *The County Courts in Antebellum Kentucky*. Lexington: University Press of Kentucky, 1972.

——. "Frenzied and Fallen Females: Women and Sexual Dishonor in the Nineteenth-Century United States." *Journal of Women's History* 3 (Winter 1992): 95–117.

——. "The Libertine Must Die: Sexual Dishonor and the Unwritten Law in the Nineteenth-Century United States." *Journal of Social History* 23 (Fall 1989): 27–44.

Isaac, Rhys. "Evangelical Revolt: The Nature of the Baptists' Challenge to the Traditional Order in Virginia, 1765–1775." In *Colonial America: Essays in Politics and Social Development*. 3d ed., edited by Stanley N. Katz and John M. Murrin, 518–40. New York: Alfred A. Knopf, 1983.

——. *The Transformation of Virginia, 1740–1790*. Chapel Hill: University of North Carolina Press, 1982. Reprint, New York: W. W. Norton, 1988.

Jackson, Luther Porter. *Free Negro Labor and Property Holding in Virginia, 1830–1860*. New York: D. Appleton-Century, 1942.

Jennings, Thelma. " 'Us Colored Women Had to Go through a Plenty': Sexual Exploitation of African-American Slave Women." *Journal of Women's History* 1 (Winter 1990): 45–74.

Johnson, Guion Griffis. *Ante-bellum North Carolina: A Social History*. Chapel Hill: University of North Carolina Press, 1937.

Johnson, Kerry. "The Fever Breaks: Virginia Lynchings, 1885–1895." Honors seminar paper, Virginia Commonwealth University, 1980.

Johnson, Michael, and James Roark. *No Chariot Let Down: Charleston's Free People of Color on the Eve of the Civil War*. Chapel Hill: University of North Carolina Press, 1984.

Johnson, Walter. "The Slave Trader, the White Slave, and the Politics of Racial Determination in the 1850s." *Journal of American History* 87 (June 2000): 13–38.

——. *Soul by Soul: Life inside the Antebellum Slave Market*. Cambridge, Mass.: Harvard University Press, 1999.

Johnson, Whittington B. "Free African-American Women in Savannah, 1800–1860: Affluence and Autonomy amid Adversity." *Georgia Historical Quarterly* 76 (Summer 1992): 260–83.

Johnston, James Hugo. *Race Relations in Virginia and Miscegenation in the South, 1776–1860*. Amherst: University of Massachusetts Press, 1970.

Jones, Jacqueline. *Labor of Love, Labor of Sorrow: Black Women, Work, and the Family, from Slavery to the Present*. New York: Basic Books, 1985.

——. "Race, Sex and Self-Evident Truths: The Status of Slave Women during the Era of the American Revolution." In *Half-Sisters of History: Southern Women and the American Past*, edited by Catherine Clinton, 18–35. Durham: Duke University Press, 1994.

Jones, Norrece T., Jr. *Born a Child of Freedom, Yet a Slave: Mechanisms of Control and Strategies of Resistance in Antebellum South Carolina*. Hanover: University Press of New England, 1990.

Jones, Robert B. "Comment: Reason of Slavery: Understanding the Judicial Role in the Peculiar Institution," part 1, *Vanderbilt Law Review* 32 (January 1979): 219–23.

Jordan, Winthrop D. *Tumult and Silence at Second Creek: An Inquiry into a Civil War Conspiracy*. Baton Rouge: Louisiana State University Press, 1993.

——. *White over Black: American Attitudes toward the Negro, 1550–1812*. 1968. Reprint, New York: W. W. Norton, 1977.

Kantrowitz, Stephen. "Ben Tillman and Hendrix McLane, Agrarian Rebels: White Manhood, 'The Farmers,' and the Limits of Southern Populism." *Journal of Southern History* 66 (2000): 497–524.

——. *Ben Tillman and the Reconstruction of White Supremacy*. Chapel Hill: University of North Carolina Press, 2000.

Karcher, Carolyn L. "Rape, Murder and Revenge in *Slavery's Pleasant Homes*: Lydia Maria Child's Anti-Slavery Fiction and the Limits of Genre." *Women's Studies International Forum* 9, no. 4 (1986): 323–32.

Kay, Marvin L. Michael. "The North Carolina Regulation, 1766–1776: A Class Conflict." In *The American Revolution: Explorations in the History of American Radicalism*, edited by Alfred F. Young, 71–123. DeKalb: Northern Illinois University Press, 1976.

Kay, Marvin L. Michael, and Lorin Lee Cary. " 'The Planters Suffer Little or Nothing': North Carolina Compensations for Executed Slaves, 1748–1777." *Science and Society* 40 (Fall 1976): 288–306.

——. *Slavery in North Carolina, 1748–1775*. Chapel Hill: University of North Carolina Press, 1995.

Keller, Morton. *Affairs of State: Public Life in Late Nineteenth-Century America*. Cambridge, Mass.: Belknap, 1977.

Kennedy, Randall. "The Enforcement of Anti-Miscegenation Laws." In *Interracialism:*

Black-White Intermarriage in American History, Literature, and Law, edited by Werner Sollars, 140–62. New York: Oxford University Press, 2000.

Keve, Paul W. *The History of Corrections in Virginia.* Charlottesville: University Press of Virginia, 1986.

King, Deborah. "Multiple Jeopardy Consciousness: The Context of a Black Feminist Ideology." *Signs* 14 (1988): 42–72.

King, Wilma. *Stolen Childhood: Slave Youth in Nineteenth-Century America.* Bloomington: Indiana University Press, 1995.

Klein, Rachel N. "Frontier Planters and the American Revolution." In *An Uncivil War: The Southern Backcountry during the American Revolution,* edited by Ronald Hoffman, Thad W. Tate, and Peter J. Albert, 37–69.

Koehler, Lyle A. *Search for Power: The "Weaker Sex" in Seventeenth-Century New England.* Urbana: University of Illinois Press, 1980.

Kolchin, Peter. *American Slavery, 1619–1877.* New York: Hill and Wang, 1993.

Kousser, J. Morgan. "Revisiting *A Festival of Violence.*" *Historical Methods* 31 (Fall 1998): 171–80.

Kovel, Joel. *White Racism: A Psychohistory.* New York: Columbia University Press, 1984.

Kulikoff, Allan. *Tobacco and Slaves: The Development of Southern Culture in the Chesapeake, 1680–1800.* Chapel Hill: University of North Carolina Press for the Institute of Early American History and Culture, Williamsburg, Virginia, 1986.

Lack, Paul D. "Slavery and Vigilantism in Austin, Texas, 1840–1860." *Southwestern Historical Quarterly* 85, no.1 (1981): 1–20.

Landers, Jane. " 'In Consideration of Her Enormous Crime': Rape and Infanticide in Spanish St. Augustine." In *The Devil's Lane: Sex and Race in the Early South,* edited by Catherine Clinton and Michele Gillespie, 205–17. New York: Oxford University Press, 1997.

Laquer, Thomas. *Making Sex: Body and Gender from the Greeks to Freud.* Cambridge, Mass.: Harvard University Press, 1990.

——. "Orgasm, Generation, and the Politics of Reproductive Biology." *Representations* 14 (1986): 1–41.

Larson, Jane E. " 'Even a Worm Will Turn at Last': Rape Reform in Late Nineteenth-Century America." *Yale Journal of Law and the Humanities* 9 (1997): 1–71.

Lawson, Steven F., David R. Colburn, and Darryl Paulson. "Groveland: Florida's Little Scottsboro." *Florida Historical Quarterly* 65 (July 1986): 1–21.

Lebsock, Suzanne. "Free Black Women and the Question of Matriarchy." *Feminist Studies* 8 (1982): 271–92.

——. *The Free Women of Petersburg: Status and Culture in a Southern Town, 1784–1860.* New York: W. W. Norton, 1984.

Lecaudey, Hélène. "Behind the Mask: Ex-Slave Women and Interracial Sexual Relations." In *Discovering the Women in Slavery: Emancipating Perspectives on the American Past,* edited by Patricia Morton, 260–77. Athens: University of Georgia Press, 1996.

Lee, Harper. *To Kill a Mockingbird.* Philadelphia: J. B. Lippincott, 1960.

Lewis, Jan E. *The Pursuit of Happiness: Family and Values in Jefferson's Virginia.* New York: Cambridge University Press, 1983.

——. "The Republican Wife: Virtue and Seduction in the Early Republic." *William and Mary Quarterly*, 3d ser., 44 (October 1987): 689–721.

Lewis, Jan Ellen, and Peter S. Onuf, eds., *Sally Hemings and Thomas Jefferson: History, Memory, and Civic Culture*. Charlottesville: University Press of Virginia, 1999.

Lindemann, Barbara S. " 'To Ravish and Carnally Know': Rape in Eighteenth-Century Massachusetts." *Signs* 10 (1984): 63–82.

Link, William A. "The Jordan Hatcher Case: Politics and 'A Spirit of Insubordination' in Antebellum Virginia." *Journal of Southern History* 64 (November 1998): 615–48.

Lionnet, Francoise. *Autobiographical Voices: Race, Gender and Portraiture*. Ithaca: Cornell University Press, 1989.

Litwack, Leon. *Been in the Storm So Long: The Aftermath of Slavery*. New York: Alfred A. Knopf, 1979.

——. *Trouble in Mind: Black Southerners in the Age of Jim Crow*. New York: Alfred A. Knopf, 1998.

Lockley, Timothy J. "Crossing the Race Divide: Interracial Sex in Antebellum Savannah." *Slavery and Abolition* 18 (December 1997): 159–73.

——. "Trading Encounters between Non-Elite Whites and African Americans in Savannah, 1790–1860." *Journal of Southern History* 66 (February 2000): 25–48.

Lockridge, Kenneth A. *On the Sources of Patriarchal Rage: The Commonplace Books of William Byrd and Thomas Jefferson and the Gendering of Power in the Eighteenth Century*. New York: New York University Press, 1992.

Logan, Frenise A. *The Negro in North Carolina, 1876–1894*. Chapel Hill: University of North Carolina Press, 1964.

Lowe, Richard. "The Freedmen's Bureau and Local White Leaders in Virginia." *Journal of American History* 80 (December 1993): 989–98.

——. *Republicans and Reconstruction in Virginia*. Charlottesville: University Press of Virginia, 1991.

Luker. Ralph E. *The Social Gospel in Black and White: American Racial Reform, 1885–1912*. Chapel Hill: University of North Carolina Press, 1991.

MacLean, Nancy. *Behind the Mask of Chivalry: The Making of the Second Ku Klux Klan*. New York: Oxford University Press, 1994.

——. "The Leo Frank Case Reconsidered: Gender and Sexual Politics in the Making of Reactionary Populism." *Journal of American History* 78, no. 3 (December 1991): 917–48.

MacKinnon, Catherine A. *Toward a Feminist Theory of the State*. Cambridge, Mass.: Harvard University Press, 1989.

MacPherson, Robert, ed. "Georgia's Slave Trials." *American Journal of Legal History* 4 (1960): 257–84, 364–77.

Mann, Coramae Richey, and Lance H. Selva. "The Sexualization of Racism: The Black as Rapist and White Justice." *Western Journal of Black Studies* 3, no. 3 (1979): 168–77.

Marten, James. *The Children's Civil War*. Chapel Hill: University of North Carolina Press, 1998.

——. "Fatherhood and the Confederacy: Southern Soldiers and Their Children." *Journal of Southern History* 68, no. 2 (May 1997): 269–92.

Martin, Charles H. "The Civil Rights Congress and Southern Black Defendants." *Georgia Historical Quarterly* 71 (Spring 1987): 25–52.

———. "Oklahoma's 'Scottsboro' Affair: The Jess Hollins Rape Case, 1931–1936." *South Atlantic Quarterly* 79 (Spring 1980): 175–88.

Masur, Louis P. *The Rites of Execution: Capital Punishment and the Transformation of American Culture, 1776–1865*. New York: Oxford University Press, 1989.

Matthews, Jean. "Race, Sex and the Dimensions of Liberty in Antebellum America." *Journal of the Early Republic* 6 (Fall 1986): 275–91.

McConnell, John P. *Negroes and Their Treatment in Virginia from 1865 to 1867*. Pulaski, Va.: B. D. Smith and Bros., 1910. Reprint, New York: Negro Universities Press, 1969.

McCurry, Stephanie. "The Two Faces of Republicanism: Gender and Proslavery Politics in Antebellum South Carolina." *Journal of American History* (March 1992): 1245–64.

McElroy, Guy C. *Facing History: The Black Image in American Art, 1710–1940*. San Francisco: Bedford Arts, 1990.

McGovern, James R. *Anatomy of a Lynching: The Killing of Claude Neal*. Baton Rouge: Louisiana State University Press, 1982.

McKelvey, Blake. *American Prisons: A Study in American Social History Prior to 1915*. Montclair, N.J.: Patterson, Smith, 1968.

McLaurin, Melton A. *Celia, a Slave: A True Story of Violence and Retribution in Antebellum Missouri*. Athens: University of Georgia Press, 1991.

McMillen, Neil R. *Dark Journey: Black Mississippians in the Age of Jim Crow*. Urbana: University of Illinois Press, 1989.

McPherson, James M. *Battle Cry of Freedom*. New York: Ballantine, 1988.

Meaders, Daniel E. "South Carolina Fugitives as Viewed through Local Colonial Newspapers." *Journal of Negro History* 60 (1975): 288–319.

Menard, Russell R. "From Servant to Freeholder: Status, Mobility and Property Accumulation in Seventeenth-Century Maryland." In *Colonial America: Essays in Politics and Social Development*. 3d ed., edited by Stanley N. Katz and John M. Murrin, 71–93. New York: Alfred A. Knopf, 1983.

Messner, William F. "Black Violence and White Response: Louisiana, 1862." *Journal of Southern History* 41 (1975): 19–38.

Miller, Elinor, and Eugene D. Miller, eds. *Plantation, Town, and County: Essays on the Local History of American Slave Society*. Urbana: University of Illinois Press, 1974.

Mills, Gary B. "Miscegenation and the Free Negro in Antebellum 'Anglo' Alabama: A Reexamination of Southern Race Relations." *Journal of American History* 68 (June 1981): 16–34.

Milton, George F. "The Material Advancement of the Negro." *Sewanee Review* 3 (1894): 37–47.

Mitchell, Reid. *Civil War Soldiers*. New York: Viking, 1988.

———. *The Vacant Chair: The Northern Soldier Leaves Home*. New York: Oxford University Press, 1993.

Moger, Allen W. *Virginia: Bourbonism to Byrd, 1870–1925*. Charlottesville: University Press of Virginia, 1968.

Moore, Louis. " 'The Elusive Center': Virginia Politics and the General Assembly, 1869–1871." *Virginia Magazine of History and Biography* 103 (April 1995): 207–36.

Morgan, Edmund S. *American Slavery, American Freedom: The Ordeal of Colonial Virginia*. New York: W. W. Norton, 1975.

——. "Slavery and Freedom: The American Paradox." In *Colonial America: Essays in Politics and Social Development*. 3d ed., edited by Stanley N. Katz and John M. Murrin, 572–96. New York: Alfred A. Knopf, 1983.

Morgan, Philip D. "Slave Life in Piedmont Virginia, 1720–1800." In *Colonial Chesapeake Society*, edited by Lois Green Carr, Philip Morgan, and Jean Russo, 433–84. Chapel Hill: University of North Carolina Press for the Institute of Early American History and Culture, Williamsburg, Virginia, 1989.

Morris, Thomas D. "Slaves and the Rules of Evidence in Criminal Trials." *Chicago-Kent Law Review* 68 (1993): 1209–40.

——. *Southern Slavery and the Law, 1619–1860*. Chapel Hill: University of North Carolina Press, 1996.

Morton, Oren F. *A History of Rockbridge County, Virginia*. Baltimore: Regional Publishing, 1973.

Moynihan, Daniel Patrick. *The Negro Family: The Case for Action*. Washington: U.S. Department of Labor, 1965.

Murphy, Edgar Gardner. *Problems of the Present South*. New York: Macmillan, 1904.

Myrdal, Gunnar. *An American Dilemma: The Negro Problem and Modern Democracy*. New York: Harper and Bros., 1944.

Nash, A. E. Keir. "Fairness and Formalism in the Trials of Blacks in the State Supreme Courts of the Old South: The State Supreme Courts of the Old South." *Virginia Law Review* 56 (1970): 64–100.

——. "A More Equitable Past?: Southern Supreme Courts and the Protection of the Antebellum Negro." *North Carolina Law Review* 48 (February 1970): 197–242.

——. "Reason of Slavery: Understanding the Judicial Role in the Peculiar Institution." *Vanderbilt Law Review* 32 (1979): 7–218.

——. "The Texas Supreme Court and Trial Rights of Blacks, 1845–1860." *Journal of American History* 58 (December 1971): 622–42.

National Association for the Advancement of Colored People. *Thirty Years of Lynching in the United States, 1889–1918*. New York: National Association for the Advancement of Colored People, 1919. Reprint, New York: Arno, 1969.

Nemeth, Charles P. "Character Evidence in Rape Trials in Nineteenth-Century New York: Chastity and the Admissibility of Specific Acts." *Women's Rights Law Reporter* 6 (Spring 1980): 214–25.

Nevins, Allan. *The War for the Union: The Improvised War, 1861–1862*. New York: Charles Scribner's Sons, 1959.

Newby, I. A. *Jim Crow's Defense: Anti-Negro Thought in America, 1900–1930*. Baton Rouge: Louisiana State University Press, 1965.

Nieman, Donald G. "Black Political Power and Criminal Justice: Washington County, Texas, 1868–1884." *Journal of Southern History* 55:3 (April 1989): 391–420.

Nolen, Claude H. *The Negro's Image in the South: The Anatomy of White Supremacy*. Lexington: University Press of Kentucky, 1967.

Oakes, James. *The Ruling Race: A History of American Slaveholders*. New York: Alfred A. Knopf, 1982.

Odem, Mary E. *Delinquent Daughters: Protecting and Policing Adolescent Female Sexuality in the United States, 1885–1920*. Chapel Hill: University of North Carolina Press, 1995.

Olds, Madeline Joan. "The Rape Complex in the Postbellum South." D.A. diss., Carnegie-Mellon University, 1989.

Owens, Leslie Howard. *This Species of Property: Slave Life and Culture in the Old South*. New York: Oxford University Press, 1976.

Painter, Nell Irvin. "Of *Lily*, Linda Brent, and Freud: A Non-Exceptionalist Approach to Race, Class, and Gender in the Slave South." *Georgia Historical Quarterly* 76 (Summer 1992): 241–59.

———. " 'Social Equality,' Miscegenation, Labor, and Power." In *The Evolution of Southern Culture*, edited by Numan V. Bartley, 47–67. Athens: University of Georgia Press, 1988.

———. "Soul Murder and Slavery: Toward a Fully Loaded Cost Accounting." In *U.S. History as Women's History: New Feminist Essays*, edited by Linda K. Kerber, Alice Kessler-Harris, and Kathryn Kish Sklar, 125–46. Chapel Hill: University of North Carolina Press, 1995.

———. "What People Just Don't Understand about Academic Fields." *Chronicle of Higher Education*, July 12, 2002, B4, B6.

Parker, Kathleen R. " 'To Protect the Chastity of Children under Sixteen': Statutory Rape Prosecutions in a Midwest County Circuit Court, 1850–1950." *Michigan Historical Review* 20 (1994): 49–79.

Parramore, Thomas C. *Southampton County, Virginia*. Charlottesville: University Press of Virginia, 1978.

Partington, Donald H. "The Incidence of the Death Penalty for Rape in Virginia." *Washington and Lee Law Review* 22 (Spring 1965): 43–75.

Pascoe, Peggy. "Miscegenation Law, Court Cases, and Ideologies of 'Race' in Twentieth-Century America." In *Sex, Love, Race: Crossing Boundaries in North American History*, edited by Martha Hodes, 464–90. New York: New York University Press, 1999.

Patterson, Orlando. *Slavery and Social Death: A Comparative Study*. Cambridge, Mass.: Harvard University Press, 1982.

Peiss, Kathy. " 'Charity Girls' and City Pleasures: Historical Notes on Working-Class Sexuality, 1880–1920." In *Powers of Desire: The Politics of Sexuality*, edited by Ann Snitnow, Christine Stansell, and Sharon Thompson, 74–87. New York: Monthly Review, 1983.

———. *Cheap Amusements: Working Women and Leisure in Turn of the Century New York*. Philadelphia: Temple University Press, 1986.

Peiss, Kathy, and Christina Simmons, eds. *Passion and Power: Sexuality in History*. Philadelphia: Temple University Press, 1989.

Phifer, Edward W. "Slavery in Microcosm: Burke County, North Carolina." In *Plantation, Town, and County: Essays on the Local History of American Slave Society*, edited by Elinor Miller and Eugene D. Genovese, 71–95. Urbana: University of Illinois Press, 1974.

Phillips, Ulrich B. *American Negro Slavery: A Survey of the Supply, Employment and Control of Negro Labor as Determined by the Plantation Regime*. New York: D. Appleton, 1918. Reprint, Baton Rouge: Louisiana State University Press, 1966.

———. "Slave Crime in Virginia." *American Historical Review* 20 (June 1915): 336–40.

Pivar, David J. *Purity Crusade: Sexual Morality and Social Control, 1868–1900*. Westport, Conn.: Greenwood, 1973.

Pleck, Elizabeth. "Feminist Responses to Crimes against Women, 1868–1896." *Signs* 8 (Spring 1983): 451–70.

——. "Rape and the Politics of Race, 1865–1910." Working Paper no. 213. Wellesley: Wellesley College Center for Research on Women, 1990.

Prather, H. Leon. *Resurgent Politics and Educational Progressivism in the New South, North Carolina, 1890–1913*. Rutherford, N.J.: Fairleigh-Dickinson University Press, 1979.

——. *We Have Taken a City: The Wilmington Racial Massacre and Coup of 1898*. Rutherford, N.J.: Fairleigh-Dickinson University Press, 1984.

Pratt, Janette B. "The Demise of the Corroboration Requirement: Its History in Georgia Rape Law." *Emory Law Journal* 26 (1977): 805–39.

Preyer, Kathryn. "Crime, the Criminal Law and Reform in Post-Revolutionary Virginia." *Law and History Review* 1 (1983): 53–85.

Rable, George C. *But There Was No Peace: The Role of Violence in the Politics of Reconstruction*. Athens: University of Georgia Press, 1984.

——. *Civil Wars: Women and the Crisis of Southern Nationalism*. Urbana: University of Illinois Press, 1989.

Raboteau, Albert J. *Slave Religion: The "Invisible Institution" in the Antebellum South*. New York: Oxford University Press, 1978.

Reinders, Robert C. "Slavery in New Orleans in the Decade before the Civil War." In *Plantation, Town, and County: Essays on the Local History of American Slave Society*, edited by Elinor Miller and Eugene D. Genovese, 365–76. Urbana: University of Illinois Press, 1974.

Richardson, Joe M. *The Negro in the Reconstruction of Florida, 1865–1877*. Tallahassee: Florida State University, 1965.

Richter, William L. "Slavery in Baton Rouge, 1820–1860." In *Plantation, Town, and County: Essays on the Local History of American Slave Society*, edited by Elinor Miller and Eugene D. Genovese, 377–96. Urbana: University of Illinois Press, 1974.

Ripley, C. Peter. *Slaves and Freedmen in Civil War Louisiana*. Baton Rouge: Louisiana State University Press, 1976.

Rise, Eric W. *The Martinsville Seven: Race, Rape, and Capital Punishment*. Charlottesville: University Press of Virginia, 1995.

——. "Race, Rape, and Radicalism: The Case of the Martinsville Seven, 1949–1951." *Journal of Southern History* 58 (August 1992): 461–90.

Roark, James, and Michael Johnson. "Strategies of Survival: Free Negro Families and the Problem of Slavery." In *In Joy and Sorrow: Women, Family and Marriage in the Victorian South, 1830–1900*, edited by Carol Bleser, 88–102. New York: Oxford University Press, 1991.

Robertson, Stephen Murray. "Sexuality through the Prism of Age: Modern Culture and Sexual Violence in New York City, 1880–1950." Ph.D. diss., Rutgers University, 1998.

——. "Signs, Marks, and Private Parts: Doctors, Legal Discourses, and Evidence of Rape in the United States, 1823–1930." *Journal of the History of Sexuality* 8 (1988): 345–88.

Rogers, Joel A. *Sex and Race: A History of White, Negro and Indian Miscegenation in the Two Americas*. 1942. 7th ed., New York: Helga M. Rogers, 1980.

Rosen, Hannah. " 'Not That Sort of Women': Race, Gender, and Sexual Violence during the Memphis Riot of 1866." In *Sex, Love, Race: Crossing Boundaries in North American History*, edited by Martha Hodes, 267–93. New York, New York University Press, 1999.

Rosenberg, Charles E. "Sexuality, Class and Role in Nineteenth-Century America." *American Quarterly* 25 (May 1973): 131–53.

Ross, John Raymond. "At the Bar of Judge Lynch: Lynchings and Lynch Mobs in America." Ph.D. diss., Texas Tech University, 1983.

Ross, Kristie. "Arranging a Doll's House: Refined Women as Union Nurses," In *Divided Houses Gender and the Civil War*, edited by Catherine Clinton and Nina Silber, 97–113. New York: Oxford University Press, 1992.

Rothman, Joshua D. "James Callender and Social Knowledge of Interracial Sex in Antebellum Virginia." In *Sally Hemings and Thomas Jefferson: History, Memory, and Civic Culture*, edited by Jan Ellen Lewis and Peter S. Onuf, 87–113. Charlottesville: University Press of Virginia, 1999.

——. *Notorious in the Neighborhood: Sex and Families across the Color Line in Virginia, 1787–1861*. Chapel Hill: University of North Carolina Press, 2003.

Royster, Charles. *The Destructive War: William Tecumseh Sherman, Stonewall Jackson, and the Americans*. New York: Alfred A. Knopf, 1991.

Russell, John H. *The Free Negro in Virginia, 1619–1865*. Baltimore: Johns Hopkins University Press, 1913. Reprint, New York: Dover, 1968.

Russell, Marion. "American Slave Discontent in Records of the High Courts." *Journal of Negro History* 31 (October 1946): 411–34.

Salmon, Emily J., and Edward D. C. Campbell Jr., eds. *The Hornbook of Virginia History: A Ready-Reference Guide to the Old Dominion's People, Places, and Past*. 4th ed. Richmond: Library of Virginia, 1994.

Salmon, John S., and Emily J. Salmon. *Franklin County, Virginia. 1786–1986: A Bicentennial History*. Rocky Mount, Va.: Franklin County Bicentennial Commission, 1993.

Sanday, Peggy Reeves. "The Socio-Cultural Context of Rape: A Cross-Cultural Study." In *Confronting Rape and Sexual Assault*, edited by Mary E. Odem and Jody Clay-Warner. Wilmington, Del.: Scholarly Resources, 1997.

Saunders, Robert M. "Crime and Punishment in Early National America. Richmond, Virginia, 1784–1820." *Virginia Magazine of History and Biography* 86 (1978): 33–44.

Schafer, Judith Kelleher. "The Long Arm of the Law: Slave Criminals and the Supreme Court in Antebellum Louisiana." *Tulane Law Review* 60 (June 1986): 1247–68.

——. "Open and Notorious Concubinage: The Emancipation of Slave Mistresses by Will and the Supreme Court in Antebellum Louisiana." *Louisiana History* 28 (Spring 1987): 165–82.

——. *Slavery, the Civil Law, and the Supreme Court of Louisiana*. Baton Rouge: Louisiana State University Press, 1994.

Schechter, Patricia A. *Ida B. Wells-Barnett and American Reform, 1880–1930*. Chapel Hill: University of North Carolina Press, 2001.

Schulman, Gary I. "Race, Sex and Violence: A Laboratory Test of the Sexual Threat of the Black Male Hypothesis." *American Journal of Sociology* 79 (1974): 1260–77.

Schwarz, Philip J. *Slave Laws in Virginia*. Athens: University of Georgia Press, 1996.

——. "The Transportation of Slaves from Virginia, 1801–1865." *Slavery and Abolition: A Journal of Comparative Studies* 7 (1986): 215–40.

——. *Twice Condemned: Slaves and the Criminal Laws of Virginia, 1705–1865*. Baton Rouge: Louisiana State University Press, 1988.

Scott, Anne Firor. *The Southern Lady: From Pedestal to Politics, 1830–1930*. Chicago: University of Chicago Press, 1970.

Scott, Arthur P. *Criminal Law in Colonial Virginia*. Chicago: University of Chicago Press, 1930.

Scully, Diana, and Joseph Marolla. " 'Riding the Bull at Gilley's': Convicted Rapists Describe the Rewards of Rape." In *Confronting Rape and Sexual Assault*, edited by Mary E. Odem and Jody Clay-Warner, 109–24. Wilmington, Del.: Scholarly Resources, 1997.

Scully, Pamela. "Rape, Race, and Colonial Culture: The Sexual Politics of Identity in the Nineteenth-Century Cape Colony, South Africa." *American Historical Review* 100 (April 1995): 335–59.

Sellers, James B. *Slavery in Alabama*. University: University of Alabama Press, 1950.

Senese, Donald J. "The Free Negro and the South Carolina Courts, 1790–1860." *South Carolina Historical Magazine* 68 (July 1967): 140–53.

Shingleton, Royce G. "The Trial and Punishment of Slaves in Baldwin County, Georgia, 1812–1826." *Southern Humanities Review* 8, no.10 (Winter 1974): 67–73.

Shorter, Edward. "On Writing the History of Rape." *Signs* 3, no. 2 (1977): 471–82.

Silber, Nina. *The Romance of Reunion: Northerners and the South, 1865–1900*. Chapel Hill: University of North Carolina Press, 1993.

Simkins, Francis Butler. "Ben Tillman's View of the Negro." *Journal of Southern History* 3 (May 1937): 161–74.

Simon, Bryant. "The Appeal of Cole Blease of South Carolina: Race, Class, and Sex in the New South." *Journal of Southern History* 62 (1996): 57–86.

Singal, Daniel. *The War Within: From Victorian to Modernist Thought in the South, 1919–1945*. Chapel Hill: University of North Carolina Press, 1982.

Sirmans, M. Eugene. "The Legal Status of the Slave in South Carolina." *Journal of Southern History* 28 (1962): 462–73.

Sizer, Lynn Cullen. "Acting Her Part: Narratives of Union Women Spies." In *Divided Houses Gender and the Civil War*, edited by Catherine Clinton and Nina Silber, 114–33. New York: Oxford University Press, 1992.

Slaughter, Thomas P. *Bloody Dawn: The Christiana Riot and Racial Violence in the Antebellum North*. New York: Oxford University Press, 1991.

Slotkin, Richard. "Narratives of Negro Crime in New England, 1675–1800." *American Quarterly* 25 (1973): 3–31.

Smead, Howard. *Blood Justice: The Lynching of Mack Charles Parker*. New York: Oxford University Press, 1986.

Smith, Cyril J. "History of Rape and Rape Laws." *Women Lawyers' Journal* 60 (September 1974): 189.

Smith, Daniel Blake. *Inside the Great House: Planter Family Life in Eighteenth-Century Chesapeake Society*. Ithaca: Cornell University Press, 1980.

Smith, Douglas. "Virginia during Reconstruction, 1865–1870: A Political, Economic and Social Study." Ph.D. diss., University of Virginia, 1960.

Smith, Lillian. *Killers of the Dream*. 1949. Reprint, New York: W. W. Norton, 1961.

Smith, Merril D., ed. *Sex and Sexuality in Early America*. New York: New York University Press, 1998.

——. *Sex without Consent: Rape and Sexual Coercion in America*. New York: New York University Press, 2001.

Smith-Rosenberg, Carroll. *Disorderly Conduct: Visions of Gender in Victorian America*, 1985.

——. "The Female World of Love and Ritual: Relations between Women in Nineteenth-Century America." *Signs* 1 (1975): 1–29.

Snitnow, Ann, Christine Stansell, and Sharon Thompson, eds. *The Powers of Desire: The Politics of Sexuality*. New York: Monthly Review, 1983.

Sobel, Mechal. *The World They Made Together: Black and White Values in Eighteenth-Century Virginia*. Princeton: Princeton University Press, 1987.

Sommerville, Diane Miller. " 'I Was Very Much Wounded': Rape Law, Children, and the Antebellum South." In *Sex without Consent: Rape and Sexual Coercion in America*, edited by Merril D. Smith, 136–77. New York: New York University Press, 2001.

——. "Rape, Race and Castration in Slave Law in the Colonial and Early South." In *The Devil's Lane: Sex and Race in the Early South*, edited by Catherine Clinton and Michele Gillespie, 74–89. New York: Oxford University Press, 1997.

——. "The Rape Myth in the Old South Reconsidered." *Journal of Southern History* 61 (August 1995): 481–518.

——. "The Rape Myth Reconsidered: The Intersection of Race, Class, and Gender in the American South, 1800–1877." Ph.D. diss., Rutgers University, 1995.

Spellman, Elizabeth. *Inessential Woman: Problems of Exclusion in Feminist Thought*. Boston: Beacon, 1988.

Spindel, Donna. *Crime and Society in North Carolina, 1663–1776*. Baton Rouge: Louisiana State University Press, 1989.

Stampp, Kenneth M. *The Era of Reconstruction, 1865–1877*. New York: Alfred A. Knopf, 1972.

——. *The Peculiar Institution: Slavery in the Ante-Bellum South*. New York: Alfred A. Knopf, 1956.

Stansell, Christine. *City of Women: Sex and Class in New York, 1789–1860*. New York: Alfred A. Knopf, 1986.

Stanton, William. *The Leopard's Spots: Scientific Attitudes toward Race in America, 1815–1859*. Chicago: University of Chicago Press, 1960.

Steinberg, Allen. *The Transformation of Criminal Justice: Philadelphia, 1800–1880*. Chapel Hill: University of North Carolina Press, 1989.

Stember, Charles H. *Sexual Racism: The Emotional Barrier to an Integrated Society*. New York: Elsevier, 1976.

Sterkx, Herbert E. *The Free Negro in Antebellum Louisiana*. Rutherford, N.J.: Fairleigh-Dickinson University Press, 1972.

Stevenson, Brenda. "Distress and Discord in Virginia Slave Families, 1830–1860." In *In Joy and Sorrow: Women, Family and Marriage in the Victorian South, 1830–1900*, edited by Carol Bleser, 103–24. New York: Oxford University Press, 1991.

Stoler, Ann L. "Making Empire Respectable: The Politics of Race and Sexual Morality in Twentieth-Century Colonial Cultures." *American Ethnologist* 16, no. 4 (November 1989): 634–60.

Stowe, Steven. *Intimacy and Power in the Old South: Ritual in the Lives of the Planters*. Baltimore: Johns Hopkins University Press, 1987.

Styron, William. *The Confessions of Nat Turner*. New York: Random House, 1966.

Sumler-Edmond, Janice. "The Quest for Justice: African American Women Litigants, 1867–1890." In *African American Women and the Vote, 1837–1965*, edited by Ann D. Gordon, 100–119. Amherst: University of Massachusetts Press, 1997.

Sutherland, Daniel E., ed. *Guerillas, Unionists, and Violence on the Confederate Home Front*. Fayetteville: University of Arkansas Press, 1999.

Sydnor, Charles S. *Gentlemen Freeholders: Political Practices in Washington's Virginia*. Chapel Hill: University of North Carolina Press, 1952.

Tannenbaum, Frank. *Slave and Citizen: The Negro in the Americas*. New York: Vintage, 1946.

Tate, Thad W., Jr. *Negro in Eighteenth-Century Williamsburg*. Charlottesville: University of Virginia Press, 1972.

Taylor, Alrutheus A. *The Negro in the Reconstruction of Virginia*. Washington, 1926. Reprint, New York: Russell and Russell, 1969.

Taylor, R. H. "Humanizing the Slave Code of North Carolina." *North Carolina Historical Review* 2 (1925): 323–31.

Taylor, Robert A. "Crime and Race Relations in Jacksonville, 1884–1892." *Southern Studies*, new ser., 2 (Spring 1991): 17–37.

Teeters, N. K., and Jack H. Hedblom. *Hang by the Neck: The Legal Use of Scaffold and Noose, Gibbet, Stake, and Firing Squad from Colonial Times to the Present*. Springfield, Ill.: Charles C. Thomas, 1967.

Thornton, J. Mills, III. *Politics and Power in a Slave Society: Alabama, 1800–1860*. Baton Rouge: Louisiana State University Press, 1978.

Thorpe, Earl E. *Eros and Freedom in Southern Life and Thought*. 1967. Reprint, Westport, Conn.: Greenwood, 1979.

——. *The Old South: A Psychohistory*. 1972. Reprint, Westport, Conn.: Greenwood, 1979.

Tindall, George Brown. *The Emergence of the New South*. History of the South Series, vol. 10. Baton Rouge: Louisiana State University Press, 1967.

——. *South Carolina Negroes, 1877–1900*. Columbia: University of South Carolina Press, 1952.

Tolnay, Stewart E., and E. M. Beck. *A Festival of Violence: An Analysis of Southern Lynchings, 1882–1930*. Urbana: University of Illinois Press, 1992.

Tong, Rosemarie. *Women, Sex, and the Law*. Totowa, N.J.: Rowman and Allanheld, 1984.

Tourgee, Albion W. *A Fool's Errand*. New York: Harper and Row, 1961.

Trelease, Allen W. *White Terror: The Ku Klux Klan Conspiracy and Southern Reconstruction*. Westport, Conn.: Greenwood, 1971.

Tushnet, Mark V. "The American Law of Slavery, 1810–1860: A Study in the Persistence of Legal Autonomy." *Law and Society Review* 10 (Fall 1975): 119–84.

——. *The American Law of Slavery, 1810–1860: Considerations of Humanity and Interest*. Princeton: Princeton University Press, 1981.

Viano, E. C. "Rape and the Law in the United States: An Historical and Sociological Analysis." *International Journal of Criminology and Penology* 2 (November 1974): 317–28.

Waldrep, Christopher. *Roots of Disorder: Race and Criminal Justice in the American South, 1817–1880*. Urbana: University of Illinois Press, 1998.

——. "Women, the Civil War, and Legal Culture in Vicksburg, Mississippi." *Journal of Mississippi History* 61 (Summer 1999): 137–47.

Wallace, Michelle. *Black Macho and the Myth of the Superwoman*. New York: Dial, 1979. Reprint, London: Verso, 1990.

Wallenstein, Peter. "Law and the Boundaries of Place and Race in Interracial Marriage: Interstate Comity, Racial Identity and Miscegenation Laws in North Carolina, South Carolina and Virginia., 1860s–1960s." *Akron Law Review* 32 (1999): 557–76.

———. "Race, Marriage, and the Law of Freedom: Alabama and Virginia, 1860s–1960s." *Chicago-Kent Law Review* 70 (1994): 371–437.

———. "Race, Marriage, and the Supreme Court from *Pace v. Ala.* (1883) to *Loving v. Va.*" (1967). *Journal of Supreme Court History* 2 (1998): 65–86.

Walters, Ronald G. "The Erotic South: Civilization and Sexuality in American Abolitionism." *American Quarterly* 25 (May 1973): 177–201.

———. "Sexual Matters as Historical Problems: A Framework of Analysis." *Societas* 6 (Summer 1976): 157–75.

Ware, Lowry. "The Burning of Jerry: The Last Slave Execution by Fire in South Carolina." *South Carolina Magazine* 91, no. 2 (April 1990): 100–106.

Washburn, Wilcomb E. "Law and Authority in Colonial Virginia." In *Law and Authority in Colonial America*, edited by George Athen Bilias. New York: Dover, 1970.

Watson, Alan D. "North Carolina Slave Courts, 1715–1785." *North Carolina Historical Review* 60, no.1 (1983): 24–36.

Watson, Harry L. *Liberty and Power: The Politics of Jacksonian America*. New York: Hill and Wang, 1990.

Wayne, Michael. "An Old South Morality Play: Reconsidering the Social Underpinnings of the Proslavery Ideology." *Journal of American History* 77 (December 1990): 838–63.

Weisberger, Bernard A. "The Dark and Bloody Ground of Reconstruction Historiography." *Journal of Southern History* 25 (1959): 427–47.

Wharton, Vernon Lane. *The Negro in Mississippi, 1865–1890*. Chapel Hill: University of North Carolina Press, 1947.

White, Deborah Gray. *Ar'n't I a Woman?: Female Slaves in the Plantation South*. New York: W. W. Norton, 1985.

———. "Female Slaves: Sex Roles and Status in the Antebellum Plantation South." *Journal of Family History* 8 (1983): 248–61.

———. *Too Heavy a Load: Black Women in Defense of Themselves, 1894–1994*. New York: W. W. Norton, 1999.

White, G. Edward. "The Appellate Opinion as Historical Source Material." *Journal of Interdisciplinary History* 1 (Spring 1971): 491–509.

Whites, LeeAnn. *The Civil War as a Crisis in Gender: Augusta, Georgia, 1869–1890*. Athens: University of Georgia Press, 1995.

———. "Rebecca Latimer Felton and the Wife's Farm: The Class and Racial Politics of Gender Reform." *Georgia Historical Quarterly* 76, no. 2 (Summer 1992): 354–72.

Whitfield, Stephen J. *A Death in the Delta: The Story of Emmett Till*. Baltimore: Johns Hopkins University Press, 1988.

Wiecek, William M. "The Statutory Law of Slavery and Race in the Thirteen Mainland Colonies of British America." *William and Mary Quarterly*, 3d ser., 34, no.2 (1977): 258–80.

Wiencek, Henry. *The Hairstons: An American Family in Black and White*. New York: St. Martin's, 1999.

Wiener, Jonathan M. "The 'Black Beast Rapist': White Racial Attitudes in the Postwar South." *Reviews in American History* 13 (June 1985): 222–26.

Wiethoff, William E. *A Peculiar Humanism: The Judicial Advocacy of Slavery in High Courts of the Old South, 1820–1850*. Athens: University of Georgia Press, 1996.

Wigmore, John Henry. *The Principles of Judicial Proof or the Process of Proof as Given by Logic, Psychology, and General Experience and Illustrated in Judicial Trials*. 1813. 2d ed., Boston: Little, Brown, 1931.

Wiley, Bell Irvin. *The Life of Billy Yank: The Common Soldier of the Union*. Indianapolis: Bobbs-Merrill, 1952.

———. *Southern Negroes, 1861–1865*. New Haven: Yale University Press, 1938.

Williams, Jack Kenny. *Vogues in Villainy: Crime and Retribution in Antebellum South Carolina*. Columbia: University of South Carolina Press, 1959.

Williams, Lou Falkner. *The Great South Carolina Ku Klux Klan Trials, 1871–1872*. Athens: University of Georgia Press, 1996.

Williamson, Joel. *After Slavery: The Negro in South Carolina during Reconstruction, 1861–1877*. Chapel Hill: University of North Carolina Press, 1965.

———. *Crucible of Race: Black-White Relations in the American South since Emancipation*. New York: Oxford University Press, 1984.

———. *New People: Miscegenation and Mulattoes in the United States*. New York: Free Press, 1980.

———. *Rage for Order: Black-White Relations in the American South since Emancipation*. New York: Oxford University Press, 1986.

Wilson, William Julius. "Class Conflict and Jim Crow Segregation in the Postbellum South [1865–1900]." *Pacific Sociological Review* 19 (October 1976): 431–46.

Wolfe, Margaret Ripley. *Daughters of Canaan: A Saga of Southern Women*. Lexington: University Press of Kentucky, 1995.

Wood, Betty. "White Women, Black Slaves and the Law in Early National Georgia: The Sunbury Petition of 1791." *History Journal* 35 (September 1992): 611–22.

Wood, Forrest G. *Black Scare: The Racist Response to Emancipation and Reconstruction*. Berkeley: University of California, 1968.

Wood, Peter H. *Black Majority: Negroes in Colonial South Carolina from 1670 through the Stono Rebellion*. New York: W. W. Norton, 1974.

Woodward, C. Vann. *The Burden of Southern History*. Baton Rouge: Louisiana State University Press, 1960.

———. *Origins of the New South, 1877–1913*. Baton Rouge: Louisiana State University Press, 1951.

Wooster, Ralph. *Politicians, Planters and Plain Folk: Courthouse and Statehouse in the Upper South, 1850–1860*. Knoxville: University of Tennessee Press, 1975.

Wriggins, Jennifer. "Rape, Racism, and the Law." *Harvard Women's Law Journal* 6 (April 1983): 103–41.

Wright, A. *Criminal Activity in the Deep South, 1700–1930: An Annotated Bibliography*. New York: Greenwood, 1989.

Wright, Gavin. *Old South, New South: Revolutions in the Southern Economy since the Civil War*. New York: Basic Books, 1986.

——. *The Political Economy of the Cotton South: Households, Markets and Wealth in the Nineteenth Century*. New York: W. W. Norton, 1978.

Wright, George C. *Racial Violence in Kentucky, 1865–1940: Lynchings, Mob Rule, and "Legal Lynchings."* Baton Rouge: Louisiana State University Press, 1990.

Wyatt-Brown, Bertram. "Community, Class, and Snopesian Crime: Local Justice in the Old South." In *Class, Conflict, and Consensus: Antebellum Southern Community Studies*, edited by Orville Burton and Robert McMath Jr., 173–206. Westport, Conn.: Greenwood, 1982.

——. *Southern Honor: Ethics and Behavior in the Old South*. New York: Oxford University Press, 1982.

Wyne, Charles E. *Race Relations in Virginia, 1870–1902*. Charlottesville: University Press of Virginia, 1961.

Yanuck, Julius. "Thomas Ruffin and North Carolina Slave Law." *Journal of Southern History* 21 (November 1955): 456–75.

Younger, Richard D. "Southern Grand Juries and Slavery." *Journal of Negro History* 40 (April 1955): 166–78.

Zangrando, Robert L. *The NAACP Crusade against Lynching, 1909–1950*. Philadelphia: Temple University Press, 1980.

INDEX

absence of force in rape, 43–44, 46; and evidence of force, 55, 154; in rape appellate cases, 91–93, 112; in statutory rape cases, 43

Fornication, 13, 22–24, 26

Fox-Genovese, Elizabeth, 231

Frankfort, Ky., 194

Franklin, William B. O., 116–17

Franklin County, Va., 60, 137–40, 177, 181

Fraud used in rape, 92–93, 297 (n. 38). *See also* Consent; Force requirement in rape law

Frazar, Douglas, 170–72, 174

Frederick County, Va., 59, 107

Fredericksburg, Va., 66–68

Fredrickson, George, 206, 243–44, 259

Freedmen's Bureau, 148, 161, 165–74, 185, 186, 194; and advocates for blacks, 166; and judicial control, 161, 321 (n. 56); monitoring courts, 171–72, 174; as watchdog, 161, 163, 170, 193

Freedom. *See* Emancipation

Freedpeople, 147–75. *See also* Men—African American; Women—African American

Free people of color: in antebellum society, 300 (n. 7); difficulty in documenting, 299 (n. 2); and labor, 103, 108, 111, 112

—men, 16, 88; accused of rape, 59, 78, 90, 91, 92, 102–14, 118–19; convicted of rape, 304 (n. 37); industrious, 103, 106, 111; supported by whites, 302 (n. 23)

French and Indian War, 75–76

Freud and Freudianism, 12, 226–29, 262 (n. 20)

Fulmer, Sophia, 97–98

Fusionist politics, 243

Gabriel (slave, Wythe County, Va.), 58, 61–63

Garrand County, Ky., 193

Gaston County, N.C., 164, 193, 210

Gayle, John, 91

Gender: bias, 88; constructions of, 88, 119, 125, 132; relations, 11; sympathy, 88, 97, 100, 118, 152, 182, 266 (n. 10)

Genovese, Eugene, 14, 68, 80

George (slave, Halifax County, Va.), 24

George (slave, Henry County, Va.), 51

George (slave, Mississippi), 65–66

George (slave, Prince Edward County, Va.), 28–29, 32–33

Georgia, 39, 52, 61, 66, 76, 123, 149, 163, 164, 187, 190, 195, 196, 197, 201, 208–9, 215

Georgia Supreme Court, 44, 88, 94, 216

Gilliam, E. W., 212

Gilmore, Glenda, 213, 214, 235, 246–47, 252

Givens, Horace, 204

Gloucester County, Va., 19

Goochland County, Va., 78

Gordon, Betty, 66–68

Gordonsville, Va., 208

Gossip, 13, 26

Governors, 85; in antebellum cases, 15, 20, 21, 22, 23, 24, 29, 31–32, 34, 35, 37, 86, 105, 106, 109, 111, 114, 115, 116; in colonial cases, 79, 86; in post-Reconstruction cases, 204, 205, 220; in Reconstruction cases, 151, 152, 154, 181, 182, 189, 191, 193; in wartime cases, 125, 132, 134, 140, 144

Granville County, N.C., 148, 182

Graves, Blair, 153–54

Green, Nathan, 89

Green, Rosanna, 58, 61–63

Greenville, S.C., 186

Greenville County, Va., 192

Gregory, Samuel F., 28

Griffin, Nash, 200

Griffith, D. W., 177, 234

Grizzard, Ephraim, 253

Gross, Ariela, 7

Guilford County, N.C., 63

Hale, Lord, 100

Halifax County, Va., 24, 39, 127–30, 151, 192

Hall, Jacquelyn Dowd, 231, 244, 245, 246, 251, 253, 259

Hampton, Va., 186, 206

Hanover County, Va., 24, 206

Harper, Frances Ellen Watkins, 253

Harpers Ferry, Va., 29

Harris, Mary, 55
Hartsock, Martha, 205–6
Haygood, Atticus Green, 212, 232
Hayley, Jackson, 187
Hearsay evidence. *See* Testimony: hearsay
Henrico County, Va., 50
Henry (slave, Davidson County, Tenn.), 40
Henry County, Va., 21–22, 136
Higginbotham, Lucy Jane, 153
Hodes, Martha, 8, 12, 123, 178, 229, 249, 255, 256, 258
Hoffman, Frederick L., 238
Holeman, John, 108–11
Holloway, Mary Jane, 53
Holmes, Jacob, Jr., 155–56
Honor, 49, 62, 66, 87, 191, 217, 231, 234, 271 (n. 69)
Hooker, Patsy, 24
Howard, O. O., 173, 185, 186
Hudgins, Sally, 54–55
Humanitarianism, 36, 79, 81–82, 87, 118, 129
Hunt, Henry, 104, 111
Hunter, William, 150–51, 152

Identity of accused. *See* Evidence: identification of accused
Ideology, 4, 10; of blacks and innate immorality, 156; of black women and sexual laxness, 154, 155, 157; of childhood, 43, 69; of poor white women and credibility, 18, 26, 27–28, 35, 62, 96, 108, 181; of poor white women and depravity, 6, 11, 14–16, 19–28, 33–39, 40, 61–63, 73, 96, 100, 108, 111, 132, 179, 181, 182, 184; of womanhood and purity, 2, 27, 28, 73, 87, 122, 179, 225, 255
Illegitimacy, 34
Incest, 59, 281 (n. 74), 336 (n. 19)
Indianola, Miss., 225
Indians, 75
Industrialism: effects of, 243, 255, 345 (n. 104)
Infidelity. *See* Adultery
Intent: as standard in rape cases, 214–15
Interracial sex. *See* Miscegenation; Sex—

between black men and white women; Sex—between white men and black women
Irish defendants, 114–15, 305 (nn. 57, 65), 334 (n. 73)
Isle of Wight County, Va., 78

Jack (slave, Wood County, Va.), 53
James, Sarah, 78
James, Thomas D., 32–33
Jefferson (slave, N.C.), 98
Jefferson County, Va., 29
Jefferson, William, 208
Jeffrey (slave, New Orleans, La.), 40
Jemmy (slave, Goochland County, Va.), 77
Jenkins, Arlenia, 137–40
Jesse (slave, Buckingham County, Va.), 55
"Jezebel" defense, 157
Jim (slave, Leesburg, Va.), 30
Jim (slave, Davidson County, N.C.), 33–36, 109
Jim Crow, 10, 221, 207, 208, 217, 235, 254
John (slave, Pittsylvania County, Va.), 130–32
John (slave, Chesterfield County, Va.), 143–49
Johnson, Benjamin, 156
Johnson, David, 205
Jordan, Robert, 206
Jordan, Sydney, 104
Jordan, Winthrop, 12, 74, 227–31, 244, 245–46, 259, 262 (n. 20); influence of, 228–29, 263 (n. 24)
Josiah (slave, Tenn.), 77
Judges, 15, 71, 73, 87, 89, 91, 95, 99, 144, 154, 159, 202, 220
Juries and jurors: antebellum, 20, 22, 23, 27, 31, 32, 34, 37, 40, 55, 59, 66, 71, 73, 85, 86, 91, 95, 96, 105, 106, 107, 108, 109, 110, 111, 112, 115, 117, 118, 220; improperly impaneled, 87, 91, 134; post-Reconstruction, 202, 203, 204, 206, 208, 214, 330 (n. 19), 336 (n. 18); Reconstruction, 153, 154, 155, 156, 159–69, 180, 181, 182, 183, 190, 191, 192; wartime, 129, 132, 139
Justices. *See* Appellate judges; Judges

Odem, Mary, 254
Orange County, N.C., 196
Orgasm, female, 273 (n. 77)
Osborne, Edward, 22
Overseer, 133, 135

Page, Thomas Nelson, 177, 234, 238
Painter, Nell Irvin, 8, 246, 258
Pardons: of African American men, ante-
    bellum, 7, 10, 21, 22, 23, 27, 36–37, 50, 52,
    103, 105, 110, 220, 295 (n. 10), 301 (n. 15),
    309 (n. 23), 327 (n. 112); of African Amer-
    ican men, colonial, 79, 81, 290 (n. 45);
    and character of white women, 21, 22, 23,
    36–37, 63, 79, 105; perceptions about
    abuses of, after Reconstruction, 205, 208,
    209; perceptions about abuses of, during
    Reconstruction, 150, 151, 152, 154, 163, 173,
    177, 181, 182, 183, 189, 193, 326 (n. 110);
    wartime, 125–27, 129, 132, 134
"Passionlessness," 230–31, 244, 246, 262
    (n. 20), 269 (n. 44)
Paternalism, 1, 3, 10, 13; African American,
    153; antebellum, 15–16, 63, 64, 66, 70–71,
    87, 102, 109–10, 111, 112, 113, 119; judicial,
    70, 87, 100, 295 (n. 14); postbellum, 179,
    199, 212; and protection, 125, 127, 129, 135,
    178; wartime, 121–22, 124, 129, 130
Patriarchy: antebellum, 6, 113, 121; impact of
    Civil War on, 124, 135; postbellum, chal-
    lenges to, 150, 255
Patrick (slave, Henrico County, Va.), 50, 58
Patronage, 103, 104, 111, 118–19, 183–84
Peabody Fund, 212
Pearson, C. J., 214
Pedophiles, 57
Penetration, penile, during rape, 56, 155,
    156, 204, 279 (n. 44), 280 (nn. 47, 53), 317
    (n. 33)
Penitentiary, 83–84; Georgia, 84; impact on
    capital crimes, 83–84, 286 (n. 16), 292
    (n. 73); North Carolina, 18; Virginia, 150,
    154, 156, 164, 181, 183, 190, 191, 192
Penn, Peter, 136
Pennsylvania, 75

Peppinger, Abraham, 33, 35–36
Personalism, 36, 102, 118, 179
Peter (slave, Hanover County, Va.), 24
Peter (slave, La.), 94
Petitions: antebellum, 7, 20, 22, 23, 24, 31–33,
    34, 36–37, 86, 105, 106, 111, 113, 114–15, 116,
    117; colonial, 79–85; post-Reconstruction,
    204, 208; Reconstruction, 150, 151, 154,
    182, 192, 193
Phil (slave, Ark.), 91
Phillips, Ulrich B., 1, 2, 52, 237
Pierson, Mary, 208
Pike, James, 197
Pillory, 61, 78
Pittsylvania County, Va., 130, 138, 140–41,
    189
Planter class, 10, 30
Pleasant (slave, Ark.), 97–98
Political equality, black, 177, 195–98
Political power, black, 243
Politics, 4; and interracial cooperation, 248;
    and lynching, 201–2; and Reconstruc-
    tion, 147–75, 194–99, 231–37; and sec-
    tionalism, 125, 126; and sex between black
    men and white women, 194, 195–99, 201–
    2, 328 (n. 11). See also Democratic Party;
    Populism; Reconstruction
Poor whites. See Whites: poor; Women—
    poor white
Populism, 243; as cause of rape fears, 250–
    51
Powell, Edward, 154
Pregnancy, 33–39, 137–39, 185, 191; and "cry
    rape," 242; and rape, 33, 34, 108–9, 272
    (n. 77)
Preston, Elizabeth, 193
Price, John, 172, 181
Prince Edward County, Va., 28
Princess Anne County, Va., 153
Prison sentences, 45, 46, 61, 66, 83, 110, 114,
    115, 117, 118, 150, 152, 155, 156, 159–60, 172,
    174, 179, 181, 182, 183, 189, 190, 191, 192,
    193, 203, 205, 206
Procedural fairness: accorded to black rap-
    ists, 9, 21, 22, 40, 81, 87–101, 129, 144–45,

tion, 166–75, 180–84, 188–94; by free
black men, 16, 78, 102–14, 118–19; from
slaveholding class, 29–30, 37–39, 48; by
slaves, 1, 2, 9, 16, 19–40, 42–71, 120–46,
293 (n. 75); and white anxiety, 3, 4, 201–2;
by white men, 292 (n. 68), 293 (n. 74),
305 (n. 65)
"Rape complex," 223–24, 227, 243, 339
(n. 4); in twentieth century, 264 (n. 30),
339 (n. 3)
"Rape-lynch scenario," 221
"Rape myth," 3, 4, 9, 10, 178, 223; exposed
as ruse, 241–43; lack of, in antebellum
South, 21; in postbellum South, 178;
psycho-sexual motives for, 12
—historiography of, 18, 178–79, 263 (n. 24),
275 (n. 11), 339 (n. 3); Cash-Jordan thesis,
263 (n. 24); centrality of white men, 245–
46; class, 246; gender war interpretation,
245–46; historians' identification with
black males, 246; link to changes in gender roles and sexuality, 245; "masculine"
interpretation, 226–27; origins at turn of
the century, 243–44, 341 (n. 26); origins
in emancipation, 230, 249, 341 (n. 26);
origins in mid-1880s, 208; origins in slavery, 225–29, 243, 263 (n. 24), 340 (n. 24);
postbellum assumptions, 229; promotes
female reliance on white males, 246;
"psycho-sexual" interpretation, 225–29,
244–45; role of industrialism, 243, 257;
ties to education, 248; in twentieth century, 256–57; use of elite sources, 225,
244; women as passive, 246
Rape rhetoric, 3, 200–202, 256
Ravenal, Henry William, 123
Readjusters, 248
Reconstruction, 9–10, 16, 147–75; blamed
for "Negro problem," 232–37; federal
control of South during, 161–62, 166, 174;
historical treatment of, 177–78, 231–37,
327 (n. 7); impact of, on southern legal
terrain, 162; and origins of black rape
anxiety, 176–78, 231–37, 249–50; pardons
during, 163, 179, 181, 182, 183; politics, 17,

160, 165, 196–98. See also Reconstruction
South
Reconstruction Acts, 161
Reconstruction novels, 233–36, 327 (n. 17)
Reconstruction South: black political par-
ticipation in, 163, 195; competing courts
in, 161, 316 (n. 17); feelings of political
impotence in, 163, 165; injustice for
blacks in, 161–62, 170, 172, 173, 321 (n. 55);
loss of faith in legal process in, 163, 165,
166, 207; military occupation, 162, 207,
208. See also Reconstruction
—and white southerners: discontent with
federal control, 162, 164, 165, 166, 167,
174, 207; frustration with legal system,
164, 165, 166, 207; frustration with political system, 164, 165, 166, 207; perceptions
about black criminality, 163–64, 195, 196;
perceptions about blacks manipulated by
Northerners, 176–77; perceptions about
corruption, 147, 162, 164, 165, 175, 176–77;
perceptions about pardon abuses, 163,
164, 173, 174, 322 (nn. 72, 78); perceptions
about Republican governors, 163;
resistance to black civil and political
rights, 164, 166, 176, 195
Red Rock, 177, 234
Reese, Maggie, 253
Reprieves: antebellum, 16, 27, 29, 30, 35, 37,
49, 50, 57, 68, 86, 90, 100, 102, 105, 113;
colonial, 79, 80, 85; post-Reconstruction,
209, 221; Reconstruction, 152, 153, 154, 181,
182; wartime, 125–27, 129, 132, 134, 135,
140, 144
Republican Party, 150, 151, 158, 161, 163, 174,
176, 182, 193, 195, 236, 240, 243
Reputation of accuser, 155, 181, 183, 188
Resistance. See Consent; Evidence at rape
trials; Force requirement in rape law;
Rape: resistance to
Retrogression theory, 343 (n. 68)
Reynolds, Tabitha, 130–32
Rhetoric, racist, 103–4, 179
Richmond (Va.) Board of Education, 248
Rives, Hallie Erminie, 176, 233

Robertson, Stephen, 60
Rockbridge County, Va., 92, 112, 166, 172
Rockingham County, Va., 115
Rodman, J., 214
Rogers, Elizabeth C., 98
Rogers, Hamilton, 30–31
Rome, Ga., 30–31
Rosen, Hannah, 149
Rothman, Joshua, 8, 72, 184
Rowan County, N.C., 29, 181, 202
Rowsey, Elizabeth, 142–43
Ruffin, Agnes, 153
Ruffin, Edmund, 123
Ruffin, Thomas, 90–95
Russell County, Va., 191

Sam (slave, Halifax County, Va.), 127–30
Sam (slave, N.C.), 47
"Sambo" stereotype, 199
Sampson County, N.C., 181
Sands, Sarah, 21–22
Scalawags, 176, 177, 233
Schmidt, Caroline, 182
Schwarz, Philip, 76, 81
Scott, W. W., 170
Scottsboro trial, 217, 224, 256
Sectionalism, 125, 126
Segregation, 206, 221, 243; contributing to rape fears, 251; elasticity of, 257. See also Jim Crow
Servants, 33, 35, 69, 204
Sex, 25; outside of marriage, 22–24, 26; pre-marital, 13. See also Adultery; Bastardy; Fornication; Marriage, interracial; Mis-cegenation; Rape; Sexuality
—between black men and white women, 13, 22–23, 33–39, 54, 98, 107, 110, 186–90; consensual, during Reconstruction, 165, 183–89, 191, 194; discussed by whites, 26, 38–39; frequency of, 184; knowledge of, by whites, 26, 38–39; politicization of, 166–75, 178, 194; post–Civil War, 167, 184–191; and post–Civil War politics, 187, 194, 201–2, 231–37; post-Reconstruction,

200; as taboo, 179; in wartime, 133–36, 137–40, 145–46
—between white men and black women, 8, 12, 26, 185, 186
Sex discrimination, 85, 98
Sexual agency
—of black males, 174, 195, 215; linked to education, 212; linked to political agency, 194–98, 236–37
—of white women, 216–17, 254. See also Desire
Sexuality, 9, 13; and black women and black male prerogative, 157; bourgeois notions of, 185, 245, 254; and chastity, 56–57, 96, 97, 169, 183, 185; and childhood, 43, 58, 63, 69, 254; and desire, 12, 100; fear of black, 12, 180; and gendered double stan-dard, 244, 253; ideas about girls', 1; and male prerogative, 11, 44; modern notions of, 252, 254; and white ideology about white women, 2, 11, 27, 28, 36; and working-class culture, 60, 69. See also Anxiety, white, about black rape; Orgasm, female
—of black males, 12, 15, 18, 196–99, 204, 212; constructed notions of, 3; link between class and, 212; link between education and, 212
Shaler, Nathaniel Southgate, 239
Shenandoah County, Va., 108–11
Shenandoah Valley, 108–11
Shoulders, Susannah, 114–15
Showalter, Abraham, 115
Slater Fund, 212
Staunton, Va., 187
Slave crime, 76, 81–82; during wartime, 135, 140, 142, 143. See also Breaking and enter-ing; Slave theft
Slave insurrection, 123–24, 309 (n. 15)
Slave-master relations, romanticized, 231–32, 308 (n. 5)
Slave owners/masters, 30, 55, 65, 85; ability to control slaves, 5, 76–77, 125, 132; dur-ing Civil War, 121, 125, 133–35; economic self-interest, 5, 30–31, 32, 35–36, 40, 72,

Titus (slave, N.C.), 78

To Kill a Mockingbird, 6, 219, 223–24

Toler, Monroe, 188–89

Toleration, 6, 17; limits of, 107–8; as response of whites to sex between black men and white women, 9, 107, 230, 272 (n. 75), 332 (nn. 43, 47)

Tom (slave, Gloucester County, Va.), 19–21

Tom (slave, Mecklenburg County, Va.), 90

Tom (slave, N.C.), 78

Tom (slave, Spartanburg, S.C.), 40

Tomkins, A. A., 252

Transportation (of convicted slaves): colonial and antebellum, 20, 21, 22, 23, 24, 28, 32, 35, 38, 63, 79, 85, 267 (nn. 12, 20); wartime, 125, 129, 132, 144

Trent, Margaret, 112–13

Trowbridge, J. T., 160

Turner, Nat, 104

Tushnet, Mark, 93

Tutson, Mark, 93

Union League, 195

United States Congress, 240

Van Evrie, John H., 198

Vardaman, James K., 241

Vaughn, Mary Jane, 24, 28

Venereal disease, 64

Vigilantism. *See* Extralegal violence; Lynching

Violence: racial, 2, 301 (n. 17); slave, 124. *See also* Castration; Domestic violence; Extralegal violence; Ku Klux Klan; Lynching; Murder; Rape

—sexual, 11, 27, 31, 44, 54, 60, 66, 96; within African American community, 157; politicization of, 166, 172

—white, after Civil War: toward blacks, 148–50, 166, 195, 201–2, 323 (n. 81), 334 (n. 78); toward white women, 30, 54, 55, 95, 105, 136–37

Virginia, 14, 23, 24, 30, 32, 38, 50, 52, 63, 66, 74, 75, 79, 105, 124, 125, 151; courts, 16, 92

Virginia Supreme Court, 88, 89, 106, 112, 113

Wakefield, Va., 208

Walton, Joe, 200

Ware, Jourdan, 190

Warrick (slave, Anson County, N.C.), 36–37

Washington County, Va., 112

Watson, William, 205

Watts, Caleb, 105–6

Weaver, Elizabeth, 78

Wells, Henry Horatio, 150–51, 193

Wells-Barnett, Ida B., 120–21; on agency of white women, 255; and antilynching activism, 120, 242; attacks sexual and racial double standards, 253; on black rape, 243; on black women and white men, 122; and white violence, 242

Wesley (slave, Elbert County, Ga.), 39

West, Stephen, 191–92

Weston, Nancy, 29, 32–33

Whipping, 32, 40, 51, 61, 62, 66, 78, 79, 93, 149, 155, 181, 190. *See also* Ku Klux Klan

White, Deborah Gray, 157

"White Caps," 208–9

White men. *See* Men—white

Whiteness, 37, 42, 61, 96, 107, 149, 206, 217

Whites: elite, 3, 10, 96, 110, 111, 113–14, 119, 145, 188–90, 192; lack of unity among, 220; poor, 5, 6; response to black-on-white rape, 13

White supremacy, 9, 10, 18, 120–21, 173, 201, 220, 243, 251

White women. *See* Women—poor white; Women—white

Widows, 38, 181, 192, 205

Wilkins, John, 192

Will (slave, Mecklenburg County, Va.), 77

Willard, Frances, 241

Williams, Elizabeth, 78

Williams, Washington, 192

Williamson, Joel, 1, 196, 206, 212, 243–46, 250–52, 259

Wingfield, Lelia, 50–51, 58

Winky (slave, Gloucester County, Va.), 23

Wise, Henry A., 68

Woman: legal definition of, 46, 47, 106

Women. *See also* Rape; Sex; Sexuality

—African American: and accusations of rape, 17, 147–58; and credibility as accusers, 153, 154, 156, 179; sexual exploitation of by white men, 185, 319 (n. 43). *See also* Children—African American; Freedpeople; Free people of color

—poor white, 125, 166; contempt for, 131, 179, 181, 182, 188, 329 (n. 18); and illicit behavior, 6, 20–21, 22, 23, 24, 25, 27–28, 33–37, 40, 61, 73, 96–101, 105, 117, 118, 139, 179, 181, 182, 183, 188, 190, 204, 205, 217; and illicit behavior in family, 24, 28, 40, 42, 59, 63, 106, 107; place of in southern society, 6; rape accusations by, 5–6, 19, 21, 33–37, 142, 179, 181, 182, 187–88; unmarried, 6, 21, 23, 24, 25, 37–38, 142

—white: and agency in sex with black men, 217; credibility as accusers, 106, 108, 109, 116, 117, 138–39, 179, 181–82, 205; as depraved, 10, 21, 88, 132, 179, 181, 182, 183, 188; motivations of in sex with black men, 97; planter-class, 38; and politics and purity, 2, 28, 73; rape accusations by elite, 29, 165–72, 188–90, 192; rarity of rape accusations by elite, 5, 37–38, 166, 275 (n. 97), 311 (n. 32); and reputation, 5, 7, 21–22, 24, 25, 27–28, 37, 40, 61, 96–101, 103, 117, 118, 179, 181, 182, 183, 188, 190, 205, 217

Wood, Martha, 180
Wood, Peter, 12
Woody County, Va., 53
Wright, George, 194, 195
Wyatt-Brown, Bertram, 36, 75
Wythe County, Va., 62

Yeoman, 77
Young, Thomas, 151, 192